Madison in the Sixties

Madison
IN THE SIXTIES
STUART D. LEVITAN

Wisconsin Historical Society Press

Published by the Wisconsin Historical Society Press
Publishers since 1855

The Wisconsin Historical Society helps people connect to the past by collecting, preserving, and sharing stories. Founded in 1846, the Society is one of the nation's finest historical institutions.
Join the Wisconsin Historical Society: wisconsinhistory.org/membership

Front cover images (clockwise from top left): State Street ca. 1961, courtesy of the author; National Guardsmen during the 1969 Black Strike, courtesy of Capital Newspapers Archives; Camp Randall ca. 1966, courtesy of the author; William Wesley Peters's "Lake View of Law Park" ca. 1967, © Taliesin Associated Architects; antiwar protesters in 1965, courtesy of Capital Newspapers Archives. Back cover images (left to right): Fred Harvey Harrington speaks to a crowd on Bascom Hill, May 18, 1966, WHI IMAGE ID 136679, photo by David Sandell; poster announcing the May 3, 1969, Mifflin Street block party, courtesy of Tom Simon, International Were Wolf Conspiracy, University of Wisconsin–Madison Archives S000104. Spine image: Madison in 1969, University of Wisconsin–Madison Archives S17020.

Frontispiece image: Black Strike supporters return to campus after marching to the Capitol, February 14, 1969. Courtesy of Capital Newspapers Archives, photo by Roger L. Turner.

Epigraph from "The Times They Are A-Changin'" by Bob Dylan. Copyright © 1963, 1964 by Warner Bros. Inc.; renewed 1991, 1992 by Special Rider Music. All rights reserved. International copyright secured. Reprinted by permission.

Printed in the United States of America
Designed by Percolator Graphic Design

22 21 20 19 18   1 2 3 4 5

Library of Congress Cataloging-in-Publication Data

Names: Levitan, Stuart D., author.
Title: Madison in the sixties / Stuart D. Levitan.
Description: Madison, Wisconsin : Wisconsin Historical Society Press, [2018] | Includes bibliographical references and index.
Identifiers: LCCN 2018013993 (print) | LCCN 2018022681 (e-book) | ISBN 9780870208843 (e-book) | ISBN 9780870208836 (pbk. : alk. paper)
Subjects: LCSH: Madison (Wis.)—History—20th century. | University of Wisconsin—Madison—Students—Political activity—History—20th century, | Madison (Wis.)—Politics and government—20th century.
Classification: LCC F589.M157 (e-book) | LCC F589.M157 L47 2018 (print) | DDC 977.5/83043—dc23
LC record available at https://lccn.loc.gov/2018013993

∞ The paper used in this publication meets the minimum requirements of the American National Standard for Information Sciences—Permanence of Paper for Printed Library Materials, ANSI Z39.48-1992.

For my family, my friends, and my city, with love and thanks.

Come senators, congressmen
Please heed the call
Don't stand in the doorway
Don't block up the hall
For he that gets hurt
Will be he who has stalled
There's a battle outside and it is ragin'
It'll soon shake your windows and rattle your walls
For the times they are a-changin'

—Bob Dylan

State Street, 1961. WHI IMAGE ID 138228, PHOTO BY RICHARD VESEY

State Street, 1969. COURTESY OF CAPITAL NEWSPAPERS ARCHIVES, PHOTO BY ROGER L. TURNER

Contents

Introduction   ix

1960	1961	1962	1963	1964	1965	1966	1967	1968	1969
1	35	67	101	135	169	209	247	301	353

Appendix: Madison City Limits Maps   406

Acknowledgments   411

Notes   413

Index   493

State Street, December 23, 1959. WHI IMAGE ID 138841

Introduction

"Talking about 'the sixties' is just decadism," counterculture clown prince Wavy Gravy said at a UW–Madison symposium in 1978.[1]

He's right, of course. "The Sixties" is an artificial construct, evoking something that didn't begin on January 1, 1960, and end on December 31, 1969. But this book does. Because even when you're writing about the era of sex, drugs, and rock 'n' roll, there have to be limits.

Not that there is all that much sex, drugs, and rock 'n' roll in this book; there's some, of course, but this is primarily a civic and political history of the period from New Year's Day 1960 to New Year's Eve 1969 rather than a cultural one. While there's a very entertaining book to be written about Madison's social scene in the sixties, this isn't it. Nor is this the Encyclopedia of the Sixties.

This is primarily the history of the five forces that drove the decade—civil rights, the University of Wisconsin, student antiwar protests, urban renewal, and Frank Lloyd Wright's Monona Terrace civic auditorium. The book also covers issues that drive every decade—politics, land use planning and development, public schools, highways and transportation, crime and disorder, and death.

I'm not trying to explain what the sixties meant to Madison, or what Madison meant to the sixties. My purpose is more fundamental—to chronicle the reality of the civic and political sixties in Madison, beyond myths and false memories.

I didn't live this history; I was born in November 1953, spent the sixties growing up on Long Island, and didn't get to Madison until August 1975. But I did cover the decade's aftermath as a newspaper reporter and spend five years as a Dane County Supervisor representing a downtown district; and, since 1982, I have served as a member and chair of several city commissions discussed herein. I leave the reader to assess whether this has made me either unduly sympathetic to, or critical of, my predecessors.

Readers should know that although I was not present for the events described in this book, I have since become friends with several of the leading participants. I hope this has helped me understand the events better, rather than undermine my intellectual independence. Of greatest concern is that several (but not all) of my commission appointments were made by Mayor Paul Soglin; I've done my best to portray his role in, and actions during, the decade honestly and objectively, and again accept each reader's determination as to how well I've met these standards.

The book is written in the present tense, because that is how it was lived. When the narrative involves a park, street, or building that has since been renamed, its current name is noted in brackets. Similarly, when a person in the narrative subsequently attained public office, did something noteworthy, or received a high honor, that is noted in parentheses. Otherwise, almost without exception, the book limits itself to matters occurring at the time of the narrative.

As to terminology: although the correct titles are *Common Council* and *Board of Education*, the text occasionally uses the more common terms *city council* and *school board*. And although *Afro/African American* and *black* did not come into vogue until late in the decade—*Negro* was the standard term until about 1967—the book uses modern terms to avoid offending modern ears. The text also conforms to current style book guidance and refers to *American Indians* rather than *Native Americans*. The text does *not* conform to any style book guidance or rules of punctuation in the items headed "Roundy Says," which capture as printed the unique stylings of legendary *Wisconsin State Journal* columnist Joseph Leo "Roundy" Coughlin, whose words I am delighted to bring to a new generation of readers.

About Madison

There was a lot less of Madison in 1960 than there is today. On the west side, much of the land beyond what is now Whitney Way was farmland outside the city, either in the town of Madison or the town of Middleton; on the east side, much of the land east of Monona Drive was in the town of Blooming Grove—though not for long.[2]

There were three commercial television stations and seven commercial radio stations, plus the University of Wisconsin's WHA radio and TV, and seven movie theaters—two of them drive-ins. There were 108 houses of worship and 126 taverns.

The city's transportation infrastructure in 1960 consisted of 357 miles of streets (308 of them paved); a local bus service provided by the private Madison Bus Company and regulated by the state Public Service Commission; six intercity bus lines; the Madison Municipal Airport, where Northwest, North Central, and Ozark Airlines flew sixty-four flights daily; and two railroad terminals, serving the Chicago, Milwaukee, St. Paul & Pacific, Chicago & Northwestern, and Illinois Central lines. There was no causeway across Monona Bay, so all traffic heading into the city from the south and west came up South Park Street. The entire length of University Avenue was a two-way thoroughfare, and its inbound traffic did not connect to West Johnson Street. State Street was crowded with cars, from the Capitol Square to Park Street.

Beyond the obvious disparities in scope, power, and expertise, the basic mechanics of city government were different then, both administratively and legislatively. When the decade began, the city did not employ a director of finance, public works, or transportation, and the mayor was provided a single administrative assistant. Despite the modest staff support, mayors throughout the decade routinely chaired the Plan Commission, Board of Estimates, and Auditorium Committee.

There was also a significant difference in membership on boards and commissions, with ranking city employees sitting on the statutory bodies that would ostensibly have oversight over their departments; for example, the public works director, city engineer, and building inspector were at one time all voting members of the Plan Commission.[3]

Three important statutory bodies featured in this narrative were established under federal urban renewal laws—the Madison Redevelopment Authority, the Citizens Advisory Committee, and the Local Committee on Urban Renewal. The formation of an Auditorium Committee, also prominent and powerful, was purely a local matter.

The Common Council met on the second and third Thursday but did its real business two nights prior at the Committee of the Whole, chaired by the council president; that was where the alderpersons heard from staff and the public, engaged in debate, and voted on a recommendation to the council, which the council routinely—but not always—adopted two nights later. The idea was that information could be most efficiently shared among the public, staff, and council if all matters were heard by the entire council sitting as one committee on one set evening, rather than by several committees meeting at various times. Debate at the council meeting was usually perfunctory, if it happened at all; council rules limited alderpersons to five minutes at the council meeting, and only if they had new information to share. For the most part, the mayoral and aldermanic quotes herein come from the Committee of the Whole; binding votes were taken at the council meeting.[4]

The public also played a different role, both by attending council and school board meetings in much greater numbers than in recent years, and by making more active use of the referendum/direct legislation process.

City government took an archaic approach to public access. Despite the availability of the new City-County Building, the city routinely held committee and other official meetings in restaurants and hotels—even the full council did so on occasion. And for much of the decade, the school board held committee meetings in members' homes and didn't publicly distribute board agendas before meetings.[5]

The schools had different rules as well. Before Madison became a unified school district in 1971, its schools were referred to as the Madison Public Schools, with a Board of Education that was only semiautonomous. The seven members of the board, elected for three-year terms, could not set their own budget, levy taxes, or schedule bond issues, and could make spending choices only within the amount of money or bonds the city council authorized. It did not always go well.

With twenty-five elementary and three high schools for its twenty-one thousand pupils, the board began the decade facing an immediate and costly building program, thanks to the same demographic destiny—the onslaught of the baby boomers—facing school boards everywhere. But in 1960, Madison added its own unique wrinkle to this challenge—a series of major annexations that would soon turn an urgent situation into a crisis.[6]

The city the board sought to educate was young and daily growing. As the decade began, 33,444 children under the age of fourteen (26.5 percent of the city's population) and 43,763 youths under the age of twenty lived in Madison. And planners projected that the expected population growth over the next ten years would create eight to twelve new neighborhoods, each averaging six thousand people, for an additional twelve thousand pupils by 1969.[7]

The board facing that challenge certainly had well-seasoned leadership. Superintendent Philip Falk, UW class of 1922, became superintendent in 1939, and the seven members of the board had more than 104 combined years in office. But by the end of the decade, the board's combined tenure would be barely a tenth of that—just one of the many things that was about to change.[8]

One thing not about to change is the enormous impact the university has on the city's economic, cultural, social, and intellectual life. With 18,786 students and 7,129 full-time employees on campus at the start of the decade, and the first wave of baby boomers about to arrive, it will be the university more than anything else that defines Madison in the sixties.

Bascom Hill, June 2, 1960. WHI IMAGE ID 138839, PHOTO BY RICHARD VESEY

Madison in the Sixties

Among downtown's prominent structures as the decade dawns: (1) Bank of Madison, (2) Levitan building, (3) illuminated Fauerbach beer sign, (4) Jackman building, (5) Park Hotel, (6) Wisconsin Telephone building, (7) YMCA, (8) Hotel Loraine, (9) Grace Episcopal Church, (10) Wisconsin Power and Light [Hovde] building, (11) Madison Gas & Electric building, (12) Capitol Theater, (13) Yost's-Kessenich's department store, (14) Gay [Churchill] building, (15) Wolff, Kubly & Hirsig hardware store [Wisconsin Historical Museum], (16) Holy Redeemer Church, (17) Orpheum Theater, (18) Hill's department store, (19) YWCA, (20) Commercial State Bank, (21) Wisconsin Life building, (22) Vocational School, (23) Central High School, (24) Kennedy Manor, (25) Manchester's department store. UNIVERSITY OF WISCONSIN–MADISON ARCHIVES IMAGE S17018

1960

Auditorium

No building since the Capitol has meant more to the city of Madison than Frank Lloyd Wright's Monona Terrace auditorium and civic center. And no building ever meant more to Wright. In 1960, this shared dream comes closer than ever to being realized.

Wright first had the grand vision in 1938, but it was not until November 1954 that city voters approved three referenda to spend $4 million on a Wright-designed auditorium and civic center in Law Park at the end of Monona Avenue. In July 1956, Wright, eighty-nine, and Mayor Ivan Nestingen, thirty-four, finally signed a contract for the greatest architect of his time to cap his career in his boyhood hometown.[1]

But in the summer of 1957, the Republican-controlled legislature passed a bill drafted by Representative Carroll Metzner (R-Madison) setting a twenty-foot height limit for any building on the Law Park lakeshore, effectively killing Monona Terrace—until Metzner and the Republicans were defeated in elections the following fall, and the height limit was repealed.

On February 15, 1959, Wright initialed his final set of Terrace plans—the eighth iteration of the project since 1938. A few weeks later, he delivered the preliminary plans and specifications for a large and small theater, exhibition/banquet hall, art gallery, and parking ramps (see image on page 2), along with his first formal Monona Terrace invoice in thirty-one years—for $122,500.

But even that heavily discounted rate couldn't be paid during any lawsuits, so shortly after Wright died on April 9, 1959, his longtime enemy Joseph W. Jackson brought a tax-payer suit against the city, once again putting all plans on hold.[2]

When Wright died, he left five great champions of his project: Mayor Nestingen, who had been elected in a special election in April 1956 and had been easily reelected twice since; William T. Evjue, editor and publisher of the *Capital Times*, who had first met Wright in 1914; and citizen activists Mary Lescohier, Professor Harold Groves, and his wife, Helen Groves.[3]

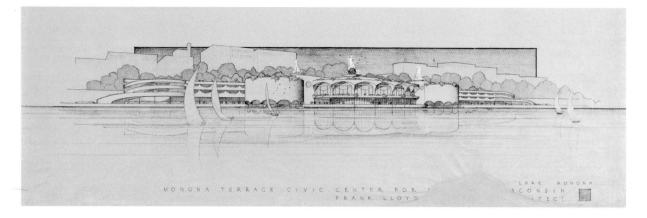

MONONA TERRACE CIVIC CENTER FOR
FRANK LLOYD

LAKE MONONA
SCONSIN
TECT

Frank Lloyd Wright's final rendering of Monona Terrace, finished on February 15, 1959, seven weeks before his death. COPYRIGHT 2018 © FRANK LLOYD WRIGHT FOUNDATION, SCOTTSDALE, AZ. ALL RIGHTS RESERVED. THE FRANK LLOYD WRIGHT FOUNDATION ARCHIVES (THE MUSEUM OF MODERN ART, AVERY ARCHITECTURAL & FINE ARTS LIBRARY, COLUMBIA UNIVERSITY, NEW YORK)

Implacable and resourceful opponents of the project remain after Wright's death as well, led by former representative Metzner; venerable economic development activist Jackson, who once said he "thoroughly detested Wright as a man and despised him as an American citizen" because Wright was a leftist libertine who didn't pay his bills; former alderman Henry Reynolds, president of his family's trucking and storage company; Marshall Browne, civic leader and founder/publisher of the *East Side News*; and south side alderman Harold E. "Babe" Rohr, a construction union leader who wants the project in his Fourteenth Ward, across the water at Olin Park. They've been working for years to kill Monona Terrace and aren't going to stop now.[4]

The new decade, however, brings good news for the "Terracites"—on January 21, 1960, Circuit Judge Norris Maloney dismisses Jackson's lawsuit and ends the eight-month delay.[5] Three weeks later, the council votes, 16–5, to authorize immediate payment of the outstanding bill; William Wesley Peters, lead architect at Taliesin Associated Architects (and widower of Wright's stepdaughter, Svetlana), resumes work on the project and continues working even when Jackson appeals to the state Supreme Court.[6] In June, the Auditorium Committee authorizes Taliesin Architects to begin final working drawings for construction bids.[7]

But while Peters and the Auditorium Committee are making progress, opponents are making trouble. In February, Alderman Rohr introduces a resolution for a referendum to choose between Olin Park and Law Park as the site of the auditorium; Jackson, the former business manager at his family medical clinic, mails about three hundred postcards to pack the March 10 public hearing on the Rohr referendum resolution. About that many people show up, demanding a new referendum and heckling Mayor Nestingen and other supporters so aggressively that Nestingen threatens to call the police. "I've been scared by bigger guys than you, Ivan," Jackson sasses from the gallery when the mayor tries to restore order. The crowd jeers when the council rejects Rohr's resolution and denies a new referendum, 13–6.[8]

In late May, opponents open a new front. Declaring a "crusade" against the project and the start of a petition drive for a new referendum to kill it, Browne, Reynolds, and

The launch of the Citizens'
Realistic Auditorium
Association in the Crystal
Ballroom of the Hotel
Loraine on May 24.
WHI IMAGE ID 136605, PHOTO BY
DAVID SANDELL

about seventy others launch the Citizens' Realistic Auditorium Association (CRAA). In September, the CRAA files close to ten thousand signatures on a petition for a referendum to "terminate all plans for an auditorium and civic center at the so-called Monona Terrace site" and find another location. City attorney Harold Hanson reiterates his legal opinion that the petition is improper because site selection is not subject to a mandatory referendum.[9]

The council's October 11 public hearing on the CRAA request for a new referendum draws an overflow crowd of about a thousand—the year's largest political gathering other than for a presidential candidate—to the auditorium at Central High School. After a tense six-hour session, with speakers on each side about evenly split, the council rejects the request, 13–7. "A slap in the face from the city council," the staunchly anti-Terrace *Wisconsin State Journal* editorializes on October 13, calling on voters to express their disapproval "at the coming elections, when the aldermen and the mayor seek office again."[10]

In December, Browne and others file a writ of mandamus petition with Judge Maloney to force the council to place the CRAA referendum on the April 5 ballot. Alderman Rohr and four other alderpersons refuse to join the city's defense against the lawsuit.[11]

The year ends with two pieces of good news for the project's proponents. Engineers report "very favorable" results from a twenty-four-hour load test of the structural steel supports, and Peters promises final working drawings and bid specifications by January 20.[12]

It appears that Wright's "long awaited wedding between the city and beautiful Lake Monona" is about to be consummated. But appearances can be deceiving.

Madisonians listen intently at the October 11 public hearing on the CRAA's petition for a referendum to "terminate all plans" for Monona Terrace and find another site for the auditorium and civic center. WHI IMAGE ID 136606, PHOTO BY DAVID SANDELL

Civil Rights

It's not a large black population that makes civil rights one of the ongoing, overriding civic issues in Madison as the decade begins; only 1,489 of the city's 126,706 residents are African American. It must be the country's zeitgeist that powers Madison's civil rights movement—that, and the combined efforts of the "Mother Watch" of South Madison, West side liberals, the small group of black professionals and clergy, and white leftist students, a disproportionate number of them nonresident Jews.[13]

Of the city's twenty-one wards, eight are all white, with 76 percent of the two hundred black households concentrated in the Ninth (Triangle/Greenbush) and Fourteenth (South Madison) Wards.[14]

This segregation isn't voluntary. With no laws at any level banning racial discrimination in housing, most of Madison's housing options are not available to blacks. Of 8,595 total rental units, African Americans have access to only 2,298; of the 10,179 houses for sale, they can buy only 1,180. There's also an economic factor: black Madisonians have almost equal access to rentals and homes for sale at low prices, but have access to only a small fraction of the city's more expensive housing, whether for rent or for sale.[15]

White households have a higher median income ($6,799) than black ones ($4,725), and the percentage of white households with income over $10,000 (20.9%) is more than double that of blacks (9.4%). And blacks are more likely to be impoverished; the percentage of destitute blacks with an income under $2,000 (18.1%) is more than triple that of whites (5.4%). The black rate for poverty (income up to $3,000) is higher as well.

Nonwhites in 1960 have "a disproportionate representation in certain occupational categories," according to a 1966 analysis.

DISTRIBUTION OF OCCUPATIONAL CATEGORIES OF NONWHITES, 1960

	Male	Female
Total	**571**	**286**
Professional/Technical	239	63
Service worker	120	101
Laborers	38	3
Craftsman/Foreman	36	8
Clerical	34	33
Private household	0	40[16]

THE DECADE IS ONLY three days old when the housing officer at Truax Air Field yields to Lloyd Barbee (State Representative, D-Milwaukee, 1965–1977), chair of the Mayor's Commission on Human Rights who just stepped down as head of the Madison chapter of the NAACP, and agrees to stop using segregated housing lists for Air Force personnel. Until now, landlords included in Major James Dodd's listing service could indicate whether they would accept black tenants. Barbee, an attorney with the state Industrial Commission, had written to Dodd in December 1959, urging him to end the practice, which Dodd agrees to do on January 3, 1960.[17]

The sit-in movement challenging lunch counter segregation in the southern outlets of national chain stores begins in Greensboro, North Carolina, on February 1, 1960. Before the month is over, it prompts Madison's first political demonstration of the decade— about a hundred students from two separate groups picketing two chains on the Capitol Square, part of a nationwide sympathy strike for desegregation.

Organizers of the main, publicly announced action at the F. W. Woolworth Company include former Wisconsin Student Association (WSA) president Gary Weissman, National Student Association delegate Judy Cowan, and several UW Socialist Club members and leaders, including chair Franklynn Peterson, and Fred Underhill; *Studies on the Left* editor Saul Landau opposes the action but participates when it is held.[18]

Madison NAACP president Odell "Tally" Taliaferro tries to stop the picketing on Saturday, February 27, even as it's happening. "I appreciate the interest of these young people," he says afterward, "but on behalf of our many friends of human rights, I regret my inability to avert this action." Taliaferro, UW class of 1934 and a chemistry laboratory assistant there, wishes they had focused on local job discrimination instead. The local

The decade's first picket, in support of the southern lunch counter sit-ins, in front of F. W. Woolworth's, 2 W. Mifflin St., on February 27, 1960. WHI IMAGE ID 104780, PHOTO BY ARTHUR M. VINJE

NAACP itself later endorses Taliaferro's statement but also commends the picketers for "a gesture of support which will lighten the spirit of free men everywhere."[19]

Unfortunately, the smaller group of picketers, led by an art student, is already at Woolworth's when the larger political group arrives. This small group, which has been distributing leaflets accusing store patrons of a "limp and smirking hypocrisy" by shopping there, moves across the Square to the W. T. Grant store, 21 S. Pinckney St., but their public relations damage to the cause has already been done.[20]

Marshall Colston, who had been a student at North Carolina Agriculture and Technical State University, where the student sit-ins started, disagrees with Taliaferro and endorses the picketing, which continues into the summer. "There are people who ought to know better who are indifferent," Colston says. In December, Taliaferro is reelected president of the NAACP chapter over Colston, 35–20.[21]

That Monday night, the Peterson-Weissman group, which also includes leaders from the campus NAACP, Young Democrats, and Inter-Fraternity Council, decides to join the National Student Association's cross-country demonstration on Thursday protesting the arrest in Nashville over the weekend of eighty-one lunch counter activists by marching up State Street to the Capitol.[22]

Both UW president Conrad Elvehjem and dean of students LeRoy Luberg publicly oppose the idea when it's announced on Tuesday. "We teach our students to look into the facts and get the information and not to put on demonstrations," Elvehjem says. The group agrees to stay on the sidewalk but says they're still going to the Capitol—unless the WSA Senate endorses a Library Mall rally instead.[23]

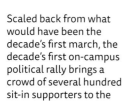

Scaled back from what would have been the decade's first march, the decade's first on-campus political rally brings a crowd of several hundred sit-in supporters to the UW Library Mall in front of the Memorial Library on Thursday, March 3. WHI IMAGE ID 104787, PHOTO BY ARTHUR M. VINJE

History professor George Mosse thinks the march would be a teaching moment. "Whatever good it will do for the cause," he says, "I'm sure it will be good for the students."[24]

In an intense two-hour Senate debate in Great Hall before about eighty students on Wednesday afternoon, former WSA vice president William Steiger (US Representative, R-Oshkosh, 1967–1978)—chair of the national Young Republicans and son of the president of the UW Board of Regents—argues forcefully for the march; WSA treasurer Ed Garvey, worried that a march would be unfairly tainted by association with the chain store picketing of a few days earlier, supports a rally instead. By a vote of 19–10, the Senate refuses to endorse the march; organizers are disappointed but proceed with plans for the rally.[25]

This time, Taliaferro endorses the more aggressive action: "It is unfortunate that the democratic rights of our students to demonstrate in a quiet, orderly fashion have been limited," he says. Governor Gaylord Nelson (US Senator, D-Wisconsin, 1963–1981) sends a strong endorsement, while Elvehjem's milder statement, read by Underhill, draws some boos for the gratuitous comment that "there is some inconsistency in a stand which favors taking organized marching out of the ROTC and proposing a disorganized march through the city—regardless of the importance of the cause." The next week, the regents make a point of praising Elvehjem for his handling of the matter.[26]

Through cold rain and snow flurries on Saturday, April 30, about fifty university students picket the Woolworth's, Grant's, and Kresge's on the Square for six hours, in further support of the sit-in movement; they'll keep it up each Saturday throughout the summer. First Unitarian Society's Reverend Max Gaebler endorses the picketing, but Dean of Students Luberg denounces it, saying the local merchants "should be commended for their non-discriminatory practices rather than be embarrassed" over things they can't control.[27]

This same weekend, Cowan and the WSA's Human Rights Committee bring twenty-four southern black students, including Nashville sit-in activist Diane Nash, to bear witness. Some supporters are concerned that the local chain-store picketing is so unpopular among the community at large that the action will tarnish the students' visit; they needn't have worried. "When we saw the picketing, it really touched our hearts," a student from Tennessee A&I says. Many of the southerners bunk with sororities and fraternities, broadening Greek support for the sit-ins. On Sunday, about a hundred UW students on the Union steps are deeply affected as the visitors share their own stirring stories of lunch-counter confrontations.[28]

The last major civil rights action of the year is commemorative—about 350 students walking in silence from the Memorial Union to the Capitol on May 17 as part of another national demonstration, marking the sixth anniversary of *Brown v. Board of Education* striking down segregation in the public schools. The students stay on the sidewalk in a single-file line that stretches four blocks, in the first march up State Street since a 1954 action supporting higher faculty pay. Another three hundred or so supporters join the marchers at a Capitol rally featuring celebratory remarks by Governor Nelson, President Elvehjem, and others. The WSA continues its opposition to off-campus action, voting 19–7 against supporting the march, a stand the *Daily Cardinal* applauds. The new Student Council for Civil Rights, led by African American law student and Korean War veteran Jim McWilliams, sponsors the march instead.[29]

Baseball great and human rights activist Jackie Robinson, flanked by Lloyd Barbee, chair of the Mayor's Commission on Human Rights (left), and UW senior Dave Obey (right), before Robinson's appearance in support of presidential hopeful Hubert Humphrey in the Memorial Union's Great Hall, March 31. WHI IMAGE ID 108739, PHOTO BY EDWIN STEIN

In August, the Mayor's Commission on Human Rights adopts a report from its chairman, attorney Barbee, finding grounds to believe the Log Cabin tavern at 529½ State St. has discriminated against black people by refusing them service. A commission delegation plans to discuss this with the owners, two university students who have acknowledged trying to stop "beatniks" from patronizing the bar.[30]

Robinson, Du Bois, Abernathy, and Paige

Four historic black men come to Madison during a four-week period in 1960, for quite different reasons. On March 29, ageless baseball pitcher Satchel Paige entertains the annual high school basketball banquet at the West Side Businessmen's Club. Two nights later, baseball and human rights immortal Jackie Robinson, sponsored by the WSA's Human Rights Committee and introduced by Governor Gaylord Nelson, endorses Senator Hubert

Humphrey in the Democratic primary for president before an overflow Great Hall crowd of more than five hundred. But the event goes awry for the Humphrey campus coordinator Dave Obey (US Representative, D-Wausau, 1969–2011) when Robinson says that, if Humphrey loses the nomination, he'll vote for Richard Nixon over John Kennedy.[31]

On April 9, scholar and activist W. E. B. Du Bois, ninety-two, praises the Soviet Union and the People's Republic of China at a packed Socialist Club meeting in Great Hall, and attends a dinner held in his honor at Troia's Steak House on State Street. On April 25, Dr. Ralph Abernathy, cofounder of the Southern Christian Leadership Conference, extols Madison's recent sit-ins at the annual meeting of the Wisconsin Civil Liberties Union at the Hillel Foundation.[32]

Urban Renewal

Madison Plat Map (West Part), 1904. Although some would come to use the terms *Triangle* and *Greenbush* (a.k.a., "the Bush") interchangeably after urban renewal, most of the Greenbush Addition is not in the Triangle urban renewal area. Much of the Triangle is actually Pregler's Addition.
WHI IMAGE ID 37394

As the sixties open, the Madison Redevelopment Authority (MRA) is moving in fits and starts on two urban renewal projects that will displace Madison's primary immigrant, ethnic, and nonwhite community—the sixty-year-old greater Greenbush neighborhood (a.k.a. "the Bush")—and open almost sixty acres of land less than a mile from the Capitol for development.

The Greenbush Addition—from Mills Street east to Murray Street, and Regent Street south to Erin Street—was platted in 1854, two years before Madison became a city; by the end of the nineteenth century, it held many fine homes and shops, some of high design. But the land east of Greenbush was too wet for development until rail yard coalman George Pregler hauled ashes and trash into the marshy area just across from the railroad lines and stock yard and platted nineteen acres of buildable lots there as Pregler's Addition in 1901. He moved some old houses from uptown, built some others, and marketed the area to poor Italians, Albanians, Sicilians, Jews, and blacks. It was low-rent housing for those who couldn't afford, or weren't allowed, to live many other places— Madison's first neighborhood on the other side of the tracks.

Over the decades, Greenbush immigrants developed Madison's strongest intergenerational and multicultural community, rich in family and faith, containing many civic and business leaders. A few Greenbush immigrants also developed Madison's deadly bootlegging industry during Prohibition, prompting some native Madisonians (including many policemen) to join the anti-immigrant, anti-Catholic Ku Klux Klan.[33]

As the century neared its midpoint, the violent crime had ended, the housing stock had been improved, and residents' sense of community had been strengthened even further. But many in Madison still believed that life in the Bush was substandard.

Then the availability of funds from the Federal Housing Acts of 1949, 1954, and 1961 presented a city-changing opportunity—and challenge.

Under plan director Walter K. Johnson's ambitious vision, the city in 1954 created the seven-and-a-half-acre Brittingham project, in the area between West Washington Avenue and West Main Street. Already interrupted by litigation, legislation, and budget cuts, Brittingham in 1960 becomes the flash point where race and urban renewal meet.

Johnson's 1957 Triangle project—the fifty-two acres between West Washington Avenue, Regent Street, and a little past Park Street—has also been beset by litigation, along with bad data and poor planning. Now, the MRA is making questionable commitments to the 1,155 residents it will displace regarding their relocation.

The city received final federal approval of the Brittingham plan in 1956, and began buying and razing the area's twenty-eight residential and nine commercial structures on August 22, 1957. But a Milwaukee County decision the following February curtailing the use of eminent domain without a jury's determination on the need to acquire the property caused the federal Housing and Home Finance Agency (HHFA) to restrict activities

The greater Greenbush neighborhood in June, 1960. Most of the buildings have already been razed for the Brittingham urban renewal area; demolition for the Triangle urban renewal area will start in 1962. WHI IMAGE ID 137503, PHOTO BY JOHN NEWHOUSE

on all Wisconsin urban renewal projects—just weeks after the HHFA allocated $1.75 million for land acquisition in the Triangle area. The Wisconsin legislature quickly enacted the Blight Elimination and Slum Clearance Act, delegating to municipalities the state's power to condemn property without necessity; a unanimous council vote on July 10, 1958, created the Madison Redevelopment Authority, the first redevelopment authority under the new law, and the projects resumed.[34]

But land acquisition was halted again when Dane County judge Edwin Wilkie ruled in late February 1959 that the blight law itself was unconstitutional. In June, the state supreme court agreed the law's provisions on condemnation were unconstitutional but let stand the creation of local redevelopment authorities. Property acquisition resumed through negotiation and jury trials, until voters approved a constitutional amendment in April 1961 permitting condemnation without a jury verdict of necessity.[35]

Meanwhile, across West Washington Avenue, the sixties began in the afterglow of a milestone Christmas present from the HHFA—final approval of the Triangle application and plans on December 24, 1959.[36]

It hadn't been easy—in addition to the litigation, the MRA struggled for almost two years to convince federal officials to allow complete clearance of the area, rather than require rehabilitation and some relocation of non-substandard structures.

Confidential correspondence and private memoranda reveal federal frustration. "You will take immediate steps to restudy the project area with the thought of excluding sound structures from acquisition and demolition," HHFA regional director Ivan Carson directed MRA executive director Roger Rupnow in November 1958, just weeks after city voters comfortably passed the $1 million bond issue to help pay for land acquisition in the Triangle. "The project may become one of clearance and rehabilitation" instead of complete clearance, he wrote.[37]

As late as June 1959, federal planners still did not agree with the MRA that the Triangle was a full bulldozer project, stating, "The evidence so far indicated that this was a rehabilitation project, not a clearance project." The planner, a Mr. Wilcox, was not impressed with the city's lack of progress: "You may damn well lose this project if you don't get going on it," he told Mayor Nestingen's aide Lyle Schaller, strongly urging the city to convert the project to rehabilitation.

As Schaller related in a memo to the mayor, Wilcox was also very unimpressed with the quality of the city's application. "You would have a rehabilitation project now if we could have made heads or tails out of your statistics," he told Schaller.

A federal relocation specialist added that the city would be required to commit to five years of housing subsidies for displaced families not qualifying for welfare. Not much was said about where the money would come from for that, Schaller reported; "However, it was pointed out that the Authority already is spending beyond its budget for unapproved items."[38]

But in its final *Eligibility and Relocation Report* in November 1959, the city dismissed any disagreement, claiming, "The fact that the Triangle Area needs an organized program of renewal activities is considered basic."[39]

Streets and parcels of the Greenbush and Pregler Additions, before urban renewal turned them into the Triangle. MADISON REDEVELOPMENT AUTHORITY

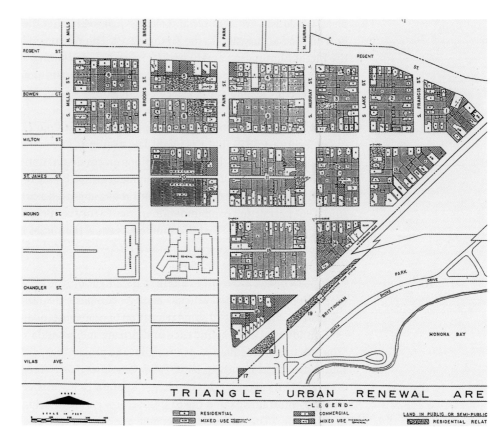

The city did not claim dilapidated housing as the primary reason for a clearance project, citing only 84 of the 233 residences as substandard (along with eight of the thirty-three commercial- and industrial-use buildings). Instead, the city focused on a range of land use, transportation, and infrastructure concerns.

According to the city, the neighborhood held incompatible uses, including a meat-packing plant, several junkyards, six taverns, and seven liquor outlets; the six-inch sewer and water mains were more than fifty years old and inadequate, as were the storm sewers, leading to periodic flooding; two-thirds of the structures failed to provide minimum yard areas; many first-floor residents got inadequate air and light; an "excessive proportion" (44.7%) of the area was devoted to poorly constructed streets and alleys; with many blind or awkward intersections, driving and parking was difficult if not hazardous; the need to widen South Park Street and West Washington Avenue required the abandonment of property along both frontages; settling had caused sidewalks and streets to become cracked and uneven because the neighborhood was built on swamp and landfill; and most of the buildings were more than fifty years old, and many had been moved.

"Complete reconstruction is considered to represent the only feasible method of correcting these conditions," the application concluded.

But that was not quite what the MRA had told residents in a brochure from earlier that spring: "Q: Will all the existing buildings be torn down? A: No. A number of buildings in good condition will be left undisturbed," although "a considerable number of those which are in good condition, but which do not fit in with the new land use plan for the area, will have to be removed."[40]

The brochure also stated that "the redevelopment area will be cleared in 'stages,' one portion at a time." The MRA will later explicitly disavow this approach.

In the November report, the city again assured the federal government that "the relocation of families living in the Triangle area into decent, safe, and sanitary housing within their means can be successfully accomplished."[41]

The new report worked; the HHFA approved the eligibility and relocation report and a final planning application the day before the last Christmas of the fifties.[42]

Nowhere in the application or any related report does the city recognize that the project would mean the destruction of a three-generation immigrant and ethnic neighborhood, nor does it discuss the personal, social, and cultural impact the project would have on those communities. The reports mention buildings and streets and sewers in detail, but not people—demographic data, but no sense of community.

In 1960 and beyond, this proves to be a problem—as does the city's overly optimistic outlook concerning housing for the displaced.

As 1960 opens, the Madison Redevelopment Authority is completing the assessments on the 233 residential and thirty-three commercial/industrial buildings it plans to buy in the Triangle area, and preparing to relocate the 1,155 residents it will displace. It's also deciding what it wants to do with the fifty-two acres once the land is cleared.

At the Brittingham site, two outstanding issues remain—relocating the last three businesses (all taverns) and deciding whether to include public housing for Triangle residents, as the Madison Housing Authority has urged.

And the MRA has even more redevelopment projects in store for the city. In early April, MRA executive director Roger Rupnow outlines a $32.5 million urban renewal program, targeting the South Madison, Williamson-Marquette, and Tenney-Lapham neighborhoods, and the UW campus from Broom Street to Camp Randall.[43]

In its May application to the HHFA's Urban Renewal Administration for $4.5 million in loans and grants to buy the Triangle properties, the MRA admits errors in its earlier analysis of how much affordable housing would be available. "Certain methodological errors had been made in making the earlier projections," the authority discloses in its Urban Renewal Plan in May, "resulting in an overstatement of the number of units expected to be generally available." But the MRA assures the feds that "standard housing is expected to be available in sufficient quantity during the relocation period to meet the relocation needs of low-income families displaced from the project area."[44]

That remains to be seen.

In mid-June, a standing-room-only crowd of close to three hundred packs the Longfellow School's auditorium for the public hearing on the Triangle urban renewal

The Triangle's preliminary zoning and land-use plan, endorsed by the Plan Commission on April 11.
CITY OF MADISON PLANNING

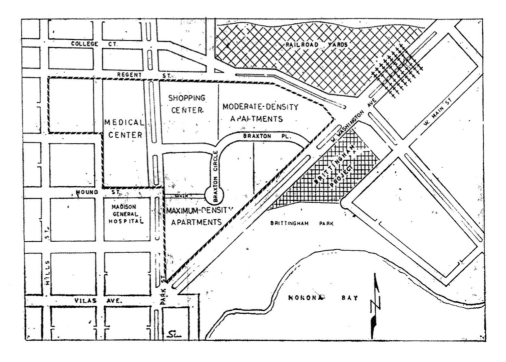

This federal form for reporting housing resources accepts that a certain portion of the housing stock will not be available to nonwhite households. In Madison in 1960, a high percentage of rental and for-sale units is available only to whites, especially those at higher prices.[45]
MADISON REDEVELOPMENT AUTHORITY

PROJECT NAME: Triangle Urban Renewal Area		PROJECT NUMBER: Wis. R-2					
ESTIMATED HOUSING RESOURCES							
TYPE OF HOUSING	NUMBER OF UNITS EXPECTED TO BE PLACED ON MARKET (Turnover plus Construction)		NUMBER OF UNITS EXPECTED TO BE AVAILABLE TO FAMILIES DISPLACED FROM THIS PROJECT				
			TOTAL			AVAILABLE TO NON-WHITE FAMILIES	
	TOTAL	AVAILABLE TO NON-WHITE FAMILIES	1 BEDROOM	2 BEDROOMS	3 OR MORE BEDROOMS	1 BEDROOM	2 BEDROOMS	3 OR MORE BEDROOMS
	(a)	(b)	(c)	(d)	(e)	(f)	(g)	(h)
A. PUBLIC HOUSING								
1. Federally aided	-0-	-0-	-0-	-0-	-0-	-0-	-0-	-0-
2. State or locally aided	100	100	-0-	100	-0-	-0-	100	-0-
B. STANDARD PRIVATE RENTAL HOUSING								
TOTAL	8,595	2,298	2,407	3,718	560	790	882	111

plan. The attendees learn the MRA will pay the higher of two appraisals for buildings on the lot (subject to legal challenge and federal approval), and provide up to $200 in moving expenses, subsidies, and mortgage assistance for new purchases to the buildings' owners. Carlo Caputo, 2103 Madison St., asks if the purchase price of his Triangle income property will enable him to purchase a similar property in another Madison neighborhood; MRA chair Albert McGinnis says yes, barring unusually high interest rates. Mayor Nestingen sends a statement acknowledging that "some temporary hardships and inconveniences will be worked to some people who are directly affected by this project," but insisting that "these inconveniences and hardships, however, are of a temporary nature, and in the over-all the general city future is benefitted many times over by way of comparison."[46]

Afterward, Rupnow says he expects the MRA to start buying Triangle properties by November. But when setting prices to purchase project area property, the MRA will be under tight federal oversight; the Urban Renewal Administration has already rejected the MRA's option of $55,000 for two Brittingham area properties, requiring a reappraisal that lowered the offer to $54,250.[47]

In early July, Chester Zmudzinski, the influential executive director of Madison Neighborhood Centers Inc. (MNCI), proposes that the MRA contract with MNCI for relocation services to displaced Triangle residents. The MRA agrees, but the Urban Renewal Administration regional office in Chicago says it's not an eligible project cost. So in August the MRA makes its own hire of a relocation specialist, on a "ten day emergency basis"—Zmudzinski's wife, Florence, a veteran social worker. On September 1, the MRA hires her as a provisional social worker for another ninety days, renewable until a permanent position is created.[48]

On October 20, the HHFA's regional administrator, John P. McCollum, summons Mayor Nestingen to Chicago to discuss "a number of serious problems" in Madison's urban renewal program, some of which "seem urgent."

McCollum writes again a week later, telling Nestingen to get to Chicago ASAP. "We are withholding certain actions in regard to the Madison projects until such time as we can apprise you fully of some of the implications" of his reaction to the city's application, McCollum writes. "We believe we have a serious responsibility to discuss these matters with the chief governmental authority of the community."[49]

When Nestingen finally makes it to Chicago on November 16, McCollum's deputy Ralph Herod demands more information on about twenty items in the Triangle application, and says the city has to get moving on both projects, even if that means hiring additional staff.

But Herod's news is mostly good—at least for the MRA. First, he slams the door on the MHA's call for public housing in Brittingham, saying that would cause unacceptable delays. Then, even though a city building inspector has determined that forty of the fifty-six structures in the three affected blocks west of Park Street between Regent and Mound Streets are either new or in good condition, and only four in poor condition, Herod determines that the area is "eligible for clearance and conversely [is] ineligible for rehabilitation." This finding will enable the construction of the two medical centers, a new Neighborhood House, and an expansion of Madison General Hospital.[50]

On December 1, the MRA uses the federal opposition as a reason to reject the MHA's bid for public housing in Brittingham. That causes the Local Committee on Urban Renewal (the federally mandated body of project-area residents and interest groups) to announce two weeks later that it will drop its support for the MHA demand on condition that public housing be included in the Triangle itself. At a public hearing, Chester Zmudzinski, who is chair of the Local Committee in addition to being head of the Madison Neighborhoods Center, warns that failure to provide public housing when residents are displaced could have dire consequences.[51]

The year ends with good news for the MRA—six years after the city initiated the Brittingham project, the Urban Renewal Administration approves the final plans. Quick council concurrence will enable the MRA to advertise the land for sale in February and receive bids in April 1961. But such easy approval does not prove possible, once urban renewal meets race at Trotter's Tuxedo Café.[52]

Trotter's Travails

Race and urban renewal meet in 1960 at Zachary Trotter's Tuxedo Café, Madison's only black bar, which Trotter had owned and operated at 763 W. Washington Ave. for twenty-two years without any complaints about his conduct or his character. But now the MRA wants his land for the Brittingham urban renewal project.[53]

As the year opens, only one local hurdle remains for the Brittingham project—relocating three taverns, the last structures standing out of the twenty-eight residential and nine commercial buildings that had been in the area when the project began.

Joseph Licari and the Frank Vitale estate have little trouble transferring their licenses. Trotter, seventy-three, who lives above the bar with his wife, Maxine, has lots. All three were among the plaintiffs in the 1959 lawsuit over the blight law; all three have since waived the necessity finding and had their property values set by court commissioners.[54]

By summer, Trotter finds a place at 1044 S. Park St., formerly Plaenert's Flower Shop, which is already properly zoned for a tavern. Walter Plaenert gets a number of vulgar, racist calls protesting the sale, but he stands by his offer; all Trotter needs is city council approval to transfer the license.[55]

Harold E. "Babe" Rohr, the powerful alderman of the Fourteenth Ward and an anti-civil rights labor leader, doesn't want the transfer to happen. The longtime business agent for the Painter's Union and president of the Construction and Building Trades Council, Rohr organizes a petition drive that collects an extraordinary 736 signatures opposing the transfer—seven times the number opposing any previous liquor license transfer in Madison. He packs the council meeting of July 14 with about three hundred constituents; many loudly boo Trotter's attorney, Maurice Pasch, when he refers to their stated concerns about parking and traffic as "fiction."[56]

"I can see prejudice," Ald. Thomas Stavrum says at the meeting. "I can see it in the faces of the people here."

"Keep your nose out of the Fourteenth Ward," Rohr responds. "We can handle this."

Lloyd Barbee, chair of the Mayor's Commission on Human Rights (MCHR), asks for referral, to study the situation, but the council denies his request and rejects Trotter's request for the transfer, 15–2. Only then, immediately after the vote, does the city council ask Barbee to see if there's any bias involved.[57]

According to the MCHR, there is at least some—as Rohr himself admits. While most who signed were sincere in opposing any tavern there, a special MCHR investigative committee concludes after extensive interviews that "racial prejudice was a motivating factor among a substantial minority of the petition signers." The committee report, which the commission adopts, calls Rohr's petition drive "a highly organized effort . . . which went beyond the ordinary bounds of neighborhood concern about the location of a tavern. Racial prejudice intensified the organizational effort that went into circulating the petition and the response to it."[58]

When the council receives the MCHR report, it files the document and takes no action.[59]

On July 14, the same night that the council rejects Trotter's transfer, it approves transferring the Vitale family's liquor license for the Shack restaurant, at 753 W. Washington Ave., to a corporation represented by former Greenbush-area alderman Joseph Genna, who plans to move the restaurant to the former location of Jimmie Schiavo's restaurant, 3519 E. Washington Ave. "A brazen example of trafficking in liquor licenses," Ald. James Marks of the Twenty-First Ward protests in vain.[60]

Mayor Ivan Nestingen, who had called the neighborhood concerns "puzzling" and unprecedented, worries about the consequences for failing to relocate Trotter.

"If they bog down on this," he warns, "you can kiss urban renewal goodbye."[61]

But the MRA doesn't bog down. It issues Trotter a check for $23,500, takes title to the property, and starts charging him $200 a month in rent. Trotter doesn't accept the check or pay the rent.[62]

Trotter keeps looking for a new location, but by year's end, he hasn't found one. And the Brittingham project, which the MRA had planned to have ready for bid, remains on hold.[63]

Madison's Housing Inequalities

A survey of the Triangle urban renewal area reveals there are 204 white households with 786 individuals and 97 nonwhite households with 369 persons. The white households are slightly poorer; nearly half have a monthly income under $350, while nearly three-fourths of the black households have a monthly income above that level. More than one-third of the nonwhite households have an income above $500 per month.[64]

Whites and nonwhites have almost equal access to rent or buy housing at low prices; nonwhites have access to only a small fraction of the more expensive houses for rent or for sale. Despite the prevalent (and legal) racial discrimination, the city continues to assert that "no special problems are anticipated with respect to the relocation of minority group families."

MADISON HOUSING AVAILABILITY, WHITE/NONWHITE, 1960

	Total Units Available	Units Available to Nonwhites
Private Rental Housing	**8,595**	**2,298**
Under $40 per month	190	152
$40–$90 per month	1,120	896
$60–$90 per month	5,340	1,134
Over $90 per month	1,945	116
Housing for sale	**10,179**	**1,180**
Under $5,000	60	54
$5,000–$8,000	450	405
$8,000–$12,000	3,670	482
Over $12,000	5,999	239

MONTHLY INCOME, TRIANGLE HOUSEHOLDS, 1960

Monthly Income	White Families	Nonwhite Families
Under $200	20	1
$200–$350	69	25
$350–$500	66	34
Over $500	49	37

FAMILIES DISPLACED BY TRIANGLE RELOCATION PLAN

Families Displaced	Rent	Own
Total	**213**	**88**
White	129	75
Nonwhite	84	13

Campus and the heart of the University Expansion Area in June. At center, the sixteen-acre southeast dorm area, where 388 structures will be razed and replaced by six high-rise dormitories, provoking a bitter battle between the city and university regents over control of related development. Around the Carillon Tower at center top is the soon-to-be-decimated Muir Woods. To the lower left, across the tracks and out of frame, is the Bush. WHI IMAGE ID 137319, PHOTO BY JOHN NEWHOUSE

UW

COMMENCEMENT, JUNE 6
- ▸ Baccalaureate: 1,700
- ▸ Master's/PhD: 700
- ▸ JD/MD: 130[65]

FALL ENROLLMENT
- ▸ Total students: 18,811[66]

HOMECOMING
- ▸ Show: Count Basie with Joe Williams; Lambert, Hendrick, and Ross; Don Adams[67]
- ▸ Dance: Skitch Henderson

The University of Wisconsin is in pretty good shape as the sixties begin. Its leaders are intelligent, dedicated, and well-meaning; its faculty respected, accomplished, and influential; its students engaged, engaging, and smart. It's enjoying a federally funded building boom in a beautiful location in a vibrant city.

What could possibly go wrong?

Campus Calendar

January 1—The Badgers begin the decade suffering a whomping defeat on New Year's Day, losing the Rose Bowl to the Washington Huskies, 44–8. Two hundred loyal fans greet the returning team at Truax Field, but they don't get much of a response from the sub-dued players. In February, the faculty renews its strong opposition to the Big Ten renewing the just-expired Rose Bowl contract with the Western Conference. "The worst part of this arrangement is that it amounts to crude commercial exploitation of the Big Ten schools for the benefit of business interests on the West Coast," the *Capital Times* editorializes on February 6 in support of the faculty's vote.[68]

January 4—At its first meeting of the decade, the faculty vindicates the longest-running social/political protest on campus by voting overwhelmingly to abolish the 1942 requirement that all male students take two years of military training in the Reserve Officer Training Corps (ROTC)—just as a decisive all-campus vote had asked for in 1949. In late February, the regents adopt former governor, now regent, Oscar Rennebohm's proposal for a two-year trial, with ROTC remaining voluntary only if enrollments over the next two years are at least 75 percent of what they were in 1959. Enrollments will go on to far surpass this minimum, and compulsory military training at UW ends after eighteen years.[69]

February 13–17—Former British prime minister Clement Atlee headlines the first Wisconsin Student Association Symposium, "The Sixties: Challenge to Our Generation," which draws about fifty-six hundred attendees to its seven programs. Among the nine speakers are six-time Socialist Party presidential nominee Norman Thomas, ABC newscaster Edward P. Morgan, and the provocative pairing of conservative *National Review* editor William F. Buckley and the liberal *Saturday Review* editor Norman Cousins, whose debate draws a full house of thirteen hundred at the Union Theater.[70]

March 17—Thirty-four-year-old Hal Holbrook presents as twice his age and captivates a capacity crowd with his engaging portrayal of the greatest American humorist in "Mark Twain Tonight!"[71]

March 18—Madison native and UW alumnus Sen. Wayne Morse (D-OR) gives an emphatic endorsement of Adlai Stevenson—and a sharp putdown of Sen. John F. Kennedy—when he keynotes the Mock Democratic convention; the six hundred delegates agree, choosing the former Illinois governor over the Massachusetts senator by better than two to one. Stevenson's strong campus support is evident when his October campaign appearance for Kennedy draws an overflow crowd, also in the Union Theater.[72]

March 25—Governor Gaylord Nelson liberalizes the Board of Regents, appointing Milwaukee trade union leader Jacob Friedrick to succeed Sun Prairie agribusinessman Wilbur Renk.[73]

April 7—Robert Penn Warren, the only person to receive the Pulitzer Prize for both fiction and poetry, lectures on "The State of Poetry: A Reassessment of Modernism" to a group of English instructors and majors.[74]

April 8–9—The spring social season opens with the campus ROTC units' Forty-Fourth Military Ball in the Great Hall and Tripp Commons, the only all-campus formal of the year and the only 2:30 curfew night for female students. Saturday night, it's the Student Peace Center's fourth annual Anti-Mil Ball, a much less formal affair. The Mil Ball has the Kai Winding Orchestra and Badger Beauties; the Anti-Mil Ball, which has grown from one hundred attendees in 1957 to four hundred last year, draws almost six hundred for records, and a satirical skit about Cuba by Marshall Brickman (1978 Academy Award winner, Best Original Screenplay for *Annie Hall* with Woody Allen), Saul Landau, and Lee Baxandall.[75]

April 10—About five hundred people attend the dedication of the $3.5 million Elm Drive Dorms—three four-story lakeshore buildings on the western campus for 443 men and 270 women, with a shared commons, which opened in the fall of 1959.[76]

April 12—Ed Garvey (Executive Director, National Football League Players' Association, 1971–1983; Wisconsin Deputy Attorney General; Democratic nominee for governor and US Senate) from Burlington, Wisconsin, is elected president of the Wisconsin Student Association on the Badger Party ticket, advocating strong ties with the National Student Association.[77]

May 9—The faculty gives and takes students' personal freedoms. It ends the ban on male students "bringing unchaperoned young women (students or non-students)" into off-campus apartments, but it also extends to men under age twenty-one the requirement to live in university-approved housing, already the rule for women.[78]

May 16—Varsity male athletes name Madison native and East High School grad Dale Hackbart "Athlete of the Year." In June, the three-sport star, who had been drafted as a defensive back by the Green Bay Packers in 1959, signs a contract to play outfield for the Pittsburgh Pirates.[79]

July 29—Jazz pianist Ahmad Jamal makes his Madison debut at the Union Theater.[80]

August 3—An era of expansion opens with the ceremonial groundbreaking for the first campus construction south of University Avenue, the first unit of the $2.8 million chemistry building (the Marshall laboratory in the Daniels chemistry building), part of the UW's $9 million construction budget in 1960.[81]

September 10—Anticipating a coming wave of baby boomers in the next five to ten years, the regents continue the university's march south of University Avenue by unanimously approving a ten-year, $24 million dormitory plan for up to four thousand residents in the sixteen-acre area bounded by Park, Johnson, Dayton, and Frances Streets. Nearly four hundred buildings in the area are slated to be bought and razed. Mainly nineteenth-century rooming houses, apartments, taverns, and small stores, the buildings are assessed as a group at $1.7 million; at the current mill rate, the buildings account for about $70,000 in property taxes. No one doubts the university's need for more space; there are nineteen thousand students, with thousands more on the way, and University Housing can accommodate only 4,300 single men and women and 700 married couples. The independent dorms and houses can hold 1,600 single women, with 8,410 single men in private apartments, and 130 single women living in spare bedrooms in private homes, made available after a public plea from campus housing officials. There are about 1,100 in the fraternity houses and about 500 sorority sisters, with the twenty-eight fraternities and fourteen sororities pledging 364 and 400 new members, respectively, in the fall.[82]

September 30—The Dave Brubeck Quartet headlines the second annual Wisconsin Union Jazz Festival, which also features dynamic South African singer-activist Miriam Makeba and a showing of the film *Jazz on a Summer's Day*.[83]

October 3—A fourteen-thousand-volt circuit breaker blows at 8:38 p.m., plunging much of Madison into darkness for about ten to thirty minutes. Calm prevails, except on Langdon Street, where an egg-throwing crowd of about three thousand is so boisterous that police declare an unlawful assembly and report several young men for university discipline.[84]

October 4—The faculty's Student Life and Interests Committee holds a special meeting and strongly reprimands the Socialist Club for sending and publicizing unauthorized speaking invitations to Soviet premier Nikita Khrushchev and Yugoslavian president Marshal Tito, and suspends its right to present speakers for two months. Club president Ron "Ronny" Radosh (Marquis Lifetime Achievement Award winner, 2007) calls the discipline "fair."[85]

October 17—An overflow crowd gathers in Great Hall for French literature professor Germaine Bree's first lecture as a faculty member on her friend, the late Nobel laureate Albert Camus.[86]

October 18—Kenosha-born Daniel Travanti (Emmy Award winner, 1981 and 1982) wins raves as the stage manager in the Wisconsin Players production of the Pulitzer Prize–winning *Our Town*, by Madison native Thornton Wilder. Travanti, a first-generation Italian American, turned down scholarships to Harvard and Princeton to attend UW.[87]

October 30—Former UW history teaching assistant Saul Landau, now a national spokesman for the Fair Play for Cuba Committee, extols Fidel Castro and the revolution to an enthusiastic, standing-room-only Tripp Commons crowd. Over the Christmas break, a group of nine students will take a committee-sponsored tour of the island, with eight coming away very supportive of the revolution.[88]

November 7—President Conrad Elvehjem permits students to miss their first two class periods so they can attend the Richard Nixon presidential campaign rally at the municipal airport at Truax Field; several hundred students join an enthusiastic crowd of more than seven thousand.[89]

Bascom Hill, December.
WHI IMAGE ID 1786, PHOTO BY DUANE HOPP

December 7—Dean of students LeRoy Luberg, a Korean War–era recruitment officer for the Central Intelligence Agency, warns students in a *Daily Cardinal* interview that they may be jeopardizing their professional futures by joining leftist political groups. There are many campuses, he cautions, that don't have "the level of toleration which is generally accepted here."[90]

December 9—The regents approve a faculty proposal to tighten admission standards for out-of-state students by requiring a top 40 percent ranking rather than the top 50. The out-of-state students displaced likely come from families with more education and higher income than their in-state replacements; according to a new UW study, almost 40 percent of out-of-state men and 60 percent of out-of-state women attending the university come from households in the top 5 percent income bracket ($15,000 and above), compared to 10 and 15 percent of Wisconsinite men and women at UW who come from households in the same bracket. And while half the fathers of nonresident students have a college degree, only 35 percent of the fathers of resident women and 27 percent of the fathers of resident men share that educational attainment.[91]

A Lord of the Ring Falls

As the decade opens, Wisconsin's Charlie Mohr is one of the country's best, and nicest, collegiate boxers. In 1959, the devout Catholic from the south shore of Long Island was voted outstanding boxer of the NCAA and was the reigning NCAA champ at 165 pounds. He also won the NCAA award for sportsmanship and conduct, and probably had more friends than anyone in Madison.[92]

In the spring of 1960, the stylish southpaw leads a fabled squad; since its intercollegiate start in 1933, boxing has been the UW's best athletic program by far, with nine undefeated seasons and an NCAA-record-setting eight national championships under coach John Walsh, who retired after the 1958 season.

NCAA Championships, UW Field House, April 9, 1960, shortly before Stu Bartell of San Jose State (right) strikes Wisconsin All-American Charlie Mohr with the blow that kills him and leads to the end of intercollegiate boxing. WHI IMAGE ID 105057, PHOTO BY ARTHUR M. VINJE

On April 9, just a few days after he's named first-team All-American, Mohr battles Stu Bartell of San Jose State before a crowd of ten thousand to determine the NCAA team championship. Mohr wins the first two-minute round. Then, about halfway through the second, Bartell lands a terrific right cross, flush on Mohr's left forehead. Mohr gets up at the count of two, takes the standing nine count, and is cleared to continue. The boxers spar and clinch a bit; then Mohr's legs buckle, and his hands hang limp. The ref stops the fight at 1:49 of the second round.

Mohr makes it back to the dressing room unaided, and apologizes to coach Vern Woodward and the team for losing. He says his head hurts and lies down. Then the convulsions begin.

By the time Dr. Manucher Javid operates at University Hospital, Mohr is already in a coma, with a tear in a major vein and a blood clot in his brain. The operation stops the bleeding and drains the clot, but Javid knows there's little hope and says so. A score or more of Mohr's teammates and friends maintain an around-the-clock vigil at his bedside.[93]

Later, influential fans of the program claim boxing wasn't to blame—they say Mohr had an aneurysm that could have burst at any time and just happened to do so during a bout. Whether they believe that or just say it, it isn't true; but with boxing already on the ropes in Madison and around the country, they hope to convince others it is.

At 8:40 a.m. on Easter morning, April 17, Mohr, twenty-two, is pronounced dead.[94]

Two days later, reporter Elliott Maraniss reveals in the *Capital Times* that Mohr had suffered from depression, was questioning his life as a boxer, saw a psychiatrist a few times, and even had electroshock treatment. Team and university officials never say whether they knew about these issues before the fatal bout.[95]

On May 9, the UW faculty meets in Music Hall. Without consulting Woodward or considering the Athletic Board's formal request for referral, the faculty overwhelmingly adopts a resolution from political science professor David Fellman to discontinue boxing at UW, declaring that it is "not an appropriate intercollegiate sport, and . . . so should be discontinued." And since the NCAA requires that faculty have total control over athletics, the resolution stands, with no recourse for the regents.[96]

On May 11, the *Daily Cardinal* publishes an angry editorial: "The faculty has abolished our intercollegiate boxing. After less than 20 minutes of discussion, they ended 27 years of boxing tradition. They didn't rely on committees, they relied on their immediate whims and fancies. It is dangerous to give such an irresponsible group so much power."[97]

Other schools soon follow suit, and in January 1961, so does the NCAA.[98]

There would never be another NCAA boxing tournament after the night that Charlie Mohr fell at the UW Field House.

In Memoriam—UW

Madison native Thomas E. Brittingham Jr., son of the great lumberman/philanthropist, suffers a fatal heart attack at age sixty-one while driving near his home in Wilmington, Delaware, on April 16. A founding trustee of the Wisconsin Alumni Research Foundation in 1927, Brittingham became its president in 1955 and oversaw its successful investment strategy.[99]

Economics professor emeritus Edwin E. Witte, former department chair and namesake of the second southeast dorm, dies May 20 at age seventy-three. Witte began his UW career as a teaching assistant in the history department, became an economics lecturer, and worked eleven years as head of the state's Legislative Reference Bureau. He became a full professor of economics in 1933. Two years later, he was the principal author of the Social Security Act.[100]

Schools

GRADUATION, JUNE 17
- West: 414
- East: 379
- Central: 155[101]

FALL ENROLLMENT
- Total students: 21,174[102]

NEW SCHOOLS
- Samuel L. Gompers Elementary School, 1502 Wyoming Way[103]

School Days

January 18—The Board of Education allocates $100,000 to increase teacher pay, but the Madison salary schedule still lags behind that in most major cities in Wisconsin and northern Illinois. Even after the starting salary for beginning teachers goes from $4,260 to $4,500 for the 1960–1961 school year, Madison ranks fifteenth out of twenty school systems; the new $4,760 minimum pay for a teacher with a master's degree ranks fourteenth. The new maximum rates, after twenty-four years, are $8,479 and $9,121, respectively. The board wanted to spend $125,000 on raises this year, but the council cut its budget. In December, another council budget cut forces the board to limit systemwide raises in the 1961–1962 school year to $40,000.[104]

April 5—Ray Sennett, president of Security State Bank, and Arthur "Dynie" Mansfield, UW baseball coach and professor of physical education, are easily reelected to their fifth and second three-year terms on the Board of Education, respectively.[105]

April 5—A $3.975 million bond issue for funds to remodel junior and senior high schools and build a north side elementary school off North Sherman Avenue passes 21,934 to 4,420, the high-water mark for a series of successful school bond votes.[106]

May 4—Members of the Mayor's Commission on Human Rights have an inconclusive meeting with Superintendent Philip Falk about why he has not offered a full-time position to African American substitute teacher Sloan Williams or any other black teachers. Falk says that two offers had been made to another black teacher, which she declined, alleging past discrimination. A member of the campus Ku Klux Klan interfraternity when he was at UW in the early 1920s, Falk insists that the board doesn't discriminate and would hire an African American if the most qualified applicant, but won't engage in affirmative action.[107]

July 1—The 9,500 pupils of the Madison Vocational, Technical, and Adult Schools get a new leader as Norm Mitby, director of the Green Bay vocational school, succeeds R. W. Bardwell, who retires after twelve years.[108]

November 27—About two hundred fifty persons attend the dedication of the Samuel L. Gompers Elementary School, named after the founding president of the American Federation of Labor. Marv Brickson, executive secretary of the Madison Federation of Labor, presents a framed photographic portrait of the school's namesake for display.[109]

Law and Disorder

The new decade finds the Madison Police Department undergoing a dramatic change under Chief Wilbur H. "Bill" Emery, thirty-seven, whom the police and fire commission named on November 1, 1959, to succeed disgraced chief Bruce Weatherly. The commission had fired Weatherly in April for smashing his squad car on January 8, after he had spent several hours drinking with his secretary at the Hoffman House, 514 E. Wilson St. Mayor Ivan Nestingen filed the misconduct charges himself, which the commission sustained by a vote of 4–1. Weatherly, who had been a reformer police chief in his native San Antonio, was a divisive leader, and so rigid and suspicious that he bugged police headquarters and even his own home. Emery, a former marine of formal bearing, brings a somewhat militaristic attitude to community relations and is not forthcoming with information. Captain of the patrol division under Weatherly, Emery did not apply for the position.[110] Emery spends most of his first year trying to restore some pride and cohesion to the force after its difficult decade under Weatherly. His second priority is reducing traffic offenses and accidents.[111]

	1959	1960
Homicide	1	4
Burglaries	324	347
Auto theft	143	162
Robbery	12	23
Rape	3	2
Aggravated assault	9	9[112]

The Police and Fire Commission (PFC) is now led by a political odd couple—President Marshall Browne (twice the unsuccessful Republican candidate for the Assembly) and Vice President James E. Doyle Sr. (former chair of the Wisconsin Democratic Party and husband of former Democratic state representative Ruth B. Doyle). Mayor Nestingen has appointed Browne to the PFC twice, even while the printer/publisher has been one of the leading opponents of Nestingen's highest priority, Monona Terrace. Browne was also the only commissioner to vote against firing Weatherly, on the charges brought by Nestingen. A past president of the Chamber of Commerce, Browne was also involved in organizing Madison Neighborhood Centers. Doyle is an attorney in private practice and a leader of this year's unsuccessful effort to draft Adlai Stevenson for president.[113]

The prim and proper Emery cites consorting with a divorcée as one of the reasons he asks the PFC in June to fire policeman Paul Lysaght, along with other conduct unbecoming an officer. The divorcée had filed a complaint alleging that Lysaght had gotten her pregnant and refused to marry her; she tries to withdraw the complaint when she learns she's not pregnant, but it's too late. The PFC fires Lysaght on July 14.[114]

The PFC fails, however, in its effort to force the retirement of assistant fire chief Edward P. Durkin for undisclosed health reasons. The commission, in a secretive, coordinated campaign to oust senior fire department officers, is able to encourage several to go quietly, but not Durkin. On August 31, the Firemen's Pension Fund Board unanimously finds the fifty-eight-year-old veteran fit for duty and rejects the PFC's request that he be involuntarily retired. Durkin's son Edward D. Durkin is also a Madison firefighter.[115]

Later in the year, the Weatherly scandal continues, even after he joins Northwest Airlines as a security officer. In December, the state Industrial Commission awards him

$3,611 in worker's compensation and medical costs for injuries sustained in the drunk-driving accident of January 8, 1959. The city appeals the commission order and sues Weatherly for the cost of the car's repairs.[116]

Disturbing Deaths

Dr. J. S. Supernaw, sixty, former chief of surgery at Madison General Hospital, shoots himself with a .22-caliber target pistol in his third-floor office in the Tenney Building, 110 E. Main St., on March 2. Supernaw, a founder of the Madison Astronomical Society in 1930, had been suffering for about two years from severe arthritis. His will provides for both his widow and his first wife, whom he describes as "the only woman I ever really loved."[117]

After a Saturday night drinking with underage friends, Jon "Mickey" Hayes, nineteen, shoots and kills his father, Henry Vilas Zoo director Harold Hayes, and another man at the Hayes home, 1317 Wingra Dr., on March 12. In September, Fond du Lac Circuit Judge Russell Hanson rules Hayes not guilty by reason of insanity and sentences him to remain at Central State Hospital for the Criminally Insane at Waupon until cured.[118]

Judge Joseph W. Bloodgood, 1820 Jefferson St., hangs himself from a shower rod in a Madison hospital on July 7. The great-grandson of a US Supreme Court justice, Bloodgood, thirty-four, was elected in April as the first judge in Dane County's new Family Court after eight years as county coroner and district attorney, and a term in the State Assembly representing the city's east side. He had been under a psychiatrist's care since suffering a breakdown while presiding over a juvenile delinquency hearing on May 17. He leaves a wife and seven children, all under eleven years of age.[119]

Highways and Transportation

NEW ROADS
- ▸ The Fish Hatchery Road interchange on the W. Beltline[120]
- ▸ Segoe Road, from Odana Road to University Avenue[121]

Transportation Milestones

January 6—The Milwaukee Road discontinues train service from Madison to Iowa and South Dakota.[122]

January 28—The council receives a report from the Mass Transit Study Committee recommending the city buy the Madison Bus Company and merge it with the Parking Utility, but takes no action. Traffic engineer John Bunch argues against municipal ownership, supporting instead increased cooperation between the city and the company.[123]

April 12—The council puts downtown residents above intercity bus companies, unanimously reversing the traffic commission's recommendation and refusing to allow buses on the 200 and 300 blocks of West Mifflin Street. The companies had claimed that getting to and from the union station at 122 W. Washington Ave., at the top of the North Henry Street hill, could be difficult and dangerous; they wanted the flat access to West Washington that Mifflin would provide. But Eighth Ward alderman Wendell Phillips says his constituents oppose the plan, so the council does, too.[124]

April 28—City and university officials agree on a two-phase $15 million improvement project for University Avenue and West Johnson Street. The first phase includes expansion to eight lanes from Bassett Street to Breese Terrace, with a new road—to be known as Campus Drive—swinging west along the Milwaukee Road right-of-way and out to Merrill Springs on the far west side. In 1980, a submerged University Avenue freeway is to be built, ten feet below grade, through the campus. The plan also makes University Avenue one-way westbound in the campus area—with the exception of a bus lane headed east on the southern side of the avenue, separated from other traffic by a low cement strip. The project will now go to the council, regents, the Village of Shorewood, and the railroad for their approval.[125]

November 8—Voters approve, by more than three to one, $1.8 million in bonds for the city's share of three east side highway projects: creating the East Side Connector (Aberg Avenue, connecting East Washington Avenue and Packers Avenue), adding lanes on Highway 30, and expanding Northport Drive (Highway 113) from Knutson Drive to Packers Avenue and down to East Johnson Street.[126]

Planning and Development

GENERAL STATISTICS
- ▸ Population: 126,706[127]
- ▸ Area: 38.97 square miles (end-of-year total)[128]

MADISON WORKFORCE (59,000 TOTAL JOBS)
- ▸ Government: 20%
- ▸ Trade (Retail/Wholesale): 19.3%
- ▸ Manufacturing: 17.5%
- ▸ UW: 8.9%
- ▸ Medical: 6%
- ▸ All other: 28.3%[129]

Business Wire

January 7—At an organizational meeting of the State Street Association at Troia's Steak House, 661 State St., Howard Stuck of Montgomery Ward, 311 State St., is the first president of the organization chartered to improve the downtown business climate.[130]

June 9—The city annexes the 520-acre, $11 million urban heart of Blooming Grove, a tiny part of the more than eight square miles—most of the land between Monona Drive and the interstate—the city takes from the town this year under Mayor Nestingen's aggressive annexation policy. The thirteen annexations, adding a record 9.78 square miles to the city landmass, also give Madison almost six thousand new residents, helping push the city's total population to an estimated 136,432. No wonder census data shows Madison growing much faster than most Midwestern cities, keeping it neck-and-neck with Rockford as the largest Midwest city outside the major metropolitan centers. And thanks in part to the $19.5 million in assessed valuation in the Blooming Grove annexation, the city's valuation soars from $400 million to $460 million; the 15 percent increase is three times the recent average.[131]

June 29—The thirty-eighth annual East Side Businessmen's Association festival starts at Voit Field in the 3400 block of Milwaukee Street. About a hundred thousand attend the six-day carnival and business display, raising money for college scholarships for east side youth.[132]

The annexed area south of Cottage Grove Road (seen here in dark shading) becomes the city's new Twenty-Second Ward; the area to the north is added to the Fifteenth Ward.
DAVID MICHAEL MILLER

September 6—Labor Day sees things going well for the 81,995 working men and women of Dane County. Thanks largely to the 25,000 or so union workers, the average weekly pay of a production worker ($108.44) is now higher than in Milwaukee ($106.87). The 10,000 county residents working in retail have an average weekly wage of about $62. About 20,000 county residents work in manufacturing.[133]

December 29—W. T. Grant, 21 S. Pinckney St., announces it will close on January 14 after thirty years on the Capitol Square and relocate to an area shopping center.[134]

Shopping Center Ping-Pong

The shopping center developments move back and forth:[135]

March 12—With construction of the new Northport Road (which will cut through the one-hundred-acre, ninety-three-year-old Bruns family farm) set for summer, developers announce a mixed-use development featuring housing and the east side's third shopping center—the twenty-acre Sherman Plaza.[136]

March 24—More than twenty thousand people brave biting-cold temperatures for the opening of the Westgate Shopping Center. Anchored by a J. C. Penney department store and a Piggly Wiggly supermarket, Westgate is, for now, the city's largest shopping center at fourteen acres; a Montgomery Ward opens in July, and a Manchester's department store on Halloween.[137]

June 7—Back on Sherman Avenue, construction begins on the North Gate Shopping Center.[138]

December 2—The state Supreme Court rejects, 6–1, the last legal challenges to the complex corporate structure of the Hilldale Shopping Center, a unique public-private partnership regent (and former governor) Oscar Rennebohm devised to keep profits for university research and scholarships rather than have them go to a private developer. The residential aspect of the regents' six-hundred-acre Hill Farms development, begun in 1957, is already successful; all but ten of the eight hundred lots have been sold, and 510 homes have been constructed.[139]

Miscellanea

January 11—The Madison Council of Parent-Teacher Associations ends its sponsorship of Saturday movies at the Strand and Eastwood because the children keep misbehaving.[140]

April 3—More than fourteen hundred attend the grand opening of the new Sequoya branch of the Madison Public Library in the Midvale Plaza shopping center. Named for the American Indian silversmith who created the written language for the Cherokee Nation, Sequoya—the first air-conditioned branch in the city system—starts with ten thousand volumes, which it eventually plans to double. But news is not good for all city libraries; a special committee found last fall that Madison's main library on North Carroll Street remains "cramped and obsolete," soon to become "grossly inadequate." And the library system as a whole has .9 books per person, compared with a national goal of 1.75. There are hopes, but no plans, for a new central library.[141]

April 26—The city council rejects, 16–3, an ordinance banning off-premises alcohol sales to anyone under twenty-one, proposed as a way to stop eighteen-year-old high school students from buying beer for their younger classmates. The ordinance's sponsor, alderman Harold "Babe" Rohr, argues the ordinance would force eighteen-year-olds to do their drinking in beer bars, "where they should be," but police chief Wilbur Emery disagrees, telling the council he'd rather have them take a six-pack back to their rooms.[142]

June 13—The first of eight weekly early-evening concerts on the Capitol Square kicks off, jointly sponsored by Madison Musicians Association Local 166 and the downtown committee of the Chamber of Commerce.[143]

(1) Edgewater Hotel; (2) Kennedy Manor; (3) Home of Senator William Freeman Vilas (1839–1908), 12 E. Gilman St., a magnificent mansion that his daughter Mary Esther Vilas (Lucien) Hanks loaned to the American Association of University Women as a residence for women graduate students in 1923, while she lived in the adjacent property (4). Upon her death on December 18, 1959, her children, Lucien and Sybil, put the property up for sale for $310,000. After an unsuccessful fund-raising effort by the State Historical Society, a new Madison nonprofit corporation, Senior Citizens of Wisconsin Inc. (SCW), acquires an option on the property. On December 17, SCW unveils its plans for Vilas Towers—350 apartments for the elderly in three high-rise buildings. Thanks to two exemptions from the Zoning Board of Appeals—granted a few days before the plans even become public—the buildings are allowed to be up to twelve stories high, from the Gilman Street elevation. Construction on the $2 million project is expected to start once financing has been secured from the initial life tenants.[144] WHI IMAGE ID 137302, PHOTO BY JOHN NEWHOUSE

June 28—About sixty children and a few mothers watch a dozen handlers use a hook and chain to get the 7,500-pound elephant Winkie to move the 150 feet from winter to summer quarters at the Vilas Zoo. Officials say she needs a larger, more secure pen.[145]

July 2—Five inches of rain and gusting winds do $500,000 of damage in the worst flood in Madison's history. Sections of University Avenue are impassable; the Shorewood shopping center is inundated, and Smart Motors, 2621 University Ave., loses twenty-one new Studebaker cars. Boys paddle a kayak down East Johnson Street, while residents of Eastmorland deal with rats being flushed out of drainage ditches.[146]

July 3—Ideal weather and the city's largest fireworks display ever bring a crowd of fifty thousand to Vilas Park for the Fourth of July celebration sponsored by the Madison Lions Club. The finale is historic—fireworks portray a fifty-star American flag, which has just become official on this day.[147]

July 7—City Forester George Behrnd announces a fourth case of Dutch elm disease, all on the east side. Last year, eight of Madison's 55,000 elm trees were affected.[148]

July 27—The City Health Department reports that it has used almost all of its special $10,660 appropriation to fog mosquitoes with DDT in nine areas of high concentration.[149]

August 4—Thirty-six rhesus monkeys owned by the UW Psychology Department escape from the monkey house at Vilas Park Zoo; most are recaptured after spending several days in the trees of Monkey Island (a zoo attraction), but the last one remains free until December 5.[150]

September 8—The city council votes to send volunteers door-to-door on a voter registration drive. The one-month effort—which city clerk A. W. Bareis opposes, the League of Women Voters boycotts, and local Republicans claim is partisan—uses 444 special deputies to register more than five thousand new voters.[151]

November 8—A record 88 percent of Madison's registered voters cast ballots in the presidential election.[152]

November 18—Mayor Nestingen and Civil Defense head Richard Wilson attend the dedication of a federally funded fallout shelter demonstration model at the home of Albert Hamann, head of UW Protection and Security, 457 Togstad Glen. The shelter, with provisions to sustain a family of five for three weeks, will be open for public viewing for two years.[153]

JFK in Madison

Presidential hopeful Senator John F. Kennedy starts his intense Wisconsin primary campaign at 5:30 a.m. on February 16, greeting workers arriving for the first shift at the Oscar Mayer plant, then holding a press conference at the Eagles Club, 123 Jenifer St., which his wife, Jacqueline, attends. In a futile effort to gain the *Capital Times's* endorsement, he also pays respects to editor William T. Evjue at his Castle Place home (where Jackie purportedly uses the john).[154]

Kennedy returns to Madison four times in the next five weeks, drawing large crowds at the east and west side businessmen's clubs, holding a very crowded press conference in the Union's Old Madison room, taping an interview for WHA-TV, making brief remarks at the University Dames fashion show in Great Hall, and concluding the campaign before an overflow crowd of more than twelve hundred in Music Hall (with another fifty outside in the freezing cold, listening to a loudspeaker). Kennedy's three sisters also appear at a series of coffees in homes all over town, and his youngest brother, Ted, participates in a panel discussion at the Lutheran student center.[155]

But it's not enough to match the local appeal and deeper liberalism of Senator Hubert Humphrey from neighboring Minnesota; while Kennedy carries six of ten congressional districts in the April 5 primary, he polls only 45 percent in Madison.[156]

On October 1, Republican nominee Vice President Richard Nixon beats Kennedy in a campus mock election, 3,940–3,057, decisively sweeping the seven Big Ten schools participating.[157]

Wisconsin residents agree, giving Nixon the state's twelve electoral votes on November 8. But Kennedy does narrowly carry Madison and Dane County, aided perhaps by the city's door-to-door voter registration drive engineered by Mayor Nestingen. Kennedy's election soon brings profound and lasting change to Madison.[158]

In his only local appearance during the general election campaign, and his last time in Madison, Senator John F. Kennedy captivates a very enthusiastic crowd of about fifteen thousand at the UW Field House on October 23.[159] COURTESY OF CAPITAL NEWSPAPERS ARCHIVES, PHOTO BY EDWIN STEIN

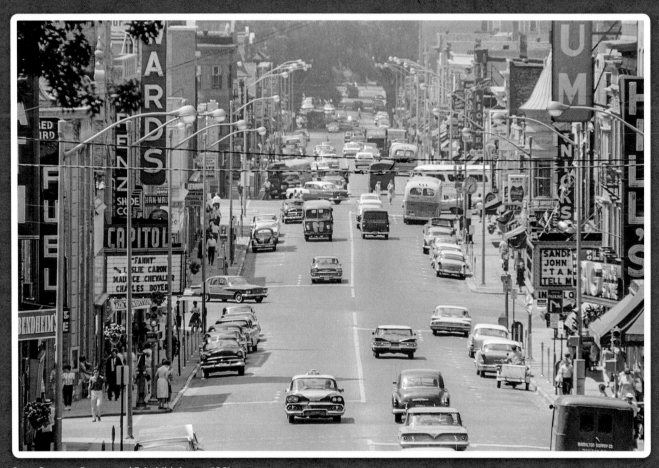

State Street at Dayton and Fairchild, August 1961. WHI IMAGE ID 137719, PHOTO BY RICHARD VESEY

1961

Auditorium

Nineteen sixty-one sets the high-water mark for the Monona Terrace auditorium and civic center—the closest Frank Lloyd Wright's vision will ever come to construction. The year also marks the beginning of the end for the Terrace, due to a most consequential mayoral election.[1]

The year starts well for project proponents. On January 10, the state Supreme Court unanimously affirms Judge Norris Maloney's decision to dismiss Joe Jackson's taxpayer lawsuit.[2] On the twenty-fifth, the Auditorium Committee unanimously approves the Frank Lloyd Wright Foundation's plans and specifications for the Terrace, and schedules council action for the thirtieth. It looks like Mayor Ivan Nestingen will be entering his reelection campaign on a high note.[3]

But the very next day, President Kennedy appoints Nestingen Undersecretary of Health, Education and Welfare. And Monona Terrace, which had seemingly been settled, becomes a political issue again.

The council caps Nestingen's mayoral career at his last meeting on January 30 with a 16–6 vote putting his cherished Monona Terrace out to bid. Now it's up to contractors and campaigns.[4]

Everyone knows that the $4 million approved in 1954 will no longer be enough; inflation alone has seen to that. And the Auditorium Committee has made the project bigger and fancier. So supporters plan an April referendum to ask voters for more money. To know just how much more, the council sets a March 7 return date on the bids—primary day for the mayor's race. But five weeks proves not enough time for such a complex project, and several major contractors decline to bid.[5]

The project achieves another legal victory on February 23, when Judge Maloney dismisses the Citizens' Realistic Auditorium Association's (CRAA's) petition to force a referendum on abandoning the Monona Terrace site.[6]

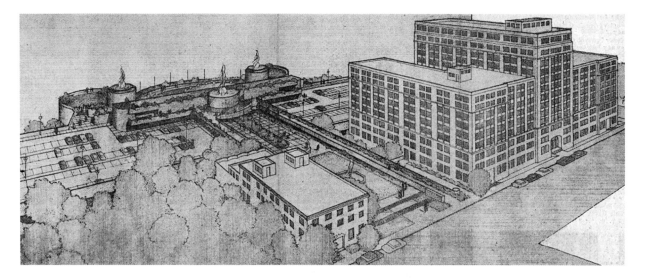

Bird's-eye view of the rooftop gardens, fountain, and parking area for Monona Terrace, from renderings that the Frank Lloyd Wright Foundation releases a few weeks before the March 7 bid opening. Flanking the entrance along Wilson Street are the Madison Club and the State Office Building.[7] COURTESY OF CAPITAL NEWSPAPERS ARCHIVES

It's the last good news the project will get all year.

Most observers are expecting an updated price tag of $7 million to $8 million, but the city gets only one qualified bid, from the Perini construction company of Boston, and it's for a staggering $12.1 million. The anti-Terrace activists pounce.[8]

"The people who promoted this unwise and ill-planned project should be ashamed of themselves," says mayoral candidate Henry E. Reynolds, who resigned as CRAA vice-chair and entered the campaign only when Nestingen announced he was quitting. It's a devastating development for Reynolds's opponent—Nestingen's administrative assistant, Robert Nuckles.

Lead Wright Foundation architect William Wesley Peters calls the bid reasonable, and discloses that he had advised Nestingen via letter in 1960 that "the considerable increase in space and the delay would result in costs far in excess of the contract costs." There is no record of Nestingen sharing this letter with the Auditorium Committee.

At the council meeting on March 9, gleeful aldermanic opponents wear black crepe paper armbands stenciled "Monona Terrace." The council rejects the Perini bid, 14–8, and sends the whole thing back to the committee.[9]

In late March, Terrace opponents try to kill it by putting a $6.6 million referendum on the April ballot, which would be sure to lose, but the council opts instead, 15–7, to send the referendum resolution back to the committee as well. The maneuver keeps the project alive, but only barely. Supporters rally and plan a $2 million private fund-raising campaign so the referendum can be reduced to $4.5 million, but time is not on their side.[10]

Promising that he could build a downtown cultural center for $4 million "or a little more"—but not saying exactly where such a center would be located—Reynolds cruises to a convincing victory on April 4.[11]

"I consider my election a rejection of the Terrace project," he declares, and promptly turns that belief into action. Taking office on April 18, Reynolds ousts the pro–Monona

Terrace citizen members of the Auditorium Committee, including Professor Harold F. Groves. New anti-Terrace members of the committee—which Reynolds chairs—include the retired director of physical plant planning for the university, Albert F. Gallistel, who was a founding member of the anti-Terrace CRAA, and retired state architect Roger C. Kirchhoff.[12]

A few weeks later, Reynolds finally reveals his preferred location for the center—the city waterworks site on East Gorham Street, across from Conklin [James Madison] Park. City staff will later rate that the lowest out of four sites reviewed, with the 300 block of East Washington Avenue and Monona Terrace ranked one and two, respectively. Reynolds would also reverse the plan to move the Madison Community Center, used primarily by youths and seniors, into the facility.[13]

As Reynolds wants, the reconstituted committee votes on June 14 to recommend that the city terminate the contract with the Frank Lloyd Wright Foundation, find another architect, and "proceed with plans to erect an auditorium and civic center at some other suitable site." If the council agrees, Reynolds says, the city could have an auditorium "in less than three years."[14]

One problem—unlike virtually all architectural contracts, this one has no provision defining the basis or process for termination. In August, Reynolds makes an emphatic plea for cancellation of the contract but falls just short.[15]

"You are personally blackmailing the city," says alderman Bert Hutchinson, of the far-east Twenty-Second Ward, as the council again sends the resolution back to committee. "We're exactly where we were five years ago," sighs Vilas-area alderman Harrison Garner, Thirteenth Ward.

There's a glimmer of hope for Terrace supporters in mid-September, when architect Peters tells the committee he could reduce the project costs to $9 million, about $5 million more than had been authorized in the 1954 referendum.[16]

Peters doesn't know it, but the Board of Education has quietly just made a major policy change that would reduce costs even more—the one proposed by Reynolds, and endorsed by school board member Dynie Mansfield, months ago. Recognizing the "drastic changes" in residential patterns since the community center was created in 1947, and that "parents living at the outer edges of the City will probably be increasingly reticent to permit their youth to attend a center in the downtown area," the board on September 5 accepts Superintendent Philip Falk's recommendation that it decentralize its functions into several schools rather than spend $1.42 million to move into the new civic center. That decision, which the board inexplicably does not convey to the Auditorium Committee, will eliminate 36,808 square feet, or 15.3 percent, of the space needs in Monona Terrace.[17]

But when the council considers scheduling a November referendum to approve the additional funds, Reynolds blocks action by threatening a veto; he wants to use the referendum politically during the council elections next spring. "I will not permit a referendum until next April," he declares, and "then only on the basis of a realistic proposal." Again, the project goes back to committee.[18]

Then the project goes back to the council, which on October 10 defies Reynolds and votes, 13–9, to put a $9 million referendum on the November ballot, but then falls two votes short of the supermajority needed to authorize the $4,000 to run the election. Some think the pro-Wright Citizens for Monona Terrace will foot the bill, but the group's president, now-former Auditorium Committee member Harold Groves, rules that out as "a dangerous and undemocratic precedent." City attorney Alton Heassler also says that it would be illegal.[19]

But that point becomes moot when Reynolds vetoes the referendum resolution, which he terms "misleading . . . a direct fraud on the people."[20]

Reynolds and the Auditorium Committee try once again to cancel the contract; this time, the council favors termination, but the 11–10 tally on November 9 is one vote short of the majority needed.

"If the Council doesn't want to break the contract now," Reynolds says, "I'm perfectly willing to wait until a referendum in April."[21]

In April of 1962, half the council will also be up in the spring election, and Reynolds has a not-so-secret weapon—the Citizens' Realistic Auditorium Association. The eight-hundred-member organization, which got ten thousand signatures for an anti-Terrace referendum in 1960, has just reactivated itself with the explicit purpose of electing an anti-Terrace Common Council.[22]

Peters has finally had enough. On November 15, the Wright Foundation files a demand for arbitration of its $600,000 bill for services rendered. And Peters makes clear he intends to continue operating under the contract. Despite the arbitration clause in the contract, the council authorizes city attorney Alton Heassler, at his urgent request, to challenge the arbitration demand in court.[23]

At year's end, an injunction blocking the Foundation's demand for arbitration is in place, with an election and a likely referendum—its terms as yet unknown—ninety-three days away.

Civil Rights

Bias is big news again this year, especially on campus. Sometimes it's accepted; sometimes it's banned.

In April, the regents vote 5–2 to accept a $100,000 bequest from the late Ida B. Altemus of Stoughton to help "worthy and needy Gentile Protestant students" in their junior or senior year. Although consistent with the university's current informal practice of accepting restrictive conditions that are stated in a positive rather than negative fashion, the regents' action draws public criticism.[24]

"The incident indicates again how the dollar consciousness at the University permeates virtually everything it does," the *Capital Times* editorializes, making it "a party to attitudes that weaken democracy." Concerned about the "moral and legal issues this type of bequest raises," the Governor's Commission on Human Rights formally requests that the regents rescind their acceptance.[25]

From left, Mrs. L. E. Pfankuchen, Madison NAACP president Odell Taliaferro, Mrs. Emery Styles, and Dr. Samuel Williams of Friendship Baptist Church of Atlanta view membership drive materials for the upcoming Freedom Fund benefit.[26]
WHI IMAGE ID 113671, PHOTO BY RICHARD SRODA

Stung, the regents consider the matter more closely, and learn in September that the university has bequests pending for students of "backward, colored, minority races" and "Caucasian, Christian students of unqualified loyalty to the United States," and already administers bequests specifically restricted to:

- "Needy, Protestant Christian high school students of the Caucasian or white race"
- "A Jewish girl in economics"
- "[Students] able to speak one of the Scandinavian languages"
- "[Students] whose thoughts and actions are motivated by a Christian character"
- "[Students] of Negro blood" (the scholarship provision in the bequest of Senator William Freeman Vilas)[27]

In October, the regents direct the administration to draft a policy statement against accepting gifts with restrictive covenants. In November, the regents receive, but don't act on, a proposed policy from the faculty Human Rights Committee: that the university "should neither accept nor administer funds [that are] restricted in terms of the race, religion, or ethnic background [unless] the clear intent of the donor is to alleviate current social and educational inequities in opportunities acting to the detriment of a particular group identifiable on racial, religious, or ethnic bases."[28]

At the October meeting, the regents approve the faculty's resolutions, based on the Human Rights Committee's recommendations, that an owner of private housing included on university housing lists "state on the application blank that his house aims at integration" and that "no photographs be requested of housing applicants prior to their acceptance."[29]

Civil Rights Dateline

May 17—Governor Gaylord Nelson and others address about four hundred students at a Union Theater rally commemorating the fifth anniversary of the Supreme Court's *Brown v. Board of Education* decision outlawing school segregation. The annual rally, sponsored by the Wisconsin Student Association and the Student Council for Civil Rights, also features folksingers Dan Kalb (cofounder of the Blues Project) and Marshall Brickman.[30]

June 23—About 150 supporters of the Student Council for Civil Rights rally and march to the Capitol to ask Governor Nelson to petition Mississippi governor Ross Barnett to release Congress of Racial Equality (CORE) Freedom Riders jailed in his state. Nelson is at a conference in Hawaii, but administrative assistant James Wimmer tells the group that Nelson is "in full accord with the demonstrators" and condemns the recent arrests. But the *Daily Cardinal* is not impressed, deriding the council's "integration agitation" as meaningless. "Let them be happy and satisfied with their harmless, and purposeless parade," the June 22 editorial proclaims. "Perhaps someday someone will really do what needs to be done instead of remaining content with merely participating in childish publicity stunts."[31]

July 21—A month after the mocking *Cardinal* editorial, four Freedom Riders from the UW Student Council for Civil Rights are arrested trying to integrate the lunch counter at the Greyhound terminal in Jackson, Mississippi. Imprisoned at the notorious Parchman Farm, the four are separated from the other prisoners and denied mattresses and toilet paper; they spend their time singing freedom songs and playing chess with sets made out of bread. Several other current and former Wisconsin students are also arrested and imprisoned over the summer, both before and after the *Cardinal* editorial. Upon their release and return to Madison, they spread the word at various public forums; among their number is Paul Breines, about to start a two-year term as president of the Socialist Club, who serves three weeks of a four-month sentence, later recounting his experience to a packed Tripp Commons.[32]

July 26—The Mayor's Commission on Human Rights creates a special subcommittee to help relocate minorities forced to move due to urban renewal. Commissioner John McGrath says finding housing for minorities is "becoming a problem

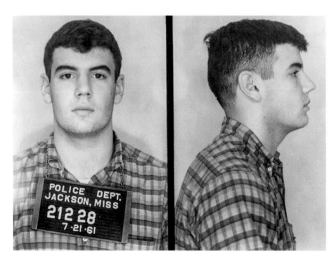

Mugshot of UW Freedom Rider and Socialist Club president Paul Breines taken after his arrest in Jackson, Mississippi. MISSISSIPPI STATE SOVEREIGNTY COMMISSION[33]

September 9, members of the UW Student Council for Civil Rights move the furnishings of a UW couple who were evicted from their flat at 540 W. Mifflin St. after they let a black UW economics instructor and his wife, just arrived from Jamaica, stay there a few nights while they were student teaching in Pennsylvania. A few days later, the Mayor's Commission on Human Rights finds racial bias was behind the elderly landlord's action and asks the UW housing bureau to delist the property until the landlord commits to nondiscrimination.[34] WHI IMAGE ID 114785, PHOTO BY RICHARD SRODA

so large" that the commission—formed as an ineffectual sop to activists after the last attempt to pass a fair housing code was defeated in 1952—can't handle it anymore; he suggests asking the council to pass an ordinance prohibiting discrimination in housing. And there's growing concern about the difficulty black airmen at Truax Field are having finding housing; commission chair Lloyd Barbee is also troubled by reports that the base has resumed using segregated housing lists, contrary to its pledge in 1960.[35]

September—After the men of Sigma Chi validate the faculty's one-year extension from the 1960 deadline by getting their fraternity's discriminatory clause removed at the national convention over the summer, the Human Rights Committee finds the fraternity in compliance with the "1960 Clause" and allows it to remain on campus.[36]

September—Stuart Hanisch, an instructor in the Bureau of Audio-Visual Instruction, begins secretly filming a group of black and white actors posing as would-be renters as they respond to apartment listings around Madison. Over the next four months, he records at least thirteen incidents of landlords lying to black apartment seekers about unit availability. The film of these undercover housing discrimination tests, "To Find a Home," is produced by UW–Extension in conjunction with the Madison Citizens Committee on Anti-Discrimination in Housing; Lloyd Barbee, now president of the Wisconsin NAACP but acting only as chair of the Citizens Committee, raises $3,000 of the film's $4,000 budget. After Hanisch and Barbee (Wisconsin State Representative, 1965–1977) explain the project and the use of hidden microphones and telephoto lenses, Bureau of Audio-Visual Instruction director Professor Fredrick A. White and Extension dean L. H. Adolfson provide the final funding. A rough cut is expected to be available early next year.[37]

October 16—The Student Council for Civil Rights presents $1,150 to pay Freedom Rider fines and bail to James Farmer, the Congress of Racial Equality national director, who says it's "the largest of any college organization." The council raised the money in a two-week campaign that found its sole success on campus. "We tried to reach the Madison area but couldn't," council chair Ron Corwin says.[38]

November 17—The regents vote 7–1 to affirm the faculty decision banning the university's oldest fraternity, Phi Delta Theta, for violating the antidiscrimination clause. Although the Wisconsin Alpha house, cofounded in 1857 by William F. Vilas and whose past members included Frank Lloyd Wright, had shown good faith in working to rid the national organization of discriminatory pratices, the president of the fraternity's general council explained in the fraternity's official publication that national policy bars "Jews, Negroes, and Orientals" because "many chapters do not regard them as acceptable."[39] The fraternity is immediately banned from pledging new members, and barred from campus next September, "unless and until" it demonstrates compliance with faculty anti-discrimination legislation.[40]

Urban Renewal

As 1961 opens, Madison's housing and development agencies are fighting each other as much as they're fighting substandard housing and blight. The Madison Housing Authority (MHA) is pushing hard for 150 units of public housing to be constructed for the residents being displaced from the Triangle, preferably in the Brittingham area, or the northeast corner of the Triangle itself, at the juncture of West Washington Avenue and Regent Street. The Madison Redevelopment Authority (MRA) is pushing back, claiming neither location is practical.[41]

Of the 301 Triangle households being relocated, fifty need subsidized elderly housing and forty-five need low-income housing; another forty-five eligible families are living in MHA's converted tar paper and wood barracks at Truax Field, which need to be torn down. But ever since the decisive defeat of a public housing referendum in 1950, the subject has seemingly been off-limits—until now.[42]

A survey by the Madison Neighborhood Centers in late 1960 reveals 130 Triangle residents over age sixty and 370 under twenty-one. Thirty-five units are occupied by UW students and sixteen by Air Force families—fifteen of them black. There are sixty-four welfare cases, including nineteen recipients over sixty years old. There are thirty-nine families with at least six members, some with as many as fifteen. There are more non–English speakers living in the Triangle than in any other neighborhood in the city.[43]

In late January, the council approves the MRA's proposed land use and zoning for the Brittingham project—150 units in buildings of up to three stories. The development criteria assure that the units will be market rate, providing no help to low-income Triangle residents.[44]

At a joint MHA/MRA meeting on February 2, the Madison Neighborhood Center's Chester Zmudzinski blasts them both. "There seems to be little or no coordination among the city agencies that should be responsible," he says. Reminding the authorities that the city was acquiring the land "at the expense of the people in the Triangle," Zmudzinski warns, "If you don't build some public housing, you will see the last of redevelopment in this community—your public relations will be so bad."[45]

"What the devil are we going to do with the people of the Triangle while we're clearing it?" asks MRA commissioner Joseph Roberts. New city planning director Kenneth K. Clark replies it would take two years to develop public housing on the Triangle, making it impossible to provide public housing there for residents being displaced.

"The question was raised," the meeting minutes relate, "as to what would happen to the people within the Project in the interim." No answer is recorded. The Brittingham project goes on sale the next day, advertised through a generously illustrated brochure.[46]

Then MRA commissioner Alderman Rohr, already under fire for blocking Zachary Trotter's liquor license transfer, mixes up the MRA with race and religion.

On April 3, he appears without notice or invitation at a board meeting of the South Shore Methodist Church, 610 W. Olin Ave., to ask the board "to reconsider its decision to sell" the building to the Second Baptist Congregation, a black church. It won't. The South Shore Methodists are merging with the Italian Methodists; while their new building on West Badger Road is under construction, the two will occupy the Italian Methodist Church at 103 S. Lake St.—among the Triangle buildings to be razed by Rohr's MRA.[47]

When Rohr's action becomes public ten days later, local NAACP chair Odell Taliaferro calls for his ouster for the good of the agency. The MRA "soon will face the responsibility of relocating many colored families," notes Taliaferro, himself a Triangle resident at 11 S. Murray St., and "if [Rohr] were to resign these people would more willingly deal with MRA, thereby insuring more rapid completion of the project." Rohr ignores him. Two weeks later, the NAACP chapter itself calls for Rohr's removal; Reynolds meets with Rohr but takes no action, other than urging the NAACP to "turn the other cheek" and "be forgiving." Reynolds denies that Rohr's support in the recent election has any bearing on this matter. In June, the First Unitarian Society makes the same request as the NAACP, for the same reason and with the same result.[48]

On May 4, the MRA accepts two negotiated bids: $150,000 from the First Development Corp. of Milwaukee for Sampson Plaza—twelve three-story brick and glass buildings on stilts around a sixty-foot swimming pool and central mall opening onto Brittingham Park, named after the company president—and $12,000 from the Marshall Dairy Laboratory for a small commercial parcel on Proudfit Street.[49]

Second Ward alderman Franklin Hall protests and vows to force the MRA to reconsider public housing on the site. If Triangle residents are not relocated in the immediate vicinity, he says, "you'll destroy the neighborhood unit that's down there." MRA chair Albert McGinnis reiterates the authority's long-standing opposition to public housing on the site, pointing out that the Brittingham residents have all already been relocated and reopening the planning would delay the seven-year-old project for another six months.

The MHA tries Hall's approach again a few days later in a joint meeting with the MRA, but things don't go any better—especially after McGinnis says the MHA plan for 150 units of public housing would create a "ghetto" filled by residents who cause social and civic problems and rely heavily on social workers. The MHA chair, attorney Roland Day (Wisconsin Supreme Court Justice 1974–1995; Chief Justice 1995–1996), and executive director Robert Callsen bristle at this contention. Press accounts call the meeting a "two-hour battle of words" filled with "sharp argument" and "considerable stone-throwing."[50]

The Madison Neighborhood Center's Zmudzinski, as chair of the Local Committee on Urban Renewal, pleads with the MRA to take "the human aspect" of the project as seriously as the "physical and economical aspects," and warns that the committee will oppose selling the Brittingham land for private development unless something is done for the Triangle residents.

Mayor Reynolds, a former member of Zmudzinski's Neighborhood Centers board of directors, offers his solution—city subsidies of low-income persons relocating into private housing. But he does not pursue or fund such a program.

Later that week, a meeting between MRA director Roger Rupnow and the Madison NAACP also deteriorates into acrimony and accusation. Taliaferro claims Rupnow said increasing the tax base is more important than taking care of the residents, and warns of a possible lawsuit; Rupnow flatly denies saying or implying anything like that, and maintains that the MRA is doing far more to relocate residents than federal law requires. "There is probably no authority in the country that is doing as much as we are for these families," he asserts.[51]

The MHA is not impressed, and repeats its request that the council reject the Brittingham bids for private market-rate apartments and prepare a new plan calling for public housing. But on Tuesday, May 23, the MHA is soundly beaten and roundly rebuked as the council's Committee of the Whole votes, 17–5, to reject its plea for public housing and accept the bids from First Development and Marshall Dairy.[52]

"The housing authority would serve their people better by proceeding in an orderly fashion," Mayor Reynolds remarks. MRA chair McGinnis says the MHA had "ample opportunity" to request public housing, and charges the agency with engaging in "delaying tactics." Alderman Bert Hutchison accuses the MHA of "harassment" of the MRA.

But Zmudzinski supports the MHA's play, again telling the council that the city's failure to provide adequate housing for those displaced from the Triangle will mean the end of the city's urban renewal program. "We are not without influence in this community," he says. "If we can't relocate these people you will have the greatest fiasco you have ever seen. Where's the coordination in this program? There is none. There is no leadership."

Zmudzinski accuses the authority of showing "tremendous hostility" toward Triangle residents, though his wife, Florence, remains an MRA social worker. And Alderman Hall, whose ward includes the long-standing black community in the Old Market Place area, says public housing is needed because blacks and other minorities in the Triangle "are not welcome in many areas in our city."

The next day, a *Capital Times* editorial mourns the outcome of the committee vote:

It is almost unbelievable that the Madison city government should be as indifferent to the plight of displaced persons in the Triangle area as was indicated Tuesday night. What, one wonders, do these city officials intend to do with the people made homeless? Do they think that people in these income classifications and minority groups can find homes easily around this city?[53]

Mayor Reynolds, whose permanent (if not full-time) residence is in the integrated Old Market Place area on East Mifflin Street, has had enough. On Thursday, May 25, he calls in the four authority principals—the MRA's McGinnis and Rupnow, and the MHA's Day and Callsen—plus Zmudzinski and hammers out a deal for sixty units of public housing for the elderly within the Triangle area and one hundred units of public housing at sites to be determined, all built as soon as possible. The MHA will later propose public housing to be built on the Triangle, in South Madison, at Webb and Rethke Avenues, and adjacent to the MHA's Truax Park apartments. But the agency drops its plans for twenty units on Aberg Avenue—in alderman Leonard Porter's ward—due to neighborhood and aldemanic opposition.[54]

On Thursday night, agreement notwithstanding, Zmudzinski continues to challenge Rupnow at the council meeting. Zmudzinski calls the MRA's 1960 housing survey "obsolete"; Rupnow insists figures on availability of units "are realistic and that we could relocate the people from the Triangle in housing at rentals they could afford to pay without recourse to public housing."[55]

The *Wisconsin State Journal* is not sanguine about Rupnow's assurances, editorially blasting him for his "subtle evasions [which] indicate either a lack of wisdom or of honesty in basic planning."[56]

Once the dueling critiques have ended, the council unanimously approves the Brittingham project as the MRA proposed. The MRA approves preliminary project plans in late September, with construction expected to start next spring.[57] The council endorses the agreement for 160 public housing units, 17–2, in late July.[58]

On May 29, the MHA makes a major decision—it administratively converts its 112 units of permanent housing off Wright Street and the 135 units in the converted Truax barracks from veterans housing to low-income housing. Adopting the federal income standards will force the eviction of sixty-five families, opening the units for Triangle families by September. By that time, the MRA expects to start land acquisition of the Triangle, after the preliminary approval by the Urban Renewal Administration of $5.9 million in loans and grants in late June.[59]

Base commander Colonel Olin E. Gilbert requests that the agency reconsider its policy regarding veterans housing, but MHA director Callsen vows to continue the policy "of taking care of our own Madison in need of public housing before considering military personnel."[60]

Odell Taliaferro still has the Triangle on his mind. Despite federal approval of a full clearance project, he continues to denounce the project as a "subterfuge" to move low-income residents out of a "choice geographical location."[61]

"This we believe to be morally wrong," he writes Mayor Reynolds and the council in late July, "since no housing shortage exists for the affluent class and many of the [present residents] have pioneered the settlement of this area, have wrestled it from Monona Bay."

Taliaferro renews his attack before the council on August 24, saying the redevelopment's "sole purpose is the expropriation of a choicely located area which will be made available to the wealthy." But with Zmudzinski mollified by the public housing commitment, the stiffest opposition now comes from Madison Gas & Electric, which fights the MRA's requirement that it put utilities underground. Over its strenuous objection, the council approves the Triangle plans on August 24, 19–1.[62]

In mid-September, the MRA approves a land acquisition policy of paying the higher of two appraisals, and sets purchase offers for 121 Triangle parcels. It quickly buys its first property in the Triangle—an income property at 120 S. Lake St., owned by former Greenbush resident Peter Vitale, for $13,000. The federal government has approved the purchase price for sixty-six other parcels, so MRA acquisition will now start in earnest.[63]

But by then, Rupnow has realized that the warnings from Zmudzinski, Taliaferro, Hall, and others were valid. At a September luncheon, he tells the Madison Board of Realtors that MRA officials "have been amazed" at how many times realtors have told them certain housing was off-limits to blacks. Rupnow asks the realtors to show houses to African Americans in nontraditional areas, but the Board of Realtors president says that's not likely to happen.

"No matter what our moral convictions are," Realtors president Vern Halle says, "when a colored person purchases a house next door, it's going to have economic ramifications." He insists that he personally opposes the unofficial policy of realtors alerting neighbors about the possibility of a black person moving in next door, but says the board has no official policy on the widespread practice.[64]

In early November, the MRA hears firsthand how that practice affects Triangle residents when Taliaferro's sister, jazz singer Dimetra Shivers, and her husband, Stanley, 113 S. Park St., convey a series of "bitter complaints," in person and in writing, about recalcitrant realtors and uncooperative redevelopment staff. "No realtor salesman would show us property on the east side of Madison," Mr. Shivers writes on November 30. He says one realtor made an appointment, then "contacted the owner of the home telling him not to sell to my son because he was Colored."[65]

At that same meeting, the authority learns that "there had been some police problems in respect to the selling of liquor after hours in the basement of the house" at 120 S. Lake St., and that tenant Charles Collins "had been very uncooperative in respect to seeking other quarters"; it promptly moves for eviction.[66]

At Mayor Reynolds's request and the council's direction, the MRA reluctantly agrees to assume responsibility for relocating Triangle residents. On December 1, Florence Zmudzinski—Chester's wife—becomes its first relocation supervisor.[67]

In the year's final days, the MRA and MHA take another stab at better coordination. They each unanimously endorse Mayor Reynolds's plan for a joint housing and redevelopment authority, headed by Rupnow, to provide the MHA the technical support it needs to administer its new 160-unit public housing program. MHA executive director Robert Callsen would become director of housing management, and Rupnow's assistant, Eugene Gangstad, would become director of urban renewal. Although personnel would be better coordinated, each board would continue setting policy independently. Sol Levin, an expert in federal housing and redevelopment regulations, turns down a better-paying job with the Milwaukee planning department to become deputy director under the new management, which the city expects to formally create in early 1962. At least, that's the plan. But there may be some internal tensions, as the mayor appoints Ald. Porter, an open foe of public housing, to the MHA board.[68]

Trotter's Travails, Continued

As the year opens, Zachary Trotter still hasn't accepted the MRA's check for his Tuxedo Café and still refuses to pay the $200 monthly rent. MRA director Rupnow says it would be unfair to allow him to stay when Licari's Spot Tavern at 767 W. Washington Ave., the only other structure remaining in the Brittingham project area, has been paying rent. So on February 1, the MRA gives Trotter a three-day notice to either pay the rent or vacate the premises. Trotter's attorney, Maurice Pasch, challenges the notice, calls the rent "ridiculous, unfair, and outrageous," and rebukes Rupnow and the MRA for not helping Trotter find a new location. "You sat on your hands," Pasch says.[69]

In March, Trotter makes an offer for two lots at 1717–1719 Beld St., with plans to build a bar and grill with two apartments above. But the property would need to be rezoned from residential to commercial (as already happened with the property across the street). With Chester Zmudzinski leading the opposition, and new mayor Henry Reynolds vowing a veto if it's approved, the Plan Commission recommends against the rezoning in late April. Reynolds, presiding at his first Plan Commission meeting, cuts the public hearing short when the comments become racially tinged.[70]

A few days later, neighborhood opposition doesn't matter much as Ald. Rohr supports and the council approves Jeanne Licari's request to transfer her license for the Spot Tavern to 1405 Emil St., near the city's southern border. About forty neighborhood residents protest in vain that the site is too near the Silver Springs School and that Emil Street is a gravel road without sidewalks.[71]

Only thirty-five Beld Street neighbors come to the next council meeting to oppose Trotter's transfer, but they're more successful. Zmudzinski, whose wife, Florence, is still an MRA social worker, again leads the successful fight against the transfer, which would have allowed the MRA to proceed with the Brittingham redevelopment. He acknowledges Trotter's predicament but says it should not be solved "at a sacrifice of this neighborhood by transferring in the problems that existed in the other neighborhood." He does not elaborate on how Trotter and his customers would constitute "problems."[72]

Trotter gets one piece of good news in late May—Judge Norris Maloney finds there is "no conventional landlord-tenant arrangement" between him and the MRA, and dismisses the MRA's suit to evict him for nonpayment of rent.[73]

Three days later, on Ald. Rohr's motion, the MRA votes to start a new proceeding for immediate eviction. The Trotters "have taken advantage of every legal technicality they can," MRA chair Albert McGinnis complains. In early June, Judge Horace Wilkie rules in favor of the MRA, ordering the Trotters to vacate by August 1. Pasch, who has just been appointed to the UW Board of Regents, describes it as "a sordid story that has left a black mark on the city of Madison."[74]

But on June 20, Trotter has a breakthrough—he finds a site that Reynolds calls "a good location" at 1616 Beld St. It's properly zoned for a tavern, so he'll only need the council to approve the license transfer. In early July, he gets even better news—Ald. Rohr, who rallied neighborhood opposition to kill the 1960 transfer, says he will not oppose this one. But Rohr still slams Trotter for insisting on "implausible sites" and expresses dismay that Trotter "insists on relocating in our wards.[75]

The third time proves the charm. Despite opposition from more than 150 property owners and residents in the area, the council, meeting as the Committee of the Whole, approves the transfer on July 11, 14–3. Ald. Rohr, under fire from the NAACP and the Unitarians, is absent.[76]

But the fireworks aren't over. Two nights later, with Rohr again absent, the council adopts the report of the Committee of the Whole without debate or separation of the Trotter matter; when neighbors who had come to protest the transfer realize this, they break out in angry shouts and curses, accusing the council of collusion and corruption. Reynolds tries in vain to gavel the chamber to order as more than a dozen men and women disrupt the proceedings for more than five minutes.[77]

Reynolds promptly signs the transfer, but Trotter is still facing imminent eviction on August 1, with almost no time to ready his property for the move. Although Judge Wilkie criticizes the MRA for using his eviction order to force a settlement of the rent issue, he does not change the August 1 deadline.[78]

Out of legal options and out of time, Trotter finally agrees to pay the full back rent, and the MRA agrees to let him stay until December 1.[79]

On September 29, more than fifteen months after Trotter submitted his first transfer request, the city issues him a building permit for a $25,000 two-story building at 1616 Beld St. [Eugene Parks's Mr. P's Place].[80]

Race for Mayor

The most significant mayoral campaign of the decade almost didn't happen.

As the head of the Kennedy for President Club during the successful Wisconsin primary campaign, and chair of the state delegation to the national convention, Mayor Ivan Nestingen was presumed to be in line for a job in the new administration. But when two months pass after the election without any word from Kennedy's headquarters in Hyannis Port, Nestingen turns to his mayoral reelection campaign.[81]

It looks like a cakewalk. The thirty-nine-year-old attorney was first elected in a special election in 1956—at thirty-four, the city's youngest mayor—then elected to a full two-year term in 1957 by a 3–1 margin; in 1959, he was reelected without opposition. He has no declared opposition when he starts circulating nomination papers on January 13.[82]

But two weeks later, just six days before the filing deadline, still unopposed, an appointment as Kennedy's Undersecretary of Health, Education and Welfare comes, and Nestingen goes.[83]

The council names retiring city attorney Harold Hanson as acting mayor, and the city settles in for a pitched battle between two highly qualified candidates who are former council colleagues with very different agendas: Henry E. Reynolds, fifty-five, former alderman (1947–1954) and council president, founding vice chair of the anti–Monona Terrace Citizens' Realistic Auditorium Association, and president of his family's trucking company, and Robert "Bob" Nuckles, forty-three, Nestingen's administrative assistant, also a former alderman (1953–1958). Reynolds, on the council when Madison had a city manager and seven aldermen, is also a director of Madison General Hospital and the Madison Bus Company; before joining Nestingen, Nuckles was an engineer with Oscar Mayer & Co. and Ray-O-Vac.[84]

Although Reynolds resigns from the CRAA in early February, Monona Terrace is clearly the campaign's dominant issue. But it's not the only one on which the candidates differ. Reynolds calls the Monona Causeway a priority; Nuckles does not. Nuckles would continue the city's aggressive annexation policy; Reynolds would not. And Reynolds vows explicitly to curtail the considerable City Hall influence of the liberal, pro-Terrace *Capital Times*. They do agree on some things—both would build a new central library and an east side hospital.[85]

An issue arises for the first time in a Madison mayoral election—a candidate's residence. The house at 616 E. Mifflin St. has been Henry Reynolds's family home since his widowed grandmother, Anna Gault Reynolds, moved there with her nine children in 1873 and started a livery stable and hauling firm in 1888, with the backyard serving as the barnyard and truck storage. Reynolds himself was born in a small house in the back in 1906, moving into the main house in 1913. Reynolds's father, Edward, who was twice elected alderman without opposition, bought his first horse and wagon at age sixteen. Henry Reynolds assumed control of the Reynolds Transfer and Storage Co. upon his father's death in 1929. He also assumed control of a second house and two hundred acres on the north shore of Lake Mendota in the town of Westport, which his father had purchased in 1910, and where he had summered every year as a child. Reynolds acknowledges he "lived at the cottage a good deal of the time," but insists his legal city residence is in fact his primary home. The *Capital Times* bestows the sobriquet "Squire of Westport" on Reynolds, and Nuckles hits the issue hard, but they can't overcome Reynolds's broad and deep community ties and solid reputation, especially with Nuckles being outspent $8,754 to $6,825.[86]

On election day, April 4, Reynolds wins by large margins on the high-turnout west side, and Nuckles carries the less active east side. Ald. Rohr, a fellow Terrace opponent, supports Reynolds vigorously, and turns out high numbers on the south side, helping push Reynolds to a 7 percent win, 20,491–17,865. In May, Nuckles returns to Oscar Mayer & Co. as a project engineer in the general machine development department.[87]

The *Wisconsin State Journal* editorially exults, while the *Capital Times* bemoans the election's implications for Monona Terrace.[88]

Taking office on April 18, Reynolds lists eight "immediate goals" for the city, including building an auditorium/civic center, constructing a new central library, improving streets and covering all open storm water ditches, and advancing the Monona Causeway. Among the long-range issues: improving the municipal airport and providing housing for "people in the low-income groups" displaced by urban renewal. "A policy which takes to heart the welfare of these people must be established," he tells the council. Reynolds also resigns from the board of the bus company, as he did when he served on the council.[89]

Reynolds, who decides to do without the one administrative assistant he's entitled to, has a rocky start in his relations with the council. Although he successfully stacks the Auditorium Committee with anti–Monona Terrace appointees, his attempt to appoint the three male losing aldermanic candidates to various boards and commissions while not appointing any of the three unsuccessful female candidates doesn't go over so well, and he's forced to withdraw them.[90]

Reynolds's relationship with the council worsens with his successful June veto of a "selfish" aldermanic pay raise from $100 to $150 a month. "Any other action the City Council may take during my term of office will not be as disappointing to me," he says in his veto message.[91]

A month later, the council responds with a stinging rebuke, rejecting Reynolds's appointment of Edwin S. Conrad—a former law professor at Syracuse University and current lecturer at the UW with a private practice—as city attorney; the council favors current assistant city attorney Henry Buslee, who finished first on the civil service exam thanks to veterans' preference points. "You are making a bad mistake in not working toward cooperation with the council," Ald. Rohr warns Reynolds during council debate.[92]

Reynolds doesn't take Rohr's advice, and nominates Conrad again in August; the council again rejects him. Eventually, Reynolds surrenders and appoints acting city attorney Alton S. Heassler, who fell to fourth because he lacked veterans' points. Quickly confirmed, Heassler hires a new assistant city attorney—Edwin S. Conrad (Madison Alderman, 1981–1982).[93]

Miscellanea

January 10—The council rejects, 20–1, an ordinance amendment that would allow consumption of alcohol in a bowling alley, so league and tournament bowlers could drink while bowling.[94]

April 4—The spring election brings good news for the city library system: approval by better than 2–1 of a $2.2 million bond issue for a new central library, at an as-yet-unspecified site. But the three women seeking election to the Common Council receive disappointing results. Frances (Mrs. Willard) Hurst, former president of the League of Women Voters, loses to attorney and UW–Extension associate professor William Bradford Smith; Phyllis Smolen, former executive director of Fellowship House, fails to unseat incumbent Thomas Stavrum; and Gertrude Casey Fuelleman, a dormitory operator and housemother, loses to Edward A. Wiegner, a UW senior and part-time accountant.[95]

April 8—The Newspaper Guild names Velma (Mrs. Harry) Hamilton, UW MA '48 and Phi Beta Kappa graduate of Beloit College, Citizen of the Year. Hamilton, who in 1950 became the first African American teacher (of English) at Madison Vocational, Technical, and Adult Schools, has served six years on the Governor's Commission on Human Rights and is currently in her second three-year term on the Wisconsin Committee for Children and Youth. She is the first black woman to receive this honor.[96]

April 18—Tenth Ward (University Heights) alderwoman Ethel L. Brown, the first and only woman yet elected to the Madison Common Council, is elected its president, 12–10, over alderman Leonard Foust, the candidate of the pro–Monona Terrace faction.[97]

May 5—Twelve-year-old David Lease, of 905 Fairmont Ave., wins the city marbles championship, held at the Camp Randall Memorial practice fieldhouse.[98]

August 30—Madison civil defense director Richard C. Wilson tells area builders that Madison is a likely target in case of nuclear war because it "is surrounded by targets," especially Truax Air Field. He suggests every homeowner build a fallout shelter in the southwest corner of their basement, and stock it for the two weeks or so it will take for radiation to drop to a safe level. City assessor Norman Poorman and building inspector Raymond F. Burt say they will waive assessments and building permit fees for shelters that meet federal standards, but not building permits, or the need to follow zoning regulations. Civil defense officials estimate about five thousand area homes have some sort of fallout shelter, ranging from improvised shelters in cisterns to full facilities. In December, thirty-seven faculty and civic leaders will issue a statement bemoaning the fallout shelter program as a "tragic misdirection of our thinking and energies and a dreadful distortion of our Western values and morality."[99]

September 28—Flamboyant entertainer Liberace has dinner and a nap at the modest home of his father and stepmother, Salvatore "Sam" and Zona Liberace, 1106 E. Johnson St., before his well-reviewed, near-capacity show at the Orpheum Theater. Sam and Zona are former musicians with the Madison Civic Orchestra, on French horn and cello, respectively.[100]

October 24—A troop train pulls out of the Milwaukee Road depot, taking Madison and area men in the Thirty-Second Infantry Division of the Army National Guard to Ft. Lewis, Washington, and into at least a full year of active military duty, due to the Berlin crisis.[101]

October 25—City health commissioner Charles Kincaid reports that cases of venereal disease are increasing rapidly, now up to about one a day. Patients who need

This life-size nativity scene is placed at the State Street entrance of the Capitol in late November by the Madison Chamber of Commerce, and complemented each weeknight throughout the holiday season by carolers from area churches.[102] WHI IMAGE ID 137720, PHOTO BY RICHARD VESEY

hospitalization may be out of luck—the combined city and county bed count of 408 is only a little more than half the current need.[103]

October 27—The *Wisconsin State Journal* announces it will reject certain movie advertising that "a large number of our readers find salacious and prurient."[104]

October 31—Someone—probably teenagers—spray paints swastikas and the word *Jew* on the walls and window of Selig's Meats, a kosher delicatessen at 301 S. Mills St., owned by Selig Iwanter, the only survivor of a family wiped out by the Nazis in Vilna, Lithuania.[105]

November 8—The city begins its annual fall spraying of DDT—which is cheaper and less damaging to car finishes than the alternative, methoxychlor—to combat Dutch elm disease. Parks superintendent James Marshall acknowledges that DDT is more toxic to birds, but says most have left the area by this time of year.[106]

December 13—Nearly two hundred freezing firemen battle a five-alarm blaze that rages out of control for six hours in subzero cold on the north side of the 400 block of State Street, doing about $500,000 in damage. The 1.5 million gallons of water firefighters use in their daylong efforts freezes into such a thick sheet of ice that city workers need almost a ton of calcium chloride salt to make the street passable. Fire inspectors blame the blaze on faulty wiring strained by two space heaters left on overnight. Victor Music and the Tellus Mater gift shop are among the sixteen businesses damaged or destroyed.[107]

UW

COMMENCEMENT, JUNE 5
- ▸ Baccalaureate: 1,600
- ▸ Master's/PhD: 700[108]
- ▸ JD/MD: 165

FALL ENROLLMENT
- ▸ Total students: 20,410[109]

HOMECOMING
- ▸ Show: Johnny Mathis
- ▸ Dance: Billy Lang Orchestra, Paul Winter Sextet[110]

NEW BUILDINGS OF NOTE
- ▸ Lowell Hall, 610 Langdon St.[111]

Dylan in Madison

Bob Dylan, nineteen, his direction still unknown, blows into town in early January and falls in with the leftist/folkie/theater crowd. He's got the number for Socialist Club president and banjoist Ron "Ronny" Radosh, but his apartment at 444 Hawthorne Ct. is too small for Dylan to stay there. So Radosh sends him over to freshman Danny Kalb, an exceptional young folk and blues guitarist, who puts Dylan up in his Huntington Court rooming house for a day or two until housemother "Ma" Peterson kicks him out. That night, Kalb takes Dylan to a party, where two couples—Fred Underhill and poet Ann Lauterbach (Woodrow Wilson, Guggenheim, and MacArthur Fellowships recipient), whose Greenwich Village music teacher had been Pete Seeger; and actor Jennifer Warren (Theater World Award winner, 1972; Short Documentary Academy Award winner, 1989), who was also a student of Seeger's (as was graduate student Radosh), and director Fritz DeBoer—take him under their collective wing and back to their flat at 430 W. Johnson St., where Dylan crashes for about a week.

THE PAD
ESPRESSO COFFEE HOUSE
527 STATE

Exotic Coffees and Teas

Spontaneous Entertainment
FEATURING MADISON'S MOST FAMOUS
SUBMARINE SANDWICH
(Free Delivery)

OPEN 8 P.M. TIL ? NITELY—SUNDAYS OPEN 4:30 - ?

The hipster's hangout— a dark and dank hole-in-the-wall where Bob Dylan accompanies Danny Kalb, and they pass the hat.
DAILY CARDINAL

"I've been broke and cold," he writes friends back in Minneapolis, and was lucky to meet a "bunch of New York people" in Madison.

Dylan spins tales of a made-up past, predicts his wondrous future, but mainly talks about and plays a lot of Woody Guthrie. His closest relationship is with Kalb, eighteen, who teaches him Dave Van Ronk's version of "Poor Lazarus" in the Johnson Street kitchen and takes him to Marshall Brickman and Eric Weissberg's place at 1028 Clymer St., the local stop on the folk music underground railroad. For a few nights at the beatnik coffeehouse the Pad, Dylan blows harmonica while Kalb sits atop the old upright piano, playing the blues, and they collect a few coins. Someone records the two at a party, but no one's really knocked out by Dylan's incessant performing (or its quality). Socialist Club stalwart Fred Ciporen chides him at a party one night for playing, unbidden, while people in his small and crowded apartment just want to talk politics and hang out. After Dylan's been in town about ten days, the charismatic and complex Underhill offers him a spot as a relief driver in a car headed for New York. It's just what Dylan's been waiting for. Arriving uptown on a brutally cold January 24, they hop the subway to Greenwich Village, where Dylan is soon onstage at the Café Wha?

Dylan returns to Madison as he's turning twenty in May, taking over Warren's room on West Johnson Street—*taking* being the operative word—for another freeloading week or two. Then he spends a few more days at Kalb's pad, where he meets the soon-to-be-imprisoned Freedom Rider Paul Breines. By now, Dylan's aura is starting to grow; he's gigged around the Village and spent time with the hospitalized Guthrie (and written "Song to Woody," which he'll record in November for his debut album). Young women are calling and coming on to him when he hangs out behind the Union—he even gets in some time on the piano at Grove's Women's Co-op—and kids are calling him King of the Folkies. He isn't, not yet, but when he plays Guthrie's "New York Town" with Radosh at the Pad, or sings with Kalb and the crowd on a Mifflin Street balcony, some see signs of the transcendent artist soon to emerge.

And then he's gone, back to New York and his destiny—taking Underhill's guitar case with him.[113]

Campus Calendar

February 8–16—The Wisconsin Student Association's second symposium series, "Ethics in Our Time," features CBS correspondent and commentator Edward Sevareid, author Ayn Rand, and philosopher/educator Sidney Hook.[114]

February 15—Famed choreographer Agnes de Mille tells a small Union Theater audience that the "excessive demands" of theatrical unions are "pricing our best audiences out of the theater."[115]

March 2—The *Daily Cardinal* publishes a front-page story exploring the attitudes of in-state students towards out-of-staters. "The reason why many New Yorkers, who seem to be mostly Jewish and Negroes, come here is that the school has a liberal attitude," says a Racine senior quoted in the paper, who cites the Socialist Club as an example of the fact that "they get away with things here they couldn't get away with anywhere else."[116]

April 17—Five days after Soviet cosmonaut Yuri Gagarin becomes the first human to travel into space and the first to orbit the globe, rocket scientist Wernher von Braun cancels his April 20 campus appearance to stay at work at the George C. Marshall flight center in Alabama.[117]

April 21—Several hundred fraternity men and other students identified as "Goldwater Conservatives" engage in Madison's first disruptive protest of the decade, breaking up a Socialist Club Union Theater rally protesting American involvement in the failed Bay of Pigs invasion of Cuba. The disrupters, who also hang an effigy of Cuban president Fidel Castro from a tree at the corner of Langdon and Park Streets, create a scene of complete chaos for nearly an hour by shouting, chanting, and loudly heckling and booing the club's speakers until former WSA president Ed Garvey restores order. At Dean of Students LeRoy Luberg's suggestion, Garvey turns the rally into an impromptu debate pitting Cuban émigré Luis Valdes against the Socialist Club's Radosh, among others. It was the threat of such disruption that caused Luberg, a former recruitment officer for the CIA, to move the rally into the theater and then order that the anti-Castro demonstrators be admitted into the Socialist Club event. Luberg later describes the event as being conducted with "dignity and care," and having a good expression of opinion.[118]

April 30—The American Legion district conference formally protests the May 4 appearance by leftist author Max Lerner, and calls for a "patriotic" speaker to be scheduled in rebuttal.[119]

COMMITTED TO ACTION

"The Wisconsin student is far from silent on the issues that dominate our time. Above all things, it is encouraging to note that he is concerned with the manifestations of his world. Although he may often trouble and bewilder his elders, the Wisconsin student of 1961 is fully aware of the hazards of the future yet thrilled by its challenge and promise, and hopeful that he may have some role in shaping the America and the world of today and tomorrow."
—*Wisconsin Alumnus*, April 1961

Anti-Castro conservatives stage Madison's first disruptive protest of the decade on April 21 in the Union Theater. WHI IMAGE ID 137721, PHOTO BY RICHARD SRODA

May 7—Senior Dan Travanti goes home empty-handed from the Wisconsin Players awards banquet despite winning his customary raves as Brick in its production of *Cat on a Hot Tin Roof.* However, the Kenosha native does score two major postgrad academic opportunities: a one-year Woodrow Wilson fellowship and a three-year National Defense Education Act fellowship. He declines both to attend the Yale School of Drama and pursue an acting career.[120]

May 22—Sophomore Pat Richter (inductee, the College Football and the Wisconsin Athletic Halls of Fame) is an easy winner of the *Daily Cardinal* "Outstanding Athlete of the Year" contest. The Madison native, who letters in baseball, football, and basketball, continues his athletic heroics in the fall, as he sets or ties four Big Ten football records, is twice the national Player of the Week, and is a consensus first- or second-team All-American. Richter isn't the only homegrown Badger to make his mark—kicker Jim Bakken (four-time selectee, National Football League Pro Bowl) ties a Big Ten record with two field goals in one game (against Indiana). Unfortunately, another teammate, junior quarterback Ron Vander Kelen, is dropped from the team in June due to "scholastic deficiencies."[121]

June 2—Governor Gaylord Nelson names Madison attorney Maurice Pasch to the Board of Regents, succeeding former governor Oscar Rennebohm.[122]

June 5—President Conrad Elvehjem celebrates "our drive to use education as a tool for military defense" in his commencement address to about twenty-five hundred graduates and twelve thousand spectators.[123]

July 18—Harvard professor Henry A. Kissinger, special consultant to President Kennedy, discusses the difficulty in negotiating with Communists in a Great Hall talk on "American Policy and Disarmament."[124]

August 30—Ed Garvey, immediate past president of the Wisconsin Student Association, is elected president of the National Student Association (NSA) at a stormy ten-day NSA convention held on campus. Garvey, a sharp critic of the House Un-American Activities Committee who vows to continue the NSA's support for the Southern civil rights actions, was considered the moderate in a campaign against an alumnus of Oberlin College.[125]

September 14—The organizational meeting of the campus chapter of the liberal group Americans for Democratic Action is held.[126]

September 25—The thirty social fraternities pledge a total of 330 new members, led by Sigma Chi with twenty-six.[127]

October 6—Jazz pianist Oscar Peterson headlines the university's third annual jazz festival, which also features local trumpeter Doc DeHaven and another showing of *Jazz on a Summer Day*.[128]

October 16—The country's most beloved poet, eighty-seven-year-old Robert Frost, captivates a capacity crowd at the Union Theater with anecdote, observation, and poetry, especially his closing piece, "Birches."[129]

October 31—Madison attorney and broadcast personality William Dyke (mayor of Madison 1969–1973; 1976 vice-presidential nominee, American Independent Party; Iowa County Circuit Court Judge 1996–2016) tells the Young Republicans that General Edwin Walker, reprimanded in June for calling former president Harry Truman a communist sympathizer, and set to resign two days later, is a man of "unquestionable ability who dearly loves his country" and had no other way to expose this infiltration.[130]

November 26—Mayor Reynolds, other dignitaries, and a cheering crowd of more than two thousand are at the municipal airport to welcome the Wisconsin football team home after it ends a mediocre season with an upset victory over archrival Minnesota. Miss Madison, Ann Gibson, presents cocaptains Bakken and Don Shade with the keys to the city, and all the players and coaches are introduced. It's a far cry from campus sentiment on September 30, when three effigies of coach Milt Bruhn dangled from Langdon Street trees following a thumping loss to Michigan State.[131]

Panty Raid of the Year

It's just after midnight Sunday morning on October 8 and more than a thousand beer-and-hormone-soaked young men are out on State Street, celebrating the football team's victory over Indiana and delighting in a twenty-year-old German model in a tight blue dress playing toreador in the street. Suddenly a group of celebrants set up a ladder, which their leader ascends; he leads the crowd in cheers and college songs—until he suddenly shouts, "Let's go on a panty raid!"

The crowd becomes a mob and surges toward the new Lowell Hall; the horde chants "We want panties" as a group mounts the first-floor roof and breaks a window before being driven off by a broom-wielding janitor. They're similarly thwarted at Ann Emery Hall. The mob fills State and Langdon Streets, pushing cars and even rocking an unmarked police car; some toss stones and cups of beer at the lawmen. After a large firecracker breaks a squad car radiator, police bring out (but don't use) tear gas and fire hoses, and the crowd disperses. Police make five arrests for disorderly conduct—two students; two locals, ages eighteen and twenty-four; and a Truax Field airman. Charges against two are eventually dropped; three forfeit bail. Five students, not all of whom were arrested, are placed on disciplinary probation and/or suspended for the spring semester and ordered to apologize by letter to police chief Wilbur Emery. UW officials reaffirm a 1959 policy statement that any student in a mob, regardless of what he or she does, is fully responsible for all of the mob's actions and is subject to discipline.[132]

Campus Planning

Thanks to federal funds and financing, the campus building boom continues in 1961 with $14 million spent on construction, including the social sciences, chemistry, and Extension buildings. And there's a lot more to come, especially as the Southeast Dorm project gets under way—much to the dismay and anger of area property owners.[133]

The university moves quickly. The State Building Commission gives final state authority to build the first unit, at the corner of North Park and West Johnson Streets, on February 6; five days later, the regents authorize A. W. Peterson, vice president for business affairs, to start buying the necessary property, which he completes by mid-September.[134]

On May 12, the regents approve state architect Karel Yasko's studies for that first dorm, a two-tower, ten-floor home for 1,134 male and female students. Regent Ellis Jensen is not impressed and tells his colleagues he has "a number of serious questions about the entire project." At a regent meeting, he says it seems "to be a club instead of a dormitory for serious purposes," especially because the facilities "provide space for television viewing, the desirability of which I question. These young people are at the crossroads of life, where they will either learn to work or learn to loaf." He also opposes the proposed parking areas because, he says, "the use of automobiles is detrimental to the health of students." He suggests that eliminating elevator service for the first four floors "would be desirable, to provide the students with another good form of exercise." The rest of the regents reject his analysis and approve submitting the plans for financing by the federal Housing and Home Finance Agency, effectively ending serious opposition to the entire project. The new units are definitely needed; residence hall director Newell Smith has already announced that between six hundred and seven hundred out-of-state students will lose their dorm housing to meet statutory requirements for housing Wisconsin students.[135]

That same day, a new urban renewal battle begins quietly with the regents' unanimous adoption of a consultant's report recommending the university ask the city and the Madison Redevelopment Authority for political and technical support in creating a 436-acre General Neighborhood Renewal Program (GNRP), to guide development from

Wisconsin Avenue to Highland Avenue. The $16.5 million urban renewal program, anticipating both clearance and rehabilitation, would encompass 67 acres around the previously designated dorm expansion area, another 94 acres in a UW planning area, and 275 acres jointly planned by the university, city, and MRA. Mayor Reynolds calls the so-called "University City" project "very beneficial to the city" and says "the city should cooperate with the university in every way to make it possible." The council endorses the concept in late July, but not before campus-area alderman Edward A. Wiegner criticizes the university for disregarding the families being displaced and warns of political trouble "if relocation problems aren't met."[136]

While the university has had to make an urgent plea for rooms for men, the private sector is helping the women. Lowell Hall, a seven-story, $2.5 million luxury dorm for 298 UW women—the largest privately owned dormitory in the state—opens in June at 210 Langdon Street. Built by J. H. Findorff & Son, it's partially funded by the Teamsters' Union Central State Pension fund.[137]

On December 8, the regents approve in principle the North Lower Campus Development Plan (below), featuring an underground auditorium and high-rise guesthouse on the site of the Red Gym/Armory, underground parking, a large Memorial Plaza, two pedestrian skywalks over a one-way Langdon Street (which would be lowered), and a lakefront location for the Wisconsin Alumni Association. Some details may change, says Professor Kurt F. Wendt, dean of the College of Engineering and chair of the Campus Planning Committee, "but we don't plan to make any wholesale departure from the basic concepts we have established."[138]

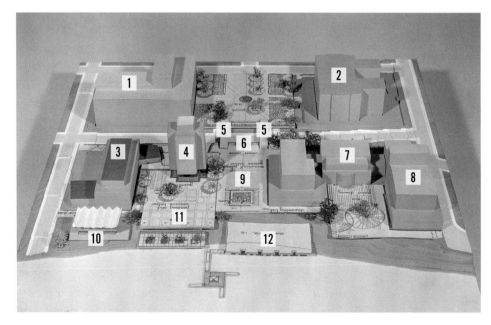

The North Lower Campus Development Plan, looking south from above Lake Mendota. (1) Memorial Library, (2) Historical Society, (3) Wisconsin [Pyle] Center, (4) Guest House (replacing the Red Gym/Armory), (5) pedestrian bridges, (6) submerged Langdon Street, (7) Memorial Union, (8) Union Theater, (9) Memorial Plaza, (10) Alumni House, (11) parking, (12) Sundeck.
UNIVERSITY OF WISCONSIN–MADISON ARCHIVES

Schools

GRADUATION, JUNE 16
- ▶ West: 478
- ▶ East: 449
- ▶ Central: 166[139]

FALL ENROLLMENT
- ▶ Public: 24,337[140]
- ▶ Catholic: 4,500[141]
- ▶ Lutheran: 271

NEW SCHOOLS AND MAJOR ADDITIONS
- ▶ Lake View Elementary, 1802 Tennyson Ln.
- ▶ Glenn W. Stephens Elementary, 120 S. Rosa Rd., named after the current board president
- ▶ West High School junior high addition and swimming pool, 30 Ash St.
- ▶ Hawthorne Elementary addition, 3344 Concord Ave., including its first proper library; a nine-by-twelve-foot closet previously served that function.[142]

Central Student Losses

The city has grown from fourteen to forty-four square miles since 1947. The impact of that peripheral growth on the pupil count in the central area (between the Yahara River and Randall Avenue and down to Haywood Drive) since then is stark:

CHANGE IN SCHOOL CENSUS, 1947–1961

	East	West	South	Central
Preschool	+4,483	+3,692	+419	−676
Kindergarten	+758	+846	+64	−83
Elementary	+3,766	+4,823	+282	−293
Junior High	+1,404	+1,950	+139	−88
Senior High	+580	+1,084	+84	−413
Total	+10,991	+12,395	+988	−1,552

If the trend continues, Superintendent Philip Falk says, there is a "remote possibility" that Central High will be closed.[143]

Growing Pain

The bill comes due for Madison's aggressive annexation policy on July 1 as the two primary schools from the former Blooming Grove area—Frank Allis at 4201 Buckeye Rd. and Glendale at 1400 Tompkins Dr.—become part of the Madison school system. This brings the total of Madison schools to twenty-seven and an immediate $413,125 hike in the school budget, just for the remainder of this year. It also adds $1.5 million to the city's bonded debt. And there are looming future obligations as well, including the need for speech therapy and counseling at both schools, and a gym and library for Glendale.[144]

Because the annexed areas had low valuation, Superintendent Philip Falk says, the city faces a stark choice: "Whether it will dilute the present school offering to the city's school children or increase the city school tax to provide for these annexed areas." The Board of Education opts for the latter option, asking the city to schedule a $9.3 million bond referendum for the April 1962 ballot (including $4.4 million for the annexed area alone), which it does.[145] But the board has its limits; when families living south of Highway 30 ask for a school bus to help their children avoid the hazardous intersection at Fair Oaks Avenue on their way to Hawthorne Elementary School, the board says no.[146]

School Days

January 27—The senior class of Wisconsin High School registers its opposition to the civil rights record of Daughters of the American Revolution by voting against participating in the organization's annual statewide citizenship contest.[147]

March 27–28—Police crack down on chronic student misbehavior, issuing forty-seven jaywalking and loitering tickets to students and adults from West High, and twenty-seven to East High students crossing East Washington Avenue against the light. West students have also been disrupting area merchants by shoplifting, loitering, roughhousing, and showing "lack of common courtesy." Police chief Emery isn't happy that the Regent/Allen area is one of only three areas (State and East Wilson Streets are the others) where officers walk a beat. "These children should not be such a problem to us that we need an officer there full time," he says.[148]

May 13—"Madison is blessed with a large number of intellectually gifted youngsters," director of the Department of Child Study and Service Carl H. Waller says, reporting that mental maturity tests of 1,536 Madison fifth graders show an average IQ of 113 and an achievement level well above the national average. In fact, in every area of study, Madison children who took the test in November 1960 scored higher on achievement tests than the national norms, often substantially.[149]

September—William "Willie" Taylor becomes Madison's first African American teacher, teaching physical education at Silver Springs school on the south side.[150]

October 16—The school board buys thirty-five acres of the Monona Golf Course from the Parks Department for $105,000, for the new, as-yet-unnamed Twenty-Second Ward high school. Parks will use the funds to buy land beyond the East Beltline for a future golf course.[151]

November 6—The school board places two seventeen-year-olds on probation for the school year after they brought stolen whiskey to school to sell to their classmates. The five students who bought it are also put on probation until the principal takes them off.[152]

Law and Disorder

State Street's not quite the asphalt jungle this summer, but it's not a peaceful place, either, with young university students and teenage townies engaging in obnoxious and offensive loitering and incessant cruising, often at high speeds. And with 178 policemen for a city of over forty square miles—the same size force it had five years ago, when the city was about twenty-eight square miles—police chief Wilbur Emery says he doesn't have the manpower to handle it, especially with thirty-two officers whose duties keep them at headquarters, unavailable for patrol. One beat cop walks State Street from 3 p.m. to 11 p.m., with two covering State Street and the Square for the next eight hours. In August, the public outcry is so great that Mayor Reynolds tells Emery to blanket the downtown, bringing peace to the streets—at least for a while.[153]

October 31—Halloween brings a night of malicious mischief as police respond to more than a dozen complaints of vandalism, property destruction, and hooliganism. At the McDonald's drive-in, 3317 University Ave., more than two hundred youngsters throw firecrackers, eggs, and vegetables at cars—even the squad cars sent to the scene. The restaurant closes at the cops' request but reopens an hour later; when it does, the barrage resumes, and it continues until police return and threaten the troublemakers with arrest.[154]

November 9—The council outlaws the use or possession of a slingshot, with the exception of homemade units used under adult supervision. It also bans minors from carrying pistols, and anyone under eighteen from buying or carrying other firearms or ammunition.[155]

November 10—Chief Emery suspends Lieutenant Donald Mickelson for five days for directing that a false report be filed after he released (without charges) three Democratic assemblymen from Milwaukee who were arrested for throwing beer cans from the eleventh floor of the Belmont Hotel at about two in the morning. Emery maintains that the reports are confidential and refuses to release them.[156]

December 26—Two of the three Chicago-area men awaiting a February trial for killing a Sauk County patrolman and seriously wounding the Lake Delton police chief escape from their cell at the Dane County jail, jump two jailers—knocking one unconscious and taking his keys—and make it to an outer courtyard on the sixth floor of the City-County Building before they are apprehended by Madison police officer August Pieper.[157]

Planning and Development

GENERAL STATISTICS

- ▸ Population: 136,432[158]
- ▸ Area: 40.85 square miles (end-of-year total)[159]

Madison's economy continues to thrive in 1961. The unemployment rate in January is 3.6 percent, half the state's level; at $6,530, the average household income is above the national average. Home ownership is at 52 percent, up from barely half in 1950. Factories employ about 6,500 production workers (about the same number, but a far lower percentage of Madison's workforce than were employed just prior to the Great Depression). In fall, the city's value hits $486 million, up $29 million from a year prior, with another $20 million in city-shaping construction under way in the Hilldale/Hill Farms area. But the accelerating pace of suburbanization poses challenges for downtown; in May, the Board of Review slashes property assessments on the Capitol Square by a quarter-million dollars.[160]

In the late summer of 1961, Monona Avenue [Martin Luther King Jr. Blvd.] ends at Olin Terrace and the train tracks, and the Monona Terrace site is an unpaved waterfront parking lot. The Park Hotel, across from the Capitol at the corner of South Carroll and West Main Streets, has been razed and gutted, to be replaced by a motor hotel with underground parking.[161] COURTESY OF CAPITAL NEWSPAPERS ARCHIVES, PHOTO BY JOHN NEWHOUSE

Business Wire

January 4—The Parks Commission names a new twenty-seven-acre park on Lake Mendota after the current parks superintendent, James G. Marshall, who has headed the parks department since 1937.[162]

January 6—Walter A. Frautschi, president of the Democrat Printing Co., announces appointments of sons John Jones Frautschi and W. Jerome Frautschi as vice presidents.[163]

March 1—Frederick J. Mohs Jr. purchases the Kennedy Manor apartment building at 1 Langdon St.[164]

May 12—The Park Hotel, which opened in 1871 and was updated in 1912, closes at midnight to be razed and gutted and replaced by the Park Motor Inn.[165]

May 26—J. H. Findorff and Son Inc. buys the historic Vilas property overlooking Lake Mendota at Wisconsin and Gilman Streets from Senator William Vilas's grandchildren, Lucien M. Hanks and Sybil Hanks, picking up the option taken out on behalf of Senior Citizens Inc., for its Vilas Towers high-rise apartment complex for the elderly; project financing remains elusive.[166]

June 1—International Brotherhood of Electrical Workers goes on strike, shutting down up to $20 million in construction for almost four weeks.[167]

November 20—The Plan Commission approves controversial plans for a racially integrated fifteen-building apartment complex with 148 units, sponsored by the American Federation of State, County and Municipal Employees on Sherman Avenue, just north of Northport Drive.[168]

December 14—To replace the Monona Golf Course, which the Board of Education bought for the new Twenty-Second Ward high school, the city buys five hundred acres on Highway 12/18 for two eighteen-hole courses; the $331,104 cost is subsidized by the first federal grant under the Urban Open Space grant program, for $99,331.[169]

Highways and Transportation

NEW ROADS
- ▸ The fifty-two-mile, $29 million I-90/94 highway from Madison to Wisconsin Dells opens October 6.[170]

Transportation Milestones

June 9—Traffic through Vilas Park is reversed to a counterclockwise pattern, with the entrance now off Edgewood Boulevard.[171]

June 27—Traffic lights are installed at four busy Beltline intersections: the East Beltline at Milwaukee Street and at Buckeye Road, Monona Road at the South Beltline, and Gilbert Road at the West Beltline.[172]

Expressway, proposed in 1956, along the Illinois Central rail bed and Regent Street/College Court corridor. WHI IMAGE ID 33732, PHOTO BY JOHN NEWHOUSE, PHOTOMONTAGE BY CITY OF MADISON

July 15—City planners report that State Street suffers from traffic congestion, inadequate parking, and bad design and recommend a coordinated, three-phase improvement plan.[173]

September 14—The council renames East Beltline/Highway 51 as Stoughton Road, with Milwaukee Street the north-south dividing line.[174]

October 26—Five years after city planners proposed a divided expressway from Proudfit Street to Midvale Boulevard, the council takes its first action to build the road. It sets a sixty-six-foot setback on College Court to create a matching one-way road with Regent Street from North Murray Street to Monroe Street, where cars will connect through a roundabout with the freeway built on the old Illinois Central rail bed. The same night, there is a big win for Mayor (and trucking company president) Henry Reynolds as the council votes, 14–6, to designate Midvale Boulevard for heavy truck traffic. Citywide, 20 percent of the 379 miles of streets remain unpaved.[175]

November 22—City department heads vote overwhelmingly to install seat belts in city-owned vehicles; of the nineteen city managers, none vote against the plan, although Reynolds and several others abstain. The city also considers requiring employees to buy belts for all private automobiles used for city business.[176]

In Memoriam

Two leading businessmen take their own lives this year—one due to failure, the other to success.

Frederick J. Meyer, fifty-one, founder and president of Red Dot Foods, 1435 E. Washington Ave., owned plants in eight cities and thirty-five thousand retail outlets in twelve Midwestern states. On May 5, he merges his company with H. W. Lay & Co. (which would merge with the Frito Co. later in the year). Although he's set to continue as president of Red Dot and become vice president and a director of the Lay company, Meyer is despondent over the loss of ownership. On May 9, while his wife Kathryne is downstairs at 415 Farwell Dr. baking cookies, he turns his sixteen-gauge hunting shotgun on himself. The house is so big, she does not hear the shot. Meyer leaves an estate of $2.3 million.[177]

Charles H. Gill, forty-nine, developed the west side plats Arbor Hills, Meadowood, and Orchard Ridge. But in late 1961, he's heavily in debt and in trouble with state regulators. He sells his showcase homes at 1222 Gilbert Rd. and in the Fox Bluff section of Waunakee, and moves with his family (his wife, Marcella, is a past president of the Madison League of Women Voters and active in local Republican party affairs) to 1210 W. Beltline. The Wisconsin Real Estate Examining Board suspends, then revokes his realtor's license on November 17; on the twenty-second—the day before Thanksgiving—Gill drives his 1960 Chevrolet station wagon into an abandoned gravel pit in the undeveloped section of Arbor Hills and kills himself with carbon monoxide.[178]

Death is good for charity this year.

Harry L. French, seventy-four, retired general agent for Northwestern Mutual Life Insurance Co. and a civic leader, dies on February 2, leaving his $541,495 estate to create a college scholarship program for Madison high school students administered through the Rotary Club, of which he was a past president.[179] William E. Walker, sixty-six, 357 Lakewood Blvd., president of radio station WISM and other regional stations and former assistant to Governor Oscar Rennebohm, dies on September 14; when "Walker the Talker" falls silent, he leaves the bulk of his $900,000 estate to religious, charitable, and educational organizations.[180]

Sister Mary Jane Frances Weber, fifty-three, O.P., UW PhD '43 and dean of Edgewood College since 1950, dies on October 2. She leaves very little in the way of an earthly estate.

Death comes even to the one who knew it best: Dane County Coroner Mike Malloy, fifty-six, who dies in his sleep at 2618 E. Lawn Ct., on November 28. Malloy had just signed an option to sell 73 acres of his family homestead to supplement the 160-acre Madison School Forest near Verona; Mr. and Mrs. Walter A. Frautschi provide the funds for the purchase in memory of her father, Jerome J. Jones.[181]

November 29 marks the final exposure for pioneer photographer Melvin Diemer, seventy-four, 4900 Lake Mendota Dr., UW PhD '11. Longtime official photographer for the UW and veteran employee of the federal Forest Products Laboratory, Diemer brought the first motion picture camera to Wisconsin in 1913 and made several breakthroughs in scientific photography. He was a thirty-third-degree Mason and past master of Lodge No. 5.[182]

State Street and the Capitol, viewed from the new Van Vleck Hall, August 22. Among the landmarks: (1) Madison Hotel, the oldest building on the Capitol Square; (2) Manchester's department store; (3) Vocational School; (4) Lake Monona; (5) Holy Redeemer Catholic Church; (6) First National Bank building; (7) the Towers, a women's private dorm; (8) Orpheum Theater; (9) Tenney building; (10) YWCA; (11) Capitol Theater; (12) Gay building; (13) Grace Episcopal Church; (14) Wisconsin Power and Light building. WHI IMAGE ID 137502, PHOTO BY RICHARD VESEY

1962

This is the year Mayor Henry Reynolds kills Monona Terrace. The threat of a single signature on a veto message proves more powerful than a petition with ten thousand names.

Nineteen sixty-two does not start well for the mayor. The city's excuse for not arbitrating the fee dispute with the Frank Lloyd Wright Foundation—that the contract itself is invalid—fails to impress Judge Richard W. Bardwell at a mid-January hearing. "You aren't really serious, are you," Bardwell asks city attorney Alton S. Heassler, "that this is an illegal contract?" With the mayor looking on, the attorney tells the judge he most certainly is.

"It shocks me," Bardwell says, itching to give an immediate decision from the bench. But he sets a briefing schedule instead, keeping on hold both the foundation's request for arbitration and the city's request that the contract be voided. A decision is not expected until after the April referendum.[1]

Exactly what the advisory referendum will ask, though, is up in the air. For the first time, supporters and opponents of the project want a referendum at the same time—they just don't agree on the question. And the fate of Monona Terrace likely depends on its wording.

At the end of January, the anti-Terrace Citizens' Realistic Auditorium Association (CRAA) again asks for the language it unsuccessfully proposed in October 1960: Shall "the City of Madison terminate all plans for an auditorium and civic center at the Monona Terrace site, and immediately take steps to select an alternative site for the auditorium and civic center?"[2]

A few days later, the Citizens for Monona Terrace offers: "Shall the city proceed with the construction of the Wright-designed civic center at the Monona Terrace site?"

A week later, the pro-Terrace faction on the city council, led by north side alderman Richard Kopp, offers its language: "Shall the City of Madison redraft the present plans and specifications and proceed to construct an auditorium and civic center at the Monona Terrace site?"[3]

Musicians and music lovers assemble for Eugene Ormandy and the Philadelphia Orchestra at the UW Stock Pavilion on May 10, 1962—a stark example of the "cow barn culture" the *Capital Times* routinely bemoans in a Madison without Monona Terrace. Thirty years earlier, university president Glenn Frank called the Medieval English and Tudor Revival building the "Cowliseum." Built by president Charles Van Hise in 1909 to house university horses and stage statewide livestock shows, the pavilion has fixed seating for two thousand, with room on the packed sawdust floor for fifteen hundred more, making it Madison's largest indoor gathering place until the Field House opened in 1930. The acoustics are excellent and there's usually no bad smell (despite the forty horse stalls under the seats), but mice sometimes scurry about and train horns are an all-too-frequent disruption.[4] WHI IMAGE ID 136607, PHOTO BY DAVID SANDELL

With twelve sponsors, Kopp's draft should pass—except that Reynolds says it's "not a fair and honest referendum" because it doesn't acknowledge realistic project costs. Reynolds wants the language he first supported as CRAA vice president in 1960.

"No one scares me with his little club of a veto," responds Terrace supporter Ald. Lloyd Foust, Sixteenth Ward, as the council's Committee of the Whole on February 20 recommends the Kopp version, 12–10—enough for council adoption, but five votes short of overriding a Reynolds veto.[5]

The morning of February 22, the mayor's media organ derides the "phony referendum" and the "fumbling and bumbling" aldermen who approved it. "The council has a shortage of honest men," the *State Journal* editorializes. "It looks as though only by getting aldermen to pledge to cancel the contract with the Wright Foundation can we get back to good government in Madison."[6]

Terrace supporters don't like it, but they can count and read; when Reynolds insists on the CRAA text at the council meeting two nights later, he prevails, 16–6.[7]

The language approved not only forces supporters to explain that to vote for Monona Terrace you have to vote *against* the referendum, but it also lets opponents piggyback on the popular (and very expensive) $9.3 million school bond issue, with "vote yes on both referendums" campaign ads.[8]

Reynolds reaps his reward on Election Day, April 3, as the resolution to kill Monona Terrace passes with about 54 percent of the vote. And as an added bonus, Foust and two other pro-Terrace aldermen are defeated (albeit over local issues, not Monona Terrace). For the first time since the project was proposed in 1953, Madison has a unified anti–Monona Terrace government.[9]

Although the 35,425 votes cast in the referendum represent a healthy 59.4 percent of the registered voters, *Capital Times* editor/publisher William T. Evjue is apocalyptically apoplectic that "the decision to remain in the cow barn era" was made by only 31 percent of the electorate (the 19,056 who voted "yes.")

"The people of Germany were indifferent to their responsibilities and tired of making decisions," he declares in his weekly "Hello, Wisconsin" statewide radio address on April 8. "They abdicated and turned things over to Hitler, who left their country in ruins."[10]

The mayor moves fast, calling a meeting of the Auditorium Committee three days after the vote to start the process of formally terminating the contract with the Wright Foundation. Ald. Frank Ross's draft blames the foundation, declaring it in breach of contract for refusing to redraft the project to bring it within the budget. It passes unanimously; even the pro-Terrace Kopp, who was easily reelected while his ward voted heavily against the project, votes yes.[11]

Reynolds wants the outgoing council to take up the measure at its final meeting—largely to embarrass the pro-Terrace aldermen—but it's referred to a future meeting, so acting city attorney Edwin Conrad (Madison alderman, 1981–1982), who took over after Alton Heassler's death in a car crash on March 30, can review various legal issues, including potential personal liability for the council.[12]

Reynolds presses his advantage when the new council is sworn in on April 17, removing Kopp from the Auditorium Committee and stacking it with three aldermanic Terrace opponents. Kopp pleads for reappointment, but Reynolds is unmoved and says Kopp "could not work too constructively" on the new committee. Kopp calls Reynolds "vindictive," and other aldermen support his cause.

Reynolds explodes. "I will not appoint Kopp under any consideration," he declares. "That's my prerogative, and that's settled!" It is, as the council confirms the new committee appointments, 17–5.[13]

The next day, the *Capital Times* returns to a theme. "A dictator takes over in city hall [and] asserts he has been given a mandate to suspend minority rights," it editorializes, denouncing Reynolds's refusal to reappoint Kopp as "a display of petulance and anger."[14]

ROUNDY SAYS

"Madison went 'Yes' yesterday I hope they get the auditorium up now they have been voting on it for six years. Why don't they go some place now where they can park about 5,000 cars and put it up. I don't care where they put it."
—*Wisconsin State Journal*, April 5

"I read about the auditorium but I still don't understand it."
—*Wisconsin State Journal*, July 7

On Thursday, May 10, six years after Mayor Ivan Nestingen and Frank Lloyd Wright signed a contract for Monona Terrace, the council officially terminates it, 16–3.[15]

The following Monday, Reynolds calls an Auditorium Committee meeting to consider a big new question: "whether it's going to be built downtown or in some outer area," such as Olin Park. Reynolds proposes having the internationally renowned consultant Ladislas Segoe pick a site—something Joe Jackson, who hired Segoe in 1938 to draft a city master plan for the Madison and Wisconsin Foundation after the unexpected death of John Nolen, has been advocating since 1960. By the end of May, the city has hired Segoe and also retained a team from the International Auditorium Managers Association. Reynolds repeats his vow to build a facility "as large as we planned at the Monona Terrace project, for $4 million."[16]

But just one week later, the Segoe consultancy isn't going well. "One thing that has bothered me at the outset," Segoe's principal associate, Charles Matthews, tells the committee in early June, "is that the function or functions of the building haven't been fully set." He rejects Reynolds's idea that the building's functions should follow the form of its site.[17]

Ald. W. R. Carnes warns against the city "getting too ambitious about attracting conventions" to the city. "There's a seamy side to convention life," he says. "Big conventions cheapen a town."

The auditorium managers weigh in, recommending a single flat-floor auditorium facility "adequate" for conventions, ice shows, and conversion to a theater using portable seats and bleachers. Their suggested site is the surface parking lot on Block 53, bounded by North Henry, Broom, West Mifflin, and Dayton Streets.[18]

It's a far cry from the comprehensive cultural facility the city had been planning for several years, and no one is too impressed. "I certainly wouldn't corrupt my building by designing it primarily for convention purposes," Segoe says.[19]

In early August, Segoe makes his site selection—the very same place he proposed in the master plan Jackson commissioned in 1938: four acres just west of Conklin [James Madison] Park, fronting 520 feet on East Gorham Street and 400 feet on Lake Mendota. With more than a dozen residences and an assessed value of $400,000, the land acquisition would cost close to $1 million.[20]

Reynolds, who expected Segoe to side with him in favoring the old waterworks site across the street from the park, isn't happy. The lakeside location is "a beautiful site," he says—maybe too beautiful. "It's so large and pretentious," he argues, "it would demand a different type of building than what I had been thinking of." He keeps pushing for the waterworks site.[21]

Unable to choose between the mayor who appointed them and the consultant he hired, the auditorium committee punts—in late August, it unanimously recommends an unspecified three-acre location in the general Conklin park area, covering both the waterworks and waterfront sites. But the council balks at endorsing an unknown site and, after an inconclusive three-hour debate in mid-September, sends it all back to committee.[22]

Ladislas Segoe's site for the civic auditorium, just west of Conklin [James Madison] Park; at right, the city waterworks site that Mayor Reynolds favors. COURTESY OF CAPITAL NEWSPAPERS ARCHIVES, PHOTO BY JOHN NEWHOUSE

In early October, the committee sides with Segoe, selecting a two-acre site just west of the park, an area within his larger proposal. Reynolds still likes his waterworks plan but says "this site seems to be ideal." Jackson concurs.[23]

So does the council, voting 15–6 on October 25 to locate the civic auditorium on the two-acre site just west of the park, and to select an architect to design it.[24]

But in mid-November, just as the Auditorium Committee is interviewing the prominent Chicago architect Alfred P. Shaw—his firm Shaw Metz & Associates designed Chicago's huge McCormick Place convention center—Judge Bardwell drops a bombshell on the project. In a sweeping decision, he finds the city's contract with the Wright Foundation valid and enforceable. "In good conscience," he holds, the city cannot avoid the foundation's call to arbitrate the fee dispute. The council promptly appeals.[25]

The Auditorium Committee presses on, recommending in early December that the city retain Shaw Metz. But it fails to consult with the Board of Public Works, which was given concurrent jurisdiction over architect selection by an earlier resolution. "That was an error on my part," a rueful Reynolds says. The public works panel led by Ald. Rohr refuses to ratify Shaw's selection, or to relinquish its authority.[26]

The year ends with the city mired in an internal jurisdictional dispute, and back in court. Again.

Urban Renewal

This is the year the Madison Redevelopment Authority (MRA) starts tearing down the Bush.

The first building to go is Clifford Bass's former two-story home at 15 S. Murray St., in mid-January. By December, the MRA will raze 122 of the 268 structures, paying an average of about $12,000 for the average residence. Compensation is set by federal regulations, which do not permit appraisals to include hardships suffered by an unwilling seller or loss of a seller's ancillary rental income.[27]

As 1962 opens, the MRA has relocated eighteen families, and executive director Roger Rupnow tells the MRA he's "most encouraged about the progress" made to date. By its close, the authority will relocate 244 individuals and families and be under scathing attack from both within and without.[28] Relocation efforts are also set back by racism and the lack of legal protection against housing discrimination; white households are relocated faster than those of non-whites.[29]

The transformation of a neighborhood into urban renewal projects is well underway by late 1962, with construction of Sampson Plaza about to start in the Brittingham renewal area and nearly half the buildings in the Triangle area already razed. Among the remaining and remembered area landmarks: (1) Frances Court apartments, (2) stock yards, (3) Roundhouse, (4) feed mill, (5) Paley's junk yard, (6) Di Salvo's grocery, (7) Gervasi's store, (8) Italian Methodist Church, (9) Adas Jeshurun Synagogue, (10) Pastime Theater, (11) Neighborhood House, (12) Gerke's junk yard, (13) future Sampson Plaza apartments, (14) Standard gas station, (15) St. Joseph's Church, (16) St. Joseph's School, (17) St. Joseph's convent, (18) Schwartz Pharmacy, (19) Agudas Achim Synagogue, (20) Madison General Hospital, (21) Sinclair gas station, (22) Longfellow Elementary School. WHI IMAGE ID 137505, PHOTO BY JOHN NEWHOUSE

Two committees assume new importance this year, each required under the federal urban renewal laws. The mayor's Citizens Advisory Committee (CAC) is city government's all-star committee of civic, business, religious, and other leaders with essentially unlimited jurisdiction to investigate and comment on all municipal activities. The Local Committee on Urban Renewal, comprising representatives from the Italian Workmen's Club, Bersaglieri Fraternal Organization, Mt. Zion Baptist Church, Calvary Methodist Church, NAACP, Adas Jeshurun Congregation, Second Baptist Church, African Methodist Episcopal Church, and the Longfellow PTA, plus some property owners and residents in the urban renewal area, has formal standing to comment on how renewal projects are proceeding. Chester Zmudzinski, the respected and influential executive director of Madison Neighborhoods Inc., and husband of MRA relocation director Florence Zmudzinski, chairs the Local Committee.[30]

The year starts with good news for the Triangle—US Representative Robert W. Kastenmeier (D-Watertown) announces on January 4 that the federal Urban Renewal Administration has approved a $2.87 million grant and $4.65 million loan for the acquisition and clearance of the fifty-two-acre site.[31]

Mayor Henry Reynolds's proposal to combine the joint housing and redevelopment authorities moves forward in late January, to take effect February 15. Both authorities unanimously endorse the plan, which involves shared staff and unified management under Rupnow, but separate boards. The MRA also pencils in pay raises for Rupnow, deputy director designee Sol Levin, and assistant Eugene Gangstad. But the plan falls apart a week later when Reynolds objects to Rupnow's raise. Sol Levin, the city's urban renewal expert who declined a job in Milwaukee to become deputy here, decides to relocate after all.[32]

The wrecking ball finally swings against Trotter's Tuxedo Café the first week of February, leaving Licari's Spot Tavern the only structure standing in the Brittingham redevelopment area, until it, too, falls in early June.[33]

On March 8, Chester Zmudzinski, in his capacity as chair of the Local Committee on Urban Renewal, tells the MRA that it should follow the plan set forth in its 1959 brochure and acquire and demolish property in a planned, area-by-area phasing, rather than picking up and taking down parcels individually. "This spotty approach is causing great concern," he says. Rupnow rejects his request, insisting that buildings are demolished as soon as they became vacant for health and safety reasons, "and not in an attempt to scare the residents."[34]

But not every building is razed that quickly. Shortly after the MRA purchases 120 S. Lake St. by condemnation and evicts the Collins family, it's reoccupied—by the MRA itself, for use by Florence Zmudzinski and her small relocation staff.[35]

On May 10, the Madison Housing Authority (MHA) finally wins its long battle for public housing, as the council approves, 17–4, its 160-unit plan: sixty units for the elderly on Regent Street between Murray and Lake Streets, thirty-six units near the Truax Park apartments, thirty-six units on Webb Avenue, and twenty-eight units in South Madison, in a three-block area just north of Penn Park. The MHA retains local architect Cashin & Associates to design the apartments.[36]

What a difference twelve years—and a growing sense of urgency—can make. In 1950, an MHA plan to build three hundred units on South Park Street was decisively killed by referendum. As with Monona Terrace, that referendum was also phrased negatively, requiring a "no" vote to support the project.[37]

But the MHA thinks even more public housing is needed, especially due to the planned South Madison project. MHA director Robert Callsen writes the MRA to enlist its support; the MRA reads the letter and files it away without action or response.[38]

By early summer, Rupnow's confidence is starting to fade. In June, he tells the MRA that relocation is "difficult" and "moving along slowly," and that rent delinquencies are becoming an issue. The MRA asks city attorney Conrad for help with collections, a task he considers low priority.[39]

The MHA gives displaced families preference in its Truax Park Apartments, the 1949 veterans housing off Wright Street. By the end of the year, seventeen Triangle households have moved in; continuing the city's de facto segregation, none are white.

Even as the MRA wrestles with relocation, it takes on a new task—preparing the joint application with UW for an Urban Renewal Authority grant to study a possible project in the university's immediate 71-acre expansion zone, which is within the massive 496-acre General Neighborhood Renewal Area, stretching from Wisconsin Avenue to Spooner Street. It also continues to seek federal planning funds for the proposed South Madison rehabilitation project.[40]

In July, Florence Zmudzinski alerts the MRA that relocation is becoming an "increasing problem," especially for nonwhites. "We can't find enough low-cost housing to meet standards," she says, "and we can't find housing for minority groups." By July 11, sixty-three families are still not relocated, as the MRA okays the demolition of another nineteen buildings. MRA chair Albert McGinnis directs Mrs. Zmudzinski to submit a written report "outlining the points discussed and any other suggestions and recommendations she might have."[41]

That she does, submitting in September a scathing and sweeping eleven-page critique of the MRA's relocation data and delivery. Zmudzinski tells the authority that its adopted 1959 relocation report was "unrealistic" about existing housing resources, "uninformed" about the problems of African Americans being displaced, "misinformed" about the availability of low-income housing, "misleading" regarding financing, and "overoptimistic" about developing new housing resources. And she also includes a cultural condemnation, claiming the agency was "unknowing regarding the needs of the people to be displaced."[42]

"We have advertised for units and attempted to persuade the community to at least show units to Negro families without success," she tells the CAC, revealing that out of 767 approved housing units last year, only 123 could be shown to nonwhites—and most of those were in South Madison, itself slated for a redevelopment program.[43]

And it's not just the authority, she writes, but the city itself that is "unprepared, often misinformed, and generally hostile to the [relocation] program and to the people being displaced" by a program that "placed emphasis on the physical aspects of acquisition and demolition without effectively coordinating the human aspects of the program." She charges that city and county welfare agencies "are approving sub-standard housing even less desirable" than some in the Triangle, that "code enforcement is too weak as presently constituted to achieve the goal of standard housing for every displaced family," and that units with inadequate wiring and no hot water "are not always considered substandard by the building inspector." Rupnow tells the MRA he did not edit the report and disagrees with certain parts of it.[44]

"This is a plea for a substantially increased base of public housing," Professor Kurt Wendt, dean of the UW College of Engineering, says when Zmudzinski presents her report to the CAC in late October. "Without that, we will not be able to meet the relocation demands."[45]

In November, Zmudzinski reports that while her report "did create an awareness of the problem . . . the publicity had not provided the relocation staff with many new units."[46]

"Madison's relocation effort involving Triangle residents is pretty obviously in trouble," the *State Journal* editorializes November 16. "Houses are being removed, or on the verge of removal, more rapidly than safe and decent housing is becoming available. This could leave persons with no income no place to go. The fault lies in planning mistakes made by the Madison Redevelopment Authority."[47]

Five days later, MRA chair McGinnis suggests a solution—having the MRA enter into five-year leases with private landlords, then renting the units to households being relocated. He acknowledges that having scattered sites would be less efficient than a single large project, "but if you are talking about the human equation, you have no right whatever to weigh it with efficiency."[48]

But when it comes time to talk with the MHA about its leased housing program, old antagonisms arise, triggered when McGinnis again mentions "public housing ghettos."

"That's the most ridiculous statement I've ever heard," MHA chair Roland Day snaps back. "It's so ridiculous I doubt if there's any reason for continuing this meeting. The place to build public housing is where it's needed."[49]

As the year comes to a close, the MRA begins its pilot project for leased housing—two prefabricated single-family homes and a two-flat, near Warner Park, East High, and Dunn's Marsh, with the MRA managing and leasing for five years.[50]

"There are colored families in Madison capable of paying reasonable rent, who can find no place to go," and large white families in a similar predicament, McGinnis tells the council as it considers a resolution approving the pilot.

West side alderman William Bradford Smith, Republican attorney from the Nineteenth Ward, calls on his colleagues to "face the reality that it is difficult for Negro families in this city to relocate and the city should be ashamed."

But with three aldermen absent on December 27, the council's 10–8 vote in support of the pilot is two votes short of the majority needed to approve the program. McGinnis says the agency will go ahead anyway, due to the "urgency of some of the relocation problems."

"A sad commentary," Mayor Reynolds agreed. "What Madison really needs is low cost public housing as fast as we can get it."[51]

Civil Rights

In 1962, the civil rights movement remains a major factor in campus life and city politics.

Civil Rights Dateline

February 26—Attorney Lloyd Barbee, as president of the state NAACP, releases the draft of a tough human rights ordinance, endorsed by the city NAACP chapter, that would ban bias in housing, employment, and public accommodations on the basis of race, color, creed, ancestry, or national origin, with a maximum fine of $200 or thirty days in jail for violations. The proposal, which also creates a nine-member city commission with a full-time director, is referred to the Mayor's Commission on Human Rights (MCHR), which Barbee chairs.[52]

April 17—After Mayor Reynolds declines to reappoint Barbee to the MCHR when his term expires, the commission elects Westminster Presbyterian Church pastor Rev. Richard Pritchard as its new chair. At the behest of national NAACP leaders, Barbee soon moves to Milwaukee.[53]

June 16—Concerned about alleged anti-Semitic discrimination by the Madison Club, the Madison Community Chest stops paying the $150 membership dues for its executive director. The question of the club's alleged discrimination, which the club denies, was raised by Community Chest budget committee member Ruth B. Doyle.[54]

August 14—The local Friends of the National Urban League is encouraged to establish a chapter of the fifty-year-old fact-finding organization of professional social workers. Leslie H. Fishel Jr., director of the State Historical Society, and S. A. Forbes, from the Credit Union National Association, cochair the local group.[55]

December 28—Marshall Colston, a supervisor with the Dane County Department of Public Assistance and a member of the MCHR, is elected president of the Madison NAACP without opposition. Board members elected at the meeting at the YWCA, 122 State St., include outgoing president Odell Taliaferro and Stuart Hanisch.[56]

A Race about Racism

In 1962, race and racism dominate alderman Harold E. "Babe" Rohr's campaign for a fourth term representing the South Park Street–area Fourteenth Ward. Rohr, the painting union leader, calls the NAACP a "malicious force" and his challenger Jan Marfyak its "hand-picked candidate." Marfyak, an administrative assistant with the department of motor vehicles, notes he is not a member of the association, disagrees with some of its tactics, and has never even met NAACP president Taliaferro.[57]

At a Franklin School forum, Rohr says blacks hurt themselves backing bills like the NAACP's proposed human rights ordinance. He denies being prejudiced, declaring "some of my best friends are Negroes."[58]

Then someone starts sending anonymous postcards to ward voters claiming Marfyak lives in a trailer, doesn't pay taxes, and is himself a Negro. Although none of this is true, Rohr refuses to disavow the lies; "I had nothing to do with this," he insists.[59]

At a campaign forum in late March, someone asks Rohr point-blank: "Do you think that Mr. Marfyak is a Negro?" When Rohr won't answer, Marfyak shoots to his feet. "In the sense of fair play, Mr. Rohr, will you tell me to my face that I am not a Negro?" he demands. He won't. "I'm not going to state whether you are or are not a Negro," Rohr replies.[60]

Both papers endorse Marfyak with blistering editorials. "Rohr seeks to whip up race hate and fear to divert attention from the real issues," the *Capital Times* declares. The *State Journal* denounces Rohr's "racist line" and his "plans to fan the flames of prejudice rather than work for solutions."[61]

In the campaign's waning days, Rohr's campaign literature reprints a 1960 photo of popular state senator Horace Wilkie (D-Madison) shaking hands with Rohr, much to Wilkie's displeasure. "I deplore the injection of the race issue into this year's campaign by Rohr's supporters, and I emphatically disagree with Rohr's refusal to disavow such action," Wilkie says, explicitly stating he's not supporting Rohr's reelection.[62]

But Fourteenth Ward voters do, reelecting Rohr 1,191–999.[63]

Despite its disappointment over the election, the *State Journal* still pushes politics over protest. "We can do without the marchers," it editorializes on April 27. "The picketing act has always had an element of phoniness in any nation where everyone has the vote. The recent trend has not only made it tiresome but a bit frightening. It has no legitimate place in a free society where we govern ourselves by the ballot box and not street agitation. Let 'em write to their congressman."[64]

Banning Biased Bequests

The year is not yet a week old when the regents vote, 5–3, to make the university the first Big Ten school to adopt a policy banning gifts or grants based on bias. The administration's proposal, which they've been working on since the regents accepted a $100,000 bequest to aid "worthy and needy Gentile Protestant students" last April, bans gifts with "discriminatory restrictions based upon race, color or creed" but not national origin; university vice president Fred Harvey Harrington explains that as the campus with the seventh-largest foreign student body in the United States, the university has to allow for grants for international students. Regent Harold A. Konnak mockingly moves to add a ban on bias based on sex, which he withdraws after regent A. Matt Werner calls the amendment "ridiculous" and "frivolous." Urging adoption, president Conrad A. Elvehjem says donors have the right to support any group they wish, but that "such support should not be given through the State of Wisconsin or the University, but given directly" to individuals or outside organizations. The only other Big Ten school with such a policy is Illinois, set by statute.[65]

Candid Cameras Curtailed

Stuart Hanisch, instructor with the UW–Extension's Bureau of Audio-Visual Instruction, sparks a statewide controversy in mid-March by publicly resigning to protest the university's suppression of his undercover film showing thirteen incidents of housing discrimination in Madison, "To Find a Home."

Hanisch and state NAACP president Lloyd Barbee, who raised $3,000 of the film's $4,000 budget as chair of the Citizens Committee on Anti-Discrimination in Housing, had explained the candid filming techniques to UW–Extension officials in 1960 and had gotten their approval and the final $1,000.

But when Hanisch screens a rough cut in January 1962, UW–Extension officials conclude the university cannot "in good conscience" release the footage because it violates the privacy of those lying to black apartment seekers. Hanisch and Barbee propose blocking the faces and street addresses of those engaging in discrimination, but the administrators insist Hanisch re-create the film using actors.

Hanisch writes an angry resignation letter instead and gives it to the *Capital Times* for Monday's front page, March 19. Tuesday morning, the state NAACP chapter starts picketing the Extension offices, first on the Madison campus, then around the state, their placards reading "UW Protects Bigots" and "Sifting, Winnowing and Film Burning."[66]

UW president Conrad Elvehjem, who in 1931 publicly supported a restrictive covenant barring "any person of the Ethiopian race" from living in his Nakoma neighborhood, says he has a "moral and ethical problem" with the candid camerawork and releases a statement: "The use of hidden cameras and microphones to force individuals to testify against themselves has overtones of the police state and violates a basic freedom our constitution guarantees."[67]

On Wednesday, university vice president Fred Harvey Harrington meets with Hanisch, Barbee, and other NAACP officials at the YWCA at 122 State St., trying to clear the air. Harrington agrees that Hanisch and Barbee were open about using candid footage but says that information didn't get to central administration. "We made a mistake at the university" to have allowed the hidden microphones and cameras, he says. "Having made it, we do not feel we should carry it forward."[68]

On Sunday, US Representative Adam Clayton Powell Jr. (D-NY), chair of the House Labor and Education Committee, demands a copy of the film, threatening a subpoena if it is not provided. Elvehjem refuses, sending instead a certified typewritten transcript of the film, including transcribed footage not included in the film's rough cut.[69]

The WSA Student Senate endorses the administration's action a few days later, stating that the fight against racial discrimination "is not worth effronting the same spirit of fair play that is offended by discrimination."[70]

The controversy splits traditional allies. The Wisconsin Civil Liberties Union board of directors—which includes attorney James E. Doyle, UW law professors William Gorham Rice and Abner Brodie, the Reverends Max Gaebler and Alfred Wilson Swan, and *Capital Times* editor Miles McMillin—votes unanimously to condemn hidden cameras and microphones as "an unwarranted invasion of privacy" and supports the administration; McMillin backs his board vote with an editorial on March 23, calling on the NAACP to "learn that the ends do not justify the means." The liberal group Americans for Democratic Action agrees with the NAACP and calls for the film's release.[71]

The administration doesn't budge, releasing only the eighty-page transcript of the film and directing Hanisch's colleague Jackson Tiffany, who has since been assigned the project, to re-create the undercover footage with actors. The original film is locked away.[72]

The regents take no formal action, but individual members express their approval of how Elvehjem and Harrington handled the controversy.[73]

Martin and Malcolm

The two most important black leaders in America come to campus in the spring of 1962, only a few days apart. But their schedule is closer than their messages.

On Friday, March 30, Dr. Martin Luther King Jr. delivers the second annual Jonas Rosenfield lecture before a very supportive capacity crowd at the Union Theater on "The Future of Integration." "Segregation is on its death-bed," the Baptist preacher declares, "and the only problem is how expensive the nation will make its funeral."[74]

On Monday, April 2, Malcolm X takes a different tack, calling for racial separation in a Great Hall address on "Black Nationalism in America." "We reject integration—period," the Black Muslim leader declares. "We've outgrown it."[75]

White Editor, Black Power

The overwhelmingly white New Left has a profound impact on emerging black political consciousness thanks to the brilliant history grad student Marty Sklar, one of the founders and editors of the journal *Studies on the Left*. In late 1961, Sklar edited an unsolicited hundred-page submission from a black former Communist Party functionary and would-be playwright named Harold Cruse, arguing that black nationalism and not integration was the prevailing black position, into a powerful thirty-page essay, "Revolutionary Nationalism and the Afro-American."

The Cruse essay becomes the centerpiece of the *Studies* spring 1962 issue on "The New Radicalism and the Afro-American" and sparks a new debate among young black intellectuals. It becomes a proximate cause for Huey Newton and others at UC–Berkeley to form the Afro-American Association, which would later beget the Revolutionary Action Movement, which helped beget the Black Panthers. The publication is so important that when Malcolm X comes to Madison in April, he breaks his own rules about not visiting a white person's residence and spends two hours after one of his speeches in deep discussion with a mainly white group at Sklar's small house at 908 W. Dayton St. After a lengthy colloquy on the relative significance of race and class in the Cuban revolution with Fred Ciporen, Malcolm embraces Ciporen and says, "Freddy, if it was up to me, you could have an X."[76]

The Silent Greek March

Madison's largest and most successful civil rights demonstration to date occurs on October 4, 1962, as about fourteen hundred sorority and fraternity members march silently in the rain from Langdon Street to Bascom Hall to protest various university human rights regulations.

Some march against a proposed ban on the Delta Gamma chapter over alleged discriminatory practices by its national board. Some march against a rule proposed by the faculty Human Rights Committee (HRC) that all campus social organizations "shall have complete autonomy" over membership, "subject only to restriction not inconsistent with the policies and regulations of the university," which the protesters contend is both too broad and too vague. Some don't know why they march, other than that their brothers and sisters do.[77]

The Silent Greek March, October 4. WHI IMAGE ID 137906, PHOTO BY EDWIN STEIN

The Delta Gamma's Omega house is in hot water because its national council suspended the house at Beloit College shortly after it pledged Patricia Hamilton, a 1959 honors graduate at Madison West High School, president-elect of the Beloit Association of Women Students, and daughter of Madison's most accomplished African American couple, Harry and Velma Hamilton. National officials insist the suspension is due to the chapter's administrative shortcomings unrelated to Hamilton, and the local house, founded in 1881, notes that it has pledged Jewish women and a nonwhite woman (from the South Pacific) without repercussions from the national council. But the HRC finds the suspension a violation of the 1960 clause banning discrimination. In September, the committee recommends the sorority's ouster by July of 1963.[78]

After delivering a petition to Dean of Students LeRoy Luberg against the proposed ban, the marchers continue down State Street and home to Langdon Street. "It's a long way on heels," says Luberg, who had waived the forty-eight-hour notice requirement to allow the march, which he calls "unprecedented."[79]

And unimpressive, the *Daily Cardinal* says, calling the march "an unwise endeavor" because its leaders were "so obviously confused" about its purpose that participants also showed "befuddlement." It's about this time that persons unknown phone in a death threat or two to editor Jeff Greenfield.[80]

Two days after the silent march of fourteen hundred students, four hundred gather for a single moment of silence at the Lincoln Terrace, showing support for James Meredith's attempt to enroll in the University of Mississippi.[81]

In late November, after Delta Gamma's national president finally gives written assurance that the sorority has no discriminatory restrictions and that all chapters are free to pledge women without regard to race, color, creed, or national origin, the HRC rescinds its recommendation. Faculty and regents grudgingly agree to let the sorority stay.[82]

The Inter-Fraternity Council also succeeds in narrowing the scope of the local autonomy provision to apply explicitly to race, color, creed, or national origin, which they endorse. "They don't have to pick members from minority groups if they don't want to, but if they want to they should be allowed to do so," President Harrington explains to the regents as they approve both the new autonomy rule and the Delta Gamma resolution in early November.[83]

But there's no reprieve for the men of Phi Delta Theta; banned from campus activities in 1961 because a national leader declared that its constitution's "socially acceptable" clause aimed to bar Jews and nonwhites, the Madison chapter members quit their national organization on September 17 and go local as Phi Delt after failing in their efforts at the summer convention to have the clause removed. They say they'll keep working on it.[84]

UW

COMMENCEMENT, JUNE 4
- Baccalaureate: 1,674
- Master's/PhD: 721
- JD/MD: 167[85]

FALL ENROLLMENT
- Total Students: 21,733

HOMECOMING
- Show: Ella Fitzgerald and the Glenn Miller Orchestra
- Dance: The Glenn Miller Orchestra[86]

NEW BUILDINGS OF NOTE
- Social Sciences Building, 1180 Observatory Dr.
- Chemistry Research Building, 1101 University Ave.
- Extension Building, 432 N. Lake St.[87]

Campus Calendar

January 3—The Student Life and Interests Committee votes to allow undergraduates over the age of twenty-one to live in the same apartment building as unmarried students of the opposite sex, effective immediately—something only graduate students were previously allowed to do.[88]

Start of construction of Southeast Dorm #1 (Sellery Hall), March 1962. Chadbourne Hall is at lower left. WHI IMAGE ID 137322, PHOTO BY JOHN NEWHOUSE

January 13—Twenty percent of UW students depend on rail transportation to get between home and Madison, Dean of Students Luberg tells the Interstate Commerce Committee in testimony opposing the proposed abandonment of four Chicago & North Western trains.[89]

February 4–13—The third annual WSA Symposium features Nobel Peace Prize winner Dr. Ralph Bunche, US Representative Adam Clayton Powell Jr., the Pulitzer Prize–winning editorial cartoonist Herbert "Herblock" Block, and a debate between US Senator Eugene McCarthy and conservative author Russell Kirk.[90]

February 5—The *Daily Cardinal* Board of Control names eighteen-year-old Jeff Greenfield the first sophomore editor-in-chief in the paper's sixty-nine-year history. A philosophy major from New York City, Greenfield (Emmy Award winner, 1985, 1990, and 1992) will step down as vice president of the campus Americans for Democratic Action to assume his new position.[91]

March 2—Saul Bellow (Nobel Prize in Literature recipient and Pulitzer Prize for Fiction recipient, 1976) speaks to creative writing students and later gives a public lecture in 165 Bascom Hall; Bellow was a UW graduate fellow in 1937 but withdrew to get married and begin his writing career.[92]

NO TESTING!

PEACE AND DISARMAMENT OR NUCLEAR ANNIHILATION

COME TO DEMONSTRATION PROTESTING
THE U. S. RESUMPTION OF NUCLEAR TESTING

TODAY, MARCH 26

STEPS OF THE WISCONSIN HISTORICAL SOCIETY

12:30 P.M.

TODAY

UNIVERSITY OF WISCONSIN STUDENTS FOR PEACE AND DISARMAMENT

This demonstration draws a crowd of about 350, including a small but noisy group of counter-demonstrators. Danny Kalb provides the entertainment.[93] UNIVERSITY OF WISCONSIN–MADISON ARCHIVES IMAGE S01276

March 3—There's pandemonium in the Field House as the Badger basketball team overwhelms top-ranked, Big 10 defending champion Ohio State (led by All-Americans Jerry Lucas and John Havlicek), 86–67.[94]

March 16—A shy twenty-one-year-old with long black hair and no makeup, barefoot in a blue jumper, folksinger Joan Baez captivates a capacity Union Theater of thirteen hundred with her achingly pure soprano voice. And the Great Folk Scare makes itself felt throughout the year, with performances by Peter, Paul and Mary; the Weavers; Odetta; Theodore Bikel; Ramblin' Jack Elliott and Jesse Fuller; and the Chad Mitchell Trio (for two shows, with future Byrds founder Roger McGuinn, then called Jim, on backing guitar and banjo).[95]

March 16—The Socialist Club forms a resolution committee to draft a policy statement opposing American intervention in South Vietnam and warning of a possible war there.[96]

March 27—More than five hundred students pack Great Hall for a candid sex education talk by Milwaukee gynecologist Dr. Andrew Boyd, second in the University YMCA's series on "Ethics and Sexual Maturity."[97]

April 1–2—Violinist Isaac Stern performs outstanding programs at two sold-out Union Theater shows (competing, on the second night, with Malcolm X's appearance elsewhere in the building).[98]

April 5–6—Duke Ellington and his fifteen-piece orchestra headline the Military Ball in the Great Hall, which is also the site the next night for the Student Peace Center's Anti-Military Ball.[99]

April 11—The *Daily Cardinal* editorializes on "our right to know" what Americans are doing in Vietnam: "It is pretty clear by now that the American effort in South Viet Nam is of a far more serious nature than has been indicated by our government. The administration has in effect thrown American military might into South Viet Nam without consulting and without informing the American people or their representatives."[100]

April 14—The UW Board of Visitors reports to the regents that it has examined the *Daily Cardinal* and "noted a number of instances of a low standard of taste and an equally low concept of good citizenship."[101]

April 14—*National Review* editor William F. Buckley returns to campus for his third appearance, attacking the "sentimental pacifism" of liberals as a threat to national security.[102]

May 7—Gus Hall, general secretary of the American Communist Party, draws a respectfully skeptical overflow crowd of about eighteen hundred to the Union Theater.[103]

May 14—Supporting Dean Luberg's assurance to the regents that "we have extremists from both sides," John Birch Society leader Clarence Manion delivers a May 14 rebuttal (to a much smaller and even more skeptical crowd than heard Hall).[104]

May 18—US Supreme Court Justice Tom C. Clark speaks to a Great Hall crowd of about three hundred.[105]

June 15—The Class of 1962 graduates into a very good job market; more than five hundred companies, organizations, and government agencies interview on campus this year, a 7 percent increase over last year's record number.[106]

October 29—South African singer and activist Miriam Makeba, filled with passion and power, returns to the Union.[107]

November 19—After consulting with the University Committee and the Athletic Board, President Fred Harvey Harrington says the university will accept an invitation to play in the Rose Bowl, notwithstanding the faculty's ongoing opposition to the Big Ten Conference's contract to participate. Nobody's happy about it; the committee unanimously adopts a resolution stating that it feels "obliged to accept the invitation," and Harrington tells the regents that "post-season games involve a type of over-emphasis that is undesirable."[108]

November 24—A jubilant crowd of ten thousand celebrates Wisconsin's 14–9 victory over Minnesota by parading to the Capitol and back behind the UW Band, blocking State Street with impunity. The Badgers not only retain Paul Bunyan's Axe and win the Big Ten title, but also finish the season ranked second in the nation, their highest-ever ranking. Everyone starts making plans for New Year's Day, when Wisconsin will take on top ranked USC—the first time the two top teams will face each other in a bowl game. Badger fans hope for a better showing than the debacle against Washington in 1960.[109]

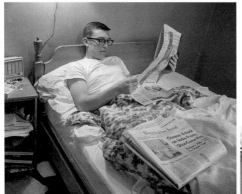

Two days before the Badgers' big game with rival Minnesota, Pat Richter reads the morning *State Journal* at home, 2034 Yahara Pl. WHI IMAGE ID 137918, PHOTO BY RICHARD SRODA

Badger victory celebration, State Street, November 24. WHI IMAGE ID 115774, PHOTO BY RICHARD SRODA

December 3—The Washington football team makes Pat Richter the first Badger taken in the first round of the NFL draft since Alan Ameche in 1955. He also joins other All-Americans in appearances on *The Ed Sullivan Show* and the two-month old *Tonight Show with Johnny Carson*. The senior, the first Badger to earn nine varsity letters since Rollie Williams in 1920–1923, had another stellar season, capped by his unanimous selection to both the AP and UPI All-American teams.[110]

December 6—Associated Women Students' Co-Ed Congress calls for a drastic revision in the curfew hours for women on campus (currently 10:30 p.m. on weeknights, 12:30 a.m. on weekends, and 11:00 p.m. on Sundays). "The restrictiveness of the present hours is an affront to the maturity and intelligence of girls who are pursuing advanced academic studies," the congress declares in a report asking the Student Life and Interests Committee for unlimited hours for senior women and liberalized hours for all others. It's a change for which the *Daily Cardinal* has long been pushing: "There are women on this campus who are simply fed up with the restrictions placed on them, who cannot understand why they are not entitled to the same privileges that are granted to intelligent high school students," it editorialized in April. "They are fed up with the absolute prohibition on free social life, even with parental consent. They do not agree that an institution of higher learning must treat every one of its co-eds as irresponsible children."[111]

December 12—"Let's make this Rose Bowl trip the last one," the *Daily Cardinal* editorializes, complaining that "the attention of students is diverted away from education toward 'the Big Game' to a degree that upsets the precarious balance between the scholastic and social life."[112]

December 16—Supporters of the House Un-American Activities Committee (HUAC) shout obscenities and edge toward violence against members of the University Students for the Abolition of HUAC trying to distribute literature at the lakeshore dorms' Kronshage Hall. A similar scenario unfolds the following night when the anti-HUAC forces are heckled at a meeting of about fifty dorm residents.[113]

December 20—A group of high-powered friends of the university, including builder Milton Findorff, banker Lucien Hanks, and meat magnate Oscar G. Mayer Jr., form the University Park Corp. to acquire and develop land on the south side of the 700 and 800 blocks of University Avenue, in close cooperation with the university.[114]

Panty Raid of the Decade

Beer bars, women's dorms, and warm moonlit nights make for a bad brew October 13–14, the weekend of UW's big game with Notre Dame. On each night, about three thousand young men go on panty raids that become near riots—the worst campus disturbances since the panty raid of May 1952, when police made twenty-one arrests.

It starts at bar time, a quarter to one on Saturday morning. As the six beer bars in the lower three blocks of State Street empty and the suds-soaked crowd builds, the men's thoughts turn to coeds, who were forced to return to their rooms by the 12:30 curfew.

The boys make their way to the new Allen Hall on the north corner of State and Frances Streets, calling for bras and panties. "We want silk!" the lusty fellows bellow, and several young women oblige, waving and dangling undergarments from their windows. Excitement builds.

Soon, a car driving through the packed intersection knocks down a boy. Then a policeman clubs a student. Flying beer bottles break windows at the Madison Inn and Allen Hall before the mob moves on to Lowell Hall, where custodian Merlin Marti, cut by flying glass from a broken door, opens the fire hose to hold the students back. Things are now out of control.

The mob blocks traffic all the way to the Capitol Square, bouncing cars and cavorting in the intersections. Students throw cans and bottles, even rocks and stones, at the police. Seven are injured, including three policemen and a fireman.

The police make thirteen arrests, including the students who roll a parked car off the end of Lake Street and into the water, pushing it thirty feet from shore. Thankfully, the Notre Dame student sleeping in the Chevy's backseat wakes up in time to escape injury.

Early Sunday morning, after quarterback Ron Vander Kelen and All-American end Pat Richter lead the Badgers to a 17–8 victory over the Irish, it starts again. But this time police are ready, and twenty officers are on the scene by midnight. With their active use of billy clubs and the paddy wagon, property damage is down but arrests are up—thirty-four young men are taken away, mainly for getting in drunken, bloody brawls.

On Monday afternoon, the faculty committee on student conduct summarily suspends twenty students, reinstating fifteen of them the next day. A handful of students pay fines of $105, but almost all have their charges dismissed by a sympathetic Criminal and Traffic Court judge, William Buenzli.

"I can realize from my own experience in the past that this was a case of your being in the wrong place at the wrong time," he says.[115]

The Death of President Elvehjem

In 1958, Conrad A. Elvehjem became the first alumnus named president of the University of Wisconsin since Charles Van Hise in 1904. Like the geologist/metallurgist Van Hise, Elvehjem was a leading scientist, attaining international renown in 1937 by isolating the vitamin niacin and discovering that it could cure the debilitating dietary disease pellagra, particularly prevalent among the world's poor.[116]

On July 27, 1962, Elvehjem becomes the first UW president since Van Hise to die in office, profoundly affecting town as well as gown.

A first-generation Norwegian American and graduate of Stoughton High School, Elvehjem was modest and somewhat shy, his administration frugal and efficient. He cared more about graduate education and faculty research than undergraduate education or daily student life.

Elvehjem's first administrative decision in 1958 was to name the former history department chair Fred Harvey Harrington (a close runner-up for the presidential appointment) vice president for academic affairs, and later vice president of the university. They were a successful team for four years, but this spring the ambitious Harrington accepts an offer to become the president of the University of Hawaii, to start September 15.[117]

July 27–28 is set to be a special weekend involving summer prom and a concert by jazz pianist Oscar Peterson. On the morning of Friday, June 27, Elvehjem sits at his Bascom Hall desk. Already troubled by high blood pressure, he's been dealing for over a year with his controversial dismissal of School of Medicine dean John Z. Bowers. At 8:15 a.m., Elvehjem has a heart attack and dies at about 9:15 a.m. at Madison General Hospital, with his wife, Constance, and son Robert at his side. The *Daily Cardinal* is out hours later with an "extra" edition; prom and concert are canceled.[118]

Harrington is in Kyoto, Japan, teaching an American Studies seminar in the month before he moves to Honolulu. He rushes home, and on July 29, the Regents' Executive Committee makes him acting president; two days later, hours after Elvehjem's simple graveside service at Forest Hill Cemetery, the regents consent to make the appointment permanent—if only the Hawaii regents will release him from his contract. They do, and on August 6, the full board unanimously confirms Harrington as the fourteenth president of the university.[119]

Before the university created the position of chancellor, the president was both the local and statewide face of the university, and this sudden transition from Elvehjem to Harrington affects the city in two ways. Scientist Elvehjem would not have named as chancellor the three humanities-based educators—Robben Fleming, William Sewell, and Edwin Young—whom historian Harrington does; all three have a major impact on

At the UW Field House on October 20, Fred Harvey Harrington and about a thousand guests celebrate his inauguration and the centennial of the Morrill Land-Grant Act, which fostered the university's early development. In Harrington's address, he predicts fifty thousand students will attend the combined campuses of the university by the end of the decade and a hundred thousand by the end of the century. Inaugural dinners throughout the state are linked by radio broadcasts from the State Radio Network and some twenty other Wisconsin radio stations.[120] WHI IMAGE ID 116010, PHOTO BY RICHARD SRODA the city during the protest era. And Harrington was made for this time; aggressively expansionist, he accelerates the university's growth, putting ever-greater pressure on city land use and housing. It was a noble thing for the Hawaii regents to let Harrington out of his contract fewer than seven weeks before his starting date; had Elvehjem died just two months later, after the school year started, they likely would not have done so, and everything would have changed.

In Memoriam—UW

George C. Sellery, UW PhD '01, dean of the College of Letters and Science from 1919 to 1942, dies on his ninetieth birthday, January 21. A scholar of Renaissance history, Sellery, 2021 Van Hise Ave., came to Wisconsin for his doctorate at the invitation of the legendary historian Frederick Jackson Turner. An educational conservative, Sellery was acting president after the regents fired President Glenn Frank in 1937.[121]

Carson Gulley, sixty-five, supervising chef for the UW residence halls from 1927 to 1954, creator of its famed fudge bottom pie, and master of seasons and spices, dies November 2 from complications of diabetes. The Arkansas native was cooking at the Essex Lodge summer resort in Tomahawk, Wisconsin, where a vacationing D. L. Halvorsen, then director of UW dormitories and food service, recruited him. Gulley directed a

State Street, just west of Lake Street, November 23.
WHI IMAGE ID 137853, PHOTO BY DAVID SANDELL

training course for Navy cooks and bakers during World War II, which he expanded into a two-year UW training course for chefs. Active in the local chapter of the NAACP, Gulley was listed in the 1950 edition of *Who's Who in Colored America*. From 1953 to 1962, he and his wife, Beatrice, hosted the weekly *What's Cookin'* on Madison's WMTV, apparently the first African American couple in America with their own television show.

Unable to find decent housing due to racially restrictive covenants and practices, the Gulleys lived in a basement apartment in Tripp Hall until his retirement. Gulley then sought to build a home at 5701 Cedar Pl. in the cooperative Crestwood subdivision on the west side, but was able to move in only after his neighbors voted to allow it (one-third of the neighborhood residents publicly stood up to vote against this at the meeting). At least one cross was later burned on his lawn. After serving and supervising sixteen million meals but never being promoted to director of dormitory food services, Gulley left the UW. The couple opened a restaurant/catering service at 5522 University Ave. on September 3; two weeks later, Gulley fell ill and was hospitalized until his death.[122]

Schools

GRADUATION, JUNE 15
- East: 423
- West: 409
- Central: 226[123]

FALL ENROLLMENT
- Total Students: 26,151[124]

NEW SCHOOLS AND MAJOR ADDITIONS
- Marquette School, junior high addition, 1501 Jenifer St.
- Conrad A. Elvehjem Elementary School, 5106 Academy Dr.

The building boom barrels on in 1962, as an educational era ends and another begins.

The year begins with another school board request for a bond issue—the largest in its history at $9.3 million, and the first bond to finance four years of construction instead of two. About $4.4 million will go to serve the 2,400 pupils brought into the Madison school system in the new Twenty-Second Ward, the area annexed from Blooming Grove, including $3.1 million for the newly named Robert M. La Follette High School. Schools are bursting at their seams, and Superintendent Philip Falk warns that if the bond issue fails, they may need to run double shifts of classes. East High School, slated for a $1.9 million junior high addition, swimming pool, and remodeling, is only twenty-six pupils short of its 2,600 capacity, with projections for 2,815 in fall of 1962 and 3,041 in September 1963. At West, four hundred will graduate in spring of 1962, and eight hundred enroll in September.[125]

Board of Education, 1962, in its lakefront offices in the old Doty School at 341 W. Wilson St. Standing, left to right: Arthur W. "Dynie" Mansfield (five years service), Ray Sennett (fourteen years), Superintendent Philip Falk (twenty-nine years), A. H. Younger (twelve years), Herbert J. Schmiege (eleven years) and vice president Dr. Ray W. Huegel (twenty-eight years). Seated, left to right: Helen S. Samp (thirteen years) and board president Glenn W. Stephens (thirty-five years). On April 3, the most hotly contested board race in several years ends with the reelection of Younger, Schmiege, and Huegel by their smallest margins ever. The fourth-place finisher is frequent Socialist candidate William Osborne Hart.[126] WHI IMAGE ID 137179, PHOTO BY DAVID SANDELL

Supporters of Monona Terrace suspect the large size of the bond issue, which will pay for five thousand classrooms, is intended to imperil the auditorium referendum, set for the same ballot. "This whopping bond issue is on the ballot," the *Capital Times* editorializes on January 25, "not so much because of the desire of the Reynolds Administration to build schools, but because it wants to kill the Monona Terrace project."[127]

On April 3, voters pass the referendum by better than 4–1 (and, indeed, kill Monona Terrace). The sixth successful bond referendum since the end of World War II, it is approved by a substantial majority in all thirty-three voting precincts. But there's a limit to how many buildings the board will boost; it endorses Superintendent Falk's plan not to significantly remodel or renovate the 1908 Central High School, even though they project the school will stay open for at least another ten years. "I don't think we can justify large expenditures in an area of decreasing populations," Falk tells the board. He also proposes moving the board offices from the old Doty School, 351 W. Wilson St., into the Washington School, 545 W. Dayton St.[128]

School Days

January—Louisiana native Geraldine Bernard becomes the first African American classroom teacher in the Madison school system, substituting during the spring semester in several elementary schools before later permanent assignments at Silver Spring and Aldo Leopold. In fall, three black teachers are hired full-time, at schools on the south and west sides.[129]

January 2—The Board of Education votes unanimously to offer regular contracts to married couples who are both teachers; previously, either the husband or wife could have only an "emergency" contract under special circumstances.[130]

May 14—The board unanimously selects Robert D. Gilberts, UW PhD '61, school superintendent at Oconomowoc for six years, to succeed Superintendent Falk starting January 1. Gilberts, a thirty-eight-year-old Wisconsin native who was previously a teacher and vice principal in Wausau, will be paid $18,000 annually, with the contract expiring July 1, 1965.[131]

September 10—The school year opens under a new state law attaching ten suburban and rural areas to the city for school purposes only, giving the Board of Education about 1,400 elementary and 350 high school pupils, and adding $904,258 to the city's bonded debt. A summer census shows that the school-age population has jumped by 6,350 to 51,822, with the Orchard Ridge area showing the largest gain for the third straight year, and most central-area elementary schools losing students.[132]

November 19—The board unanimously approves the merger of Central and Wisconsin High School into Central-University High School, effective July 1, 1964. Superintendent Falk says this will provide Central with needed additional students and relieve pressure on West, which will soon be at capacity, requiring the city to open a new west side high school by September 1966. The regents approve the merger on December 7, ending the independent educational initiative university president Van Hise began in 1911.[133]

December 11—Several hundred people brave below-zero temperatures for the dedication of Conrad A. Elvehjem Elementary School on the far southeast side, near its eponym's boyhood home in McFarland. Constance Elvehjem tells the capacity crowd honoring her late husband that there could be "no greater tribute than to have a school named after him." The school was built in a breakneck eighteen weeks after approval of the spring bond issue.[134]

December 17—At the public hearing for his final school budget, Superintendent Falk bemoans last year's $25,000 cut in the proposed teacher salary schedule and urges support for higher pay. "Unless we can beef up the starting pay of our teachers," he says, "we are going to start loading up our schools with mediocrity."[135]

December 31—Falk retires after almost twenty-four years as the superintendent.[136]

Planning and Development

GENERAL STATISTICS

▸ Population: 140,993[137]

▸ Area: 44.35 square miles (end-of-year total)[138]

EMPLOYMENT, MADISON MARKET, SUMMER 1962[139]

▸ Government: 27,400

▸ Wholesale and Retail Trade: 15,900

▸ Manufacturing: 13,100

▸ Services: 10,300

▸ Construction: 5,000

▸ Finance, Insurance, Real Estate: 4,000

▸ Transportation, Utilities, Communications: 3,900

Citywide assessments crack the half-billion mark for the first time this year, up from $23 million to $505 million. But the future may not be as bright downtown as elsewhere—assessor Norman Poorman again lowers assessments for properties on State Street and the Capitol Square, this time by $1 million, which he attributes to "the competition of new outlying shopping centers and discount houses and temporary uncertainty about the future of the Square." And central city landlords will lose $395,000 in rent when the Hill Farms State Office Building opens in January 1964.[140]

That competition also concerns the Madison Chamber of Commerce, which in June endorses state legislation to ban retail sales on Sundays except of items necessary for health, welfare, and recreation. Chamber leaders say most retailers oppose Sunday sales but stay open out of competitive pressures from the new shopping centers; more than thirty Madison stores are now open on Sundays, up from nine in 1955.[141]

The year also brings labor strife that pauses development but ultimately provides some workers with better pay. On April 12, about 120 truck drivers, members of Teamsters Local 695, strike fifteen ready-mix concrete and building supply firms for higher wages and benefits. As picket lines go up at Findorff and other general contractors, $120 million in construction shuts down, including Hilldale Shopping Center, the Van Vleck Mathematics Building, and an addition to Madison General Hospital. At Governor Nelson's request, UW law professor Nathan S. Feinsinger mediates a settlement, which ends the strike after twenty-four days. From a starting hourly wage of $2.65, the union sought a sixty-six-cent increase over three years, and the employers offered fifty cents; the settlement is for fifty-six cents.[142]

Sacred Structures

Urban renewal claims another religious institution on April 29, as the Torah scrolls are removed from the Adas Jeshurun Synagogue, 702 Mound St., prior to the building's demolition as part of the Triangle Redevelopment. The scrolls are taken to the Beth Israel Center, 1406 Mound St., which most of the congregants will now join. Both Beth Israel and Adas Jeshurun were offshoots of the Agudas Achim Synagogue, 802 Mound St. (1904–1950). On July 11, the former Gates of Heaven synagogue, 214 W. Washington Ave., is sold to the Fiore Coal & Oil Company for use as an office. The historic Italianate sandstone building, designed by August Kutzbock, was dedicated in September 1863 but ceased to serve as a shul in 1879, when it was rented to the Unitarian society (Frank Lloyd Wright came to services here until he left town in 1886). It's been occupied since by various religious and commercial interests, most recently two dentists.[143]

Bricks and Books

In late April, the council finally settles a long-standing debate over where to locate the new central library, voting 12–7 for the 200 block of West Mifflin Street. The Library Board's preferred site in the 200 block of West Washington Avenue across from the YMCA was too costly for the $500,000 land acquisition budget, and the parking utility wants the site of the old Carnegie Library on North Carroll Street, across from the vocational school, for an expanded municipal parking ramp. So the library gets its third choice.[144] On May 27, more than a thousand people visit the new Monroe Street Library open house, as the street has a branch library for the first time since October 1960. The $75,000 building holds eleven thousand volumes and will add about four thousand through the year.[145]

Housing Initiatives

The sixty-six-unit Chalet Gardens cooperative housing project for the elderly, on a ten-acre site out on Verona Road, opens May 30. Co-op president Bjarne Romnes says eleven units in the $1.4 million project have already been sold. In early November, the Federal Housing Administration (FHA) approves the feasibility study and higher project costs for the first unit of Vilas Towers, the apartment complex for the elderly on the site of the historic Vilas mansion at Gilman and Wisconsin Streets. The state FHA director thinks the prospects of FHA financing are "excellent" for the eight-story, 109-unit building, planned as the first of three. Building permits are issued in late November for the $1 million, 140-unit apartment project on Northport Drive sponsored by the American Federation of State, County and Municipal Employees. The integrated, rent-controlled project will be built on the former Bruns farm, just east of North Sherman Avenue, where it will have good fire protection as Fire Station #10 opens in September at 1517 Troy Dr.[146]

Annexation Attack

The new law that lets certain towns and villages have their schools brought into the Madison school system also gives the city new annexation power if they do. The city said it would use that power against any towns and villages if their schools were attached to the city school sytem; they were, and it does. It does so secretly, and without warning—or even notice—to the affected municipalities.

In a move so sudden and secret that Mayor Henry Reynolds doesn't even know it's coming until just hours before the meeting, the council on September 13 annexes twenty-nine parcels from two villages and three towns, including the Maple Bluff and Blackhawk Country Clubs, Eagle Heights, the main commercial strip in Shorewood Hills, the Lakewood School in Maple Bluff, the Sears warehouse off Sherman Avenue, the Arboretum property south of the Beltline, and more, with an assessed value of $5.5 million.

Reynolds calls the action "morally wrong" but doesn't veto the resolutions, letting them take effect without his signature. Of the twenty-nine parcels, twenty-five have no residents, so they cannot be put to referendum. But they can be challenged in court—and they are later this year.[147]

October 25 is opening day for the Hilldale Shopping Center, the largest shopping center in south central Wisconsin. Delayed by strikes and shortages, the thirty-four-acre center has twenty-six stores employing around six hundred persons—about half at the Gimbels-Schuster's department store. The morning ceremony starts with the national anthem performed by a twenty-piece brass band; freezing winds force the cancellation of a mass balloon release, but don't deter several thousand shoppers. For those who stay late, the two-thousand-car lot features incandescent lights with color-coded pastel porcelain shades to help them remember where they parked.[148] WHI IMAGE ID 137495, PHOTO BY JOHN NEWHOUSE

Highways and Transportation

NEW ROADS

▶ The Gorham Street Bend at Baldwin Street opens in late September, so inbound traffic on East Johnson Street no longer has to make a hard right turn at North Few Street and then a quick left at Gorham Street to continue heading west.[149]

▶ The thirty-mile stretch of I-90 from Madison to Janesville opens in early November, giving Madison a freeway connection to Chicago and points beyond.[150]

Monona Causeway Under Way (Maybe)

Madison's patron saint of planning, John Nolen, first proposed a parkway across the bay in 1911, and a full causeway was included in all three subsequent master plans. Alderman C. A. "Doc" Deadman tried for a half-million-dollar highway in 1927, but the council voted it down. In 1955, then–State Rep. Ivan Nestingen got a bill passed allowing Madison to fill 150 feet out from the railroad tracks, but nothing happened. In July 1960, the State Highway Commission told Mayor Nestingen that it was "not timely" to request federal highway aid, and the possibility of it becoming so, they told him, "appear[ed] quite remote." [151]

The world's only midwater crossing of competing railroad lines, with Mayor Reynolds's proposed causeway route indicated in ink. COURTESY OF CAPITAL NEWSPAPERS ARCHIVES, PHOTO BY JOHN NEWHOUSE

But Mayor Reynolds campaigned on building the causeway, and now things are starting to happen—to the great consternation of those supporting Monona Terrace, who are concerned the road would facilitate construction of the auditorium at Olin Park instead.[152]

"For various reasons, various people want to locate the auditorium in Olin Park, and it can't be done unless there is a causeway," the *Capital Times* editorializes. "That's why the project is being pushed without plans and with only the wildest idea of what it will cost and what it will do to the lake and bay."[153]

In April, the city's consulting engineers Mead and Hunt Inc. estimate that preliminary work on a two-lane roadway across Monona Bay would cost about $900,000, supporting Reynolds's claim that the road could be built for "less than $1 million," or about $2.3 million for a full six-lane highway.[154]

"Action—at last—on the causeway," the *State Journal* editorially enthuses, calling on the city to "get on with" building the road, which "everyone concedes is important to the continued health of downtown Madison."[155]

There's more for the causeway crowd to celebrate on April 20, when the Public Service Commission's chief engineer gives his tentative approval to the city's plans. Although many regulatory hurdles remain and the project is not yet financed, Reynolds pushes ahead; a week later, he makes a big show of dumping broken concrete from the Triangle and Brittingham urban renewal areas along the shoreline as the first fill.[156]

The *Capital Times* decries the mayor's "publicity gag," part of his "curiously desperate campaign" to get the causeway under way, and asks, "What's the rush?"[157]

Things slow down when about fifty lake-area residents demand a public hearing at the Public Service Commission, claiming the road will do environmental damage. Among those leading the opposition or testifying for it are Professor Harold M. Groves, president of Citizens for Monona Terrace, and Clifford S. Roberts, who narrowly failed to unseat the anti–Monona Terrace, pro–Olin Park alderman Rohr in 1960. After five days in June and July of predictably conflicting scientific testimony from dueling advocates about water flow and aquatic life, the Public Service Commission retires to consider the matter, and is still doing so as the year ends.[158]

Miscellanea

January 18—The Italian Workmen's Club celebrates the fiftieth anniversary of its founding as Club Lavoratori Italia di Mutuo Soccorso e Beneficenza.[159]

February 13—The Library Board approves a proposal by city clerk A. W. Bareis for year-round registration of new voters at the main library, all branches, and the bookmobile.[160]

April 12—The council unanimously adopts alderman Franklin Hall's work relief ordinance, requiring all able-bodied relief recipients to work on city-supervised projects or take vocational training in order to receive relief. The $1.47 hourly wage is set at 80 percent of the city's lowest pay classification, payable in vouchers for food and housing

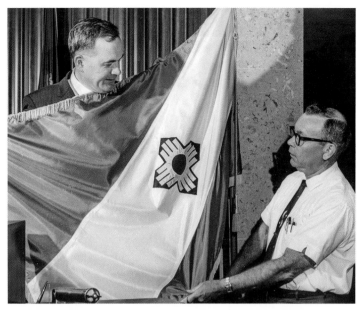

City attorney Edwin Conrad unfurls the Madison flag for mayoral administrative assistant Robert Corcoran (right) in August 1965. COURTESY OF CAPITAL NEWSPAPERS ARCHIVES

The *Capital Times* refuses to publish this ad for the film *Tender Is the Night* on February 2 because publisher William T. Evjue finds the text and art "suggestive and objectionable." Mr. Evjue started screening ads after two school principals in northern Wisconsin complained in 1961.[161] COURTESY OF CAPITAL NEWSPAPERS ARCHIVES

rather than cash. The ordinance also creates a seven-member Board of Public Welfare in control of the program.[162]

April 12—The council adopts the first official city flag, designed by two young members of the Madison Scouts Drum and Bugle Corps, Rick and Dennis Stone, and sewn by their mother, Frances. It consists of two blue triangles representing Lakes Mendota and Monona, a stripe of white running from lower left to upper right to represent the isthmus, and the sacred sun symbol of the Zia Pueblo nation emblazoned in gold on a black background to represent the state capitol. After its approval, the flag hangs upside down in the council chambers for over three years, until city attorney Edwin Conrad notices the mistake and corrects it.[163]

May 2—Airport superintendent Robert Skuldt (Dane County Supervisor, 1985–1992) reveals that Truax Air Force Base will soon house nuclear weapons in a "virtually foolproof" warehouse, for potential use by the F-89 fighter jets stationed there. Skuldt tells the Citizens Advisory Committee that the Air Force will likely remain at Truax "for years and years," and that the airport's highest priority is a new terminal.[164]

May 13—An estimated twenty thousand people—one of the largest crowds to gather in Madison since the end of World War II—jam the Capitol Square as fifty marching units and a series of bands mark Memorial Day. "We are dedicated to the principle that we shall be neither dead nor Red," US Representative Robert W. Kastenmeier (D-Watertown) says during a solemn ceremony featuring a wreath-laying tribute, a reading of the roster of Madison and Dane County wartime veterans who died over the past year, and patriotic proclamations. At a later service at the Memorial Union terrace, flowers are strewn in Lake Mendota to honor military personnel lost at sea.[165]

June 24—An overflow crowd at St. Raphael's Cathedral celebrates a high pontifical mass in honor of the fiftieth anniversary of the priestly ordination of the founding bishop of the Madison Diocese, the Most Reverend William P. O'Connor. The sacerdotal jubilee brings together the greatest array of Catholic prelates Madison has ever seen, including four cardinals, twenty-five bishops, and fifty monsignori. The two-hour ceremony is televised from the historic 1866 cathedral a block from the Capitol.[166]

July 25—Former Madison police chief Bruce Weatherly's sad saga comes to a tragic end when he is shot to death by his wife, Inez, in the bedroom of their farmhouse in his native San Antonio, Texas. Mrs. Weatherly, who staunchly defended her husband throughout his rocky ten-year tenure in Madison and at his termination hearing in 1959, tells investigators he had been drinking heavily and was "sick, sick, sick. I couldn't stand it any longer." She had sought last year to have him committed to a state mental hospital for drug addiction before he agreed to private treatment (he had briefly committed himself to Mendota State Hospital in 1961). Charged with murder with malice and facing the electric chair, Mrs. Weatherly ignores the advice of her lawyer and appears before the grand jury for two hours. She knows what she's doing; on September 20, the grand jury drops all charges. Chief Weatherly, forty-nine, once the renowned young reformer of the San Antonio police department, had recently accepted a State Department position reorganizing the Brazilian police force; the Weatherlys were soon to leave for São Paulo.[167]

August 23—The council confirms two of Mayor Reynolds's appointees: Edwin J. Duszynski, previously the first public works director for both Appleton and Cudahy, as Madison's first director of public works, and Edwin Conrad as city attorney. Conrad, whom the council twice refused to confirm in 1961, has been acting city attorney since Alton Heassler's fatal traffic accident in March.[168]

September 11—The Library Board approves using Western Union messengers to collect library books that are especially overdue. Under the program, in effect in about forty cities, messengers will be sent after patrons who ignore three overdue notices.[169]

October 26—City Forester George Behrnd celebrates the city's "very good luck" in controlling the spread of Dutch elm disease, losing only 285 trees this year—about .05 percent of the city's 55,000 elms.[171]

Beloved WIBA radio host and writer George "Papa Hambone" Vukelich, here listening to jazz in his Plymouth Circle living room, publishes his first novel, *Fisherman's Beach*, in October.[170] WHI IMAGE ID 136874, PHOTO BY EDWIN STEIN

ROUNDY SAYS

"Who is this guy Ronald Genrick of Portage I got his name on a piece of paper on my desk. I hope he is in the fish business. I need a couple."

—*Wisconsin State Journal*, July 7

October 27—Dueling groups march around the Capitol Square to support and oppose President Kennedy's blockade of Cuba. About two hundred people, organized by the Women's International League for Peace and Freedom and several student groups, parade with placards calling for the United States to "keep its hands off Cuba," while an anti-Castro group distributes literature calling US Representative Kastenmeier a "left-wing extremist." The right-wing piece is printed by the Independent Awake America Committee and paid for by UW student Tommy G. Thompson (governor, Wisconsin, 1987–2001; US Secretary of Health and Human Services, 2001–2005).[172]

In Memoriam

Gay Braxton, eighty-five, who grew Greenbush's most important secular institution by organizing Neighborhood House as a settlement house in 1921 and serving as its resident director until her retirement in 1950, dies, after a short illness, on March 26 at the house she shared with her longtime companion and Neighborhood House assistant, Mary Lee Griggs, at 4013 Birch Ave. A native of Richmond, Virginia, Braxton attended Smith College and came to Madison from Quincy, Illinois, where she headed a settlement house known as "Cheerful Home."[173]

It's a sad year for lawyers and judges.

Wisconsin Supreme Court Chief Justice Grover L. Broadfoot dies at age sixty-nine on May 18, setting in motion events that will change Madison's political future. Governor Gaylord Nelson first offers the vacancy to his friend James E. Doyle, a highly respected attorney and the former chair of the state Democratic party. When Doyle declines, Nelson taps State Senator Horace Wilkie (D-Madison), who is quickly confirmed. With Wilkie leaving the legislature, State Representative Fred A. Risser—who only days earlier had opened his campaign for a fourth term in the Assembly—declares his candidacy for the seat. Risser is elected easily in November and will continue to get reelected well into the twenty-first century.[174]

Disgraced former judge Ole Stolen, seventy-two, a stern Progressive moralist who in 1921 suborned perjury to falsely implicate the father of a murdered eleven-year-old Greenbush girl, Annie Lemberger, then borrowed heavily from bootleggers to pay blackmail, dies on August 14 of a heart attack. The *Capital Times* eulogizes him without mentioning the scandal, for which he was disbarred.[175]

City attorney Alton S. Heassler, sixty, is killed March 30 in an auto accident at the intersection of West Lawn and Prospect Avenues. The Madison native was also a former Dane County supervisor and unsuccessful candidate for the Republican nomination for district attorney.[176]

Downtown, spring 1963. Buildings that will one day be razed include: (1) Vilas mansion, (2) Central High School, (3) First Methodist Church, (4) Christ Presbyterian Church, (5) Manchester's department store, (6) Carnegie Library, (7) Madison Gas & Electric, (8) Methodist Hospital, (9) YMCA, (10) St. Raphael's Church (due to arson), (11) First National Bank Building. At lower right, the Doty School [Doty Condominiums].

1963

Civil Rights

Thanks to a conservative white mayor, a forceful black leader, a vast citizens' support network, and strong newspaper support, Madison makes civil rights history in 1963 by adopting the state's first open housing ordinance—but only after it is inadvertently weakened by advocates, then strengthened by an opponent.[1]

By 1963, the legal ability of Madison residents to discriminate based on race has profoundly destabilized the city's housing market. As the Madison Redevelopment Authority learned in relocating residents from the Triangle, nonwhites have access to only about 19 percent of the city's housing units, almost all in their "traditional" neighborhoods of South Madison and the East Dayton Street area.[2]

Despite that, a fair housing ordinance isn't a dominant local issue as the year opens; an open housing law that would preclude the need for an ordinance is already before the state legislature. Still, the Mayor's Commission on Human Rights (MCHR), chaired by Reverend Richard Pritchard of Westminster Presbyterian Church, wants some movement on the comprehensive human rights ordinance Lloyd Barbee and the NAACP proposed in early 1962. And a local chapter of a statewide group, Madison Citizens for Fair Housing, also forms, the latest in a long list of support groups.[3]

With the main focus on urban renewal and city finances, fair housing is not critical to the mayoral campaign. Challenger Albert McGinnis supports an ordinance; Mayor Henry Reynolds, whose East Mifflin Street family home is in Madison's oldest integrated neighborhood, says he'd "like to think there isn't a need," but would support one if recommended by the MCHR. Without staff, funds, or a meaningful ordinance, MCHR can informally investigate claims of discrimination and try to conciliate a resolution, but no more.[4]

"If we can accomplish it with brotherly love, this is the way it should be done," the mayor says, telling African American leader Harry Hamilton, "You don't want to live where you're not wanted."[5]

The December 10 Committee of the Whole public hearing on the Equal Opportunities Ordinance.
WHI IMAGE ID 136614, PHOTO BY DAVID SANDELL

But in June, as state efforts appear stalled, the city's Special Committee on Minority Housing starts working to create a local ordinance. Two days later, local NAACP president Marshall Colston, vice chair of the MCHR, writes Reynolds to protest the "apathy and indifference of the city government to serious civil rights problems in Madison," as evidenced by eighteen months of inaction regarding a human rights ordinance. Colston has been trying for six months to find out the status of the Barbee/NAACP draft but hasn't even gotten a reply. Colston is also still waiting for a reply to letters he sent the city's Board of Realtors and Chamber of Commerce.[6]

In mid-July, Colston finally meets with Reynolds and is encouraged. "I think the mayor sees the need for some corrective legislation," he says afterward. "I think he's sincere about it. As long as there's the possibility of legislation, or some other way of doing it, we won't demonstrate." But if those efforts fail, Colston says, "We're very well prepared to act in that area."[7]

While Colston works for a solution, others deny that anything needs to be done. "Colston and others like him are making a big hullabaloo over a problem that doesn't exist," Darwin Scoon, the executive vice president of the Wisconsin Realtors Association, declares. Homeowners should be able to sell—or not sell—to anyone they choose, he says at a late July Memorial Union debate with Colston sponsored by the Student Council for Civil Rights.[8]

Even as Scoon champions private property rights, racial unrest simmers on the near east side over the possibility that a second black family might move into an area neighborhood. Several months of anonymous telephoned threats bring increased police surveillance of the area.[9]

Madison NAACP president Marshall Colston, wife Eva, and children Marty, Laura, and Jacqueline, August 1963. After getting his master's in social work at the National Catholic University in Washington, DC, Colston became a case work supervisor for the Dane County Department of Public Welfare in 1959, and in the midst of the summer's open housing debate is named district supervisor for the state welfare department.[10] WHI IMAGE ID 137856, PHOTO BY DAVID SANDELL

In early October, city attorney Edwin Conrad harkens back to the Civil War to conclude that the city has the authority to regulate private property to foster equality and can enact a fair housing law. He begins drafting an ordinance with extensive consultation from a subcommittee of the Mayor's Commission on Human Rights: Reverend Wright, attorney Shirley S. Abrahamson (justice of the Wisconsin Supreme Court, 1976–1996; chief justice, 1996–2015; and justice, 2015–present), and Betty (Mrs. James) MacDonald.[11]

MCHR chair John McGrath assembles the Tuesday Night Committee, including representatives of a dozen or so civil rights, civic, and religious organizations, to coordinate public support efforts, and also work with Conrad on the text. Several hundred individuals become actively involved.[12]

On October 26, the Madison Citizens for Fair Housing publishes an extraordinary two-page newspaper advertisement in the *Capital Times*—a list of more than two thousand supporters of open housing, including full names and addresses. Some anonymous activists circulate petitions in opposition.[13]

On November 4, twenty-three months after the NAACP proposed an equal opportunities ordinance, Conrad releases the draft of a sweeping ordinance banning bias in housing, public accommodations, employment, public facilities, and all activities licensed by the city. It would abolish the Commission on Human Rights in favor of a five-member Anti-Discrimination Commission, with subpoena power but no direct enforcement authority. Although the draft does not provide the commission with enforcement powers as the NAACP proposed, Colston commends Conrad for a "comprehensive ordinance, a very good job."[14]

Conrad's draft applies to the holder "of any city license or permit," with violators subject to loss of license after a council hearing, in addition to fines of from $25 to $500. The MCHR drafting subcommittee objects to that as a double penalty imposing undue hardship and recommends its deletion. The commission goes further and deletes the entire subsection on licensees and permittees. The draft introduced to the council in the commission's name does not cover permittees or licensees, and their exclusion is not deemed significant. For now. The subcommittee also changes the new commission's name to Equal Opportunities Commission but can't persuade Conrad to allow it to have enforcement powers.[15]

On November 7, the Republican-controlled State Assembly kills three civil rights bills, defeating the fair housing provisions by more than two to one.[16] On November 20, the MCHR adopts the subcommittee's final draft 12–0–1; attorney Carroll Metzner, the former state representative who wrote the 1957 law blocking construction of Monona Terrace, abstains because it covers private housing. "Some things cannot be legislated but must be left to the individual's conscience," he says.[17]

More importantly, all the groups represented in the Tuesday Night Committee endorse the measure. MCHR chair McGrath's strategy of building grassroots support throughout the process is paying off.[18]

That broad base will be necessary as the real estate industry mobilizes to fight the fair housing provision. "I can't understand why the realtors or any group would oppose [fair housing]," Reynolds says in a television interview a few days later.[19]

An angry Ald. Rohr, whose south side district includes more than 55 percent of Madison's black population, denounces the ordinance and its proponents. "This isn't going to get the colored man a place to live, and it isn't going to do him any good, either," he says. "I say there's no problem, but there will be if this is passed." Rohr confidently predicts the housing section will be defeated, as does council president Ald. Richard Kopp.[20]

Tuesday, December 10, is United Nations Human Rights Day. In the evening, more than four hundred people pack the council chambers for a six-hour Committee of the Whole meeting devoted entirely to the Equal Opportunities Ordinance. The four-hour public hearing is tense but orderly; MCHR chair McGrath and secretary MacDonald organize a coordinated presentation with fair housing supporters far outnumbering opponents—except from the real estate industry.[21]

The only realtor there to support the measure is Patrick J. Lucey (lieutenant governor of Wisconsin, 1965–1967; governor of Wisconsin, 1971–1977; US ambassador to Mexico, 1977–1979; Independent vice-presidential nominee, 1980), owner of Madison's largest real estate company and former chair of the state Democratic Party. "Negroes here are the victims of a vicious and effective conspiracy, a disgrace for which we must all share the guilt," he says, urging adoption. But the official position of the city's realtors—opposition—is expressed by Board of Realtors president Earl A. Espeseth, a member of the Madison Housing Authority; he acknowledges some discrimination but insists "city people can take care of the problems on a voluntary basis."[22]

After all their coordinated organizing, supporters face an unforeseen problem as the meeting unfolds—a young black activist from the campus Congress of Racial Equality (CORE) tells the council that even if the measure passes, his group will continue to send whites and blacks to test for compliance as was done in the university's "To Find a Home" film. Although Tom Bolden, cochair of the Madison CORE chapter, later assures the council that testing would stop if the ordinance passes, council president Ald. Richard Kopp doesn't care.

Madison Board of Realtors ad printed in the *Capital Times* on December 9, 1963, opposing the fair housing provisions of the Equal Opportunities Ordinance. A week earlier, the National Association of Real Estate Boards took out a full-page ad in the *Wisconsin State Journal* proclaiming "A Property Owners' Bill of Rights."[23] COURTESY OF CAPITAL NEWSPAPERS ARCHIVES

ADVERTISEMENT

ATTENTION!
Property Owners

Why should you oppose housing sections of the equal opportunities ordinance?

· **BECAUSE**   This Is "Forced Occupancy" Legislation

· **BECAUSE**   No specific need has been shown or proven. Our Board of Realtors has to date, one request for aid in finding housing as a result of our open invitation which appeared in both local newspapers. Furthermore, with minority groups, including colored, in basically every city ward, we believe anyone can find housing in every area of the city, commensurate with their ability to obtain financing.

· **BECAUSE**   This proposed ordinance invites harrassment.

· **BECAUSE**   In effect you are guilty of the complaint filed against you by anyone until you prove yourself innocent.

· **BECAUSE**   This ordinance will not eliminate discrimination. Those who are prejudiced will continue to discriminate!

· **BECAUSE**   This ordinance could set neighbor against neighbor — tenant against landlord. It will foster fear and uncertainty in the minds of homeowners!

TAKE ACTION — SPEAK UP

You Are The Only One Who Can Help Yourself!   ATTEND THE PUBLIC HEARING
Call or Write Your Alderman!   TUESDAY NIGHT, DECEMBER 10th, 1963

This ad is presented as a public service by the Madison Board of Realtors.

"I don't think the residents of any ward have to answer to a group of university students under any circumstances," he says.[24]

When the public hearing ends near midnight, it's still standing room only. Council president Kopp calls for a show of hands; city clerk A. W. Bareis counts 198 in support and 68 opposed.

Introduced and strongly supported by a conservative mayor, the fair housing measure also has its strongest council support from conservatives, led by alderpersons Ethel Brown, Harrison Garner, and William Bradford Smith. Its sharpest opposition comes from labor-friendly aldermen, including Rohr, Kopp, Leo Cooper, and Ellsworth Swenson.

"Let's face it," says Rohr, "the world is built on prejudice and discrimination."

North side alderman Kopp acknowledges there's some discrimination in Madison, but he asks, "Should we pass a law because there are a few bigots?"

"It's the very minimum we can do," Mayor Reynolds replies, "so that we can go on record and say that all our citizens are equal as far as the City Council is concerned."

After almost two hours of debate, the chamber is still packed when the committee votes 12–10 to delete the entire housing provision. As the conservative, pro-ordinance *Wisconsin State Journal* notes, five aldermen endorsed by the liberal, pro-ordinance *Capital Times* vote against fair housing. After a motion to kill the entire ordinance fails, 13–9, the council adjourns at 1:30 a.m.[25]

The setback is bitter but represents some progress from the 14–5 defeat a similar, weaker measure authored by then-alderman Ivan Nestingen suffered in 1952.[26]

Fair housing advocates have about forty-two hours to figure out how to get at least one vote changed, so Mayor Reynolds can break an 11–11 tie to enact the ordinance.[27]

It's the council's only female member, Tenth Ward alderwoman Ethel Brown, who crafts the critical compromise—to exempt rooming houses with four or fewer roomers and owner-occupied apartment buildings with four or fewer units. The rooming house exemption isn't just to get the eleventh vote, Ald. William B. Smith thinks, but also to "reflect the attitudes of her constituents" in University Heights, who rent rooms to UW students but wouldn't want "to open their homes to people of all races and colors where they would have to share the same bathroom."[28]

Brown's amendment is quickly adopted, starting a dizzying display of legislative freestyling that exempts absentee-landlord apartments and all single-family homes from coverage.

As a backlash to the CORE testing activities, the council also adopts Sixth Ward alderman George Elder's motion making it unlawful for anyone without a "bona fide intention" to offer to buy or rent housing "for the sole purpose of securing evidence of a discrimination practice as defined in this ordinance." Two months after the premiere of the university's controversial "To Find a Home" film, the council thus makes illegal the testing it depicts.

As distraught supporters watch the wreckage of exemption after exemption and consider pulling the matter entirely, an unexpected savior appears. For all the advocates' organizing, it takes a bewildering move by an opponent to make the measure meaningful.

Ald. Bruce Davidson—a consistent opponent of the fair housing provisions—moves to limit exemptions from the ordinance to only owner-occupied buildings. His amendment carries, without debate, 20–2. He explains he moved the amendment to strengthen the ordinance, which he still votes against.[29]

The final version satisfies far east side alderman George Reger; though he opposed it on Tuesday, he supports the ordinance as amended, creating an 11–11 tie that Reynolds breaks with an emphatic "aye." Madison has made history with adoption of the first fair housing ordinance in the state.[30]

As adopted, the ordinance makes it illegal to refuse to sell, rent, lease, or finance housing based on race, color, creed, or ancestry, with these exemptions:

- Owner-occupied single-family residences;
- Owner-occupied houses with not more than four roomers;
- Owner-occupied apartment buildings with four units or less.

Based on 1960 federal census data tabulated by the plan department, about 60 percent of the housing units in Madison are exempted from coverage:

HOUSING UNITS COVERED/EXEMPT FROM FAIR HOUSING CODE

	Total	Owner-occupied	Covered by Fair Housing Ordinance	% Units Covered
Single Family	21,595	17,550	4,045	18.7%
1–4 Apt. Units	11,075	5,845	5,231	47%
5+ Units	6,355	n/a	6,355	100%
Total Dwelling Units	39,025	23,395	15,631	40%

Davidson's amendment more than doubles the number of units covered, increasing the number of houses and apartments where nonwhites can live in Madison by 9,276. But there are still more than 23,000 units where the ordinance does not apply.[31]

Open housing advocates are restrained in their celebration. Colston calls it a "net gain" for Madison, "even with the housing section watered down in a serious manner." Pledging a "sincere effort" to make it work, McGrath says he's "greatly disappointed that the City Council found it necessary to so greatly weaken the proposed ordinance."[32]

Privately, though, they're thrilled at getting far more than they expected; McGrath, associate editor of *The Progressive* magazine, and attorney Abrahamson can hardly contain their delight at what's been accomplished.[33]

For Ald. Rohr, the fiercest foe of open housing, who thought Thursday night was a smashing success, Friday brings an uncomfortable understanding of what happened. When he reads the full account of what passed after all the amendments, he's aghast.

"My God!" he exclaims. "I had no idea what we voted for last night." As the business representative for Painters Local 802 and president of the Madison Building Trades

Attorney Shirley S. Abrahamson, a member of the Mayor's Commission on Human Rights, walking her Irish setters Betsy-B and Briscoe. Abrahamson becomes a partner with the law firm of La Follette, Sinykin, Doyle & Anderson this July, as she is helping draft the historic Equal Opportunities Ordinance.[34] WHI IMAGE ID 137633, PHOTO BY EDWIN STEIN

Council, Rohr takes some solace from a vote by the Madison Federation of Labor a few days later. After adopting a generic resolution opposing discrimination, the Fed rejects, 30–15, a motion by the Wisconsin Federation of Teachers' C. Clark Kissinger to endorse the just-enacted ordinance.[35]

At year's end, Mayor Reynolds appoints the charter members of the Equal Opportunities Commission, including MCHR members McGrath, MacDonald, Ald. James Marks, and Reverend James C. Wright. He does not appoint Abrahamson or Colston.[36]

Civil Rights Employment

Although housing is the controversial aspect of the city initiative, NAACP leader Colston presses the business community over the summer to endorse, and live by, the employment protections as well. The Madison Chamber of Commerce issues a statement affirming "the principle of equal job opportunities for all persons meeting the job qualifications," which Colston calls "a deceptive and fraudulent document which adds nothing to the solution of the problem and indeed could aggravate it."

The business community "has taken no affirmative action to integrate the personnel in its stores," Colston charges, and says he views the chamber's response as "worse than none. We are not satisfied with the puny efforts made by some merchants who hire Negroes as elevator operators and janitors and then think they have offered fair employment to the Negro." He warns that "sit-ins and picketing will be started" at stores and businesses "which refuse to raise" qualified African Americans "from menial positions."[37]

A new survey by the State Industrial Commission underlines Colston's claims; of 469 employees in three Madison restaurants, only nine are African American, all of whom have menial, back-of-the-house jobs. The story is similar in the building trades; of the 188 apprentices, none are African American, and no African Americans are on the list of apprenticeship candidates. Trades union officials insist that's not because of discrimination, but due to lack of interest. "I've never seen a colored boy apply for an apprenticeship in carpentry," says Carl Eckloff, president of the Madison Building and Construction Trades Council. There are four local building trades unions with black members—laborers, bricklayers, cement finishers, and Ald. Babe Rohr's painters. And among nine of the city's largest employers, there are only forty-seven African Americans in a total workforce of 7,706 employees.[38]

The Movement

March 4—UW faculty reject a resolution that would ban university sports teams playing schools from states that "impede or attempt to impede" civil rights enforcement. The existing policy prohibiting competition against teams from institutions that practice discrimination remains in place.[39]

Part of the Madison contingent of around forty about to leave from Memorial Union August 27 for the March on Washington for Jobs and Freedom. In the center is the Reverend George W. Vann, pastor of St. Paul's African Methodist Episcopal Church, the group leader.[40] UNIVERSITY OF WISCONSIN–MADISON ARCHIVES IMAGE S00650

June 15—Led by schoolchildren carrying the American flag, about 150 civil rights activists silently march around the Capitol for ninety minutes in tribute to slain African American leader Medgar Evers. Afterward, local NAACP chairman Marshall Colston tells reporters, "We intend to go into the streets, to demonstrate and picket" unless the Madison Chamber of Commerce commits to ending job discrimination.[41]

August 2—The regents adopt Regent Arthur DeBardeleben's motion that the UW administration "be requested to examine the whole subject of civil rights and equal educational opportunities with a view to determine whether the University is doing everything it can do in this area and what further can be done."[42]

September—At Madison Vocational, Technical, and Adult Schools, about fifteen of the ten thousand students enrolled in day and evening classes are black, and only one out of six hundred in post–high school courses; there's one black teacher, Velma Hamilton. At Madison Business College, two or three of the four hundred students are black. There are four black teachers in the Madison schools.[43]

September 22—Close to a thousand people gather at the Capitol Square in the year's largest civil rights demonstration, occasioned not by legislation or aspiration, but by tragedy—the murder in early September of four black girls in the Birmingham, Alabama, church bombing. But the march and rally sponsored by the Madison Committee for Civil Rights are temporarily disrupted by a swastika-bedecked white supremacist

As He Defends His Ideas

Negro Youth Discovers People Listen to Him

Eugene Parks
"... *a fanatic doesn't do anybody any good* ..."
—State Journal Photo by John Kreisler

A *Wisconsin State Journal* profile of Eugene Parks (Madison city alderman, 1969–1975; State Personnel board member, 1985–1990) at age sixteen, shortly after the La Follette High School junior is elected president of the Wisconsin Association of Student Councils. Last year, Parks served as a Madison Youth Council delegate to the Mayor's Commission on Human Rights.[44] COURTESY OF CAPITAL NEWSPAPERS ARCHIVES

pushing through the crowd and shouting racist epithets. Owen H. Reierson, twenty-four, harangues the stunned and silent crowd until he is arrested for disorderly conduct. The marchers, mostly white, with a high percentage of students, bear black armbands; they march around the Capitol twice, the group stretching three-quarters of the way around. Reierson, a Madison native, is on parole from San Quentin Prison in California for a second-degree robbery conviction.[45]

September 24—District Attorney William D. Byrne hires the first black assistant DA, Beloit native Donald R. Murphy.[46]

October 28—About six hundred attend the Union Theater premiere of the controversial UW film "To Find a Home," showing blacks attempting, generally without success, to rent apartments in Madison outside their "traditional" neighborhoods. The film is an acted re-creation of the film shot with hidden microphones and cameras, which the UW suppressed in 1962 out of privacy and civil liberties concerns. The *Daily Cardinal* says the film lacks "the suspense and spontaneity of the original film," but that the university's "decision not to release the original film was correct."[47]

November 10—The young black civil rights leader John Lewis, executive director of the Student Nonviolent Coordinating Committee (SNCC), tells a Union Theater gathering that the "vicious and evil system of discrimination" will be peacefully overthrown.[48]

November 13—The Friends of SNCC registers as a UW student organization, and a Madison chapter of the Congress of Racial Equality (CORE) is organized under cochairs Janet Lee—sister of Senator Gaylord Nelson and a member of the State Democratic Party executive committee—and student Thomas Bolden. Biology grad student Silas Norman is vice chair and alderman Frank Hall is treasurer.[49]

November 19—CORE national director James Farmer celebrates the new Madison chapter with a Park Motor Inn press conference and a speech at Mt. Zion Baptist Church, pledging that the fledgling local affiliate will continue its testing activities to expose discrimination in housing and employment. A UW campus chapter of CORE had held an organizational meeting in early April but never filed as a student organization.[50]

Urban Renewal

Urban renewal expands this year, even as the Madison Redevelopment Authority (MRA) gets powerful enemies both within and outside city hall and the city council flirts with a very foolish decision.

Important urban renewal groundbreakings bookend the year. On January 24, seven months after the last building in the Brittingham area was razed, the First Development Corporation of Milwaukee starts construction on what will be the state's first residential urban renewal project to be completed—the $2.4 million Sampson Plaza, 150 market-rate units in ten three-story buildings. "There is no more important program in the state than urban renewal," Governor John Reynolds says. According to federal Urban Renewal Administration commissioner William Slayton, "The relocation experience here in Madison has been excellent." On December 19, the Madison Housing Authority has a ceremonial groundbreaking of the frozen 2.5-acre parcel bounded by Regent, Lake, Murray, and Milton Streets for the sixty-unit public housing project for the elderly, part of its $1.88 million program that also includes one hundred low-income units off Wright Street, on Rethke Avenue, and in South Madison, all of which start construction.

The MRA continues to buy up and tear down the Bush. As the year opens, it has purchased 180 of the 253 parcels in the Triangle area, at a cost of $2.43 million; by October, it has purchased 229 and razed 182, about 70 percent. In November, the MRA starts condemnation proceedings on Neighborhood House, the Bush's most important secular building and the community linchpin for decades.[51]

At the year's outset, the relationship between the Madison Housing Authority (MHA) and the MRA is so bad the *State Journal* editorially pleads with the agencies to "reconcile their differences in the best interests of the city." Its call goes unheeded.[52]

In March, the MHA declines to participate in the MRA's proposed lease plan, and also tells the MRA it's not interested in undertaking a study for a low-income housing demonstration program.[53]

Campus, Greenbush, and environs, March 1963. Construction is almost complete on Sellery Hall and just beginning on Witte Hall and Sampson Plaza. On the upper campus, the Social Sciences building has replaced a stand of trees in the Muir Woods behind the Carillon Tower.
WH IMAGE ID 137491, PHOTO BY JOHN NEWHOUSE

In late May, the council reverses the long-standing MRA policy not to allow Triangle property owners to move their buildings, and directs the MRA to put Triangle buildings in good shape up to bid to be moved. "Redevelopment has had a tough enough time without giving it a black eye by putting the bulldozer to good buildings," says former alderman Reese, just beaten in his bid for reelection. After a personal inspection tour by Mayor Reynolds, the MRA in June identifies four buildings that could be moved—the properties of Vito Schiro, Paul Genna, and Robert Caruso, and its own relocation office.[54]

In June, the MRA votes against requiring the proposed Triangle shopping center to provide space for Triangle merchants because that "would restrict the feasibility of the sale." The MRA minutes also relate that "it was pointed out that the merchants could buy the site themselves or could participate in the purchase of it as an aid to their own relocation."[55]

In November, the MHA has to cut its public housing construction costs by $18,000 by eliminating refrigerators in the 100 scattered-site low-income units.[56]

A month later, while the MHA is pleading for more public housing, and former Greenbush residents are still demanding on-site replacement housing, the MRA tentatively agrees to sell a large Triangle parcel for 250 units of market rate elderly housing—the $3 million, eight-story Vilas Towers, which has failed to find financing for its Mansion Hill proposal overlooking Lake Mendota.[57]

Renewal and a Race

When MRA chair Albert McGinnis decided to run against Mayor Reynolds, he should have expected that urban renewal would become an issue in the campaign. A week after he beats Reynolds in the March 5 primary it does, with the mayor's stunning attack on the authority for its handling of Triangle razing and relocation—particularly the 1959 Eligibility and Relocation Report that stated there was adequate and affordable replacement housing. "The report was so fantastically inaccurate that anyone who had done a fair job of research would know immediately that it did not reflect the Madison situation," he says, citing Florence Zmudzinski's similar conclusion.

Although the 1959 data about housing availability and the schedule of demolition came from city staff, Reynolds holds McGinnis—chair of the MRA since its founding in 1958—personally responsible. "A great deal of needless human suffering arose out of the hasty and ill-planned removal of people from the Triangle Renewal project and reflects the bungling of my opponent," Reynolds asserts. "Due to the speed with which the authority went ahead, the problem grew worse."[58]

"I resent any implication that we have bungled the renewal program [or] caused a great deal of human suffering," State Rep. Norman C. Anderson, another charter citizen member, responds at the MRA meeting two days later. He says Reynolds attacked McGinnis for "purely political reasons."[59]

Ald. Harold Rohr, who was vital to Reynolds's 1961 election but is now backing McGinnis, blasts the comments as "uncalled-for and irresponsible. If he's got something to say, he should come here and say it."

The MRA considers Rohr's proposal to invite Reynolds, but concludes "that nothing would be served in having the Mayor appear before the Authority and read the statement that he had already released to the press."

Days after Reynolds's narrow victory on April 2, McGinnis resigns—just one week before his five-year term expires. He does not go quietly. "As a result of your own failure to make yourself aware of and be informed" of the MRA's activities, he writes Reynolds, "you have placed the redevelopment authority in an apparent emergency situation." McGinnis suggests that Reynolds start reading the MRA reports and "avoid pushing the panic button or otherwise smear a project carried on as a mandate of the people, with council approval, by non-paid citizen members."[60]

Rohr, whom the NAACP and Unitarians had tried to have removed from the MRA in 1961, also quits, blasting Reynolds for playing "campaign politics" with the authority.[61]

Reynolds blunts any political damage McGinnis was hoping to inflict, however, with his appointment of the widely respected, recently retired school superintendent Philip Falk, who is quickly elected chair.[62]

Rejecting Renewal

Madison's first urban renewal areas affected the poor and powerless. Not so the General Neighborhood Renewal Plan (GNRP), covering land from Mansion Hill to University Heights. That proves to be a problem for the MRA.

The proposed joint planning effort has been controversial since last spring, when city and university planners started work on the application for $128,582 in federal funds to prepare for the impact the university's seventy-one acres of development will have on the 496 acres buffering that expansion area, from Wisconsin Avenue to Spooner Street.[63]

The university expects to spend $17.97 million acquiring the land in the expansion area, where it anticipates $100 million in construction over the next ten years. After recouping $4.14 million by selling some parcels for private development, the university plans to adopt an urban renewal plan that would provide $9.23 million in federal funds for land costs. President Harrington comes to the council in late February to explain that the city-university study is the key to the $9 million.[64]

The council agrees, voting 15–4 to submit the application. But that doesn't end the debate; the vote ignites it.[65]

A few weeks after the council action, attorney Lowell Thronson calls a protest meeting at the Washington School, 545 W. Dayton St.; two hundred attend and form the Citizen's Watchdog Committee. Thronson tells the angry crowd that "vultures" are waiting to snatch properties at depressed prices and calls for a "massive force" to fight the study. Donald Hovde, president of the Madison Board of Realtors, echoes Thronson and predicts vast acreage being cleared. Ald. Reese tries to explain that the buffer area will focus on conservation and rehabilitation, but he is shouted down.[66]

It's not massive force that the committee applies at first, but political propaganda— a light red leaflet filled with mischaracterizations and misrepresentations about urban

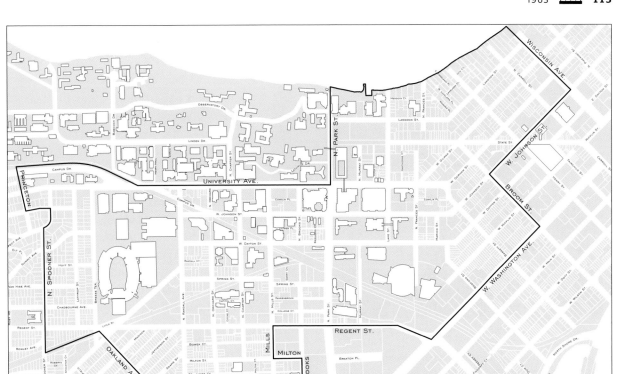

The UW General Neighborhood Renewal Plan, as initially proposed. DAVID MICHAEL MILLER

renewal and the GNRP. Coordinating with the pro-Reynolds Citizens for Better Government political action committee, of which Hovde is the secretary, the Citizen's Watchdog Committee distributes the so-called "pink sheet" in wards represented by aldermen supporting the GNRP or McGinnis. Although Reynolds introduced and strongly supports the GNRP, the committee does not criticize him for doing so, and he does not rebuke the committee for its inaccuracies.[67]

These efforts pay off on April 2 with the reelection of Reynolds and the election of four aldermen who ran on antirenewal platforms, including railroad switchman Leo Cooper, who upsets MRA member Gordon Reese.[68]

Then Rohr stirs the pot even more, resigning from the MRA and moving that the city rescind its approval of the GNRP study.[69] On April 23, the council in Committee of the Whole votes 12–7 to do just that. Reynolds, strongly urging the council to reject the rescission, thinks the gamesmanship Rohr started is personal. "I feel all of this is for my benefit," he says.[70]

When the council meets for final action two nights later, Reynolds plays his own card, vowing not to veto the rescission resolution if it passes. Aldermen can't cast the popular but irresponsible vote and count on him to bail them out.

West side alderman James Marks, a member of the UW engineering faculty, levels a blistering attack on the "watchdog committee," calling them "a fanatic group of

MRA 'Hanged' In Protest

Hanging the Madison Redevelopment Authority in effigy at the Madison Home Owners Association picnic at Brittingham Park, August 24. Greenbush-area alderman Leo Cooper, appointed to the MRA after his election in April, is in the light sport coat, fourth from the right, looking at the effigy. COURTESY OF CAPITAL NEWSPAPERS ARCHIVES, PHOTO BY TOM BARLET

extremists" who used half-truths, distortions, and McCarthyism. "Their kind of demagoguery is a real danger," Marks says.

Such exhortations—and the fear of being blamed for losing a $9 million federal grant—work; enough aldermen change their vote that the rescission fails by one vote, 11–9.[71]

But the MRA's victory is only a temporary reprieve. In August, a new threat emerges—the Madison Home Owners Association (MHOA), started by property owners in the University expansion area. It wants a referendum to ban any future urban renewal unless a project is endorsed by 51 percent of voters in the applicable wards.

To fight the next urban renewal, MHOA links with the lingering resentment from the earlier efforts and hosts a Brittingham Park picnic for former Triangle residents, who demonstrate their attitude about urban renewal by hanging the MRA in effigy. "Urban renewal in Madison represents the will of the middle-class planner who plays with the city like a child plays with his toys," says Fran Remeika, the MHOA's lead researcher and analyst. Within weeks, the association has more than four hundred members pledged to work for, and support, the referendum to end local urban renewal.[72]

Although based in the university area, the MHOA also attacks the MRA's proposed Marquette Area Redevelopment Study, which covers seventeen full or half blocks along Williamson Street from Patterson to Thornton Streets, plus the Dewey Court area. A neighborhood pro-renewal petition correctly decries "the blight and delinquency which have occurred" and continue; on six blocks along upper Williamson Street, more than half the structures are deteriorated or dilapidated.

On September 24, the council disregards the outside agitators—none of the fifty MHOA members at the meeting live in the Marquette area—and endorses the study, which is sponsored by Sixth Ward alderman George Elder. The MHOA continues its attacks while the study is under way; more than three hundred east siders come to an MHOA meeting at the Eagles Club in mid-October to hear Remeika denounce the MRA as "dishonest . . . unfair . . . cold-blooded." MRA assistant director Eugene Gangstad is present but stays silent when invited to respond.[73]

On December 26, the council rejects a full federal urban renewal project and approves a plan for strict building code enforcement and city purchase of distressed properties in the Dewey Court area as they become available from willing sellers.[74]

That doesn't stop the Home Owners Association from continuing to plan its referendum to end urban renewal, with the spring election about a hundred days away.

Survey Shows Surprising Satisfaction (Or Does It?)

In early November, the MRA releases a survey of 260 families relocated from the Triangle between October 1961 and April 1963 showing wide satisfaction with the program—173 respondents in favor, 73 opposed, the rest neutral or unaccounted for. Of the families relocated for at least one year, sixteen felt the program was basically good, except it hurt the elderly; fourteen were happy about it; nine were strongly opposed.[75]

The "Interim Report on Relocation" documents tremendous dispersion; Triangle families moved to twenty-eight of the city's thirty-three census tracts (although the largest number, 33 out of the 260, remained in the area). Relocation also increased the number of homeowners from sixty-eight to eighty-five; tenancies declined from 192 to 107.

In terms of housing quality, the report documents a clear success. While a little more than a third of the housing initially occupied by the 260 families in the Triangle was substandard (about evenly divided between housing of whites and nonwhites), all 199 units to which the families moved were inspected and found (or made) standard and up to code.

But respondents care less about the quality of their new housing than the price they got for their old. Economically, owners of income property were clear losers; of the twenty-five interviewees who owned income property, fifteen moved into single-family units—usually at higher cost, and with loss of income. Ten replaced income property at higher cost.

Minorities were also disadvantaged. Of the 1,111 units staff inspected to make sure they were

On November 5, St. Joseph's Catholic Church, 12 S. Park St., is razed, to be replaced by a medical facility. Built in 1916 as the only Madison church intended to serve a single nationality, it was the social and spiritual center for three generations of Italians living in the Bush. The church's parochial school, just across Bowen Court, was also recently razed. Originally a wooden structure, the church was bricked in 1931 by neighborhood men idled by the Depression. The church, which for many years featured a well-attended Sunday evening service, holds its last Mass on July 28. The November report on attitudes of relocated families notes that "the most concentrated negative feelings (usually among elderly or long-term Triangle residents), centered around [losing] the church."[76] WHI IMAGE ID 116030, PHOTO BY RICHARD SRODA habitable for people being relocated, 960 were available only to whites; two nonwhite families received a total of twenty-one referrals before they finally gave up and left the state.

The objective of providing decent, safe, and affordable housing in reasonably convenient locations "has been less than a total reality to all," Rupnow concedes in his cover letter forwarding the report to the MRA, especially for minorities and whites with large families.

He blames the Madison Board of Realtors for refusing to help. In December, as the council considers realtors' opposition to the Equal Opportunity Ordinance, Rupnow tells the group, "We've had almost no assistance from the real estate profession in terms of obtaining relocation housing [for minorities]. The vast majority of board members have not been the least bit interested in the relocation of minority families. Frankly, both the staff and I sincerely doubt that there is any possibility of a change of heart."[77]

UW sociology professor Jack Ladinsky later criticizes the survey sample and methods.[78]

Renewal and Race

The MRA again confronts conflicts at the conjunction of race and renewal.

In January, the MRA amends its application for the South Madison planning grant to add a prohibition on "discrimination because of race, color, creed or national origin," as required by President Kennedy's recent executive order.[79]

But in November, thirty days before the city will adopt the state's first open housing ordinance, the MRA refuses to stop using segregated lists for relocation referrals, even after a request from the city's Special Committee on Minority Housing.

Rupnow insists the authority doesn't keep segregated lists but notes only whether a unit is open to nonwhite tenants. "If the list were limited only to units available for open occupancy," he says, "our search for relocation housing would be limited and the competition for nonwhite housing would be increased." That is, whites would have 85 percent fewer relocation options, without adding any units for nonwhites. "The fact that there are a number of units in Madison that are not available to nonwhites is something over which we have no control," except in its own projects, Rupnow reminds the authority, noting that open occupancy will be required for housing built in the Triangle itself.

"As long as there is a list that is available to whites only, that is segregation, in our definition," the minority housing group chair, filmmaker Stuart Hanisch, replies.

"I am certainly in sympathy with the request," MRA relocation director Florence Zmudzinski responds, but she notes that, despite President Kennedy's executive order, the federal reporting forms still require race-based listing of available housing. The MRA votes unanimously to continue the race-based listings "until such time that the Federal Regulations are changed."[80]

State Street, November 29, 1963. WHI IMAGE ID 116041, PHOTO BY RICHARD SRODA

Race for Mayor

Henry Reynolds, fifty-seven, looks pretty good for reelection, especially when county clerk Otto Festge and alderman Lawrence McCormick pass on challenging him, leaving only east side attorney, land developer, and MRA chair Albert J. McGinnis, forty-four.[81]

In his first bid for elective office, McGinnis hits Reynolds for the city's growing debt, his rocky relations with the council, and for moving too fast on the Monona Causeway and too slow on annexations. Although the civic auditorium is no longer the dominant issue, McGinnis favors the Monona Terrace site and calls Reynolds's Conklin Park/waterworks site "ridiculous."[82] Like President Kennedy, McGinnis served in the Pacific theater during World War II and often adopts JFK's penchant for putting his hand in his suit coat pocket when he sings in the choir at Messiah Lutheran Church.[83]

Reynolds runs on his record of frugality (he never hired the one administrative assistant he could have), holding taxes at forty-two mills this year ($42 in property taxes for every thousand dollars of assessed value), and making progress on a downtown library, parking ramps, and the causeway. He wants a major expansion of the municipal airport and city acquisition of Cherokee marshland for conservation and recreation.[84]

McGinnis, who is strongly supported by the *Capital Times*, opposes the April bond issues for Monona Causeway and new sewers; Reynolds emphatically favors both, as does the *Wisconsin State Journal*, which emphatically favors Reynolds.[85]

After McGinnis's surprising 731-vote margin in the March 5 primary, Reynolds goes on the attack, accusing McGinnis of "bungling" the relocation of Triangle residents as MRA chairman. Council conservatives chime in, claiming McGinnis "juggled" MRA finances improperly (not true) and supported regulatory practices as MRA chair that he opposed in his own private land developments (true).[86]

On election day, April 2, Reynolds carries the west side, as he did in 1961, and his challenger the east; Rohr helps McGinnis carry the south side, but Reynolds's support in the Vilas, University Heights, and Nakoma neighborhoods provide the narrow victory— 19,809 to 18,605—with less than half his 1961 margin.[87]

The election night bond news is uniformly good for Reynolds, as voters approve all five referenda. Four issues worth $7 million—for the University Avenue expansion, storm sewers, airport improvements, and a two-floor addition for the vocational school— pass overwhelmingly; the $1 million bond to start construction of the Monona Causeway carries by a much closer margin.[88]

But the aldermanic returns carry cause for mayoral concern—Reynolds's political organization Citizens for Better Government supports only one of the six new aldermen, and two of his strongest council supporters are defeated.[89] And on top of that, the council elects as its new president his frequent foe, the pro–Monona Terrace alderman Kopp.[90]

Reynolds's second term is not off to a smooth start. And things are only going to get bumpier.

UW

COMMENCEMENT, JUNE 10[91]
- Baccalaureate: 1,909
- Master's/PhD: 740
- JD/MD: 150[92]

FALL ENROLLMENT
- Total Students: 24,275[93]

HOMECOMING
- Show: Dick Gregory, Maynard Ferguson, Chad Mitchell Trio
- Dance: Maynard Ferguson [94]

NEW BUILDINGS OF NOTE
- Van Vleck Hall, 480 Lincoln Dr.[95]
- Sellery Hall, 821 W. Johnson St.[96]

Campus Calendar

January 11—UW president Fred Harvey Harrington rejects a close research and development relationship with business interests. "We don't want to develop a research park," Harrington tells the regents. "We shouldn't take research off the campus, and we shouldn't bring industry on the campus."[97]

Southeast dorms and environs in the summer of 1963. Sellery Hall, a ten-story dormitory for 1,100 male and female students, opens at the corner of North Park and West Johnson Streets on September 9, the first unit in the $24 million Southeast Dormitory and Recreational Area. Witte Hall is under construction at right; it opens in the fall of 1964. The brownstone apartments of Sterling Court are between Park and Murray Streets. The new administration building is under construction at the upper center. UNIVERSITY OF WISCONSIN–MADISON ARCHIVES IMAGE S00335

January 24—The UW Protection and Security Department hires its first female investigator, Nancy Marshall, a former member of the Madison Police Department's Bureau of Crime Prevention. Campus police chief Albert Hamann says Marshall, a former home economics teacher in Sheboygan Falls, will handle investigations involving women and juveniles.[98]

February 18—Merce Cunningham and his dance company mystify most of the large Union Theater crowd with the avant-garde choreography of "Dance by Chance." The three long dances also feature musical direction and performance by John Cage.[99]

March 7—Students for Peace and Disarmament sponsors a public forum on "Vietnam: Our Undeclared War." At the time, there are more than ten thousand American soldiers in Vietnam, designated by the US government as military advisers and not as combat troops; about a hundred American soldiers have died in country.[100]

March 8—A week after playing the "Playboy Lounge" (Inn Wisconsin) at the Military Ball on March 1, pianist Ben Sidran (2012 Distinguished Alumni Award, Wisconsin Alumni Association) and His Quintet inaugurate live Friday afternoon jazz in a packed Rathskeller.[101]

March 10—W. H. Auden gives a lackadaisical, almost lazy performance of his Pulitzer Prize–winning poetry for a near-capacity Union Theater crowd.[102]

March 26–27—Guitar master Andrés Segovia awes audiences at two sold-out Union Theater shows with his survey of guitar styles over the centuries (everything but early lute music). Segovia first performed on campus in 1933 in Great Hall, only two years after his New York debut.[103]

On January 3, five thousand fans gather at Municipal Airport to greet the Badger football team, returning after its stirring Rose Bowl loss (42–37) to USC on New Year's Day.[104] WHI IMAGE ID 136611, PHOTO BY DAVID SANDELL

April 23—The third Annual UW Women's Day brings about 350 alumnae and other state women to campus for a series of seminars. "When you compare the desire of women for knowledge with the percentage of women in professional schools," President Harrington says, "you can see we have barely begun doing the things that need to be done."[105]

April 25—The Student Life and Interests Committee caps a long struggle for female empowerment by approving the Associated Women Students' proposal to liberalize women's hours. Effective November 1, seniors and women over twenty-one will have no curfew, and juniors will have no curfew on weekends—making Wisconsin one of the more lenient schools in the Big Ten. Starting with the coming Summer Session, the hours for house closings will also be extended to 1 a.m.[106]

April 28—Anthropologist Dr. Margaret Mead tells a Union Theater crowd of about four hundred that early marriages are keeping women from careers outside the home and domesticating men so they choose family needs over professional opportunities.[107]

May 2—United Auto Workers union president Walter Reuther tells a capacity Union Theater crowd that America is "smug, complacent, and indifferent" and needs a stronger sense of national purpose, including progress on civil rights.[108] Up the hill, Beat poet Lawrence Ferlinghetti reads to a rapt, overflow crowd in 272 Bascom, the last event on the Poets 1963 series sponsored by the Union Literary Committee and the Athenean Society.[109]

Steve Miller (Rock and Roll Hall of Fame inductee, 2016), with bandmates Ben Sidran and Boz Scaggs, plays a fundraiser for the Elvehjem Art Center.[110] UNIVERSITY OF WISCONSIN–MADISON ARCHIVES IMAGE S00105

YOU ARE INVITED TO A

BEAN FEED

$1.00

SUNDAY, MAY 19th
4-8 P.M.
WISCONSIN CENTER LAWN

All Proceeds to Student Campaign for Art Center

BADGER BEAUTIES—To Serve Hot Dogs, Beans, Chips, Pop.

ENTERTAINMENT—Dixieland Combo (4-5 p.m.)

Steve Miller and The Ardells (5-7 p.m.)

The D-G Combo (7-8 p.m.)

JOIN IN THE STUDENT CAMPAIGN FOR THE ELVEHJEM ART CENTER

ROUNDY SAYS

"The All-Stars worked it right Vandy didn't throw to Richter too much that left the other receivers open. As the Packers were looking for Pat to get the ball. But when Vandy found him it was over."
—*Wisconsin State Journal*, August 6, after Ron Vander Kelen and Pat Richter combined for a seventy-three-yard touchdown to lead the College All-Stars to a stunning 20–17 upset of the NFL champion Green Bay Packers in Soldier Field.

May 6—Faculty makes voluntary ROTC permanent, after the two-year trial period succeeds in maintaining participation on the Madison and Milwaukee campuses at 75 percent of the 1959 level of 195 students. Compulsory ROTC would have returned if fewer than 146 students enrolled; 178 registered in 1961, and 155 in 1962.[111]

May 19—Naval ROTC in dress blues stand guard and the university band plays "Varsity" as the outstanding young women from each living unit form a "W" and are honored during the 43rd Annual Senior Swingout ceremonies on Bascom Hill.[112]

May 21—The Student Life and Interests Committee approves letting all senior students live in apartments, effective the fall of 1964. The current rule, allowing only seniors over twenty-one to do so, affects about four hundred underage seniors.[113]

May 29—Two-time All-American Pat Richter—the only man since 1926 to earn nine varsity letters, and the holder of seventeen school, conference, or national receiving records—signs with the Washington franchise of the National Football League, where he joins fellow East High Purgolder and Badger Dale Hackbart.[114]

August 3—Senator Fred Risser secures adoption of a bill to save fraternity beer parties by reversing an earlier law that inadvertently prevented persons under twenty-one from drinking beer unless accompanied by a parent or guardian or in a beer bar. Risser's bill clarifies that persons aged eighteen to twenty-one may drink beer outside of a licensed establishment if they are in the presence of a "mature, responsible adult" who will "insure propriety at a gathering of young persons." The ban on carryout sales to unemancipated minors remains.[115]

August 6—Marking the eighteenth anniversary of the dropping of the atomic bomb on Hiroshima, demonstrators at a Capitol rally call for a nuclear test ban treaty, withdrawal of US troops from Vietnam, and cuts in the military budget. Sponsors include the Student Peace Center, Students for Peace and Disarmament, Women Strike for Peace, and the Madison Peace Center.[116]

The city's first demonstration against the war in Vietnam, Memorial Union steps, October 18.
WHI IMAGE ID 137728, PHOTO BY EDWIN STEIN

August 18—UW announces the appointment of Harvey Goldberg, UW PhD '50, specialist in French history, as professor of history. Goldberg, who did his doctoral work under President Harrington, has been at Ohio State University.[117]

September 29—Tom Hayden, who just completed his term as president of the Students for a Democratic Society (SDS), gives his "Critique of American Liberalism" to the Socialist Club meeting in Great Hall. A former editor of the Michigan *Daily*, Hayden was the primary author of the SDS's 1962 Port Huron Statement while a graduate student in Ann Arbor.[118]

October 18—About three hundred people gather on the steps of the Memorial Union for the city's first demonstration against the war in Vietnam, sponsored by Students for Peace and Disarmament, Americans for Democratic Action, Student Peace Center, Socialist Club, Young Democrats, Contemporary Affairs Forum, and Young Socialist Alliance. There are now about fifteen thousand American troops in South Vietnam, still not identified as combat forces; 122 die this year, up from 53 in 1962.[119]

December 23—Mathematics and computer science professor J. Barkley Rosser assumes his duties as director of the US Army Mathematics Research Center on campus.[120]

Schools

GRADUATION, JUNE 15
- West: 475
- East: 408
- Central: 213[121]

FALL ENROLLMENT
- Total Students: 28,969[122]

NEW SCHOOLS
- Robert M. La Follette High School, 702 Pflaum Rd.[123]
- Philip H. Falk Elementary School, 6323 Woodington Way[124]

As Robert Gilberts takes over January 1 as Madison's first new Superintendent of Schools since 1939, demographics drive the Board of Education to close one school in the central city and open two on the periphery.[125]

In the first major school redistricting in more than twenty years, the board in early March votes to close the forty-seven-year-old Abraham Lincoln elementary school, 720 E. Gorham St., after this school year. The school has only about half its capacity of 425 pupils; closing it will save about $38,000 in annual operating costs and about $15,000 in teacher salaries. The board agrees to turn the entire parcel—including 330 feet of Lake Mendota frontage—over to the city; Mayor Reynolds says it "has good possibilities as a permanent home for Madison's cultural groups," and the Parks Commission directs parks superintendent James G. Marshall to develop a plan for that purpose. The Madison Art Association quickly expresses a strong interest.[126]

Two days after voting to shutter that central city school, the board endorses the purchase of an eighty-acre site on the northeast corner of Mineral Point and Gammon Roads for a new far west side high school; it will be needed by the fall of 1966, when West High is projected to be at capacity. The board plans to spend $9.3 million on construction from 1966 through the end of the decade.[127]

In May, the board votes to allow pregnant teachers to remain at work until the twentieth week of pregnancy. Until now, teachers were required to resign three months after becoming pregnant. In October, Gilberts explains that "the biggest reason for turnover is that we have a lot of young married women who teach for us."[128]

Young Vandals

It's a summer of youthful school vandalism, with more than $2,000 in damages done to various schools—sometimes by children too young to attend them.

"This is the worst summer of school vandalism we've ever had in Madison," police captain Kenneth Hartwich says in late August, shortly after two boys, ages six and eight, heave large stones through the thermopane windows in the new East High addition.

Hartwich blames parents for not teaching their children "respect for public or other people's property," and says the city has to invoke the statute that allows assessing parents up to $300 for each act of vandalism their children commit.[129]

Coatsworth on Castro's Cuba Canned

In late October, the board votes 3–2 against renting out the Central High School auditorium for a presentation on Cuba by UW economic history grad student John Coatsworth, one of fifty-nine students who broke the federal ban on travel there this summer. James T. Sykes, a YMCA program associate at the University YMCA, had sought to rent the room for Coatsworth (Guggenheim Fellow, 1986; Columbia University Dean of the School of International and Public Affairs, 2007–2011; Columbia University provost, 2011–present) to

speak and show slides in a benefit for the Emergency Civil Liberties Committee, formed to defend four students indicted for flying to Cuba via Czechoslovakia.[130]

"I personally think all these students were wrong," board vice president and east side dentist Dr. Ray Huegel says, because of "the communism of this. I may as well get it out in the open."

After refusing the rental, the board authorizes Superintendent Robert Gilberts to grant the request anyway, if he finds it "feasible." Gilberts had earlier recommended approval, but after further review, he opposes the proposal because of the fund-raising aspect. "We must refuse requests made for private gain," he tells the board when Sykes (Dane County Supervisor, 1968–1972) renews his request. "I don't feel an open-door policy would be in the best interests of the board."

Sykes points out that several groups, from the NAACP to the Student Nonviolent Coordinating Committee to the Audubon Society, have charged admission to events held in public school auditoriums. Gilberts says this is different and would violate state law.

On November 4, the board members vote unanimously to reaffirm Gilbert's rejection.

The Wisconsin Civil Liberties Union condemns the action and adopts a resolution by its chairman, emeritus professor William Gorham Rice, calling the rejection "repressive . . . capricious . . . a discriminatory abuse of power . . . [and] a breach of the public trust."[131]

Dedications and Celebrations

March 12—Governor John Reynolds and Mayor Henry Reynolds headline the dinner banquet celebrating the fiftieth anniversary of Madison Vocational, Technical, and Adult Schools. Other jubilee events include a student dance, a food show, talks to community groups, and publication of a new brochure on the school's history.[132]

October 13—More than eight hundred attend the Sunday ceremony dedicating the Robert M. La Follette High School, 702 Pflaum Rd., in memory of Wisconsin's great Progressive governor and senator. "The finest school in the United States," board president Glenn W. Stephens says of the fifty-five-classroom, $3 million facility, the first junior/senior high school to open since West Junior-Senior High in 1930. Glass walls in halls give the school a light and airy feeling; there's reddish-brown brick and concrete block for substance, walnut paneling for style, and a copper roofline for finish. The school's 1,130 students have 51 teachers, each of whom Principal August Vander Meulen introduces.[133]

November 19—About two hundred attend the dedication ceremony for the Philip H. Falk Elementary School, on the city's far southwest. Falk, recently named chair of the Madison Redevelopment Authority, served as superintendent of schools from 1939 until his retirement on January 1.[134]

Law and Disorder

Inspector Herman Thomas, Censor

Police inspector Herman Thomas, a former foreman at the Gisholt Machine Company, college dropout, and honors graduate from the FBI academy, never goes to the movies—except on assignment as Madison's censor, to enforce the ordinance banning "any obscene or immoral picture in any theater or show house." Former chief Bruce Weatherly gave him that assignment, which Thomas calls his least desirable.

In early January, Thomas gets a tip about a foreign film at the Majestic Theater—*Phaedra*, Jules Dassin's retelling of the Greek tragedy of a second wife's illicit love for her stepson, starring Dassin's wife, the magnetic Melina Mercouri, and a young and sensitive Anthony Perkins. Thomas watches the movie and agrees that the soft-focus, blurred-image love scene is "overtly immoral" and "sickening." Thomas tells the Majestic's assistant manager to cut the offending scene or close the theater.

Wisconsin Civil Liberties Union president William Gorham Rice calls this action intolerable and a "perverse use of police power." Police chief Wilbur Emery agrees that "no one man should sit in judgment" and proposes creation of a citizen's censorship committee, though he wants nothing to do with it.

A few days after Thomas truncates the film, an ad hoc panel of citizens chosen by Emery finds the film appropriate for adults, and restores the cut footage. It is the panel's only action—city attorney Edwin Conrad later advises that the city lacks legal authority to create a censorship board.[135]

Bongo!

Dane County deputies arrest twenty-two "real beatniks," including eleven UW students, after breaking up a midnight bongo party on May 10 in the historic First Lutheran Church at the corner of Old Sauk and Pleasant Valley Roads. Members of the interracial group, including former UW football star Lowell "Gooch" Jenkins, twenty-seven, are charged with criminal trespass and disorderly conduct; some musicians slip out a window and avoid arrest. When church officials testify that the church was unlocked and essentially abandoned, and the deputies testify that the rhythm enthusiasts were polite and respectful, Judge William Buenzli dismisses all counts—but makes each defendant write a letter of apology.[136]

Dragnet Dodged

Madison police with guns drawn lock down the State Capitol over lunch on October 28 and set up a dragnet around the Square, but fail to apprehend a well-dressed young gunman trying to cash checks stolen from the Republican party headquarters at

115 S. Webster St. Officer John H. Shesky comes close to catching the outlaw behind the Belmont Hotel but has to back off in the face of a .32-caliber revolver. The gunman runs toward Wisconsin Avenue and disappears into the crowd around Manchester's department store.[137]

Edgewater Gun Death Reveals Campus Dope Ring

When Edgewater Hotel manager Austin "Augie" Faulkner asks Madison police detective Edward Daley to check up on the young man in suite 38 with a $74 room service tab, neither figures he'll find the heir to a mayonnaise fortune dead on the floor. But when Daley opens the door, he sees Hal F. Hellman, twenty-one, grandson of the condiment company founder, lying under a sheet with an accidentally self-inflicted gunshot wound to the head. Then he sees the room's registered guest—an unemployed, bail-jumping check forger from Chicago, twenty-four-year-old William "Bill" Over—leveling a loaded .38 at him, while Richard Johns, the pot-smoking, bongo-playing son of the late Republican Congressman Joshua Johns from Green Bay, skedaddles. As Over holds the gun on Daley, he takes a handful of sleeping pills and is soon subdued.

Daley knows all three because they've been under surveillance since September, part of a police investigation into a campus-area drug ring. Johns and Hellman both dropped out of the university in November.

Charged with smoking marijuana and selling dollar joints, Johns faces a ten-year prison sentence; Over pleads innocent to six charges, including reckless use of a gun and attempting to obtain morphine with a forged prescription. As police confirm that a female student is also under surveillance and suspicion, the university issues a statement assuring parents that the drug ring involves "an extremely small number of their sons and daughters." The investigation into drug use on campus continues over the Christmas break, with arraignments for Over and Johns set for January.[138]

Trouble for Moonlighting Cops

Striking workers, leftist students, and a nationally respected labor mediator combine this summer to expose and eliminate inappropriate police moonlighting.

On May 24, the twelve mechanics represented by United Auto Workers (UAW) Local 443, frustrated at the lack of progress in their contract negotiations, go on strike against Bruns Volkswagen, 1430 N. Stoughton Rd. They set up a picket line, but the company stays open with scabs from Rockford—until mathematics grad student C. Clark Kissinger, chair of the Socialist Club and organizer of the fledgling chapter of the Students for a Democratic Society (SDS), offers to "get some of my friends to come out and see if we could close the place down."

The next Saturday, thirty picketers from SDS and UAW turn away virtually every potential customer. The strikers start their own garage, and Kissinger begins printing a weekly paper, *Picket Line News*, distributed throughout Madison. "The strike would have certainly collapsed without student intervention," Kissinger tells the SDS national office, for which he would run as National Secretary in 1964–1966. "Even the strikers admit this."

With the action ongoing, accusations fly, and in July the Wisconsin Employment Relations Board (WERB) holds hearings into the company's complaint of unfair labor practices by the union.

That's when police captain George Schiro testifies that the company, claiming threats and violence from the union, is paying thirty-four policemen $3 an hour to work as private security guards while still in uniform. Madison is the only city of any size in Wisconsin to allow police in uniform to work as private security during a strike.

WERB chairman Morris Slavney tells Schiro that's a bad idea, because it gives the appearance "that the forces of law and order might be taking sides, which might just add a little more fuel to the dispute."

"Mr. Slavney's remarks were very appropriate," Mayor Reynolds responds, recommending that "police officers refrain from this sort of thing. If police protection is needed, it should be given in the normal course of duty."

Within days, Reynolds and police chief Wilbur Emery make the policy official, banning off-duty officers from strike security work. They eventually restrict off-duty work even further, requiring all in-uniform moonlighting pay to be handled through the city's payroll system.

The strike ends in mid-December, after a National Labor Relations Board examiner finds the company guilty of unfair labor practice and orders reinstatement of the striking workers. Contract talks continue.[139]

Miscellanea

March 14—The council unanimously approves Sixth Ward alderman George Elder's proposal to adopt and strengthen the state's open meetings law as city policy. All regular and special city meetings will henceforth have to be held in publicly accessible places, with proper notice, and be open, except for personnel items and a few other specified matters.[140]

March 16—The Police and Fire Commission names Ralph A. McGraw, forty-eight, chief of the Madison Fire Department. The twenty-three-year veteran of the department takes over when Chief Edward J. Page retires on July 1.[141]

May 14—The city welfare board formalizes its policy cutting off relief payments for recipients who don't try hard enough to find work. "The dole, while economically satisfying, is psychologically crippling," the board declares. Welfare director Elma Christianson says the board's policies "weren't meant to be punitive, but in some cases they have to be." The board also wants the work-for-relief policy to apply to non-Madison residents, which it currently doesn't; Christianson predicts that would cut the caseload substantially.[142]

May 20—West side schools, fire stations, and the lion house at the Vilas Park Zoo are among the first of twenty-eight Madison-area public buildings to receive supplies for

Civil Defense officials pose while men in the work relief program and county prisoners with Huber Law privileges to work outside the jail unload the first of several truckloads of supplies for Madison-area fallout shelters in late May. Officials suggest the steel drums containing supplies could be used as commodes after the supplies are emptied. WHI IMAGE ID 137739, PHOTO BY EDWIN STEIN

fallout shelters. There are approximately 150,000 shelter spaces in the city—about half in downtown public buildings that are inaccessible at night. The Citizens Committee to Eliminate Civil Defense calls the fallout shelter program "useless and futile" and a waste of money.[143]

June 5—The Madison Parks Commission officially names the recreation area on Lake Mendota between North Butler and North Franklin Streets James Madison Park, the first public facility honoring the city's namesake, the fourth president of the United States and father of the Bill of Rights. The area has commonly, but unofficially, been known as Conklin Park, after nineteenth-century mayor and coal merchant James Conklin, whose holdings included a large ice house at the lakefront end of the North Hamilton Street axial. Joe Jackson, the planning and economic development activist working to put the civic auditorium in this area instead of Law Park, got the city to buy the land from Conklin's descendants in 1939, and it was Jackson who suggested this new branding, which is not subject to council review. The city plans to acquire additional properties to extend the park farther east, to the Lincoln School property.[144]

September 30—City forester George Behrnd reports Madison had a record 388 cases of Dutch elm disease this year, as the city begins its fall DDT spraying. The city uses DDT in the fall because the alternative, methoxychlor, damages car finishes (for which the council refuses to pay claims), and there are fewer birds around to be poisoned.[145]

Highways and Transportation

On January 4, the state Public Service Commission (PSC) authorizes construction of the Monona Causeway, adjacent and parallel to the railroad tracks. On April 2, voters approve a $1 million causeway bond issue, 19,517–14,380—the only one of four bond issues that day not to pass by at least three to one.[146]

Five days after the PSC approval, Mayor Reynolds orders urban renewal rubble, which he's been piling up in Law Park, spread as a token start to the project. The *Capital Times* editorializes on January 10 that the "dumping of filth and refuse that may ruin all one side of the lake" shows that Reynolds is "trying to blitzkrieg Madison" into approving the causeway bond issue, "the result of the obsession of Mayor and the Obstructionists that the Causeway will make the revival of Monona Terrace unlikely."[147]

In May, the council authorizes further filling, which continues despite notice in July that no state or federal funds will likely be available for five years. But after new test borings, the city's engineering consultants end Reynolds's plan to use construction rubble in August, calling for at least 270,000 cubic yards of dredged granular fill. In November, consultant John Strand, estimating $896,000 for fill for a four-lane roadbed and $986,400 for six lanes, strongly urges the larger project. Once the city decides on size, Strand says the road could be open to limited traffic a year after construction starts. The Friday before Christmas, the Board of Public Works approves relocation orders for fifteen properties on Bellevue Court.[148]

Planning and Development

GENERAL STATISTICS
- ▸ Population: 148,468
- ▸ Area: 44.56 square miles (end-of-year total)

Downtown is one big construction zone this year, with work under way on the central library, an eight-story women's dorm on the northwest corner of State and Frances Streets, an addition to Bethel Lutheran Church, the Anchor Bank building, and parking ramps on North Lake and West Dayton Streets.[149]

Business Wire

May 1—Construction starts on Madison's largest multifamily development, the Allied Development Corporation's fifty-six-acre, 580-unit project on the former Tiemann farm just off Verona Road. The thirty-building Allied Terrace should be completed in the fall of 1964.[150]

May 2—The first day of full operation for the 130-room Park Motor Inn is ten days shy of two years after the Park Hotel was razed. First guests are the Wisconsin Elementary Principals Association's annual convention attendees.[151]

May 23—The 105-year-old William F. Vilas House is razed, to be replaced by a modernist black cube for the National Guardian Life Insurance Company's headquarters in 1964. Parks advocates tried to get the city to buy the historic property when the long-planned Vilas Towers elderly housing project overlooking Lake Mendota failed to find financing, but the Findorff construction company sold the site to the insurance company in early May.[152]

June 28—The Wisconsin Supreme Court unanimously upholds Judge Bardwell's ruling that the 1956 contract between Madison and the Frank Lloyd Wright Foundation is valid and its arbitration clause enforceable. Mayor Reynolds expresses hope that the fee dispute can be resolved through negotiation, but meetings between the parties are fruitless, and arbitration is set for early 1964.[153]

ROUNDY SAYS

"The Auditorium setup in this town is a joke they should tie a horse to one of the parking meters and put up a sign 'One Horse Town.' It was eight or ten years ago we voted for it they have had a thousand meetings in the meantime. The blueprints must be so worn out by now you would need a pair of binoculars to see the blueprints."
—*Wisconsin State Journal,* August 4

The razing of (1) Christ Presbyterian Church on August 12 initiates a downtown development fight that will take eighteen months to play out, while the October 29 groundbreaking for a new library sets a final due date for (2) the 1906 Carnegie Library. Also pictured: (3) Vocational School, (4) First Church of Christ Scientist, (5) Masonic Temple, (6) Central High School, (7) First Methodist Church, (8) Manchester's pigeon-hole parking, (9) Manchester's department store, (10) Woolworth's, (11) Chandler's shoes, (12) Baron's department store, (13) Baron's shoes, (14) the Hub men's clothier, (15) Wisconsin Life Insurance building, (16) Rendall's women's clothier, (17) Commercial State Bank, (18) Anchor Savings and Loan, (19) YWCA. WHI IMAGE ID 137506, PHOTO BY JOHN NEWHOUSE

June 9—The new Christ Presbyterian Church, at Gorham and Brearly Streets, is dedicated. The church's historic sanctuary, built at Wisconsin and Dayton Streets in 1891, is razed for a parking lot by its new owners, the National Guardian Life Insurance Company, on August 12.[154]

October 29—A groundbreaking ceremony is held for Madison's $1.5 million Central Library, designed by Weller and Strang Architects. The facility is expected to open in early 1965, after which the 1906 Carnegie Library across from the Vocational School will be razed for a parking ramp.[155]

November 14—Mayor Reynolds casts the tiebreaking vote to start condemnation proceedings on 536 acres of marshland owned by Cherokee Park Inc. on the city's far north side. His Westport residence and other area holdings give him a personal stake in this issue. The city will acquire the area, plus another 190 acres, for conservation.[156]

Affordable, Integrated Housing Angers North Side Neighbors

On the north side, Madison's first multifamily moderate-income housing project, the five-building, 140-unit Zander Northport Apartments, opens this fall just east of Sherman Avenue. Simultaneously, neighboring single-family homeowners fight on two fronts to block a second integrated complex kitty-corner to the Zander project across Northport Drive.

Sponsored by the American Federation of State, County and Municipal Employees (AFSCME), with Federal Housing Administration Section 221 financing, the nonprofit project is named for Arnold Zander, a Madisonian who helped found AFSCME (originally, the Wisconsin State Employees Association) here in 1932. The federal financing carries strict income limits on tenants.

Because the first phase already has five black families, and the second $1.5 million complex will be integrated as well, some assume race is a factor in the neighborhood opposition; area alderman Richard Kopp vehemently denies that's the case, calling such claims a "despicable" effort by supporters to portray opponents as segregationist. He insists opposition is over density, traffic counts, and property values for the nearby single-family homes.

In September, Kopp and neighboring alderman Leonard Porter—who both voted against the Equal Opportunities Ordinance—prevail at the Plan Commission, which rejects the necessary rezoning just east of Dryden Drive. But days later, after a stormy two-and-a-half-hour discussion, the council reverses the commission and grants the rezoning, 12–6. After reconsideration, a second session in October is even more contentious; an angry Kopp loudly denounces his colleagues after they reaffirm the rezoning, neighbors make thinly veiled political threats, and somebody turns off all the lights in the council chamber. A lawsuit filed by twenty-six neighborhood residents also fails to stop construction.[157]

> **DUELING EDITORIAL HEADLINES, MAY 6**
>
> "An Exciting Downtown Madison"
> —*Wisconsin State Journal*
>
> "Crisis Developing in Downtown Madison"—*Capital Times*

Kennedys and Madison: Seven Days in November

On November 20, President John F. Kennedy starts his last full day in the White House by sending a Western Union telegram to Madison for UW president Fred Harvey Harrington to read at the dedication of the Joseph P. Kennedy Jr. Memorial Laboratories, funded in part by a $250,000 grant from the family foundation. The president, whose sister Rosemary suffered a botched lobotomy in 1941 and is currently institutionalized in Jefferson, Wisconsin, salutes lab director Dr. Harry Waisman on his efforts to "conquer the vast field of mental retardation and its attendant problems." Senator Edward Kennedy and brother-in-law Sargent Shriver, the Peace Corps director, tour the lab, attend a symposium, and hold a dedicatory luncheon at the Memorial Union.[158]

Around 11:30 a.m. on November 22, about eight hundred festive Badger boosters board a special twenty-car Milwaukee Road train bound for Minneapolis and the

UW–Minnesota football game. Eleven months after their thrilling Rose Bowl loss, Wisconsin hopes to salvage a disappointing season by at least keeping Paul Bunyan's Axe.

In downtown Dallas about an hour later, two Madison men see the presidential motorcade go by. Holmes Tire and Supply vice president George Holmes, in town on business, watches it pass before his meeting breaks for lunch at a restaurant near Parkland Hospital. Army lieutenant Bruce Koepcke, on his way from officer training in Oklahoma home to Nakoma for a month's leave, watches from a spot on the curb a few hundred yards from Dealey Plaza. Moments later, Koepcke hears what he thinks are firecrackers.

When news of the assassination reaches Madison, music professor Gunnar Johansen can't teach—he can only choke back sobs by playing Beethoven's Kreutzer Sonata with violinist Rudolph Kolicsh. History professor Harvey Goldberg cancels his lecture to be with the students in the crowded but quiet Rathskeller. Campus religious centers hold special services.

At 2 p.m., the UW football team leaves Madison by chartered plane for Minneapolis. UW's President Harrington wants the game postponed or canceled, but the Minnesota regents say it should be played "because of President Kennedy's deep interest in physical fitness and athletics." By the time the team lands, Minnesota's president has agreed with Harrington, and the game is set for Thanksgiving morning. Harrington announces that all weekend classes and social activities are canceled, including some Monday and Tuesday.

In the Capitol rotunda, Owen Reierson, wearing his swastika armband and giving the Nazi salute, loudly celebrates what he calls a "miracle for the white race." Out on bail from his September arrest for disrupting the Birmingham church bombing memorial, Reierson tries to hand out racist and anti-Semitic literature before he's again arrested for disorderly conduct.

By evening, a hard rain is falling.[159]

November 25 is cloudy and damp for the day of President Kennedy's funeral. Everything's closed; everybody's either in church or watching TV. At 8 a.m., eight hundred pack the pews and aisles at St. Raphael's Cathedral for a Pontifical Requiem Low Mass for the first Catholic president. At the Mass at St. Matthew's Cathedral in Washington, Father Walter J. Schmitz—an alumnus of Central High School, son of the founder of the Hub clothing store, and now dean of sacred theology at Catholic University in Washington—assists Bishop Richard Cardinal Cushing. At ten, the bars of the Dane County Tavern League shut down for three hours. The Loraine hotel puts a television in the lobby; a sound system on the Capitol Square blares patriotic songs. The Gisholt machine plant is open, but nonsupervisory workers can take the day off; Oscar Mayer workers observe a moment of silence at 11 a.m. Even the bad guys take a break. During the five hours of Kennedy's funeral and burial, the police receive only six calls; fifty is the norm.

After the burial, the state's official memorial service is held at Lincoln Terrace; a silent crowd of ten thousand climbs Bascom Hill to mourn one martyr in the shadow of another. Carillon bells ring, somber and slow. Muffled drums herald the ROTC units. The university choir sings hymns, the marching band plays the national anthem. Harrington

President Kennedy's memorial service, Bascom Hill, November 25. WHI IMAGE ID 136616, PHOTO BY DAVID SANDELL

and other dignitaries make remarks. Benediction, "Taps," drums beating retreat. The crowd quietly melts away—just in time for the 5 p.m. reopening of the four downtown movie theaters. That evening, fifteen hundred overflow the First Congregational Church for a multidenominational service. "Something is wrong in our land," Reverend Alfred Swan declares. "We rely too much on violence, too many weapons are flashed before the eyes of the young." Protestant and Jewish clergy read scripture and lead prayers, and many in the crowd cry as they sing "America the Beautiful."[160]

On November 26, Dane County Judge Buenzli orders Reierson to the state hospital at Waupun for a mental exam. "For you to derive pleasure and satisfaction from such a wanton act of malicious violence," Buenzli says, "is evidence to this court that you may be deranged." Reierson says that he's entitled to his "political beliefs" and that the rotunda crowd should be charged for threatening him. Reierson's attorney quits representing him, stating, "He is now personally repulsive to me." That night, the Mayor's Commission on Human Rights introduces its Equal Opportunities Ordinance, and the Young Socialist Alliance presents a speech by its national chairman on "the United States War Machine under the Administration of President Kennedy."[161]

In February, California authorities revoke Reierson's parole, and he is extradited to finish his sentence at San Quentin.[162]

View to the east in the summer of 1964. UNIVERSITY OF WISCONSIN–MADISON ARCHIVES IMAGE S00095

1964

Urban Renewal

Anger, fear, scandal, and greed nearly kill the Madison Redevelopment Authority this year and cost two top bureaucrats their jobs, as issues of race and urban renewal poison relations among aldermen and Mayor Henry Reynolds.

The Madison Redevelopment Authority's (MRA's) year gets off to a bad start as it confirms in early January what many had long claimed—under the federal urban renewal procedures, it has been paying less for the property it acquires than the city and university have. If the MRA had paid the same rate for the 242 parcels acquired on the Triangle that the city paid for parcels bought for the library, causeway, and other projects, it would have spent an additional $890,000; had it paid the same rate that UW paid for the 109 parcels it acquired for the southeast dorms, it would have paid about $1.4 million more. MRA executive director Roger Rupnow says this probably accounts for some of the problems the authority has faced, but notes federal support is capped at the higher of two independent appraisals, and doesn't take into account inconvenience to an unwilling seller or loss of ancillary income.[1]

At that same meeting, State Rep. Norman Anderson (Speaker of the Wisconsin Assembly, 1971–1977) leads the MRA to overrule Rupnow and support the request from Madison Neighborhood Centers director (and Local Committee chair) Chester Zmudzinski to lower the price for the new Neighborhood House location at Milton and South Mills Streets from $2 to $1.50 a square foot. It's part of a three-way deal under which the MRA will pay $41,000 for the Neighborhood House at 768 W. Washington Ave., and sell Neighborhood House the Glidden paint company building at 911 Regent St. for $5,000 to move and use as its new facility. But when renovation proves too expensive, Neighborhood House decides to build new, and the paint building is moved across Regent Street for commercial use.[2]

Although Rupnow says it's "a figment of the imagination" that new housing in urban renewal areas will be reserved for displaced persons, he proposes, and the MRA approves, a plan for 150 units of low-rent housing at the point of Regent and Washington Streets, which he suggests the Madison Housing Authority should build for former Triangle residents.[3]

But the Madison Home Owners Association (MHOA) cares more about stopping the 496-acre General Neighborhood Renewal Plan (GNRP) around the university than fixing the Triangle; in late January, it begins a direct legislation petition drive for the council to "terminate all urban renewal activities" and dissolve the MRA by October 1, or submit the matter to referendum.[4]

The MRA, already vilified for the Triangle project, is now seen as complicit in the university's expansionism and becomes the target of citizens' anger. Just days before, UW's President Harrington had proclaimed an "aggressive and expansionist" policy. "I have been called a bigger imperialist" than Teddy Roosevelt, he tells the Madison Chamber of Commerce, acknowledging his reputation in the GNRP area. "But we have to look on the growth being forced on us as an opportunity."[5]

The MHOA makes some procedural mistakes that cost it three weeks of petitioning, but still files almost 1,400 more signatures than the 6,552 needed.[6] The association wants the question of dissolving the MRA on the lower-turnout April ballot, so it can target individual candidates, rather than on the November ballot with the presidential election. Supporting the MRA, Mayor Reynolds and both newspapers want the referendum in November, but after an extraordinary effort by city clerk Eldon Hoel to certify the signatures, and helpful rulings by city attorney Conrad, the council suspends the rules on February 27 to give the MHOA what it wants and allow the referendum on the April ballot.[7]

Because the legislation that created the MRA doesn't have a provision for its abolition, there's some question of how the city could fully implement the referendum. Yet it has to—Conrad rejects legal advice from a League of Municipalities attorney and rules the referendum mandatory. Passage would allow completion of the Triangle and Brittingham projects already under way, but end work on the South Madison, GNRP, and Marquette area studies.[8]

Although some in the MHOA, such as Madison Board of Realtors president Donald Hovde, have positions of influence, the MHOA is composed largely of small property owners taking on the entire political establishment. Reynolds, who a year earlier attacked the MRA and its chairman, Albert McGinnis, for "bungling" the Triangle project, now decries the "air of mistrust" surrounding the MRA and campaigns against the referendum, as does the League of Women Voters. University president Harrington highlights the importance of the GNRP, which would be lost if the referendum is approved.[9]

In rare agreement, the conservative *Wisconsin State Journal* and liberal *Capital Times* each run extensive articles and editorials explaining how much urban renewal has accomplished, and how much is yet to be done. "Mistakes were made in the Triangle," the *State Journal* editorializes on April 3, but "the MRA is a tool which the city needs and one which, it appears, it is beginning to learn how to use." The *Capital Times* agrees. "Action has sometimes been too hasty and ill-considered and the program has suffered from unconscionable political manipulations," it editorializes that afternoon. "But to make a hasty decision now to cut it off because of these past mistakes would simply be another hasty decision that could well turn out to be an even more serious mistake. We are convinced that the city has learned from past mistakes and that residents of this city need not fear a repetition of those mistakes."[10]

In late March, the council approves the MRA's proposal for 127 units of moderate-income housing on the 5.5-acre site at Regent and West Washington Streets and directs the authority to solicit proposals. The first proposal comes from Mayor Reynolds himself, announcing a few days later that he will lead a nonprofit group to build a series of two-story townhouse units, to be called the James Madison Apartments. The $1.27 million project "aimed specifically for families displaced by MRA" will be income-limited non-public housing, and will pay property taxes. Notwithstanding the new group's firepower—it includes former mayor George Forster, Judge Richard Bardwell, Madison Bank & Trust Co. president Collins Ferris, Lowell Frautschi, and labor attorney John Lawton—Reynolds says they will "gladly step aside if a better use of the land is offered." MHOA analyst Fran Remeika denounces the initiative as political grandstanding that, after forty years, would give Reynolds's group the project at no cost and with no federal restrictions.[11]

On April 7, the referendum to end urban renewal and abolish the MRA comes down to the last precinct reporting. With 36,665 votes cast—representing 70 percent of registered voters—the MRA survives by 367 votes, 18,516–18,149. The Ninth Ward (home of the Triangle and Brittingham projects) and the Sixth Ward (where many are bitterly opposed to the Marquette study) both vote heavily to end all renewal activities, while the Fourteenth Ward (where residents favor the South Madison project) votes heavily to continue. It's strong support from west side wards that keeps the MRA alive.[12]

But urban renewal itself kills the political careers of two east side incumbents, including MRA member Ald. Wilbur Carnes, Sixteenth Ward. And Williamson Street pet shop owner Pete Schmidt rides anti-MRA sentiment to a decisive victory over six-term incumbent Ald. George Elder, who sponsored an MRA study in the Williamson-Marquette area.[13]

The close call causes renewal supporters to reflect. "Perhaps Madison was negligent in the consideration of the displacements," says Citizens Advisory Committee (CAC) chair Arthur Towell, a public relations executive who did pro bono work for the MRA. "If we had built low-cost housing first instead of Sampson Plaza, this might not have happened." Mayor Reynolds thinks the city was just too ambitious. "We have set our goals a little bit too high," he tells the CAC. "We have to realize we can't have a utopia in this program."[14]

Three days after the election, the university regents take an important step in the heart of the GNRP area, which further complicates city politics and planning. They vote to seek State Building Commission approval to coordinate with the University Park Corporation, the corporation formed by friends of the university in December 1962, to build housing for eight hundred graduate students and a commercial mall on the 700 and 800 blocks of University Avenue. University vice president and trust officer A. W. Peterson, who is also president of the corporation, assures the board that the existing owners and tenants will participate, provided they get a fair price for their property and reasonable lease terms.[15]

Neighborhood House, 768 W. Washington Ave., Greenbush's most important secular building since social worker Gay Braxton made it a settlement house in 1921, is razed in late September. During construction of the new facility at 29 S. Brooks St., programming is provided at 110 S. Lake St.[16] WHI IMAGE ID 136619, PHOTO BY DAVID SANDELL

Having survived the GNRP-inspired referendum, the MRA proceeds in its pursuit during the summer and fall, getting final federal approval of the $127,000 grant in late October for the study the council authorized in February 1963.[17]

But the MRA's survival doesn't mean its troubles are over. There remains significant hostility toward urban renewal. And acrimony between aldermen and Reynolds is so bitter that they fight all year over his appointments to the MRA.

For Reynolds to name Bob Nuckles, the man who ran against him last year, to the MRA would be statesmanlike. Except Bob Nuckles just lost a bitter race against Reynolds's constant council critic, Ald. Richard Kopp. In this case, what is statesmanlike also turns out to be a mistake.

And Reynolds picks another fight, taking Ald. Harold Rohr off the Board of Public Works after eight years. No one's surprised that it's Rohr who moves to return the MRA citizen appointments to the mayor, with a request that he remove one citizen appointee and name Ald. Kopp instead. The motion passes easily, but Reynolds does not comply.[18]

In mid-May, Reynolds sends up the same three names, and the council again insists on a second alderman to join the anti-MRA Ald. Leo Cooper. So Reynolds removes one citizen appointee and names an alderman—but it's not Kopp; it's Robert "Toby" Reynolds (no relation), the fresh-faced, pro–civil rights, pro–urban renewal west sider who clashed with Rohr over civil rights in the recent campaign.

"What have you got against Kopp?" demands anti-MRA Ald. Ellsworth Swenson, Eighth Ward, whose wife is an official with the Homeowners Association. Mayor Reynolds says a lot of women have asked that he not appoint him. Kopp calls Reynolds "small-minded" and says he's "trying to jam his personal feelings down the Council's throat."

With eighteen votes needed for confirmation, Ald. Reynolds fails 15–5; Nuckles is affirmatively rejected, 10–11, and Mayor Reynolds withdraws the reappointment of the other citizen, holdover William Nemec.[19]

The mayor tries again in early July, this time pairing Ald. Reynolds with east side realtor Ralph Anderson, but falls one vote short. Two weeks later, the fourth time proves a partial success as the council confirms Anderson—but not Reynolds.[20]

The conservative Mayor Reynolds tries one last time to appoint the liberal Ald. Reynolds in early October; Swenson again leads the opposition, and the appointment fails, 14–7. It's an unprecedented and never-repeated snub by the council of a mayor and a council colleague.[21]

Reynolds doesn't try again, leaving citizen member and state representative Norman Anderson, a charter member of the MRA who is trying to step down after six years, still in place as the year ends.

The Madison Housing Authority suffers no similar disruption. It easily confirms as its new chairman Earl Espeseth, who as president of the Madison Board of Realtors led its fight against the fair housing ordinance less than five months earlier.[22]

At the end of the year, the MHA announces that some of its low-income public housing will be available by New Year's Day; with demand exceeding supply, the authority reaffirms that renting to persons displaced by MRA activities will be a high priority.[23]

IN EARLY SEPTEMBER, the Citizens Advisory Committee urges Mayor Reynolds to appoint an administrative assistant to focus on the "human" side of urban renewal, to "see that housing is available before people are uprooted." Reynolds names the Planning Department's Sol Levin "to help me in whatever way I can use him."[24]

Reynolds will need lots of help. The urban renewal agencies are about to have their worst week ever.

On November 9, barely two weeks after final federal approval of the GNRP grant, Owen Coyle of the *Capital Times* reveals that MRA executive director Rupnow and his wife own property within the GNRP area, a house and lot at 1323 Randall Ct., which they bought in April. His brother owns property, too, around the corner at 117 N. Randall Ave.[25]

Rupnow says his ownership wasn't a secret; he just didn't tell the MRA until after the grant was approved because federal conflict of interest rules applied only once the contract was signed in late October. It's a legal defense, but the MRA's problem is political; Swenson and Triangle-area alderman Leo Cooper, Ninth Ward, a member of the MRA, have already introduced a resolution freezing all new MRA activity—especially the GNRP—for two years.[26]

The next day, at city attorney Conrad's urging, the MRA unanimously declares Rupnow's action "indiscrete [*sic*] and contrary to the public interest" and tells him to find a

Bob Dylan, in black leather jacket and pointy boots, draws a less-than-capacity crowd and mixed reviews at the Orpheum on November 19. He's silent between songs as he performs old and new classics, including three—"Mr. Tambourine Man," "Gates of Eden," and "It's All Right, Ma (I'm Only Bleeding)"—not released until January 1965. Guy Lombardo, personable in a black tuxedo, delights a sold-out show with sweeter sounds four nights later.[31]
COURTESY OF CAPITAL NEWS-PAPERS ARCHIVES

solution. "You are affecting the whole structure of government if you condone his action," Conrad says. Cooper practically accuses Rupnow of being self-serving in his strong support for the GNRP.

Other ethics issues emerge. Citizen MRA member Robert Shaw, a builder, reveals he's done "some work on public housing" and wonders "if I'm doing something wrong." "From a purist standpoint," Conrad responds, "that is right."[27]

On November 12, MHA executive director Robert Callsen is jailed on two charges of driving after license revocation for two drunk driving convictions, and is sentenced to seventy-five days. Callsen attends the MHA meeting that night on work release privileges, without telling the MHA about his arrest and jailing.[28]

Friday the thirteenth brings bad news for both bureaucrats. First, Mayor Reynolds says he wants Callsen to quit as executive director and take the assistant MHA director job that's been vacant for two months. Hours later, Rupnow resigns and the MRA holds an emergency meeting to name Levin as acting director. Levin is well received, and he says he'll seek the post on a permanent basis.

"I don't know whether we should congratulate you or offer condolences," MRA member Arnold Gehner tells Levin.[29]

The following Wednesday, the MHA takes the mayoral hint and demotes Callsen to assistant, naming as director Bjarne Romnes, a twenty-five-year veteran of state and county social welfare work. Romnes's sole housing experience was developing Chalet Gardens, the cooperative housing project for the elderly out on Verona Road, in 1961; the innovative project couldn't meet its membership requirements and was taken over by the Federal Housing Administration just this August.[30]

The MRA's annus horribilis continues even into Thanksgiving week, after it ignores Ald. Cooper's opposition and reaffirms its support for the GNRP study. Cooper is more successful with his colleagues, getting the council to vote, 14–8, on November 24 for a one-year freeze—effectively rejecting the federal planning grant of $127,400 and costing UW $9 million in federal support for land acquisition. But the vote, while decisive, falls short of the seventeen needed to override the presumed mayoral veto. So, at Ald. Reynolds's suggestion, the council creates a special urban renewal committee to evaluate all aspects of the program and report by February.[32]

A few days later, Mayor Reynolds tells the MRA he'll indeed veto the freeze resolution; the MHOA immediately threatens another referendum.[33]

University president Harrington, whose institutional expansionism has helped create the crisis, is aghast at the looming loss of $9 million. He suggests Reynolds veto the freeze and ask the MRA not to spend any of the GNRP planning money until the special committee makes its report.[34]

That's what happens. Reynolds vetoes the freeze; Levin gets the federal Housing and Home Finance Administration to hold the money until the council acts on the special committee's report, and on December 10 everything's referred for three months.[35]

Reynolds appoints a largely pro-renewal committee, which elects Ald. Reynolds as chair, and gets ready for six nights of hearings in January to determine the future—if any—of urban renewal in Madison.[36]

Suddenly, a Christmas-week surprise throws the future of the two prime blocks in the GNRP up in the air, as twenty-one University Avenue merchants and property owners, organized as the Lake Park Corp., petition the MRA on December 21 to bypass the University Park Corp. and create an urban renewal district to work directly with them in redeveloping the 700 and 800 blocks of University Avenue. Area alderman James Goulette says the plan is "not to spite the university," but acknowledges he has "not consulted with university people about this."[37]

The "university people" will soon make their reaction known.

Civil Rights

After adoption of the historic, if limited, fair housing provisions of the Equal Opportunities Ordinance, Madison's primary focus returns to employment, as activists from the Congress of Racial Equality take a more confrontational approach.

The new Equal Opportunities Commission (EOC) gets its first housing discrimination case in February—a married couple with two children who allege that their recent eviction from a two-room apartment was discriminatory. Chairman John McGrath, who

The charter Equal Opportunities Commission. Seated from left: Attorney Leon Isaksen, Reverend James C. Wright, Betty MacDonald, Mayor Henry E. Reynolds, John McGrath, and William Gothard. Standing from left: Ald. George Olip, Ald. James Marks, Ald. Leonard Porter, and Chester Zmudzinski. MacDonald and McGrath are named secretary and chair, respectively, retaining positions they held on the now-defunct Mayor's Commission on Human Rights. Marks was the primary council proponent of the new Equal Opportunities Ordinance, Porter a vigorous opponent. After the spring election, Porter is replaced by an even more-implacable enemy of the commission and its work—Ald. Harold Rohr, who attends only one meeting in 1964.[38] WHI IMAGE ID 137859, PHOTO BY DAVID SANDELL

knows the landlord to have previously rented to minorities, investigates and finds the tenants were behind on their rent and had misled the landlord about the number of occupants; the EOC summarily dismisses the complaint. The potential remains for lots of housing-related proceedings—a quarter of the 1,128 foreign students at UW report being discriminated against in their search for housing, with foreign-born blacks the most frequent victims.[39]

In February, the State Industrial Commission issues a report on local employment by race, showing Madison employers, both private and public, hiring very few African Americans:

	White Employees	Black Employees
American Family Insurance	557	0
First National Bank	219	1
Gardner Baking	300	1
Gisholt	1,093	11
Madison Gas & Electric	384	0
Madison Kipp	367	0
Ohio Chemical	377	0
Oscar Mayer & Co.	3,723	31
Rennebohm	686	3
Dane County	860	4
State of Wisconsin	13,000	110 FT/90 PT
University of Wisconsin	12,476	125
State Colleges	2,224	2

"None has launched a really aggressive program to assure implementation of equal employment opportunity," the commission notes, which "tends toward perpetuating the status quo." And that current situation, the commission reports, is that few employers here "have yet to come to grips with the problem of fair employment practices."

The commission also explains why few blacks apply for employment: "Years of exclusion and the lack of affirmative assurance that job opportunity is available has persuaded Negroes there is no point in applying."[40]

Spring brings the decade's first disruptive protest, an obstructive "shop-in" of the Sears department store—the highlight of a successful campaign by the new Madison chapter of the Congress of Racial Equality (CORE) to pressure the store into integrating its workforce.

When CORE first contacted Sears last November, none of the store's 321 employees were African American; CORE asked Sears to hire some for public contact jobs—first

CORE pickets Sears, 1101 E.
Washington Ave., March 23.
WHI IMAGE ID 136621, PHOTO BY
DAVID SANDELL

for the Christmas rush, then for permanent positions—and declare itself an "Equal Opportunity Employer." The store, already under investigation by the State Industrial Commission, did not do so.

CORE increased its demand in early January, calling on Sears to hire five black sales clerks by March 15; two days before the deadline, the store hires a single black maintenance worker. That's when CORE goes public, calling for a consumer boycott and engaging in an extended "public education" campaign.

On March 21, while a picket line of about sixty-five sing civil rights songs along the sidewalk, a crew of about forty go to various departments inside, trying on clothes and feigning extensive purchases before talking to the salespersons about discrimination and canceling their orders. The action—led by CORE chair Silas Norman, Elizabeth Dennis, Bourtai Scudder, Evan Stark, and Clark Kissinger, and also including activists from the Peace Center, the Socialist Club, Students for a Democratic Society, and other groups—culminates in a singing, aisle-blocking sit-in in the shoe department. One obstructer, eighteen-year-old Stanley I. Grand, a white UW sophomore from Washington, DC, is dragged out when he refuses to identify himself to inspector Herman Thomas, becoming the first person arrested this decade at a group political demonstration (Judge Buenzli later changes the vagrancy charge to disorderly conduct and forfeits Grand's $55 bail). As the picketing and boycott continue into April, CORE publicity director Lea Zeldin says numerous customers have canceled their store charge accounts.[41]

Lloyd Barbee, president of the state NAACP, overwhelmingly approves of the demonstration and boycott; Marshall Colston, head of the Madison branch, doesn't. Echoing Odell Taliaferro's cautionary comments from February 1960, Colston says he knows of no previous complaints against Sears, and if any do arise, they should be taken to the EOC.[42]

Although CORE doesn't file a formal complaint with the EOC, the commission holds a public hearing on April 6—before a crowd of about sixty—under its plenary power to investigate possible discrimination. Testimony is compelling but inconclusive.

Store manager Fred Pomraning recounts that he offered two African Americans Christmas jobs in 1963, but they both declined. CORE chair Norman claims that the store turned away several qualified blacks. Pomraning denies that the store discriminates and says he hired an African American for the auto service station and three more for part-time jobs.

By the time the EOC closes its file without action on April 14, Sears has three full-time and four part-time black employees. Norman congratulates the store and urges it to do more.[43]

About a week later, Rev. Fred Shuttlesworth, a cofounder of the Southern Christian Leadership Conference, rouses a Capitol Square crowd of about five hundred on April 25 with his emphatic call for adoption of state and federal civil rights legislation. UW freshman Tracy Nelson (founder of the blues/rock band Mother Earth), the young folk/blues singer from Shorewood Hills, is among the entertainers at the rally sponsored by the Madison Committee for Civil Rights.[44]

Race-Based Races

Civil rights once again becomes the central issue in south side alderman Harold "Babe" Rohr's spring campaign for his fourth term, as Clifford Roberts, announcer for the *Capital Times*'s WIBA radio station, campaigns explicitly on Rohr's opposition to the Equal Opportunities Ordinance. Rohr flings the issue back in a campaign flyer attacking Roberts as a "self-avowed member" of the NAACP who "has taken part in NAACP 'sit-in' demonstrations."[45]

Even after its enactment in December, Rohr is still fighting the fair housing provisions. "What would you say if the city passed an ordinance that you would have to rent or sell to every Jew that came to your door?" he asks a group of black landlords at a South Madison Neighborhood Council meeting in February.[46]

Rohr even brings race into the basic administration of the election itself, when he prevents adoption of the list of Democratic Party poll watchers because it includes two blacks, including EOC member Rev. James C. Wright. It's only when city attorney Edwin Conrad calls the action illegal that the council confirms the city's first two black election officials.[47]

NO BIG BROTHER IN MADISON

On May 14, the Madison Common Council adopts the following resolution:

Whereas, recent technical advances in electronics and photography permit easy and common use of secret and hidden devices to obtain visual and auditory evidence from unsuspecting persons; and

Whereas, such methods are repugnant to the cherished American traditions of common decency and fair play;

Now therefore be it resolved, that the Common Council of the City of Madison opposes such secret methods of obtaining evidence as reprehensible and inconsistent with the high ethical and moral standards extant in said city, and instructs all boards and commissions of said city not to use such devices in any investigations, inquiry or hearing, without the prior knowledge of all persons concerned.

Equal Opportunities Chair John McGrath endorses the resolution for putting Madison "in the forefront in the nation in arresting the alarmingly increasing use of these dubious devices."[48]

On April 2, as about twenty CORE members protest in the cold rain, Democratic presidential candidate George Wallace, the governor of Alabama, is given a warm reception by the Madison Exchange Club at the Cuba Club. Wallace denies he is racially prejudiced and draws applause for his attack on the pending federal civil rights bill as something that "will destroy the constitutional rights of everybody."[49] COURTESY OF CAPITAL NEWSPAPERS ARCHIVES, PHOTO BY RICHARD SRODA

While Rohr is still fighting equal opportunity, council candidate Robert "Toby" Reynolds puts his political future at risk fighting for it.

In a tight University Heights primary race to succeed Ald. Ethel Brown, Toby Reynolds formally repudiates the very valuable endorsement from the AFL-CIO's Committee on Public Education (COPE) because the labor group also endorsed Rohr and fellow EOC-foe Ald. Ellsworth Swenson. "I cannot understand the position of Madison labor" on the local ordinance, Reynolds says, especially given the national AFL-CIO's support for the civil rights bill pending in Congress.[50]

"I am sorry that the Madison AFL-CIO has permitted its image to be damaged by endorsements of this kind," Reynolds telegrams Federation of Labor executive director Marv Brickson. "My beliefs do not permit me to accept an endorsement that goes only to candidates for alderman with this record."[51]

Over Rohr's strong objection, COPE reaffirms its endorsement of Toby Reynolds. Rohr vows to fight anything Reynolds, if elected, introduces to the council.[52]

Roberts, who failed to unseat Rohr in 1960, is endorsed by both newspapers, but Rohr wins handily, as does Reynolds. Rohr will soon make good on his threat.[53]

Civil Rights on Campus

On campus, as in the city, civil rights remain a big issue despite the small black population. With the university no longer keeping data on how students identify racially, EOC chair McGrath and a group of black student leaders undertake a literal head count, which reveals that about 100 of the university's 26,293 students are black, with more from Nigeria (twenty-three) than Wisconsin (twenty-one). The small number dismays UW officials, who thought the nonwhite population was higher. Among the 2,254 faculty, there are only nine blacks.[54]

For one of the few African American students, late winter brings bad news. Veteran civil rights activist Dion Diamond, twenty-two, a recent transfer to UW from Howard University, had been a Freedom Rider in 1961 and later a field secretary in Mississippi and Louisiana for the Student Non-Violent Coordinating Committee. One of his more than thirty arrests is pending—a charge of "criminal anarchy," attempting to overthrow the government of Louisiana, later reduced to disorderly conduct. In late February, the US Supreme Court dismisses the appeal of his conviction; Diamond serves his two-month sentence, returning to Madison to continue his activism and academics, graduating in June.[55]

In early May, the faculty votes to require all fraternities and sororities to certify by November that "there are no provisions in the constitution, by-laws, ritual or any other controlling rules" that prevent the membership from pledging any students on account of race, color, creed, or national origin, and to certify by 1972 that either (a) only active UW students can participate in membership decision, or (b) local members can override any veto from alumni or the national office if the local feels the veto was due to racial or religious discrimination.[56]

Seeking a special session on civil rights legislation, about thirty college and high school students from the Madison CORE chapter engage in the first civil rights demonstration to disrupt the Wisconsin legislature in the balcony of the Assembly Chambers on April 27. After Assembly sergeant-at-arms Norris J. Kellman brusquely confiscates several unauthorized signs (top), the group stands to sing "We Shall Overcome" (bottom) as the annoyed Assembly adjourns. There are no arrests as the group marches out singing. CORE chapter chair Silas Norman opposes the action and resigns, and leaves about a month later for the Selma Literacy Project. He is succeeded by Bourtai Scudder, daughter of British modernist poet Basil Bunting.[57]

WHI IMAGES ID 137731 AND 137734, PHOTOS BY DAVID SANDELL

"Adjust to freedom," Professor Walter Rauschenbush, a member of the faculty's Human Rights Committee, tells a stormy meeting of fraternity representatives in October; the next night, the Inter-Fraternity Association endorses the imminent certification but votes 37–17 against the two provisions to be completed by 1972. "This decision will make the enforcement of the policy very much more difficult," the faculty's Human Rights Committee annual report predicts.[58]

The Greeks quickly comply with the first certification, except the Acacia and Phi Gamma Delta fraternities and the Kappa Delta sorority; they don't respond to the HRC's requests for information, refuse to sign the certification, and are recommended for termination.[59]

In late June, about fifteen UW students and former UW student Andrew Goodman are among the thousand or so students venturing to Mississippi for the Freedom Summer voter registration efforts organized by the umbrella group of several civil rights organizations, the Council of Federated Organizations. On the project's first day, June 21, Goodman and local CORE workers James Chaney and Michael Schwerner investigate the burning of a Neshoba County Baptist church; returning to their home base in Meridian, they are arrested for speeding and taken into custody. That night, Ku Klux Klansmen torture and murder the three; their bodies, buried in an earthen dam outside Philadelphia, are not discovered until August 4. On June 29, about one hundred fifty students demonstrate at the Capitol demanding federal protection for southern civil rights workers. The Friends of the Student Non-Violent Coordinating Committee (FSNCC) continues its active outreach and fund-raising on campus.[60]

When former Madison CORE chapter chair and president of the Student Council for Civil Rights Silas Norman, a graduate student in microbiology, is arrested in July doing voter registration work in his native Georgia, the FSNCC want to solicit donations for bail and educational activities on the Capitol Square, but the city council rejects its request, 16–5. The group goes ahead anyway after city attorney Edwin Conrad says it doesn't need permission, but collects only $154; FSNCC leader Larry Ozanne reports that the group is heckled with racist epithets.[61]

In late November, about eight thousand students, nearly a quarter of the student body, join the National Student Association's "Thanksgiving Fast for Freedom." By putting their money where their mouths could have been, the students are able to send about $5,000 not spent on their own dinners to Mississippi to buy food for impoverished households, both black and white.[62]

Auditorium

The ninth year since passage of the Monona Terrace referendum opens with a late January offer from the Frank Lloyd Wright Foundation to settle its claim against the city for $170,000—what Judge Bardwell had proposed as a settlement in 1962, and a little less than half what it would have been due had the city accepted the $12.1 million bid in 1961 and built the project.[63]

Mayor Reynolds asserts the foundation is due nothing beyond the $122,500 it has already received because it breached the contract by designing a facility so wildly beyond the $4 million budget. However, he accepts that "the city may have a moral obligation here," and a few days later offers a final $100,000 payment to the foundation, adding another $35,000 in a closed-door council meeting to split the difference. He apparently doesn't tell the council the foundation has already rejected that offer.[64]

"I know this is not acceptable to you and your clients," the mayor writes foundation attorney Randolph Conners the next day in transmitting the $135,000 offer. Although city attorney Edwin Conrad warns that arbitration could cost more than the foundation's $170,000 request, Reynolds says that's now "the proper procedure."[65]

And Reynolds, who alienated aldermen in 1961 by appointing Conrad, now tells the council that Conrad is "afraid" of Conners and has "ruined" several negotiating sessions. He wants to hire a high-powered East Coast attorney specializing in construction disputes—Edward Cushman, whom the *Capital Times* routinely identifies as the "Philadelphia lawyer."[66]

Two weeks later, the council comes close to authorizing the $170,000, but backs off when Reynolds lectures the group on negotiation tactics. "This is what he [Conners] expects you to do," Reynolds says. "I can't save the city $35,000 if you take this approach."[67]

Chief foundation architect William Wesley Peters makes another attempt to settle, offering to redesign the project, at reduced fees, at either Monona Terrace or another downtown site, if the city pays the $170,000. Reynolds responds that the Monona Avenue site has been dead since the 1962 referendum, and that it would be "just too costly to build over the railroad tracks and over the highway" as planned. The Wright foundation "would be considered along with any other architects" to design a project at another site, he adds, rejecting Peters's proposal.[68]

Peters makes a final, futile effort. "We regret that we have no tangible evidence from the mayor which indicates a desire to expedite a solution," he telegrams on February 25; if the city does not settle at $170,000, the foundation will proceed to arbitration.[69]

In that case, replies Reynolds, the city's position will be that the foundation is entitled to nothing. In fact, he says, based on Cushman's quick review of the file, the city may even demand that the foundation return the $122,500 it has already been paid. The council agrees with Reynolds in a 12–10 vote on February 27—two years and three months after Peters first called for arbitration. A month later, the council ratifies Reynolds's decision to retain Cushman at $350 a day—a steep discount from his corporate fee, but still far more than Madison lawyers make.[70]

It takes the city and foundation until early July to pick their representatives on the three-member arbitration panel. As the parties work—not very diligently—to pick an independent third arbitrator, formal claims are filed in September. The foundation seeks $366,551; as it threatened, the city offers nothing, and demands return of the $122,500 paid in 1960.[71]

And then . . . nothing. As Reynolds prepares to step down after two terms in April, the year ends with everything in limbo. There is no progress on an alternate site, no selection of the necessary third arbitrator, and no resolution in the foreseeable future.

Perhaps the 1965 election—pitting liberal county clerk Otto Festge against Reynolds's former campaign manager, George Hall—will serve to sort things out.

UW

COMMENCEMENT, JUNE 8
- Baccalaureate: 2,165
- Master's/PhD: 765[72]
- MD/JD: 170

FALL ENROLLMENT
- Total Students: 26,293[73]

HOMECOMING
- Show: Harry Belafonte, Sonny Terry & Brownie McGhee, Nina Mouskouri[74]

NEW BUILDINGS OF NOTE
- Witte Hall, 615 W. Johnson St.
- H. L. Russell Laboratories, 1630 Linden Dr.
- Psychology, 1202 W. Johnson St.
- Engineering, 1415 Engineering Dr.
- Administration, 750 University Ave.
- McArdle Cancer Research, 1111 Highland Ave.
- Law, 975 Bascom Mall
- Primate Regional Center, 1223 Capital Ct.
- Zoology Research, 250 N. Mills St.[75]

Commencement, June 8
WHI IMAGE ID 117346, PHOTO BY
RICHARD SRODA

A specter is haunting university administrators in 1964—the specter of an ever-increasing population on a campus about to burst.

"The Madison campus figure is staggering!" University president Harrington exclaims at the February regents meeting. The campus is in the midst of its greatest two-year enrollment jump ever, with more to come; the state's educational planning body, the Coordinating Committee on Higher Education, projects enrollments of 45,000 in 1970 and 52,183 in 1973—almost 20,000 more than any other plan had projected.[76]

Believing the campus population will double in nine years, administrators start planning to double the size of the campus. In January, the regents endorse Harrington's call to increase construction of student housing from a thousand units per year to twenty-five hundred—part of his grand plan for a complex of residential and academic facilities for ten thousand to fifteen thousand freshmen and sophomores near Picnic Point, and a similar setup north of the Veterans' Administration hospital.

"The area at the base of Picnic Point is very promising," Harrington says, although he concedes that there could be some "foundation problems as the land is below lake level."[77]

In May, the regents formally designate eight acres across from the Natatorium as the site for high-rise dormitories for three thousand, similar to those under construction on West Johnson Street, and approve preliminary plans for a $4.5 million apartment complex for married students at the intersection of Tokay Boulevard and Gilbert Road, adjacent to the Westgate Shopping Center. None of the units are built.[78]

In the summer of 1964, Witte Hall (lower right) is getting landscaped and Ogg Hall is starting to rise. The new administration building (center right) where all university records will be centralized, has its grand opening June 12.[79] UNIVERSITY OF WISCONSIN-MADISON ARCHIVES IMAGE S01477

The city has been trying for several years to get the university to allow the extension of Whitney Way through its experimental farm located between Mineral Point Road and South Hill Drive, and finally complete the course from University Avenue to the Beltline. For as many years the regents have refused, citing ongoing research activity on the farm that the road would destroy, and denying they were trying to hurt the Westgate shopping center, located just down Gilbert Road [Whitney Way], competitor to the university-sponsored Hilldale Shopping Center. But the connection is needed for access to the university's Charmany and Rieder farms, which is where university president Harrington wants to build a full four-year western campus. So this summer the regents finally agree to allow the extension and also sell the wooded and grassy area for a city park. The university bought the 125-acre Rieder farm in 1938 for $20,000, and the 200-acre Charmany farm in 1946 for $65,000.[80] UNIVERSITY OF WISCONSIN-MADISON ARCHIVES IMAGE S10474

To cap it off, plans call for a four-year campus on the Charmany-Rieder Farms, on Mineral Point Road at Whitney Way, about five miles west of Bascom Hall. To Harrington, it's not if, but when a full western campus will open. "We will certainly have some sort of campus use here one day—very handsome and quite high," Harrington confidently predicts in September.[81]

The university is equally frantic over the onslaught of automobiles, scooters, bikes, and pedestrians. "Drastic action is needed," engineering dean Prof. Kurt Wendt, the campus planning chief, tells the regents.[82]

Board president Arthur DeBardeleben is particularly ambitious, asking about "development of an underground rapid transit system" to serve the campus. Cheaper to move the campus, Harrington replies. DeBardeleben suggests a monorail "so that we can eliminate all parking problems"; vice president Robert Clodius says they could look into one as had "been used at Disneyland and the World's Fair."[83]

The administration even considers banning all student cars, but Wendt says there's "some question about the legality" of doing so. The regents also consider, but don't adopt, the campus planning committee's proposal to post guards at three campus checkpoints to block all personal vehicles—including bicycles—during the workday.[84]

Evidence of the university's permissive rules on automobiles: Lot 60, on the far west fringe of campus, fall 1964. UNIVERSITY OF WISCONSIN–MADISON ARCHIVES IMAGE CLP-A0163

Campus Calendar

January 6—The faculty unanimously approves allowing all seniors, regardless of age, to live in off-campus apartments, effective this September. There are now about six thousand students who live in apartments, and about 750 seniors under the current minimum age of twenty-one who cannot. New dean of public services LeRoy Luberg says the new policy "could be considered a stepping stone" to eventually letting younger underclassmen also live in apartments.[85]

January 10—On the recommendation of President Harrington, the regents name University of Illinois law professor Robben W. Fleming, forty-eight, UW Law '41, first provost of the Madison campus. A former UW faculty member and former federal attorney, Fleming is also vice president of the National Academy of Arbitrators. Harrington picks Fleming from a slate of candidates provided by a faculty screening committee headed by Monona Terrace advocate Dr. Van R. Potter of the University Medical School.[86]

February 18–26—The fifth annual Wisconsin Student Association (WSA) Student Symposium series, "Dissent," features Senator Gaylord Nelson; Alabama governor George Wallace; the John Birch Society's US representative John Rousselot; African American author Louis Lomax; Communist historian Herbert Aptheker; and critic Dwight Macdonald—who dissents from the event. "I'm in favor of free speech," he says in a speech supporting the cultural elite, "but that does not mean anyone has a right to speak anywhere."[87]

March 2—The decade's most important campus political group, the Students for a Democratic Society, formally registers as a student organization, with economics professor Jack Barbash its faculty adviser. "We have people here who think they are socialist and people who think they are liberals," says mathematics graduate student and founding chairman C. Clark Kissinger, adding, "There is left, and there is left."[88]

March 6—A protest doubleheader, thanks to Alabama governor George Wallace and secretary of state Dean Rusk. A group from CORE pickets Wallace as he returns to Madison to announce his entry into the Wisconsin presidential primary at an afternoon press conference at the Edgewater Hotel; that evening, about thirty students from various socialist and peace groups picket Rusk's talk before an overflow crowd at the First Congregational Church, part of the centennial celebration of the university YMCA.[89]

April 17–18—While the legendary Bo Diddley rocks the Military Ball in Great Hall (with Ken Adamany's band The Knight Trains on the bill) on Friday night, folksinger Guy Carawan, who first popularized "We Shall Overcome," is singing for the Student Nonviolent Coordinating Committee (SNCC) at the University YMCA. Saturday night, it's a Bo Diddley album, and nickle bags of popcorn, for the thousand who pack Great Hall for the Student Peace Center's eighth annual Anti-Mil Ball. There's great live music, too, for the largest turnout yet—Tracy Nelson sitting in with the Johnny Kalb blues band.[90]

May 9—Comedian and activist Dick Gregory and the Freedom Singers come to campus on a national thirty-day tour raising money for Freedom Summer and SNCC. The show sells poorly and is moved from the Stock Pavilion to Music Hall.[91]

May 15—Governor John Reynolds names Kathryn F. Clarenbach, director of university education for women, the founding chair of the Governor's Commission on the Status of Women. Clarenbach, who holds a BA, MA, and PhD in political science from the UW, also chaired the first state conference on the status of women in January. She and her realtor husband, Henry, have three children—Sarah, David (Wisconsin State Representative, 1975–1983), and Janet—and are copresidents of the West High PTA.[92]

June 24—Slugging centerfielder Rick Reichardt, a two-sport star junior from Stevens Point who won back-to-back Big Ten batting championships and led the conference in stolen bases, ends a bidding war by several major league teams and signs with the Los Angeles Angels for an astronomical $205,000. The sum, which wasn't even his top offer, so stuns Major League Baseball—it's twice what future Hall of Famer Willie Mays makes that year—that the league starts an amateur draft, making Reichardt the last of the baseball "bonus babies." Son of a Green Bay Packers team physician, Reichardt came to Wisconsin on a football scholarship and was the starting fullback on the 1962–1963 Rose Bowl team and leading receiver in the conference last fall before choosing the diamond over the gridiron.[93]

September 24—Ralph Ellison, author of *Invisible Man,* reads from his novel in progress, which he says is "all autobiographical," but "not an account of my own life." The section he reads at the Union

Betty Friedan tells a predominantly female audience packing Great Hall that educators must "take the responsibility of affirming the image of woman as a person. There are more fundamental things to discuss about women on campus than problems of sex."[94] UNIVERSITY OF WISCONSIN–MADISON ARCHIVES IMAGE S00106

IS THERE "A CRISIS IN WOMEN'S IDENTITY"?

BETTY FRIEDAN,
author of
the controversial best-seller
"The Feminine Mystique"
says **YES!**

AT 8 P.M. THURSDAY, JULY 23
in the Great Hall of the Union

Mrs. Friedan will offer her views on "contemporary American woman's greatest problem" and the related challenge to education.

Present your fee, Union membership or faculty card at the Union Box Office for a FREE ticket.

Sponsored by the Forum Committee of
THE WISCONSIN UNION

Theater—about an old black man who loses his religious faith when he finds worms have been eating his coffin—is among the three hundred pages destroyed by a fire in 1967.[95]

October/November—October and November provide music for almost every taste. Violinist Isaac Stern, jazz pianist Oscar Peterson, and bluegrass pickers Lester Flatt and Earl Scruggs and the Foggy Mountain Boys delight diverse Union Theater audiences. Sitar master Ravi Shankar graces Great Hall—two years before Beatle George Harrison first hears him play. "Mayor of MacDougall Street" Dave van Ronk beats back a bout of bronchitis for a program of classic folk blues in 230 Social Science.[96]

December 13—Assistant sociology professor Maurice Zeitlin and others draft an open letter to President Johnson, signed by ninety-four faculty members, calling for the phased withdrawal of American troops from South Vietnam.[97]

December 19—NYU professor David Boroff, author of *Campus USA*, salutes the Memorial Union's Rathskeller as "the most justly celebrated hangout in academia," where "beer has corrupted no one, and where political debates flourish at any hour, class lines crisscross (freshmen girls meet *real* graduate students), and professors sit in earnest conference with students over cups of coffee." It's all true.[98]

The Built Environment

Decisions made and actions taken in 1964 profoundly affect the UW's physical presence. "We have never had anything like the building program we now have," President Harrington tells the regents in March.[99]

That month, a skeptical board approves adding a 13,103-seat second deck and a two-story press box to Camp Randall (current capacity: 63,435) and building a winter sports arena, paid for by raised ticket prices. Regent Charles Gelatt worries about the "very real danger that the commercial success of college football could decline" to the point that it is no longer on television, making the press box unnecessary; regent Maurice Pasch asks about "moving the stadium entirely." Regent and Park Falls attorney Arthur DeBardeleben questions whether this is "a proper function of the university" and warns, "We should not take on commitments that for the next fifty years we are going to be bound to a good team."

DeBardeleben is prescient; after the addition opens in 1966, the football team wins only six of thirty-eight games the rest of the decade, without a winning season until 1974.[100]

In late September, the regents approve—with some misgivings—the design for the university's most massive structure yet—the brutalist, fortress-like $9.8 million South Lower Campus Building for History, Music, Art, and Art Education [George L. Mosse Humanities Building].

"It looks like something right out of Mesopotamia," Gelatt grouses. DeBardeleben says it looks like a factory. Campus planning chief Wendt promises that "a proper treatment would be developed to improve the appearance." At least its brutalism will be balanced somewhat by the extensive trim, stone entrances, plaster covering bare concrete, and especially the interior courtyard sculpture garden (or so the plan is).

The regents also approve doubling the $5.5 million Language Building to eighteen stories, making it the tallest building in Madison, and the administration's new home. The regents later name it after the university's greatest former president, Charles Van Hise, requiring them to take his name off the Lakeshore Dorm refectory it had adorned since 1926.[101]

But the expansionist era may be over. At year's end, the university is upended by Warren Knowles's defeat of Governor John Reynolds (US District Court Judge, 1986–2002) to become the first Republican governor in six years, and with an all-Republican legislature. "The people of Wisconsin are unwilling to pay higher taxes for state education," Knowles declares, denouncing the UW's "grandiose schemes" and warning of enrollment cuts and other austerity measures. The university submits a record budget request and waits for what cuts and caps the new year might bring.[102]

Riot of the Year

Nine inches of heavy snow and a couple hundred young men from the ag campus dorms make for a spectacular frozen melee on the night of March 9, as students roll a huge snowball—eight feet around—onto Elm Drive, blocking the street just east of the new Natatorium and snarling traffic for a four-block area. As their numbers grow to about five hundred, the students drive police back with a barrage of snowballs for about ninety minutes, tip over two large flatbed trucks around the massive mound to protect it, and even block westbound University Avenue with trailers from the stock barn. Campus police finally start pulling random students into squad cars for questioning, and the crowd fades, off to study for six-week exams. There are no arrests.[103]

In Memoriam—UW

UW planning chief Albert Gallistel, seventy-five, who was known for fifty-two years as the "walking blueprint" of eighty million cubic feet of UW buildings, dies New Year's Day. Gallistel started with the UW in 1907, assisting State Architect Arthur Peabody on the campus plan of 1908; he retired in 1959, after thirty years as director of plant planning, and became a consultant on the university expansion projects. Gallistel and his wife, Eleanor, helped found St. Paul's University Chapel and for many years were resident managers of the summer tent colony for married students known as Camp Gallistela. The genial pipe smoker served many years as chair of the university Arboretum Committee; Gallistel Woods was dedicated in his honor.[104]

Martyred Freedom Summer volunteer Andrew Goodman, twenty-one, UW x64, lived at 202 N. Park St. as a freshman in 1961, but got pneumonia and withdrew after a semester and transferred to Queens College in his native New York, where musician Paul Simon became a casual friend. As a teenager, Goodman investigated conditions in West Virginia coal mines, lived with farming families in western Europe, and taught in a camp for inner-city children in New Jersey.[105]

Schools

GRADUATION, JUNE 12
- East: 550
- West: 538
- Central-University: 261[106]

FALL ENROLLMENT
- Total Students: 30,242
- K–6: 18,057
- 7–9: 6,163
- 10–12: 5,752
- Special Ed: 270[107]
- Catholic: 5,200[108]

With 75 percent of Madison pupils having above-average intelligence for their age—the average fifth-grader has an IQ about fourteen points above the national average, about on a par with sixth-graders—the school board in January adopts a restrictive homework policy for elementary school, limiting sixth graders to an hour a night, and preferably no homework over the weekend.[109]

School superintendent Robert D. Gilberts issues an administrative directive in mid-February mandating immediate suspension and possible expulsion for pupils possessing "any instrument which can be used to harm others or disrupt school routine," or committing other "anti-social acts in school or on school premises." The order follows a set of rumbles over teenage romance. But some troublemakers don't need weapons; in late October, vandals scale a ten-foot wall at East High School and do about $1,000 worth of damage to various offices, with even more costly damage being done to West High days later. Police surmise that the vandals were retaliating against a supervisor who had disciplined them.[110]

Glenn W. Stephens, school board member since 1927 and its president since 1950, and former State Representative Ruth B. Doyle are easily elected to the school board on April 7. In September, the board unanimously adopts Doyle's proposal to release itemized meeting agendas to news reporters at same time they are sent to board members.[111]

The board will have a new partner in its labor relations. In early June, with less than half the eligible voters casting ballots, Madison teachers vote to name the Madison Education Association their exclusive representative for collective bargaining, eliminating involvement by the Madison Federation of Teachers.[112] But teacher salaries remain comparatively low; in August, the board adopts the 1965–1966 salary schedule, raising pay for beginning teachers from $4,900 to $5,100 and the top salary for a teacher with a master's degree from $9,964 to $10,950. The new salaries will still be about $200 below the going regional rate, making recruitment difficult.[113] Recruiting male teachers is especially difficult, with two out of three who are offered positions turning them down. Unlike schools in several other Wisconsin cities (including Appleton, Janesville, Oshkosh, and Sheboygan), Madison does not offer more pay for heads of households. Madison officials, who believe male teachers provide greater school stability and classroom discipline, worry that the situation is approaching a crisis.[114]

On July 1, the board bypasses West High School assistant principal Douglas Krider and names Douglas S. Ritchie, principal of Port Washington High School, the third principal in West High's thirty-four-year history. A graduate of Oshkosh State College, with a master's degree from UW, Ritchie has spent his entire teaching and administrative experience in Port Washington. The Madison native, a former semiprofessional baseball player, plans on eliminating homeroom and giving clerks some administrative tasks now performed by teachers. The first semester under Ritchie brings heightened enforcement of the student code, requiring pupils to act like "ladies and gentlemen" by refraining from holding hands, wearing tight trousers, and smoking on school grounds. In late October, Ritchie also proposes a closed lunch period for West Junior and Senior High Schools, but drops the plan under heavy criticism just three days later.[115]

In early October, the board unanimously adopts a guide to help Madison teachers develop interracial understanding in their classrooms. "A magnificent job," says Madison NAACP president Marshall Colston of the program, a result of the NAACP's request last year for a study of how African Americans are treated in textbooks. *The Human Rights Curriculum Guide* will be used in daily classroom activity for all grades. But EOC chairman John McGrath says it was "a very serious oversight" for the guide to omit any mention of the commission or the new Equal Opportunities Ordinance.[116]

School expansion on the periphery and contraction downtown continues. On May 28, the city council annexes the eighty acres on Gammon Road for a far west high school. A few days later, the school board approves expanding the school from 1,500 to 1,800 pupils, and expanding the far east La Follette High School from 1,500 to 2,200 pupils. In early June, the Board of the Vocational, Technical, and Adult Schools approves a long-range expansion program, which includes taking over Central High School; city school officials say it won't happen. Vocational schools have a current total enrollment of 11,507.[117]

But the pressure for new schools and more classrooms may have peaked. Declining birth rates and a less aggressive annexation policy give Madison its smallest increase in school age population since 1954—4.83 percent (1,974 students); the total population of youths age four through nineteen is 42,784. And the schools will lose about eight hundred students—and $229,716 in federal aid—with the closing of the Truax Air Force base.[118]

What to name the new far west high school is of concern to the city council, which votes 12–7 in late August to recommend the late President Kennedy for the honor. West side alderman William Bradford Smith, Nineteenth Ward, a Republican, notes that area voters didn't support candidate Kennedy in 1960, and warns that naming the school after him could endanger the bond issue needed to build it. Ald. Harrison Garner also opposes the measure because, he says, "To name a schoolhouse in every community after President Kennedy would be to cheapen the name." The board takes no action.[119]

Planning and Development

GENERAL STATISTICS
- Population: 157,844[120]
- Area: 44.74 square miles (end-of-year total)

The Manchester Skywalk

Capitol Square is struggling in 1964, as outlying shopping centers sap its retail base and demographics change its market. It's a big problem, and Madisonians Morgan Manchester, Gerald Bartell, and Robert Brooks announce a big solution in April: Capitol Pavilion, a $2 million, five-story, five-hundred-car parking ramp with thirty thousand square feet of retail on West Dayton Street between Wisconsin Avenue and South Carroll Street.[121]

"Madison and the Square is decaying," says Manchester, president of the department store his father founded, Harry S. Manchester's Inc., and without this project there will be "more of a slum around the Capitol than we have now."

Gerald Bartell and Robert Brooks are partners in the development firm Madison Properties Inc. Bartell, an amateur thespian, was an innovative broadcast and publishing executive who reshaped Wisconsin radio and television in the forties and fifties, including Madison's WMTV, where his programming included the Carson and Beatrice Gulley cooking show. Robert Brooks, a talented watercolorist, earlier developed the Greentree neighborhood and owned the four Nakoma Road corners around the Brookwood shopping center with his Yale Law classmate Neil Woodington.[122]

But to create the Capitol Pavilion, Manchester, Bartell, and Brooks face one significant roadblock—the entire project depends, as they see it, on construction of a 132-foot-long, 16-foot-wide glass-enclosed pedestrian skywalk, 22.5 feet above Wisconsin Avenue. They say that without that direct connection from the ramp to the department store (and also to Baron's, which Madison Properties buys and quickly sells to Manchester's), the project can't get financing. And a lot of people don't like the idea of a skywalk blocking the Capitol.

Manchester releases a photomontage of the proposed skywalk and Capitol on May 8 and asks for approval within a week, but the city accedes to Governor John Reynolds's request for referral. Architects Herbert Fritz and Harold Rosenthal use the extra time to tweak the design and get critical aesthetic support from university artists Aaron Bohrod and Warrington Colescott. The project also expands to a $6 million venture, with a motel and bank.[123]

Morgan Manchester, president of Harry S. Manchester's Inc., poses in front of the former site of the Christ Presbyterian Church at Wisconsin and Dayton Streets, shortly after his company bought the hundred-car lot from the National Guardian Life Insurance Co. This is where Manchester, Gerald Bartell, and Robert Brooks want to build their Capitol Pavilion ramp, shops, and skywalk. Behind Manchester, the Dayton Street fronts of Central High and the Vocational School, and a glimpse of the Carnegie Library and the new parking ramp are visible. The white building on Carroll Street at the far end of the lots is the rear of the YWCA, 122 State St. WHI IMAGE ID 116648, PHOTO BY RICHARD SRODA

State planning director Walter Johnson—formerly Madison's chief planner—and the state engineer both recommend rejecting the proposal, but Governor Reynolds waives any state objection on May 25. "In view of the deterioration of downtown Madison, and in view of the fact that the walkway is apparently well designed," he writes the Plan Commission, "it would not serve the public well to oppose its construction."[124]

Despite the governor's endorsement, the Plan Commission's lengthy public hearing that afternoon features more opponents than supporters, and defeat looks likely—until Manchester suggests approval be conditioned on a set of standards that plan director Kenneth Clark has just drafted. Clark would rather they turned Wisconsin Avenue into a pedestrian mall, but says the Capitol Pavilion "will be more beneficial to the Square than nothing at all," provided the final design meets "most" of the standards in his policy statement—including that it be in "the public interest in community aesthetics, safety, economy, facilities and liability" and be removed "if the public finds it distasteful."

That's good enough for the commission, which votes unanimously for the conditional approval. The Board of Public Works follows suit the next day.[125] But the council does not. It rejects the skywalk on Thursday, 17–4, throwing the entire development into question.[126]

Still, the council keeps the concept alive by creating—as Governor Reynolds has been strongly urging—a Joint City-State Downtown Planning Committee to craft a skywalk policy. Resolution doesn't come easily.[127]

Mayor Henry Reynolds considers a model of the revised skywalk in late November. WHI IMAGE ID 137865, PHOTO BY EDWIN STEIN

In October, the council unanimously adopts the standards drafted by Clark in May, setting the stage for Manchester Skywalk 2.0. It comes in less than two weeks—a $5 million project for parking, a motel, and offices, with a $150,000 skywalk 17 feet above Wisconsin Avenue, 16 feet high, 22 feet wide, and 132 feet long.[128]

In late November, a special three-man ad hoc committee of experts starts its review of the new proposal, still pending at year's end.[129]

Business Wire

January 5—Edgewater Hotel manager Austin H. Faulkner announces the hotel has purchased from the National Guardian Life Insurance company 38,000 square feet of lakefront land to its east—part of the historic Hanks estate—extending its waterfront holdings to nearly a full block, for a "unique development" to be detailed later. A month later, the insurance company begins construction of its headquarters, a modernistic black cube, on the adjoining Vilas estate.[130]

April 24—With the Capitol Pavilion proposal under way, Madison Properties Inc. reveals a $12 million project consisting of twenty-six buildings along a one-mile stretch of University Avenue, with 650 apartments, a 200-room Ramada Inn, plus commercial and office space. Later this afternoon, they announce plans to build a ten-story, 225-room Holiday Inn in the 400 block of State Street, which would be the second attempt to build a hotel where Victor Music burned down in December 1961. Bartell says he has an accepted offer from Meyer Victor and hopes to begin construction by late July. Ultimately, neither of the two hotels is built, but much of the University Avenue project is.[131]

The proposed site of a Holiday Inn, at 417–423 State St., taken from the planned West Gilman Street entrance to the 167-car garage on April 25, 1964. Across the street, from left to right: Martin's Tailor Shop, Bluteau's market, Ella's Delicatessen, the Catholic Information Center, and the US Army and Air Force recruiting stations. WHI IMAGE ID 117237, PHOTO BY RICHARD SRODA

July 20—About two hundred people, most of them state employees, attend the dedication of the five-building, $12 million Hill Farms State Office Building complex, occupied since February. "There is probably not another office building in Wisconsin that houses people whose functions are so vital to the continuance of an orderly society as this one," Governor John Reynolds says, citing the Public Service Commission, Industrial Commission, and Department of Motor Vehicles.[132]

September 10—The council approves a compromise with the towns of Madison and Fitchburg over sixteen disputed annexations, under which Madison annexes Eagle Heights, the two university farms on Mineral Point Road, and the West Side Businessmen's Club, while the Town of Madison keeps twelve parcels, including the Sears warehouse on Fordem Avenue. The businessmen's association dispute dates to the city's contested annexation in 1960, the rest to the "surprise annexations" of 1962; their resolution means that for the first time in fifteen years, the city has no active annexation litigation.[133]

October 22—The council defeats, 14–6, a zoning amendment to stop absentee landlords from renting single-family homes in the university fringe area to students. The failed amendment by Vilas-area alderman Harrison Garner, which would have limited "family" to bona fide residents of Madison "bound together by ties of blood, marriage, or dependency," was supported by the Lake Wingra Community Council and recommended for adoption by the Plan Commission, but successfully opposed by the Wisconsin Student Association and the Board of Realtors.[134]

October 25—Hilldale Shopping Center, which has grown to include thirty-five stores, shops, and offices, celebrates its second anniversary; fifteen downtown merchants now have full stores at the center.[135]

November 19—Defense Secretary Robert McNamara announces that all Air Force installations and operations at Truax Air Force Base will close by July 1968, leaving only a squadron of the Wisconsin Air National Guard. The city estimates the base—with 2,708 military and civilian employees—pumps about $20 million into the Madison economy, about a third of which goes to local businesses. The airfield, headquarters for the Thirtieth North American Air Defense Command, was named after Madison fighter pilot First Lieutenant Thomas L. Truax in 1942, shortly after he was killed in a training flight. Madison Municipal Airport superintendent Robert Skuldt says he expects the land and buildings to be turned over to the city. The closing will take about eight hundred students—and about $230,000 in federal aid—out of the Madison schools.[136]

November 27—Describing the Atwood Avenue business district as an area of "old, deteriorating structures and traffic congestion" that "offers a depressing or unexciting appearance, for it is unplanned, inconvenient, unattractive and in mixed use," the city Plan Department calls for a variety of initiatives, including a shopping center at Schenk's Corners.[137]

December 21—The council approves the purchase price of $175,650 for forty-one acres of UW land at Mineral Point and Rosa Roads for the proposed "Hickory Hill Park" and files an application for a federal grant to defray some of the cost.[138]

Law and Disorder

Young Lovers Make Trouble

Teenage romance turns to trouble early in the year, as high school gangs rumble all over town. On January 31, an Edgewood High School girl entices the Verona boy she's dating and four of his friends into an ambush at Peppermint Park, the carnival area on the far west side, where they are severely beaten with clubs and rubber hoses by the West High boy she's also dating and fifteen of his friends. Police thwart a rematch rumble, set for a Verona gravel pit, after getting an anonymous tip. Another girl with two suitors becomes a catalyst that week in the 2400 block of East Washington Avenue, where eleven pupils from East, La Follette, and Monona Grove High Schools battle with fists, clubs, and switchblades. Madison police also confiscate three switchblade knives from students at Central and West after a knife fight between two young teens at West, also fighting over a girl.[139]

Young Smokers in the Clear

The January 11 release of the Surgeon General's report linking cigarettes to lung cancer reminds Madison that its own tobacco ordinance fines adults $100 for providing cigarettes to anyone under eighteen but sets no age limit on smoking. "Juveniles can walk around flaunting their cigarettes, and they don't have to tell us where they got them," police chief Wilbur Emery explains in asking for an ordinance that would making it a $20 violation for a minor to possess cigarettes. Emery also wants the legal age lowered from eighteen to sixteen because he believes "the majority of seventeen-year-olds who smoke do so with the consent of their parents, and who are we to say the parents are wrong."

The Committee of the Whole accepts Sixth Ward alderman George Elder's argument that smoking and drinking beer should have the same legal age, and recommends keeping it at eighteen. But after the Madison Youth Council calls this an infringement of personal liberty and urges education rather than enforcement, the council reverses its decision, agrees with Emery, and on April 23 lowers the legal smoking age to sixteen. Madison Youth Council vice president Eugene Parks, noting the many aldermen smoking during the meeting, says his group doesn't condone smoking, "but we feel this is the responsibility of the youth and his parents." Nadine Goff, editor of the Central High School *Mirror*, tells the council that a survey shows that almost 30 percent of Central senior high students and nearly 20 percent of junior high students smoke or had smoked.[140]

Highways and Transportation

Transportation Milestones

February 19—The privately owned Madison Bus company agrees to extend its South Park Street line a half-mile to provide service to the Burr Oaks area in South Madison, where residents have been pleading for better service—just days after Ald. Kopp introduced a resolution to study a municipal bus system because the company had "failed to provide the type of bus service which is essential to [the] welfare and prosperity" of city residents.[141]

April 12—Traffic engineer John Bunch proposes the Outer Circle as a way to facilitate parking and ease the current traffic congestion on the Square, caused by the current load of more than sixteen thousand cars a day. The plan, featuring five new sets of lights to regulate traffic moving in the opposite direction as traffic on the Square, is in place by fall and quickly gains acceptance.[142]

June—The city approves a plan to develop the 1.7-mile stretch of the West Beltline between Nakoma and Gilbert Roads as a freeway, the first section of a previously planned divided highway from Park Street to Middleton. The city will pay about $20,000 toward the $1.253 million improvement.[143]

September—The council makes North Lake Street, which had been one-way toward Lake Mendota between University Avenue and State Street, a two-way street.[144]

November 3—Voters approve, by better than 2–1, borrowing $6.5 million in three bond issues for major street projects, including the Monona Causeway, University Avenue, and Highway 113, along with improvements to the airport, and to storm and sanitary sewers.[145] Two days later, the State Public Service Commission approves the plans and specifications for dredging to create the roadbed for the causeway. Construction bids come in under budget, and the city plans to open the road by late 1966.[146]

December 2—The State Highway Commission officially approves the University Avenue Expressway. Land acquisition will cost about $5 million, with construction estimated at about $6 million; the federal government will pay about half. Construction should start in about a year and be done by 1970.[147]

December 17—It's bicycles, not cars, that concern police chief Wilbur Emery at a traffic commission meeting; he wants all fourteen thousand banned from State Street and the Capitol Square at all times, and from other main streets during morning and evening rush hours. "Bicycles slow traffic and become hazards," Emery tells the Traffic Commission, noting the fifty-two bike accidents this year, forty-one involving injuries. The commission does not act on Emery's request.[148] As the year ends, the state Highway Commission marks State Street as a scenic route and calls for the removal of overhead signs and billboards.[149]

Miscellanea

February 2—More than half of Bethel Lutheran's six thousand members attend a series of rededication services following a $1.1 million expansion project at 312 Wisconsin Ave.[150]

February 19—Madison watercolorist Lee Weiss is awarded the Medal of Honor in the national Knickerbocker Artists of New York competition for her abstract "Winter Dunes." Weiss, wife of economics professor Leonard Weiss and the mother of four daughters, won "best of show" at last year's Madison Art Association exhibit.[151]

March 8—La Follette High School senior Eugene Parks wins a medal and a $50 savings bond by taking first place in an American Legion oratorical contest with a ten-minute original speech on the US Constitution.[152]

April 1—After complaints about dogs running loose, the Parks Commission bans dogs from seven city parks. "Maybe we need a dog park," says commissioner Mrs. George Hanson.[153]

May 2—About a hundred students and residents stage a quiet and orderly picket march along Mifflin Street and around the Capitol Square protesting American involvement in Vietnam. Part of a nationwide activity, this local May Second Committee action is led by John Coatsworth and Harriet Tanzman.[154]

May 26—Temple Beth El celebrates twenty-five years as a congregation, all under founding rabbi Manfred Swarsensky, with the announcement of a $105,000 expansion project of the synagogue, 2702 Arbor Dr.[155]

July 14—Manchester's department store sells one of the controversial "topless" bathing suits designed by Rudi Gernreich but returns the remaining five it had ordered after city attorney Edwin Conrad tells store officials "that the merchants of Madison owe it to

ROUNDY SAYS

"I dropped in to see Pee Wee Kelly the other day he has been ill. I thought he was coming along good what more could be fairer?"
—*Wisconsin State Journal,* June 24.

"I will never forget Dave Condon of the Chicago Tribune he spoke at my birthday party about three years ago. He seen that beautiful looking yellow sweet corn on the cob then he set out to establish a record. So if you think I am a little nuts throw the paper away."
—*Wisconsin State Journal,* June 26

the citizens here not to perpetuate this hysterical insanity that's going on." Vowing to prosecute any woman wearing the suit in public, Conrad calls on "all the citizens of the city, and particularly the clergy, to back me up on this." Store president Morgan Manchester says, "Everybody who has any style sense at all is selling them. I personally don't think they are in very good taste, but I don't want to pass moral judgment on them."[156]

July 14—City forester George Behrnd reports that Dutch elm disease is under control, with only 214 confirmed cases this year among the city's fifty-five thousand elms, down from 277 this time last year. "The situation looks good," Behrnd says.[157]

September 16—Mayor Reynolds and 350 guests celebrate the gala opening of the Madison Art Association galleries in the new Madison Art Center in the former Lincoln School. The center's inaugural exhibit is drawn from the American Federation of Arts's recent *Banners USA* exhibit in New York City. An Aaron Bohrod lithograph, *Church in Luxembourg*, is auctioned at the gala, the first of twenty prints given by an anonymous donor for fundraising.[158]

September 24—Republican presidential nominee Barry Goldwater opens his Wisconsin campaign on the State Capitol steps with a surefire crowd-pleaser—a reading of the "sifting and winnowing" plaque on Bascom Hall. "Something that has always been in my mind since my first visit" to the university, he says. There's some chanting and heckling during the program before Goldwater's late arrival, but nothing disruptive; the crowd of about ten thousand is attentive during his speech, a generally moderate statement of conservative principles. Per university policy for local appearances by presidential nominees, early afternoon classes are canceled; several thousand students attend, in both support and opposition. About fifteen hundred picketers organized by the Ad Hoc Committee Against Extremism parade silently on the outskirts of the crowd.[159]

September 28–October 3—The Festival de France transforms the Capitol Square into Paris, with Eiffel Towers at the Washington Avenue entrances, Arcs de Triomphe at the Wisconsin and Monona Avenue entrances, and a joie de vivre in the air. In a private affair on Saturday night, September 26, 350 Madisonians in their finest formalwear feast on a lavish array of French delicacies at a champagne buffet benefit for the Madison Civic Symphony Orchestra cosponsored by the French Consul General and the Madison Civic Music Association at the Hotel Loraine. After food comes fashion; nine French models, who were guests at the Badger–Notre Dame football game earlier in the day, present more than fifty haute couture outfits from Parisian designers. The festival, coproduced by the Madison Chamber of Commerce and the French government, goes public on Monday. Restaurants adopt a continental menu, French films play at the Majestic and Capitol Theaters, the Junior Women's Club tea dance takes a French theme. The Bank of Madison

Eiffel Tower (mock) and Capitol (real), during setup for the Festival de France, September 17. WHI IMAGE ID 137744, PHOTO BY EDWIN STEIN

Part of the crowd of ten thousand awaiting Republican presidential nominee Senator Barry Goldwater's speech from the Monona Avenue [Martin Luther King Jr. Blvd.] steps of the State Capitol on September 24. In the background, the Festival de France mini–Arc de Triomphe. WHI IMAGE ID 138225, PHOTO BY EDWIN STEIN

boasts the first American display of the works of the French artist Jean Veidly, winner of the Grand Prix International, a thousand photographs of French scenes fill downtown windows, and local artists have exhibitions. The Leo Kehl School of Dance creates "The Parisienne," which it performs with the classic can-can at the Park Motor Inn. Flower carts filled with fall blossoms and newsstand kiosks with French vendors and magazines set up on the Square, under the watchful eye of an actual gendarme.[160]

December 2—Ald. Harrison L. Garner announces he won't seek reelection in April, ending thirty-five years on the council. His primary city accomplishments include the establishment of the municipal civil service system early in his career and the fluoridation of city water in the 1940s. Born in a log cabin near Lancaster, Pennsylvania, in 1883, and often called "The Colonel" in recognition of his rank during World War I, Garrison was for many years executive vice president of Anchor Savings and Loan.[161]

In Memoriam

Thomas Coleman, seventy, widely respected both as president of Madison-Kipp since 1927 and as a powerful state and Republican leader for three decades, dies of cancer on February 4. In March, his son J. Reed Coleman is named as his successor and promises to keep the plant at its east side location.[162]

Dr. Arnold S. Jackson, seventy-one, a founding member of the American Board of Surgery and director of his family's medical clinic from 1951 until this past May, dies August 30 after a brief illness. The Madison native—whose father, James, and maternal grandfather, Dr. Joseph Hobbins, were pioneer physicians in Madison—conducted groundbreaking research into the role of thyroid ailments in mental retardation. He later served as a voluntary medical adviser at St. Coletta's home in Jefferson. Jackson's home, on a ten-acre parcel at 3515 W. Beltline, was designed by his friend, Frank Lloyd Wright, whom his older brother Joseph detested.[163]

Helen Samp, seventy-six, a school board member from 1949 to 1963, dies of cancer on December 23.[164]

Madison's most famous photographer and one of its best young photojournalists both die this year. Angus McVicar, sixty, who chronicled Madison from the mid-1920s to 1942, when he joined the university photography department, dies on May 8. Richard W. Vesey, forty-one, award-winning photographer for the *Wisconsin State Journal* for nearly twenty years, dies of a heart attack on December 30.[165]

Among the major off-campus changes since the image on page xiv: (1) the National Guardian Life Insurance company headquarters replaced the Vilas mansion in 1964, (2) Christ Presbyterian Church was razed in 1963, (3) Thirty On The Square is under construction, replacing the Wisconsin Life Insurance company building, (4) the Park Motor Inn replaced the Park Hotel in 1963, (5) the Anchor Savings and Loan building and (6) parking ramp replaced the century-old Blied and Atwood buildings in 1964. The oldest building on the Square (7), built in 1855 as Bacon's Commercial School and converted in 1900 to the Madison Hotel, is razed in late June 1965 for the new Emporium.[1] UNIVERSITY OF WISCONSIN–MADISON ARCHIVES IMAGE S00046

1965

In 1965, demonstrations against the growing war in Vietnam replace demonstrations in favor of civil rights as the left's dominant political issue—a transition marked by a direct action at Truax Air Force Base in mid-October.

As President Johnson escalates American involvement in the war, some are outraged at the imperialism and militarism, some are offended by the war's dishonest and grotesque nature. But in 1965, most students, like most Americans, are neither outraged nor offended but support the war.[2]

Whether hawk or dove, nearly everyone is personally invested. In April, with the draft at ten thousand men a month, the mean age of inductees from Wisconsin is twenty-three, but as the draft more than triples by fall, the mean age drops to twenty, leaving previously protected college men, and maybe even teenagers, increasingly exposed. The state's quota of volunteers and draftees, 404 in August, jumps to 677 in September and 744 in October.[3]

Creating the Committee

The American bombing of North Vietnam on February 7 sparks the creation of the first ongoing antiwar protest organization, the Committee to End the War in Viet Nam (CEWVN or CEWV). Alternately led by students associated with the Communist and Socialist Workers parties, CEWV will engage in ongoing education and outreach, hold periodic rallies, and be the main antiwar group for about the next two years.

On February 9, the day after the executive councils of both the university's Young Democrats and Young Republicans adopt resolutions endorsing the bombing, about 250 students march through freezing rain—and an occasional hostile snowball—from campus to the Capitol for a rally sponsored by the Ad Hoc Committee for Peace in Viet Nam, organized by sophomore Daniel B. Friedlander. Among the speakers protesting the bombing raids are professors William Gorham Rice, Joseph Elder, Francis D. Hole, and Maurice Zeitlin. John Coatsworth, who violated the travel ban to Cuba in 1963, moderates the rally, which also features Hillel Foundation director Rabbi Richard W. Winograd and mayoral candidate William Osborne Hart. Leaders of the major campus organizations, including the Wisconsin Student Association, Memorial Union, Associated Women Students, and Inter-Fraternity Council, issue a statement afterward declaring that a majority of students "would not condemn the government for its recent actions in Viet Nam."[4]

Madison police film and photograph the rally from the Capitol's second-floor balcony, ostensibly for "training" purposes; some civil libertarians raise concerns, but the council blocks attempts to question police chief Wilbur Emery on the full purpose or use of the films and photographs. The overt intelligence gathering soon becomes covert, with systematic police infiltration of the antiwar movement.[5]

The group, now calling itself the Committee to End the War in Viet Nam, stages a twenty-four-hour vigil on the Capitol steps February 12–13, maintaining between fifty and a hundred demonstrators through the thirteen-degree night; several participants, including Liz Dennis and Stu Ewen, pass the time singing old rock-and-roll songs with new antiwar lyrics, while Professor William A. Williams—whose reputation as a revisionist historian of American diplomatic history attracted Coatsworth to Wisconsin—shares a flask with sociology grad student Evan Stark. Two students are arrested and charged with disorderly conduct for pelting the picketers with snowballs. There are no other incidents, as a Saturday rally of more than three hundred and another night's vigil cap the week's events. The weekend vigils continue for about two months.[6]

Friedlander and undergraduate history student Jim Hawley—who had created a stir by attending the 1962 founding convention of Students for a Democratic Society as a seventeen-year-old member of a communist-front youth group—register CEWVN (later known as CEWV) as a university student organization on February 25.[7]

On March 15, David Keene (American Conservative Union chairman, 1984–2011; National Rifle Association president, 2011–2013) registers the UW Young Americans for Freedom (YAF), an affiliate to the national conservative group, which has grown from a meeting at author and polemicist William F. Buckley's Connecticut estate on September 11, 1960, into an enduring and powerful right-wing organization.[8]

The Teach-In

The first "teach-in" about the war is held at the University of Michigan on March 24; the next day, a "Faculty-Student" CEWV announces a Wisconsin effort that draws several thousand students to cram the corridors and classrooms of the Social Sciences Building on April 1. From 2 p.m. until after midnight, twenty-six prominent faculty—including professors Merle Curti, George Mosse, and Germaine Bree—give lectures and lead discussions on the causes and effects of the war; more than a thousand pack into overflowing Room 230 for the concluding panel, starring Professor William Appleman Williams. Professor David Carr, noting the nearly unanimous opposition to the war from all the

Teach-in in Room 230, Social Sciences Building, April 1. WHI IMAGE ID 73689, PHOTO BY DAVID SANDELL

speakers, is not impressed: "The overall result was to combine lectures with political harangues," he writes in the *Daily Cardinal*. "A rational and responsible effort at constructive criticism of American foreign policy was impossible under these unfortunate circumstances." The weeklong protests culminate the next day in a noon rally of about a thousand on Library Mall, featuring remarks by sociology professor William Sewell (the primary faculty instigator of the teach-in), Williams, and former National Security Council analyst Marcus Raskin.[9]

While the teach-in is under way, acclaimed war photojournalist Dickey Chapelle, sister of geology professor Robert Meyer, tells the Committee to Support the People of South Viet Nam rally of about two hundred at the Law School that she's "honored to attend the first counter-demonstration" in support of the war. Chapelle, from Shorewood, has covered wars since World War II; she's spent more than a year in Vietnam and is soon to return on assignment for the *National Observer*, after which she plans to retire. The Committee to Support the People of South Viet Nam, led by a half-dozen students active in fraternities and campus politics, also drafts a petition in support of the American war effort; in four days, they collect six thousand signatures, which they present to presidential aide McGeorge Bundy—the national security adviser who recommended the February bombing raids that sparked the CEWV—at the White House on April 25. As they do, about 250 picket outside the gates, in a protest organized by the Students for a Democratic Society.[10]

International Days of Protest, October 15–16

In early October, the broader, community-focused Madison CEWV votes against civil disobedience during the coming weekend's International Days of Protest, orchestrated by the National Coordinating Committee and expected to draw a hundred thousand or so protesters to events around the country. Cochair Jim Hawley calls civil disobedience "impractical at this time," but doesn't rule it out in the future. A newly formed group whose members have roots in the Student Peace Center and CORE disagrees with the decision, declares itself the Committee for Direct Action to End the War in Viet Nam, and announces an action proposed by Lea Zeldin—an attempted "citizens' arrest" of Truax Air Field's commanding officer, Lieutenant Colonel Lester Arasmith. If unsuccessful in making the arrest, they will sit in until removed.[11]

On the fifteenth, a crowd of about three hundred gathers at the Memorial Union steps for speeches, with music from the Mitchell Trio (featuring newcomer John Denver) and Tracy Nelson; about fifty counterdemonstrators heckle and hassle. The next day, there's a similarly sized crowd for more speeches from Frank Emspak, Stu Ewen (Chair, Frederic Ewen Academic Freedom Center, 2006–2012), and others, and a picket on the State Street steps of the Capitol.[12]

But these events are overshadowed by the Committee for Direct Action action at Truax, where about seventy-five protesters march from East Washington Avenue down Wright Street to the main gate; awaiting them are about two hundred military and civilian police, a hundred counterdemonstrators, and scores of reporters.

Spokesman Jim Makagon asks permission to enter; it's denied. He demands Arasmith present himself for arrest "for crimes against humanity" in Vietnam; Arasmith, a Canadian, doesn't. Eleven protesters sit down in the roadway, linking arms and singing civil rights songs.

Police chief Wilbur Emery tells the group they've got five minutes to clear the road, but they don't move; when the paddy wagon arrives fifteen minutes later, the nine men and two women are arrested and charged with loitering in a public street. The Truax Eleven include early CORE activists (including Bourtai Scudder [Washington State Assistant Attorney General] and Mr. and Mrs. Stanley Grand) as well as fledgling antiwar activist Bob Cohen, twenty-two, first-semester law student from Levittown, New York. Evan Stark (Rutgers Medical School Department of Urban Health Administration professor and chair, 1995–2012; Manware Humanitarian Award recipient, 2002) is the press liaison. Five plead no contest to loitering in a public street; the others go to trial in mid-November before Judge William Buenzli, who rejects Cohen's constitutional arguments, finds them all guilty, and imposes fines of $25.[13]

The *Daily Cardinal*, whose managing editor, Jean Sue Johnson, is active in the Committee to Support the People of South Viet Nam, is again unimpressed. Calling the protesters "bigots and martyrs," the paper offers some advice: "The reliance by so many students on militant action also lessens their chance of getting what they want. The average citizen or congressman reacts negatively to picket lines and placards and is not very likely to

Police carry Bourtai Scudder, one of nine men and two women from the Committee for Direct Action to End the War in Viet Nam arrested for obstructing the road in front of the Truax Air Force Base, into a paddy wagon on October 16. PHOTO BY NEAL ULEVICH

support the protesters. If the protesters really want to accomplish something, they would do well to consider the old-fashioned technique of lobbying." The *State Journal* calls the protest movement "deplorable . . . repugnant," and counterproductive.[14]

Protest Timeline

May 4—Wisconsin Alumni Association president Robert Spitzer calls for "a lot more God and country" on campus, and fewer political demonstrations. "It seems a shame that alumni are often forced to spend more time defending the University than they do singing its praises," the Burlington businessman tells attendees at a Founder's Day dinner.[15]

May 6—CEWV delays and disrupts three military and State Department officials (the so-called "truth teams") trying to explain the government perspective, presented by the Committee to Support the People of South Viet Nam. About seven hundred students, roughly split between opponents and supporters of the war, pack the 450-seat Social Sciences room past capacity as Evan Stark and others heckle and hiss at the officials. Anti-protesters try to shout down the disrupters and the event devolves into chaos—all in front of network news crews and national reporters.[16]

The editorial backlash is swift, severe, and universal. "If the minority fringe is allowed to continue to make all of the noise on this campus without opposition," the *Daily Cardinal* warns, "academic freedom here at Wisconsin will be dealt a very serious blow." The conservative *State Journal* declares "the 'end-the-war' crowd is doing an excellent job of self-destruction of any influence it might have had on campus." Even the antiwar *Capital Times* calls the action "an offensive display of childish show-offism" and says participants "did damage to the university and have made themselves legitimate subjects of censure."[17]

May 23—Ambassador Averell Harriman suffers some satirical leafleting outside and snickering inside but is not disrupted when he speaks to a generally receptive crowd of about eight hundred at the Union Theater. A few days later, Professor Williams assures the Exchange Club that Madison remains a small, placid city, and no one should be overly concerned by the demonstrations.[18]

July 7—The UW YAF becomes the first conservative political group to stage a demonstration in Madison, picketing during a dedication ceremony for the Capitol in support of section 14(b) of the federal Taft-Hartley Act, which allows states to enact anti-union "right-to-work" laws. Thanks to the large crowd gathered for the dedication, David Keene and about a dozen YAF activists hand out a thousand leaflets in only two hours, denouncing legislative efforts to repeal 14(b).[19]

July 9—The US Senate Internal Security Subcommittee invites fifteen UW students, including CEWV leaders Hawley and Coatsworth, to testify in a closed session to respond to allegations about their political activity, which conservative commentator Bob Siegrist made in a secret session in May. They decline.[20]

July 29—General Lewis Hershey, director of the Selective Service System, tells the *Daily Cardinal* that the recent doubling of the draft to thirty-five thousand men a month puts college students at risk. "Local draft boards will first look to student deferments if they feel a manpower pinch," he says.[21]

July 30–31—US Representative Robert W. Kastenmeier (D-Watertown), denied a formal hearing on the war in Vietnam before the House Foreign Affairs Committee, holds a "grass roots" public hearing at the First Methodist Church on Wisconsin Avenue. Kastenmeier had wanted to meet in the City-County Building, but prowar alderman Harold "Babe" Rohr, a member of the City County Building Commission, blocked use of the council chambers because of the subject. Police chief Emery also urged the building commission to reject Kastenmeier's request because the hearing would "attract many not concerned with the issue and they'd be up to no good." Kastenmeier was also denied use of the State Capitol. The hearing was finally set for the federal courthouse, then moved to the larger church. Critics of American policy predominate the hearing, but the witness list also includes such young conservative leaders as the YAF's Keene and Tommy Thompson, chair of the Dane County Young Republicans. There are no disruptions during the proceedings.[22]

Early August—Inspired by the impact of a massive and mobilized student cohort at the Free Speech Movement at the University of California–Berkeley in late 1964, a coalition of peace and civil rights groups forms the National Coordinating Committee to End the War in Viet Nam and leases a three-flat at 341 W. Mifflin St. for its headquarters. Frank Emspak, cochair of the Madison CEWV, quits his job as a project assistant in Clinical Oncology—thereby losing his deferment—to chair the effort coordinating activities of dozens of antiwar groups leading up to the International Days of Protest in October. Emspak gets his draft notice almost immediately after giving a nationally televised interview, but after his physical is classified 1-Y (to be inducted only in event of war or national emergency).[23]

August 23—About fifty picketers organized by Evan Stark and the Student Peace Center protest the Union Theater appearance of Vice President Hubert Humphrey on August 23 (see front cover, lower left image). "If they can show us how to get out of Vietnam without the communists getting in," Humphrey tells cheering delegates to the National Student Association convention, "we'll put the placards around here in the hall of fame rather than the hall of shame."[24]

October 28—The council unanimously adopts Ald. Richard Kopp's resolution declaring that Madisonians "abhor the demonstrations" against President Johnson's handling of the war in Vietnam and pledging the city's "support of our country in bringing about peace in the world." "I dislike the reputation this city is getting because of a few people who come here to go to school," the Northport-area alderman says.[25]

October 30—Student antiwar demonstrations are backfiring and increasing public support for the war, journalism professor Scott Cutlip tells a hearing sponsored by the UW Young Democrats. History professor William Taylor adds that antidemonstrator sentiment is growing and creating a "neo-McCarthyism."[26]

November 12—"Wisconsin's tradition of freedom of expression has added to our national reputation," President Harrington tells the regents, adding that students don't lose their political rights as citizens. He calls the disruptive heckling of the State Department team "disgraceful," and suggests that the Committee to Support the People of South Viet Nam is stronger than the Committee to End the War in Viet Nam, "although it has not received as much publicity."[27] He's right—a survey about this time indicates that two of every three students support the American war effort without reservation, and only one in four wants American troops out.[28]

November 23—UW students decisively defeat a referendum asking if the WSA Senate should take stands on national or international issues that don't "directly" affect UW students, voting 2–1 that campus government should limit itself to campus issues.[29]

November 28—It's a blustery twenty degrees on the Saturday after Thanksgiving when about a dozen protesters from a splinter group from the CEWV called Viet Nam Dissenters, dressed in black with faces painted white, march from campus to the Capitol carrying a coffin made of paper and wood. As they near the Capitol, about fifteen members of the Citizens in Support of the United States Soldiers in Viet Nam hurl raw eggs and smash the mock coffin. Police observe the assault without response.[30]

Civil Rights

Alabama Bound (or Not)

Three busloads of Badgers bound for Alabama to support the march from Selma to Montgomery leave town on March 16, on a trip arranged by the university Friends of the Student Non-Violent Coordinating Committee (SNCC). "I am proud that our students are concerned enough about basic human rights to express their views," Chancellor Robben Fleming says, calling on instructors to treat the two-day absences as they do "other collegiate ventures which cause temporary absence."[31]

But the original destination, Selma, is getting too dangerous. The group heads for Montgomery instead, until the situation there also proves so hazardous that SNCC officials ask the 114 students to head for Washington, DC, to protest federal failure to protect civil rights workers on their ongoing march. After talking it over for more than two hours at the Chicago bus depot, the group reluctantly agrees to the new plan, which becomes a wintry four-day vigil in front of the White House. Squatting on snowy, slushy sidewalks isn't much fun, and the students are a bit bitter about not getting to Alabama, but they draw national media to the cause and feel they've done some good. At night, the students stay at the Lincoln Memorial Congregational Temple, sleeping on the pews and floor.[32]

Meanwhile, a chartered flight of about twenty-five clergy, doctors with donated medical supplies, and law students leaves Madison for Montgomery at about two in the morning on St. Patrick's Day.[33] The "Freedom Fliers" make it only to Chicago before they're snowbound by a late-winter storm and stuck for twenty-four hours. Still, their spirits stay high. "We shall overcome," one passenger is said to remark, "even the weather."[34]

A VICIOUS CIRCLE

"The principle of open housing has been generally accepted, but because Negroes do not have the economic resources to move to better neighborhoods, there has been a concentration in certain areas. Equal employment opportunities are also accepted in principle, but in many cases Negroes are not qualified for jobs available. Therefore in Madison there is not basically a question of denying civil rights as such but there is the problem of Negroes being unable to attain equal status because of lack of resources. This in turn means lack of qualifications, education, training and consequently poorer jobs and lower pay. This makes for a vicious circle. Negroes live in poorer and more crowded homes, which leads to greater delinquency and crime, more broken homes, less preparation for jobs, a higher ratio than whites on relief and in aid to dependent children. Therefore we have more than a civil rights problem; we have an economic problem, a relief problem, a slum problem, and tax base problem—all of which affect the image of the City."—Report of the Equal Opportunities Commission, April 27, 1965

As more than a hundred equality activists board buses, presumably headed south, two students show their opposition to civil rights in a provocative way.
WHI IMAGE ID 137747, PHOTO BY EDWIN STEIN

The group finally makes it to Montgomery late Thursday morning, March 18, staying about a day and a half to observe, assist, and report on the march. University YMCA program director Jim Sykes is among those walking the last miles into the capital.[35]

Four years after the *Daily Cardinal* mocked "integration agitation," editor Gail Bensinger and sports editor David Wolf are along to bear witness in Montgomery, while reporter Eric Newhouse, on the bus initially slated for Selma, reports from Washington.[36]

Civil Rights Dateline

January 19—The Equal Opportunities Commission reports it received nine complaints about alleged discrimination in housing and three about discrimination in employment in its first year, all either resolved or withdrawn. The commission continues to operate without a budget, city office, or professional staff—a situation it says is not sustainable.[37]

February 28—La Follette High School senior Eugene Parks, president of the Madison Youth Council, concludes the First Baptist Church's eighteenth annual Youth Series with a talk on "The Courage to Be a Real Leader."[38]

March 14—Close to a thousand Madison residents, most coming directly from church, mass at the State Street steps of the State Capitol for a Sunday-morning prayer vigil for civil rights. Republican governor Warren Knowles draws sustained applause when he salutes the demonstrators, including a group that marched almost two miles through biting winds from the First Congregational Church on Breese Terrace. Rabbi Manfred Swarsensky is master of ceremonies for the program organized by the Reverend George

Equal Opportunities Commission chair Reverend James Wright tracks the dispersion of Madison's approximately 1,750 black residents after enactment of the Fair Housing Ordinance in December 1963. Although 36 percent still live in South Madison, there are now only two wards (the Seventh and Eleventh) that remain all white, down from eight in 1960. But blacks are over-represented in one type of housing—making up only 1 percent of the city population, they occupy 17 percent (28) of the city's 160 public housing units.[39] WHI IMAGE ID 136687, PHOTO BY DAVID SANDELL

Vann, pastor of St. Paul's African Methodist Church. The emotional highlight is the eulogy by First Unitarian Society's Reverend Max Gaebler for the Reverend James Reeb of the Unitarian Universalist church in Boston, who died Thursday after being attacked by segregationists in Selma.[40]

April 3—In a televised "exit interview," Mayor Henry Reynolds cites adoption of the Equal Opportunities Ordinance in December 1963 as the leading accomplishment of his four years in office.[41]

August 29—St. Paul's African Methodist Episcopal Church, a spiritual cornerstone for Madison's black residents, holds its last service before being razed. The church was built for Bethel Lutheran in 1887, bought by St. Paul's and moved to 625 E. Dayton St. in 1902, and moved to 631 E. Dayton St. in 1928. The congregation will move into the former Central Lutheran Church building, 402 E. Mifflin St.[42]

November 18—More than four thousand residence hall students give up their Thursday dinner the week before Thanksgiving, raising over $3,500 in this year's Fast for Freedom fund-raiser for the Mississippi Poor People's Corporation and the National Student Association.[43]

"Profile of the Negro Student"

A head count of black students conducted by special assistant to the faculty Ruth B. Doyle identifies eighty undergraduates and thirty-eight graduate students among the UW's 24,201 students, including fourteen from Milwaukee and ten from Madison. Doyle conducts ninety-minute interviews with seventy-three; almost everyone reports they are "the only Negro whom most of their fellow students have ever met." While "only a few of the undergraduates reported any unpleasant" encounters based on their color, "many of the graduate students did report unpleasant incidents which occurred during their search for housing," prior to adoption of the city's fair housing code. Many of the undergraduates hail from integrated neighborhoods; half have at least one parent with a college degree, and "only a very small number come from backgrounds which could be described as disadvantaged."

Although the 1964–1965 census records thirty-five more black students than last year, Doyle notes that "the vast majority of our students come to college without ever having met or talked to a Negro," and leave the same way. But, she says, a modern university "cannot pretend to offer well-rounded education while this gap in social and cultural life continues." She calls for aggressive recruitment and financial assistance to

UNION FORUM COMMITTEE PRESENTS

Dr. Martin Luther King, Jr.

3:30 P.M., TUES., NOV. 23
UNIVERSITY PAVILION

"THE FUTURE OF INTEGRATION"

Tickets 75c Union Box Office

Nobel laureate in the cow barn.[44] UNIVERSITY OF WISCONSIN-MADISON ARCHIVES IMAGE S00101

bring more black students to Madison, and for white students "to undertake work, travel and educational ventures which will take them into the Negro areas of the country."[45]

Movement Orators

Although civil rights are receding as the university's primary political cause, the campus remains friendly territory for civil rights leaders.

On May 5, Floyd McKissick, national chairman of the Congress of Racial Equality, tells a Union Theater crowd of about two hundred that "it's getting harder to teach non-violence."[46]

John Lewis, national chairman of the Student Nonviolent Coordinating Committee, speaks twice on November 2—a noon rally on the Union steps, and an evening address in Great Hall, after which about four hundred students give him a standing ovation before moving up Langdon Street to Hillel for a freedom hootenanny.[47]

On November 23, the standing ovation from a near-capacity Stock Pavilion crowd of about twenty-six hundred is for 1964 Nobel Peace Prize recipient Dr. Martin Luther King Jr. Although his talk bears the same title as his 1962 address, it differs in substance, including calls for a massive program of public works, expanded public education, an increase in minimum wage to $2 an hour, and the employment of blacks in Southern law enforcement.[48]

Barring Jews Is Bad News for the Madison Club

University president Fred Harvey Harrington proves the power of one man's protest against anti-Semitism—his resignation in early October from the Madison Club results in the city's premier private club admitting its first Jewish members a month later. But a drafting decision made in 1963 limits the city's power to do more.

It had long been evident that the club, where Madison's business and legal elite entertain and intertwine, did not have any Jewish members, and the reason why was obvious as well. In 1962, the Madison Community Chest had stopped paying dues for its executive director out of concerns over anti-Semitism, and other groups had stayed away.

So in October 1964, when Collins Ferris, president of Madison Bank and Trust Company, invited Supreme Court Justice Myron Gordon and attorney Gordon Sinykin to apply for membership, they naturally were reluctant. But Ferris, a former club president, insisted that board members are "determined to put this barrier to rest."[49]

They apply in February, but months go by with no action on their applications. The news isn't public, but it's not completely private, either. Within a few months, Harrington, who joined the club at the suggestion of Wisconsin Alumni Association executive director and club board member Arlie Mucks Jr., is getting uneasy; as state chairman of Brotherhood Week for the National Conference of Christians and Jews, he's especially sensitive to anti-Semitism. He writes Mucks urging approval of the applications, and suggesting other Jews who would also make good members.

In September, the board finally votes—but the two negative votes on the nine-member board constitute rejection. The news is still not "public," but people know.

"You tried nobly, Arlie," Harrington writes Mucks on October 5. "I do thank you for your efforts to open the Madison Club to Jewish members." Harrington laments that the club directors "failed to measure up to their opportunity," and instead contributed to this "shocking story in our day."

"Feeling as I do about anti-Semitism and other forms of discrimination," Harrington tells Mucks, he's not only quitting the club, but refusing to meet there with alumni groups in the future.

It takes a week for Harrington's resignation to become public—and when it does, in an un-bylined *Capital Times* story on October 12, the outrage is immediate and widespread.[50]

Ferris expresses "disappointment and disillusionment" and others are "highly incensed." Several attorneys wonder how quickly they can resign. A petition circulates calling for the two men's admission. It's never announced which two board members cast the blocking votes. Directors Duane Bowman (of Bowman All-Star Dairy) and Bruno Stein (of Marshall Dairy Labs) publicly bemoan the rejection; construction executive George Icke snappishly refuses to comment.[51]

But the club is more than a private enclave; its members are on numerous public boards and commissions and frequently schedule official meetings there—including for city committees. Mayor Reynolds quickly reschedules the Auditorium Committee meeting scheduled for the club that week; other cancellations follow.[52]

"The righteous indignation of so many people over this disgraceful incident is a healthy thing for the community and speaks well of the high moral values of the overwhelming majority of Madison citizens," the Madison Jewish Council says in a statement.[53]

On October 14, Ald. Reynolds introduces, with fourteen cosponsors, "a resolution relating to the liquor license of the Madison Club." The intent, Reynolds says, is "to express the council's disapproval of discrimination [and] provide a legal basis for any later action." They plan to revoke the club's license if discrimination is proved—just as the 1963 draft ordinance would have let them do, until the entire licensure section was deleted.[54]

On October 28, the council votes 16–4 for a resolution declaring its "strong disapproval" of discriminatory membership practices, stating it will "deny any and all privileges granted by the city to those organizations which discriminate against others because of race, creed, color, national origin, or ancestry," and directing the Equal Opportunities Commission (EOC) to "investigate and recommend a solution" to implement the policy.[55]

As the EOC sets about its investigation, pressure continues to build on the club's directors. The petition for admission approaches one hundred signatures, including three

Supreme Court Justices (some of whom have reportedly threatened to resign). The list of canceled events grows to include a meeting of the Wisconsin Alumni Research Foundation and the Dane County Bar Association dinner dance.[56]

The club's directors note, accurately, that there are no discriminatory restrictions in the bylaws and appoint a committee to review whether two negative votes from the nine directors should be enough to kill an application. They decide it isn't, and on November 15, barely a month after Harrington's resignation became public, the board amends its membership rules to require only five positive votes for approval of an application.[57]

The board asks Gordon and Sinykin to reapply; they do and are quickly welcomed—with varying degrees of sincerity—into the club.[58]

The EOC praises Gordon and Sinykin for their "courage and good grace" through the controversy, and commends the club for its "positive action in furthering the cause of human rights." The two men thank the commission; there's no record of a response from the club.[59]

Race for Mayor

The mayoral election of 1965 gives the city a clear choice between continuity—businessman George Hall, who ran Henry Reynolds's two successful campaigns—and change—Democratic Dane County clerk Otto Festge.

Hall, sixty-four, 3826 Cherokee Dr., is chairman of Hyland Hall Co. and H & H Electric Co., president of the board of directors of Madison General Hosptial, and a member of the Rotary Club and Zor Shrine. Festge, forty-four, 4310 Herrick Ln., began his career in public service as Cross Plains town assessor in 1946 and has been county clerk since 1953; a former part-time farmer, he's a member of the Lions Club.[60]

The race is largely free of the personal invective that marked the 1963 campaign, but the candidates do step a bit beyond actual issues. Festge routinely refers to the "Reynolds-Hall administration"; Hall says Festge is too tightly entwined with "the System," the rural County Board interests that routinely disfavor Madison.[61]

Their clearest point of disagreement is Monona Terrace. Hall is absolutely against it, primarily because his top priority is an expressway from Blair Street to the Causeway through Law Park. But he wants the Wright Foundation to design for a new site, which he'd like to be within three blocks of the Capitol. Festge, a talented multi-instrumentalist who played with the Madison Symphony Orchestra while attending UW and was later a public school music teacher in Black Earth, says Monona Terrace is still the best site, but is "not unalterably committed to it," in case a different site is demanded by the public or recommended by the planners. Hall supports the ongoing arbitration over the foundation's fee; Festge favors a negotiated settlement instead. The strongest support for Monona Terrace comes from attorney William Dyke, who finishes third in the seven-man primary in March.[62]

Festge calls for Madison and the surrounding municipalities to subsidize expanded bus service, turning to public ownership if the subsidy system doesn't work. He says Hall's support for new roads rather than mass transit shows he's "living in the past."[63]

Although the campaign coincides with Selma and the bombing raids on North Vietnam, neither civil rights nor the burgeoning protest movement becomes an issue. Both candidates support the police practice of photographing crowds, including at political demonstrations, and say the current fair housing code is adequate. Hall doesn't see any need to expand the ordinance to cover more than the current 40 percent of housing units; Festge says, "We must work toward complete open housing" by eliminating the exemptions, but only after more experience.[64]

Both candidates say they'll implement plans to buy a forty-acre site at Milwaukee Street and Highway 51 for a full general hospital, possibly run by a religious or charitable organization.[65]

Festge focuses on financial issues, warning of the city's increasing debt and vowing to restore Madison's AAA bond rating, reduced to AA early in Reynolds's second term. He also proposes a comprehensive city beautification program.[66]

Hall calls for a joint City-County Health Department and wants to consolidate the villages of Monona and Shorewood Hills into Madison. A member of the board of the Vocational, Technical, and Adult Schools, Hall advocates closing Central-University High School and turning the building over to his system.[67]

There's a strong partisan tone to the nonpartisan election. Festge, elected county clerk six times as a Democrat, features a photograph of himself with US Senator Gaylord Nelson in his campaign literature; attorney James E. Doyle, former state party chair, chairs the Festge for Mayor Committee. Former GOP State Representative Carroll Metzner, the county GOP chair and a former GOP secretary of state, are among the 150 at Hall's Hotel Loraine Crystal Room kickoff, along with aldermen William Bradford Smith and George Reger and council candidates Kenneth Luedtke and attorney Milo Flaten. Ald. Babe Rohr, who broke with Reynolds last election, is supporting his chosen successor.[68]

Following Rohr's lead, the construction trade unions all support Hall; municipal employees go for Festge. The Federation of Labor's Committee on Political Education endorses both.[69]

And each candidate has his newspaper providing supportive coverage. As Reynolds ends his term attacking the *Capital Times*, Hall begins his campaign by doing the same, noting that the paper, which had railed against Reynolds for his Westport residence and had long denounced candidates who ran for one office while holding another, ignores the awkward facts that Festge has only recently moved into the city, still owns a farm in Black Earth, and is the incumbent county clerk.[70]

What little suspense exists over the outcome is over early on Election Day, as Festge carries nineteen of twenty-two wards on his way to a landslide victory, 24,811 to 16,589.[71]

In his April 20 inaugural address, Festge lays out an ambitious agenda: settle the fee dispute with the Wright Foundation and start a new auditorium process, identify and acquire land for the "sorely needed" east side hospital, meet the "great need of improved public transportation," improve relations with the university, establish a "Madison Area Planning and Policy Advisory Committee for Teamwork" to pursue greater cooperation and coordination with area municipalities, and reduce the council's role in routine personnel reclassifications.

The liberal Festge closes with a salute to his conservative predecessor, praising former mayor Reynolds for passing the Equal Opportunities Ordinance, establishing the Department of Public Works, and getting the Monona Causeway under way. "All of these have been major contributions of lasting value," he says.[72]

Auditorium

In his successful campaign for mayor, county clerk Otto Festge said he would settle the fee dispute with the Frank Lloyd Wright Foundation. Six weeks after taking office in late April, he does.[73]

As the year opens, the city seems to have given up on building the auditorium. Mayor Henry Reynolds, who says he still wants to build one on the waterworks site across from James Madison Park, hasn't even called a meeting of the Auditorium Committee since the fall of 1963. The city and foundation are ostensibly preparing for arbitration over the fee, if any, due the foundation, but the parties take several months to appoint the arbitration panel; no sessions have been scheduled.

Once again, Monona Terrace is the dominant issue in a mayoral campaign. Festge supports it, although he's not "unalterably committed" to the site and would accept an alternative if recommended by the planners or demanded by the people. George Hall, Reynolds's 1961 campaign manager, is unalterably opposed, although he would like to see the foundation stay involved at a new site. Festge favors settling the fee dispute; Hall holds to arbitration.[74]

Valentine's Day brings a bountiful bouquet for Festge and other Wrightians—a full-page ad in the Sunday *State Journal* from twenty-five of the leading downtown merchants, bankers, and property owners, calling for a $6.5 million "Cultural Center in the Center of Madison," at Monona Terrace, based on Wright's design. Foundation architect William Wesley Peters says that's an "entirely feasible" budget and offers some cost concessions.[75]

But Reynolds doesn't want to end his term at peace with the foundation. He refuses widespread calls to postpone the arbitration and discuss settlement, and makes bitter personal attacks on statement signer Gerald Bartell. For good measure, Reynolds vetoes an action to divert interest income to the auditorium bond account; after a final, angry confrontation with the council, the aldermen fail to override the veto by one vote.[76]

Two weeks before the election, longtime Wright nemesis Joe Jackson revives his strident attack on the architect's "anti-militaristic activities and associations," releasing an eleven-page screed drawn from the files of the American Legion. It's a reprise of material Jackson released shortly after Wright's death in 1959, accusing him of being a communist or fellow traveler. Festge and Hall both sharply denounce Jackson's action.[77]

Festge's landslide election on April 6 augurs well for a new approach, and the change is immediate. In his inaugural address on April 20, Festge urges adoption of a resolution putting the arbitration on hold and creating a new ad hoc committee to negotiate a settlement; two nights later, an eager council complies, voting 18–4 to suspend the arbitration, direct Edward Cushman—the Philadelphia lawyer Reynolds had hired—to stop work, and give Festge and the six-man committee two months the settle the dispute.[78]

Reynolds tells them not to try, but to proceed to arbitration. In a mid-May appearance, he maintains that the foundation's failure to design a building within the $3.5 million budget means that "from a legal standpoint and morally, the city owes nothing" and is actually entitled to a return of the $122,500 it paid the foundation in 1961. Reynolds claims that foundation attorney Randolph Conners privately agrees, and that's why he's stalled the arbitration.[79]

With matters deadlocked but perilously close to arbitration, foundation architect Peters agrees to settlement talks on June 10. Also present to observe, at Festge's invitation, is nationally renowned labor mediator and UW professor Nathan Feinsinger.[80]

The parties start talking at 9:30 a.m., but by late afternoon are still $100,000 apart. That's when they agree to have Feinsinger actively mediate; he starts a little after 9 p.m., while the scheduled council meeting is in recess.[81]

Shortly after midnight, the deal is done, at just under the midpoint between the offers first made in January 1964—$150,000 as "full payment of any claim" by the foundation against the city. The council breaks into applause and unanimously approves the settlement. Feinsinger says he'll donate his fee to the project.[82]

The *Capital Times* celebrates the settlement and says it shows that Festge "is a master of the tools and techniques of democracy." The *State Journal* says the "speedway settlement" was "the politics of the smoke-filled room, the payoff to hide unpleasant blunders."[83]

Twelve years after Madison voters endorsed it, nine years after the city and Wright contracted for it, and three years after voters killed it, Monona Terrace is formally abandoned.

By delaying the settlement for eighteen months, Reynolds succeeded in saving $20,000—less than the city spent on Cushman (who also offered to waive some billings) and the unconsummated arbitration.

Financially, it's a devastating result for the foundation, capping its total compensation since Wright launched the idea in 1938 at $272,500 for more than sixty-three thousand hours of work.[84] But Peters maintains that the foundation still wants to work with the city to make Wright's dream come true. "The foundation has been devoted to this project since Mr. Wright first proposed it, and we are still devoted to it," he says.

Whether the foundation will remain involved, though, is largely up to the Auditorium Committee Festge appoints in late June. He does his best to make that result likely, returning pro-Terrace alderman Richard Kopp to the panel from which former mayor Reynolds unceremoniously removed him four years prior. And while he puts a few anti-Terrace aldermen on the panel, the citizen appointees are all supporters—he even names

Professor Van Potter the president of Citizens for Monona Terrace. "Like dangling a red flag in front of a bull," first-term alderman Milo Flaten says in voting, in vain, against Potter's confirmation. Festge later adds some anti-Terrace members, including former mayor George Forster.

Robert Studt, the president of what would be one of the auditorium's primary users, the Madison Theater Guild, is also confirmed as a voting member, without discussion of any potential conflicts.[85]

But the same day Festge names the new committee, yet another threat comes from Wright's oldest nemesis. Joe Jackson, eighty-six, who served with General John Pershing's cavalry in the Great War and was instrumental in getting the Veterans' Administration Hospital established, gets a bill introduced to make Law Park a state memorial for Wisconsin veterans, blocking it for the auditorium project. It's recommended by a Senate committee in June but defeated in October.[86]

By November, the committee makes several major decisions for a phased development. Phase one would address cultural needs—a building with an auditorium for about twenty-five hundred and a smaller theater for a thousand, to cost no more than $4 million. Phase two would cover convention facilities, including a banquet hall for twenty-five hundred and exhibition space. And there are three acceptable areas featuring nine separate sites—Law Park, Olin Park, and James Madison Park. The committee also agrees that the architect should be a Wisconsin resident.[87]

Marshall Browne, a leader in the 1962 referendum, is not happy that a Monona Terrace site—part of the Law Park options—is back in the mix and threatens to revive the Citizens' Realistic Auditorium Association. The referendum banning that site still stands, he asserts, "and it seems unbelievable that the present Auditorium Committee could decide on its own that the will of the people is to be ignored and we are again to dredge up the dreary controversy of Monona Terrace."[88]

But the committee doesn't back down and directs planning director Kenneth Clark to provide a detailed analysis of all three areas. The committee plans to consider his report in early 1966.[89]

Urban Renewal

Madison celebrates two Triangle milestones and solves two thorny problems caused by campus-area development.

As the year opens, so too do Madison's first public housing units, the Madison Housing Authority's 160 units at four sites, which Mayor Henry Reynolds pushed through in April 1961. They may already be oversubscribed: 62 applications have already been approved, with another 150 being processed.[90]

The Gay Braxton Apartments, the first new housing units in the Triangle urban renewal area, are occupied entirely by former residents of the old neighborhood. Most of them express delight with their new accommodations. "The change is wonderful. It's

Dedication of the Gay Braxton Apartments, June 24. Mary Lee Griggs, longtime companion and valued colleague of the late Neighborhood House director Gay Braxton, is the guest of honor at the dedication of the Madison Housing Authority's sixty units of public housing for the elderly. At left, Mayor Otto Festge and former MHA chair Roland Day, each of whom recognizes former mayor Henry Reynolds for leadership on this and other public housing projects. To Griggs's left, the federal Public Housing Authority's P. F. Papadopulos and current MHA chair, Realtor Earl Espeseth. In the background, the new residents—all from the old neighborhood.[91] WHI IMAGE ID 138227, PHOTO BY DAVID SANDELL

like a dream," says Mrs. Salvatore Amato, whose former flat at 30 S. Murray St. had space heaters and a shared toilet in the basement. Maria Gervasi now occupies an apartment on the exact site where Gervasi's store and tavern once stood. And everyone was thankful that the Madison Home Owners Association's Fran Remeika, who had sought to end urban renewal, was able to organize the successful effort to save Josephine Brasci's glorious thirty-seven-year-old grapevine; grown from a cutting her late husband, Giorgio, brought from Sicily to 611 Regent St., the vine was preserved and replanted onsite, at the Redevelopment Authority's expense.[92]

The Triangle also restores the legendary community resource, Neighborhood House, but with a new mission. Unlike the Americanization efforts of the original Neighborhood House, programming for the twenty-seven hundred households in the area from Proudfit Street to Edgewood Avenue will seek to address socio-economic stress. The area's average household income of $5,500 is $1,000 below the city average, and one in twelve households has a single parent, compared to a city average of one in sixteen; of the two-parent households, one in four finds both parents working. One of three centers owned and operated by Madison Neighborhood Centers Inc., and funded by the United Community Chest, the $200,000 three-level, two-story building also houses a clinic of the Dane County Mental Health Center.[93]

There's good news for the council's Special Committee on Housing, Relocation, and Welfare; despite the furor over urban renewal in late 1964, only six residents register to speak at its first public hearing on January 6, and the committee doesn't hold all six scheduled sessions.[94]

The Madison Redevelopment Authority (MRA) has good financial news to report—assessments in the Brittingham urban renewal project increased from about $250,000 in 1956 to $1.24 million, with a corresponding jump in taxes paid from $10,450 to $52,063. The gross cost for land acquisition and preparation was $826,044; after the land was sold for $162,900, the federal government paid two-thirds the net cost of $633,144, leaving the city's share about $152,152, which it should recoup in less than four years.[95]

There are encouraging signs in the Triangle as well. Interest in the proposed shopping center set for the southeast corner of Park and Regent Streets is so strong that in November the MRA votes for a design competition; rather than simply selling the land to the highest bidder, the MRA will set a price and have a panel of experts judge the submitted designs, then negotiate with the firm with the best plan and highest economic value. At least four firms have formally expressed interest in building the center, which is to include a grocery store and various neighborhood retail businesses. "Developer interest is of such extent," MRA director Sol Levin says, "that it would be difficult to justify limiting negotiations to just one developer. There is no question we will be able to install an excellent center which will service the area."[96]

In late November, the federally financed improvements to West Washington Avenue—on former neighborhood land taken under urban renewal—are topped by a new pedestrian skywalk, which crosses in front of the Capitol and has its western terminus just about where Neighborhood House once was.[97]

The city even finally gets started on the South Madison Renewal Plan.[98]

So it's no wonder the MRA names Sol Levin its permanent director in April, five months after he became acting director in the wake of Roger Rupnow's forced resignation. Levin, respected by both renewal and antirenewal leaders, coordinated the committee that resolved the General Neighborhood Renewal Plan crisis and represents the city in negotiations over development on University Avenue, in addition to handling the ongoing activity in the Triangle and South Madison.[99]

Mayor Otto Festge heads the list of a dozen speakers as about two hundred attend the October 31 dedication of the Madison Neighborhood Center's new Neighborhood House, 29 S. Mills St. In the background, construction continues on the $1.5 million Madison Medical Center, the first for-profit development in the Triangle. WHI IMAGE ID 137915, PHOTO BY EDWIN STEIN

Campus-Area Crisis Averted I—GNRP

The city starts the year under its self-imposed March deadline to approve a new university-area General Neighborhood Renewal Plan (GNRP) or undergo another risky referendum. Fortunately, Ald. Reynolds and the special eighteen-member Housing, Relocation, and Welfare committee he proposed, and now chairs, meet the challenge, crafting a new GNRP about half the size of the controversial 496-acre original proposal. Instead of extending to Spooner Street on the west, south to Mound Street, and as far east as Wisconsin Avenue, the proposed new boundaries go only to Randall Avenue, Regent Street, West Washington Avenue, and Bedford/Frances Streets.

On February 25, the issue that almost caused the abolition of the MRA and a two-year halt to urban renewal last April is settled by the council's unanimous voice vote approving the new boundaries; both advocates and opponents of urban renewal credit the successful outcome to first-term Ald. Reynolds. But despite the happy ending, the delay caused by the Homeowners Association's threat of a referendum to stop the original GNRP does do damage; federal authorities ultimately refuse to hold the $127,000 grant, which had already been approved. The funds lapse, and the city has to reapply. And there are limits to Reynolds's influence—in August, his committee flatly rejects his call to discuss merging the MRA and the Madison Housing Authority.[100]

Campus-Area Crisis Averted II—Murray Mall

Sandwiched between the 3,260 residents of the southeast dorms and the campus proper, the 700–800 blocks of University Avenue (between Lake and Park Streets) have more development potential than any two blocks in the city. That's why the area becomes the focus of a protracted battle among the university, the city, and the area's property owners; they all want to control its development. The university, which already owns the half-blocks directly across from the dorms, plans to use its standby dummy corporation, the Wisconsin University Building Corporation, to buy the rest, though it will use eminent domain if necessary. After construction of housing and offices for graduate students, the remaining land would be turned over to the University Park Corporation, a nonprofit controlled by the university for commercial development. They call the project Murray Mall.

But the current merchants and restaurateurs aren't keen to lose and then lease the land they already own; instead, they want the MRA to create an urban renewal project under which it would buy their land, then sell it back to their Lake Park Corporation for a coordinated development. University administrators are sympathetic; the regents are not, rejecting in January the request from President Harrington and university vice president A. W. Peterson—who's also president of the University Park Corporation—to join the city's urban renewal application.[101]

The city moves ahead with its application anyway.[102] And it throws a little shade on the university, adopting area alderman James Goulette's resolution to halt all development in the two blocks for six months. The statement is only symbolic; the university wouldn't be starting any construction within that period anyway.[103]

In June, the city learns that the university's opposition has real, not just symbolic, repercussions; the Housing and Home Finance Agency withholds approval of the planning grant because its financing presumes university cooperation. As long as the regents maintain their opposition, the city is foreclosed from federal funds. And the regents, knowing that the city's handling of the larger GNRP has now twice threatened the university's anticipated $9 million in federal support for land acquisition in the expansion zone, are firm in their opposition.[104]

Echoing Harrington's initiative to solve the GNRP crisis last December, it's Chancellor Fleming who solves the Murray Mall mess in mid-August. His plan: satisfy the city by creating an urban renewal project, satisfy the university by reserving the 700 and 800 blocks for academic and related use, and satisfy the merchants by adding the 600 and 900 blocks for commerce and parking.[105]

Within a week, the council meets in special session to endorse the concept. Two days later, on August 20, the regents agree, voting unanimously to join the city and MRA in applying for a $125,529 urban renewal planning grant for the four blocks. The application, which the council unanimously approves on October 14, also seeks $2.6 million in federal funds if the plan is approved and developed.[106]

Harrington's appointment of one of the country's leading mediator/arbitrators (Fleming will serve as president of the National Academy of Arbitrators 1966–1967) has paid off in an unexpected, but not unprecedented, way.[107]

South Madison—a Pocket of Poverty

The MRA's preliminary report on the South Madison rehabilitation area, prepared by Urban Planning Consultants of Chicago, documents the pocket of poverty in the area south of Wingra Creek and east of South Park Street, where one-third of the 202 households are considered impoverished, with annual incomes of less than $3,000; the countywide figure is 12.8 percent. Unemployment is 24 percent, ten times the Dane County figure. Fifty-nine percent of the 721 individuals are nonwhite and just over half of the total population is under nineteen. It's a stable neighborhood—15 percent have lived there all their lives or more than twenty-five years, and almost two-thirds have been residents more than five years. But more than 25 percent say they moved there because it was the only area a black family could find housing; 15 percent say it was all they could afford. Support for a renewal project in South Madison is overwhelming—88 percent think it's a good or very good idea.[108]

UW

COMMENCEMENT, JUNE 7
- ► Baccalaureate: 2,225
- ► Master's/PhD: 766
- ► JD/MD: 166

FALL ENROLLMENT
- ► Total Students: 29,170[109]

HOMECOMING
- ► Show: Bob Hope (two shows)[110]

NEW BUILDINGS OF NOTE
- ► Ogg Hall, 835 W. Dayton St.
- ► Gordon Commons, 770 W. Dayton St.
- ► Veterinary Science, 2015 Linden Dr.[111]

Campus Calendar

February 14–24—*New York Times* editor James Reston questions American policy in Vietnam as he keynotes the ten-day Wisconsin Student Association "Decisions in Diplomacy" Symposium, which also features six-time Socialist Party presidential candidate Norman Thomas and the ambassadors from Israel, India, and Kuwait.[112]

February 24–25—The American Ballet Theatre returns for a two-night engagement, with choreography by George Balanchine and Agnes de Mille.[113]

March 4—The Hillel Foundation on Langdon Street hosts a coffee-and-cookies reception for folk singer Pete Seeger in a fund-raiser for the University Friends of the Student Nonviolent Coordinating Committee; a minimum contribution of seventy-five cents is requested. The highlight of Seeger's Orpheum show that night is a driving rendition of Bob Dylan's "A Hard Rain's A-Gonna Fall" that delights and excites the near-capacity crowd.[114]

March 26—Ralph E. Hanson, who left the State Patrol in his native Maine to become safety officer at Truax Air Field, is announced as director of the Department of Protection and Security, a unit of the physical plant division.[115]

March 28—Though her lustrous voice is not the wonder it once was, world-renowned contralto Marian Anderson still thrills a capacity Stock Pavilion crowd of three thousand—her third "Cow Barn" concert since 1938—with a program of classical songs and Negro spirituals. Madison is one of only fifty stops on her international farewell concert tour, and the only one where a train whistle interrupts her performance of "Ave Maria."[116]

April 2—Count Basie headlines the Military Ball in the Great Hall; admission is $3.50 per couple.[117]

Murray Mall and environs, late summer, 1965. As the 3,260-student southeast dormitory area expansion is finished with the fall openings of Ogg Hall and Gordon Commons (foreground), the battle to control the south side of the 700 and 800 blocks of University Avenue dominates—and almost destroys—city-university relations. This is the last photo taken of the Sterling Court brownstones at upper center left; other than the University Club, the entire block bounded by Park, State, and Murray Streets and University Avenue is razed this summer for the Humanities building and Elvehjem Arts Center. COURTESY OF CAPITAL NEWSPAPERS ARCHIVES

April 9—Jerry Lee Lewis proves he's still "The Killer" at the Alpha Epsilon Pi "Ape Party," featuring a bevy of "Jungle Maidens."[118]

April 28—*National Review* editor William F. Buckley condemns the left's "ideological rigidity" before a Great Hall crowd of about 350, half of whom give the conservative intellectual a standing ovation.[119]

July 15—Joseph F. Kauffman, forty-three—a former Peace Corps training director, Brandeis University dean of students, and Anti-Defamation League worker—assumes his duties as the first dean of student affairs, with jurisdiction over all matters relating to student life, interests, health, safety, and welfare.[120]

August 24—The State Building Commission approves construction of the $3.8 million Gymnasium Unit II on the western campus, paving the way for the razing of the Red Gym/Armory, as long sought by the administration for a high-rise guest house and underground auditorium.[121]

September 3—Among the fraternity brothers returning for the 133rd convention of Alpha Delta Phi is two-time Academy Award–winning actor Fredric March, known as Fred Bickel when he was president of the Class of 1920 and a member of the Inter-Fraternity Ku Klux Klan. March returns to a thriving fraternity scene, as the thirty-two fraternities pledge 507 new members—a record 23 percent increase over 1964. Total fraternity membership is projected at about 2,260, more than 10 percent above the 1963 membership.[122]

"SOME REFLECTIONS UPON BECOMING A HAS-BEEN"

"I don't really understand just why students are so generally disliked here. But people are antagonistic and make no effort to hide their resentment. The most obvious way they take this out is economically. Compare the standards of housing near the campus with those of the rest of the city—the deplorable conditions and the outrageous rents—and you'll see just how soft a touch students are considered. Compare the prices in the grocery stores and restaurants and drug stores. I can't begin to count the times I've been insulted by total strangers as I've walked around downtown. We students are hated and criticized by many—and we pay through the nose for it."
—Gail Bensinger, outgoing editor-in-chief, *Daily Cardinal*, April 15

October 22—Bob Hope gets plenty of laughs at homecoming but earns his loudest ovation with a tribute to soldiers serving in Vietnam. "They are fighting to stop communism," he says to thunderous applause at the Fieldhouse. "And if we don't stop them there we may have to stop them in Lodi." Demand for tickets is so great that Hope becomes the first homecoming headliner to perform two nights. Hope also makes an appearance during halftime of the Badgers' homecoming loss to Ohio State, telling a few jokes and kissing homecoming queen Linda Cowan.[123]

October 23—Tragedy strikes during the first half of the Badgers' homecoming game, as A. W. Peterson, sixty-six, university vice president and trust officer, suffers a fatal heart attack in the stands at Camp Randall. A top and trusted administrator for more than forty years, Peterson had announced he was retiring next June and had been honored with a testimonial dinner just the night before his death. On June 14, 1968, the regents vote to rename the new administration building the Alfred Walter Peterson Office Building in his honor.[124]

November 8—US Senator George McGovern (D-SD), recipient of the Distinguished Flying Cross during World War II, calls for a stop to the bombing in Vietnam, but not a military withdrawal, during his daylong appearance as the university's "politician-in-residence."[125] That night, jazz multi-instrumentalist Roland Kirk dazzles a capacity crowd at Turner Hall in a benefit for the Committee to End the War in Viet Nam and the Madison Citizens for Peace in Viet Nam.[126]

November 23—After one of his two opponents is disqualified for a false campaign poster, history graduate student Paul Soglin (alderman, 1968–1973; mayor of Madison, 1973–1979, 1989–1996, 2011–present) is narrowly elected to the Student Senate of the Wisconsin Student Association. He campaigned for "a radical approach to student government . . . one that challenges the decadent order" in which "the student joins with the administration in determining curriculum, tenure, and other major decisions."[127]

December 8—The *Capital Times* reveals the Athletic Board has secretly voted, 4–3, to dismiss football coach Milt Bruhn, three years after he had the number two football team in the country. But the Badgers went 3–6 in 1964 and won only two of nine games this past season, and the alumni want him fired. There's economics involved, as well as ego—attendance this year has averaged 56,427 per game, about 20,000 under Camp Randall's new capacity. But President Harrington and Chancellor Fleming give Bruhn their strong support, and two days later the regents renew him for another year.[128]

The Campus Loosens Up

Student life gets a little more relaxed in 1965. In April, University Residence Halls eliminates most dining hall dress regulations, allowing "ordinary street wear," except for Sunday dinner. According to a letter from Paul Ginsberg, the residence halls social-educational coordinator, footwear is required and headscarves, swimsuits, and short shorts are banned; otherwise, students need only pay heed to "cleanliness, modesty, etc." and "the desire for a pleasant atmosphere" in the dining halls.[129]

> **ROUNDY SAYS**
>
> "Anybody should know we are going to have a better team than last year predicts. I never want to see Wisconsin as bad as they were last year again."
> —*Wisconsin State Journal*, June 4

In October, the faculty vote to lift curfews for both junior and sophomore women. Junior women, already without weekend curfew, no longer have a 1 a.m. weeknight curfew; sophomore women, who previously had to be back in their living units by 11 p.m. on weeknights and 1 a.m. on weekends, now have no hours on weekends and a 1 a.m. curfew on weeknights. Women who are under twenty-one years of age need parental permission to enjoy the new hours. The rules requiring students to be twenty-one to live in off-campus apartments remain.[130]

Other restrictions also still apply—students must register with the university all motor vehicles that they operate in the city of Madison, and may not operate motor vehicles east of Babcock Drive or Breese Terrace during weekday work hours or on Saturday mornings, even when school is not in session. There are more than 14,000 vehicles registered on campus this year, up from 13,233 in 1964.[131]

Things are getting looser in the arts as well. In the spring, civil rights, antiwar, and cultural activists Stu Ewen, Bob Gabriner, Paul Breines, and Russell Jacoby (Guggenheim Fellow, 1980) form the Ad Hoc Committee for Thinking (ACT) and become anti-authoritarian cultural pamphleteers with a mimeograph machine, distributing quirky commentaries on the politics of everyday life, signed simply "ACT Tract Number 1, 2," and so on.[132]

And in October, English grad students Betsy and Morris Edelson publish the first issue of the illustrated thirty-two-page literary magazine *Quixote*, financed by their teaching assistant stipends and Morris's GI Bill benefits. The December issue, with contributions from both faculty and students, jumps to sixty-four pages, with a press run of four hundred.[133]

A few hundred students smoke pot, but not in the dorms or frat houses; most who toke live in the Mifflin Street area. Most of the marijuana is mediocre, brought in by students from the East Coast and Chicago returning from break, but some is quite good. A nickel bag, one-tenth of an ounce for $5, is the most common size; a dime bag has a

quarter of an ounce, and a full ounce goes for $25. Hashish is also available, and there are also some pockets of peyote use. By the end of the school year, drug use will be up considerably.[134]

Cardinal Controversy

An unprecedented attack on the *Daily Cardinal* by a prominent conservative commentator and powerful state senator backfires and ends with the governor, regents, and administration giving strong support for the newspaper.[135]

On January 28, right-wing radio talker Bob Siegrist reveals that *Cardinal* managing editor John Gruber rents a room at 515 W. Johnson St. from Gene Dennis Jr., the son of the late head of the Communist Party USA, and that another renter, Michael Eisenscher, was both the son of the former chair of the state Communist Party and a Communist himself. And Siegrist claims to see a disturbing pattern of the *Cardinal* covering the same stories as the Communist Party's *Daily Worker*.

The next day, Republican state senator Jerris Leonard writes Regent president Arthur DeBardeleben that he's "very much disturbed" to learn about Gruber's rooming house relationship "with known political leftists," a situation that "has reached the point of absurdity . . . clearly appalling."[136]

Denouncing what he considers the *Cardinal's* "left-oriented journalism," Leonard calls on the regents to "investigate Mr. Gruber's associations and intensively review the editorial policy" of the *Cardinal* and report to the governor and legislature. "If it is determined that Mr. Gruber's reported association influences the political tone of the *Cardinal*," Leonard writes, "it is clear that his removal must be sought."

As assistant majority leader and chair of the powerful State Building Commission, which controls major university construction, Leonard issues a not-so-veiled threat. The situation is of "such a serious nature," he writes, that if the regents don't investigate and report within two weeks, he will call for a "special legislative committee to study this matter and take appropriate action. This situation cannot be allowed to continue for even one more month."

As Siegrist hammers away every night at the *Cardinal* staff and their friends, personally as well as politically, campus groups of all stripes rush to the paper's defense, including the Young GOP and Inter-Fraternity Council.[137]

When the regents meet on February 5, it's Leonard's letter, not Gruber's housing, that they find clearly appalling. Democrats and Republicans alike—labor leaders and industrialists—denounce what one calls a witch hunt and another equates with McCarthyism. Then they unanimously adopt a resolution that Regent Kenneth L. Greenquist—a former state commander of the American

A RESOLUTION

"It would be destructive of the essence of *The Daily Cardinal* if any authority, whether a Regent, a legislator or other, could prescribe what shall be orthodox and therefore acceptable for publication and what shall be unorthodox and therefore interdicted. In reaffirming the dedication of the Regents to freedom of inquiry and expression, this Board deplores attempts to subject any student editor or writer to denunciation because of his associations or the ancestry of his associates."
—Board of Regents, February 5

Legion—likens to the famed "sifting and winnowing" statement from 1894. Harrington later adds that he's "proud" of the *Cardinal*, "one of the best student newspapers in the country."[138]

"We are personally gratified that the Regents have endorsed the editorial freedom of the paper and educational freedom of the University in such decisive terms," the *Cardinal* responds the next day. "It is men like these who will create a new generation capable of confronting the world in a realistic manner."[139]

Blustery right-wing state senator Gordon Roseleip tries to get the House Un-American Activities Committee to investigate—at the same time he demands a free subscription for all legislators—but Governor Knowles, a Republican, ends the controversy by endorsing the regents' action a few days later.

"This is America," he says. "Let's continue to have the right of free speech and free press."[140]

Schools

GRADUATION, JUNE 18
- ▸ West: 715
- ▸ East: 620
- ▸ Central-University: 270
- ▸ La Follette: 244[141]

FALL ENROLLMENT
- ▸ Total students: 31,968
- ▸ Senior high schools: 5,940
- ▸ Junior high schools: 6,626
- ▸ Elementary schools: 19,008[142]

NEW SCHOOLS
- ▸ Abraham Lincoln Junior High, 909 Sequoia Tr.[143]

Beginning of the End for Central?

On September 8, the fifty-seventh anniversary of Central High School's first day, the school receives a warning that it's approaching its last and will likely close due to declining enrollment. "We cannot conclude but that the central area of the city will not furnish enough junior and senior high school pupils to maintain Central High School in its present role," chief district analyst Clifford Hawley reports to a special tripartite city-schools committee.[144] Which fits perfectly the plans of vocational school director Norman Mitby and board president George Hall, already with 717 full-time and 1,902 part-time students and needing new space for the many more on the way.[145]

On November 1, a group opposing the closing presents petitions signed by 1,290 residents pledging "a concerted fight to defeat any plan" to close the school. And the NAACP warns that closing Central could lead to de facto racial segregation, and vows to monitor the move closely. The board promises to consider the petitions and the concerns when deciding the school's fate and sets a special meeting for next January 13 to do just that.[146]

A Rough Start for Lincoln Junior High

Within weeks of its opening in the fall, the new Abraham Lincoln Junior High School is rocked by reports of violence, widespread theft, and harassment, even a schoolwide extortion ring forcing pupils to hand over nickels and dimes for protection. A group of about eighty parents meets on September 30 to form an advocacy group; more than two dozen say their own children have been threatened or hit, or had items stolen. Lincoln's founding principal, Jack Stickels, acknowledges that his experience as principal of Lakewood School in Maple Bluff did not fully prepare him to handle the ethnic and economic diversity on the south side; although the misconduct is not race-based, close to a third of the new school's pupils are black. There are material problems as well—the school opened with construction still under way in the gym, commons, and library, preventing adequate instruction to occur in the school's innovative modular system. Stickels modifies the schedule to make it a bit more structured, while the board applies for $35,500 in federal funds to hire guidance counselors and a social worker.[147]

There's more discouraging education news. A new study by an Urban League researcher reports a "low level of performance among Negro students" in Madison overall and on standardized tests; 54 percent score below the norm in mathematics, and 39 percent score below the norm in reading. Only 74 percent of all black students entering Madison high schools graduate, and those who do rarely do so with honors. Only three black university students give Madison addresses, and only one graduated from a Madison high school in 1965. Madison has barely a handful of blacks among its 1,500 teachers; Superintendent Gilberts is trying to hire more, but they are in such high demand and Madison's pay is so low that recruitment is difficult.[148]

School Days

April 6—Voters approve by better than 3–1 (29,111–8,192) the third large school bond issue of the decade, $6.45 million to build a new high school and elementary school on the far west side, a far east elementary school, and several additions. Personal redemption and generational shift mark historic school board elections as former MRA chair and failed mayoral candidate Albert McGinnis and law professor James B. MacDonald upset Herbert Schmiege (on the board since 1950) and A. H. Younger (a member since 1949). Board vice president Dr. R. W. Huegel, on the board since 1934, is the only incumbent reelected.[149]

September 8—West High institutes a closed lunch period, following continuing complaints from area residents and businesses about disruptive pupils; four groups of 520 students eat lunch in twenty-seven-minute blocks from 11:20 a.m. to 1:20 p.m. Principal Douglas Ritchie also enforces a stricter dress and behavior code, banning smoking and ordering several boys to get haircuts. The designated founding principal of James Madison Memorial High School, Richard Gorton, says he'll also institute a closed lunch when the school opens in 1966.[150]

September 20—The school board votes, 5–2, to distribute a list of fallout shelters and other civil defense information in sealed envelopes brought home by schoolchildren. City civil defense director Richard Wilson proposed the plan because the shelters in the public schools can accommodate only 14,129 people, less than half the total enrollment, and parents need to know what other protection is available.[151]

December 6—The Madison Bus Company threatens to cancel service to Van Hise Elementary and West High schools due to rowdy students. Pupils, particularly from Van Hise, have been shooting heavy paper clips and other objects at drivers' heads, and a bus nearly jumped a curb after the driver was conked on the noggin with a potato.[152]

December 21—Superintendent Robert Gilberts proposes a "Citizens Education Advisory Council," comprising representatives of civic and service organizations, to recruit and support candidates and serve as a liaison between the public and the Board of Education. The board shows little interest in the idea, and Gilberts does not pursue it. It dies a quick and quiet death.[153]

Naming Rights and Wrongs

Martyred presidents make problems for the school board when it comes to naming new schools.

On May 17, the board names the system's first free-standing junior high school on the spur of the moment, without the item even appearing on the meeting's agenda, because building committee chair and board vice president Dr. Ray Huegel says contractors have to finish the wall where the plaque would be installed to meet the July 28 completion date. At least it's a popular and appropriate choice—ratifying the request from the steering committee of the South Madison Neighborhood Council for "Abraham Lincoln Junior High School."[154]

About a month later, Huegel, presiding in the absence of the ailing president, Glenn Stephens, has the board vote by secret ballot to name the new high school under construction at Mineral Point and Gammon Roads. The public has made several suggestions.[155]

Echoing last year's formal recommendation by the Common Council, the Madison Federation of Labor wants to honor the late President Kennedy, as does fireman Edward D. Durkin. Many suggest legendary Wisconsin naturalists—a group led by *Capital Times* reporter Irv Kreisman proposes John Muir; Professor Hugh Iltis and others counter with Aldo Leopold. It's Joseph W. Jackson, who prompted the 1963 renaming of Conklin Park to pay tribute to the city's namesake and the country's fourth president, who proposes "James Madison Memorial High School."

Board member Ruth B. Doyle warns that the intended tribute will quickly fade, with the school "bound to wind up being known as just 'Memorial.'" However, "Little Jemmy" gets a 3–2 victory on the second ballot.

The council, which controls the school board budget and bonding authority, is not happy at the vote; fifteen aldermen, claiming to be acting only as "citizens, taxpayers and parents," write the board, urging it to reconsider. They agree with Doyle that "as a practical matter the new high school will be known as Memorial."[156]

"That argument is a lot of hokum," board member Arthur "Dynie" Mansfield says, and the board stands by its decision. But Doyle and the aldermen are right—James Madison Memorial High will indeed come to be known as "Memorial."[157]

Christmas Curtailed

Madison's growing cultural and religious diversity causes several schools to reduce and even eliminate their traditional Christmas programs this year.

Requiring students "to sing praises to Jesus was not quite right," Silver Spring school principal Dorothy McClinnon determines, so she cancels the program entirely.

"I've felt this need for many years," she says, "but could not screw up enough courage to do so until this year." The school's staff and PTA support her decision.

Other schools seek a balance between sacred and secular songs of the season. "Once in a while some people of the Jewish faith have a reaction to the Christmas program," Orchard Ridge principal Ron Fox says, "but most go along with it because they don't want to be different."[158]

In Memoriam—Schools

It's a sorrowful year for the school board.

Attorney Glenn W. Stephens, seventy-three, 1102 Sherman Ave., a member of the Board of Education since 1927 and its president since 1950, dies July 31 after a long illness. A native of Chicago Heights, Stephens remained in Madison following his graduation from UW Law School in 1916. The new elementary school on Rosa Road was named in his honor in 1961. On August 24, Mayor Otto Festge appoints attorney Richard Cates to succeed Stephens. Cates, who served with the US Marines in World War II and the Korean War, is a former chief deputy district attorney and special prosecutor in a state John Doe proceeding. In 1958, he unseated GOP state representative Carroll Metzner but did not seek reelection.[159]

Herbert J. Schmiege, sixty-seven, 1824 Yahara Pl., a member of the Board of Education from 1950 until his narrow defeat in April, dies on May 20 after a brief illness. A former alderman and president of the East Side Businessmen's Association, Schmiege retired in 1962 as director of the State Bureau of Purchasing.[160]

Miscellanea

March 3—As Mayor Henry Reynolds prepares to step down after four years, he gets in a final jab at the city council, telling the Citizens Advisory Committee that it "seems to be more interested in its own political expediency and how its actions sound to the press" than solving problems. "The people do not disagree with me when they know the facts," he says.[161]

Renowned combat photojournalist Dickey Chapelle (seated at center) and other participants prior to the thirty-fifth annual Matrix dinner on March 30, where she tells the five hundred guests in Great Hall that America is losing the war in Vietnam. Dr. Kathryn F. Clarenbach (seated to Chapelle's right), toastmistress for the Theta Sigma Phi event, speaks on the need for every woman to become active in her community and fulfill her own potential. Joyce (Mrs. Gerald) Bartell stands between them.[163] WHI IMAGE ID 136676, PHOTO BY DAVID SANDELL

March 25—The council rejects, by voice vote, a request from American Federation of State, County and Municipal Employees Local 236 that city employees get the whole afternoon off on Good Friday. The city will continue to allow employees to attend church services, but they must return to work at 3 p.m.[162]

April 29—President Johnson ends a long and embarrassing struggle over the federal judgeship for the Western District of Wisconsin by appointing James E. Doyle, 21 N. Prospect Ave., former vice president of the Madison Police and Fire Commission. As a highly respected attorney and former chair of the state Democratic Party, Doyle had been seen as the obvious choice after Judge Patrick Stone died in January 1963. But Doyle had chaired the national committee trying to draft Adlai Stevenson for president in 1960—a permanent disqualification to President Kennedy and his attorney general brother, Robert. The appointment went instead to Green Bay labor lawyer David Rabinovitz, but the Senate never voted on his confirmation, and his appointment expired when Congress adjourned in late 1964. The seat has been vacant for over six months before Johnson finally names Doyle, husband of former state representative and current school board vice president Ruth B. Doyle, on April 29. Doyle is confirmed three weeks later and sworn in June 22.[164]

May 27—The council adopts an ordinance making it illegal to recruit, use, or be a professional strikebreaker, defined as "any person who customarily and repeatedly offers himself for employment in the place of employees involved in a labor dispute." The ordinance, which does not affect the use of scabs who don't "customarily and repeatedly" cross picket lines, carries fines of $50–$500.[165]

August 27—Mayor Festge issues a series of guidelines for how discotheque dancers should dress at the city's four clubs employing go-go girls. "Sensual elements," the new rules state, "should not become so blatant that they completely overshadow all other elements of the dancing, or become the dominant interests of the spectators." Also, dancers should be covered at least to the level "as is acceptable on city beaches." Police chief Wilbur Emery, citing what he calls "a breakdown in moral standards" due to the growing number of discotheques, had asked Festge to issue the standards.[166]

Newly minted US Judge James E. Doyle; Ruth B. Doyle; and their children (left to right) Anne, Katherine, James E. Doyle Jr. (attorney general of Wisconsin, 1991–2003; governor of Wisconsin, 2003–2011), and Mary.
WHI IMAGE ID 137864, PHOTO BY EDWIN STEIN

October 28—The council ends the practice of city bodies meeting in private homes, ordaining that all meetings be held in the City-County Building or another building to which the public has access. But it accepts Festge's suggestion to allow meetings in hotels and restaurants because members are sometimes so busy they have to meet over lunch. Ruth B. Doyle tells the school board the ordinance doesn't apply to it, but city attorney Conrad overrules her.[167]

November 9—Central High alumna Tracy Nelson, who turns twenty-one next month, releases her first folk-blues record album, *Deep Are the Roots,* on the Prestige label. But the Shorewood Hills native, who volunteers at the Plymouth Congregational Church's day care center and has completed two years of studies in social work at UW, isn't planning on a career in music; she thinks she'll go into teaching.[168]

Common Council Confused by Women Bartenders

The council ignores city attorney Edwin Conrad's warning against "beginning the year of the Great Society by discriminating against women" and adopts an ordinance, 14–7, on January 14 barring the issuance of a bartender's license "to a member of the female sex, or to any person afflicted with a contagious or venereal disease."[169]

"This is not discrimination," Mayor Henry Reynolds, longtime trucking company president, replies. "It's setting qualifications. You're saying a woman isn't qualified to be a [licensed] bartender, it's a class of work a woman shouldn't be doing."

Current ordinance allows women to serve as bartenders when there is a licensed operator on the premises. But due to a drafting error, it also permits women to be licensed. Conrad not only urges the council to accept that, but also to amend the 1963 Equal Opportunities Ordinance by prohibiting discrimination on the basis of sex. The council ignores its lawyer on both accounts, precluding that employment and leaving the discrimination unaddressed. It accepts instead legal commentary from police chief Wilbur Emery, who requested the legal prohibition.

Sponsor Ald. Harold "Babe" Rohr references the council's gender exclusivity. "I think we're all men enough on this council to take the position that a woman's place is not behind the bar," the painter's union leader says to his all-male colleagues.

Not necessarily so, says railroad switchman Ald. Leo Cooper, Ninth Ward. "Any woman behind the bar won't cause half as much trouble as some on the other side of it," he says.

But on November 11, the council reverses itself and adopts an ordinance from "Pet Shop" Pete Schmidt, Sixth Ward, expressly allowing women to be licensed bartenders. This time, the council ignores former Marine Emery, who warns in vain that licensing women as bartenders will likely harm public safety.[170]

State Street, from just west of Gorham, November 13.
UNIVERSITY OF WISCONSIN-MADISON ARCHIVES IMAGE S05353

State Street Struggles

As students return this fall, it's not bartenders, but rather bar patrons who have people upset about the state of State Street. Some worry that the plethora of beer bars catering to college students and townies—seven on State between Gilman and Murray Streets, and a total of fourteen within easy walking distance of State—is endangering health, safety, and welfare.[171]

The bars also require lots of law enforcement resources. Weekend nights, four officers walk a beat in just the 500–700 blocks; football weekends, the force is doubled.[172]

On September 1, State Street merchants and friends form a self-help group, the Campus Area Improvement Association, to fight the establishment of any additional beer bars in the 400–600 blocks and to demand even more police protection.[173]

"We're completely fed up with drunkenness, the rowdiness, the broken glass and the drag racing," says the association's president, furrier Stanley Hershleder, "and it has got to the point where it is not safe for persons to walk on some of the side streets." Within a week, membership is up to 350 and growing.

City officials take notice, and take some action, adopting an ordinance forbidding minors from possessing open containers of beer when not accompanied by parents. One of the major complaints of State Street merchants has been teenagers drinking beer, legally, on the sidewalk outside the bars.

The city even says no to three restaurants—Italian Village, Caputo's Uptown, and Gargano's Pizzeria—seeking beer and liquor licenses. Even though none of them is a beer bar, the council unanimously rejects all three applications in early November.[174]

Council Conflicts

The year opens with a proposal by socialist mayoral candidate William Osborne Hart that elected city officials be required to disclose their business and professional associations; two months later, three aldermen introduce a draft ethics code requiring disclosure of financial interests and abstention in cases of conflicts, but carrying no penalty for violations.[175]

They should have done more, sooner.

In July, the *State Journal* reveals that four respected and influential aldermen who voted to spend $93,000 in city funds installing lights and improving the stands at Warner Park are on the board of the for-profit Madison Mustangs Football Club Inc., which plays there for the same $150 nightly fee the city charges area high school teams.[176]

To make matters worse, the president of the Mustangs is attorney John Fox, vice president of the north side development Cherokee Park Inc. (CPI), which had been involved in a long-running, contentious battle with the city over ownership of the wetlands in the Cherokee Marsh. And three of the four aldermen—Richard Kopp, Don Smith, and Robert "Toby" Reynolds—are on the council's special committee negotiating with CPI. Aldermen Kopp, Smith, and John Connell, who all represent north side districts, are among the seven incorporators of the team, whose cofounder and vice president is Joseph C. "Buffo" Cerniglia. The aldermen are also on the team's executive committee, and will receive between two hundred and seven hundred shares of the dollar-a-share stock when it is issued. West sider Reynolds had not subscribed to the stock offering.

The aldermanic involvement should have been made known a few days before the spring election, but the Mustangs' first annual report was filed more than a month after the statutory April 1 deadline.

The aldermen contend there's no conflict because the team's directors had agreed to distribute profits to other city recreational activities rather than its shareholders (a policy they could change at any time). Still, Kopp offers to give his stock to the city because the football team "is such a good deal for the entire city that the city should not only support the team, it should own part of it."

Kopp concedes he did not consider such a donation prior to the *State Journal* story. But he attacks the *State Journal* for "witch-hunting and character assassination" and insists he cleared his involvement with Mayor Otto Festge before voting for the new bleachers. Reynolds thinks critics may have "a valid point," and asks city attorney Conrad "to set out guidelines on this matter."[177]

The Mustangs, meanwhile, have their own concerns—on August 27, Coach Hank Olshanski quits after a season-opening defeat and is replaced by former UW fullback Merritt Norvell. A three-time letter winner and starting fullback on the 1962–1963 Rose Bowl team, Norvell is also a UW grad student and probation officer for Dane County.[178]

The draft ethics code remains in committee at year's end.

Planning and Development

GENERAL STATISTICS

▸ Population: 160,281[179]
▸ Area: 45.11 square miles (end-of-year total)[180]

Business Wire

January 6—As the year opens, the door closes on the Manchester Skywalk. The special design committee appointed by Mayor Reynolds emphatically rejects the project due to the "unfortunate visual interference with the Capitol." The committee—state architect James Galbraith, UW artist-in-residence Aaron Bohrod, and consulting engineer Adolph J. Ackerman—declares the view of the Capitol from the sixteen streets that converge on the Square "part of the public domain" that must be "preserved as an inspiration for future generations" as "the heritage of a great city."[181] On January 25, the Plan Commission also recommends against the skywalk, 5–4, with Mayor Reynolds breaking a tie vote. Among those voting no is J. E. Nissley, an employee of a competing store a block away, the Emporium. Morgan Manchester says he will continue to operate Baron's department store but that the ambitious Capitol Pavilion, now proposed as a fourteen-story mixed-use project, is on hold during a study of underground parking and connecting tunnels.[182] In June, Mrs. Manchester buys the parking lot behind Baron's, ending the involvement of Madison Properties on the block.[183] Capital Pavilion is never built, and the land remains available for construction of the Concourse Hotel.

January 14—Resolving a long-standing dispute, the council ignores objections from Mayor Reynolds, unanimously approves a 350-acre preliminary plat for Cherokee Park Inc., and agrees to pay $136,000 for 450 acres of Cherokee Marsh for parks and recreation.[184]

January 19—The Allied Development Corporation, developer of the large plat just off Verona Road, files for bankruptcy after charges of securities fraud filed against its top officers, Neil Woodington and Robert C. Kelly, cause a severe curtailment of its credit.[185]

January 28—The council votes to start buying forty acres of land east of the East Beltline Highway (Highway 51) between Milwaukee Street and Highway 30 for the long-proposed east side hospital.[186]

February 11—The council rezones the site of the former Capital Hotel, 208 King St., for a ten-story motel and apartment house, only four days after the request is introduced. The motel is never built, and the site remains available for a state office building.[187]

Spring—Land annexed in 1960 is developed as Midland Realty's first east side project, Meadowood-East, at the juncture of Cottage Grove Road and Acewood Boulevard. Company president Gilbert S. Rosenberg says the first homes will be available before school starts.[188]

June—Developers announce a new 247-acre Parkwood Hills plat, extending the city another half-mile to the west, to Gammon Road. The plat, which borders the newly named James Madison Memorial High School now under construction, will convert three family farms into the site for 440 single-family homes and 440 multifamily units.[189]

June 23—A crowd of about 175 celebrates the dedication of the new $2.2 million Central Library at 201 W. Mifflin St. Mayor Otto Festge notes that the work was undertaken under Mayor Henry Reynolds but says he's "happy to accept the credit."[190]

June 25—Modern commerce claims the oldest structure on the Square when the 1855 Bacon Building, at the corner of Pinckney and Mifflin Streets, remodeled in 1900 as the Madison Hotel, is razed for the new Emporium department store.[191]

September 3—Local labor has lots to celebrate as it marks its day. There are only eighteen hundred unemployed job-seeking adults in the Madison/Dane County market of 113,100, a rate of 1.6 percent—far below the national rate of 4.4 percent.

	September 1963	September 1964
Manufacturing	14,300	14,700
Construction	6,300	6,800
Transportation/Communication/Utilities	4,700	5,000
Wholesale & Retail Trade	18,200	19,300
Finance/Insurance/Real Estate	4,700	4,900
Services	12,600	13,200
Government	29,200	30,100[192]

Highways and Transportation

NEW ROADS

▸ Gilbert Road interchange, 1.5-mile four-lane divided highway and overpasses over Whitney Way[193]

▸ Packers Avenue Phase One, one mile from Aberg Avenue to Northport Drive[194]

Transportation Milestones

February 22—The east side was where Madison's transit system began in 1892, and it's where the Madison Bus Company experiment in express bus service starts, from the Capitol Square to South Stoughton and Buckeye Roads in twenty minutes, for thirty cents. The route is soon serving close to two hundred riders per day on nine round trips—popular enough that the company adds a bigger bus, and the city and Public Service Commission approve a west side route to Nakoma Road and Midvale Boulevard. Service will start once the widening of West Washington Avenue from Proudfit to Park Street—part of the Triangle and Brittingham urban renewal projects—is completed in late September. On tap for 1966: express service north to the hospital grounds.[195]

May 23—Madison enters the jet age at 4:50 p.m., as Northwest Airlines begins daily 727 fan-jet service through Milwaukee to New York's LaGuardia Airport. More than twenty-five hundred area residents are on hand at Municipal Airport to tour the innovative aircraft before fourteen passengers take off on the first flight. Mayor Otto Festge presides at the ribbon-cutting ceremony for the Reynolds administration project, presenting a package of Wisconsin cheese to a stewardess who is said to deliver it to New York mayor Robert Wagner.[196]

June 21—An era in train travel ends when the Chicago & North Western Railroad suspends use of its historic Blair Street depot, built in 1910 at a cost of $250,000, and shifts to a new facility at 1898 E. Johnson St. A week later, Madison Gas & Electric announces it has paid $390,000 for the depot and adjoining property, which it will use for offices, storage, and propane production.[197]

November 18—Almost a year after his request, police chief Emery finally gets some satisfaction in mid-November when the Traffic Commission endorses an ordinance banning bicycles from the Capitol Square and State Street, and restricting their use on several major traffic arteries during rush hour. A special study committee is also considering making bike registration mandatory, as well as education and licensure of bicyclists, and designating bike routes on streets and sidewalks. Although the City-University Coordinating Committee endorses the ordinance in principle, Mayor Festge calls the proposed ban an imperfect solution and promises to give "careful consideration" to student opposition.[198]

December—Monona Causeway falls a year behind schedule when equipment failures and the onset of winter force crews to stop working before sufficient fill is dredged and placed, preventing construction of the bridges. The causeway, which former mayor Henry Reynolds said would cost $1 million, is now projected to cost twice that; its 1966 opening is pushed back to at least late 1967, maybe 1968.[199]

Law and Disorder

March 19—White Madison patrolman Richard C. Osterloth, twenty-eight, is severely beaten and kicked by a half-dozen black men on the 600 block of State Street as he attempts to break up a fight and arrest one of the combatants shortly before 10 p.m. Although the street is jammed with crowds in town for the high school basketball tournament, no one goes to Osterloth's aid; as the group pummels him, Lorenzo Miller, on probation for a statutory rape charge involving a fourteen-year-old girl, escapes through the crowd. Osterloth is hospitalized for nine days with head and internal injuries, and five men are convicted of various offenses and sentenced to terms of up to nineteen months.[200]

April 4—It's a good thing Detective Dominic Schiro has his badge in his inner coat pocket when filling in for his nephew Joseph "Buffo" Cerniglia at the sales counter of his brother Frank's Regent Liquor Store after work on Sunday night. Otherwise, the bullet fired by masked gunman Nathan Lee Thomas would have made its way into his chest instead of being stopped by the leather-encased metal shield. Thomas is sentenced to eight years for armed robbery but found not guilty of attempted murder. Incensed that the verdict was influenced by press reports of Schiro's stationhouse comments after the incident that apparently differed from his trial testimony, police chief Wilbur Emery restricts press access at the police headquarters for the foreseeable future.[201]

June 27—Decrying that "policemen are meeting more resistance in enforcing the law," Chief Emery announces the return of two-man patrol cars, discontinued in 1950, "for the safety of our officers and the protection of people involved at arrest scenes." To provide for the twenty two-man squads patrolling from 7 p.m. to 3 a.m., Emery ends the overnight walking beats on the Capitol Square and east side.[202]

October 18—City attorney Edwin Conrad declines police chief Emery's request that the October issue of *Playboy* magazine be banned from sale in the city. Emery and chief inspector Herman Thomas objected to "The Official Sex Manual" and an interview with atheist activist Madalyn Murray O'Hair—contents of the issue both men claimed were of "questionable moral significance." But Conrad explains that the "manual" is satire and not obscene under current Supreme Court rulings, and that O'Hair is an important, albeit controversial, public figure. "I would agree with you that maybe these types of articles should not be included in such a magazine," Conrad writes. "However, this does not mean that the articles per se are pornographic."[203]

In Memoriam

Oscar G. Mayer, seventy-six, whose family visit to Madison in 1919 led to the founding of the city's most important private employer, dies in his sleep of a heart attack at his home in Evanston, Illinois, on March 5. Mayer was general manager of his father's Chicago packing plant when his brother-in-law, banker Frederick W. Suhr, told him about an auction for a failed meatpacking co-op near the sewage plant on the northeast side of town. Mayer was eager to decentralize his operations through a rural slaughterhouse, and he liked what he saw; his father, Oscar F. Mayer, authorized him to offer $300,000 for the facility, which co-op members overwhelmingly accepted. A few months later, the company subsidized the extension of streetcar tracks from the east side to the plant, so its workers could get to the remote site; it also built fifty modest homes for workers. Mayer became chairman and moved the company headquarters to Madison upon his father's death at age ninety-five in 1955; at the time, the company employed close to five thousand workers, about one-third of the city's entire industrial workforce. Mayer and several executives, especially Adolph C. Bolz, also became important local philanthropists.[204]

William J. Meuer, seventy-nine, founder and operator of Meuer Photoart House for forty-seven years, dies on April 8. A Central High School and UW alumnus, and graduate of Harvard Law School, Meuer purchased his store at 411 State St. in 1929; he sold his interest in 1961.[205]

Dudley Montgomery, eighty-two, former president of the Madison Bus Company, dies on October 26. Son of the owner of Madison Railways Company, the bus company's predecessor, Montgomery's career spanned the eras of horse-drawn cars, electric trolleys, and motor-powered buses. He retired in 1962, after fifty-six years in transit.[206]

J. Jesse Hyman, seventy-nine, president of the Emporium Company, and of the Beth El congregation during construction of the synagogue on Arbor Drive, dies on December 9. It was Hyman, long active in civic and philanthropic causes, who made the Emporium "the friendly store for thrifty shoppers."[207]

War Dead

Army captain Humbert "Rocky" Versace, twenty-eight, whose parents formerly lived at 5110 Flambeau Rd., is the first casualty of the war in Vietnam with local ties when he is executed on September 27 in reprisal for South Vietnam's execution of three Communist sympathizers. An Airborne Special Forces intelligence officer and a 1959 graduate of West Point, Versace was the son of a career military man stationed at Truax in the late fifties. The Mass of St. Martin is offered for him at St. Paul's University Catholic Chapel; Versace planned to study for the priesthood with the Maryknoll Fathers when his Army commitment was over.[208]

Marine staff sergeant Roscoe Ammerman, thirty-seven, a member of the Central High School class of 1946, becomes the first native Madisonian casualty when he is killed in action in Quang Nam province on October 3. Ammerman quit school and joined the Marines at seventeen in August 1945; he saw combat in the Korean War, later served in Lebanon, and died an infantry unit leader. He is survived by his mother, a sister, and two brothers, all of whom live in Madison.[209]

Acclaimed photojournalist Dickey Chapelle, forty-seven, sister of UW geology professor Robert Meyer, becomes the first female American war correspondent to be killed in action in Vietnam when a Marine trips a booby-trapped land mine while she is covering a large Marine operation near the Chu Lai air base on November 4. A Shorewood, Wisconsin, native who covered wars from Iwo Jima to Da Nang, Chapelle was in Vietnam on assignment for the *National Observer,* after which she had planned to retire. A strong supporter of the American war effort, Chapelle spoke in Madison this past spring at a rally for the campus Committee to Support the People of South Vietnam and the Matrix banquet for female journalists. The committee quickly organizes a fund campaign in her honor, raising $1,600 to provide CARE relief packages for Vietnamese villagers.[210]

The Madison skyline from Lakeside Street, December 26. WHI IMAGE ID 137860, PHOTO BY DAVID SANDELL

1966

Protest

Nineteen sixty-six starts in the shadow of December's draft of 40,200 men and a warning from Selective Service System director General Lewis B. Hershey that "marginal" students could soon be drafted, putting about 10 percent of university freshmen and sophomores at potential risk. With no clear definition of "marginal," the American Council of Educators recommends that Hershey reinstitute the policy in place during the Korean War, using class rank and/or a standardized test to determine 2-S student deferments; he adopts the policy in late January.[1]

Draftees serve two years, subject to the vagaries of the Army placement practices; each volunteer enlists for a three-year stretch at a chosen assignment in his preferred service. College men are at risk when a draft exceeds 30,000 men.

Thanks to volunteers, February's anticipated draft of 32,900 is reduced to 22,400; April is better still, a final draft of 21,100, the lowest in six months. There are so many enlistments that the local Navy and Air Force recruitment offices start a waiting list. Most area National Guard and Army Reserve units, which require six months of active duty and six years of weekly meetings, are all also filled or nearly so.[2]

UW dean of students Joseph Kauffman, a World War II veteran, calls the policy to base deferments on academics "fair and equitable." But a very vocal segment of his student body disagrees with the entire concept of college deferments; they argue that protecting privileged college students unfairly burdens the poor and nonwhites, and insulates the politically powerful middle class from the war's true impact. They also warn that academic integrity suffers when grades literally become a matter of life and death.

In April, dean of student affairs Martha Peterson reaffirms the existing confidentiality policy established a year earlier, that a student's academic records are not available to draft boards unless the student personally authorizes their release.[3] Between eight and nine thousand of the UW's approximately 12,500 male students have returned the IBM "blue card" authorizing the university to furnish their full records.[4]

The Draft Sit-In

The most successful antiwar action to date takes place indoors in mid-May—a sit-in, led by Students for a Democratic Society (SDS), at the new administration building protesting university policies on the draft.[5]

As two thousand alumni gather for their weekend, about two hundred students meet in the Memorial Union lobby on Friday, May 13. They approve a set of demands, issued later that night by the ad hoc Committee on the University and the Draft (CUD):

- That the faculty hold a special meeting "to discuss the relation of the University to the Draft,"
- That the administration "publicly protest the use of class rank and intelligence tests as criteria for military exemption and the interference of the Selective Service System (SSS) with the freedom of the academic community," and
- That the university "refuse to cooperate with the Selective Service System" by releasing class rank and/or grades or allowing SSS exams to be held in university facilities.

"Present regulations foster social inequality and violate basic tenets of the academic community," The Committee to End the War in Viet Nam's (CEWV's) Jim Hawley and Lowell Bergman (recipient of numerous Emmy, Peabody, and other awards for print and broadcast journalism) and outgoing SDS president Marty Tandler write university president Fred Harrington, which the university "has an obligation to make clear to the Selective Service System and to society at large."[6]

Some of the twenty or so SDS activists picketing the draft deferment exam on May 14, as about two thousand of their test-taking classmates file into the Field House. UNIVERSITY OF WISCONSIN–MADISON ARCHIVES IMAGE S00899

Saturday morning, about two dozen SDS activists picket and distribute literature outside the Field House as another group of college men, a hundred times as large, files in to take the three-hour, 150-question test that could determine their lives and deaths. Several protesters reportedly finish picketing and join the test takers.[7]

Early Monday afternoon, May 16, Harrington, Chancellor Robben Fleming, Kauffman, and other administrators meet in Bascom Hall with fourteen representatives of the CUD. "The university's official position must be the protection of individual choice" to either accept or decline the university's services in maintaining a student's deferment, Harrington says in rejecting the CUD's demands. The current system will continue, he says, unless the faculty decides otherwise at its meeting on May 25.[8]

While that meeting is going on, a rump group of about two hundred fifty assembles on the lawn outside the two-year-old, as-yet-unnamed administration building, where the student records at issue are kept. A larger group had voted the night before against occupying a building, but when word comes down the hill that the administration has rejected CUD's demands, math teaching assistant Hank Haslach and sophomore Bob Zwicker, the new SDS leaders elected only a few days earlier, and John Cumbler move to take over the building. The group agrees by acclamation, and they all walk in.[9]

Across Murray Street, workers start construction of the Humanities building.[10]

At first, it's just about twenty-five or thirty individuals, but news zooms around campus, and scores of students start showing up, suddenly needing transcripts or new ID cards. The group keeps growing, and by late afternoon more than five hundred are jamming the lobby and hallways, with an equal number outside. By midnight, close to fifteen hundred students are taking part in the peaceful occupation.[11]

Bob Cohen urges active obstruction, but the group collectively agrees to occupy, but not disrupt, administrative operations. It's a wise decision.[12]

Madison police chief Wilbur Emery wants to clear the building, but Fleming says the protesters can stay "so long as there is no interference with property in the building or with the conduct of business." Governor Knowles says it's an "internal matter" for the university administration to handle.[13]

The only disruption inside comes from some "uncontrollable individuals" not part of the protest; the main lobby is briefly cleared at 11 p.m. so they can be removed, then the protesters are let back in. There's a showing of Charlie Chaplin's *Modern Times* for the 175 or so who stay all night. Outside, some who oppose the action hurl insults and eggs;

campus police chief Ralph Hanson, protecting the protesters, catches a few—not always with his hands.

Through the day, into the night, and throughout the whole week, a unique sense of community develops, something few there had ever experienced before in such a large setting. They're not just sharing their space and their food, or studying together for next week's finals, but really discussing the issues. For many, this new level of communication and collaboration is the highlight of the sit-in.[14]

They're also frequently debating, sometimes at great length, and rejecting, by overwhelming vote, initiating interference. And the leadership wisely keeps the focus on the draft and not the war, which most students still support.[15]

Several faculty come by, some to stay awhile. History professor George Mosse is a calming presence, his colleague Harvey Goldberg his usual intense self. Professor William Appleman Williams gives a disjointed discourse comparing the sit-in to a baseball game, with the faculty soon coming to bat, to win the day; it's not his finest moment. The only professor to actually sit in is sociology professor Hans Gerth.[16]

The action breaks through to groups previously completely hostile to the antiwar movement. Tuesday night, the Wisconsin Student Association (WSA) Senate adopts a resolution, 20–11, incorporating most of the protesters' demands.[17] On Wednesday, the Inter-Fraternity Council overwhelmingly approves a parallel bill calling the draft inequitable and college deferments bad for education, and endorsing the CUD's demands. For the first time, at least some of the denizens of Langdon and Mifflin Streets are on the same side.[18]

Inside the administration building during the sit-in, May 17. WHI IMAGE ID 136681, PHOTO BY DAVID SANDELL

Protesting the protesters, May 18. UNIVERSITY OF WISCONSIN–MADISON ARCHIVES IMAGE S00094

Some, of course, are still on the other side. The University Young Republicans vote, 21–20, to "condemn" the demonstration, which they liken to "mob rule." The Ad Hoc Committee for Student Choice wants the university to facilitate whatever each student decides for himself.[19]

Tuesday night, around the same time that the WSA Senate is endorsing the sit-in before about two hundred people in Great Hall, a slightly larger group of angry, jeering students packs a sweltering Wisconsin Center auditorium past capacity for a raucous eighty-minute confrontation with a four-man State Department "truth team." The meeting, broadcast live on closed-circuit TV to two overflow rooms, dissolves in chaos after one official charges the students with following the Communist Party line.[20]

At 4:00 p.m. Wednesday afternoon, May 18, there's another unprecedented event—Harrington and Fleming appear at Lincoln Terrace atop Bascom Hill before a crowd estimated at between six and ten thousand.

"Dissent and protest are in the Wisconsin tradition, as are protection of individual rights and majority rule," Harrington says. "This University—perhaps more than any other institution in this nation—is one in which students and faculty and administrators work together with mutual respect—though certainly not always in complete agreement."[21]

"You, by your disciplined behavior throughout the demonstration, have proven once again that the right to protest, which is essential in a democratic society, can be handled in a responsible manner at the University of Wisconsin," Fleming adds. "We, by our willingness to meet and discuss issues which trouble you, have, I hope, also demonstrated that

President Fred Harvey Harrington speaks to a crowd of about seven thousand on Bascom Hill, May 18. Fred Ciporen is in the front row at right, with coat and glasses. WHI IMAGE ID 136679, PHOTO BY DAVID SANDELL

we will try to understand another point of view."[22] Fleming draws cheers by announcing a special faculty meeting on the draft on Monday, May 23, two days before the regularly scheduled session. "We have won," CEWV's John Coatsworth says. Professor Williams tells the protesters they "have functioned as the conscience of the university."[23]

WSA senator Paul Soglin, weeks away from graduating, sends Harrington a handwritten note, telling him that he was "thrilled at seeing so many people discuss, debate and resolve a difficult problem." It's the "first time," he says, that he's "proud to be a student" here, and he salutes Harrington and his administration for having "created the atmosphere in which I have obtained this feeling."

Harrington thanks Soglin for his "warm note" and sends him back a copy of the letter, "since you may later want to recall your feelings."[24]

The sit-in, reduced to a token force late Thursday, ends at 4:30 Friday afternoon, after the chair of the powerful University Committee writes protest leaders that "its continuation is bound to prejudice the point which the students are attempting" to make. "It is not advantageous to remain in full force in the light of the faculty meeting Monday," agrees CUD spokesman Lowell Bergman. And don't come back, Fleming adds.[25]

On Saturday, another seventeen hundred students take the deferment test; a few protesters hand out leaflets, but there are no pickets.[26]

It's a dark and stormy Monday afternoon, May 23, when a record 892 faculty pack the Music Hall auditorium for the special meeting that convenes at 3:50 p.m. About an equal number of students, listening to the proceedings in the Great Hall and other Union rooms, are stunned when Chancellor Fleming proposes to end debate and vote at 5:45 p.m.—and they're outraged when the faculty makes it 5:30. That's barely a minute of meeting for each hour of sit-in.[27]

Chancellor Robben Fleming speaks at Lincoln Terrace, May 18. Seated behind him are WSA president Gary Zweifel and university president Harrington; taking notes at the pedestal is *Capital Times* reporter John Patrick Hunter. WHI IMAGE ID 136684, PHOTO BY DAVID SANDELL

After hearing from three students—WSA president Gary Zweifel, CUD chair Evan Stark, and James Greenwald from the antiprotester Ad Hoc Committee for Student Choice—the faculty considers four resolutions.[28]

Professor Goldberg moves that the UW not release class rank "in any form to anyone," that it only notify draft boards that a student is or isn't currently enrolled, and that it continue to provide academic transcripts to students; his motion is silent on the use of university facilities for draft exams.[29] Professor Williams presents the CUD's resolution that the university "not cooperate with the Selective Service System" by releasing class rankings to them or permitting the use of campus facilities for the deferment examination, and that it not provide transcripts directly to students.[30]

The Williams and Goldberg variations are both rejected by voice vote, as is one offered by Professor Michael Petrovich on behalf of teaching assistants.[31] With little debate, the faculty overwhelmingly adopts the University Committee's version—that class rank "should not be transmitted" to draft boards but only be available directly to the students, for whatever purpose they wish, and that campus facilities should remain available for the draft deferment exams. The resolution also creates a faculty-student committee, as urged by the WSA, "to review all Selective Service problems and procedures facing the University."[32]

The University Committee's resolution also denounces "illegal and unauthorized" means of protest, declaring the faculty "unalterably opposed to coercive methods which interfere" with normal university operations. But, at Professor Mosse's insistence, the faculty deletes those two paragraphs.[33]

The activists can't believe the faculty let them down, that it was all for naught. "A total defeat," Stark says, as the movement's trust in the faculty evaporates in an instant.[34]

After repeated denunciations of what they consider the faculty's betrayal, the protesters decide to resume the sit-in; finding the administration building locked, about a thousand go back up the hill to Bascom Hall, which they occupy throughout the night.[35]

Although Fleming had earlier forbidden further sit-ins, he doesn't roust them. But Tuesday morning, he tells the leaders that he's "deeply disturbed" by the occupation and warns of "serious disciplinary action" if it's not ended promptly. It ends at about 10:30 a.m., by vote of the remaining two hundred activists. That night, about 120 students vote to make the CUD permanent, with Stark and Bergman as cochairs.[36]

Thursday, finals start.

Harrington and most of the regents praise the protesters. Harrington calls the leaders "predominantly high-level students," explains that the protest was not because students were trying to *avoid* the draft but because they were against their own special privilege, and describes their decorum inside the administration building as "quite extraordinary."[37]

Regent Kenneth L. Greenquist, a past commander of the state American Legion, does voice a complaint—not with the administration or the students, but with press photographs that he says unfairly represent the protesters as unwashed and unkempt. "It comes with ill grace," he says, "for the press to degrade the ideas or philosophies on the grounds that the advocating students have a poor appearance by our social standards. Ideas are not related to how men dress, shave or cut their hair." He tells his colleagues that the university "has come out of this particular situation with greater prestige than it had going into it."[38]

And with greater internal cohesion, too. On a campus with several distinct subcultures of students and academics, history professor William Taylor says in September, the most important result of these nine days in May was "the discovery that a university could operate as a community."[39]

At least for a while.

Protest Timeline

February 4–5—The Committee to End the War in Viet Nam (CEWV) marks its first anniversary with a twenty-one-hour Capitol vigil and picket on another bitterly cold night. The gathering, ranging from a handful to about two hundred, draws some counterdemonstrators—mostly high school students throwing snowballs from the top of the new Thirty On The Square building.[40]

March 24—American Communist Party theoretician Herbert Aptheker tells a receptive Union crowd of about nine hundred that the Johnson administration's Vietnam policy exploits the same "anti-Communism psychosis" that Hitler used in acquiring power, and that the US is doing to Vietnam what Hitler did to Europe.[41]

March 26—After two days of workshops and seminars, Yale history professor Staughton Lynd closes the International Days of Protest weekend with a nighttime address to a chilled Bascom Hill crowd of almost a thousand. Recently returned from Hanoi, the former director of the Student Nonviolent Coordinating Committee-organized Freedom Schools of Mississippi criticizes the antiwar movement for failing to mobilize around the draft, and calls for organized actions against the upcoming Selective Service examinations.[42]

March 31—Nobel Peace Prize winner Ralph Bunche, undersecretary of the United Nations, tells a large Union Theater crowd of his "deep feeling of frustration" over the lack of diplomatic communication on the war.[43]

July 4—CEWV tries to mix protest with patriotism in a two-pronged action under new cochairs Robin David and Lowell Bergman. While a group of about fifteen stages a fast on the Memorial Library mall, Walter Lippman (no relation to the famous columnist) and a small group distribute and sell antiwar pamphlets in Vilas Park. Heckled by a handful of high school students and harassed by a parks worker who threatens to tip over their table, they're ordered to leave by a policeman who says their presence is creating a dangerous disturbance. Chancellor Fleming challenges police priorities, writing Mayor Otto Festge that their "responsibility [was] to quell any disturbance rather than stop the distribution of this literature which may have been unpopular with some of the people at the park." But Festge, contending that "tension was building" toward a possible "riot," with a hundred angry persons surrounding the antiwarriors, defends the police for "fulfilling their sworn duty to preserve the peace." The council later enacts an ordinance prohibiting the sale, but not the free distribution, of literature in city parks.[44]

July 14—West side alderman William Bradford Smith, Nineteenth Ward, an attorney and the Republican candidate against Representative Robert W. Kastenmeier (D-Watertown), secretly flies to Saigon with press credentials from the Vietnamese Information Agency on behalf of newspapers in Beaver Dam and Monroe, and tours the country for eight days as a self-styled "working newsman." Smith pays for himself and adviser Professor Russell Edgerton, listing the $3,000 as a "personal campaign expense." As a campaign tactic, it backfires—the Republican *Portage Daily Register* calls the trip "ill-conceived, ill-timed . . . a trick to deceive the voting public." And it's unsuccessful, as Kastenmeier rolls to an easy reelection.[45]

October 13—The city council rejects a request from the Women's International League for Peace and Freedom to set up a card table at 613 University Ave. to solicit signatures on a petition protesting the use of napalm in Vietnam. "The Council doesn't want to go on record for use of sidewalks for such a purpose," says Ald. Milo Flaten in moving to reject the request. But the council does approve a request from the East Side Kiwanis Club to raise money by selling candy on the sidewalk in front of the Security State Bank at Schenk's Corners.[46]

November 8—Bourtai Scudder, Lea Zeldin (Wisconsin Hospital Rate Review Program Appeals Board member, 1979–1980), and three young men are arrested, their thirteen picket signs confiscated, for campaigning too close to the City-County Building polls on election day. The Committee for Direct Action members were handing out literature for Scudder's write-in campaign for Congress against US Rep. Kastenmeier. Scudder, arrested at the Truax demonstration last October, claims Kastenmeier, one of the most dovish members of Congress, is as bad on the war as his GOP challenger, Ald. Smith. SDS and CEWV both chip in for their legal bills. A year later, they're fined $28 each.[47]

December 2–5—Friday's joint SDS–CEWV–Young Democrats rally on Library Mall to support demonstrations at Berkeley and Michigan, and to demand a series of referenda on the war and draft, grows into a Monday night meeting of about four hundred, which Bob Cohen convenes and Evan Stark chairs. Fred Ciporen—who told Dylan to put away the guitar in 1961, and discussed race and class in Cuba with Malcolm X in 1962—makes the motion to create a political party to campaign in both campus and city elections on issues like jobs, housing, transportation, and poverty. The party is named United Campus Action, then quickly changed to University Community Action.[48]

December 15—Students at Madison West High School form a Vietnam discussion group for an objective analysis of the war. "We who will soon graduate face the uncertain future of mounting war," the group accurately notes.[49]

Heckling Ted Kennedy

Five months after the most popular political action to date comes the least—the CEWV's heckling of Senator Edward Kennedy at a packed Stock Pavilion campaign rally for Democratic gubernatorial candidate Lieutenant Governor Patrick J. Lucey on October 27, which sparks a political backlash and new disciplinary rules.

The Committee to End the War in Viet Nam photobombs Sen. Edward Kennedy's appearance for Lieutenant Governor Patrick J. Lucey's gubernatorial campaign at the Stock Pavilion on October 27. From left: State Senator Martin J. Schreiber, Attorney General Bronson La Follette, Kennedy, and Lucey. PHOTO BY NEAL ULEVICH

It also marks a new level of confrontation by war protesters. Disrupting anonymous State Department truth teams was one thing—preventing President Kennedy's youngest brother from speaking at a political rally in a university facility is another.[50]

CEWV had announced in September that it wouldn't allow speakers from the federal government to speak on campus undisturbed. So even though Kennedy is here to tout old family friend Lucey as a student-friendly governor, and not to make a pitch for the administration's war program, the CEWV executive committee decides to implement that policy. With about ten days' notice before Kennedy's appearance, the leaders plan the action without involvement or notice to the full membership.[51]

As the crowd files in that Thursday afternoon, thirty or forty CEWV members quickly position themselves among the crowd behind the stage; their signs appear in Kennedy's photos, and their voices are picked up by his microphones. Out in the crowd of three thousand, the eight CEWV executive committee members are set to call out their questions. Mimeographed sheets with a dozen questions have been distributed to CEWV supporters, for those who will join in.

Rising to speak to a standing ovation, Kennedy is immediately peppered with questions from the CEWV leaders, which he repeatedly ignores. Many CEWV members throughout the crowd and others begin catcalling and shouting for Kennedy to "talk about the war."

Unable to proceed, Kennedy invites CEWV chair Robin David to speak from the podium; David reiterates the Socialist Workers Party slogan, "Bring the troops home now," but is unprepared to debate a United States Senator and obviously outmatched by the charismatic Kennedy.

CEWV leader Robin David demands Sen. Kennedy "talk about the war" during his campaign appearance at the Stock Pavilion, October 27. WHI IMAGE ID 138229, PHOTO BY ROGER L. TURNER

Aware that Kennedy has won the room, CEWV leaders quickly decide to disrupt his speech with continued heckling, which spreads.[52] Down front, Lea Zeldin provides some of the loudest and most urgent shouts of the afternoon. "I have four sons," she cries out, "and I don't want them to die in Asia." A student tosses a coat over her head; she throws it off and keeps it up. Others, CEWV and not, join in, and the heckling continues for nearly half an hour. Kennedy finally gives up, unable to finish his remarks. "Certainly, a spirited occasion," he says later, as he flies to La Crosse for a more orderly appearance.[53] Although CEWV did not direct the widespread heckling after David was dismissed by Kennedy, the group initiated the overall action, and so gets the blame.[54]

Reaction is swift and harsh. President Harrington calls the event "disgraceful." Chancellor Fleming says, "It's a sad day," and asks the WSA and faculty to "investigate this matter further and report to me." More than eight thousand students sign an apology. That evening, the city council unanimously passes a resolution, sponsored by all twenty-two aldermen, apologizing to Kennedy and inviting him to come back and speak on city-owned property.[55]

The faculty's Student Conduct and Appeals Committee holds a special Saturday session and declares that deliberately interfering with a university-sanctioned speech "may constitute grounds for university disciplinary action, not excluding the possibility, in flagrant or repeated cases, of suspension of expulsion." Sunday, the University Committee holds a special session and votes to create new policies and procedures to protect the rights to speak and hear.[56]

Calling the action "a defeat for the national anti-war movement," Bob Cohen and two others issue a blistering attack on Robin David and call for the ouster of the entire CEWV executive committee.[57]

In a marathon seven-hour meeting Sunday night, November 13, in which professors Harvey Goldberg (the CEWV faculty advisor), Germaine Bree, and others participate, the membership defeats Cohen's motion of no confidence, 128–13, and adopts a statement from the executive committee apologizing only for failing to make its case "effectively." The statement also defiantly declares that CEWV "will not succumb to the attempts to make us capitulate and to divide us with empty allegations concerning our denial of free speech."[58]

The WSA committee, sympathizing "with the frustrations that would prompt" the heckling, finds "a technical violation of the principle of free speech." But because the university had been inconsistent in enforcing policies and procedures, the WSA doesn't suspend any CEWV rights, opting instead to put the committee on "provisional status" for the rest of the semester.[59]

WSA's Senator Soglin opposes even that punishment, telling the Senate students should be proud that CEWV insisted that Kennedy honor the university rule requiring a question period. Kennedy had in fact agreed to do so, but that was not made publicly known. Not that that would have mattered; CEWV still would have heckled.[60]

The WSA also reaffirms as "fundamental to freedom of speech" on campus "the right of each member of the audience to hear what the speaker is saying," and "the obligation of members of the audience to let that person be heard."

Most of the regents are not happy with the WSA's response. "This problem needed stronger action," regent Maurice Pasch declares at the board meeting the next day. Regent Greenquist agrees that the action was "juvenile and completely disgraceful," and that the hecklers "don't deserve to be associated with the heritages of the university." But board president DeBardeleben cautions his colleagues to avoid "over-reacting to this."[61]

The chancellor sides with the president and concurs in Kauffman's conclusion that no further action be taken.[62]

Although he doesn't impose any discipline, Fleming is contemptuous of the disrupters, comparing their reliance on "the moral imperative" to the argument used by the Ku Klux Klan, Nazis, and Chinese Red Guards. And he warns that actions like this threaten free speech on campus. "People do not accept harassing a speaker so he cannot speak," he tells a meeting of the Wisconsin Civil Liberties Union in late November. "This more than anything else will bring action down upon us."[63]

He's right. On December 12, the faculty overwhelmingly adopts an antiobstruction policy, section 11.02 of the University Rules and Regulations, with no ambiguity about its cause. "This may be called the Ted Kennedy section," says its chief drafter, political science professor David Fellman, 1960's antiboxing activist.[64]

The resolution adopting the rule, immediately binding on the Madison campus, states that those attending a program sponsored by a campus group "have the duty not to obstruct it, and the university has the obligation to protect the right to listen and participate." Exactly what those terms mean, Fellman says, will be up to the dean of students and the Student Life and Interests Committee.

The *Daily Cardinal* denounces the "disgraceful display" at the Stock Pavilion and endorses the faculty action as a way to ensure free speech. "When student heckling impairs the ability of others to listen," it editorializes, "this is an abuse of the right of free speech. No one has a monopoly on truth and no one has a monopoly on rights. The 'Ted Kennedy section' makes this quite clear." Most students, the paper declares, "were disgusted" by the CEWV's action, which "disgraced" the university.[65]

And the backlash isn't confined to campus. State Senator Fred Risser warns that conservatives controlling state government will cite this incident in pushing to cut the university's budget. He's right, too—they do.

CEWV faculty advisor Goldberg takes the long view. "A violation of the free forum took place, which must exist for all," he acknowledges, but it was in an "urgent attempt to focus attention where attention belongs."[66]

War Dead/War Hero

Marine Lance Corporal Jean Pierre Dowling, twenty-two, East High class of 1962, whose parents live at 4509 Darby Ln., is killed by small-arms fire in Quang Ngai province in Vietnam on January 29. In order that Dowling can be buried in the soldiers' section at Forest Hill Cemetery, the council quickly adopts an ordinance expanding eligibility from the World Wars and the Korean War, to any combat area or American police action.[67]

Staff Sergeant James R. Neubauer, thirty-four, whose parents and brother live on the east side, is killed in Vietnam on February 5, when he steps on a booby-trapped grenade. The nineteen-year Army veteran, who had been in country for about four months, was set to retire late next year. He is the first Portage native to die in the war.[68]

Greenbush native Marine Lance Corporal Jeffrey M. Fields, Central High School class of 1963, receives the Navy Commendation Medal with combat distinguishing device for "heroic achievement" in late March for rescuing an injured comrade during an encounter with the Viet Cong near Chu Lai. Fields, whose parents, sister, and brother live at 120 S. Mills St., is cited for "completely disregarding the risk to his own life" by braving intense small-arms fire to successfully rescue a wounded squad leader, shielding him with his own body until the situation was secure. Fields, recruited to join the Marines at Chesty's bar in the early spring of 1964, was less than three months from the end of his combat tour at the time.[69]

And Marlborough Park neighbors both lose their sons in Vietnam in a two-month period.

Marine Corporal Michael Joseph Banovez, twenty-one, 4342 Crawford Dr., is killed by small-arms fire in Quang Tri province on July 18, seventeen days after his twenty-first birthday; he's on a four-month extension after his three-year tour of duty ended June 28. A record-setting hurdler at West High School, he joined the Marines shortly after his graduation in 1963 and was his platoon's honor man at graduation. The Madison native was a member of Bethel Lutheran Church and the Madison Scouts Drum and Bugle Corps.[70]

Marine Private First Class Donald Dingeldein, twenty-one, whose parents live at 4346 Crawford Dr., is accidentally shot and killed by a fellow Marine near Da Nang on September 18. Dingeldein, a machine gunner who lettered in football in the class of 1963 at Waukesha High School, entered the Marine Corps in February.[71]

Auditorium

Governor Warren P. Knowles opens the year with a blast at local indecision, telling five hundred guests at a service club luncheon at the UW Field House in late January that Madison must "pick a spot and build" its auditorium and civic center. The city, he says, "is missing great opportunities as an international convention center." The GOP chief executive also says Madison should use the Capitol Square for concerts and other cultural events.[72]

The city Plan Department tries to move things along a few days later, recommending that the civic auditorium be located in the first two blocks of East Wilson Street—currently home to the Bellevue Apartments, the Diocese of Madison Chancery and building, and some of the Madison Club's land. Notwithstanding that the site is set back far from the lake and would overlook four sets of train tracks and the four-lane North Shore Drive, the sixty-page report cites its "commanding location [with an] . . . exceptional view of Lake

Monona" as one of the site's highlights, along with easy accessibility and the availability of parking. The report gives a middling assessment of Olin Park and virtually eliminates the James Madison Park area from further consideration.[73]

Mayor Festge gives a thirty-five-minute presentation to the Auditorium Committee in mid-March supporting the Wilson Street site but falls just short; after four hours of acrimonious debate, his own appointees fail to approve the site, 7–8. The other three sites—Law Park, James Madison Park, and Olin Park—all fail as well. Two longtime aldermanic supporters of the Monona Terrace plan at Law Park are particularly frustrated. "This committee has got to make a decision," snaps Ald. Toby Reynolds. "This committee is incapable of selecting" a site, adds Ald. Richard Kopp.[74]

"It will be a long time before Madisonians witness a sorrier spectacle than the deliberations Tuesday of the Auditorium Committee," the *Capital Times* editorializes March 16. "If there is an award for evasion and neglect of responsibility, the group has won a special tin plate medallion. What, in Heaven's name, needs to be done in order to get some action out of this Administration and this City Council? Will there ever be an end to this stalling and lack of courage to make a decision?"[75]

On April 7, Festge issues a statement firmly rejecting Olin Park, and again endorsing the Wilson Street site—a proposal he tries to sweeten by expanding it to include part of the original Monona Terrace site in Law Park. Festge notes that the committee has "constantly emphasized" that both the auditorium and civic center should be downtown. But that afternoon, Festge's committee ignores its established criteria and his detailed critique of the site and votes, 8–7, to put the entire auditorium and civic center complex at Olin Park. The committee never votes on the Wilson Street or Law Park sites but does give one sop to advocates of Monona Terrace—the designation of the Wright Foundation's William Wesley Peters as the preferred architect, subject to negotiations.[76]

The committee's action is not well received, and its acceptance by the council seems doubtful. "They toss out their criteria, we can toss out their recommendation," says Ald. Robert McMurray, Second Ward. "They have not functioned along the lines the council approves."[77]

Peters tells Festge in a phone conversation the next day that he's willing to discuss trying again, but he wants city negotiators to have explicit authority—in writing. And he makes it clear he thinks the committee made a mistake.

"Olin Park is a magnificent, beautiful site that should be part of the development of the whole of Lake Monona," he tells a reporter, but Law Park is "far superior," especially for the downtown economy.[78]

Peters's reference to a comprehensive lakefront development isn't spontaneous, but rather is the result of a suggestion made by Auditorium Committee member and ardent Monona Terrace advocate Dr. Van Potter, when the two men met secretly a few weeks prior. Indeed, at about the same time Peters is talking to a reporter on April 9, Potter is holding an invitation-only press conference at his McCardle Laboratory for Cancer Research to propose that Peters prepare a master plan covering the whole shoreline from Olin Park to B. B. Clarke Beach.[79]

Although Potter still holds to Law Park as the proper site for all facilities, he suggests a sweeping plan with the auditorium and theater at Olin Park, with exhibition hall and related functions at Law Park.[80]

Just four days later, the Auditorium Committee endorses Potter's plan, voting 12–1 for "immediate construction of a cultural center" with auditorium and theater at Olin Park, and "immediate planning" for such "urgently needed" facilities as a convention facility and art gallery at Law Park, all pursuant to a master shoreline plan designed by Peters.[81]

Not everyone is sold on the notion, though. Planning director Kenneth Clark says a unified downtown Monona Avenue site "is the only location if we are concerned about city planning and development," and the Plan Commission agrees, refusing to endorse the grand plan on May 9, 5–3.[82]

But that doesn't matter to the mayor or the council. On May 12, when the council deadlocks 11–11 on a motion to refer it all back to the committee with explicit instructions to choose a single site downtown, the mayor has the chance to break the tie by voting aye. But Festge, who said in the 1965 campaign that he favored the Monona Terrace site unless the planners recommended otherwise, inexplicably lets the tie vote stand, and thereby fail, dooming a unified downtown site. The council then ratifies the Potter proposal, 12–10. The *State Journal* is delighted, the *Capital Times* outraged.[83]

Now the committee has to negotiate a contract with Peters; it's easier said than done. The architect, who has been working on Monona Terrace almost since his late father-in-law first proposed it in 1938, tries to prod the city into reconsidering the split-site concept.

"It does not seem logical or sound city planning," he writes Festge on May 30, "to separate the auditorium and convention facilities." He also notes, with considerable understatement, "some trepidation about entering into a contract with the city" to design for a site the Plan Commission has opposed.[84]

Festge is unmoved; site selection is settled, he says, and he cancels a scheduled meeting with Peters. Peters says Festge is playing games for "strictly personal political implications" and refuses to deal with him outside of the committee.[85]

Peters doesn't go any easier on the committee. "Important decisions appear to have been made for reasons of political expediency," he tells the group on June 10, "in many cases seemingly affected by an irrational fear of an unprincipled opposition," namely the anti-Monona Terrace "Obstructionists."[86]

Desperate for the prestige of a Wright-related design, and recognizing the political realities, the committee buckles—a bit. It approves, 9–3, a resolution to hire Peters to do schematic drawings and cost estimates for a master plan featuring the auditorium and theater at Olin Park and exhibition and other facilities at Law Park, "unless the city agrees, at the suggestion of the architect, to change the priorities and to shifting the facilities from one spot to another."[87]

Peters is interested but won't commit. Separating the major functions "is a serious mistake which could well prove fatal to the ideal development of Madison and most certainly to the best interests of the downtown area," he reiterates, telling the committee that "as the plan is now," he would not be the architect. He says he's done talking, and the committee almost lets him abandon the project over what anti-Terrace former mayor George Forster calls his "arrogant contempt" for the mayor and committee.[88]

But cooler heads prevail—Festge and Peters even resume direct communications—and shortly before 2 a.m. on June 24, the council votes 17–5 to endorse negotiations with Peters for a comprehensive plan for the entire Monona Basin.[89]

The final resolution, approved 12–5 on July 14, is a model of equivocation, allowing Peters "the freedom to recommend the location of the facilities" and delaying the final decision "until after a thorough and objective study" has been made and approved by the committee and council. The resolution sets a maximum total cost of $9 million for both the auditorium and civic center, with the initial buildings limited to the $4 million approved in the referendum of 1954.[90]

Now negotiations are just down to money. Peters proposes a basic fee of 9.8 percent of construction costs; Forster says he's "trying to gyp the city." But by the end of September, there's a deal—$102,000 for a schematic master plan and construction drawings, plus 9 percent for the first $9 million of construction costs, and 9.8 percent for everything beyond that. The foundation also gets ten years of exclusivity for basin development.[91]

> ## ROUNDY SAYS
>
> "I got a letter a man wanted to know who was going to be in the Rose Bowl this year. That is like me trying to find out when Madison is going to get an Auditorium."
> —*Wisconsin State Journal*, August 21

In another dead-of-night vote on October 14—again, at about 1:45 a.m.—the council ignores a threatened lawsuit and votes 15–7 to approve the contract for a Monona Basin Master Plan, to include an auditorium for up to twenty-five hundred, exhibition and banquet space for up to three thousand, and a small theater, recital hall, and art gallery of ten thousand square feet.[92]

Festge and Peters sign the contract on November 7, ten years and four months after former mayor Nestingen and Frank Lloyd Wright signed the contract for Monona Terrace. Three weeks later, longtime Terrace foe Carroll Metzner files his lawsuit, claiming that the city's abuse of discretion in approving the contract invalidates the agreement and places city officials at personal risk for the $102,000. He doesn't really expect to win—he just wants to delay things long enough for a new mayor and council. After all, that's how the "Obstructionists" killed Monona Terrace.[93]

Despite the risk, Festge and the council don't back down but have Peters proceed with his user group interviews. The year ends like so many others—architects drawing plans, lawyers preparing for litigation.

Civil Rights

The Movement

*March 15—*A bad economy and good information have helped reduce the number of housing discrimination complaints, Equal Opportunities Commission chair Reverend

James Wright reports, as high vacancy rates and greater understanding of the fair housing code have led landlords to seek, not shun, black tenants.[94]

May 5—The *Madison Sun*, a newspaper aiming to be the voice of Madison's black community, debuts. Publisher Lawrence Saunders says the paper will be published every other Thursday and distributed free to more than ten thousand homes in Madison.[95]

May 14—The Newspaper Guild of Madison names Reverend Wright, also the assistant minister at Mt. Zion Baptist Church, its Citizen of the Year.[96]

May 31—The Madison Board of Realtors, which campaigned against the city's fair housing code in 1963 and the similar state statute in 1965, joins the Wisconsin Realtors Association in a newspaper ad attacking the proposed fair housing section to the federal Civil Rights Act as "forced" housing. "Because we are concerned about the human rights of all Americans," the ad reads, "we protest a law that gives one person the right to force another to enter into a contract against his will."[97]

June 30—As a delegate to the federal Status of Women conference, UW director of continuing education Dr. Kathryn Clarenbach plans to introduce a resolution demanding that the federal Equal Opportunities Commission enforce the gender-based provisions of the Civil Rights Act of 1964; she's "absolutely appalled" when the women running the conference won't let her, for risk of offending the Johnson administration. It crystallizes her understanding of the need for a national lobby like the NAACP to apply outside pressure. So she organizes a like-minded group of activists, starting with Betty Friedan, to sit together at the closing luncheon that noon, and founds modern feminism. The eight women dream up the name National Organization for Women (NOW), which Friedan writes on a napkin. The organization's goal: "To take the actions needed to bring women into the mainstream of American society." Others at the luncheon join the effort; by dessert, twenty-seven women have put down five dollars each, which Clarenbach collects (along with the napkin), becoming NOW's first secretary. Clarenbach organizes the temporary steering committee that organizes NOW's founding conference in October, where she is elected chair of the board.[98]

July 1—South Madison native Richard Harris, twenty-nine (Rev. James C. Wright Human Rights Award winner, 1997), becomes director of the South Madison Neighborhood Center. Harris, UW class of 1961, has a master's degree in social work from the University of Illinois and has worked for the Hyde Park Neighborhood House and the Illinois Youth Commission.[99]

Reports on Race

Nineteen sixty-six is a year of reports.

In April, a two-man research team from the US Conference of Mayors paints a stark but ultimately hopeful picture in "Enlarging Equal Opportunity in Madison," a thirty-nine-page analysis commissioned by the city. It finds, "If you are non-white in Madison, you are twice as likely as your white fellow citizen to be poor. Despite Madison's prosperity and sophistication, the poverty rate is surprisingly close to that of the nation as a whole."

The report challenges Madison's effort to understand and address problems plaguing the minority community:

> There appears to be insufficient data about the Negro population and the problems they face in Madison. Too little is known by those responsible for public action about the social and economic characteristics of Madison's Negro population. Those in a position to plan and program for Madison's future and growth could not provide simple facts about Madison's 500 Negro families.
>
> Unfortunately, there is a paucity of occupational data about Negroes in Madison, but it is clear that affirmative action is required to ensure that Negroes make the fullest possible contribution to Madison's future.

The report raises disturbing questions about interracial communication, despite the fact that "Madison is making a conscious effort to improve the condition of people who are poor as well as Negroes and other minority groups. Disadvantaged groups do not yet, however, appear to have sufficient confidence in the sincerity of these efforts nor do they appear to have much sense of participation in this effort. Whenever possible people from disadvantaged groups must be recruited to participate in the shaping and actual conduct of programs."

The same situation applies in the schools: "Madison's educational institutions appear to be of uniformly high quality [and] the vocational school has demonstrated unusual flexibility. The high quality school staff with a relatively liberal budget has been incorporating the latest ideas into its educational programming, yet persons in the community do not seem to have any sense of involvement or participation in the development or implementation of these new ideas."

The report finds that the (newfound) support for fair housing by the realty and finance communities, enactment of state and local fair housing laws, low unemployment, and relatively small number of blacks make "the housing problems of Negroes in Madison much less severe than in many cities, even of comparable size. With a relatively small amount of special effort major improvement can be made."

The report calls for hiring more black teachers and a full-time executive director for the Equal Opportunities Commission, which the report suggests has floundered somewhat since enactment of the Equal Opportunities Ordinance in December 1963.

Madison has "relatively small remaining problems of racial discrimination and poverty," the report concludes, and a "unique combination of circumstances which provides Madison with an excellent opportunity. Madison can and should become a leader and a model for other communities."[100]

Another April report relates the "deep feeling of rejection and a desire for belongingness among lower-income Negroes who do not feel close to the rest of the community" because of their "rather involuntary isolation."

This report, compiled by Urban League of St. Louis researcher Naomi Lede, calls Madison's private housing market "geared to moderate or middle-income families, a sort of 'no man's land' as far as low-income nonwhites are concerned." It cites other problems that also continue, especially in "the area of adoption and illegitimacy. The agencies who are directly involved in giving these kinds of services seem to be somewhat apprehensive about Negro children."

The report, prepared in support of the Madison Friends of the Urban League application for funding from the Community Chest, a forerunner to United Way, concludes that "there is no prevailing atmosphere of racial conflict in Madison. The majority of both whites and Negroes felt that the climate of race relations was good, and most expressed the belief that the races would continue to 'always get along' in the city. There were minorities in both groups, however, who felt that this was not really the case. It is very likely that a substantial part of those who see racial friction is speaking of subtler aspects rather than open conflict."[101]

This relatively good news, though, causes an unfortunate reaction. Although more than three-fourths of Madison's black citizens are unaware of the services provided by public and private welfare agencies, creating a need for an agency like the Urban League to coordinate and promote services, the Community Chest twice rejects the League's application to become a participating "Red Feather" agency. Board president Collins Ferris explains in December that "discrimination as it is known in other communities doesn't exist in Madison."[102]

The Equal Opportunities Commission (EOC) issues its own annual report in late September, with mixed conclusions. Racial prejudice "is more widespread than many people realize," it finds, "and will yield only very gradually to the increased occasions for human contact which are now developing." The EOC says that "the employment picture for the Negro in Madison is fairly bright in terms of opportunity," but there remains a great need for education, training, and apprenticeship opportunities "to help bridge the gaps created by discrimination, deprivation and denial of opportunity in the past." The report states that the city's fair housing code has "facilitated movement out of the traditional neighborhoods," but that African Americans are still finding "some resistance on the part of private home sellers," as the ordinance does not cover the sale of private homes.[103]

Banning Bars in Biased Clubs

In late June, the council approves recommendations from the EOC to bar new liquor licenses for private organizations with discriminatory membership policies, and to prevent the renewal of existing licenses for such organizations at some point after 1969. "Because of the present climate in Madison," state NAACP leader Marshall Colston tells a state Industrial Commission hearing, "organizations which discriminate will not in the future receive licenses to operate. I think the Council will go all out in this effort."[104]

Three private clubs in Madison—the Elks, the Moose, and the Eagles—have clauses in their national charters barring nonwhites from membership and will face a challenge in renewing their licenses if their policies do not change by the deadline. At least three

Dane County judges—Norris Maloney, William Byrne, and William Buenzli—belong to one or more of the discriminatory clubs. Mayor Otto Festge formerly belonged to both the Eagles and the Moose but resigned because he was too busy to attend meetings. The EOC reports no evidence of discrimination in the use of the clubs' bars or dining facilities by members or guests. The clubs also report that they support the ongoing national efforts to remove the discriminatory membership clauses.[105]

Barmaid Battles

The city continues to struggle with the concept of licensing women bartenders.

In February, the Common Council ignores advice from Mayor Otto Festge and a warning from police chief Wilbur Emery, and votes 16–6 to issue the first-ever bartender's licenses to five women applicants. Festge wants the council to wait for an attorney general's opinion on the legality of refusing to license women due to the nature of the work; Emery claims that the introduction of go-go dancers has led to increased prostitution, which would be worsened by licensing women bartenders. Ald. Babe Rohr agrees, asserting that licensing women will depress industry wages and "create the same kind of situation as now confronts our community because of the go-go girls. We have a moral obligation to the city to exclude women bartenders," he says, because they should be home taking care of their families.[106]

Capital Times editor/publisher William T. Evjue, who has railed against alcohol since he supported Prohibition as a member of the State Assembly in 1917, zealously opposes the "rush to abandon a historic policy and start licensing women bartenders."[107]

Despite granting the five licenses, the council and its special operator's license review committee still don't treat the genders alike—interviewing every female applicant, but interviewing male applicants only if they have criminal records or when there is a question about their residence.

In July, the council refuses to issue a license to Ruth Sharon Fey, a twenty-six-year-old divorcee with a five-year-old son. Although the council never formally explains the reason for the refusal, the only questions at her two public interviews are about her marital status and child care.[108]

Fey sues, but Circuit Judge William Sachtjen, a Madison alderman from 1947 to 1960, rules that she isn't entitled to a license or an explanation. "Maybe they didn't disclose the reasons because they didn't want to embarrass her," he says in dismissing her claim in late August.[109]

Fey fares better in her complaint before the state Industrial Commission, which unanimously rules in late September that the city did discriminate by forcing female applicants to meet standards not set for men, and must either issue Fey a license or reconsider her application using a nondiscriminatory process.[110]

The city appeals, even though it has already ended its practice of interviewing all women. Ald. James Pfefferle, chair of the license review committee, says the city has "a right not to issue licenses to women" at all, and may rescind the ordinance authorizing women to be licensed as a result of the ruling. But Ald. Rohr's proposal to repeal the ordinance fails in early September, 12–8.[111]

"The girl didn't get a fair hearing," Judge Richard Bardwell says during the hearing on the city's appeal in late December. "Not to give any reason seems to be arbitrary on its face."[112]

But equity aside, Bardwell is clearly impressed with the jurisdictional challenge raised by assistant city attorney Bruce Kaufmann—that the state antidiscrimination law applies only to housing and employment, giving the commission no authority over municipal licenses. Bardwell's decision is expected in early 1967.[113]

The council is less conflicted when it comes to liberalizing another aspect of city nightlife, voting unanimously on December 8 to end a long ban and legalize dancing in taverns. Bars with a dance area no larger than 625 square feet will need a cabaret license, which requires a $100 annual fee; the current dance hall license will still cover larger establishments. On December 22, the council issues thirty-seven new cabaret licenses, including to the Shuffle Inn, 967 S. Park St., and Bob and Gene's, 619 University Ave.[114]

Civil Rights on Campus

February 14—Lewis "Les" Ritcherson, a successful high school coach in Waco, Texas, is named the first black assistant coach on the UW football team. Ritcherson, whose son is a quarterback, will coach ends and backs.[115]

May 5—Student Nonviolent Coordinating Committee (SNCC) cofounder Julian Bond, recently elected to but denied a seat in the Georgia House of Representatives due to his opposition to the war, speaks to a capacity Great Hall crowd on "Containment Abroad and Social Unrest at Home." He jokingly reveals what he calls SNCC's First Law of Civil Rights Movements: "a rights movement is successful in direct proportion to the number of white college students who are locked up in the course of activities."[116]

September 4—The first cohort of twenty-four black students in the Special Five-Year Program for Tutorial and Financial Assistance, created and run by Ruth B. Doyle, begins classes.[117]

September 21—NAACP national field director Charles Evers, brother of slain civil rights worker Medgar Evers, tells a Union Theater audience of about five hundred that racism must be uprooted "where it starts—in the white community." Evers's talk, "Black Power vs. Non-Violence," is sponsored by the Union Forum committee and Young Democrats.[118]

November—Freshman Willie Edwards of Chicago and Milwaukee junior Walter Ward form a new black power group, Concerned Negro Students, with initial membership limited to black students. On December 14, they submit to the university office for student organizations the constitution of "Concerned Black Students" without the racial exclusivity—"founded on the belief that, for the actual realization of his liberty, social and economic freedom, the Afro-American himself must assume the role of determining the most advantageous use of his political and economic resources."[119]

Urban Renewal

Nineteen sixty-six brings big personnel changes for housing and urban renewal.

On Valentine's Day, the Madison Housing Authority (MHA) relieves Robert Callsen of his duties as assistant director, making him half-time accountant, at his request. Callsen, who served as director prior to his arrest and incarceration for driving after suspension in December 1964, began with the MHA as an accountant in 1946.[120]

In April, Mayor Otto Festge appoints former Madison and state NAACP president Marshall Colston as a commissioner of the Madison Redevelopment Authority (MRA).[121] At the MRA's organizational meeting in May, in its first contested leadership election since its creation in 1958, Ald. James Pfefferle ousts chairman Philip Falk, the seventy-seven-year-old retired superintendent of schools who had served since Albert McGinnis resigned after the 1963 mayoral election.[122]

The first week of June is a good week for former UW football star and former coach of the Madison Mustangs, twenty-five-year-old Merritt Norvell (Michigan State University athletics director, 1995–1999)—he receives his UW master's degree in social work and is named the MRA relocation director and assistant community services officer.[123]

Triangle Update

More than two years after then-MRA director Roger Rupnow proposed 150 units of moderate-income housing in the Triangle at Regent Street and West Washington Avenue, the project finally gets a nonprofit sponsor—the Bayview Foundation. Under current Federal Housing Administration regulations, tenant income limits will range from $6,000 for a family of two to $9,300 for a family of seven or more.[124]

In May, the first private development in the Triangle, the $1 million, five-story Madison Medical Center, opens; Sam Schwartz, whose pharmacy at Park and Mound Streets was a popular teen hangout before it was razed for the redevelopment, leases the first-floor pharmacy as a member of the corporation that owns the building.[125]

With twenty-three acres in the fifty-two-acre Triangle still to be sold, late August is a busy time in the medical quadrant west of South Park Street. The MRA sells a forty-thousand-square-foot lot at the northeast corner of Milton and South Brooks Streets to Madison General Hospital at $2 per square foot for a $3 million, three-story, sixty-thousand-square-foot medical research facility.[126] And several parties are interested in a larger, 1.7-acre parcel on the south side of Regent Street between Mills and Brooks Streets, just west of the medical center, including a group proposing a 128-bed nursing home and the Davis Duehr eye clinic.[127]

The Triangle's commercial node also makes progress as the MRA starts negotiating with Kohl's Food Stores in November to develop and anchor the long-planned shopping center at the southeast corner of Park and Regent Streets.[128]

But across West Washington Avenue, all is not well in the Brittingham renewal area, which is already three years late in closing its books—much to the displeasure of federal officials. In mid-November, developer Sampson Enterprises Inc. tells the MRA its market-rate housing complex is at 98 percent capacity but still not covering costs; warning that the project could fail and be taken over by the Federal Housing Authority, it asks for approval to build a hundred-unit addition to generate new revenue. Out of the question, says MRA director Sol Levin, listing the regulatory and planning obstacles. Sampson withdraws its request.[129]

Murray Mall 2.0

The great city/university flash point is back on track.

In mid-March, US Representative Robert W. Kastenmeier (D-Watertown) announces approval of the $125,529 planning grant for the twenty-one acres in the 600–900 blocks of University Avenue, and that $2.6 million has been reserved for the federal share of the cooperative effort of the UW, the city, and the Lake Park Corp.[130]

But the project—under which the university gets the 800 block for its $6.3 million communication arts building, and all of the 900 block except the First National Bank Building and the Rennebohm Drug Store; the merchants get the 600 block through their Lake Park Corp.; and they split the 700 block—still needs the regents' blessing. It finally comes in early October, about ten months after Chancellor Fleming proposed the four-block solution. The agreement also closes Murray Street for a mall between Johnson and University, with a city promise to complete the mall up to State Street.[131]

Housing Update

In May, the council approves the MHA's application for federal funds for 210 units of public housing. The plan calls for the construction of 130 units for the elderly and conversion of 80 of the 120 units for military families at Truax Park into low-income housing.[132] There are about twenty-five hundred families (about one thousand of them elderly) that qualify for low-rent public housing but whose needs are unmet—even as the overall vacancy rate rises to an unhealthy 7.1 percent in 1965, up from 2.8 percent in 1963.[133] The MHA approves construction of 130 low-rent units for the elderly on two sites—the Richmond Hill property between Lakeside Street and Olin Avenue, and parcels at East Johnson and North Baldwin Streets—and solicits proposals.[134]

UW

COMMENCEMENT, JUNE 6
- Baccalaureate: 2,300
- Master's/PhD: 1100
- JD/MD: 216[135]

FALL ENROLLMENT
- Total Students: 30,287[136]

HOMECOMING
- Show: Tony Bennett and Woody Herman
- Dance: Tommy James and the Shondells[137]

NEW BUILDINGS OF NOTE
- Van Hise Hall (partial), 1220 Linden Dr.
- Camp Randall Addition, 1440 Monroe St.
- Molecular Biology and Biophysics, 1525 Linden Dr.
- William S. Middleton Medical Library, 1305 Linden Dr.[138]

Campus Calendar

February 13–24—US Supreme Court Justice William O. Douglas headlines the sixth annual WSA Symposium in February on "The Direction of American Democracy," featuring lectures and seminars by Senator Albert Gore (D-TN), broadcasters Edward P. Morgan and David Schoenbrun, Washington columnist Marquis Childs, and editor of *The Nation* magazine Carey McWilliams.[139]

February 20—A doubly historic event takes place as the university dedicates the refectory serving the Lakeshore dorms, where Carson Gulley (1897–1962) was Residence Halls head chef from 1927 to 1954, as Carson Gulley Commons. It's the first time a UW building has been named for a nonwhite individual, and the first time a civil service employee has been so honored.[140]

February 26—Saxophone immortal John Coltrane challenges two near-capacity Union Theater audiences with his avant-garde second quartet.[141]

March 4—University vice president Robert Clodius reports to the regents that out-of-state freshmen have higher grades than Wisconsin resident freshmen, except for males from New Jersey and Pennsylvania; out-of-state women do better than men across the board.[142]

March 15—James Dickey, writer-in-residence at the university, is awarded the National Book Award for his fifth volume of verse, *Buckdancer's Choice*. The poet, conducting a class in poetry this semester, conducts an open session the next week analyzing the work of aspiring poets and gives a free reading in Tripp Commons. Dickey also discusses with the twelve seminar students in the small South Hall classroom ideas for his work in progress—his first novel, published in 1970 as *Deliverance*. The famed "Dueling Banjos" composition in its 1972 film adaptation is arranged and performed by former UW student Eric Weissberg.[143]

April 1—Athletic director Ivan Williamson names Bob Johnson (inductee, Wisconsin, United States, and International Hockey Halls of Fame), thirty-five, head hockey coach at Colorado College the past three seasons, to lead the Badger's fledgling hockey program. "Wisconsin has made tremendous improvements in the three years it has had hockey," Johnson says. "I see no reason why we can't keep the program moving all the way to the top." A three-sport star, the Minnesota native led the Minnesota Gophers to two consecutive Western Collegiate Hockey Association titles in the early fifties and played minor league baseball for the Chicago White Sox.[144]

April 30—Dave Brubeck engages a capacity Stock Pavilion crowd with his classic quartet. The Greek Week presentation raises money for scholarships for foreign students.[145]

May 8—Speeches, songs, and dinner for five hundred in Gordon Commons, the largest common dining room in the nation, highlight dedication ceremonies for the four-building, $24 million southeast dormitory complex, now home to 3,260 students.[146]

May 13–14—Alumni weekend (celebrated by about two thousand alums) opens Friday afternoon with the ceremony designating the university's first building, North Hall, a registered national historic landmark.[147] Saturday night, the First Lady of Song, Ella Fitzgerald, returns to the Field House, swinging everything from "Bill Bailey" to "A Hard Day's Night."[148]

Spring—Despite the national upsurge in venereal diseases, the campus is relatively clean, with only two cases of syphilis and three of gonorrhea this year, all of them cured. "There's no venereal disease problem at the university," Health Services director John D. McMaster says when his report is released.[149]

August 9—At 2:45 a.m., Detective Thomas McCarthy executes a search warrant at 511 W. Mifflin St. and arrests a twenty-three-year-old junior from New York for a few grams of marijuana and hashish. Deputy district attorney James C. Boll says the student bought some of the drugs and won the rest in a gin rummy game with two other students. Charges are later dismissed due to errors in the warrant.[150] Large quantities have driven good-grade marijuana down to $20 an ounce, and a hit of LSD goes for $5; there's also a lot of hashish and methedrine, with some cocaine, heroin, DMT, and opium as well.[151]

Fall—Thanks to one of the country's loosest vehicle registration policies, there are about ten thousand student-owned cars, motorcycles, and scooters on and around campus. As the fall semester starts, so too does a four-year experiment in pedestrian habits—will students going between the Union and Bascom Hill use a new $26,500 wooden bridge arching over North Park Street to avoid the heavy traffic? Experience soon proves the vast majority of students will not. So in December, the City-University Coordinating Committee asks for, and police chief Wilbur Emery and traffic engineer John

Bunch agree to provide, a police officer and sign directing students to use the bridge. "Friendly persuasion hasn't worked," Emery says.[152]

September–November—A new Union film series presents famed directors Jean-Luc Goddard, George Stevens, and King Vidor to screen and discuss their movies *Les Carabiniers, Shane,* and *War and Peace,* respectively.[153]

September 30—The San Francisco Mime Troupe's first performance in Madison is its most controversial production yet, a full-blown minstrel show featuring an interracial cast in blackface—three of whom had just been arrested in Denver for lewdness and bad language. Here, the capacity Union Theater crowd delights in the performance without interference. *Civil Rights in a Cracker Barrel,* cowritten by Saul Landau, is sponsored by *Quixote* literary magazine and raises enough money to print future issues.[154]

October 7—Fall rush results in 377 men pledging the thirty campus fraternities.[155]

October 13—Radical organizer Saul Alinsky, whose Industrial Areas Foundation recently organized poor blacks in Rochester, New York, discusses the politics of poverty and the meaning of black power with a capacity Union Theater crowd.[156]

November 14—Radical attorney William Kuntsler tells a Union crowd of about 150 that America has only "surface freedom" and is on the verge of a new McCarthyism.[157]

November 16—The Martha Graham dance company exhilarates and exhausts a capacity Union Theater audience, with the sixty-six-year-old Graham dancing the title role in *Judith;* the young Judith is portrayed by UW alumna Mary Hickson, who also dances the leading role in *Circe.*[158]

November 17—After another dismal losing season (3–6–1) drives the average game attendance in the 75,935-seat Camp Randall down to 51,725, and the alumni to open anger, President Harrington can't protect football coach Milt Bruhn any longer. The Badgers' most successful coach of this century submits his resignation to the Athletic Board chairman, Professor Frank Remington, and becomes Ivy Williamson's assistant athletic director. Bruhn's boys make sure he goes out a winner, ending the season two days later with a come-from-behind upset victory over his alma mater, Minnesota. Then the team carries their coach off the field on their shoulders. On the recommendation of Chancellor Fleming and the Athletic Board, the regents give former Badger star quarterback and Bruhn's assistant, John Coatta, thirty-seven, a three-year contract as the new head coach. A side benefit—Coatta can get no-show jobs for his players at the trucking and storage company owned by his father-in-law, former mayor Henry Reynolds.[159]

Rise and Fall of the Second Campus

Working to implement President Fred Harrington's long-standing plans for a second full four-year Madison campus, Chancellor Robben Fleming issues a report in mid-February picking the old Charmany and Rieder farms flanking Whitney Way on Mineral Point Road, the university's experimental farms since 1957. Fleming suggests that students on the new campus "could doubtless participate in central campus activities in exceptional situations like intercollegiate activities," but that "social and recreational life would have to be localized [through] a relatively self-contained campus life." Although Fleming insists the administration is not actually proposing the second campus "as another college responsible to the Madison chancellor as are the other colleges," he calls the second campus concept "our best judgment of what could be done after 1971–1972."[160]

Legislators are not impressed. Assistant Majority Leader and State Building Commission cochair Jerris Leonard (R-Milwaukee) compares the university to his three-year-old toddler asking for another piece of candy. Democrats aren't any more supportive.[161]

The political problems grow insurmountable when the original enrollment projection of 41,350 in 1971 is reduced a few weeks later to 36,424, which the influential University Committee says has "removed some of the urgency for making a decision" to establish a second campus. In September, Harrington concedes that his dream of western expansion is likely dead. The enrollment slowdown has been more successful than expected, he says, so Madison "won't have to face the question of a second campus for a few years," if ever.[162]

Schools

GRADUATION, JUNE 17[163]
- West: 657
- East: 495
- Central-University: 298
- La Follette: 283

FALL ENROLLMENT
- Total Students: 32,768[164]

NEW SCHOOLS
- James Madison Memorial High School, 201 S. Gammon Rd.
- Ray W. Huegel Elementary School, 2601 Prairie Rd.
- Samuel Gompers Junior High School, 1502 Wyoming Way
- John F. Kennedy Elementary School, 221 Meadowlark Dr.[165]

The Vote to Close Central

Madison High School—the sturdy Municipal Gothic structure designed by prominent Minneapolis architect Cass Gilbert, renamed Central High School in 1922 when the East Side High School opened, then Central-University High School on the closing of Wisconsin High in 1964—was the city's crowning educational achievement when it opened September 8, 1908. But now its days are numbered.[166]

For more than a year, the board of the Vocational, Technical, and Adult Schools has been after the Board of Education to turn over some of Central's classrooms, and to make a quick decision on the building's future. Its efforts succeed on February 7 with the school board's 6–1 vote to close the school in June 1969.[167]

"There appears to be no advantage in further delaying a decision which must ultimately be made," says school board member Arthur "Dynie" Mansfield, reading from a five-page statement before making the momentous motion. "The indecision in this matter may be causing more trouble than the problem itself."[168]

Mansfield argues that the building's needs are so great—a new library, modern labs and science rooms, a better gym—and the downtown demographics declining so steadily, that the school is not worth modernizing, especially with the vocational school board pressing for the classrooms and land.

Albert McGinnis casts the lone vote against closing, precisely to protest that pressure; he says the vocational school doesn't understand how the new eleven-county vocational school system will soon make this site obsolete for it as well, even with its proposed high-rise classroom building. "I don't think the vocational system has examined its long-range needs enough," he says.

Other members are more concerned about how the decision will affect students. "I hope the students now there will continue," superintendent Robert Gilberts tells the board, "but we expect there will be a decline in enrollment." Since the board has vowed to keep Central functioning at its full academic level, he says, "We will have to make a greater investment to assure continuance of the programs" and waive the policies on minimum class size. Those tenth graders who choose not to start at Central in the fall will go to East High or the new James Madison Memorial High.

Ald. James Pfefferle, Third Ward, a candidate for the school board in the spring election, says the decision "was railroaded through," but won't say by whom. Noting that twenty-one aldermen had called on the school board to hold off on closing Central, Pfefferle warns of "drastic cuts" in future school board budgets, which remain under the city council's control.[169]

But voters apparently endorse the school board's action. Pfefferle and Dr. Paul Candlin each campaign vigorously against UW baseball coach Mansfield and his fellow veteran incumbent, Security State Bank president Ray Sennett, over the decision but don't even come close to carrying a precinct in Central High's attendance area in the April election; voters reelect Sennett for his seventh three-year term and Mansfield for his fourth, both by almost two-to-one. The same day, voters approve a $750,000 bond issue for a new vocational school building by better than three-to-one.[170]

The vocational school's effort to achieve community college status—and outgrow its downtown facility—is further advanced when UW announces in mid-September it will accept at full value credits from its academic programs.[171]

Schools Days

February 7—The same day the school board votes to close Central, it further angers the council by rejecting a special $2,000 appropriation the board had asked for to provide bus service for South Madison children attending Franklin Elementary School. The board objected to the council's requiring it to provide service to children beyond third grade as a condition for getting the money. Area alderman Babe Rohr also makes an impassioned plea for the board to provide a hot lunch program at Franklin, but a motion to do so is ruled out of order.[172]

March 3—The Lapham School principal resigns hours after being acquitted on charges of indecent behavior with a ten-year-old boy.[173]

March 7—Superintendent Gilberts grudgingly agrees to stop requesting photos of job applicants, shortly after state industrial commissioner Carl Lauri and Attorney General Bronson La Follette say doing so is discriminatory and would tend to discourage non-white applicants. The school system has nine black staff members and several interns. Gilberts says administrators never discriminated against applicants, and that photos were "a valuable clue" to help officials remember the thousand teacher applicants they interview each year for the three hundred or so openings. "The loss of pictures will create a handicap for both applicants and us," Gilberts says. "But the use of pictures is apparently not acceptable," he says, "so we shall comply with the ruling."[174]

July 11—The school board again names a new elementary school after its incumbent president—this time, Dr. Ray W. Huegel, namesake for the innovative round school on the far west side. Huegel, a dentist, has been on the board since 1934 and its president since the death last July of the first such honoree, Glenn W. Stephens. And the board names the two new elementary schools after the late President Kennedy (far east) and naturalist John Muir (far west), one year after declining to name the new far west high school in either's honor.[175]

October 13—The council unanimously approves Mayor Festge's appointment of former *Capital Times* reporter Herbert Marcus, now a publicist for the CUNA Mutual Insurance Society, to succeed attorney Richard Cates on the school board. Cates, whom Festge had appointed to succeed the late Glenn W. Stephens in 1965, unexpectedly resigned due to the press of legal work.[176]

October 16—Two juvenile boys using illegal slingshots break fourteen Lapham School windows. After a warning from police, the offending east side store owner where the slingshots were purchased removes the forbidden items from his counter.[177]

November 8—Voters approve a $26.5 million bond issue to fund a building program to accommodate the six thousand new pupils expected to enter the school system over the next five years, including the new far east side high school, twelve new elementary schools, five new junior highs, and numerous additions. The 2–1 margin is down substantially from the 3–1 margin for the 1962 referendum.[178]

December 5—The new James Madison Memorial High School gets an early holiday gift—board approval of plans for a $500,000 football stadium, including concrete bleachers for forty-eight hundred and a heated press box with room for thirty persons and two television cameras.[179]

Dollars and Census

Due to a salary schedule that is $400–$500 below that of other Midwestern school systems, and competition from such popular federal programs as Project Head Start and VISTA, Madison still has a handful of teacher vacancies as the new school year starts, and only about fifty substitutes on call; it usually has five times as many subs. "We knew about the salary problems," district teacher recruiter John Reynoldson says, "but we never anticipated the federal programs would cut into the marketplace as much as they have." Despite the low pay, Madison has the highest school tax rate of any major city in Wisconsin; while the portion of the tax bill for city, county, and sewer has decresed steadily since 1961, the tax levy for the schools has increased by an even larger margin. And there's no immediate relief in sight; next year's school budget calls for an additional 197 teachers and staff to handle fifteen hundred new pupils. But the pressure will likely recede in a few years—new census data shows the smallest increase of school-age population since 1949 and an actual decline in the preschool population.[180]

Planning and Development

GENERAL STATISTICS
- Population: 164,700[181]
- Area: 45.33 square miles (end-of-year total)[182]

Business Wire

January 13—The council completes the most staff-intensive task the city has undertaken in the last twenty years when it unanimously adopts a comprehensive new zoning ordinance; it becomes effective with the adoption of the new zoning map in late June.[183]

February 8—Oscar Mayer and Company names P. Goff Beach Jr. the fourth president in its fifty-three-year history, and the first outside the Mayer family. He succeeds the founder's grandson, Oscar G. Mayer Jr., who succeeds his late father as chairman of the board.[184]

February 25—The council votes unanimously to vacate a block and a half of South Baldwin Street, from East Washington Avenue to the railroad tracks, to allow the Gisholt Corporation to plan a ten-year, $10 million expansion program. Gisholt executives, who had earlier hinted that the company might leave Madison if the request were denied, say they will add 600 employees to the current workforce of 1,558 (making the annual payroll $11 million). "If we wish to attract new industry," Mayor Otto Festge says in urging approval, "we must ensure that industry here now is happy with our city." Baldwin Street is closed in late October, with fencing and gates, in anticipation of construction starting in early 1967.[185]

June 6—Henry Turville, whose family has owned the wooded sixty-five-acre Turville Point on the southwest shore of Lake Monona since 1854, proposes a multimillion-dollar development there with three ten-story apartment buildings, townhouses, a luxury hotel, and a twenty-thousand-square-foot shopping center. The plan, drawn by Professor Leo Jakobson, chair of the university's Department of Urban Planning, would leave about thirty-five acres for public parkland. But the city, which has been eying this property—the largest undeveloped lakeshore land in Madison—since 1938, wants it all; in September, the council votes 21–1 for immediate acquisition, using condemnation if necessary. With the land appraised at $650,000, a $391,000 federal "open spaces" grant in late December gets the parties close, but negotiations remain unconsummated as the year ends.[186]

Summer—There's a substantial drop in new housing compared to 1965, probably due to the high (6.5%) interest rate. From May to August, the building department issues permits for 175 housing units, down from 423 the same time last year. But thanks to the 106 units in the Monona Shores Apartments on the South Beltline, 148 permits are issued in September, up from 91 a year prior. A survey conducted for the Madison Housing Authority finds the city's median rent the highest among large Wisconsin cities, and a vacancy rate of 7.1 percent—several points higher than is healthy.[187]

August 24—Park Plaza, on the 2300 block of South Park Street, has its grand opening. The three-hundred-thousand-square-foot center, featuring a Kroger supermarket, Rennebohm Rexall drug store, and Ben Franklin variety store, was developed by a doctor's group from Chicago.[188]

September 14—More than six years after it was proposed, Cherokee Park, the largest single real estate development in the city's history at 942 acres, opens with the sale of the first 27 of its 605 lots. Years of contentious dispute between the city and developer John Fox ended last year when the city purchased 260 acres of Cherokee Marsh for conservancy, supplemented by deed restrictions and later state purchases.[189]

September 15—City forester George Behrnd reports that close to six hundred trees are afflicted with Dutch elm disease, the most in the city's history, with the worst-hit areas around Camp Randall and Olbrich Park.[190]

October 17—The six-story, fifty-six-hundred-square foot Emporium department store at the corner of East Mifflin and North Pinckney Streets celebrates its grand opening as the largest retail store built on the Square in the past fifty years. Among its mechanical innovations—the first automatic sliding doors in Madison, and high-speed self-service elevators.[191]

Library News

Six decades after it opened, and a year after it closed, the Madison Free Library is razed on June 28 to allow expansion of the parking ramp across from the vocational school. Funded by Scottish industrialist Andrew Carnegie and designed by the Philadelphia architect Frank Miles Day, the Elizabethan Gothic structure featured Bedford limestone, handsome wainscoting with quarter-sawn oak, and a basement auditorium for 350. It opened

February 23, 1906, and has been vacant since the new Central Library opened at 202 W. Mifflin St. last June. As the city is tearing down the historic main library, it's opening two new branches in peripheral shopping centers. On March 4, the Lakeview branch of the Madison Public Library opens in Sherman Plaza, the day after about ten thousand residents attend its open house. On November 20, the Silas U. Pinney Library, named for the mayoral father of the Madison library system, opens in the C and P Plaza on Cottage Grove Road—an area not yet in the city during Pinney's administration (1874–1876).[192]

Atwood Area Struggles

It was in 1892 that Frederick and Wilhelmine Schenk opened their general store at the juncture of two historic American Indian trails now known as Atwood Avenue and Winnebago Street. Five decades later, the Schenk's Corners neighborhood had become Madison's first major commercial node east of Capitol Square. At its height in the postwar years, it had all the trappings of a small downtown—library, movie theater, fire station, restaurants, drug store, two banks, funeral parlor, flower shop, post office, radio station, and even a weekly newspaper, the *East Side News*, published for thirty-seven years by anti–Monona Terrace activist Marshall Browne. But then shopping centers with plenty of parking opened on East Washington Avenue (1953), Cottage Grove Road (1962), and First Street (1963), and neighborhood retail died.[193]

By the spring of 1966, the vicious circle of disinvestment, decline, and decay has left fifteen vacant storefronts on the nine-block stretch from Winnebago Street to Fair Oaks Avenue. In fall, city consultants craft what they hope is a solution—a supermarket and shopping center in the triangle bounded by Winnebago, Atwood, and the Milwaukee Road railroad tracks. To make the area more pedestrian-friendly and allow for the return of needed on-street parking, the planners also propose a new road along the railroad right-of-way from First Street to Division Street, to divert outbound traffic headed for Monona Village and the far southeast.[194]

But as the Plan Commission begins its review of the proposals, city planners aren't overly optimistic; as a 1964 analysis concluded, "There is no one way to miraculously overturn the trends of declining business and increased competition that have been at work for the last ten or more years."[195]

Highways and Transportation

Transportation Milestones

April 28—After complaints of motorcycles and motor scooters doubling up in metered parking spaces, the council unanimously bans their daytime parking on State Street and parts of University Avenue. The council reverses itself somewhat in August, allowing a limited number of motorcycle-only spaces. And as increased traffic on State Street leads to increased midblock accidents—fifty-nine in under eight months—city officials propose prohibiting all parking during morning and afternoon rush hours. But when State Street merchants warn that will turn the street into a blighted area like Atwood Avenue, the council in late August refers the issue to next March.[196]

July 1—A summer of vandalism besets the Monona Causeway, including destruction of $3,000 worth of sensitive gauges used to measure when fill is compacted enough for further construction. In the construction area near downtown, swimmers and boaters have also broken down some of the diking material used to prevent erosion of the road that's already there. The city posts a notice: "Please don't knock this dyke down because literally you could be instrumental in washing away part of the causeway." The highway long touted as the vital link between downtown and the southwest is already a year behind schedule and a million dollars over budget.[197]

September 6—The private Madison Bus Company starts its fourth express bus route, to the southeast and Monona Village, providing service from Tompkins and Monona Drives to the Square in twenty minutes. Madison opened the year with one of the country's most successful private bus companies. In 1964 and 1965, bus systems in other cities with populations ranging from 100,000 to 250,000 lost about 8 percent in revenue; the Madison Bus Company gained more than 6 percent. The company operates sixty buses, thirty-four of them the large forty-five-passenger model, part of the company's $635,000 investment since 1960. Madison's twenty-cent fare is lower than in fifty of the seventy-eight cities in Madison's population range, and higher than only twenty-two. The company's president, William Straub, credits city officials for the successful public/private partnership: "When I tell bus operators in other cities of the cooperation we get," he says, "they find it hard to believe."[198]

November 4—Six years after the $15 million University Avenue expressway was proposed, city crews under traffic planner Warren Somerfeld race to open its first element, the curve connecting inbound University Avenue with West Johnson Street, the day before the homecoming game. They make it, only a few hours later than planned, and Johnson Street becomes four lanes eastbound.[199]

November 18—The full $2.3 million first phase of the University Avenue expressway opens, four lanes one-way westbound from Broom Street to Breese Terrace, with an eastbound bus lane on the south side of the street. Mayor Festge calls the wrong-way bus lane, separated by a low cement divider, an experiment that "may prove useful elsewhere if successful here." All does not go entirely smoothly at first; motorists illegally use the bus lane, and the lack of traffic lights makes it hard for pedestrians to cross. City traffic engineers hope the installation of lights on Johnson Street at Randall Avenue and Mills Street in mid-December will solve pedestrians' problems.[200]

December 13—The new $2.36 million Madison Municipal Airport terminal opens as a crowd of five hundred watches Mayor Otto Festge, acting ground control, call in its first scheduled flight, Northwest Airline Flight 224 from Minneapolis (already safely on the tarmac). Full service begins with the 6:15 a.m. North Central flight to Chicago on December 15. The terminal is a mile and a half closer to downtown than the existing terminal on Highway 51, and eight times as large, with a five-hundred-car parking lot out front. It offers the latest in automatic baggage delivery, as well as a Hoffman House cocktail lounge and restaurant.[201]

December 14—The Wisconsin division of the American Automobile Association (AAA) proposes a controlled-access freeway through downtown to provide nonstop travel from Verona Road to Aberg Avenue and I-94 on the far east side. The freeway would follow the Illinois Central right-of-way, down the Regent Street/College Court corridor, to North Shore Drive, up to Pennsylvania Avenue, Packers Avenue, and the East Side Connector. "Freeways enhance property values," AAA traffic engineer William Marvin maintains.[202]

Miscellanea

Winkie and Ruth Ellen

Three-year-old Ruth Ellen Freedman was spending the summer in Madison because her father, Ralph, an English professor at Princeton University, was about to start a guest lectureship at UW. On June 28, around 4:30 p.m., she's at the Vilas Zoo with her mother, brother, and some other children. They all want to see the famous elephant Winkie, brought here by the pennies and nickels of children in 1950. The mothers warn the children to stay back, but several crawl through a ten-inch opening under a cyclone fence to approach the cage itself. Erected in 1926 as temporary quarters, the cage has bars that are ten inches apart. Ruth Ellen goes with them, unknowingly teasing Winkie by stretching out her hand with popcorn, then bringing it back. Suddenly, the 7,500-pound pachyderm grabs the girl's wrist with her trunk and pulls her through the bars, flinging her down like a doll and stomping on her as everyone screams. Keeper Melvin Bollig comes running as the elephant trumpets, but it's too late. Two days later, the zoo begins blocking the opening.

Friends and neighbors spontaneously send $75 to the Freedmans, which they donate to the Madison Public Library in Ruth Ellen's memory, to purchase preschool picture books for the Main Library Children's Room; a special bookplate will mark each volume indicating the gift. In fall, the zoo trades Winkie and $3,500 to a breeding farm in Woodland, Washington, for a 420-pound, ten-month-old elephant, whom they call Winkie Two. Winkie is later moved to the Portland Zoo, where she resides until 1977, when she is moved to the Wildlife Safari in Winston, Oregon, where she dies in 1982 at age thirty-five.[203]

City Council Ethics

Declaring its "confidence in the competence, integrity and ethical conduct" of current city officials and employees, but mindful that "their conduct in both their official and private affairs should be above reproach," the council unanimously adopts its first-ever ethics code on September 8, establishing guidelines for avoiding "actions that are incompatible with the best interests of the city." The ordinance, based on a model code from the International City Managers Association and the product of four years of sporadic consideration, addresses conflicts of interest, civil service appointments, political activity, campaign contributions, and more. The code does not establish specific penalties but suggests that suspension, removal from office, "or other disciplinary action" may be taken, depending on the circumstances. The ordinance establishes a seven-member Ethics Board to administer the ordinance, which drafters acknowledge leaves much to future interpretation. Ultimately, says Ald. Thomas Consigny, First Ward, "It's a matter of your own judgment."

This council action follows the revelation in January that attorney and UW regent Maurice Pasch had quietly given Ald. Andrew S. Herfel a $50 campaign contribution in 1963 right after Herfel supported Pasch's client on a liquor license application. At the strong urging of then-mayor Henry Reynolds, Herfel returned the check by registered mail, and the matter has only now become public three years later. When district attorney Michael Torphy declined to prosecute, the council renewed its efforts, now successful, to establish a code.[204]

In Memoriam

Daniel P. Parkinson Jr., thirty-three, 1208 Vilas Ave., becomes the first Madison fireman to die in the line of duty since 1947, and the fourth in the city's history, when a falling timber knocks him unconscious and dislodges his oxygen mask as he is fighting a State Street fire on January 8. He dies of smoke inhalation. A Greenbush native, Central High

Mrs. Christine Parkinson, flanked by her daughters Anne and Linda; to her left fire chief Ralph McGraw, Captain Ed Durkin, and other mourners, St. James Church, January 11. COURTESY OF CAPITAL NEWSPAPERS ARCHIVES, PHOTO BY EDWIN STEIN

School graduate, and combat medic during the Korean War, Parkinson was a big, athletic fellow, but so soft-spoken he was nicknamed "Monk." Along with his wife, Christine, Parkinson was a knowledgeable and enthusiastic jazz aficionado; after a 1959 trip to Ripon to see pianist Dave Brubeck, they developed a friendship with his saxophonist, Paul Desmond, and were eagerly awaiting the upcoming Brubeck and John Coltrane concerts. Hundreds of Parkinson's friends and family, and firemen from around the state, fill St. James Church for the funeral on January 11; among the pallbearers is his boyhood friend, restaurant owner Tony Lombardino, who gave Parkinson his nickname. Since survivor benefits from the city end after fewer than eight years, a scholarship fund is established for Daniel P. Parkinson III, age four, and his two sisters, ages seven and five. The council adopts a resolution that when a new central fire station is built, it will be dedicated in Parkinson's memory. Fire chief Ralph McGraw blames faulty wiring for the fire, which does $250,000 in damage and destroys Sergenian's carpets and a hearing aid store at 227–229 State St. For days, thousands of Madisonians drive past the scene of the tragedy, creating traffic jams with their rubbernecking, until cold rain and snow drive them away. There's ice on the sidewalk for weeks afterward.[205]

Ralph A. Hult, seventy-five, who only last December turned his long-standing Chevrolet dealership over to Clarence Thorstad, dies unexpectedly on February 20, ten days after his birthday. Hult's father started selling Chevrolets in 1915, three years before General Motors acquired the line, making the franchise at 608 E. Washington Ave. one of the oldest in the nation.[206]

Monona Causeway under construction, July 1967. COURTESY OF CAPITAL NEWSPAPERS ARCHIVES, PHOTO BY JOHN NEWHOUSE

1967

Protest

Getting the Dow Chemical Company to stop making the incendiary gel Napalm B for use in Vietnam has been a Students for a Democratic Society (SDS) priority ever since the Michigan chapter launched the protest campaign against the Michigan-based company in August 1966. Two Madison protests against Dow this year have profound and lasting impacts on Madison and the university.[1]

Dow 1—The Skirmish, February 21–22

A two-day Madison SDS action against campus recruiting by Dow in February makes history and creates the conditions for the pivotal political event of the decade, the Battle of Dow on October 18.[2]

On Tuesday morning, February 21, about 150 students meet at Lincoln Terrace; SDS president Hank Haslach leads a group of about forty to the Chemistry Building, and SDS vice president Robert Zwicker and Bob Cohen take the rest to the Commerce Building. They've got placards of photos from *Ramparts Magazine* of Vietnamese children with horrifying napalm burns, which they intend to use to confront the students interviewing with Dow about the work of their prospective employer. The publicly announced plan, as proposed by Cohen (who's not an actual SDS member), is to stand inside with signs aloft but not obstruct the interviews. Disrupt some minds, perhaps, but not university operations.[3]

But there's some confusion, and a bit of university misinformation, over whether their signs are allowed inside the buildings. Sergeant Brown of UW Protection and Security confronts Haslach, claiming the signs are dangerous; the men have a verbal confrontation that escalates until Brown puts Haslach up against the wall and under arrest for disorderly conduct. At about the same time, the same thing is happening at Commerce—Cohen is also arrested and forcibly removed. The first political protesters arrested on campus, Haslach and Cohen, are quickly released on bail, while the picketing and leafleting in each building continues.

In Commerce, police try to arrest Zwicker when he won't put down his placard but back off when he drops to the floor and is covered by a handful of other protesters. They all get up and continue picketing, with placards, Zwicker participating, until early afternoon, when they regroup and decide to hold an obstructive sit-in the next day. University Community Action representative John Coatsworth considers the week's events counterproductive for the antiwar movement and tries to arrange a forum featuring all parties, but the Dow recruiters decline.[4]

Wednesday, February 22, will be Madison's most momentous Washington's birthday since the first City Hall opened on the holiday in 1858, with the first mass arrests on campus and a tense occupation of administrative offices—with administrators inside.[5]

The day starts with protesters marching to the Engineering Building, where UW police chief Ralph Hanson falsely claims that the Dow recruiters have left; the protesters march back up to Bascom Hall, where they sit in at several administrators' offices, including that of President Fred Harvey Harrington (who's not there). After almost an hour, about twenty members of the Committee for Direct Action (CDA) slip out of Bascom and head back to Engineering, where they force their way past Engineering professor James Marks and noisily occupy various offices and hallways. Although they don't actually prevent any Dow interviews, they are certainly disrupting normal office operations. Professor Marks—the liberal former west side alderman who's in charge of the building—calls for the campus police. At about 4:45 p.m., they arrest eleven protesters for sitting in—including Zwicker, Bourtai Scudder, and Lea Zeldin—and six more who throw themselves under squad cars in a futile attempt to foil the arrests.[6]

When word of the arrests gets back to Bascom Hall, the sit-in becomes a blockade, as about 350 protesters block the hallways while Cohen and others engage Harrington, Chancellor Robben Fleming, and Dean Joseph Kauffman in the dean's office for close to three hours. The group demands that charges against the seventeen be dropped and that Dow and the CIA be banned from campus before they'll let the two men leave; Fleming rejects all demands and warns that anyone who prevents him from leaving will face assault charges. None of the administrators feel as if they're held captive; they are choosing to stay and talk. But it's hot and smoky and increasingly tense as they go back and forth over the competing moral imperatives of peace, free speech, public responsibility, and individual choice, until someone accuses Fleming of "duplicity," and he walks out. The group agrees to take a break at 7:45 p.m. and meet again in the building's auditorium in about an hour.[7]

When they all get back together Fleming announces that in the interval he's written a personal check for $1,155 for bail for eleven of the arrestees; to Haslach's disgust, the six hundred student protesters erupt in cheers. The seventeen defendants, all represented by attorneys Percy Julian Jr. and Edward Ben Elson, all plead innocent and are set for trial. Fleming later tells Harrington he never got the bail money back.[8]

Thursday morning, antiwar protesters open a new front with the unveiling of the Wisconsin Draft Resistance Union (WDRU) through publication in the *Daily Cardinal* of a full-page "We won't go" ad. Haslach, Zwicker, Coatsworth, Stu Ewen, Jim Rowen, and

Anti-Dow protesters occupy the office of university president Fred Harvey Harrington and block Bascom Hall hallways on February 22. UNIVERSITY OF WISCONSIN–MADISON ARCHIVES IMAGES S17026 AND S00130

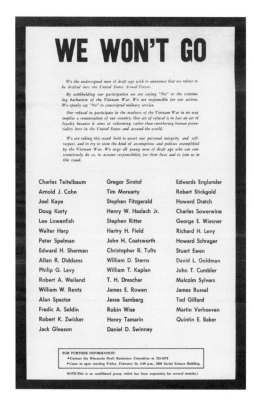

WE WON'T GO

We the undersigned men of draft age wish to announce that we refuse to be drafted into the United States Armed Forces.

By withholding our participation we are saying "No" to the continuing barbarism of the Vietnam War. We are responsible for our actions. We openly say "No" to conscripted military service.

Our refusal to participate in the madness of the Vietnam War in no way implies a renunciation of our country. Our act of refusal is in fact an act of loyalty because it aims at redeeming rather than smothering human potentiality here in the United States and around the world.

We are taking this stand both to assert our personal integrity and self-respect, and to try to stem the kind of assumptions and policies exemplified by the Vietnam War. We urge all young men of draft age who can conscientiously do so, to assume responsibility for their lives and to join us in this stand.

Charles Teitelbaum	Gregor Sirotof	Edwards Englander
Arnold J. Cohn	Tim Morearty	Robert Stickgold
Joel Kaye	Stephen Fitzgerald	Howard Dratch
Doug Korty	Henry W. Haslach Jr.	Charles Sowerwine
Lee Lowenfish	Stephen Ritter	George E. Wiesner
Walter Harp	Hartry H. Field	Richard H. Levy
Peter Spelman	John H. Coatsworth	Howard Schrager
Edward H. Sherman	Christopher R. Tufts	Stuart Ewen
Allan R. Diddams	William D. Sterns	David L. Goldman
Philip G. Levy	William T. Kaplan	John T. Cumbler
Robert A. Weiland	T. H. Drescher	Malcolm Sylvers
William W. Rentz	James E. Rowen	James Russel
Alan Spector	Jesse Samberg	Tod Gilford
Fredic A. Seldin	Robin Wise	Martin Verhoeven
Robert K. Zwicker	Henry Tamarin	Quintin E. Baker
Jack Gleason	Daniel D. Swinney	

FOR FURTHER INFORMATION:
• Contact the Wisconsin Draft Resistance Committee at 255-6575
• Come to open meeting Friday, February 24, 4:00 p.m., 2206 Social Science Building.

NOTE: This is an unaffiliated group which has been organizing for several months.

The public start of the Wisconsin Draft Resistance Union, February 23, 1967.
UNIVERSITY OF WISCONSIN–MADISON ARCHIVES IMAGE S00110

John Cumbler are among the forty-seven signatories who declare their refusal to be conscripted, and call on others to do likewise. It's a legally and academically risky thing to do and becomes a mark of distinction for those on the list. In one of the first signs of feminism in the predominantly sexist antiwar movement, another "We won't go" ad in May will include about fifty women, including Rowen's wife, Susan McGovern, daughter of dove Senator George McGovern.[9]

Later that morning, a group of about sixty conducts a peaceful, nonobstructive sit-in for several hours near the Dow interview room in Agriculture Hall. But the powers that be focus on the disruption instead.

That afternoon, 833 faculty vote overwhelmingly to adopt a resolution reaffirming the "Kennedy" rule 11.02—that students can protest and petition only "by lawful means which do not disrupt the operations" of university facilities. Fleming warns before the vote that "if we reach a showdown, the restoration of order cannot be accomplished without the importation of a substantial outside force," but he says he doubts "very much" that he will ever have to ask the governor to send the National Guard.[10]

That night, the city council unanimously adopts a resolution calling the demonstrations "irresponsible and reprehensible" and calling for UW officials to take "stringent measures" against the demonstrators. The council also wants an investigation into whether the divorced Scudder, thirty-five, and widowed Zeldin, thirty-seven, are receiving public assistance from Dane County for their families. "If some of the demonstrators learned the facts about these female pied pipers," says west side alderman William Bradford Smith, "they wouldn't be so eager to follow them."[11]

Friday morning, February 24, an "appalled" *Daily Cardinal* attacks the SDS for "denying student rights and freedoms" and engaging in "gross language and incoherent, emotional babbling. The protesters have defeated their cause by their action."[12] A little later, Governor Warren Knowles says the action was "far beyond the area of reasonable conduct" and calls on the university to "lay down some strict disciplinary rules" and enforce them.[13]

That afternoon, a group of about eight hundred protests the protesters through subzero weather at a Bascom Hill rally called by the newly formed "We Want No Berkeley Here" committee, organized out of the Kronshage dorm. Then they pack the Bascom Hall auditorium, by invitation, giving Fleming another standing ovation: "This is the first time I haven't felt lonely in a crowd in days," he says to cheers and applause. "No minority can dictate its views to the university," he declares.[14]

Sunday morning, about twenty CDA members led by Cumbler, and including Scudder and Zeldin, attend morning worship at the First Congregational Church, standing quietly against the walls bearing antiwar signs throughout the sermon, part of a

recurring CDA action. About 250 parishioners remain afterward for an hourlong discussion with them.[15]

The political backlash that began with the obstruction of Ted Kennedy grows, with the cochairmen of the legislature's budget-writing Joint Finance Committee explicitly threatening to cut the university's budget over the episode. "Let's be honest," says Senator Walter Hollandale (R-Rosendale). "If you feel unkindly toward them, they won't get as much money." And the criticism continues to spread as the State Assembly votes, 82–15, to demand that the university explain how it's maintaining "a responsible intellectual and social climate" following "offensive" articles in the *Daily Cardinal*.[16]

On March 2, the WSA Senate votes, 19–11, to ban SDS from campus until at least next fall; Senator Paul Soglin, part of the Bascom Hall hallway occupation on February 22, argues against the suspension, which Assembly Speaker Harold Froelich applauds in a telegram to President Harrington attacking the administration. "Your telegram astounds me," Harrington replies, calling the powerful legislator "totally in error" in his criticism. The proposed ban, which Haslach calls "childish" and the Student Court quickly overturns, greatly enhances SDS's popularity and expands its "membership" to about three hundred overnight.[17]

On March 6, Fleming issues Faculty Document 122, detailing that he will continue to use whatever force is necessary to ensure compliance with rule 11.02: "Given the traditions of this campus, it is fair to assume that the faculty wants to preserve dissent, but without anarchy, and that it wants order, but without oppression."[18]

At a special meeting two days later, the faculty rejects, 249–62, a motion by Sociology professor Maurice Zeitlin to ban job interviews by "corporations involved in producing war materials," and adopts the Report of the Committee on Placement Services allowing "any bona fide employer" to recruit on campus. Among those voting for the ban is the Vilas professor of sociology, William Sewell.[19]

The regents commend the administration "for its courageous, reasoned and far-seeing actions, [exemplifying] 'sifting and winnowing' in the search for truth."[20]

Cohen and Zwicker are convicted in late September and sentenced to short jail terms, which attorney Percy Julian appeals, as he does the charges against Haslach.[21]

In Midland, Michigan, Dow executives make plans for their return to campus in mid-October. Protesters do, too.

Protest Dateline

February 14—*Ramparts Magazine*, whose editor, Robert Scheer, spoke on campus the previous week, publishes an explosive expose of the CIA's long-term secret funding of the National Student Association (NSA). The CIA's role in this effort to enlist American college students in the crusade against communism had been known only to the NSA's highest officers, including former WSA and NSA president Ed Garvey.[22]

March 21—A WSA referendum shows students reject extreme positions for or against the war in Vietnam, with the greatest number (2,744) favoring phased, negotiated withdrawal more than any other single policy:

WSA REFERENDUM, MARCH 21

	Yes	No	No Opinion
Favor immediate unilateral withdrawal of all US armed forces?	1,853	4,420	397
Favor application of whatever force necessary to accomplish total military victory?	2,427	6,920	397
Should university stop compiling class rank for draft purposes?	4,989	3,972	1,045
Should the draft be abolished?	3,980	5,260	780[23]

April 11–12—A coalition led by SDS, University Community Action (UCA), and Committee to End the War in Viet Nam (CEWV) conducts an orderly rally and picketing of CIA recruitment interviews at the Law School. About 150 students, mostly young women, sit in without obstructing, while up to eight hundred rally on Bascom Hill. About fifty students interview with the agency, although some, like former SDS leader Marty Tandler—who lists another SDS officer as a reference—are not actually seeking employment.[24]

May 3—Betty Boardman, who defied a State Department ban by sailing with eight other Quakers into Haiphong Harbor in March with $10,000 in medical supplies for North Vietnamese citizens, tells a large Belmont Hotel luncheon of the Dane County Democratic Party that North Vietnam is fighting for its freedom. That night, popular

Dane County undersheriff Vernon "Jack" Leslie and his wife, Jane—whose two sons are both Marines in combat—resign from the county party in protest.[25]

May 16—The WSA Student Senate votes, 16–4, to oppose the compilation of class rankings "for the purpose of cooperating with the Selective Service System." The resolution, from NSA delegate Soglin, "demands that the faculty take immediate and appropriate action."[26]

July 14—A Bastille Day paint-in of the North Park Street skywalk bridge by the Memorial Union results in UW police arresting eight students, including editor Stu Ewen and two staff writers from the state's first underground newspaper, *Connections.*[27]

November 7—Beating back a bid by the American Legion to block their appearance at the Dane County Memorial Coliseum, world-renowned pediatrician Dr. Benjamin Spock presents a lengthy antiwar lecture, leavened by the sharp satire of Harvard mathematician / pianist Tom Lehrer. The crowd of over seven thousand also witnesses the public unveiling of Madison Citizens for a Vote on Vietnam, a new group seeking a spring referendum on the war.[28]

November 13—A University Forum discussion of the CIA among new chancellor William Sewell who has replaced Robben Fleming; professors Anatole Beck, Frank Remington, and Kenneth Dolbeare; a representative of the pro-CIA interview Committee to Defend Individual Rights; and Soglin ends when Soglin declares the discussion a "dialogue of the absurd" and leads a walkout of about five hundred from the Union Theater.[29]

November 17—After Madison SDS and the UW Young Democrats call for obstruction of CIA interviews, scheduled for campus November 27–28, the agency moves the interviews off campus, then postpones them until at least next February.[30]

November 20—With an overwhelming force of police officers and deputies in reserve, and the circuit court order barring obstruction in force, Navy and Marine Corps interviews at Camp Randall Memorial Building are conducted without incident.[31]

December 4—More than one hundred Madison women, mostly students, mark the national antidraft week by marching from the Capitol to Camp Randall for speeches and a flagpole ceremony, and then on to the Dane County draft board, 1619 Monroe St., where they are refused admission.[32]

December 8—Ten days after announcing his candidacy for president, Senator Eugene McCarthy draws an enthusiastic overflow crowd of more than fourteen hundred at the Union Theater in his first campaign appearance for any of the five primaries he's entered. Predicting he'll win the Wisconsin primary next April, McCarthy says starting the state-wide campaign on campus made sense "because it was here on this campus that the first banner was raised." And McCarthy is pleased as he snips the ribbon to open the campaign office at 116 E. Mifflin St. "This is a better headquarters than I have in Washington," he tells office manager Marjorie "Midge" Miller (Wisconsin state representative, 1971–1985), a former assistant dean in the College of Letters and Science, now coordinator of religious activity on campus.[33]

December 22—Sociology professor Zeitlin, chair of the Madison Citizens for a Vote on Vietnam, files 8,410 signatures on petitions for a spring referendum to determine if "it is the policy of the people of the city of Madison that there be an immediate ceasefire and withdrawal of troops from Vietnam, so that the Vietnamese people can determine their own destiny."[34]

Dow 2—The Battle, October 17–18

Dow would have had trouble recruiting on any campus during the national "Stop the Draft" week leading up to the March on the Pentagon on October 21.[35] But on October 16, Dow recruiter William "Curly" Hendershot returns to a Madison especially on edge, due not only to the late-winter arrests during his first visit, but also a spring of costly strikes by construction unions, a summer of racial strife, and now four weeks of a disruptive strike by Teamster bus drivers.

And Hendershot comes back to a campus under new management: Chancellor William Sewell, a surprise pick after predecessor Robben Fleming accepts the presidency of the University of Michigan.[36]

The return engagement ends with a more radicalized student body, a more hard-line university administration, a more hostile state government, a more concerned and divided local community, and a more aggressive police force.[37]

Anti-Dow activists—from SDS, CEWV, UCA, Concerned Black People, and other groups—start planning for Dow 2 as soon as the *Daily Cardinal* publishes the fall's interview schedule in late August. To accommodate all the groups—and shield them all from university discipline—they create the Ad Hoc Committee to Protest Dow Chemical, which holds a protracted series of public meetings to devise a unified strategy. Bob Cohen, freshly shaved by Dane County deputy sheriffs while briefly jailed for his Dow 1 conviction (now on appeal), and Evan Stark push for an obstructive sit-in, to prevent the job interviews from taking place; Coatsworth and others argue the CIA (set to return in November) is a more appropriate target for a disruption, and the Dow action should be a purely educational picket.

By early October, the more radical faction has prevailed, and the Ad Hoc Committee has endorsed the idea of a disruptive occupation, something explicitly forbidden by the "Kennedy" rule 11.02 just reinforced by Faculty Document 122.[38] Expanding the national SDS slogan "From protest to resistance," Stark writes a leaflet explaining the action: "Before, we talked. Now we must act. We must stop what we oppose. We will enter the arena of action to make the kind of history we want. We will enter a building in which Dow is recruiting and stop them."[39]

If you do, Dean Kauffman warns at Sewell's direction on October 11, the university "will not hesitate to invoke university discipline, including disciplinary probation, suspension or expulsion whether or not arrests are made." President Harrington assures the anxious regents that "there will be a tightening of controls."[40]

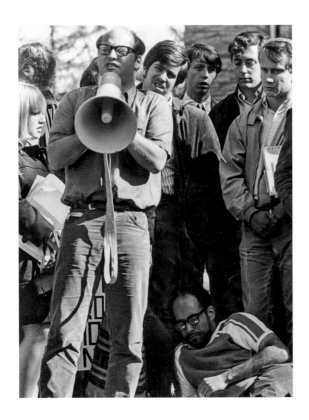

Evan Stark with bullhorn, but without his customary cap; Bob Cohen reclining. Commerce Building plaza, October 17. UNIVERSITY OF WISCONSIN–MADISON ARCHIVES IMAGE S00129

For any student, the threat of expulsion is highly significant; for men in 1967, it's potentially life-threatening. It's also threatening to organizations; the Concerned Black People can't risk having its leaders expelled, and on Friday, October 13, the group withdraws from the demonstration.[41]

What Kauffman saw as fair warning, Soglin sees as prior restraint; he becomes the lead plaintiff in a federal lawsuit movement lawyer Percy L. Julian Jr. files Monday morning to prevent Kauffman and the university from carrying through.[42]

Monday night, a mass meeting of about three hundred—including undercover police—finalizes the two-step plan: an informational picket on Tuesday, October 17, a disruptive sit-in on Wednesday. Everyone planning to sit in knows they could get arrested, and they even expect to; they plan to go limp and be carried off, one by one, just like in the civil rights sit-ins of the early sixties. It will take the cops all day to clear the corridor, they imagine.[43]

They know they could face university discipline, too. But no one even contemplates the thought of being physically beaten. But if that does happen, the response will likely be different than in those earlier actions.

"They were told not to even accidentally strike a policeman," an undercover officer reports to Chief Emery in his account of the meeting of October 16, "but that if they were struck first, they had every right to defend themselves even if it meant decking the policeman attempting to hit them." The spy puts the department on notice, and on edge: "It would not surprise me at all if some of these protesters did take a few swings at policemen."[44]

UW police chief Ralph Hanson also finalizes his plans, including that there will be "no mass arrests." Hanson figures that arresting a handful of protesters will cause the remainder to dissipate.[45]

"Everyone is waiting with great expectations for the coming clash," the *Daily Cardinal* editorializes Tuesday morning, October 17.[46]

It doesn't come Tuesday afternoon, which proceeds as planned—a peaceful informational picket and rally by about four hundred outside the Commerce Building, and another dozen or so inside. There's confrontation but not disruption.[47]

That night, there's an unplanned but entirely natural convergence of culture and politics, as *Quixote* literary magazine brings back the San Francisco Mime Troupe for another night of political commedia dell'arte—with pointed localized references—in the Union Theater.[48]

"This is your school, and if you don't like it, you should try and change it," director Ron Davis tells the capacity crowd after the curtain call. "And if you can't change it, then you should destroy it. See you at the demonstration."[49]

Early Wednesday morning, Hanson briefs the twenty off-duty Madison police officers he's hired, directing them to remove the bullets from their guns and not carry riot sticks. He assures them they're "not facing a hostile group. The kids are too sophisticated for this sort of thing." He also distributes a statement of policies and procedures, including the mandate that police "exercise patience, tolerance and restraint." He also directs that if someone resists being taken into custody after an arrest, to abandon the effort and issue a warrant later.[50]

About three hundred protesters meet at 10:30 a.m. at the base of Bascom Hill; it's the same number as met on the Union steps exactly four years earlier for the first antiwar protest, but this group has a mindset that would have been unfathomable on October 18, 1963.

The Mime Troupe is there for spectacle and moral support (except for actor Peter Coyote, who "overslept after a bawdy night with an undergraduate Valkyrie"); with tambourines and trumpets, they march up the hill, heading for the Commerce Building just past Bascom Hall.[51]

The first forty protesters enter Commerce at 10:48 a.m. and surround the four officers stationed by the interview room, 104; they sit down, and the narrow hallway, about fifty yards long, is soon filled with another two hundred or so who sit and block the corridor. Dozens more stand by in support. Among those briefly pinned against the walls before he gets out is assistant director for student organizations Joel Skornicka (mayor of Madison 1979–1983).[52]

Soon it's so packed you can't raise your arm to check a wristwatch. The crowd chants and sings, raucous noise bouncing off the tile and glass, a cacophony of protest.

A young woman tries to get through for an interview; protesters physically stop her. Others try and are also repulsed. Hanson calls Kauffman to tell him the crowd is "willfully" and "purposefully" obstructing the interviews by blocking the corridor, violating rule 11.02.

On the plaza, pickets, speeches, and more spectacle from the Mime Troupe attract a crowd of more than a thousand. Veteran civil rights and peace activist Vicki Gabriner, wife of activist and *Connections* cofounder/editor Bob Gabriner, snakes through the crowd in whiteface and leggings. In sarcastic tribute to the regents' idealistic statement of academic freedom from 1894, she bears a sign proclaiming herself "Miss Sifting and Winnowing."

At 11:15 a.m., Chief Hanson tells three linked-arm protesters blocking the door to room 102 they're under arrest; but when his officers attempt to take one into custody, the crowd grabs the protester and holds on until Hanson halts the arrest, pursuant to his guideline.

The university had believed the obstructers would accept arrest. Though almost all in the hallway planned to submit if arrested, administrators and officers now see that not all will. Later, it will become an accepted belief among university administrators that the violence about to come was perpetrated by a small clique who willfully planned and tried to precipitate it.[53]

Hanson tries to leave but can't; Cohen tells him to jump out the window. Hanson telephones Sewell and gets his okay to call Madison police chief Wilbur Emery for his promised support. Emery sends officers from the traffic bureau, most of them native Madisonians simmering with class and political resentment. Emery reportedly tells them not to swing their riot sticks, and to keep both hands on the stick when using it.

Hanson finally makes his way out of the building and back to Bascom where he, Sewell, and the others agree that police should not attempt to empty the entire corridor, but only clear a path to room 102 to relieve people trapped there.

At about noon, Emery and the Madison officers start arriving at the parking lot behind Bascom, adjacent to Commerce, drawing more students to the plaza. The sight of police with helmets and riot sticks jolts the crowd inside, long before police are ready to move; women remove their jewelry, men move closer to the doorway to beef up the front.

At 1 p.m., Hanson goes back into Commerce with only four unarmed university police, to declare the gathering an unlawful assembly and demand that the crowd disperse or be arrested. Jeered and defied, then and again, Hanson makes a bold move and asks the students if they would leave if the Dow recruiter did, too.

Some respond encouragingly, some are skeptical. Hanson agrees to withdraw his men while a four-man delegation, including Stark, Ewen, and Carlos Jolly, meet with Sewell and Kauffman. The thought of a negotiated victory electrifies the crowd.[54]

But it's not to be. Sewell can't possibly accept Stark's offer, which would involve Sewell signing a statement directing Dow to leave and not return, in order for the four-man delegation to recommend, but not guarantee, that the sit-in end.[55]

Sociologist Sewell, who's had sociology research assistant Stark in seminars, considers him "the master strategist of the whole thing [but] essentially unprincipled." Stark thinks Sewell is immobilized, "frozen still . . . just staring at the wall."[56]

Sewell gives his matter-of-fact assessment about imminent arrest: "You guys better get out of that building," he says, "because people are going to come in and get you out if you don't."[57]

About 1:30 p.m., Hanson returns to Commerce one last time alone, to announce it's an unlawful assembly and deliver the warning, "We are going to clear the place out." But he's got a cold, and although he uses a bullhorn, there's so much crowd noise that only the front rows can hear him. Those who do link arms, and some wrap their belts around their fists; someone shouts that women should kick officers "in the balls."[58]

Hanson crosses to the Carillon Tower, where the riot squad is restless; the Madison officers have removed their badges, either for security or to conceal their identities. Hanson fails to tell them that the intent is merely to make a path to room 102, not to clear the entire corridor. Hanson and his four men, all without helmets and riot sticks, followed by thirty Madison officers with both, march back in to Commerce. Less than three minutes have elapsed since his last warning—not nearly enough time for protesters to leave, even if so inclined (which very few are).[59]

Protesters prepare as police enter the Commerce Building, October 18. At far left, Jonathan Stielstra; at right, with sheepskin coat, Paul Soglin. UNIVERSITY OF WISCONSIN–MADISON ARCHIVES IMAGE

The police make it about twenty-five feet past the doors before they start using their batons to try to dislodge the linked-arm protesters.

Suddenly the police are overwhelmed by the crowd surging forward; although many, probably most, are simply pushed forward by involuntary crowd dynamics, the police interpret the act as a hostile one. Hanson, the only officer who knows the plan is just to make a path to room 102, is knocked out of the building and rendered unable to command during this critical moment.[60]

A policeman falling backward breaks a huge window with his baton, and the loud crash adds to the panic. He keeps swinging his stick to clear the sharp shards out of the window frame, spraying glass; when the protesters see the baton in use, they press forward, pushing police out.[61]

The Madison officers, outnumbered by about ten to one, regroup outside and charge back in. Hanson and Emery are both outside, and neither gives a signal to use batons, but the officers come in swinging, flailing away with the two-foot wooden nightsticks. Untrained in the proper prod-and-poke method, they use their batons as clubs, engaging in indiscriminate overhead swinging; they club protesters still sitting on the ground, some trying to leave, some even uninvolved in the protest.[62]

Nightsticks rise and fall with frightening frequency. The thwack of wood on skull sounds like a bouncing basketball, or a watermelon hit by a baseball bat.[63]

Police clubbing protesters in the Commerce Building hallway, about 1:45 p.m., October 18. UNIVERSITY OF WISCONSIN–MADISON ARCHIVES IMAGE

Some students fight back, kicking and spitting. Fear and panic and pain turn to hysteria as chaos engulfs the corridor.[64]

Police aren't even arresting the protesters. "We didn't have enough men for that," Emery later explains.[65] They're just beating them, passing them down the hallway, and throwing them out into the Commerce courtyard, where the growing crowd is stunned by the spectacle and turning into a mob. Police arrest some people in the crowd outside, including Vicki Gabriner.[66]

Police clear the building in about thirteen minutes but haven't yet won the day. Thousands of students fill the plaza, enraged at seeing their classmates beaten bloody. One group surrounds and rocks a paddy wagon until police release several detainees, including Gabriner.

The plaza has become a battleground, kids against cops, far beyond the initial catalysts of napalm and the war. "Seig heil!" cry the angry protesters, striking at officers as bricks and bottles, even concrete pavers, fly. Something, a rock or a shoe, slams squarely into Detective Tom McCarthy's nose, knocking him unconscious with serious facial fractures.[67]

The 1:20 p.m. classes get out at 2:10 p.m.; now there are about five thousand students in the area. At 2:15 p.m., Madison police chief Emery calls for reinforcements from the Dane County Sheriff and orders the use of tear gas. It is the first time tear gas is used to

Arresting Vicki Gabriner, "Miss Sifting and Winnowing." WHI IMAGE ID 123717, PHOTO BY SKIP HEINE

quell an antiwar protest on a college campus. But police aren't trained in its deployment, and it is carried by the wind whipping off Lake Mendota, affecting many who were not part of the protest but are becoming radicalized in the moment.[68]

As the chaos continues, protester Jonathan Stielstra strikes a symbolic blow, mounting the roof of Bascom Hall to cut loose and let fall the American and Wisconsin flags atop it. Photographed in the act, he's eventually caught and sentenced to thirty days.[69]

Governor Warren Knowles offers to send for the National Guard and is quite upset when Sewell refuses to request its mobilization.[70]

The battle rages across the plaza and over the hills for more than an hour, until 150 officers establish a firm perimeter around Commerce. By about 4:30 p.m., it's all over.

Sewell has been watching from his Bascom Hall office—frozen, traumatized, knowing he has all but ruined his reputation and the university's. He thinks the police and students both "went nuts," and that "it was just lucky that somebody wasn't killed."[71]

Confrontation on the Commerce Building plaza, a little after 2:00 p.m.
WHI IMAGE ID 3780

By the time it's over, forty-six students and six nonstudents are treated at University Medical Center, mainly for scalp lacerations. Among those beaten was Soglin. His sheepskin coat protected his head for a while, but with four cops working him over, he received enough blows to his back and legs that he was bloody and dazed. Once he was tossed out into the maelstrom, he was off for stitches on his leg at the emergency room.[72]

Seventeen officers also suffered injuries ranging from black eyes and broken bones to a permanently damaged larynx. More students than police were hurt, but the police were hurt more seriously.[73]

Stark, who slipped out of Commerce as the assault was beginning, visits his wounded troops after the battle. "Afraid and paranoid," he will quit school in mid-November and leave the state. He soon gets a job directing a federally funded community center in Minneapolis, and in 1969 hires Committee for Direct Action mainstay Lea Zeldin.[74]

Mayor Festge later praises the police "for the excellent manner in which all members of the department conducted themselves," which he says "exemplifies the finest traditions of the Madison Police Department."[75]

But the police are embarrassed at the beating they've taken and vow it will never happen again. Emery resolves to take a tougher approach next time, and respond with superior force at the outset. The university takes a similar lesson—that protesters will actively resist arrest, not just go limp.[76]

Still, officers take pride in what they've been through; they call the cops who stormed Commerce "the Dirty 30," and some even wear uniform patches with that moniker.[77]

Sewell suspends further Dow interviews pending a special faculty meeting and announces he'll seek charges against the protest leaders.[78]

Later on the eighteenth, the State Assembly adopts, 94–5, a resolution denouncing the protest as "a flagrant abuse of the treasured traditions of academic freedom" and urging the expulsion of its leaders "whenever necessary." Some legislators propose more extreme action: "We should shoot them if necessary," says Senator Leland McParland (R-Cudahy). "I would. Because it's insurrection." The Senate unanimously establishes a special fact-finding committee.[79]

There's also a backlash on campus, where Dow later announces that at least 150 students—a record—have signed up for a new round of interviews. The university chapter of the conservative Young Americans for Freedom also reaches record membership in 1967.[80]

Even some who oppose the war are incensed at the protesters' attempt to prevent others from exercising their rights. "When the principle that the end justifies the means prevails, freedom is destroyed," *Capital Times* editor Miles McMillin thunders in a front-page editorial. When it's even attempted, he writes, "it results in the kind of violence we all deplore."[81]

Connections fires back that the paper "has been venomous yet confused," reflecting that the progressive image of Madison and the university "is hollow and irrelevant to the crisis which we are confronting."[82]

It is not the last time that Madison liberals and radicals will challenge each other's integrity and strategy.

Wednesday night at 9 p.m., a mass meeting of three thousand students on the Library Mall, facilitated by the Mime Troupe's Ron Davis, votes to strike classes until the faculty bans city police from campus and gives amnesty to the sit-in leaders.[83]

Thursday morning, a Lincoln Terrace rally held by the newly formed Committee for Student Rights (CSR), chaired by Soglin, draws a crowd of about two thousand before setting out picket lines at major buildings on campus. While the picketing is under way, the university announces it has suspended thirteen protest leaders, including Stark and Cohen; seven return for the second semester, and the rest either withdraw or are expelled.[84]

The nascent Teaching Assistants Association supports the strike, and about 160 of the university's 2,000 TAs choose not to hold their classes; among those continuing to teach as usual is English teaching assistant Lynn Cheney (National Endowment for the Humanities chair, 1986–1993), whose husband, Dick (US Representative, R-WY, 1979–1989; US Secretary of Defense, 1989–1993; vice president of the United States, 2001–2009), also continues his work as a political science graduate assistant. In November, the regents defeat by one vote, 5–4, a motion to fire all TAs who failed to perform.[85]

The strike has only modest success, and only in the College of Letters and Science, where the four thousand or so absences are about four times more than usual.[86]

On Thursday afternoon, 1,350 angry, bitter, and confused faculty members hold an emotional six-hour meeting in the Union Theater (with a two-hour dinner break). About an equal number of angry, bitter, and confused students listen to the proceedings piped into several Union rooms and onto the Terrace. A noose hangs over the theater stage, left over from the recent production of *Marat/Sade*.[87]

Sewell—who wants to quit the administrative job he never sought—firmly blames "the tragic events [on] those who unlawfully disrupted the functions of the University and defiantly continued to do so despite repeated warnings and efforts to get them to cease and desist." But he finally reminds the faculty that they're the ones who reaffirmed both strict enforcement of the antidisruption rule and Dow's right to interview—over his opposition. "You don't have the guts to admit I did exactly what you wanted," Sewell says to cheers and a standing ovation. The faculty endorses his action calling in police

Mass meeting Wednesday night, Library Mall. COURTESY OF CAPITAL NEWSPAPERS ARCHIVES "to enforce the mandate of the faculty as expressed" in rule 11.02 and Faculty Document 122, 671–378.[88]

Protesters even lose on the question of police brutality. "We know enough to say there was police brutality and we ought to have enough guts to say it," law school professor Ted Finman declares, but the faculty disagree, voting 562–495 against a resolution condemning the use of "indiscriminate violence" by the police.[89]

Students had been disappointed at the lack of faculty support following the 1966 draft sit-in; now they feel totally betrayed. It wasn't so shocking that police would beat protesters, but that they would do so with the university's apparent blessing is shattering. As the faculty file out of the theater shortly before midnight, about a thousand students stare stonily, some muttering "shame."[90]

By Friday noon, the strike is sputtering. A crowd of about a thousand gathers at Lincoln Terrace for a CSR rally; after a three-hour debate, the group agrees to end the strike and hold a funereal "march of sorrow" the next day, demanding a ban on police and military recruiters on campus and amnesty for the protest leaders.[91]

Saturday morning, at about the same time as the historic Pentagon protest, two thousand students meet on Library Mall for two hours, to debate again whether to start a new sit-in at Bascom Hall or end the episode with the mournful march. Perched on the Historical Society building's balustrade, Soglin, his fellow University Community Action party leader Ira Shor, and the CEWV's Frank Emspak do a rough count; the call could go either way, but they conclude the group favoring the march is slightly larger. They're happy to bring it to a dignified end.[92]

Up State Street they go, many in coats and ties or wearing black armbands; the orderly and grim procession is heckled by football fans heading the other way for the Iowa game at Camp Randall. Soglin and Shor tape the CSR demands to the Capitol door and make some remarks before the protest quietly ends.[93]

Sunday night, after a Bascom Hill prayer vigil, about three hundred students meeting on the mall vote to end the strike. Upset at the CSR's exclusive focus on police brutality rather than the war, Soglin quits that night as chair and turns his attention to off-campus organizing. The situation seems promising; the riot has jolted the broader Madison community, making it want to find out more about the war and the people opposed to it.[94]

The next weekend is homecoming; among those returning is former WSA senator Chuck Robb, now a Marine Corps major, and his fiancée—Lynda Bird Johnson, the president's eldest daughter. There are no protests.[95]

On November 17, the regents vote 7–2 to continue employment interviews as "an important service to the students," declaring that obstructing such interviews "is considered misconduct meriting the most severe disciplinary penalties of the University."[96]

A disciplinary hearing for five students begins on November 28 but is disrupted by heckling and the clanging of cowbells.[97] Two days later, Cohen and two others walk out of their disciplinary hearing before the Student Conduct and Appeals Committee and are summarily expelled. The next day, while about seventy-five students stage a twenty-minute Bascom Hall rally in their support, Cohen is "relieved" of his TA duties. The

Standing in profile in a dark suit, leading movement attorney Percy L. Julian Jr., talking with client, Bob Cohen. Seated, left to right: protester/defendant Carlos Jolly, an unidentified man, and UW law student Cheryl Rosen. COURTESY OF CAPITAL NEWSPAPERS ARCHIVES

three also face criminal charges.[98] More than two thousand students—and at least one professor—sign a statement declaring themselves "equally responsible" for the demonstration, published in the *Daily Cardinal* on December 6.[99]

Cohen ends two years of antiwar activism on campus on December 15, pleading no contest to the disorderly conduct charge and agreeing to leave the state; Judge William Sachtjen fines him the maximum $100. The former philosophy TA marries a recently withdrawn senior in history from northern Wisconsin and leaves town.[100]

Also on December 15, a Dane County jury convicts five Dow protesters, including two of the three Hanson tried to arrest and *Connections* photographer Michael Oberdorfer, for disorderly conduct. "I'm only sorry I can't give you more than thirty days," Judge W. L. Jackman says as he imposes the maximum sentence. Jackman, whose son is an Army captain in Vietnam, makes them start their sentence six days before Christmas, but the state Supreme Court releases them pending appeal. An appointee of GOP governor Warren Knowles, Jackman will be facing his first election in the spring.[101]

War Dead

Major Charles Thoma, thirty, East High 1954, UW class of 1958, dies on January 12 after being shot in the head by a sniper while leading a search-and-destroy mission of the "Black Lion" Second Battalion, Twenty-Eighth Infantry, First Infantry Division, in the jungle northwest of Saigon. The son of retired Army colonel Henry C. Thoma, 4182 Nakoma Rd., and Mrs. Clifford Engle of San Francisco, Major Thoma was captain of the cross-country team, a member of the track and wrestling teams, and a member of Phi

Kappa Sigma at UW. Recipient of the Army Commendation Medal with Oak Leaf clusters, he is survived by his parents and his wife, the former Beverly Hubbard, and three sons.[102]

Army Private First Class Thomas E. "Pete" Matush, twenty-one, East High class of 1964, son of Mr. and Mrs. Joseph J. Matush, 1959 E. Washington Ave., was drafted shortly after high school graduation and sent to Vietnam three weeks before his twenty-first birthday. Four months later, on January 12, he's killed when the truck he's in goes over a land mine.[103]

Army Private First Class James Clifcorn, twenty-two, Edgewood Academy class of 1962, is fatally shot on April 14 while serving with the First Cavalry Division in the An Lo Valley of South Vietnam. Clifcorn was three months shy of graduating from Maryknoll Seminary and entering the priesthood when he dropped out to join the Army and go to Vietnam.[104]

Army Specialist 4-C Leonard D. Thompson, twenty-one, 42 Wirth Ct., is killed when his tank battalion is ambushed in Quang Tri province on April 25. A member of Plymouth Congregational Church, he worked at Sub-Zero before entering the Army shortly after his graduation from East High in 1965; he had served in Vietnam for about six months.[105]

Marine Lance Corporal Gordon Wayne Stoflet, twenty, East High class of 1965, dies June 29 of wounds received in action with the First Marine Regiment of the First Marine Division on May 13 in Quang Tin province. A member of Holy Cross Church, he is survived by his parents, grandparents, and seven siblings. Stoflet entered the Marines in January 1966, arriving in Vietnam that July.[106]

Army Specialist 4-C Vernon J. Stich, twenty-one, son of Vernon Stich, 2112 Atwood Ave., a heavy truck driver, is killed in a vehicle crash in Cam Rahn Bay on August 7, ten weeks after arriving in Vietnam.[107]

Army Corporal Mark W. Neuman, twenty, West High 1965, a paratrooper with the 101st Airborne Division, is killed while on patrol on August 25. Neuman, whose father, Master Sergeant Willard F. Neuman, 1833 Baker Rd., is the supervisor of Army recruiting in Wisconsin, had volunteered for six months' extra duty in Vietnam.[108]

Navy Hospital Corpsman Ronald Reinke, twenty, of 1618 National Ave., Middleton, is killed in action near Da Nang on September 6. A noncombatant responsible for rescue and aid, he had just been awarded a Purple Heart for wounds received in earlier action when he was ordered back into action following a heavy enemy attack. Reinke, who worked at Oscar Mayer before joining the Navy in January 1966, and whose paternal grandparents live on the east side, is killed in the same general area where Corporal Stoflet, his wife's cousin, was fatally wounded.[109]

Army Specialist 4 Robert P. Casperson II, twenty-four, East High 1962, of 3418 Home Ave., is killed in action on November 15, six months after arriving in country. A Big Eight conference wrestling champion, Casperson had recently recovered from wounds received on October 27 and just been reassigned to the front lines.[110]

Marine Corporal James Donn Plecity, nineteen, West High 1966, of 5743 Kroncke Dr., is killed in action in Quang Tri province on December 6, four months after arriving in country. The last time the rifleman was home on leave, he had talked about how angry he was at the student protesters and the antiwar movement.[111]

Auditorium

Publicly, nothing much happens in the city's ongoing struggle to build a civic auditorium through early 1967. William Wesley Peters conducts user group interviews while the city prepares for the taxpayer lawsuit from Carroll Metzner, who claims the city abused its discretion by paying the Wright Foundation at a rate (9.8%) much higher than Wisconsin's standard 6 percent.

In July and August, there's a nine-day trial of dueling witnesses before Circuit Court Judge Edwin Wilkie, whose brother, former state senator and current state Supreme Court Justice Horace Wilkie, had introduced the bill repealing Metzner's anti–Monona Terrace height restriction law in 1959. September 12 marks a complete legal victory for the city, as Wilkie rejects all of Metzner's arguments and finds the contract with the foundation valid.[112]

Two weeks later, Peters excites and somewhat intimidates the Auditorium Committee with a sixty-six-page progress report that identifies forty separate elements to the project, and tentatively places the civic auditorium and convention facilities at Law Park.[113]

Monona Basin, aerial view.
COPYRIGHT 2018 © FRANK LLOYD WRIGHT FOUNDATION, SCOTTS-DALE, AZ. ALL RIGHTS RESERVED. THE FRANK LLOYD WRIGHT FOUN-DATION ARCHIVES (THE MUSEUM OF MODERN ART, AVERY ARCHITEC-TURAL & FINE ARTS LIBRARY, COLUMBIA UNIVERSITY, NEW YORK)

On December 6, Peters makes it official with the release of his eighty-nine-page master plan and an impressive five-hour presentation. It's quite an early civic Christmas present—a staggering statement of architectural ambition that extends Wright's design over nearly three miles of lakeshore and causeway.[114]

At Law Park/Olin Terrace, the proposed core complex of three buildings will include a 2,350-seat civic auditorium, a 1,000-seat Wisconsin State Theater, and a twenty-thousand-square-foot exhibition space/2,000-seat banquet hall. In order to survive economically, Peters says, the auditorium, theater, and convention facilities all have to be together downtown.

OVERALL AERIAL PERSPECTIVE

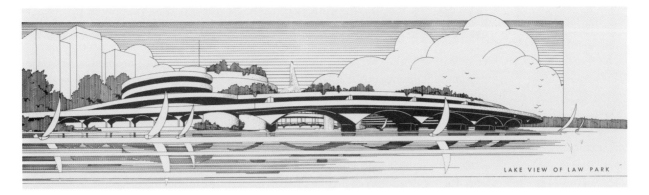

LAKE VIEW OF LAW PARK

Lake view of Law Park Auditorium, Monona Basin Plan. WILLIAM WESLEY PETERS, TALIESIN ARCHITECTS, LTD.

To the east of Law Park, Peters proposes a public marina and large community center, updating a Wright concept from 1893 that was scuttled by the economic panic that year.

Across the water at Olin Park, the cultural complex would feature another thousand-seat theater, a small recital hall, a sixty-seven-thousand-square-foot art center, a natural amphitheater, and a pond/boat-launching facility.

In the central facility, Peters has improved on one of Wright's basic concepts—he places the convention center in the middle, rather than the large auditorium, so he can lower the building's profile and preserve the lake view from the street.

Unfortunately, Peters also incorporates the worst element of Wright's earlier designs—an inability to provide parking without ruining the view from inside. Peters puts three levels of parking around the banquet room and lobby, between building and water; there's hardly a view from inside of either lake or sky. Peters omits the parking structure, which at its apogee extends five hundred feet over the lake, from some of the presentation illustrations.[115]

Still, the response is almost uniformly positive. Those who hated Wright for personal reasons (such as octogenarian economic development activist Joe Jackson) or the Law Park site for political reasons (such as south side alderman Harold "Babe" Rohr) maintain their opposition, but most support the stunning proposal.[116]

Mayor Otto Festge calls the plan "even better" than the original Monona Terrace and says it puts Peters "on the same plane with the great Frank Lloyd Wright." The *Capital Times* is predictably enthusiastic, and the national publications *Architectural Forum* and *Progressive Architecture* praise the plan as a milestone. Even the *State Journal*, while critiquing the plan for having "many of the original basic weaknesses" of Monona Terrace and a price tag "frightening to the Madison homeowner," says the proposal is "beautifully done" with "flashes of architectural genius."[117]

Peters estimates full build-out will take decades and cost about $25 million but identifies three options the city can build now with the $5.5 million already available from the 1954 bond issue for construction and parking.[118]

The council schedules a public hearing for late January, in anticipation of quick action and—finally—a successful resolution of the long-running saga.[119]

Civil Rights

Four years after the successful fight for the state's first fair housing ordinance, Equal Opportunities Commission (EOC) chair Reverend James C. Wright moves to fix the weakness in that landmark legislation—that exempting all single-family houses and owner-occupied apartment buildings of four units or less leaves the ordinance covering only about 40 percent of the housing in the city.[120]

In March, Wright has the commission reaffirm its position for totally open housing—while warning that the matter "should not become a political issue" before the April election. He decides not to challenge the ban on testing for housing discrimination, which the council had imposed during the original enactment. And he appoints commission vice chair Mary Louise Symon (chair, Dane County Board of Supervisors, 1974–1980) to chair an amendment committee, which reports in August that "it is imperative" that the commission work to eliminate all exemptions.[121]

Wright explains to the commission in early September that a white family seeking to buy a house usually looks at about twenty homes, but black families have only a handful of options.[122]

Newly appointed EOC member Ald. James Crary, Fifteenth Ward, tries to deter his commission colleagues, telling them his council colleagues (and their constituents) feel the ordinance is "fine the way it is," with "no need to do anything more." Ald. Thomas Consigny, First Ward, supports eliminating the exemptions but worries about a council backlash that will harm the commission's long-standing request to finally get a paid executive director.

The commission considers making the politically expedient gesture of supporting an exemption for owners of single-family homes who take in up to two roomers, and delaying implementation for six months. But at the urging of Wright and Symon, the commission reaffirms its policy of no exemptions and an immediate effective date.[123]

"It is appalling in this day and age," Wright declares, "that in the matter of basic shelter, a Negro's choice is restricted." The influential Mayor's Citizens Advisory Committee agrees, endorsing full open housing 11–1.[124]

Days before council action on the EOC's proposed ordinance amendment, a terrorist attack strikes at the heart of open housing—the second firebomb attack in two months on the home of Professor A. C. Jordan, 4405 Tokay Blvd. The black South African scholar, whose son Pallo left the United States under threat of deportation earlier this year due to his political activism, also has had a swastika burned on his front lawn.[125]

The full fair housing bill is scheduled for a Committee of the Whole public hearing on September 26. About 6 p.m. on September 25, Reverend Wright is working on his presentation in the commission offices in the City-County Building when he takes ill. Rushed by ambulance to St. Mary's Hospital with an undisclosed ailment, he is still hospitalized the next day, unable to attend the hearing.[126]

But more than 250 do, 213 registering in support and 17 in opposition. Mayor Festge plays a sympathy card in noting Wright's absence and urging adoption in his honor.[127]

Longtime EOC enemy Ald. Harold Rohr, who bitterly opposed the commission's creation in 1963, does all he can to delay and annoy, calling the bill's supporters civil rights "pretenders" and "hypocrites" and again moving for a referendum, which is rejected, 17–5. "We are overlooking the majority of property owners," Rohr complains.

"There is too much of this going on in the country today," Ald. Crary adds. "Everything is going along fine and then somebody rocks the boat and tips it over." Crary, a Dane County deputy sheriff, votes for the referendum and against passage. Ald. Pete Schmidt, Sixth Ward, warns that the city might be liable if welfare recipients damage apartments they're able to rent only because of this amendment. "There is no such thing as a colorless or transparent welfare recipient," he says.[128]

Schmidt is unaware that the EOC's end-of-year report on its recent series of public hearings will also highlight "discrimination against welfare clients" by both individuals and public agencies. "This problem has become acute to the degree of denying the basic human right to have a place to live, and to be considered a citizen equal to other citizens," it will declare.[129]

Mayor Festge, who cosponsors the EOC initiative, says the concept isn't complex. "The issue is purely and simply equality," he says.

The Committee of the Whole does add two minor exemptions to the EOC proposal—housing belonging to religious organizations, and owner-occupied residences with up to four roomers—before endorsing the sweeping measure, 16–6. The vote is the same for final passage on September 28, as Madison once again adopts the most comprehensive open housing ordinance in the state.[130]

Reverend Wright remains hospitalized for more than a month and is too ill to attend a farewell service in his honor in early November before he leaves for a planned two-year course at Garrett Theological Seminary in Evanston, Illinois. Symon becomes acting chair upon his resignation from the commission.[131]

The Movement

February 20—The university's office of student organizations registers Concerned Black Students (formerly Concerned Negro Students), with Willie Edwards as president. The group is also referred to as Concerned Black People, and later the Black People's Alliance.[132]

March 28—A six-year campaign by the Friends of the Urban League, including two years of direct negotiations and controversy, finally succeeds as the United Community Chest accepts the Urban League as a "Red Feather" member agency.[133]

July 18—The EOC issues its annual report, finding that "discrimination in housing still exists and the choice of housing is still limited because of the shortage of low and moderate-income rental units and the significant proportion of owner-occupied units."

Overall, though, it's been "a good year for the commission," with only eighteen formal complaints, none of which resulted in a finding of discrimination.[134]

August 22—The EOC approves a new brochure—"When Members of a Minority Group Move into Your Neighborhood."[135]

December 19—The EOC stuns civil rights advocates by endorsing the use of racial identification codes on Madison school records. "I have never seen a commission on equal opportunities propose such a thing," says recent Madison arrival Dr. Nathaniel O. Calloway, a former president of the Chicago chapter of the Urban League and former member of its national board, warning of legal action from the NAACP. "There is no reasonable excuse or justification for keeping any racial records."[136]

Public and Police Speak Out

After a summer sizzling with "tension-filled incidents with racial overtones," the EOC holds a series of public hearings in neighborhoods with large minority populations, hoping to gain some understanding and tamp down tensions. A later report documents more than a dozen racial conflicts all over town in 1967, including "numerous hostile confrontations" resulting in fights between white and black students near East High, with "conflict and hostility spread[ing] to Central High Negroes." There's "evidence of white apprehension and hostility when a Negro family" moves to the Monroe Street area, and "vandalism to homes and cars of Negro families" living around Odana Road and Tokay Boulevard. In Sherman Village, a white woman pickets the new home of an African American family.[137]

"RACIAL DISCRIMINATION UNDENIABLY EXISTS"

"Hostility and distrust of police. Police brutality was cited. Specific incidents revealed that although there were some incidents of actual excessive force, the major portion of the incidents were again of a subtle sort—inconsideration, racial slurs, excessive pick-ups, singling out, lack of an active policy of hiring minority group members which would overcome a past reputation for discrimination, and general denial of the respect for the dignity of the Negro citizen. There is real fear of harassment and retaliation. A serious lack of rapport exists between Madison minority group members and the police. Rapport between the citizens—particularly the poor and minority group members—and police must be established. Active recruitment and hiring of Negroes and other minority group members on the police force should be done to dispel the attitudes created by past actions of the Madison Police Department. Intensive and extensive training and education for officers at all levels in minority problems, the sensitive role of the police, the prevention and control of racial incidents must be instituted. Efforts must be made by the Police Department to ensure the unbiased treatment of all citizens regardless of race, creed, color or economic status."—Report and Recommendations, Madison Equal Opportunities Commission, December 1967[138]

About 150 east side residents, about twenty of them African American, attend an emotional hearing at Marquette School on August 2, telling commissioners and Mayor Festge about alleged race-based police brutality and other discrimination. The next night, a comparable crowd tells similar stories at Lincoln School on the south side. Mayor Festge rejects calls for a civilian review board of police actions, saying that's already a function of the Police and Fire Commission.[139]

Sometime on August 3, the police department takes an important step toward someday hiring its first nonwhite officer—for the first time, it adds the statement "An Equal Opportunity Employer" to its job advertisement running that week in the daily newspapers. The statement was not included when the ad was placed but added as a "correction" after the department's all-white hiring practices came under fire at the August 2 public hearing.[140]

On August 4, the commission and public hear from inspector Herman Thomas and the six policemen who patrol the South Madison and Williamson Street areas, all of whom insist they have never hassled or hurt any black residents. "I'm amazed at the small number of incidents and the ease with which we can communicate with the colored people," says South Madison patrolman Gerald Eastman. Everyone downplays the possibility of violence.[141]

In mid-December, the commission reviews the hearings and the state of race relations in Madison in a disturbing thirteen-page report (a portion of which is on page 270).

Race for Mayor

Mayor Otto Festge was elected to his first term in 1965 by eight thousand votes. But election night 1967, he's ahead by only about thirty votes with just one precinct left to report. That's what happens when the tax rate rises five mills, crime is up, college students are causing trouble, the building trades go on strike the day before the election, and everything feels like it's breaking down.

Festge, forty-six, almost gets to run unopposed, but attorney and former broadcast personality William Dyke, who finished third in the seven-way primary in 1965, enters the race just hours before the January 31 deadline.[142] Dyke, thirty-five, campaigns almost exclusively on Festge's spending, taxes, and purported failures of leadership, and avoids culture and crime.[143] A former aide to GOP lieutenant governor Olson, Dyke enjoys active support of local and state Republican officials, while the Dane County Democratic Party doesn't even endorse Festge, even though he had been elected county clerk six times as a Democrat. At least the Madison Federation of Labor's Committee on Political Education endorses the incumbent.[144] Festge cites as his primary accomplishment the recent acquisition of a site on Milwaukee Street for the long-sought east side hospital, making progress on the Monona Basin auditorium and civic center, and forming the Alliance of Cities to lobby for better state shared revenue. And he notes that most of the tax hike has been for the schools, not city services.[145]

Festge runs moderately well throughout the city; Dyke wins wards by larger margins, especially his Nakoma neighborhood. It all comes down to University Heights, a precinct with a thousand votes. About 10 p.m., the last numbers come in: Festge 511, Dyke 474. Festge gets his second term by just seventy-five votes—reduced to sixty-two after a recount, 17,261 to 17,199.[146]

Chastened by his political near-death experience and sensing the brewing tax revolt, Festge vows to keep the tax rate at forty-seven mills. "I believe we can provide for our needs through the normal increase in the city's valuation," he tells the council in his inaugural message on April 18. It's a statement he will soon regret.[147]

Citing economic expansion as "perhaps the single most vital consideration" the city faces, Festge reiterates his call for an industrial land bank and proposes creating a transportation commission. He says there's a "crying need" for better social services planning and delivery and asks the council to create an advisory committee on housing and social services, to help develop community services for the growing number of elderly and low-income public housing residents.

Festge, who had made more progress on the auditorium/civic center in two years than immediate predecessor Henry Reynolds had made in two terms, also takes a bold swipe at the diehard anti-Wrightians: "The attempt by a small obstructionist minority to once again delay this project is a grave disservice to our city, and deserves forthright condemnation from the leaders of this community—including the morning newspaper and candidates for public office." Like Reynolds did before him, Festge removes persistent critics from the Auditorium Committee—former mayor George Forster and west side alderman William Bradford Smith.[148]

Festge closes his inaugural address by calling the narrowness of his victory "a challenge to me, my administration, and to this Common Council."[149]

He has no idea of the challenges to come.

Budget Blunderings

Madison city government fails at one of its fundamental tasks in 1967, ending the year without an adopted 1968 budget. It is, one alderman says, "the city's darkest moment."[150]

The crisis begins in early November when the Board of Estimates cuts $500,000 from the $25.4 million school budget. School officials are blindsided and outraged, especially since city finance director Andre Blum had said he would support the budget as "realistic." Superintendent Douglas Ritchie says Mayor Festge has been duplicitous, and board member Arthur "Dynie" Mansfield accuses aldermen of "looking forward to the next election more than to the welfare of children."[151]

The people support their school board, overflowing the council budget hearing on November 20 with the largest crowd in years—about 350 interested and agitated persons, the overwhelming majority of whom support restoring the funds. Some say the city should pay for it through the property tax; some say it should impose the $9 auto registration fee the legislature had enacted a few days earlier, but they almost all say the city should pay for it.[152]

The council gets the message and restores the $500,000, but can't decide whether to put it all on the property tax (a two-mill increase, to a levy of forty-nine mills), or to put half of it on a wheel tax they have reason to believe might be invalid.

Because, as the attorney from the anti–wheel tax American Automobile Association (AAA) points out, the enabling legislation has an effective date of January 1; city attorney Edwin Conrad thinks the council can adopt the tax prior to then but isn't entirely sure.

Sometime after midnight, the council takes the warning from the AAA's A. Roy Anderson to heart and votes 11–9 against the wheel tax; sometime around three in the morning, it thinks again about a tax rate of forty-nine mills, reverses itself, and adopts the wheel tax, 12–8.[153]

But a week later, Attorney General Bronson La Follette says Anderson was right—the city can't adopt a wheel tax until the state legislation takes effect. The city suddenly has a half-million-dollar hole in its budget—with only about two weeks before the deadline for mailing the tax bill.[154]

Mayor Festge, who had vowed to hold the line on property taxes after raising them five mills during his first two-year term, calls a special council meeting to adopt a comfort resolution expressing the council's intent to readopt the wheel tax after January 1. It quickly descends into chaos and confusion. "I can't remember a worse situation or a worse meeting," says seventeen-year veteran alderman Lawrence McCormick.[155]

First, the council votes, 12–10, against Festge's comfort resolution solution. Then it votes against raising the mill rate to cover the shortfall, and votes, 14–8, to direct city clerk Eldon Hoel to issue tax bills with the levy at forty-eight mills. But then it rescinds that action, too, and recesses until December 12—even though Hoel says the tax bills have to be issued by December 8.[156]

"This is the night the city of Madison stopped meeting its obligations," west side alderman Robert "Toby" Reynolds says. "I say God help our town and God help those of you who vote seven ways on one issue."[157]

A semblance of order is restored on December 12. First, the legislature passes a new bill enabling cities to enact the wheel tax prior to January 1. That night, Festge casts the tiebreaking vote to adopt the comfort resolution the council had earlier rejected, clearing the way for Hoel to issue tax bills at the forty-eight-mill rate, which he does.[158]

But when the council returns on December 28 to make good on its pledge to readopt the auto tax, the wheels fall off. With three aldermen absent, including pro–auto tax alderman Milo Flaten, the council votes 11–8 for its enactment—one vote short of the twelve votes needed. Festge pleads with the eight opponents, but none will change his vote. And the tax bills have already been sent out at 48 mills, making it impossible to raise the levy.

With the budget thus still half a million dollars out of balance, the council then delivers the final blow, voting 18–1 to rescind the budget entirely. For apparently the first time since Madison's incorporation in 1856, the city enters a new year without an adopted budget. With no council meeting scheduled until January 12, no one knows what further chaos the new year's first fortnight might bring.[159]

UW

COMMENCEMENT, JUNE 5
▸ Baccalaureate: 2,350
▸ Master's/PhD: 1,075[160]
▸ JD/MD: 240

FALL ENROLLMENT
▸ Total Students: 32,859

HOMECOMING
▸ Show: Nancy Wilson, Harper's Bizarre
▸ Dance: Freddy and the Freeloaders, ? and the Mysterians[161]

NEW BUILDINGS OF NOTE
▸ Van Hise Hall, 1220 Linden Dr.
▸ Gymnasium Unit #2, 2000 Observatory Dr.
▸ Daniels Chemistry Building, 1101 University Ave.[162]

The 600–800 blocks of University Avenue, with the southeast dorms looming just beyond the parking lots. Among the important establishments visible on the south side of University Avenue: Kroger grocery (615), Bob & Gene's tavern (619), A&P grocery (623), Goeden's fish market (635), Hialeah cocktail lounge (647), Kingburger restaurant (665), Madison Suzuki (719), Three Bells tavern (763), Lorenzo's restaurant (813), and Paisan's restaurant (821).[163] UNIVERSITY OF WISCONSIN-MADISON ARCHIVES IMAGE S01475

The Bus Lane Protest

Many campuses have been having demonstrations against the war, the draft, and the CIA. But only Madison has a disruptive protest over a wrong-way bus lane.[164]

The reconstruction plans for University Avenue had always featured an eastbound bus lane on the south side of the street, set against four westbound lanes, ever since the project was first proposed in 1960. But when the reconstructed avenue opens in November 1966, the entire university community warns it's a potential hazard. Several intersections don't have traffic lights, and students focused on crossing the four lanes of cars heading west sometimes forget about the one lane heading east.

That's what happens on March 1, when campus beauty queen Donna Schueler walks into the side of a bus and is injured so badly her left leg has to be amputated.[165]

Students, faculty, administration, and regents all plead with the city to move the bus lane over to the newly expanded, one-way eastbound Johnson Street. But the city refuses.[166]

Chancellor Robben Fleming warns that "challeng[ing] the city's authority will encourage retaliatory measures." The students take to the streets on Wednesday, May 17—the anniversary of the first full day of the 1966 draft sit-in—anyway.[167]

It's actually a professor who plans the demonstration, computer sciences professor Leonard Uhr, on behalf of the Committee to Save the Bus Lane for Bicycles. It's to be a lawful demonstration, with students massed at the intersections of University Avenue and Brooks and Charter Streets, where the lack of a traffic light gives pedestrians the right-of-way; when a bus approaches, they'll pack the crosswalk.[168]

As Fleming warned, the council moves toward a crackdown, through a special $200 fine for obstructing a bus. "Every time a group disagrees with something, there is an immediate move today to lay their bodies in the street, to march and to demonstrate, instead of negotiate," says sponsor Ald. Richard Kopp. Ald. Toby Reynolds, whose late father was a distinguished professor, urges the council not to "overreact to the unwise acts of these people." Mayor Otto Festge breaks an 11–11 tie on the Kopp proposal by voting no; if Festge had declined to vote at all, it still would have failed.[169]

The demonstration begins as planned at 3 p.m. on May 17, with Professor Uhr and a few hundred students walking west on the University Avenue sidewalks, crossing—slowly—at every intersection to hold up traffic. But then an advance squad breaks away and encounters an eastbound bus at Brooks Street.

Chanting "illegal and immoral," several students spontaneously drop their bikes to block the bus and get on the ground themselves. Hundreds of reinforcements rush up in support, both on their feet and on the ground. Forcibly clearing a path for the bus to escape, police arrest fifteen, including Bob Cohen.

The crowd of participants and supportive observers is now about three thousand. For the next three hours, students use their bodies and their bicycles to block the buses; when the buses reroute to Johnson Street, students follow. And back again. There are

Students eye westbound traffic while crossing University Avenue on March 2, the day after campus beauty queen Donna Schueler walked into an eastbound bus (the lane at left) and lost her left leg. COURTESY OF CAPITAL NEWSPAPERS ARCHIVES, PHOTO BY TOM BARLET

about two hundred protesters who stop traffic by walking—slowly, legally—in the cross-walks, and about fifty who drop to the ground to block eastbound buses.

Police make twenty-five arrests, including Cohen (for a second time) and Soglin. Some are arrested for blocking buses, some for cursing out the cops; a half-dozen are arrested after a group of three hundred surrounds a squad car and accosts the officer inside. Most end up paying small fines.[170]

Late that night, about three hundred boisterous young men stage a combination panty raid/march to the Capitol. They rock a city bus, break a window, and block University Avenue. There are no arrests.[171]

On Thursday, May 18, the City Traffic Commission votes unanimously to continue the bus lane, with new safeguards—two more traffic lights, a wider walkway, and a barrier to prevent midblock crossing. Madison Bus Company president William Straub, a voting member of the commission, does not participate in the discussion or decision.[172]

Unfortunately for the political demonstrators, another panty raid and water fight Thursday night grows into the biggest campus disorder in several years. Police make six arrests as they battle up to twenty-five hundred students who smash lights on State Street and at the State Capitol, invade women's dorms, and disrupt traffic throughout downtown. Although this second disturbance is entirely unrelated to the bus demonstration, neither the public nor politicians make any distinction.[173]

The start of the Bus Lane Protest, University Avenue at Mills Street, May 17.
COURTESY OF CAPITAL NEWS-PAPERS ARCHIVES, PHOTO BY SKIP HEINE

When demonstrations and disruptions continue Friday morning, Teamster union officials order the bus drivers not to drive through campus, and the company routes buses down Regent Street instead. At about 2:30 p.m., with chaos still raging, they stop driving all routes—a complete shutdown of all bus service throughout the city until Saturday morning, when cops on every corner restore order.[174]

"The people of the city are furious at the university," says Mayor Otto Festge, perhaps regretting his symbolic vote against the Kopp measure a week earlier. The Common Council certainly is furious, unanimously adopting resolutions that the university "take direct disciplinary action with respect to students who deliberately and flagrantly violate state law and city ordinances," and reimburse the city $2,717 for special police services.[175]

Reflecting the growing political threat from the legislature, the State Assembly jumps in, voting 86–9 for a harshly worded resolution condemning both students and the administration.[176]

And at least one powerful regent wants the administration to find "some way to reprimand" Professor Uhr for his activism. "While we may not have the legal right to discipline," says Regent Dr. James Nellen, team physician for the Green Bay Packers, "we have the moral right" to do so. "A completely shocking concept," replies Regent Arthur DeBardeleben.[177]

Festge says police will "crack [students'] heads together" if necessary to restore order and demands the university "obtain copies of the police arrest reports and call these students in" for discipline. Fleming, who's already announced he's leaving to become president of the University of Michigan, says he will neither discipline students for non-academic offenses nor crack their heads.[178]

A week later, the council votes to retain the bus lane and implement the commission's safety recommendations. In June—seven months after the wrong-way bus lane opened—the city installs traffic lights at Charter and Brooks Streets.[179]

That same week, police finally ticket flamboyant attorney Ken Hur, who's been driving in the bus lane since it opened; now he can challenge the privatized lane in court.[180] Festge doesn't help matters, either legally or in his relations with the campus community, by issuing an executive order days later allowing cabs to use the lane as well.[181]

Campus Calendar

February 6—Stokely Carmichael, chairman of the Student Non-Violent Coordinating Committee, tells a near-capacity Union Theater crowd of more than twelve hundred students, almost all of them white, that black Americans must end their dependence on the "white supremacist power structure. Our purpose is to fight white supremacy, not to integrate." Carmichael's talk, sponsored by the University Young Democrats, is delayed a day when his plane is unable to leave Chicago due to winter weather; "even black power was unable to overcome white snow," he jokes.[182]

February 7—Paul Soglin announces his resignation from the Student Senate, effective April 1, to work on campus-community relations through the University Community Action party.[183]

February 12–19—Pulitzer Prize–winning cartoonist Bill Mauldin keynotes the eighth annual WSA Symposium, "Revolution '67," with the contrarian message that "this is not a revolutionary society, and never really has been." Sex researcher Dr. William Masters assures capacity Union Theater and Great Hall crowds that penis size does not matter (associate Virginia Johnson does not appear due to illness); Harvard professor and State Department consultant Henry Kissinger says that conditions in the USSR and Red China increase the chance for negotiations to end the war in Vietnam; Episcopal bishop James Pike, accused and cleared three times on charges of heresy, lambasts organized religion before an overflow crowd at the First Congregational Church; and LSD guru Dr. Timothy Leary tells an overflow crowd in the Union Theater to "turn on, tune in, and drop out." UW president Harrington later tells the regents that he thinks listening to Leary's talk would make someone "less inclined to use LSD, but I recognize that there are differences of opinion."[184]

February 13—Mandolin great Bill Monroe, the "Father of Bluegrass" music, gives a dazzling performance with his Blue Grass Boys, featuring Peter Rowan.[185]

February 17—With thousands of students using drugs, especially in the dorms, and the price of pot dropping to $15 an ounce, the *Daily Cardinal* calls for the legalization of marijuana and the licensure of dealers.[186]

March 3–7—The radical literary journal *Quixote* and the Students for a Democratic Society present the anti-LBJ adaptation of *Macbeth*, *MacBird!*, in Ag Hall. It's just days after the world premiere in Greenwich Village, and playwright Barbara Garson makes a special appearance.[187]

March 7—The first underground newspaper in the state, *Connections*, is published as Bob Gabriner and Stuart Ewen expand their 1965 counterculture commentary *ACT Tracts* into sixteen edgy and irreverent pages. It's experimental at all levels, from layout to distribution, and "dedicated to remaining underground, rather than being buried above ground." The paper is delayed a day when North Shore Publishers in Milwaukee refuses to print it; the Courier Hub Publishing Company takes the job but insists on blanking out certain words. The editors agree that an expurgated paper is better than having no paper at all.[188]

March 11—R&B great Smokey Robinson and all the Miracles bring Motown to the Stock Pavilion for Greek Week.[189]

March 13—With Governor Warren Knowles and a crowd of close to five hundred looking on at the forty-fourth Gyro Club banquet in Great Hall, the Wisconsin basketball team names junior forward Joe Franklin the squad's most valuable player for leading the fourth-place Badgers to their first .500 season since 1962.[190]

March 17—The Paul Butterfield Blues Band plays two blistering Union Theater sets, earning cheers from the crowd and a condescending review in the *Capital Times*. The Chicago-based band returns for a week's residency in mid-May at the Loge, 514 E. Wilson St., and an October date at the Factory, 315 W. Gorham St.[191] In late October, Butterfield's former guitarist, Mike Bloomfield, unveils his new Electric Flag band, also at the Factory.[192] Local favorites White Trash Blues Band opens for both groups, and also for the Animals in March (the occasion for another condescending review).[193]

March 22—Assembly Speaker Harold Froelich urges the legislature's Joint Finance Committee to cut the UW's budget as punishment for "the moral and social degeneration on the campus." Froelich is especially incensed at the *Cardinal's* publication of a photo taken inside a bathroom.[194]

March 28—A week after being offered the presidency of the University of Minnesota, Chancellor Robben Fleming accepts the presidency of the University of Michigan, effective September 1.[195]

April 2—Legendary bebop trumpeter Dizzy Gillespie brings his quintet for two shows at the Union Theater.[196]

April 3—The faculty approve a new residence hall visitation plan allowing each supervised living unit to decide by a two-thirds vote whether to allow visitors of the opposite sex in their rooms between noon and 10 p.m. on either Saturday or Sunday. Visitations are voided if the living unit serves beer at a social function before or during the visitation period. House officers will be responsible for enforcing the requirement that doors "must be left ajar" during visits.[197]

April 8—The Student Peace Center presents the largest Anti-Military Ball yet, featuring satirical skits and music by Ben Sidran and Johnny Kalb.[198]

May 12–13—*Quixote* literary journal jump-starts the Summer of Love, bringing Allen Ginsberg and the Fugs to the Stock Pavilion, where they entrance and excite a near-capacity crowd of seventeen hundred with "Third Coast Sutra." It's an evening of profane and profound beat poetry and avant-garde rock; Ginsberg reads "Kral Majales (King Of May)," his ode to Beatlemania "Portland Coliseum," and "First Party at Ken Kesey's with Hell's Angels," and the Fugs perform "Slum Goddess of the Lower East Side" and "Wet Dream over You." The next day, a chanting Ginsberg dressed in white, the Fugs, and a crowd of hundreds venture to Picnic Point to dance, sing, eat, love, and get high at Madison's most successful be-in of the season, sponsored by *Quixote*, the Wisconsin Film Society, and Zach Berk's Open Arts Group.[199]

June 24—Ella Fitzgerald, backed by Skitch Henderson conducting the Chicago Symphony, delights and excites a near-capacity Field House crowd with an all-Gershwin concert.[200]

July 7—The regents give President Harrington a $3,500 "stay here" raise, so he won't be tempted to pursue the vacant presidency of the University of California.[201]

August—Richard Becker is arrested for selling a $10 bag of marijuana to police officer Terry Ninneman, who grew a beard and hung out at Lorenzo's Restaurant, at 813 University Ave., to infiltrate drug groups. His successful prosecution leads the police to rely increasingly on young undercover officers rather than paid informants, increasing the conviction rate.[202]

September 15—Regents approve the sale of beer with up to 5 percent alcohol content in the Memorial Union; the era of 3.2 "near beer," which began with the end of Prohibition in 1933, ends November 1.[203]

September—The fall fraternity and sorority rush, which numbered about three thousand prospective pledges in September 1965, dwindles to barely a third of that this fall.[204] A second black fraternity, the twelve-member Omega Psi Phi, organizes in October, joining the twenty-two-member Kappa Alpha Psi.[205]

October 26—Eugene Parks, twenty, is named leader of the UW YMCA's Washington–United Nations Seminar on "Problems in the Urban Community" next spring. Parks, a La Follette High School grad, is a UW junior majoring in economics.[206]

November 8–9—The world premiere of Michael Smuin's *The Catherine Wheel* highlights the American Ballet Theater's two-night return to the Union Theater.[207]

November 17—Ali Akbar Khan, master of the sarod, presents a program of Indian ragas at the Union Theater.[208]

December 13—UW Community Cooperative founding president Rob "Zorba" Paster announces that the membership drive has surpassed its target of 4,000, hitting 4,800. The co-op, focusing on books and student supplies, is set to open January 31 at 401 W. Gorham St.[209]

ROUNDY SAYS

"Johnny Coatta should be quite a coach I think I might be off from first base when I say this but I think he is going to be one of the best coaches that ever coached a Wisconsin team.—If he makes me look bad I'll have to get a job on one of Reynolds trucks that is his father-in-law.— I hope Johnny does pretty good I don't know how to drive a truck."
—*Wisconsin State Journal*, April 26

Chancellor William H. Sewell

On June 9, the regents confirm president Fred Harvey Harrington's surprise pick for chancellor—the esteemed Vilas professor of sociology Professor William Sewell, age fifty-eight. Sewell was not even mentioned among possible candidates, and his name is misspelled on the next morning's front page, but he appears to be the ideal candidate for the time. His opposition to the war and to Dow interviewing on campus, and his leadership in the 1965 teach-in, should give him credibility with student protesters. As a former chair of the sociology department, he understands academic politics. A former football recruit at Michigan State University who still does daily calisthenics, he should relate well to regent Dr. James Nellen, the conservative team physician for the Green Bay Packers. And Sewell even has a unique insight into and relationship with the man who has run the draft since World War II, General Lewis B. Hershey—he worked with Hershey as assistant director of research for the Selective Service System during the war.[210]

Yet Soglin, who has quit the Student Senate, been elected representative to the National Student Association, and become a *Daily Cardinal* columnist, is not optimistic. "He appears to be in sympathy with the left," he writes a few weeks later. "Unfortunately, he has never been in a position of power, forced to make split second decisions. Sewell's liberal rhetoric may fail him when the pressure's on or he may simply become an administration tool, exercising no independent power; in either case," Soglin predicts, "the pot is going to blow up in his face." Sewell doesn't think much of Soglin, either.[211]

Although the *Wisconsin Alumnus* identifies "increased student agitation" as one of the most pressing challenges facing him, the pipe-smoking, sherry-drinking Sewell disclaims that as being one of his priorities. "I didn't become chancellor of this university to become dean of students," he tells a reporter. That's why the university hired Dean of Students Joe Kauffman.[212]

Sewell tells Harrington he'll take the job on a one-year basis, to see if he likes being an administrator.[213]

Razing the Old Red Gym

As 1967 opens, it appears the Old Red Gym will soon be closing and coming down, just as called for in the 1960 North Lower Campus Plan. It was a matter of statewide pride and celebration when the armory/gymnasium was dedicated in 1894, but now it's badly deteriorated, and administrators think the lakeside site begs for better use.[214]

"It will be razed this summer," university president Harrington tells the regents in January. Once the massive new gym out by the western playing fields opens that fall, he says, it won't be needed. There's "considerable disagreement" over whether the site should be used for a faculty lounge, guest house, or some other purpose, but the building "should be razed."[215]

"Unfit for anything other than sweaty exercise," adds university vice president Robert Clodius.[216]

Exactly the point, say the students in the southeast dorms and Langdon Street, outraged at the threat to their athletic facility, and by the notion they should have to go a mile out Observatory Drive for their recreation.[217]

Harrington holds firm. "There is a University commitment to pull down the old red gym," he reiterates for the regents the next month. But he acknowledges there's "a rather active movement to save the gym."[218]

Chancellor Robben Fleming accurately warns that "we will meet a good deal of faculty resistance if we take it down without any replacement" recreational facility. But he disavows any interest in the building itself, which Alan Darst Conover and Lew Porter designed as a Norman Revival fortress due to widespread fear of civil disorder. "I don't feel attracted to the aesthetic value," he tells the regents, who generally share his disinterest in the only building on campus with crenellated towers and wall slits.[219]

There's also no discussion of the cultural or social aspects of the building, which until the Stock Pavilion opened in 1915 housed the largest auditorium in Madison. In its second-floor hall, seating several thousand, Robert La Follette was twice nominated for governor, William Jennings Bryan spoke, and Isadora Duncan danced.[220]

In May, engineering dean and campus planning chief Professor Kurt Wendt presents the planner's proposal for the site—a "multi-purpose campus community center," featuring dining, social, recreational, and meeting facilities for students, faculty, and alumni; a four-hundred-seat auditorium; a guest house of thirty to sixty rooms; and underground parking. The plan also calls for a major recreational facility on the southwest corner of Park and Dayton Streets.[221]

"We believe the red gym should be eliminated as soon as possible," Wendt tells the regents, calling the former fortress "a firetrap" that has "started to slide into Lake Mendota."

Several regents are among the three generations of young men who took their physical education and military drills in the building; regent James Nellen asks if the exterior could be preserved "for sentimental reasons." Wendt says it can, but "the cost would be completely fantastic."

Then the influential Board of Visitors sides with the students that the old gym be maintained until there's a new recreational facility in the area. Although Harrington insists "the gym should be pulled down this summer," he agrees.[222]

But once a new gym goes up, the old gym will come down. Wendt tells the regents he hopes that will be within two years, but thinks it might take three.

In Memoriam—UW

Beloved scholar Professor Helen C. White, seventy-one, dies on June 7, a month before her retirement after forty-eight years on the UW faculty. Known around campus for her purple attire, White was a two-time chair of the English department, the recipient of twenty-three honorary degrees, and an author of thirteen books. A devout Roman Catholic, White was a staunch foe of Senator Joseph McCarthy and in 1957 gave the main address at the rededication of the famed "sifting and winnowing" plaque on Bascom Hall.

In 1970, the regents will name the massive lakefront building housing the English department, undergraduate library, and parking ramps in her honor.[223]

Professor Harry Steenbock, eighty-one, who saved millions of youngsters from the dreaded bone disease rickets by discovering vitamin D in 1924, and then made millions of dollars for UW, dies on Christmas Day of complications after a heart attack. The Quaker Oats Company offered Steenbock a million dollars for his patent for radiating food with ultraviolet light, but he wanted to endow UW's research activities, so he worked with Dean Charles S. Slichter to create the Wisconsin Alumni Research Foundation, and gave it his patent. By the time the patent expired in 1945, rickets had been eliminated from the United States, and the Wisconsin Alumni Research Foundation was established as the critical funder of UW research in the natural sciences.[224]

Schools

GRADUATION, JUNE 9
- West: 677
- East: 512
- La Follette: 339
- Central-University: 271[225]

FALL ENROLLMENT
- Total students: 33,522 in fifty-four schools[226]
- Thirteen elementary schools: 19,277
- Twelve junior high schools: 7146
- Five high schools: 6,443

FIRST DAY HIGH SCHOOL ENROLLMENT
- East: 1,847
- West: 1,443
- Memorial: 1,264
- La Follette: 1,251
- Central-University: 638

As the Madison school system gets a new leader and wages a budget battle with the city, it also suffers under two big labor strikes. The building trades strike keeps John Muir Elementary School on the far west side from opening through the end of the year, forcing the board to rent classroom space for 157 pupils in the nearby parochial St. Thomas Aquinas School. The school board has not rented church space for classrooms since it was needed for Central High students prior to construction of East High in 1922. And the two-month strike by Teamsters bus drivers at the start of the school year forces the board to scramble to find enough nonunion drivers to convey the children—a situation particularly galling to board president Ray Huegel, a member of the Madison Bus Company's board of directors.[227]

And in 1968, a Department of Public Instruction analysis will reveal that Madison received the smallest percentage of state school aid among Dane County's fifteen consolidated school districts for the 1967–1968 school year, with the second-highest percentage coming to the district on its border:

STATE AID, 1967–1968 SCHOOL YEAR

	Aid per Pupil	Aid, % of School Operating Budget
Madison	$70.36	11.5%
Monona Grove	$309.06	47.3%[228]

School Days

January 1—The seemingly traditional New Year's Day vandalism strikes Orchard Ridge School, where juveniles smash forty-four windows and eighteen shades; their parents pay about $400 of the $761 in damages. Sixty-seven more cases of school vandalism are reported by May, causing thousands of dollars' worth of damage to several west side schools.[229]

January 9—The school board ends a lengthy stalemate in early January by approving a contract with Madison Teachers Inc. that keeps teachers among the lowest-paid in the area but establishes the union's right to compulsory arbitration of grievances. Madison schools will pay starting teachers $5,800 in the 1968–1969 school year; most area systems will pay $6,000.[230]

January 9—The board also approves $408,265 in contracts for an athletic facility and grandstand at James Madison Memorial High School, which veteran board member Arthur "Dynie" Mansfield extols as a year-round multisport complex to be available for public use. Deviating from its standard practice, the board lets Roberta Leidner (chair, Dane County Board of Supervisors Highway and Transportation Committee, 1982–1994), representing the Capital Community Citizens, raise questions about the proposal. "A citizen can't just stand up and ask to be heard," superintendent Robert Gilberts says, but the board lets Leidner speak before overriding her concerns and agreeing with Mansfield; the legendary university athlete, in his thirtieth year as the Badger baseball coach, advocates forcefully for the facility, which will be named in his honor after his death in 1985.[231]

January 27—It's the cost of schools, Mayor Otto Festge tells a League of Women Voters luncheon, that has almost single-handedly caused the city tax rate to rise over the last eleven years, from 36 to 47 mills. The cost of city services and the cost of non–city services (such as the metropolitan sewerage system and the vocational school) have stayed at about $10 per thousand dollars of property value, while school costs have jumped from

15.7 mills in 1957 to 26.3 mills this year. Festge and the council continue to oppose creation of a unified school district, which would give the school board independent budget authority.[232]

February 16—West High School's student senate votes that students should not be required to say the pledge of allegiance or stand while others are doing so, as is currently required daily at Memorial High School.[233]

February 20—A commission of the National Institute of Mental Health selects Madison's pupil services division—115 professionals serving about twenty-five hundred handicapped students—as one of the twenty best such programs in the country.[234]

March 16—Superintendent Gilberts upholds the decision by La Follette High principal August Vander Muelen to prevent graduate student Mark Greenside, UW 1966, from serving as an unpaid student-teacher because he won't shave his goatee. Gilberts says the trim facial hair "would not have a desirable effect on students." Greenside, who must perform student-teaching to obtain his license, accepts an offer from the Verona schools.[235]

March 28—Teen vandals with slingshots and rocks cause about $2,000 in damage, breaking twenty-one windows and several reinforced doors at Van Hise School at 4801 Waukesha St. It's the seventh instance of window breaking at Van Hise, Odana, and Orchard Ridge Schools since September, accounting for nearly $10,000 in damages. Police nab five youngsters, who explain they did it "for lack of anything better to do."[236]

April 4—Ruth B. Doyle, project assistant for the dean of student affairs focusing on recruitment and support of black students, and wife of federal judge James E. Doyle, is easily reelected to her second three-year term on the board. Herbert Marcus, whom Mayor Festge appointed to the board last October when attorney Richard Cates resigned, also wins a full term.[237]

April 20—Superintendent Gilberts, who succeeded Philip Falk in January 1963, accepts appointment as the superintendent of the Denver public school system. On July 5, the school board votes, 4–3, to name West High School principal Douglas S. Ritchie superintendent. Doyle, who cast the only vote against Ritchie's appointment as principal in 1964, leads the opposition, saying Madison is too big to be a starter district for a first-time superintendent.[238]

August 7—Ritchie tells the board he wants a "cosmopolitan staff embracing all nationalities and races," but that there is a "shortage of Negroes in the professions and a lack of applicants." A federally mandated survey in the fall shows that only thirteen of Madison's 1,623 instructional staff are black and sixteen of the fifty-four schools have no black pupils. Of the 512 black pupils enrolled in the thirty-nine other schools, Franklin (101), Central High (50), Marquette Elementary (49), and Lincoln Junior High (48) have the highest populations.[239]

August 31—Five Madison teachers are arrested for unauthorized use of the Dane County Fairgrounds—handing out antiwar leaflets at a teacher convention outside the new Dane County Memorial Coliseum. They are quickly released on order of district attorney James Boll, after Ritchie gives permission for the distribution.[240]

September 5—Throughout the school system, a majority of teachers have no class-room experience as the school year begins. And due to the continuing pay gap, only 36 percent of the individual teaching contracts offered are accepted. The new school year brings new disciplinary problems—in the first four months of the 1967–1968 school year, there are 346 suspensions from high schools, up from 144 over the same period the year before.[241]

November 7—Superintendent Ritchie writes to principals and teachers, urging them to take "immediate steps" to stop the "irresponsible defiance by troublemakers under the popular guise of independence and rightism." Decrying "actual refusals to obey, disgusting outbursts of foul language, and threats," Ritchie warns that the number of arrogant and defiant students "is increasing in number and in intensity. The most alarming feature of this is parental attitude which actually borders on approval of irresponsible behavior."[242]

December 4—Staggered by the board of estimates' surprise $500,000 cut to its budget, the school board starts studying whether to seek financial independence by becoming a unified school district.[243]

December 19—Fifteen-year-old Robin Zeldin, son of activist Lea Zeldin, is suspended for three school days from James Madison Memorial High School for refusing to shave his mustache. In mid-December, the five senior high school principals "unanimously reaffirm their intentions to ban students who appear with extremes in dress and grooming, including unshaven conditions such as mustaches, sideburns and beards."

Madison Area Technical College

On June 12, at its last meeting before ending its fifty-five years as an independent city vocational school, the Madison Board of Vocational, Technical, and Adult Schools adopts a statement declaring academic freedom "essential to the purposes of our school and society."[244]

On July 1, the Madison vocational school becomes part of the newly created four-county Vocational, Technical, and Adult Education District No. 4. The new District 4 board, chosen by the chairmen of the Dane, Sauk, Columbia, and Jefferson County boards, names former Madison vocational school leaders Norm Mitby and Marv Brickson district director and chairman, respectively. The new board also assumes control of Central-University High School, which the Madison vocational school is buying from the Board of Education for $605,000; it will lease some classrooms back to the school system until Central-University closes in two years. In November, the state Board of Vocational, Technical, and Adult Education approves a new name for the school—Madison Area Technical College—effective January 23, 1968. The state had earlier rejected the school's first choice, Madison Community College.[245]

Law and Disorder

May 11—Madison police officers name the Wisconsin Professional Police Association as their exclusive agent for collective bargaining, ending the seventeen-year representation by Madison Police Union Local 553.[246]

May 17—Attorney Stuart Becker, former chair of the county Republican Party, is named president of the Police and Fire Commission. President of the Madison Salvation Army Advisory Board, a director of the Madison Chamber of Commerce, and a former alderman (1942–1946), Becker pledges "moral support" to the police and fire departments and criticizes the news media for publicizing demonstrations "to a point that is very distressing to our citizenry."[247]

September 19—The police department unveils a small walnut and gold-colored plaque dedicating its new $62,000 communications center to the memory of disgraced former police chief and office bugger Bruce Weatherly, "who was co-developer of this system and spent his life working toward our common goal of better law enforcement."[248]

November 23—Patrolman Michael Ponty becomes the first Madison Police Department officer to use the chemical spray Mace, subduing two persons who become unruly and threaten him when he tries to issue a Thanksgiving Day traffic ticket. A week later, after another deployment of the concentrated tear gas during a crowd disturbance allegedly causes a woman to suffer facial burns, lose control of her legs, and become hysterical, Wisconsin Civil Liberties Union chairman William Gorham Rice asks Mayor Otto Festge for a policy statement on its use. Festge replies that Mace is "a more humane tool for police to use" than "billy clubs, muscle power, or even firearms," and he trusts in each officer's discretion about when to use it. And he says he's convinced that "the manufacturer's claim that it causes no permanent discomfort or harm is true."[249]

December 6—As stage and screen legend Ginger Rogers and her hairdresser execute a quick costume change before the finale of the musical comedy *Hello, Dolly!* at the Orpheum Theater, a thief slips into the star's unlocked dressing room, steals about $300 from the hairdresser's purse, and makes a clean getaway.[250]

Urban Renewal

Triangle

In late February, the Federal Housing Authority (FHA) gives preliminary approval to the Bayview Foundation as the nonprofit sponsor of the low- and moderate-income housing project set to be constructed on a six-acre site at the juncture of West Washington Avenue and Regent Street, and reserves $2.2 million for the 173-unit project. Bayview president, attorney Paul Gartzke, says the foundation, which includes three aldermen appointed by

Mayor Festge, expects substantial local support since the land and buildings will revert to city ownership after forty years.[251]

But city plans for about a thousand housing units elsewhere in the Triangle are derailed on August 14 by FHA state director Leonard Katz, who says the FHA will not guarantee mortgages for the proposed fifteen- to seventeen-story buildings because construction costs would put the monthly rents beyond the target population's ability to pay. "Madison is not a high-rise town," Katz says, urging the city to plan townhouse-style buildings instead. The next day, the Madison Redevelopment Authority (MRA) amends the Triangle plan to allow for either high-rise or townhouse units, depending on developer interest and financing.[252]

In mid-October, the council approves the MRA's sale of the 1.7-acre parcel on Regent Street between Mills and Brooks Streets to the Davis Duehr eye clinic. It is the fifth of eleven Triangle parcels to be sold.[253]

Across West Washington Avenue, the Brittingham Urban Renewal project, the state's first completed residential urban renewal project, is officially administratively closed out on April 14. The final project cost is $674,271 for land acquisition and preparation, with the city's cash outlay $69,755. Area property taxes have gone from about $10,000 before the project began in 1957 to about $53,000. But the project has not been as financially successful for the First Development Corporation; its 150-unit, ten-building Sampson Plaza complex has lost $30,000 in each of the past three years.[254]

Five summers after the MRA started razing property, the Triangle consists of the Madison Medical Center (left) and Gay Braxton Apartments public housing for the elderly (center), and only a few segments of the old neighborhood streets. South Park Street has now been improved and expanded, under the same urban renewal financing and eminent domain as West Washington Avenue; its pedestrian skywalk terminates about where Agudas Achim synagogue used to be. WHI IMAGE ID 137499, PHOTO BY JOHN NEWHOUSE

South Madison

In late June, the US Department of Housing and Urban Development (HUD) cancels the grant reservations for the long-stalled South Madison project because the city failed to make sufficient progress during the three-year planning period. But HUD officials say they expect the funding to be restored, so the city continues work; in August, the council unanimously approves the seventy-two-acre, fifteen-block project that will rehabilitate 155 of the area's 221 substandard structures, reconstruct several streets to Madison standards, and improve Penn Park. The local share of the $2.7 million project is $780,000, with another $322,000 for the purchase of the land where the sixty-six houses will be razed.

In early October, HUD approves the plan and authorizes the MRA to begin work on the project before the $1.6 million federal grant is fully processed. By late fall, the MRA has acquired about twenty-five of the properties it will raze, putting the project so far ahead of schedule that street reconstruction and park development are moved up to the spring of 1968. MRA relocation officer Charles Hill tells the MHA there will be about seventy-five families needing public housing due to the South Madison project alone.[255]

GNRP

The Madison Home Owners Association attack on the MRA in 1963–1964 results in the loss of a $3.7 million federal grant in June as HUD cancels the grant reservations for the 198-acre General Neighborhood Renewal Plan (GNRP) because the city failed to make sufficient progress over the past three years. HUD officials expect the planning grant to be restored but say there's little chance that the federal funds will be enough for full implementation.[256] The MRA decides to push ahead and hope for the best; HUD approves a $225,555 planning grant in late August, with no commitment to further project financing.[257] The next day, the MRA releases initial plans for a $7.2 million, twenty-acre project in the 600–900 blocks of University Avenue; the university will build its Communication Arts building in the 800 block and other academic structures on most of the 900 block, with the 600 block and almost all the 700 block devoted to the Lake Park Corporation's private commercial ventures. The university also plans to develop North Murray Street into a mall.[258]

Planning and Development

GENERAL STATISTICS
- Population: 169,600[259]
- Area: 46.19 square miles (end-of-year total)[260]

Labor Strife

Plumbers Union Local 167 isn't fooling around when it goes on strike on Saturday, April 1. Because a strike by any one of the Building and Trades Council unions is honored by all the other trade unions, the Plumbers Union knows that it's shutting down $120 million in major public construction projects in the city and a ten-county area. On the morning of Monday, April 3, the members of Sheet Metal Workers 560, Steamfitters 394, Ironworkers 383, the Bricklayers, and the Cement Finishers also put their feet on the street, and stay there until June 8.[261]

The strike takes its toll—the school board has to rent parochial school space for three months because the new John Muir School isn't ready; the Monona Causeway isn't open for the World Food Exposition at the Fairgrounds; and major campus projects, including the massive Humanities Building and the Elvehjem Art Center, are stalled. The strike succeeds—the unions get about everything they want, including elimination of the hated "industry fund," which forced independent contractors to inflate their bids for kickbacks to the trade associations.[262]

Ald. Harold "Babe" Rohr, Painters Union business agent and president of the Building Trades union council, does not comment on the impact of the strike on the municipal projects.

The strike and war-related high interest rates combine to depress local new construction. The year's total of $23.4 million is only $1.1 million above the 1966 level, and about 30 percent lower than 1965's $32.7 million.[263] But other sectors pick up the slack, and unemployment drops from 2.6 percent in January to 1.6 percent in September and October, all well below the state and national averages. About fifty-five hundred jobs are added this year.[264]

Atwood Angst

The planning department continues its work on the Atwood Avenue business district, issuing a bleak report in April on its "depressing, unexciting appearance . . . that is unplanned, inconvenient, unattractive . . . a commercial district of old, deteriorating structures" and skyrocketing vacancies. City consultants Midwest Planning and Research Inc., find a majority of buildings in poor or fair condition, and a "declining community spirit, especially among the young people living and working in the area, evidenced by a lack of local focus" on neighborhood problems.[265]

Their seventy-two-page solution is a private urban renewal plan, starting with a forty-thousand-square foot shopping center featuring a full-service supermarket and chain drugstore on the lakeside corner of Atwood Avenue and Winnebago Street. In order to provide a more pedestrian-friendly environment by diverting cars from Schenk's Corners, the consultants propose a new road aligned with the railroad tracks, from First Street to Division Street. The report also says the venerable East Side Businessmen's Association has become "too diffused to be effective" in promoting the area's revitalization and recommends a new nonprofit corporation be created to acquire and redevelop properties.[266]

Despite concerns over small commercial nodes like the Atwood business district, Madison moves in 1967 to create the next generation of mass retail by annexing, zoning, and building the roadways necessary for the J. C. Penney Co. to build the $10 million East Towne and West Towne regional shopping malls. Pleased with the city's $850,000 improvements to East Washington Avenue, the company kicks in a quarter million for land acquisition and road alignment.[267]

As the city grows by the most acreage since 1962, it undertakes several other vital annexations, including the American Family headquarters on East Washington Avenue, American TV on the West Beltline, 187 acres along Milwaukee Street for the long-sought east side hospital, and eighty acres across Gammon Road from Madison Memorial High School.[268]

The city plan department tries to get downtown on the shopping mall bandwagon, proposing in late September that the two blocks of Mifflin Street on the Capitol Square be converted to a covered mall. But the concept of an air-conditioned arcade with attached parking ramp and a skywalk or underpass to cross Wisconsin Avenue is not well received.[269]

Nor is developer Floyd Voight's proposal for the empty lot on the north side of State Street's 400 block—a fourteen-story, two-hundred-room hotel with a 150-seat movie theater and parking for a hundred cars, which meets the same fate as Madison Properties' hotel proposal in 1964. The lot, vacant since Victor Music burned down in December 1961, remains so.[270]

Park Plans

On April 13, Madison receives a $411,628 federal grant underwriting half the cost to purchase lakefront properties on East Gorham Street for expansion of James Madison Park. The city plans to acquire the properties as they become available over the next seven or eight years, without using its condemnation power.[271]

And the city finally strikes a deal with Henry Turville for his heavily wooded sixty-five acres on the southwest shore of Lake Monona, adjacent to Olin Park. He isn't happy about losing the 4,300 feet of lake frontage that's been in his family for almost a century, but he agrees to sell once the city starts condemnation proceedings. The city will pay $480,000, supplemented by a federal grant of $390,000 and a state grant of $25,000; at $13,700 an acre, the city is paying $2,300 an acre less than the county paid in June for fifteen acres adjacent to the fairgrounds. The city also agrees to name the area Turville Park.[272]

Dedications and Openings

March 26—On a rainy Easter afternoon, barely four and a half years after Dane County decided to build a sports and entertainment arena, a crowd of about four thousand

attends the dedication of the Dane County Memorial Coliseum. At 312 feet around and 98 feet high at its center, with 7,670 permanent seats and up to 3,330 temporary ones, the coliseum was designed by the firm Law, Law, Potter and Nystrom and built by the Anthony Grignano Company. Some finishing touches remain, but coliseum manager Roy Gumptow vows everything will be ready for the inaugural event next weekend—the Zor Shrine Circus. On April 12, Paul Revere and the Raiders perform as the arena's first music act.[273]

September 13—The dedication of Amund Reindahl Park, 1818 Portage Rd., honors the two-term register of deeds and one-armed bachelor farmer who, at his death in 1946, bequeathed one hundred acres of his family's land to the city for a park and school.[274]

December 19—Mayor Otto Festge and officials from Twentieth Century Theater attend the opening of the former Eastwood Theater as the sleek new Cinema Theater [Barrymore Theater] at 2029 Atwood Ave. A $250,000 remodel has replaced the faux Spanish stucco from 1929; in its place are walnut and white panels, blue carpets, and a brass and glass chandelier. The theater's first film is John Huston's *The Bible*.[275]

Highways and Transportation

NEW ROADS:
- The city adds 7.54 miles of streets this year, for a total of 464.13 miles.
- Expanded South Park Street between Regent Street and West Washington Avenue
- Highway 113 between Commercial Avenue and East Washington Avenue
- South Stoughton Road (Hwy 51) between Highway 30 and East Broadway
- Odana Road, westerly from Whitney Way
- John Nolen Dr.

Transportation Milestones

January 26—The council bans scooter and motorcycle parking on State Street and most of University Avenue, except in specially designated stalls.[276]

March 23—The council lifts parking meter restrictions on Monday and Friday nights, making street parking free after 6 p.m.[277]

May 8—The city ethics board rules that William H. Straub, president of the Madison Bus Company, has no conflict of interest serving on the City Traffic Commission, provided he does not vote on matters "related directly" to the bus company.[278]

November 22—John Nolen Drive, stretching 8,300 feet from North Shore Drive to Olin Avenue—with 3,200 of those feet over water—is dedicated and opened. Railroads started crossing Monona Bay in 1854; now cars can, too, giving everyone access to a striking view so far enjoyed by only a few—the Lake Monona approach to downtown Madison. Mayor Festge gets to celebrate another accomplishment of former mayor Henry Reynolds, who campaigned for its construction more than six years prior, but who declines, without explanation, to join the ceremony. Perhaps his reticence is because the causeway is opening a year late and at double its proposed $1 million budget. As promised, the two-lane road (with room for four more lanes) is soon diverting about ten thousand cars a day from South Park Street and the Bayview neighborhood.[279]

Bus, Stopped

In early May, Teamsters Local 695 takes the 108 drivers and 32 mechanics of the Madison Bus Company away from the Amalgamated Transit Workers Union. At 1:30 a.m. on September 20, it takes all 140 employees out on strike.[280]

The union wants a raise of forty-seven cents an hour over two years, plus full company payment for health insurance; the company offers twenty-seven cents over three years, plus a partial increase in insurance coverage. Current starting pay is $1.45 an hour, which the union wants increased by a dollar; average pay is $2.68 an hour. The company, which carried about seven million passengers on its ninety-one buses in 1966, reported a net income last year of $33,768 on revenues of $1.33 million; company president William Straub—still a member of the City Traffic Commission—says he'd have to raise fares from twenty to twenty-five cents to meet the union demand.

Within the strike's first week, there's a noticeable impact on downtown merchants, some of whom start layoffs. Workers, most seriously hospital workers, are having trouble getting to their jobs. High school and university students are hitchhiking to class. Everyone's life is predictably complicated.[281]

Dismayed at the lack of progress under mediation conducted by the Wisconsin Employment Relations Commission, Festge on October 4 turns again to the man who mediated the Monona Terrace fee dispute in 1965—UW law professor Nathan Feinsinger, who announces he hopes to have the strike settled by the following midnight.[282]

But as the clock is striking twelve, so too remain the Teamsters. Feinsinger repeats his prediction the next day, with the same result. And again the next day. He puts in more than thirty hours of mediation over the next week, with no progress.[283]

On October 13, Feinsinger offers a proposed settlement that comes very close to the union demand—a forty-cent raise over two years, plus increases in health insurance and other fringe benefits. The Teamsters quickly approve the proposal; Straub says it would cost $287,600, aside from strike costs and future ridership loss—about three times what the nickel fare increase would bring—and rejects it.[284]

Four days later, about the same time as the bloody police confrontation with Dow protesters at the Commerce Building, Madison Bus Company announces it has petitioned the Public Service Commission (PSC) to abandon service and has set a special stockholder meeting for October 23 to dissolve the corporation. The city, which holds about 7 percent of the company stock, votes no, but the owners of the remaining 93 percent vote yes.[285]

Auditors and appraisers start preparing the company for sale, while Straub tells Festge he'll never sign a contract with the Teamsters. The city petitions the PSC to order immediate resumption of service. Festge warns of a winter without mass transit and reveals plans for a possible spring referendum on municipal ownership or operation.[286]

There's a possible breakthrough on November 2 as downtown merchants offer to raise $65,000 for a subsidy to cover the difference between the company offer and the Feinsinger proposal for a year. But company officials quickly reject the offer and prepare for the abandonment and dissolution hearing before the PSC on November 10.[287]

Festge levels an uncharacteristically harsh response. "I am shocked at the company's disregard for the public welfare," he says, calling the company "the biggest obstacle to a strike settlement." He launches a petition drive to support the city's request that the PSC order the immediate resumption of bus service.[288]

More than thirteen thousand petitions pour into the PSC offices, and hundreds of spectators jam the commission hearing on November 10. They hear some surprisingly good news from the mayor—the bus company would agree to the Feinsinger proposal, provided the city guarantees the $65,000 supplemental contribution. Chamber of Commerce executive director Irv Lackore assures Festge that "the Madison business community would immediately raise" the money.[289]

That's good enough for the company, and after another marathon mediation managed by Feinsinger and Wisconsin Employment Relations Commission chair Morris Slavney, the fifty-three-day strike ends on the afternoon of November 11. Feinsinger, who also mediated the bitter 1966 transit strike in New York City, calls this the "toughest" labor dispute in his long and storied career.[290]

With Festge chairing the supplemental fund drive, company and union officials anticipate service will resume in two or three days, a week at most.

It doesn't. After a quick $5,000 from the First National Bank, contributions dribble in; after nearly a week, the fund is still $50,000 short. Feinsinger isn't happy that the business community hasn't fulfilled its commitment; "The public is entitled to an explanation," he says. Festge says he hopes for service to be restored by Thanksgiving, still a week away.[291]

Monday, November 20, donations hit $23,500 and the PSC approves the nickel fare boost. Under pressure from Feinsinger and Festge, the buses finally roll again on November 21—sixty-two days after the strike started, and ten days after it was ostensibly settled. That night, the council authorizes hiring a consultant to help the city plan for the future of its mass transit. UW transportation expert Professor William Dodge, who assisted Feinsinger in the mediation, endorses the move; "It is reasonable to assume," he says "that another crisis will arise."[292]

At the end of the year, the motion to dissolve the company is still in effect, and Madison Bus Company president Straub is complaining about being "libeled and slandered" during the strike. The company has rescinded the petition to the PSC to allow the dissolution but can refile at any time.[293]

Miscellanea

January 20—Judge Richard Bardwell voids, on jurisdictional grounds, the 1966 Industrial Commission ruling that Madison discriminated against Ruth Fey when it denied her a bartender's license. Bardwell finds it "clearly reasonable" to conclude that the city denied Fey a license "because she was a female," but holds the Industrial Commission jurisdiction limited to employment relationships and does not cover the issuance of licenses.[294]

March 24—Most Madison stores, all banks, and all government offices except the post office are closed, as in other years, from noon to 3 p.m. for Good Friday. Unlike other years, there are antiwar demonstrations inside the First Methodist Church, Covenant Presbyterian Church, and Bashford Methodist Church during services.[295]

April 25—Bishop Cletus Francis O'Donnell, forty-nine, formerly the auxiliary and vicar general to the Archbishop of Chicago, is installed as new Bishop of Catholic Diocese, succeeding Bishop William P. O'Connor, who retired at age eighty after leading the Diocese since its founding in 1946.[296]

July 4—The Lions Club's sixteenth annual shower of sparklers at Vilas Park is likely the last to take place there after a Parks Commission decision in April to deny future fireworks permits for fear of spooking the animals.[297]

September 23—Arriving at Truax Air Field to avoid picketers, First Lady Lady Bird Johnson extols rural life to a World Food Exposition crowd of about twenty-five hundred at the Dane County Coliseum.[298]

November 11—About twenty-five of the seventy-five veterans marching in the Veterans Day parade are from the new Veterans for Peace in Vietnam group. As some from the more traditional units mumble and grumble and about a hundred spectators watch quietly, Roberta Leidner, a Marine Corps Women's Reserve veteran of World War II, places a large Veterans for Peace wreath on a temporary memorial cenotaph at the State Street entrance to the Capitol.[299]

November 11—More than five hundred attend a dinner dance honoring seventy-five-year-old Jimmy Demetral, who has raised about $50,000 for handicapped children's activities through his benefit wrestling matches. Demetral, who emigrated from Greece as a small boy, was a featured attraction for more than twenty years at the Wisconsin State Fair, wrestling all comers; he later operated Gulessarian's rug store on State Street and served as athletic director at Oscar Mayer. The council recently named a new city park near the plant in his honor.[300]

November 17—Former vice president Richard Nixon, expected to enter next spring's presidential primary, calls for mining North Vietnam's Haiphong Harbor in an appearance before seven hundred university students at the Wisconsin Center. There are no demonstrations or protests against the GOP front-runner, who decisively beat Senator John Kennedy in a campus mock vote in 1960.[301]

December 13—Camp Indianola, one of the oldest boys' summer camps in the country, located on thirty-one acres with 1,791 feet of shoreline on the northwest banks of Lake Mendota, closes after sixty-two years. Among its generations of campers was a ten-year-old Orson Welles, who performed an astonishing one-boy version of *Dr. Jekyll and Mr. Hyde* in 1925.[302]

DDT

It was in 1963, the year after Rachel Carson exposed the environmental hazards of DDT in *Silent Spring*, that the city stopped using the insecticide to kill the beetle spreading Dutch elm disease. In 1967, the year the Environmental Defense Fund is formed with the goal of banning DDT, both the Parks Commission and the Board of Estimates vote to resume its use, recommending that the city spend $8,400 to spray ten thousand of the twenty-seven thousand city-owned trees from helicopters.[303]

About 55,000 of the city's 130,000 shade trees are elms, and about half of those are on public property. By 1967, the city has lost about 3,000 trees since the fungus was found in 1958, and the infestation is quickening; elm fatalities increased from 376 in 1965 to 766 in 1966 and over 1,000 in 1967.

The only way to save the trees, parks superintendent James Marshall says, is to switch from methoxychlor back to DDT. West side alderman Robert "Toby" Reynolds believes Marshall's priorities are misplaced. The elms are nice, he says, "but I just don't think it's a good idea to go out and fill the air with poison." The first time the council considers the commission proposal in the Committee of the Whole, it deadlocks—eleven members vote to approve the plan, one vote short of the number needed for approval, but not enough votes to adopt an ordinance banning its use, either. But two nights later, on October 26, environmentalists win a clear victory—a 14–8 vote to ban the use of DDT on trees.[304] But it can still be applied on shrubs.

In Memoriam

Thomas R. Hefty, eighty-one, the son of Swiss immigrants who rose from being a part-time bookkeeper to become president and chairman of the First National Bank, dies January 19 after breaking his hip in a fall at his home in Maple Bluff.[305]

District attorney Floyd McBurney, twenty-nine, West High National Honors Society class of 1955, Phi Beta Kappa UW class of 1960, UW Law class of 1963, a brilliant and personable quadriplegic paralyzed since a diving accident at age sixteen, dies February 20 from a lung infection that set in after an operation for a bleeding ulcer. It's not yet been four months since he became the first Republican since 1948 elected to a partisan Dane County office. Close to four hundred people (including three Supreme Court justices serving as honorary pallbearers) brave a snowstorm to attend McBurney's funeral at St. John's Lutheran at 322 E. Washington Ave., where he had been confirmed two years before his accident. The McBurney Disability Resource Center on the UW campus will be founded in 1977 with funds from his memorial account, largely through the efforts of McBurney's faculty mentor, the noted real estate professor James Graaskamp (himself a quadriplegic).[306]

Herman Loftsgordon, eighty-four, east side civic leader and banker, dies at his home, 1407 Morrison St., on September 14. One of the founders in 1918 of Anchor Savings and Loan and its chairman from 1953 until his death, Loftsgordon was president of the East Side Businessmen's Association when it built the Eastwood [Barrymore] Theater in 1929. He was the first president of the East Side High School PTA when the school opened in 1922, and he ran unsuccessfully for mayor in 1925.[307]

Milton B. Findorff, seventy-three, former president, now chairman of the board of Madison's largest construction company, dies September 19 after a half-century with the firm his father, John H. Findorff, founded in 1890.[308]

Leo T. Kehl, sixty-seven, internationally renowned dance instructor, dies on October 18 after a brief illness. Director of the school his father, Frederick William, founded in 1880, Kehl taught not only thousands of Madison children to dance, but thousands of dance instructors as well, including future film stars Gene Kelly and Vera Ellen. A cofounder of the Madison West Lions Club, Kehl wrote books on dance that are used by thousands of schools and dozens of major universities.[309]

Thomas H. Moran, sixty, an East High Purgolder who advanced from payroll clerk to chairman of the board of the General Telephone Company of Wisconsin, dies October 23, six hours after falling from a ladder while cleaning leaves from the eaves of his Maple Bluff home.[310]

Otis Redding

"King of the Soul Singers" Otis Redding was one of the breakout stars at the 1967 Monterey Pop Festival in June, and in October he dethroned Elvis Presley as the British music magazine *Melody Maker*'s top male vocalist. So there's a big buzz about his first Wisconsin appearance—two shows at Ken Adamany's club, The Factory, 315 W. Gorham St., on Sunday, December 10. The early show isn't sold out, but it looks like the late show will be.[311] Opening act is a band Adamany manages from Rockford called the Grim Reapers, the nucleus of what will later become the band Cheap Trick.

The dynamic singer is poised to move beyond clubs like the fifteen-hundred-capacity Factory, where his contract is for $3,000 plus 50 percent of the gross revenue over $7,000. He's got dates scheduled on the Ed Sullivan and Johnny Carson shows as well as a duet album with Aretha Franklin in the works, and he's just accepted Vice President Humphrey's invitation for a Christmas trip to entertain American troops in Vietnam.[312]

Redding and his party—pilot Richard Fraser; five members of his backing band, the Bar-Kays; and a teenage assistant—are flying in from Saturday night shows in Cleveland in the green-and-white Beechcraft 18 airplane he had just bought used for $78,000. James Brown told him the twin 450 engines weren't big enough, but it's Redding's pride and joy. It's raining so heavily in Cleveland on December 10 that some flights are grounded, but Otis doesn't want to disappoint his fans.[313]

Fraser knows he'll need to make an instrument landing in Madison because of a low ceiling and poor visibility, so the Georgian sets the plane to autopilot—and doesn't realize that ice is building up on the frame. Redding is in the copilot's seat, probably asleep.[314]

Bernard Reese, president of the Gardner Baking Company, is on the lake side of his home at 4709 Tonyawatha Trail when he hears the plane. He doesn't think the motors sound strong enough for an instrument landing.[315]

At 3:25 p.m., the plane is four miles south of the airport, about twelve hundred feet above the lake. Fraser gets clearance to land and lowers the landing gear. Suddenly, with no call of distress, the plane sputters and stalls, and falls into the wintry water, killing all aboard but Bar-Kays trumpeter Ben Cauley.[316] Reese watches in horror, then races inside to call police.

Mrs. H. R. Dickert, 4643 Tonyawatha Trail, also sees the plane hit the choppy surface; she, too, calls police, and Reese heads out in his boat with her son, Chris. As police divers begin the difficult and dangerous job of recovering the bodies, Chris finds Otis's grey attache case bobbing in the water.[317] Although police later report it contains between $3,000

Otis Redding's shattered Beechcraft 18 is pulled from Lake Monona on December 11, the day after its crash, his name visible on its fuselage.
COURTESY OF CAPITAL NEWS-PAPERS ARCHIVES, PHOTO BY ROGER L. TURNER

and $4,000—part of the payments for the show in Cleveland and a fraternity dance at Vanderbilt University in Nashville—it's not returned to Redding's widow, Zelma, or his father when they come to Madison on Monday, shortly after Redding's body is found, still strapped in his seat. Record company road manager Twiggs Lydon is successful, however, in getting coroner Clyde Chamberlain to overlook the small bag of marijuana found in Otis's pocket.[318]

Late Sunday afternoon, as the damp and chilled crowd waits impatiently outside, it falls to Gary Karp, keyboardist with the White Trash Blues Band, to go to the club's second-floor window to announce that the show's canceled. At first, many are suspicious and start to boo. But when Karp repeats the awful news, the terrible reality sets in, and a stunned silence falls over the crowd.[319]

It's not quite two months since the Dow riot, and police worry what might happen; they ask Adamany to open the club so people can focus on music rather than grief and anger. Adamany offers refunds and lets the crowd in for free; while the Grim Reapers play, he quickly books the R&B band Lee Brown and the Cheaters to come over from Milwaukee.[320]

Before leaving his home in Macon, Georgia, for the short tour, Redding had completed the vocal track on a softer, contemplative song, written on a houseboat in Sausalito shortly after the Monterey festival. Stax Records vice president Al Bell worried about its marketability, but Redding trusted his own artistic instinct: "This is my first million seller, right here," he said on December 6.[321]

Redding underestimated. Released on January 8, 1968, "(Sittin' On) The Dock of the Bay" soon tops both the R&B and pop charts, wins two Grammy Awards, and sells about four million copies.[322]

The National Transportation Safety Board lists the cause of the crash as "miscellaneous—undetermined."[323]

Marching in memory of a drum major for justice, peace, and righteousness, April 5. UNIVERSITY OF WISCONSIN-MADISON ARCHIVES IMAGE S00103, PHOTO BY SHERESHEWSKY

1968

Civil Rights

Nineteen sixty-eight is the worst year yet for race relations in Madison, with tensions turning increasingly physical, and relations between blacks and the all-white police force hitting a new low.

Mourning Dr. King

Once again, thousands gather to grieve atop Bascom Hill, just as they did in 1963. But this time the mourning is different.

The morning after Dr. Martin Luther King's April 4 assassination in Memphis starts with a heated disagreement between Chancellor William Sewell and a group of about twenty black student leaders over their dueling plans for a service that noon at Lincoln Terrace.

Sewell, who has already canceled that afternoon's classes, wants the students to speak as part of the official university program, an idea they emphatically shout down. "Black people must lead the memorial," not just speak as part of the program, declares Sidney Glass, head of Concerned Black People; when things get tense, Sewell yields. He agrees to make introductory remarks, announce that he's keeping several buildings open for students to gather in later, and then allow the black students to run the program.[1]

The program itself is full of bitterness and anger. Clara Meek, one of five students to speak during the twenty-minute program, breaks into tears: "I have a dream, too," she says to the crowd of about ten thousand, almost all white, "that one day every darn one of you is going to pay." Kenneth Irwin says, "There is no other course the black people can take" but to riot.[2]

Also unlike during President Kennedy's memorial service, there's a march; at an estimated fifteen thousand, fully filling six blocks of State Street, it's the largest demonstration in Madison's history to date, other than to celebrate a Big Ten championship or the end of a war.[3]

Rows of black Madisonians up front link arms and alternate between freedom songs and militant chants—"Ain't Gonna Let Nobody Turn Me Around" interspersed with "Black power!"

They march around the Capitol and up Wisconsin Avenue, heading down Langdon Street to the foot of Science Hall, where they sing two choruses of "We Shall Overcome," then move, in large numbers, to the buildings that Sewell has kept open.[4]

Once there, they stay for hours, black and white, engaging in the most candid conversation about race the campus has ever seen. Sewell, observing the packed auditorium in Social Sciences, thinks it's the capstone to "the greatest day for education that had ever hit the campus."[5]

The regents aren't so impressed; they pass a rule requiring permission of the president and the regents' executive committee to declare a campus holiday.[6]

Sunday afternoon, April 7, is dark and windy as a crowd of three thousand gathers at the Capitol for the community's program, highlighted by stinging comments from Concerned Black People's Ardinette Tucker. She condemns "the Madison community which still believes there are no race problems here. I will break some windows to make you care."

Four white men—Reverend Alfred Swan, Professor Maurice Zeitlin, businessman Jack von Metterheim, and Father Joseph Hammer—lead the silent march down State Street and out University Avenue to the First Congregational Church for a memorial service, attended by Governor and Mrs. Warren Knowles, Mayor and Mrs. Otto Festge, and other dignitaries. Equal Opportunities Commission (EOC) director Reverend James Wright speaks, Reverend Swan recites Lincoln's second inaugural address, Rabbi Manfred Swarsensky preaches scripture, and Reverend Robert Borgwardt reads from King's "Letter from Birmingham Jail." Reverend Richard Pritchard, the only Madison cleric to have spent time in the South for civil rights, is not invited to participate in the program. A special offering for Dr. King's Southern Christian Leadership Conference collects over $1,000.[7]

The Breese Stevens Field Incident

On the night of August 3, fights between whites and blacks at a Breese Stevens Field dance and their aftermath highlight, and worsen, the city's racial tension.

There are about four hundred teens at the dance, about 85 percent white, most from the east and far east sides. Most of the fifty to seventy-five black teens are from downtown and the south side. Most everyone comes to dance and hang out; some, both white and black, come to make trouble, and do. Some have been drinking.[8]

By 10:30 p.m., there are fights going on all around. Some come out of nowhere, some from past grudges, some are the sum of ongoing bad blood between black students from Central and white students from La Follette. Some fights are white-on-white; some are because a black boy asked a white girl to dance. The fights are broken up by five off-duty police officers, who make no arrests inside the stadium. Kids and cops both use racial epithets.[9]

But when a mixed-race group turns on a cop and threatens him, Sergeant James Morgan decides things are out of control and ends the dance early at 11 p.m.[10]

Though most of the crowd moves away, some fights move to Patterson Street and continue.

Suddenly a car containing four white youths, its lights off, lurches forward through the group; the driver slams on the brakes but hits Willie James, of 1735 Baird St., breaking his leg. In a flash, three or four black teens are atop the car, and another half dozen or so alongside, smashing windows and denting the body. Some of the passengers had already tussled with black students that evening; one of the occupants is David Crary, son of the Fifteenth Ward alderman. Police make no arrests but focus on dispersing the crowd, then taking James to the hospital.

The white kids scatter, but scores of black youths take to East Washington Avenue, where someone breaks a window at Ridge Madison Motors. Some are disrupting traffic as they head to the Square to catch a bus back home. A young black male is said to shout, "Let's burn white city down." Four officers on foot follow closely behind, and four squad cars cruise at walking speed alongside them.[11]

A cop tells them to quiet down; a black youth curses and gets arrested for using obscene language. When he resists, an adult and three juveniles try to interfere and are also arrested, all for disorderly conduct. Charges against the adult will later be dismissed after trial; the juveniles are never charged.

Around midnight, a caravan of cars filled with white youths descends on the south side. As they cruise the streets hollering racial epithets, the black youths erect makeshift barricades; the east siders have to smash through them to get back home.[12]

Word quickly spreads through the minority community that the police used racial epithets and arrested only blacks, letting whites go free.

EOC director Wright, fearing tensions are so high that a full-scale riot could erupt, convenes an extraordinary public hearing in the city council chambers Sunday afternoon. The chaotic session is dominated by charges of police racism, and Wright seems to agree. "There does appear to be a double standard" regarding arrests, he says afterward.[13]

The commission commends Wright for acting with alacrity, but the rest of Madison's political and law enforcement community is not happy with the emergency public hearing or the ad hoc committee Wright appoints to investigate further. Police inspector Herman Thomas denies any double standard and says any racial trouble in Madison is caused by "agitators from outside."[14]

Stuart Becker, president of the Police and Fire Commission, calls on Wright to "cease and desist from further ventilating your complaints through the news media," which he says "can only lead to heated racial tensions in the community."[15]

A group of eighteen prominent African American professionals—including state equal rights division chief Clifton Lee, *Madison Sun* editor/publisher Lawrence Saunders, attorney Percy L. Julian Jr., the Madison Redevelopment Authority's Merritt Norvell, assistant UW football coach L. H. Ritcherson, and Dr. N. O. Calloway—responds by charging that racism is prevalent in the Madison Police Department.[16]

"In the execution of racial justice," they write the EOC, "Madison is in many instances as negligent as those notorious southern cities which have made a tradition of ignoring the rights and needs of the black citizen. This thinly disguised contempt for the comparative value of a black life has made a mockery of the phrase 'equal protection under the law.'"

Noting that Madison still has no black officers, the signatories warn about the "growing anger in the black community" over police/community relations.

The police heatedly deny any racial bias or improper actions, citing Sergeant Gerald Thorstensen's April act of saving a black teen from a mob of thirty whites kicking and hitting him, during which Thorstensen was also punched and kicked.[17]

Mayor Festge admits things are bad. "There has been a severe disruption, if not a complete breakdown in communications between the so-called establishment and Madison's minority community," he says. He promises a full and complete investigation.[18]

"It is not news there is bigotry in the Madison police department," the *Capital Times* editorializes on August 15. "The racial bigotry that exists in the department was bound to get this community in trouble sooner or later. It is a good thing for the whole community that the racism in the department has come to a head and we can get the ugly thing out on the table and look at it."[19]

On August 20, the council spends over an hour interrogating, criticizing, and sometimes defending Wright over the emergency hearing and his plans for an ad hoc committee investigation. "I feel you stirred up a lot of turmoil in this city," says Ald. James Crary, whom Festge did not reappoint to the EOC in April. Ald. Harold "Babe" Rohr, who led the fight against the Equal Opportunities Ordinance in 1963, tells Wright, "You have failed to accomplish the duties entrusted upon you."[20]

Mayor Festge counsels the commission to go along with whatever plan the council adopts, lest the aldermen think that the EOC "was acting like a defiant child."[21]

Two nights later, the council changes course and votes, 18–1, to allow the EOC to conduct the inquiry into "alleged racial tension" to "determine if such tension exists, its causes and its effects on the welfare of the city." But the fifteen-member commission is strictly barred from determining whether there were any violations of the Equal Opportunities Ordinance or police department rules and regulations. The only dissenting vote comes from Ald. Ralph Hornbeck, Twelfth Ward, a former policeman.[22]

Two days before the EOC hearings begin, police chief Wilbur Emery releases the results of his own investigation, which clears all officers of any wrongdoing. The reason officers followed groups of blacks and not whites, he says, is because they "apparently left in fairly large groups and their attitude appeared to indicate trouble afoot, whereas the officers report that the white youths dispersed without creating any problem."[23]

Emery also denies that any officer used his flashlight or baton, an assertion challenged by Central High School junior Callie Franklin, who later testifies under oath she was hit by a flashlight as she was beating on a white girl inside the car.[24]

Emery goes on the offensive as the leadoff witness at the first hearing on September 17. Relations between black youths and police have worsened since August 3, he says, "because of the blowing up of this incident. I think there has been more damage in the last six weeks, as far as black-police relations are concerned, than in the past few years." Emery alludes to outside "black agitators" who have come here to cause trouble, but declines the EOC's request for more information.[25]

Merritt Norvell, community services director for the Madison Redevelopment Authority, disagrees. The tensions are the same, he tells the EOC at the next hearing two nights later, it's just that "black people are now letting their feelings be known." The greatest problem in race relations, Norvell says, is that "the majority of our citizens do not believe that racial bigotry and discrimination exist in Madison."[26]

After the president of the Madison Professional Policemen's Association, patrolman John T. Randall, declines the EOC's invitation to testify, friends of the force start spreading the word that the EOC is just out to smear the police. That's when the abusive phone calls to commissioners start.[27] And Ald. Thomas Kassabaum, credit manager at Manchester's department store, takes things a step further, introducing an ordinance to abolish the EOC in retaliation for the hearings.[28]

But when an overflow crowd comes to the council's November 12 meeting to support the commission, Kassabaum moves to reject his own proposal; the only alderman voting to support the proposal to kill the EOC is its former member, Ald. Crary.[29]

By the end of the year, the EOC conducts seventeen hearings into the incident and its aftermath, seven in closed session, taking sworn testimony from fifty-six witnesses—several of whom it has to subpoena, an unprecedented act by a city commission. Four more hearings are scheduled for January, with the EOC's final report expected in late February.[30]

The Movement / Racial Strife

January 28—Extensive racial discrimination in Madison has caused black residents to lose hope in the American dream, Madison Redevelopment Authority community services director Charles Hill tells a First Methodist Church program on race relations. Hill, recently named secretary of the state Department of Local Affairs and Development, also says city welfare services are inadequate.[31]

January 29—Advertising and outreach have failed to persuade sufficient numbers of nonwhites that past discrimination has ended and that City Hall is truly an equal opportunity employer, city personnel director Charles Reott says. Reott's pledge to "just keep hammering away" at minority recruitment may be paying off; with only twelve minority employees among the city's 2,100 employees on February 1, the minority census jumps to twenty by the end of March.[32]

February 16—Black comedian-turned-activist Dick Gregory warns an overflow crowd of white university students at the First Congregational Church that America must end the injustices that cause revolution "because we will burn your neighborhood down to the ground, house by house, if you don't."[33]

March 28—Seeking support for a paid executive director, the EOC reports to the council that there have been at least eighteen instances of overt racial conflict in the past eleven months.[34]

April 2—Native Madisonian (Central High class of 1951) Edwin Hill Jr., the first black person to seek election to the Common Council, fails to unseat south side alderman Harold "Babe" Rohr, who led the fight against the creation and expansion of the Equal Opportunities Ordinance. Hill, thirty-four, is a building superintendent for Anchor Savings and Loan and is on the board of Madison Neighborhood Centers and in the Madison Jaycees. Rohr, the business representative for Painters Local 802 and president of the Madison Building Trades Council, is reelected to his seventh term by a comfortable margin.[35]

April 5—After a teen dance at the East Side Businessmen's Association (ESBMA) clubhouse on Monona Drive, some black youths beat up a white youth near Olbrich Park; in response, about thirty whites chase three black teens for several blocks, finally catching one on Johns Street, whom they kick, hit, and threaten to kill. Madison police sergeant Gerald Thorstensen pushes his way through the mob to rescue the youth and is himself kicked and hit; while other officers rescue the two other black youths, Thorstensen calls for reinforcements to break up the mob.[36]

April 16—A job fair at the South Madison Neighborhood Center attracts thirty-three local employers (including the all-white police department) and five hundred residents.[37]

May 7—After more fights between whites and blacks spark incidents along Atwood Avenue, Monona police chief Walter Kind orders the ESBMA teen dances shut down. "Things were just getting out of hand," he says.[38]

May 21—Mayor Otto Festge asks Madison's 125 employers with more than fifty employees to declare themselves equal opportunity employers by signing the "Plans for

Progress Alliance" pledge that the EOC has sent them.[39] In late September, EOC employment chair Merritt Norvell reports that 113 of the firms have done so.[40]

May 27—The EOC premiers an hourlong documentary, "Madison's Black Middle Class," produced by radio personality and writer George "Papa Hambone" Vukelich, highlighting the plight of middle-class blacks in Madison. "Madison is ostensibly liberal but people are rather complacent," one interviewee says. "The white middle-class people in Madison live in a Never-Never land," another says.[41]

Late August—Nelson Cummings (commissioner, Madison Redevelopment Authority, 1969–1979), the first director of the new Madison Urban League, files complaints with city and state officials alleging housing discrimination. Cummings, thirty-four, has been living in a motel while his family remains in South Bend, Indiana, and he tries to rent a three-bedroom house in Madison. He says he may have to quit in October if he can't find proper housing, but he eventually does find a house on Odana Road.[42]

September 21–22—Police investigate four separate reports from whites alleging that groups of black men accosted and threatened them, and broke their car aerials.[43]

December 3—Five teenagers burn crosses—five feet high, wrapped in gasoline-soaked rags—at the Johns and Hargrove Street homes of two white girls dating black boys. The one eighteen-year-old involved pleads no contest to disorderly conduct charges and is sentenced to thirty days in jail; four juveniles are released to their parents, awaiting Juvenile Court action.[44]

The EOC Gets an ED

The EOC, having failed twice since 1965 to get paid professional staff, tries again; there are so many issues to address that it's becoming "almost impossible" for the all-volunteer commission to do its job.[45]

But the commission knows where to focus its attention. "The attitude of white people toward Negro neighbors is the problem we have to be most concerned with now," EOC chair Mary Louise Symon tells the Board of Estimates in late March, urging its support for a paid executive director.[46]

On April 11—a week after Dr. King's assassination—the council finally agrees, voting, 19–2, to create and fund the position. Mayor Otto Festge says it's "a matter of the highest priority," as "the events of the past week have lent a special sense of urgency" to the issue.

The only alderman to speak in opposition is a member of the EOC, Ald. James Crary, a Dane County deputy sheriff. "I don't think we have a serious [racial] problem in Madison," Crary says, "but within five years, with a director, we will have one." When Crary's term on the commission expires two weeks later, Festge does not reappoint him.[47]

As expected, Festge on May 18 names as the EOC's first executive director its former chair, Reverend James C. Wright. Wright, forty-two, who ranked first among the forty applicants for the $10,000-a-year post, cuts short his studies at the Garrett Theological Seminary in Evanston, Illinois, to start work in May. A native South Carolinian, Wright holds a BS degree in psychology from UW, formerly served as associate pastor at Mt. Zion

The Champ makes a point at the Stock Pavilion, April 26. COURTESY OF CAPITAL NEWSPAPERS ARCHIVES, PHOTO BY J. D. PATRICK

Baptist Church, 2019 Fisher St., and operated a nearby barbershop. This spring, he has also been attending the Urban Training Center at the University of Chicago, focusing on police-community relations.[48]

Muhammad Ali

It's been ten years since Cassius Clay lost the Pan American Games championship at the Field House, three days short of a year since Muhammad Ali refused induction in the armed forces and was stripped of his title, and ten months since he was convicted of draft evasion and sentenced to five years in prison. Now, on April 26, the Champ is headlining the International Students against War, Racism and the Draft program at the Stock Pavilion. But he only wants to talk about one of those things.

"I'm not promoting anything anti-draft, and I'm not here to talk about the war," he says. "I'm here on behalf of the honorable Elijah Muhammad" to present "The Black Muslim's Solution to Racism."

At first, Ali dominates the stage, just as he did the ring. The crowd chuckles when he says he doesn't have "the complexion or the connection" to talk about his conviction while it was under appeal. And they roar when he sets forth what he calls the Black Muslim economic program: "We don't want no pie in the sky when we die," he says. "We want something sound on the ground while we're still around."

But Ali's call for "complete separation" between blacks and whites doesn't go over as well. The largely white student crowd grumbles when he calls integration "hypocritical" and hiss, even boo, when he declares "intermarriage and race mixing should be prohibited."[49]

A Madison police officer, on an undercover special assignment, is not impressed. "Much of Ali's speech was repetitive and not particularly revealing," he reports in a confidential filing filled with misspellings—even including botched versions of the names Muhammad Ali and Cassius Clay. "Many times Ali was hissed by the audience and in fielding questions, he often showed a very infantile mentality."

The undercover officer adds he's "certain that a large number were there only to hear the great boxer, not the Muslim preacher. This because I recognized a number of students who I know to be non-radical."[50]

Race on Campus

Race relations on campus continue to worsen, even as the university tries to improve them.

April 24—"Wisconsin is a terribly bigoted place," says UW junior Gene Parks, director of the University YMCA's Project TEACH, and, "If progress toward racial equality is going to be made, it will have to come within the white communities." Parks is hoping to train and pay forty-five white students to go into their home communities with that message.[51]

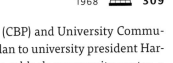

May 3—Representatives of Concerned Black People (CBP) and University Community Action Party (UCA) present a six-part racial equity plan to university president Harrington, requesting courses in black history and culture, a black community center, a year's pay for professors taking leave to do civil rights activity, and that the university sell its shares in Chase Manhattan Bank to fund a black scholarship program. UCA chairman Bill Kaplan says "no commitments were made."[52]

May 16—Chancellor Sewell creates a special fourteen-member faculty committee, chaired by Professor Wilson B. Thiede, to initiate an "action program" to address "race relations in America" through existing courses, special lectures, or new curricula.[53]

May 17—The regents direct the administration to expand efforts to provide equal education opportunity for the disadvantaged and to "include as a high priority" for the next budget funds to meet "the problems of poverty, prejudice and equal opportunity." President Harrington projects a $4 million budget for the 1969–1971 school year. The board also creates the Martin Luther King Scholarship Fund, supported by money transferred from the Wisconsin Student Association (WSA) Scholarship Fund, which Harrington says the university will match.[54]

May 17–20—A year to the day since they took to the streets to block the buses, students take to the suites in an unprecedented confrontation of the board. A hundred students from CBP, UCA, and the WSA demand the university sell its 3,300 shares of Chase Manhattan Bank stock (valued at $230,000) because the bank helped the apartheid government of the Union of South Africa survive a financial crisis in 1961, with proceeds from the sale to be used for minority scholarships. It's the same meeting at which the regents create the King Scholarship Fund and endorse other aid to the disadvantaged, but the students are not satisfied. "As long as the university is involved with the Chase Manhattan Bank, it is the enemy of Concerned Black People," CBP leader Willie Edwards says. "If you don't sell, we'll take further action." UCA chairman Kaplan makes an insistent demand for the action, which, he says, "The university can afford and the country needs."[55]

The regents deliberate in closed session for about ninety minutes and decline to comply or to reconsider. The students actively consider a hostile occupation of the room but are dissuaded by Edwards and other black leaders. Instead, they return to the scene of the antiwar movement's high-water mark precisely two years prior, peacefully occupying the administration building with up to four hundred protesters until 1:20 a.m. on Saturday, when they depart peacefully.[56]

But about twenty minutes later, somebody tosses three Molotov cocktails through a first-floor window in historic South Hall, starting a blaze that heavily damages about fifteen thousand student records, melts fixtures, and causes smoke damage on all four floors of the second-oldest building on campus. University officials caution against linking the firebombing to the protest over Chase Manhattan stock.[57]

At a Monday noon rally of five hundred students at Bascom Hall, some militant whites favor another confrontation with university administrators, but CBP leader Edwards says obstruction would just "give the administration an excuse to come in and

An office in South Hall after the firebombing on May 18. COURTESY OF CAPITAL NEWSPAPERS ARCHIVES, PHOTO BY CARMINE A. THOMPSON

knock some heads." The rally features a surprise appearance by former protest mainstay Bob Cohen, who loses the crowd by rapping on student power rather than racism.[58]

After the protest, CBP leaders meet with Harrington and learn the university has formally agreed to three of their demands: hiring a black assistant director of the minority scholarship program headed by Ruth B. Doyle, giving students an equal voice in the program's operations, and starting an orientation for black freshmen run by black students. But the regents resolutely refuse to reopen the question of selling the Chase stock, and the UCA's Kaplan calls the concessions "meaningless."[59]

June 14—On Harrington's recommendation, the regents name the distinguished educator Dr. Samuel D. Proctor as the university's first dean of special projects, coordinating the program they mandated in May. Proctor, former president of historically black colleges in Virginia and North Carolina, assumes his duties July 1.[60]

November—The Afro American and Race Relations Center, 929 University Ave., opens, as recommended by the Thiede Commission on Studies and Instruction on Race Relations. Center director Suzanne Lipsky is seeking volunteers to turn the five empty rooms on the third floor of an old house into an attractive site for coffee and conversation.[61]

November 1–2—The university's first black homecoming is a milestone for black Greeks—two nights of dances and more put on by the Black People's Alliance, Alpha Kappa Alpha sorority, and Kappa Alpha Psi fraternity.[62]

November 6—Dean Proctor celebrates the success he's found in the university's recruitment and retention of black students. "The major substantial program development has been the Special Scholarship Program, directed by Mrs. Ruth Doyle," Proctor says, citing her program's growth from twenty-four students admitted in 1966 to sixty-one in 1967, and 106 new students this year—about sixty from Wisconsin, by far the highest percentage yet. The 175 current students each receive tutoring and about $2,000. There are now about five hundred black students on the Madison campus.[63]

November 13—In a talk to a Democratic party luncheon, Ruth B. Doyle decries the growing racial separatism on campus, and warns that "we should resist the development of a black curriculum with a black staff. This could turn us back 100 years. Integration is painful and difficult, but we must see it through."[64]

November 14—Vice chancellor Robert H. Altwell informs Chancellor Edwin Young that President Harrington has "completely reneged on his promise to provide funds to match the student's contribution" to the King Scholarship Fund. "We have yet to [prove] to ourselves and certainly to the black students that we are committed," Atwell writes, warning that unless and until such proof is provided, "We can expect major political confrontations, and even violence."[65]

November 15—The University Committee on Financial Aids approves an additional two hundred scholarships for the Special Program of Tutorial and Financial Assistance. At a later meeting with Young, at which Doyle is present, a group of about twenty-five black students demand that she be fired and that a special black curriculum be established, along with other recruitment and retention initiatives for black students.[66]

November 16—Saturday afternoon at about 3 p.m., university police arrest a black nonstudent, Terrence Calneck, in the Rathskeller after he gets into a shouting match and threatens an elderly female worker who allegedly used a racial epithet when he complained about the portion of ice cream she served and refused to pay for it. The arrest gets physical, as four officers wrestle with Calneck and handcuff him. He's charged with disorderly conduct, resisting arrest, and battery; the WSA pays half of Calneck's $500 bail.[67]

November 19—Students protesting Calneck's arrest stage a noisy eight-hour picket and boycott of the Rathskeller. Although the picketers don't physically obstruct business, tensions between protesters with drums and bullhorn and patrons who want dinner get so great that Union director Ted Crabb closes the Rat's serving lines from 5:30 to 8:30 p.m. Cafeteria revenue drops about $600 from the normal $1,700, while Rat revenue drops from $1,400 to $400.

At lunch and dinner, SDS/Wisconsin Draft Resistance Union (WDRU) runs a "liberation food service" in the Trophy Room across from the Rat, providing free sandwiches, chili, and more "food without the bitter salts of racial epithets." Later, about seventy-five students, predominantly white, issue a set of demands, including Calneck's freedom, student control of a police-free Union, and the opening of the Union to nonstudents.[68]

November 20–21—The boycott and SDS/WDRU feed-in continues, cutting cafeteria and Rathskeller revenue in about half; it ends by order of the University Health Sanitarian and the start of Thanksgiving break. There are no incidents or arrests, and no satisfaction on the part of the protesters after their action.[69]

November 20—"Inasmuch as Mrs. Doyle or any white person is incapable of relating" to the black students in the Special Scholarship Program, the Black People's Alliance tells a special meeting of the program's advisory committee, "We demand the removal of Ruth Doyle immediately and the replacement of her with four administrators—two Black, one American Indian, and one Mexican." It's not personal; most of the black students like Doyle and find this step necessary but ironic and sad.[70]

November 21—Almost all the hundred or so black students attending Oshkosh State University are arrested after a sit-in and destructive rampage through the Dempsey Hall administration building. Angered at president Roger Guiles's refusal to accede to their demands for black courses and programs, a black cultural center, and removal of the financial aid director, the Black Student Union members ransack offices, topple furniture, and smash typewriters. The university suspends classes for ten days and tentatively expels ninety-one students. Returning to Madison from a support demonstration, black leader Edwards and the SDS's Michael Rosen discuss strategy for a possible black strike on the Madison campus.[71]

November 22—The Black People's Alliance (BPA) presents the Special Scholarship Advisory Committee with a proposal to expand and improve the university's affirmative action program, beyond firing Doyle, by doubling the current black student population of five hundred, putting black students on admissions committees, and paying black students to attend a summer program for basic skills in writing and math. The BPA later publicly issues the demands.[72]

November 23—A group of seventeen black students go to Chancellor Young's home, 122 Shepard Ter., to present additional demands to the BPA proposal presented on November 22. Young is in bed with the flu but invites one student into his bedroom to talk, which they do at considerable length. Young thinks the exchange is very constructive, and indicative of how most blacks believe the university is making a reasonable attempt to start meeting their needs.[73]

November 25—Black students stage a series of brief disruptions during the afternoon and evening in support of their demands and the Oshkosh black students—they interrupt classes in several buildings, chant "Oshkosh hey" while marching through the library, hamper traffic on State Street, and turn in false fire alarms. The action is organized by the "Wapenduzi Weusi"—Swahili, more or less, for "black revolutionary"—a closed and confidential black leadership group formed to frustrate police surveillance and infiltration.[74]

That afternoon, the Special Scholarship Advisory Committee votes 4–3 to recommend to Young that Doyle "be removed from all capacities" connected with the program she created. The discussion is so disquieting that the committee chair, Professor Archibald Haller, resigns. Chancellor Young appoints a special committee to review the BPA demands, chaired by Dean Proctor and including BPA leaders Willie and Liberty Edwards.[75]

November 26—BPA members and supporters continue their actions the next day with a mild disruption in the library during which they mix up card files, move books, and put pepper in the ventilation. Campus police chief Ralph Hanson says the disruptions do not rise to the level of acts prohibited by the rules the regents recently enacted.[76]

November 28—Thanksgiving.

November 29—The Proctor Committee gives Mrs. Doyle twenty minutes to defend her program and reputation. Among those about to pass judgment, she bitterly notes, is the man she holds responsible for engineering her ouster, Willie Edwards.[77]

December 2—The Proctor Committee recommends that the university accede to almost all the BPA demands, including that Doyle be dismissed and the tutorial and financial aid programs be run by black administrators. The committee also urges that the black students expelled from Oshkosh be allowed to stay in school, either there or at Madison, and that the university create a black cultural center, hire more black faculty, and double the current black student body of about five hundred.[78]

December 16—"If I were not here, there would be no program to restructure," Doyle writes Chancellor Young. "If I were black and male, there would be no need to restructure, except for the expansion of staff. But I am here, and on the job. Until I am satisfied with the direction which the program will take and with my own prospects, I intend to stay at my job."[79]

White and Black Make Big Red Blue

Just as black unrest flares across campus, racial tensions explode at Camp Randall, deepening the woes of a winless football team.

On November 20, Ray Arrington, a black UW track star and member of the Athletic Board, meets privately with the board to convey a series of grievances that black football players hold, including a lack of rapport with coaches, the need for academic counseling for athletes, and the status of athletes whose eligibility ends before they receive their degrees.[80]

Some of the accusations are very personal, arising from Coach John Coatta's mandate to black players that they not date white women. The black players ignore that directive with impunity, leading to resentment from white players and coaches. White players also get most, though not all, of the easy jobs with the trucking company owned by Coatta's father-in-law, former mayor Henry Reynolds; more black players work on the line at Oscar Mayer.[81]

The black players are also upset that quarterback Lew Ritcherson, son of the team's only black coach, was benched in favor of a white player. And they want several assistant coaches fired, or at least "reviewed."

The Athletic Board chair, Professor Frederick Haberman, says the board takes the concerns seriously and promises "honorable, peaceful and fruitful negotiations" after Thanksgiving break.[82]

Two days before the break, eighteen black players boycott the team banquet at the Field House; four freshmen attend, and four others are excused. "This is just a football thing," one boycotter says, "not a general protest against the University administration."[83]

The next day, white linebacker Ken Criter, the team's MVP, says racial tension is "definitely part" of the reason the Badgers have lost their last fifteen games, with an 0–19–1 record in the two years since Coach Milt Bruhn was forced out and Coatta hired. Another white defensive player, Tom McCauley, says, "There are guys who should have been kicked off the team" but "were not because they are black. They are the ones who discriminated against us."[84]

On December 3, athletic director Ivan Williamson and the Athletic Board hold a lengthy closed-door session with the black players, whose complaints are more about disrespect than overt racial discrimination.[85] And the next day, about forty white players—almost all the whites on the team—meet with the Athletic Board to share their perspective. They agree with some of the black players' concerns but are "strongly supportive" of the coaching staff.[86]

Double-barreled bad news is delivered on Thursday the fifth at a special joint meeting of the regents and the Athletic Board. First, news is shared of the $250,000 deficit the winless football team has caused the Athletic Department. Then comes the stunning race-based resignation by popular assistant coach Gene Felker, star end for the 1951 Big Ten champion Badgers, in protest of the administration's "policies of handling the student unrest on this campus as well as the handling of the Football situation."

Black players "committed treason against the coaching staff [and] the ring leaders must be fired," Felker says in a lengthy statement to the boards. The onetime Green Bay Packer also blasts the "frightened administrators who will not take a firm stand but would rather try to appease the minority groups on this campus."

"White coaches have not had an equal opportunity at this institution to succeed," Felker charges, noting that black assistant coach Les Ritcherson has a five-year employment agreement from President Harrington, while Coatta has a three-year contract and all his other assistants have only one-year guarantees.[87]

On December 6, the regents call in Coatta and pledge their "complete cooperation" in helping him return the Badgers to being "competitive in Big 10 football." He's got one year left on his contract to do so.[88]

Protest

Dow Redux

The year opens with the surprise return of Bob Cohen, who drops his appeal and serves out his fourteen-day sentence from his disorderly conduct conviction for Dow 1.[89]

With Dow about to return to campus, an SDS meeting of forty-three students on February 7 decides to obstruct the interviews.[90] Five days later, Chancellor Sewell indefinitely defers the interviews, along with those of the Navy and Marine Corps.[91] The regents are upset; "I thought we had the riot thing pretty well-settled, that when an interview is scheduled it will be held," Regent Walter Renk snaps at Sewell at the regents' meeting on the sixteenth. Sewell explains he's waiting for the report from the special faculty-student committee chaired by Professor Samuel Mermin, and says he'd need "350 policemen from seven counties" to preserve order. Harrington stands by his chancellor.[92]

A Dow 1 prosecution ends about a week later when assistant district attorney Andy Somers, who's running for the council in the Sixth Ward, reduces the February 1967 charge against math TA and former SDS president Hank Haslach to a civil disorderly conduct. Haslach pleads no contest, and Judge William Sachtjen fines him half of the $100 maximum.[93]

A petition protesting Sewell's postponement of the Dow interviews as "a discriminatory policy [which] has infringed on our right of free choice to interview these bona fide employers" is signed February 27 by 1,096 engineering students and fifty-eight faculty. The students are especially concerned about having job interviews as soon as possible because the higher draft calls, coupled with the loss of their student deferments, are causing many to consider employment opportunities with the armed services.[94]

"Bascom Memorial Cemetery, Class of 1968," March 18. UNIVERSITY OF WISCONSIN-MADISON ARCHIVES IMAGE S00892

Dow protest leader Evan Stark, who has quietly returned from Minnesota for an unannounced Madison visit, is spotted and tailed at the Union by two undercover Protection and Security officers on his way to the Play Circle on March 2. Arrested on the outstanding disorderly conduct warrant for Dow 2, he spends a few hours in jail, then returns to Minneapolis.[95]

Sewell reschedules the Dow interviews for March 30 so they're held just days before the presidential primary, figuring that activists who are supporting Senator McCarthy won't risk embarrassing him by a disruptive protest. Some of Sewell's liberal friends are upset, but the strategy works; the interviews at Camp Randall Memorial Building go off without a major hitch. Half a dozen antiwar activists, led by Betty Boardman, distribute leaflets; seventeen students have interviews, and two individuals are calmly arrested for disorderly conduct for blocking a doorway. The Navy and Marine interviews on April 10 are similarly subdued, with nine demonstrators and no arrests.[96]

When Dow returns on November 7, potential confrontation turns to communication as protesters and engineering students engage in conversation in and around the Engineering Building during the interviews. There are no attempts to disrupt or obstruct, and no arrests.[97]

Viet Vote

Once Professor Maurice Zeitlin and the Citizens for a Vote on Vietnam turn in 8,140 signatures on petitions for a referendum on Vietnam, the council has only two choices—adopt the statement calling for "an immediate cease-fire and the withdrawal of United States troops," or put it on the spring ballot. Yet on January 25, eight aldermen ignore the city attorney's advice and vote against doing either. "I find it extremely repugnant to deal with this question in any way," says Ald. Dick Kopp, on the losing side of the 13–8 vote to proceed with the referendum. Ald. James Crary even blames North Korea's recent seizing of the spy ship *Pueblo* on "these same pacifists" giving "the impression that our country is divided." Council president Ald. George Gill calls them out: "You objected to [student protesters'] acts of civil disobedience, you should support this legal action." Having put the referendum on the ballot, the council then restores its patriotic self-image by voting 20–0 to urge the public to vote "no"; west side liberal Ald. Toby Reynolds abstains.[98]

Polling shows the referendum might pass, until President Johnson's disavowal of candidacy two days before the vote changes the dynamic; on April 2, the referendum is defeated, 27,755–21,129. Zeitlin notes that 43 percent support is better than other antiwar referenda have done in San Francisco; Cambridge, Massachusetts; and Dearborn, Michigan, which received from 32 to 38 percent support. "I consider the vote a major victory," Zeitlin says.[99] Despite its defeat, the referendum helps spur turnout, which is critical to history graduate student Paul Soglin's defeat of incumbent Ald. Ellsworth Swenson.[100]

New Students, Old Issue

The 1968–1969 protest season starts on September 14 with the return of an issue from years ago, as about 250 students meet on Library Mall and proclaim themselves the "Freshman ROTC Resistance." They vote to boycott the mandatory Reserve Officer Training Corps (ROTC) orientation classes, which are still required of freshmen males even after ROTC itself was made voluntary in 1960 (when professor Edwin Young, now chancellor, chaired the University Committee).

About thirty of the three hundred students walk out of the first ROTC orientation Monday morning, September 16; another sixteen do likewise at the noon session.[101]

Monday night, about two hundred students meet and endorse engaging in prolonged disruptive discussions during the class sessions, which continue through the week. Thursday night, the Student Senate endorses making the orientation voluntary and schedules a referendum.[102]

The voluntary ROTC program itself is already hurting; combined enrollment for the Madison and Milwaukee campuses last fall fell to 1,257, its lowest level since 1,951 signed up in 1962.

The first women-directed antiwar action takes place Saturday morning, September 21, when about sixty women and a handful of men rally at Lincoln Terrace and march on Agricultural Hall to invade a Naval ROTC class. After freshman Laura Rosen reads a statement (Captain C. E. Olson gives her his microphone) denouncing the military presence on campus and the war, the program resumes—but that's when the hissing, hollering, foot stomping, and clapping begin. Olson twice warns that "further disruptions will not be tolerated," but he takes no action to expel the protesters.[103]

At the rally, Naomi Puro urges the start of what she calls a "women's liberation movement" on campus, focusing on issues beyond ROTC, including abortion, birth control, and discrimination in employment. After the action, she takes names and numbers.[104]

Protest Timeline

February 15—The ever-growing campus opposition to the war becomes more personally urgent for some after draft director Lieutenant General Lewis B. Hershey ends almost all deferments for graduate students. Between 70,000 and 175,000 students starting graduate school in the fall will be drafted.[105]

March 4—The faculty-student committee chaired by Professor Mermin approves, eight to six, continuing on-campus job interviews, without discrimination, for all bona fide employers. They should be scheduled "so as to minimize the possibility of disruption and violence," with the chancellor having discretionary authority to postpone or relocate a particular interview.[106]

March 21—In late afternoon, about seven hundred students pack the Agricultural Hall auditorium to heckle and hiss US secretary of agriculture Orville Freeman so severely he cuts short his talk. Two days later, Chancellor Sewell cites this action, and the immediate backlash, as evidence that disrupters are doing "incalculable damage" to the university, and calls on the leaders of campus organizations to help stop them. Early the next morning, someone sets fire to the side door in Bascom Hall, with no lasting physical damage. It's one of a raft of firebombings and small fires set on campus in the months after Dow.[107]

That night, while a large and happy crowd packs the Dane County Youth Building to greet Republican presidential hopeful Richard Nixon, the South Central Federation of Labor's political action committee, Committee on Political Education, votes against endorsing any aldermanic candidate who supports the Vietnam referendum.[108]

In the aftermath of Dow, the city yearns to learn about what's going on down on campus. One forum features two future mayors. UNIVERSITY OF WISCONSIN–MADISON ARCHIVES S00102

April 25–27—Madison's participation in the International Student Strike Against War, Racism and the Draft begins with a Thursday night "camp-in" by about forty activists on Bascom Hill; in the morning, a handful of picketers urge students to boycott classes, without noticeable effect.[109]

Friday afternoon, close to three thousand students pay seventy-five cents for a full program at the Stock Pavilion, starring Muhammad Ali. The Champ preaches black separatism; Professor William Appleman Williams makes the kind of politically pointed remarks the students are expecting, calling for a "reconstruction of this society [to] change this mess."[110]

The strike itself largely fizzles, with only a handful of picketers outside classrooms—although organizers say that the entire crowd at Ali's speech was essentially on strike, since the rally was during the day.[111]

One likely reason most students go to class—twelve-week exams are under way.

On Saturday, a peaceful crowd of about four hundred marches from campus to the State Capitol, where they sit in the spring sun for about two hours of speeches from leaders of several antiwar and antiracism organizations.[112]

May 15—It's epithets and eggs for Selective Service chief Hershey when the draft director arrives at the Hotel Loraine for an Armed Forces Day talk to the Downtown Rotary club. The Wisconsin Draft Resistance Union (WDRU) action draws about three hundred noisy protesters, their line stretching from West Washington Avenue to West Main Street. Most are orderly, chanting "Hell no, we won't go!" and other antidraft slogans as about fifty Madison police officers and two dozen helmeted Dane County deputies with Mace and riot sticks stand by—one with a very menacing axe handle. But a handful throw about twenty eggs, coating Hershey's black station wagon (and a few officers); WDRU leaders reproach the egg tossers and seize their remaining stockpile, but the public relations damage has been done. Greeted with a standing ovation by the five hundred business and professional men in the Crystal Ballroom, the seventy-four-year-old military man avoids a second confrontation afterward by slipping down a back alley and out through a dry-cleaning store on the far side of the block. Hershey does not visit his old research director from World War II, Chancellor Sewell.[113]

May 20—The US Supreme Court upholds the constitutionality of the Wisconsin disorderly conduct statute and the convictions of Bob Cohen and Robert Zwicker at Dow 1; on the twenty-eighth, the seventeen remaining Dow 1 arrestees plead no contest and are fined $50 each.[114]

June 10—About a hundred protesters, many wearing white armbands or bearing signs, stage a silent demonstration near the end of the UW commencement ceremony.[115]

September 18—About seven hundred activists meet in 6210 Social Sciences for the merger meeting of the Madison Students for a Democratic Society (SDS) and the WDRU. The WDRU's John Fuerst, a former chairman of the SDS chapter at Columbia University, says the unified group will focus on organizational activity rather than the previous strategy of confrontation.[116]

September 21—Students heckle US Supreme Court Justice Thurgood Marshall, the first African American on the High Court, when he refuses to denounce or even discuss the war during a well-attended Union Theater appearance. Marshall is able to finish his talk, which is part of the Law School's observance commemorating the hundredth anniversary of the Fourteenth Amendment to the Constitution.[117]

October 1—Sometime around 1 a.m., arsonists with glass-cutting tools pour gasoline through the window of the state headquarters of the Selective Service System at 1220 Capitol Ct., lighting a gas-soaked towel as a fuse. The explosion blows out a window; some draft records are destroyed, fixtures melt, and there's smoke damage. Draft officials suspect the incident is related to last week's attack on the draft office in Milwaukee.[118]

October 7—Male freshman vote 775–292 for ROTC orientation to be voluntary. In early December, the All-University ROTC Policy Committee agrees, recommending that the five class-hours of orientation become optional, starting next fall. The recommendation will now go to the full faculty and the Board of Regents.[119]

October 12—About three thousand march from the mall to the Army–Air Force recruiting office, 429 State St., for a series of speeches but cancel plans to continue on to Camp Randall (for fear of violence when the football game ends). Police chief Emery had denied the parade permit request from WDRU, SDS, CEWV and CDA, but Mayor Festge overruled him and issued the permit.[120]

Rules and Regulations

February 3—The new Faculty Assembly—fifty representatives elected by the 3,700 faculty members on the thirteen university campuses—adopts a rule that students "may support causes by lawful means which do not disrupt the operations of the University or of organizations accorded the use of university facilities."[121]

April 19—The regents approve new administrative rules restricting use of the Memorial Union to members and their invited guests (with guest cards), preventing the use of amplified sound within 175 feet of a campus building without prior permission, and making it illegal to block campus offices, classrooms, or other facilities.[122]

July 19—The regents adopt tough rules subjecting students to discipline—up to expulsion—for "intentional conduct that seriously impairs University-run or University-authorized activities," including blocking building entrances or interrupting classes, speeches, or programs by heckling or "derisive laughter or other means." The code permits the immediate suspension of a student, pending a hearing, if it appears the misconduct will be repeated. A student who is expelled has to wait a full year before reapplying for admission; Regent Walter Renk's motion to bar students who are expelled from ever applying for readmission loses, 9–1.[123]

September 6—The regents adopt an emergency administrative rule making it illegal for anyone to attend a class or other instructional session unless enrolled or with the instructor's consent.[124]

October 16—Governor Warren Knowles tells the Madison Downtown Rotary Club that the university needs "firm disciplinary measures" so that "the taxpaying public" is assured it remains "a center of academic discipline—not a never-never land of perpetual adolescence. We should tell the disrupters, the hippies, the narcotics and LSD users, the pornography peddlers, that they are not welcome [at the UW]." That the cautious, moderate Knowles—a former president of the university alumni association—would make such a speech is seen as a bellwether of statewide public opinion. The downtown businessmen cheer his attack on "students raised in a prevailing attitude of permissiveness—from pampering parents to over-promising political leaders."[125]

November 2—New Chancellor Edwin Young assures the Wisconsin Alumni Association board of directors that the university "will catch, punish and separate from the University those who obstruct its function." Young warns the SDS/WDRU not to go through with their threatened takeover of another campus building. But, he says, "If it's confrontation that some of these students want, then they will get it."[126]

November 5—Protesting the day's presidential election and the imminent return of Dow, about two thousand students stage a boisterous but orderly march up State Street. Afterward, about thirteen hundred attend a mass meeting in the Union Theater and overwhelmingly reject calls to take over a campus building.[127]

December 13—Federal Judge James E. Doyle sides with Ald. Paul Soglin, the SDS, and eight other students in their October 1967 challenge to university rule 11.02, implementing the "Kennedy Rule" on disruptions. Doyle declares the rule unconstitutional because its ban on "misconduct" is "vague and over-broad." The university appeals.[128]

War Dead

Army Private First Class Edgar Gerlach, twenty, a tank driver, is killed January 30 at the Pleiku base camp during a mortar attack. A 1965 graduate of Robert M. La Follette High School, Gerlach was a counselor at the Monona Grove YMCA and a Life Scout in Boy Scout Troop 150, where he received the God and Country Award and was elected to the Order of the Arrow. He entered the Army in October 1966 and had been in country since August 1967.[129]

Army Corporal Bruce Knox, twenty, whose parents live at 1862 Fisher St., is killed in combat February 4. A graduate of Central High School and member of St. Joseph's Catholic Church, Knox worked at Gisholt Machine Company before being drafted. A member of the First Cavalry Division, he had been in Vietnam nine months. In September, the Army posthumously awards Knox the Purple Heart, Silver Star, Bronze Star, Air Medal, and other commendations, particularly for his action moving through hostile fire near Hue to rescue and administer first aid to a wounded comrade.[130]

Marine Private Thomas J. Blaha, nineteen, who attended West High School, is killed in action February 8. His parents, who live at 621 Pickford St., learn of his death on Valentine's Day—two years to the day after he joined the Marines. Blaha, who also attended Stoughton High School, was sent to Vietnam in December 1967.[131]

Marine Lance Corporal Lawrence J. Herfel, nineteen, is killed in action in Quang Tri Province on February 24. Herfel, whose parents live at 922 Nobel Ln., joined the Marines in August 1966, two months after graduating from Robert M. La Follette High School, and arrived in Vietnam a year later.[132]

Marine Private First Class Daniel Lloyd Meysembourg, eighteen, 117 S. Marquette St., is killed in action in the Quang Tri area on March 11. Meysembourg joined the Marines a month after graduating from Central High School in 1967; he had been in country seven weeks at the time of his death. Born in Rice Lake, Meysembourg grew up with his family at 821 Regent St. in the Greenbush neighborhood, attending St. Joseph's Catholic Church and School; the family moved to the east side when their house was razed for urban renewal and joined St. Bernard's Catholic Church.[133]

Army Specialist 4 Bernard "Bernie" Mazursky, twenty, whose mother and sisters live at 314 S. Orchard St., is killed in an ambush in Kontum on May 4. A 1966 graduate of Central-University High School and member of Beth Israel Center, Mazursky was a freshman at UW when he gave up his student deferment and enlisted along with his best friend in December 1966; he visited home before being transferred from Germany to Vietnam on March 23.[134]

Army Specialist 4 James Leahy, twenty-five, an information specialist with the 39th Army Engineer Combat Battalion, and the only son of the head of the Madison draft board, dies August 8 of wounds received when his vehicle struck a land mine near Chu Lai, just south of the supply base at Da Nang. A graduate of Queen of Peace School and Edgewood High School, he enlisted in the Army after graduating from Milton College in 1967 so there wouldn't be accusations of favoritism related to his father's job; his father, Maurice, 4114 Meyer Ave., a safety specialist at Oscar Mayer and a World War II veteran, is head of Draft Board Thirteen, which handles conscription for city residents.[135]

Army Lieutenant Harry B. Hambleton III, twenty-four, formerly of 4213 Odana Rd., dies on September 14 on board the hospital ship *Repose* of wounds received when his encampment came under heavy fire seven days prior. Hambleton graduated from West High School in 1963 and UW in 1967, where he was in the ROTC program. In his nine months in Vietnam, he had been awarded three Purple Hearts, a Presidential citation, the Army Commendation Medal for heroism, the Bronze Star for valor, the Air Medal, the Soldier's Medal, and several other commendations.[136]

Navy Hospital Corpsman Third Class Dan Michael Bennett, twenty-one—whose wife and eighteen-month-old son, Dan Jr., live at 11A Wright Ct.— is killed by rifle fire on Foxtrot Ridge December 11 after he leaves his secure position to administer aid to a wounded Marine. A native Madisonian whose parents and nine siblings all live on the east side, and a 1965 graduate of East High School, Bennett had been in country about five months at the time of his death.[137]

Auditorium

Once again, the year begins with good courthouse news for Monona Terrace proponents—the announcement on January 10 by longtime Terrace foe Carroll Metzner that he's not appealing Judge Edwin Wilke's ruling upholding the city's Monona Basin contract with the Frank Lloyd Wright Foundation.[138]

It's not entirely smooth sailing yet, though. A week later, three former mayors—Henry Reynolds, Harold Hanson, and George Forster—denounce the entire Monona Basin plan as an "impractical and unnecessary white elephant" for "small special interest groups" that will create "an intolerable traffic and parking mess," block lake views, and provide a "Taj Mahal complex for an art club."[139]

But Mayor Otto Festge puts the full weight of his office behind the plan, with Law Park auditorium as the first facility to be constructed. Making for another newsworthy Washington's birthday, the council on February 22 votes 15–4 to approve the master plan, make the Law Park auditorium the first priority, and direct foundation architect William Wesley Peters to proceed with a schematic design for the auditorium. Although zealous Olin Park supporter Ald. Babe Rohr attacks the Law Park site as a proposal that "has torn the city apart," he vows to support the decision after the vote—as long as the building stays within its $4 million budget.[140]

In early August, the council approves by voice vote the schematic plan for the auditorium, which includes a 2,360-seat theater that can be converted to a smaller facility for 1,100 attendees, and 16,280 square feet of flat floor space for convention use. Ald. Rohr praises Peters for following the contract "to the letter" and urges his colleagues "not to nit-pick, which I have done in the past."[141]

"I look forward to groundbreaking next spring," the mayor says, hopefully.[142]

A month later, Peters unveils for the Auditorium Committee the full development drawings for what he calls "a great circular drum," eighty feet high, sheathed in "soft golden brick" and designed to "achieve the sense of joyous pageantry natural to a theater,

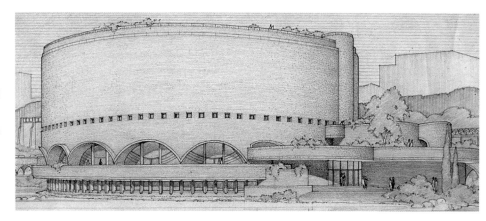

William Wesley Peters's "great circular drum" of a civic auditorium, presented September 9. COPYRIGHT 2018 © FRANK LLOYD WRIGHT FOUNDATION, SCOTTSDALE, AZ. ALL RIGHTS RESERVED. THE FRANK LLOYD WRIGHT FOUNDATION ARCHIVES (THE MUSEUM OF MODERN ART, AVERY ARCHITECTURAL & FINE ARTS LIBRARY, COLUMBIA UNIVERSITY, NEW YORK)

yet combined with the noble dignity of a building representing the cultural and civic aspirations of the capital city of a great state."

Peters concedes, however, that the limited construction budget means the building will be "very usable," but unfinished. And even though Peters echoes Frank Lloyd Wright in extolling the project for connecting downtown Madison "with the priceless heritage of lake and water, freed from the intrusion of mechanistic expediency," his parking ramp—like Wright's—still blocks the view from inside.[143]

But none of this matters to the council, which promptly approves Peters's plan and authorizes him to prepare construction documents. Peters says he hopes to have working drawings by February 1 and bid documents issued two weeks later. Presuming the bids come in within budget, the schedule calls for an April groundbreaking and completion in the fall of 1970.[144]

UW

COMMENCEMENT, JUNE 10
- ▸ Baccalaureate: 2,435
- ▸ Master's/PhD: 1085
- ▸ JD/MD: 274[145]

FALL ENROLLMENT
- ▸ Total Students: 33,976[146]

HOMECOMING
- ▸ Show: John Gary, the Brothers Four, the Fifth Dimension, Godfrey Cambridge
- ▸ Dance: Syndicate of Sound, the Outsiders[147]

NEW BUILDINGS OF NOTE
- ▸ Nielson Tennis Stadium, 1000 Highland Ave.[148]

Campus Calendar

January 4—The WSA agrees to sponsor a Camp Randall music festival on May 4 featuring Bob Dylan, the Doors, the Association, and Bill Cosby, to be produced by promoter Frank Fried, the man who brought the Beatles to Chicago. The Doors do play the Coliseum on November 8, but the festival doesn't happen.[149]

January 9—Former UW student Steve Miller, who left Madison in 1965, returns to play the Factory as the first Bay Area musician to have signed a huge record contract.[150]

January 24—Chancellor William Sewell says he's "distressed by the growing hostility" the community is showing to students and even faculty, especially over "protest activities which are offensive to community values and expectations"—even those protests which are "perfectly legitimate and carried out in a legal manner." Speaking to a joint luncheon of twenty-one service clubs at the Field House, Sewell also derides those who treat students with "contempt, derision and censure" over their hair and dress, as though their appearance were "a major challenge to the very foundations of our society."[151]

February 1—UW dean of students Joseph E. Kauffman announces he's leaving after three years to become president of Rhode Island College; he's the fourth UW administrator to become head of another academic institution in the past year. Chancellor Sewell thinks Kauffman became "completely battle weary [and] not much good" after Dow, and isn't sorry to see him go.[152]

February 11–18—Civil rights activist/comedian Dick Gregory headlines the ninth WSA Symposium, "Crisis in Confidence—the Credibility Gap," which also features antiwar senator Wayne Morse (D-OR, a Madison native and UW alumnus), birth control advocate and head of Planned Parenthood Dr. Alan Guttmacher, Kennedy assassination conspiracy theorist Mark Lane, and author and social critic Vance Packard.[153]

March 6—Wisconsin basketball forward Joe Franklin, the team's two-time MVP, becomes the first Badger in sixteen years to be named first team All-Big Ten. The quiet Central High star, who first shot hoops in the old Neighborhood House on West Washington Avenue, holds twenty-one Wisconsin scoring and rebounding records and is the Big Ten's top rebounder. He's drafted by the Milwaukee Bucks but does not make the team.[154]

March 9—Joan Baez, who began the decade barefoot in the thirteen-hundred-seat Union Theater, performs for a capacity Stock Pavilion crowd of almost triple that, in a bright psychedelic blouse and miniskirt, her setlist updated to include Beatles, Stones, and Dylan. At a Madison Inn press conference earlier in the day, she urged students to "engage yourself in life and get out of the institutions preaching death."[155]

March 15—On President Harrington's recommendation, the regents welcome back Edwin Young, the former dean of the College of Letters and Science, as vice president of the university. Chancellor Sewell privately tells Harrington, "You're stockpiling Ed Young for when they fire me." Harrington just laughs.[156]

April 1—The faculty unanimously approves lifting the remaining curfew—11 p.m. weeknights, 1 a.m. weekends—for freshman and sophomore women, and allowing all juniors and seniors with written parental permission to live in unsupervised housing even if under twenty-one years of age.[157]

April 4—The WSA surveys its constituents on sex, drugs, and continuing on-campus job interviews:

WSA REFERENDUM, APRIL 4

	Yes	No
Provide free birth control info	7,361	760
Distribute birth control	5,501	2,512
Legalize marijuana	4,795	3,196
Work to legalize marijuana	3,166	4,632
Continue on-campus job interviews	5,537	2,357[158]

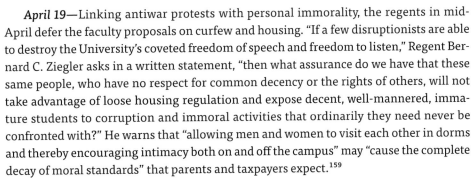

April 19—Linking antiwar protests with personal immorality, the regents in mid-April defer the faculty proposals on curfew and housing. "If a few disruptionists are able to destroy the University's coveted freedom of speech and freedom to listen," Regent Bernard C. Ziegler asks in a written statement, "then what assurance do we have that these same people, who have no respect for common decency or the rights of others, will not take advantage of loose housing regulation and expose decent, well-mannered, immature students to corruption and immoral activities that ordinarily they need never be confronted with?" He warns that "allowing men and women to visit each other in dorms and thereby encouraging intimacy both on and off the campus" may "cause the complete decay of moral standards" that parents and taxpayers expect.[159]

May 3–5—Gwendolyn Brooks, the first African American woman to receive the Pulitzer Prize for poetry, and Howard University Dean Mercer Cook, former US ambassador to several African nations, headline the three-day Madison Conference on Afro-American Letters and Arts. Sponsored by the ad hoc Wisconsin Conference on Afro-Arts, with financial and moral support from the university administration, the conference also presents the Madison Art Center Players performing *A Raisin in the Sun* by the late Lorraine Hansberry, a former UW student.[160]

May 10—Folk Arts Society and the Wisconsin Draft Resistance Union bring the Magic Sam Blues Band back to Great Hall for the last show and dance of the semester.[161]

May 17—In a serious blow to the Independent Housing Association, the regents approve, 7–3, allowing freshmen and sophomores under twenty years of age to live in unsupervised off-campus housing with the written consent of their parents or guardians. They also vote, 7–2, that "no general restrictions on student hours in supervised housing be imposed by the University"—ending hours for women. Opposition to both measures is led by Madison attorney Maurice Pasch and Sun Prairie agribusinessman Walter Renk.[162]

May 17—Tracy Nelson comes home, at least cinematically. She and her band, Mother Earth, are featured in the new hippie flick *Revolution*, opening at the Majestic. The former UW student, who went west in 1966 with a ticket won in a Milton College folksinging contest, performs the title track and two other tunes. Nelson and the band are rehearsing her new album under a new three-year contract with Mercury Records.[163]

May 21—Legendary blues singer and harmonica player Lightnin' Hopkins gives an impromptu performance in the Rathskeller to raise money for the Poor People's March in Washington.[164]

June 10—The class of 1968 graduates with 15 percent having participated in antiwar protests and less than 10 percent having participated in civil rights demonstrations, according to a four-year study of four thousand students and dropouts conducted by the Social Behavior Research Center.[165]

July 12—New York mayor John Lindsay draws a near-record crowd of six thousand to the Union Terrace for a Friday afternoon speech supporting New York governor Nelson Rockefeller's presidential candidacy—the largest outdoor speech on campus since eight thousand gathered to hear Indian prime minister Jawaharlal Nehru in 1949. The charismatic Republican suffers no pickets or disruptions, is applauded for his attacks on the war and President Johnson, and is booed only for his references to Rockefeller. Lindsay also meets briefly with law professor Nathan Feinsinger, who settled New York's crippling transit strike in 1966.[166]

September 18—History professor Harvey Goldberg, the hero of radical and revolutionary UW students, is the first professor to have a class disrupted by the History Students Association, as the group's Michael Rosen successfully diverts Goldberg's crowded European Social History class—a lecture on seventeenth-century market capitalism—into a critique of the course itself.[167]

September 19—B. B. King makes his college campus debut at the Union Theater; "Basically, he educated a lot of honkies," the *Daily Cardinal* reviewer enthuses.[168]

September 27—Harry Belafonte captivates a crowd of seven thousand as he returns to the Field House, this time with the Delores Hall Gospel Singers and singer-songwriter Jackie DeShannon.[169]

October 20—Senator Gene McCarthy makes his first Wisconsin appearance since losing the presidential nomination to Senator Hubert Humphrey at a campaign rally for Senator Gaylord Nelson and US Representative Robert W. Kastenmeier before four thousand enthusiastic admirers in the Field House.[170]

October 22—Independent presidential candidate Dick Gregory returns to Madison (with his running mate and fellow Symposium speaker, Mark Lane) to denounce the Wisconsin law that prevents counting presidential write-in ballots. After a talk about the end of the two-party system at a noon benefit luncheon at the Park Motor Inn, he comes back to campus and is met with raucous applause and a standing ovation from a packed Great Hall. In a speech piped throughout the Union, he urges students to move beyond civil rights, which he calls "an insult to me. It doesn't help the Indians or the Mexicans. Human rights frees a lot more people." But he also warns of more racial violence: "We're gonna Patrick Henry you—give us liberty, or give us death."[171]

October 24—Eldridge Cleaver, defense minister for the Black Panthers and the Peace and Freedom party candidate for president, cancels his appearance at the Stock Pavilion because he double-booked and decided to keep the other date. Tickets can be refunded or used as donations at the rally for Eugene Parks's write-in campaign for sheriff that night in the State Historical Society auditorium.[172]

October 26—Folk Arts Society presents the First Madison Blues Festival, featuring J. B. Hutto & His Hawks and Johnny Young's Chicago Blues Band, in Great Hall. Admission is $1.[173]

October 27—Two of San Francisco's best come to campus—in the afternoon, wiry acid rockers Quicksilver Messenger Service blast through "Mona" and "Who Do You Love?" for free in Great Hall; at night, tired acid troubadours Country Joe and the Fish perform "I-Feel-Like-I'm-Fixin'-to-Die Rag" and more in the Stock Pavilion, where the acoustics are not as good for rock as for orchestral music.[174]

November 3—Poet Robert Bly, winner of the National Book Award for poetry and co-founder of American Writers against the Vietnam War, reads and discusses his poetry in the Old Madison Room.[175]

November 12—Vel Phillips, the first female and first black Milwaukee alderwoman, and the first black person to serve on the national committee of a major political party, tells the Theta Sigma Phi Matrix banquet in Great Hall that "the struggle for freedom must not be viewed as an end in itself."[176]

November 17—Jazz saxophonist/flautist Charles Lloyd, the 1967 *Downbeat* jazz artist of the year, brings his quartet, featuring Keith Jarrett on piano, to the Union Theater for two Sunday night shows before small but enthusiastic crowds.[177]

November 22—Twenty-year-old mop-top violin phenom Pinchas Zukerman, the 1967 cowinner of the coveted Leventritt Award, shows a Union Theater crowd he could be the next Isaac Stern.[178]

December 9—Urbanologist, and rumored Nixon cabinet appointee, Harvard professor Daniel Patrick Moynihan tells a Union Theater crowd of about a thousand that violence used as a means would soon become an end in itself.[179]

Coach, Interrupted

When basketball coach John Erickson resigns April 3 to become general manager of the NBA's new Milwaukee Bucks, everyone knows his handpicked successor will be John Powless. Everyone, that is, except for Professor Frank Remington and the Athletic Board—at a seven-hour meeting that ends about 1:30 a.m. on Wednesday, April 24, they name Bob Knight, twenty-seven, the coach at West Point for the past three years and forward on the championship Ohio State teams of Jerry Lucas and John Halicek. The regents' executive committee signs off that afternoon. As soon as they do, Matt Pommer has the story in the *Capital Times*—before Knight, who was visiting his parents in Ohio, can tell West Point officials or even his wife. Knight throws a fit, claims he had never accepted the offer, and that he's offended by the leak; Remington knows Knight did accept the offer and there wasn't a leak, but doesn't object when Knight renews his contract with West Point Friday morning. Powless, thirty-five, gives up his appointment as tennis coach and is confirmed as the new basketball coach by midnight.[180]

Changing Chancellors

Jumping before he's pushed, Chancellor William Sewell resigns at the end of June after one troubled year in Bascom Hall and returns to his position as Vilas research professor in sociology. President Harrington admires Sewell greatly but knows he's not the chancellor the campus needs right now, and thinks it's for the best. Sewell agrees: "I was the wrong man for the times and the situation," he writes a friend six months later.[181]

As expected, and as Sewell predicted, the regents in mid-September—Friday the thirteenth—unanimously endorse Harrington's choice for his third chancellor in five years, Ed Young.[182]

But the appointment almost doesn't happen; Harrington's handpicked search and selection committee inexplicably does not include Young among its list of candidates. Harrington has to call the members in and direct them to do so.[183]

Harrington privately believes Young to be "a little stronger than I was in terms of taking positions being against the students, a crackdown type who used secret agents among the radicals." Harrington is right. "Demonstrations are appropriate behavior for students," Young tells an introductory press conference, but "we won't tolerate disruption of this university. There are always people who would like to destroy the system," he says, "but I don't regard closing down the University as a legitimate demand."[184]

Reefer Madness and More

The *Daily Cardinal* estimates seventy-five hundred or so students have used illegal drugs, mainly marijuana, and that around five thousand will again—half of them at least weekly. There's a staggering amount of good pot around Madison—the *Cardinal* estimates a thousand pounds the first six months of the 1967–1968 school year—which drives the price of an ounce down to as low as $10 to $15, effectively ending the practice of nickel and dime bags. There's lots of hashish, which holds steady at $10 a gram. Drug use is even rampant in the dorms—pot, LSD, sometimes even opium. Students who are caught smoking pot are placed on warning status and told another infraction could lead to expulsion. Sales of amphetamines are soaring, with a gram of methedrine costing between $20 and $40, and "black beauty" pills about a buck each. There are about a hundred speed freaks who use regularly, but very few of them shoot up.[185]

Police continue to use young undercover officers rather than informants to infiltrate drug-taking groups at the Rathskeller, Lorenzo's, and the Uptown Café—professionalizing the evidence-gathering and making prosecutions more successful.

In the first nine months of the year, Madison police arrest thirty-one adults and thirty-seven juveniles on 104 drug charges; on the last day of September, they team up with federal agents to execute forty-six more arrest warrants of users and sellers, aged fifteen to twenty-four, including two university women and four high school girls.

Among the estimated $75,000 in drugs seized are one thousand hits of mescaline, which a federal undercover agent bought for $3,750, with a street value of about $15,000. Detective Stanley Davenport, head of the narcotics squad, says all the undercover contacts, and all the purchases by juveniles, were made at either the Union or Library Mall.[186]

Several students with long hair and wearing hippie clothes when arrested are shorn, shaved, and dressed in jail dungarees for their initial October 1 court appearances, on order of Sheriff Franz G. Haas. Reacting to news of the arrests, Madison residents flood police phone lines throughout the day with tips about other suspected users and dealers.[187]

Later that morning, Mayor Festge issues letters of commendation to Davenport and Detective James McFarlane for their "exemplary [policework] in exposing the illegal traffic in drugs and narcotics in Madison." Festge gets a late kick at former chancellor Sewell, complaining of "less than full cooperation [from] past university administrations."[188]

On October 3, the Assembly State Affairs Committee opens hearings into "The Problem of Drugs in Wisconsin," which committee counsel James R. Klauser (Wisconsin secretary of administration, 1986–1996) proclaims "a direct attack on the University." Detectives Davenport and McFarlane testify that the university is the Midwest's best drug center, with drugs being sold openly and cheaply on Library Mall. They also back up the mayor, testifying that they've received no help from UW police chief Ralph Hanson.[189] Federal narcotics officials deny the claim that Madison's drug problem is worse than in comparable cities, and say Madison police are exaggerating.[190]

The next day, Young assures the Board of Regents that he's working on ways to restrict access to the Union but otherwise declines to address the city's allegations. Harrington acknowledges, however, that "there has been a substantial amount of friction" between the city and university "for a long time." Regent Pasch tries to use the controversy to restore the restrictions on student hours, which were lifted in May, but fails.[191]

Also on Friday, the director of the Dane County Alcoholic Referral Center reveals that 392 juveniles have been referred to him by the Juvenile Court for drinking problems over the past eighteen months, and that 78 percent of the teen drinkers were regular drug users.[192]

Meanwhile, on October 10, assistant district attorney Michael Zaleski tells around a hundred law enforcement officials that it's okay to proceed without a proper search warrant, as long as illegal drugs are seized. "All right, you lose the case, big deal," he tells a juvenile justice conference at the Wisconsin Center; the important thing "is to get the stuff off the market." He recommends uneducated jurors and notes that most Wisconsinites "don't like those people with beards and long hair." District attorney James C. Boll, up for reelection next month following his appointment in 1966, publicly rebukes Zaleski.[193]

At the upper end of State Street, some hold the adults responsible for what the children are doing. "The recent and constant revelations about drug use, demonstrations, and the nude performances on the UW campus attest to the ineffectiveness of the administration's policies," Assembly Speaker Harold V. Froelich (R-Appleton) says. "It is only a matter of time before the policies of the UW administration destroy what has become a great state university." He releases a report on October 11 titled "Administrators Fiddle as UW Self-Destructs" and warns of direct legislative involvement in campus affairs. There are bipartisan calls for the regents to fire President Harrington, who assures Governor Knowles—incorrectly—that there's no significant drug use or distribution in the dorms.[194]

Making matters worse, Detective McFarlane tells four hundred concerned parents at a West High Parent-Teacher Association meeting that drug use among city and university youth is "completely out of control" and that the police are "not equipped to handle this situation."[195]

In early December, Young reports that he has barred high school students from the Union and worked with Madison schools superintendent Douglas Ritchie to distribute about fifteen thousand leaflets to parents, asking their help in enforcing the rule. He criticizes those who "show their insolence and disregard for the rights of others" by using Union rooms without prior authorization, or disrupting normal operations. "We have some people who believe freedom means freedom only for them," he says, but warns that new rules might not solve the problem: "We have some very inventive people." But barring younger teens from the Union does little to slow drug use in the city or on campus.[196]

Another *Cardinal* Contretemps

Three years after the regents defended the *Daily Cardinal* over alleged Communist influence, the board itself attacks the paper for bad language. The paper prints a College Press Service dispatch in late October about factional infighting at a national SDS meeting involving (and naming) radical anarchists "The Up against the Wall Motherfuckers." After considering proposals to close the *Cardinal* down (which it can't do, because the paper is a private corporation) and expel its editors, the board unanimously adopts a resolution on November 1 to "reprimand" the paper for language "unacceptable for public use" and threatens "to take appropriate action whenever language standards are violated" in the future.[197]

Editor-in-chief Gregory Graze's response is not conciliatory. "The whole concept of obscene language is absurd," he says. "I think many of the Regents' meetings are obscene."[198]

A follow-up front-page editorial, "Up against the Wall, Re. . .ts" is even more confrontational, vowing to "resist in every way, legally and extra-legally, the totalitarianism" of the regents. "For if the *Cardinal* dies at the hobnail boot of the regents, the blood will be on 34,000 hands and no student group or individual will be safe from the guillotine." The paper also prints passages from works by Shakespeare, Mailer, Joyce, and Lawrence, all with four-letter words, all from works on required class reading lists.[199]

"If the paper is being clearly retaliatory in what it's printing," Regent Bernard Ziegler responds, "then the proper thing to do is begin action to expel [the paper's top editors]."[200]

At their December meeting, the regents direct the administration to find out "what action the Regents could take" to evict the *Cardinal* from its university facilities and demand that the paper's entire Board of Control appears at their January meeting. University vice president Robert Taylor says the three faculty members will be there, but he's not sure about the five students, who were elected in a campuswide election.[201]

"We expect them to be here," board president Charles Gelatt reiterates.[202]

Peter Pan

Tear-gassed and briefly jailed at the Democratic National Convention in his native Chicago that August, drama major Stuart Gordon puts a Windy City spin on J. M. Barrie's children's classic in his fifth and final Screw Theater production, *Peter Pan*. Keeping much of the text, he turns Captain Hook into Mayor Daley, the pirates into cops, and Tinker Bell's pixie dust into LSD. The critical concept of innocence, sought and soon lost, is illustrated by six nude coeds doing an eight-minute modern dance to Iron Butterfly's acid rock "In-A-Gadda-Da-Vida" under a psychedelic light show.[203]

But after photos from the dress rehearsal hit the wire services, it looks like the opening-night performance on Monday, September 23, will also be the closing performance.

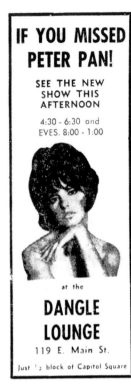

IF YOU MISSED
PETER PAN!

SEE THE NEW
SHOW THIS
AFTERNOON

4:30 - 6:30 and
EVES. 8:00 - 1:00

at the

DANGLE
LOUNGE

119 E. Main St.

Just ½ block of Capitol Square

Some cross-market advertising by Al and Tom Reichenberger, proprietors of the Dangle Lounge strip club. COURTESY OF CAPITAL NEWSPAPERS ARCHIVES

Tuesday's two performances are canceled out of concern that district attorney James C. Boll will prosecute the dancers for indecent exposure, exposing them to five years in prison and a $5,000 fine. That night, Johnny Carson cracks jokes about the event in his *Tonight Show* monologue.[204]

On Monday, September 30, an invitation-only performance takes place for about fifty university and law enforcement officials, to determine whether the play is obscene. City attorney Edwin Conrad walks out right before curtain, declaring "Madison isn't ready" for nudity on stage. "University of Wisconsin standards," Conrad says, "don't comprise community standards."[205]

Those community standards, the Republican DA declares the next day, "do not permit girls to dance nude before an audience." Facing his first election in November after being appointed to succeed the late Floyd McBurney, Boll says he won't prosecute over the two performances the week before, but vows to arrest and prosecute Gordon and any nude dancers if the production proceeds as planned that evening.[206]

Newly appointed chancellor Edwin Young thinks he's made sure that won't happen, blocking Gordon's use of the Union Play Circle, where the power is cut and the door locked. He doesn't count on the Wisconsin Film Society canceling its Buster Keaton festival in B-10 of the Commerce Building and offering Gordon the six-hundred-seat basement auditorium for two free performances.[207]

The atmosphere is electric. But the staging is disrupted, especially when four of the featured dancers drop out. So Andre De Shields (Obie Award winner, 2007), who had been playing the leader of the play's Black Panther faction, joins the dance troupe—but in a proper dance belt, and not on stage while the (white) women are nude.[208]

With plainclothes cops plainly in evidence, both performances go off without a hitch.

The production gets largely positive reviews. Assistant speech professor Robert Skloot, one of a group of professors who declared the show not obscene, calls the production "alternately dull and magnificent," with the dance sequence "a spectacle of beauty not otherwise achieved." He says the play shows pitfalls common to "new and bright directors" like Gordon but has "compensating virtues."[209]

A few days later, after a fired former Republican state senate aide named Roger Mott files a complaint, Boll (Dane County Circuit Court Judge, 1979–1989) issues an arrest warrant for Gordon on two counts, with a potential ten-year term and a $10,000 fine.[210]

That Friday is the regents' monthly meeting—Young's first full meeting after his appointment exactly three weeks before. It does not go well, as the board votes, 7–2, to "go on record as not condoning nudity in theatrical productions, and that they deny the use of University of Wisconsin buildings and facilities for such productions."[211]

Gordon and his girlfriend, Carol Ann Purdy (one of the two dancers), appear in court voluntarily a few days later and are charged with producing and participating, respectively, in a "lewd, obscene and indecent" performance.[212] Her father, a prominent Janesville physician, cuts off all financial support.[213]

A month later, Mott withdraws his complaint; police chief Wilbur Emery and a deputy sheriff sign new ones. But because they didn't see the actual performance, their testimony is worthless. Now elected to a full term, Boll withdraws the complaint on December 3, pleading in vain for someone who saw the performance to sign a complaint "so we can determine by trial by jury" if Dane County community standards "permit this type of performance."[214]

Gordon and Purdy are married December 20 at the First Unitarian Society, with the Reverend Max Gaebler officiating. Dr. Purdy walks Carolyn down the aisle but doesn't stay for the party.[215]

In Memoriam—UW

Regents president Kenneth L. Greenquist, fifty-eight, UW Law class of 1936, an eloquent and forceful advocate for the university during difficult days, is not quite six years into his nine-year term when he dies of cancer on April 5. A former two-term Progressive Party state senator (1939–1943), Navy lieutenant with World War II combat experience in both the Atlantic and Pacific, and past state commander of the American Legion, the Racine attorney was ideally suited to defend the university against conservative attacks. He fought the Legion itself in the mid-1950s when it denounced the university for allowing left-wing speakers, and pushed back against more recent Republican criticism of the *Daily Cardinal* and student protesters. His death, and the end that month of fellow liberal Arthur DeBardeleben's nine-year term, leaves only two Democrats on the board, enabling the seven appointees of GOP governor Warren Knowles to effect what DeBardeleben blasts as a "partisan takeover" of its leadership that will "harm the university."[216]

Emeritus professor Rudolph E. Langer, former chair of the mathematics department and of the humanities division, dies at his home, 822 Miami Pass, on March 11, three days after his seventy-fourth birthday. Langer joined the Wisconsin faculty in 1927 and retired in 1964; he led the Army Mathematics Research Center from its start in 1956 until 1963 and was the first mathematician to receive the Army's "Outstanding Civilian Service" award. He was also the founding president of the Madison Art Foundation and president of the Madison Art Association, and gave his vast collection of prints to the Madison Art Center, which would grow into the Madison Museum of Contemporary Art, where the highest donor group is called the Langer Society.[217]

Oscar Rennebohm, a Columbia County farm boy who got his pharmacist's degree from UW in 1911 and amassed a fortune as a Madison druggist before serving as an influential governor and UW regent, dies at his Maple Bluff home of a heart ailment at age seventy-nine on October 15, with his wife, Mary, at his bedside. It was Rennebohm, a regent from 1952 to 1961, who devised the university's wildly successful foray into urban planning, with the Hill Farms neighborhood and Hilldale Shopping Center. From a single store on the southeast corner of Randall and University Avenues in 1912, he built a chain of twenty Rexall outlets, including "The Pharm" at State and Lake Streets. Rennebohm was a charter member, director, and president of the UW Foundation; he also personally funded scholarships and created a foundation that has so far provided $2 million for civic and community projects. Rennebohm survived an eleven-man Republican primary to win election as lieutenant governor in 1944; reelected in 1946, he became governor on the death of Governor Walter Goodland the next year. Elected to a full term in 1948, he began the state's housing program for veterans and pushed through advances in public education, welfare, and state care for the mentally ill. He did not seek reelection on the advice of his physician. Governor Warren Knowles offers the state capitol for Rennebohm's funeral, which the family declines.[218]

Schools

GRADUATION, JUNE 6–7
- East: 517
- West: 410
- La Follette: 353
- Memorial: 322
- Central-University: 197[219]

FALL ENROLLMENT
- Total Students: 33,487
- Elementary schools: 19,334
- Junior high schools: 7,207
- High schools: 6,823[220]

NEW SCHOOLS
- John Muir Elementary, 6602 Inner Dr. (after a four month delay)
- Charles A. Lindbergh Elementary School, 4500 Kennedy Rd.
- Carl Sandberg Elementary School, 4114 Donald Dr.[221]

SCHOOLS CLOSING
- Sunnyside Elementary School, 3902 E. Washington Ave.[222]

Race and Classrooms

There are 544 black pupils enrolled in forty-three of the system's fifty-five schools, with all nonwhites comprising 2.3 percent of the 34,002-student body:

District Racial Composition

Negro: 544	Spanish-American: 105
American Indian: 24	White: 33,184
Oriental: 145	

Schools with More Than Ten Black Pupils

Franklin Elementary: 107	Lowell Elementary: 26
(19% of student body)	Hawthorne Elementary: 20
Lincoln Junior High: 56	East Junior High: 19
(14% of student body)	East Senior High: 18
Marquette Elementary: 45	Marquette Junior High: 16
Central High: 44	Dudgeon Elementary: 15
Silver Spring Elementary: 33	Lindbergh Elementary: 11[223]

School Days

January 2—Judge Richard Bardwell grants Lea Zeldin a temporary restraining order preventing the Board of Education from suspending her son Robin again for not shaving his mustache.[224]

January 15—West High School principal Orris C. Boettcher bans students from bringing the current issue of *Connections* into the school because he finds some of the artwork in the current issue "obscene."[225]

January 23—Overriding objections from State Assembly leaders, the State Board of Vocational, Technical, and Adult Education formally renames the Madison Vocational School the Madison Area Technical College, effective immediately. The bipartisan group of legislators worried the new nomenclature would confuse the public.[226]

January 29—John Muir Elementary School finally opens after repeated delays due to the strike last spring by construction unions.[227]

February 5—More than two hundred parents and pupils pack the school administration building auditorium for the public hearing on the proposed dress, grooming, and conduct code.[228]

February 26—Rejecting the request by the Council of Parent-Teacher Associations for more discussion, the school board adopts a dress, grooming, and conduct code subjecting boys to suspension and expulsion for wearing facial hair. "The youth of today need boundary lines," Superintendent Douglas Ritchie says in pushing for adoption of the rules, which all principals had endorsed. The board first rejects, then unanimously approves, a motion by Ruth B. Doyle that pupils facing expulsion get a written notice of charges and the right to a hearing with representation. Veteran board member and longtime UW baseball coach Dynie Mansfield says that police working on drug issues have told him that "all the boys arrested were of the long hair variety. Some say there is no connection, but our principals feel differently. Behind the mustache, the beard, the long hair and improper dress lies the real reason for their actions: a defiance of authority, lack of discipline, disrespect for rules and regulations, disobedience to their parents, as well as school personnel." The new rules also require dress that is "neat and appropriate to the occasion and in keeping with good taste," and provide that "extremes in hair length and style will not be permitted." Pupils are also required to "adhere to school rules, regulations and directives; exhibit respect for the school staff, and develop standards of personal conduct which exhibit respect and deference to authority." Amid continuing controversy, the board in fall reopens consideration of the code for further discussion. Fifteen-year-old Robin Zeldin remains in school and still wears his mustache.[229]

April 1—School research director Clifford Hawley informs the board that Longfellow School, 210 S. Brooks St., is in "critical trouble" due to a continuing decline in enrollment, which has dropped by half since 1955—mostly attributable to urban renewal.[230]

April 3—Insurance attorney Keith Yelinek and Robert DeZonia, executive director of the Wisconsin Association of Independent Colleges and Universities and a former co-director of the state Coordinating Committee on Higher Education, are easily elected to three-year terms on the school board. They succeed Dr. Ray Huegel, seventy-seven, the board president, who steps down after thirty-three years on the board, and law professor James MacDonald, stepping down after one term. Incumbent Albert McGinnis, the attorney/developer, is reelected to his second term.[231]

April 9—Superintendent Ritchie keeps schools open after the assassination of Dr. King, directing building principals to use their own judgment in deciding how to impart the significance of King's life.[232]

May 20—Superintendent Ritchie acknowledges to the Citizens Committee for the Teaching of Negro History in Madison Schools that he could "identify no thread of continuity" in how the schools present any nonwhite history and culture. "The blind spots are so vast, they're appalling," says school board member MacDonald.[233]

May 22—"Our Negro citizens are growing very discouraged, and time is running out," Betty Fey, chair of the EOC's Education Committee, says, urging the board to create a human rights curriculum supervisor and a director of human relations. Black children "are not having anywhere near an equal education," she says, due to the "climate and prejudicial attitudes" of white pupils and teachers who "don't have the background and understanding" to relate to blacks. The much-ballyhooed 1964 Human Rights Curriculum Guide is "merely gathering dust," EOC director Reverend James C. Wright adds. The job would be challenging; "There does not yet exist an American history book which includes the role and impact of the American Negro in history," Fey notes.[234]

June 11—Students for a Democratic Society (SDS) is trying to foment youthful rebellion, Madison's director of secondary education tells the Citizens Advisory Committee, citing the young activist group High School Students for Social Justice and its underground newspaper, the *High School Voice*. Conan Edwards claims the student paper shares a publishing address with the underground paper *Connections* and contains stories outside the realm of "normal decency." *High School Voice* chairman Jonathan Lipp and editor Allison Steiner deny any ties to SDS and call Edwards's charges a "reflection of a paranoid fear that local high school students are capable of organizing themselves independently against the authoritarian attitudes of school administrators." The group has about forty members, mostly from West and James Madison Memorial High Schools.[235]

June 16—A new "Human Relations Progress Report" documents the difficulty the school board is having recruiting and retaining black teachers; of the 1,850 teachers in the Madison school district, only sixteen are black. "Negroes have excellent employment opportunities," Ritchie says, "and we are unable to attract many applicants." A recent recruiting trip to historically black teacher colleges in the South was canceled when only three students signed up for interviews. Madison has just begun trying to recruit in eastern Pennsylvania, but Ritchie isn't too optimistic. The board conducts a three-day human relations workshop for all principals and administrators, and offers professional credit to teachers who take a weeklong course on "The Negro in American History," taught by State Historical Society director Leslie H. Fishel Jr., an early member of the Friends of the Urban League. The board later teams up with the local NAACP chapter on a five-point program to improve racial understanding and opportunity.[236]

July 1—John A. Matthews starts work as the first full-time executive secretary for Madison Teachers Inc. A classroom teacher from Billings, Montana, Matthews will be the group's chief administrative employee but will not set policy or necessarily participate in all bargaining sessions.[237]

August 12—The school board unanimously approves Ritchie's recommendation to create the position of director of human relations—as the NAACP, Urban League, EOC, League of Women Voters, and Citizens Committee for the Teaching of Negro History in Madison Schools have been advocating—as a way to foster interracial understanding.[238]

August 16—The school system faces a critical shortage of substitute teachers, especially for art and special needs students. Pay is $22 per day and nonlicensed personnel are eligible.[239]

August 18—Superintendent Ritchie blames permissive parents for the rise in student activism, which he says is one of his two biggest problems, along with whether or not to build a new school. "Parents have gone too far in wanting their children to try everything," he says to strong applause at an Optimist Club meeting. "There really isn't a generation gap, it's a gap between intelligence and common sense."[240]

Urban Renewal

January 8—The Madison Housing Authority (MHA) tries to solve housing problems faced by the city's increasing number of Spanish-speaking migrant families by reserving up to twenty public housing units for their use. More than thirty migrant families, most from Texas, have arrived in Madison since last fall. MHA director Bjarne Romnes meets with state and local representatives of United Migrant Organization Services to develop policies and procedures.[241]

February 2—The Federal Housing Authority approves a $1.99 million grant to the Bayview Foundation to build 144 units of moderate-income housing, just east of the Gay Braxton apartments. The foundation was formed about two years ago for this endeavor, with members from Neighborhood House, the Lake Wingra Community Council, Beth Israel Center, Memorial United Church of Christ, St. James Catholic Church, the League of Women Voters, the Parent-Teacher Association, and the Madison Home Owners Association, plus three aldermen. The foundation, which will pay the Madison Redevelopment

Authority (MRA) $123,740 for the land, will also pay property taxes and will turn the project over to the city after forty years.[242]

February 5—MRA director Sol Levin names MRA relocation supervisor Merritt Norvell, twenty-seven, as the authority's new community services director, to succeed Charles Hill, who has been appointed the new executive assistant to the secretary of the state Department of Local Affairs. But by the end of the year, just a few days before Christmas, Norvell will be hired away from the MRA by the UW to become the assistant to the first vice chancellor for student affairs, F. Chandler Young.[243]

April 18—The federal Department of Housing and Urban Development (HUD) approves a $1.5 million grant for the MRA's long-planned, oft-delayed seventy-two-acre renovation and rehabilitation project in South Madison. The project will involve razing 66 of 221 buildings, rehabilitating the remaining 155, and providing street, park, and sewer improvements. After a change in federal regulations forces the city to make an unexpected $362,000 cash outlay, the first rehabilitation work begins in mid-August—an addition and remodeling at 1711 Fisher St. When HUD rejects as too high the price the MRA is offering for several parcels, the MRA endorses using local funds to make up the difference—an initiative it had not considered when faced with the same conflict on the Triangle in 1962–1963.

In addition to physical improvements, community services are also being provided; the Friends of South Madison has started a series of paid internships for teens, the University YMCA has a program aimed at "overcoming white racism" and fostering self-esteem, the Community Welfare Council has assigned an outreach worker and plans to provide a black history course, and the Community Action Commission conducts a recreational program called "Operation Madcap," all in addition to the MRA service center on Taft Street. The MRA also sells a parcel to Foundations for Friendship Inc. for a day care center.[244]

August 27—HUD approves a $3.5 million grant for the twenty-one-acre, $5.4 million urban renewal project in the 600–900 blocks of University Avenue, to be developed cooperatively by the city, UW, and Lake Park Corporation, the organization of current property owners and businessmen with former area alderman James Goulette as its president. The federal funds will be used to buy and raze the fifty-two properties; another HUD grant of $195,762 will be used for residential relocation. The city tab of about $2 million will be spent on area infrastructure, including street improvements, storm sewers, and traffic signals. Two days later, the MRA approves spending $800,000 to purchase the first fourteen properties, with most of the rest being purchased by the end of the year.[245]

November 19—The MRA resolves a competition over the right to build housing and a shopping center on the Triangle's remaining fifteen acres by splitting the difference. David Carley's Public Facilities Associates gets 343,000 square feet to build 250 units and the shopping center at the corner of Park and Regent; Fred Mohs and Associates gets 293,000 square feet to build 350 units. The tentative deal is contingent on detailed plans for construction and financing and requires approval by HUD and the city council.[246]

December 9—The MHA approves $2.58 million in federally financed long-term bonds to build low-rent public housing. The city's first federal bond issue for $2.36 million financed the 160 public housing units, which opened in 1965.[247]

The Death of Bjarne Romnes

Bjarne Romnes, fifty-six, the executive director of the MHA since 1964, dies on April 10, two days after suffering a stroke during a meeting. Within the week, the MHA names MRA director Sol Levin acting director. In September, each agency endorses consolidating their staffs into a city Department of Housing and Community Development. On September 26, almost seven years since the first such proposal fell apart, the council creates the consolidated department and names Levin executive director and secretary; he remains director of the individual agencies, which retain their separate boards.[248]

On November 18, the MHA dedicates the 168-unit Richmond Hill public housing project for the elderly, at 540 W. Olin Ave., as the Bjarne Romnes Apartments. The tenants all seem delighted by their new housing. Mayor Festge calls the late Stoughton native, who spent twenty-five years as a state and local welfare official before developing Chalet Gardens as cooperative housing for the elderly in 1959, "a very special kind of man who worked most diligently to meet the problems of the poor and the elderly." The $1.4 million three-story horseshoe-shaped project, designed by architect Herbert Fritz, was built on the "turnkey" system by Public Facilities Associates, the development firm started in 1967 by David Carley, former Democratic national committeeman and candidate for lieutenant governor, and his brother Jim. Among those at the dedication is Green Bay Packers general manager Vince Lombardi, chairman of the board of the Carleys' firm.[249]

Law and Disorder

In addition to ongoing racially motivated skirmishes, 1968 is marked by a failed effort at gun control, debates over Mace and riot gear, increased drug use, rising crime, widespread townie attacks on students, and a brutal murder on campus that's never solved.

"We have a very serious crime increase, and I'm concerned about it," Madison police chief Wilbur Emery says, releasing statistics showing a sharp increase in several categories of crimes over 1967. The data does not include crimes committed on the UW campus.

	Jan.–June 1967	Jan.–June 1968
Homicide	0	0
Rape	7	12
Burglaries	383	534
Assaults	74	132
Auto theft	221	223
Robberies	13	24[250]

Petty theft also continues to be a major problem, with several downtown stores employing plainclothes guards and other security measures. The University Book Store has five security officers on duty but estimates it will still lose $50,000 this year from shoplifting.[251]

Attacks on university students, often by high school students, have become so frequent that a campus self-defense committee forms.[252] Some of the attacks even involve weapons; a thirty-year-old Monona man who brandished a shotgun while forcing two Langdon Street students to shave their mustaches is placed on probation, while his accomplice, who beat one of the students bloody, is fined $207.[253]

A yearlong council study into why so many policemen have resigned—sixty quit the force between 1961 and 1966, eighteen in 1966 alone—finds "a serious lack of communication between the chief of police," an "overly authoritarian working atmosphere which fails to consider the interests and needs of employees as human beings," and some "glaring weaknesses in key administrative command positions." Chief Emery says he'll "endeavor to implement" the March 26 report as soon as possible.[254]

In mid-October, Emery, forty-six, suffers a mild heart attack during a medical checkup at St. Mary's Hospital and ends up in satisfactory condition in the intensive care unit.[255]

Guns Not Controlled

The morning after Senator Robert F. Kennedy is shot, June 5, Mayor Otto Festge announces he will introduce an ordinance to require the registration of all firearms "and adequate control on their sale or transfer." The city's current mild firearms ordinance consists of a 1917 measure requiring businesses selling firearms to report daily sales, including a description of the weapon and the name and address of the purchaser, to the chief of police, and a 1966 amendment, pushed through by Ald. Harold Rohr, prohibiting persons under eighteen years of age from possessing firearms unless under adult supervision and forbidding all persons from carrying firearms in public without a permit from the chief of police. Rohr sought a stronger ordinance at the time but was unsuccessful.[256]

Two weeks later, Festge offers an ordinance requiring registration of all firearms and setting a $200 fine for noncompliance; he also voluntarily registers his own two rifles and two shotguns, which several aldermen see as gratuitous grandstanding. The mayor's proposal, which Ald. Rohr cosponsors, does not include any restrictions on the sale or transfer of guns, other than notice to the chief of police. The $1 registration fee would be valid for five years.[257]

On June 25, after antiregistration forces dominate the three-and-a-half-hour Council Committee of the Whole public hearing, voting 107–20, with another 2,159 names on a petition in opposition, the committee recommends killing the measure, 17–4. Among those voting against gun registration are the two deputy sheriffs, the former city policeman, and the assistant district attorney on the council.[258]

Two nights later, however, the council reconsiders its vote and refers the entire matter to a special committee to be appointed by Mayor Festge. The committee, chaired by Circuit Judge Richard Bardwell and including two members of the National Rifle Association, unanimously recommends a modest proposal: increasing the maximum fine for failing to report the sale of a firearm from $100 to $500, providing more specific definitions of the firearms covered, and applying its terms to individual sellers.[259]

But even that is too much for the council, which on October 10 sends it back to committee, where it remains at year's end.[260]

No Mace to the Face

City attorney Edwin Conrad gave the chemical tear gas spray Mace a clean bill of health in late 1967. But on May 7, a week after the US Surgeon General raises new concerns about it containing a kerosene by-product, Conrad stuns the police department by withdrawing his approval because he's "concerned about the city's liability in the use of a fairly potent toxic substance." Police chief Wilbur Emery disagrees, noting there have been no injuries to either officers or arrestees in the ten times it has been used in Madison so far, and maintaining the spray is "the more human way to effect an arrest than using a club, gun or fist."[261]

The next day, after a heated conference with Conrad, Emery, and public health director Charles Kincaid, Mayor Festge sides with his cautious lawyer, suspending the use of Mace pending further medical information. "As long as there's a legal doubt, I consider it wise to wait for more factual information from the Surgeon General," Festge says.[262]

The Dane County Traffic Department continues to use it; the sheriff's department has never started.[263]

Police Association secretary Captain George Schiro provides more factual information in late June, writing Festge about three officers who were attacked and injured while trying to make arrests, which he says happened only because they couldn't use Mace. He urges Festge to reconsider the ban.[264]

It's not until October 25 that Festge does, after a special committee appointed by attorney general Bronson La Follette issues a report approving its use under specific guidelines, which the mayor incorporates. The rules limit its use to trained officers, who should never aim it higher than the armpit, use it only against individuals and not in group settings, and treat recipients with "copious amounts" of water as soon as possible. Emery agrees with all the rules and notes that the training for all 224 officers includes receiving a Mace burst themselves.[265]

In mid-November, the council—eager to be seen supporting the police and concerned that another mayor could rescind the new directive—enacts Festge's authorization and guidelines into ordinance.[266]

Riot Gear

On July 11, the council approves an $8,300 appropriation for the police department to buy sixty-two riot helmets, forty-eight night sticks, and 150 gas masks. Or does it?

As newly elected Eighth Ward alderman Paul Soglin notes the next day, there were only eighteen members on the floor at the time of the voice vote; since he and fellow first-termer Ald. Alicia Ashman were both recorded as voting no, the measure could not have gotten the seventeen votes required under council rules.[267]

Among the scores of anti-Dow protesters sent to the emergency room by baton-wielding police in the Commerce Building on campus last October, Soglin says police shouldn't have additional riot equipment "because they don't know how to use it," and don't need it.

And Soglin, currently a history grad student, objects strongly to the resolution's preamble, which warns about "increased activities by certain groups," making it "imperative that the department be prepared to meet any situation that may arise."[268]

The Madison Professional Policemen's Association writes to Ashman that it is "shocked and dismayed" by her vote, coming at a time when "assaults on police are at an all-time high" and "the public is more and more condemning violence and supporting its police." Association vice president Roth Watson says the association didn't write a similar letter to Soglin because it "recognized that Ald. Soglin's constituents are not necessarily concerned with the safety of police officers."[269]

"As far as I'm concerned, the motion was not passed," Soglin says.

But as far as city attorney Conrad is concerned, it was; being recorded as voting no on a voice vote is not the same, he says, as voting no in a roll call. On Conrad's advice, Mayor Otto Festge signs the resolution appropriating the funds.[270]

On July 22, Soglin, Ashman, WIBA radio host George "Papa Hambone" Vukelich, and Professor and Mrs. Francis Hole file a taxpayer's lawsuit seeking to block the purchase as an unauthorized expenditure. "The domestic arms race has to stop somewhere," Ald. Ashman says. "Why not stop it here?"[271]

Circuit Judge Norris Maloney thinks the legal question is close enough that he issues a temporary restraining order on July 24, stopping the city from going through with the purchase.[272]

The next day, Emery unloads his frustrations at a special meeting of the Equal Opportunities Commission. "If everyone would shut up and forget about it, everything would be fine," he says, revealing that he "would have preferred to keep the whole thing secret" but had to go to the council for the money.[273]

But rather than litigate, the council simply relegislates, bringing the measure back for another vote on August 8. As the Republican convention in Miami Beach is nominating Richard Nixon for president, the council ignores a satirical skit by the Wisconsin Draft Resistance Union and approves the riot gear, 17–3. Ashman tries to attach a strict gun control measure "for the further protection" of officers, but is unsuccessful.[274]

Murder at Sterling Hall

Christine Rothschild was a quiet and studious eighteen-year-old freshman from Chicago, living in a single room in Ann Emery Hall. A member of the National Honor Society, student council president, and a part-time model, she liked to take long walks around campus in the early morning.[275]

Sometime around dawn on Sunday, May 26, she leaves her Langdon Street dorm for a walkabout. A few hours later, probably between 10:30 a.m. and noon, she's murdered and left in the bushes in front of Sterling Hall.

It's a crime of uncommon fetishisms and brutality. Her killer fractures both jaws and breaks four ribs, strangles her with an intricate garrote made from her own coat lining, forces her leather driving gloves down her throat, and stabs her fourteen times with a scalpel, piercing her heart. He does not assault her sexually.[276] Her body is found about 7:30 Sunday night.

The university offers a $6,000 reward for information leading to the killer, but police soon acknowledge they have no leads, no suspects, no murder weapon, and no motive.[277]

In fall, a strong suspect emerges—the mysterious and odd third-year medical resident Niels Jorgensen, forty-two, who worked at the UW hospital, just across Charter Street from Sterling Hall. Dismissed from the hospital five weeks after the murder, he moves to New York, where police question him for several hours in September. Not knowing he had stalked Rothschild, made obscene phone calls, and watched her as she slept, they don't think they have grounds for an arrest, and never do.[278]

Planning and Development

GENERAL STATISTICS
- Population: 164,991[279]
- Area: 46.92 square miles (end-of-year total)[280]

MADISON WORKFORCE[281]
- Government/UW: 34 percent
- Trade: 21

- Manufacturing: 15
- Service: 14
- Construction: 6
- Finance: 5

Strike!

A city already stressed by war, protest, and racial strife suffers a summer of strikes by fifteen hundred industrial workers.

On May 15, the 315 members of United Auto Workers Local 1329 and 23 members of Machinists Local 1406, with respective hourly wages averaging $2.25 and $2.90, strike Ray-O-Vac, the city's third-largest employer.[282] The strike lasts until late September, when new agreements provide for a 35-cent raise over three years, plus an increase in pensions. The United Auto Workers members settle on September 18 and say they're going back to work, whether or not the machinists have settled, which 1406 quickly does.[283]

There's far more at stake when the 1,170 members of Steelworkers Local 1401, with an average hourly wage of $3.24, strike Gisholt Machine Company, the city's second-largest private employer (after Oscar Mayer) on July 1.[284] The strike lasts until September 28 and brings the workers a 67-cent raise over three years, plus improved pension benefits.[285]

Although the strikes mean a loss of about $2 million in wages to workers whose families total about five thousand people, economists doubt that the strikes will have any major impact on the city's overall economy.[286]

Parks

The city finds out this year that expanding a downtown park is not like taking a walk in one.

In mid-June, owners of lakeside property in the 500 and 600 blocks of East Gorham Street are stunned and outraged to receive a letter from Mayor Otto Festge and parks superintendent James Marshall telling them that the city is reversing a policy established by the council in 1963, and is planning to use eminent domain to take their property by condemnation.

The city explains that it has received a $411,628 federal grant to subsidize the park's expansion, which requires that the lands be acquired by April 1969. "This very substantial financial aid and the time limits imposed require us to change the acquisition policy which has been carefully observed in the past," Festge and Marshall write.[287] The city, which already owns 1,615 feet of lakefront, is seeking sixteen parcels, to provide another 585 feet of parkland.[288]

"We sincerely want to continue negotiations," Festge tells a neighborhood meeting in October, "but if they fail, condemnation is the only route for the city to follow."[289] But the property owners fight back, and in December the council approves condemnation of only two properties, leaving the remaining fourteen to be acquired through negotiation.

Lakeside homes on the 500 and 600 blocks of East Gorham Street, where the city wants to expand James Madison Park. In the foreground is the former Lincoln School, then home to the Madison Art Center. WHI IMAGE ID 137298, PHOTO BY JOHN NEWHOUSE

Area alderman R. Whelan Burke calls the park "a disgrace, an eyesore" that's used only for improper activities in the dead of night and isn't worth expanding.[290]

Park development moves slowly but less contentiously on the far west side.

German immigrant Charles Elver, owner of the Elver House and Capital Hotel, lived and worked downtown and died in 1928. Elver's will directed that on the death of his daughter, the trustees of his estate would buy a tract of land, preferably at least seventy-five acres, to be donated as a park and named in his honor. His daughter, Ottilia Cheech, died in 1961, and after seven years the trustees finally find suitable land—fifty-two acres on high ground off Raymond Road, with an excellent view of downtown and the west side. The property turns out to be beyond city limits, about a half-mile into the Town of Madison, but when Mayor Otto Festge is presented with the deed on October 3, "Charles Elver Park" becomes the city's fifth-largest park, behind Warner (224 acres), Reindahl (92 acres), Olbrich (72 acres), and Vilas (62 acres).[291]

Business Wire

September 24—Cleveland development company Jacobs, Visconti and Jacobs Co., which developed Westgate Shopping Center in 1960, formally unveils plans for two regional shopping centers on the outskirts of town. West Towne and East Towne, both similar to the developer's Brookfield Square, which opened last fall in suburban Milwaukee, are set to open in the fall of 1970 and the fall of 1971, respectively.[292]

October 1—The Wil-Mar Center, serving the Williamson-Marquette neighborhoods, becomes the fourth member of the Madison Neighborhood Centers (MNC) when it opens in temporary quarters at the Pilgrim Congregational Church at 953 Jenifer St. The MNC had wanted to use the old Assembly of God Church at 1103 Williamson St., but the Zoning Board of Appeals denied a necessary zoning waiver in July. MNC director Chester Zmudzinski says Wil-Mar is unique among the MNC facilities—its board members "are people from the area it serves." Zmudzinski appoints Reverend David G. DeVore, former curate at Grace Episcopal Church and chaplain for the Dane County Probation Department, as the first director.[293]

October 22—Ignoring the recommendations from planning director Kenneth Clark, two rejections by the Plan Commission, and most of the Williamson-Marquette neighborhood, the council sides with Realty Associates and Sixth Ward alderman Andrew Somers and rezones 1030 and 1034 Jenifer St. and 1025 Williamson St. to allow the construction of a luxury four-story apartment building with up to seventy units.[294] On November 7, Mayor Festge vetoes the rezoning because it conflicts with the city's land use plan, would set a precedent for other high-density rezonings, and would complicate plans to widen Williamson Street if needed for an expressway corridor.[295] The veto is upheld.

Highways and Transportation

Cars—driven and parked—continue to bedevil the university. The city's got its own problems with mass transit.

Transportation Milestones

On January 11, the chair of the university's Parking Board proposes excavating part of Bascom Hill for an underground six-hundred-car parking ramp, with the entrance at Park and State Streets. Professor W. Wallace Cleland says he doesn't think there will be too much opposition, even though the excavation and landscaping would cause the loss of the hill's elm trees, because "they will have to go anyway," victims of Dutch elm disease.[296]

In late June, UW consultants seek to solve the growing conflicts between pedestrians and vehicles by a $29 million "south corridor" bypass—a four-lane below-grade highway from University Avenue east to Breese Terrace that would cut through the football practice fields southeast behind the engineering campus and rise to a fully elevated road as it bends east of Camp Randall Stadium, continuing eastward between Regent Street and College Court, crossing the railroad tracks and Dayton Street before descending to meet Johnson Street and Gorham Street at ground level.[297] As a more modest alternative, campus planners proposed an $18 million, mile-long underground tunnel, from three blocks west of the First Congregational Church to the corner of East Johnson and North Frances Streets.[298]

The city has a simpler plan—relocate the railroad tracks that cross Randall Street a bit to the north and build a highway that doesn't destroy University Heights. And with the support of GOP governor Warren Knowles, that's what's done.[299]

A representation of the university's proposed elevated highway. DAVID MICHAEL MILLER

Getting On the Bus

In mid-January, the city learns that the Madison Bus Company is "headed on a disaster course," largely due to the sixty-two-day strike by Teamsters Local 695 last fall; the company carried about 157,000 passengers weekly before the strike but has been stuck at about 104,000 since. Even with the nickel fare increase, weekly gross revenue has dropped from $26,000 to $22,500, putting the company $110,000 in debt. With only $34,000 (out of the hoped-for $65,000) raised by voluntary contributions to supplement the difference between the company's final offer and the wage hike that was ultimately granted, officials project the fund will run out by May.[300]

After disbursing $3,745 by the end of January, Mayor Festge halts further payments until the company provides more information about its operations; company president William H. Straub, whom Festge last year removed from the city Traffic Commission, refuses and calls the mayor's bluff. "The men will not work" if the city doesn't make the payments, he warns, and "the responsibility for the cessation of the bus operation will have to rest with you." Although the Teamsters vow to stay on the job, and the company reveals it's using some of the supplemental funds to pay nonunion supervisors, the mayor blinks and a week later agrees to release another $7,898. "I very much resent the pressure tactics," Festge says in mid-February.[301]

On February 22, the city finally fights back, with a unanimous council vote to put two referenda on the April ballot—one to authorize the city to own and operate a bus system, the other to issue $1 million in bonds for its purchase.[302]

Then it gets personal. On March 11, Festge says he'll dump the bus company's management if the city takes it over; that afternoon, without notice to the city, the company petitions the Public Service Commission (PSC) to discontinue service. Straub says the company, which owns ninety-three buses and employs 105 drivers, has lost $55,000 since resuming service November 23, 1967.[303]

On April 2, voters approve both referenda by three-to-one margins.[304]

A week later, Straub testifies before the PSC that the company will lose more than $100,000 this year, and that there is no "reasonable possibility in the future" that it could become profitable.[305]

On May 21, the company gives the city an option until November 1969 to purchase it for $910,000, and the city agrees to pay an average $22,000 monthly subsidy from July 1 until the option is executed. The subsidy, with Shorewood Hills, Maple Bluff, and Monona contributing a combined 7 percent, would provide the company a 5 percent operating profit; the city's consultant calls the deal "fair and reasonable."[306]

On June 4, company stockholders overwhelmingly agree, and the company withdraws its PSC petition to abandon service. On the thirteenth, after replenishing the supplemental salary fund, the council formally approves the subsidy-purchase arrangement and creates a seven-member Bus Utility Commission to oversee the system.[307]

In early September, the bus company starts new express routes to the far west and far east sides. The next month brings unexpectedly good news—for the first time since March 1967, the company makes a profit and doesn't need the city subsidy.[308]

Miscellanea

January 2—Mayor Otto Festge vetoes the council's December 28 rescission of the unbalanced budget, so the city can pay its employees while it decides whether to re-enact the $9 wheel tax or cut $550,000 in expenses. Madison's unprecedented budget madness finally ends January 11 with unanimous adoption, without debate, of a budget cutting $550,000 from streets, parks, and libraries. The council also repeals the auto registration fee.[309]

February 27—Another breakout star from the Monterey Pop Festival, Jimi Hendrix, touring behind his new album, *Axis: Bold as Love*, plays two ear-rattling, sold-out shows at the Factory (and gives a quiet backstage interview to the *Daily Cardinal*). Hendrix's equipment doesn't arrive until an hour after the first show was set to begin, leaving patrons huddled outside in the bitter winter cold, but he's worth the wait as he blazes through "Fire," "Foxy Lady," and more. "'Scuse me while I kiss this guy," he sings in "Purple Haze," pointing at bassist Noel Redding. Contrary to some reports, Hendrix does not smash or burn his white Stratocaster.[310]

March 14—Eighteen years after voters by referendum abolished the position of city manager, the council appoints Robert Corcoran, former administrative assistant to Mayor Festge, to the newly created position of city administrator, a civil service position that will have primary responsibility for the daily operations of city government.[311]

An original print of this poster by Brad Cantrell sold at auction in 2017 for $20,712. COURTESY OF KEN ADAMANY/LAST COAST PRODUCING—ALL RIGHTS RESERVED.

March 25—An enthusiastic Dane County Memorial Coliseum crowd estimated at eighteen thousand—a venue record—showers Senator Eugene McCarthy with thunderous applause as the Minnesotan gives his main Wisconsin address for the upcoming presidential primary. Before his strong but understated attack on President Johnson and the war, there's a great undercard of entertainment: Lou Gossett reading a biting antiwar letter from Mark Twain, satire from Alan Arkin and Elaine May, and songs of social commentary from Janis Ian (who, at sixteen, is still too young to vote). McCarthy wins Wisconsin with 56 percent, carrying Dane County with 62 percent. Much credit goes to McCarthy's Madison headquarters chief Midge Miller.[312]

March 27—A fitting finale at the Factory, the last big show before it closes at the end of April—the Butterfield Blues Band, with the White Trash Blues Band to open.[313]

March 30—WKOW radio changes its slogan to the "NOW sound, with NOW music, for NOW people." The station, which also extends its broadcast hours from 5 a.m. to 2 a.m., except on Sundays, will feature soul and "underground" music, along with talk shows on controversial topics.[314]

April 2—The election turnout of 79.8 percent is the highest ever for a municipal election, second all-time only to the 88.3 percent turnout for the presidential election of 1960. Among the unprecedented nine new alderpersons, a trio of new progressive leaders are voted onto the council, including the second woman in the city's history and the third student in the last decade. Former public health nurse Alicia Ashman—a veteran civic activist with the League of Women Voters, Capital Community Citizens, and Housing Opportunities—wins an overwhelming victory in the Tenth Ward (University Heights), the same district that Ethel Brown represented from 1951 to 1964. Thanks to the campus-area turnout inspired by the McCarthy campaign and the Vietnam referendum, history grad student Paul Soglin easily unseats three-term alderman Ellsworth Swenson in the downtown Eighth Ward. In a stunning upset, attorney Jan Wheeler beats former council president Ald. Richard Kopp in the north side Eighteenth Ward, by fifty-four votes. And the near east Sixth Ward opts for law and order over fur and fins, as assistant district attorney Andrew Somers ousts incumbent "Pet Shop" Pete Schmidt.[315]

Given the budget fiasco, bus debacle, and more, it's not surprising voters reject the proposal to move to a four-year mayoral term by better than two-to-one.[316]

April 11—The Belmont Hotel, which Howard, Charles, and David Piper built in 1924 for moderate-income travelers, closes and begins conversion to become the new home for the YWCA. The Y just beats its deadline to raise the necessary $250,000 purchase price.[317]

April 12—The Madison Chamber of Commerce breaks with about twenty years of tradition and allows its members to keep their shops open from noon to 3 p.m. on Good Friday; many do.[318]

April 30—The recently incorporated Taychopera Foundation, a group interested in saving Madison's historic and architecturally significant buildings, holds its first organizational meeting. Among the initial trustees are founding president and former mayor Henry E. Reynolds, *Capital Times* reporter Frank Custer, State Historical Society director Leslie H. Fishel Jr., Urban and Regional Planning Professor Leo Jakobson, construction executive George W. Icke, and attorney Robert B. L. Murphy.[319]

June 27—The council enacts an ordinance permitting all city employees, including firemen and policemen, to engage in political activity during nonwork hours, including raising campaign contributions and circulating nomination papers for city candidates. Sponsored by south side alderman and Painters Union business agent Harold Rohr, the ordinance eliminates current prohibitions on these activities. After fire chief McGraw and police chief Emery, and most department heads, voice their opposition, Mayor Festge vetoes the ordinances. The vetoes are sustained, and the council passes a revised version that maintains the ban on city employees raising money for city candidates.[320]

July 1—McDonald's opens on Lake and State Streets, falsely advertising the Madison franchise as its first with indoor seating.[321]

August 27—The new Fire Station #1 opens in the 300 block of West Dayton Street, replacing the historic station at 15 S. Webster St. The second-floor conference room is named the Parkinson Room, in memory of Dan "Monk" Parkinson, the firefighter who died in the State Street fire of January 1966.[322]

September 8—Longtime civil rights activist Reverend Richard Pritchard—who was removed as minister at Westminster Presbyterian Church in March after twenty-one years, during which its membership grew from two hundred to sixteen hundred—is installed as pastor at the city's newest church, Heritage Congregational.[323]

October—Broadcast newsman and personality Marsh "Marshall the Marshall" Shapiro buys the working-class neighborhood bar Glen and Ann's at the corner of North Frances and West Johnson Streets and converts it into the Nitty Gritty, a bar/restaurant/venue featuring Chicago and national blues acts.[324]

November—Bill Winfield, a member of the Green Lantern Eating Co-op, and his friends sign a temporary lease for the defunct White Front Grocery at the corner of Mifflin and Bassett Streets and start selling $5 memberships for a proposed grocery co-op there. The founding by-laws of the Mifflin Street Community Co-op declare that the store aims "to embody a belief in community self-determination in opposition to the dominant trends in all communities in which control is increasingly concentrated outside the community and operated for profits which are not used for the betterment of the community. Our assets, as people and money, are committed to this struggle by any means necessary." They raise about $1,500 by Christmas break and proceed with the serious work of stocking the store with equipment and goods.[325]

November 5—Vernon "Jack" Leslie, forty-eight, who quit the Democratic Party earlier this year when it honored Betty Boardman, is elected the first Republican sheriff of Dane County, unseating Sheriff Franz G. Haas, sixty, whom Leslie had served as undersheriff until being fired after announcing his candidacy. Wisconsin Alliance Party candidate Gene Parks, twenty-one, polls 7,939 votes after a brief write-in campaign; city clerk Eldon Hoel terms this a "fantastic" result given the difficulty of write-in campaigns.[326]

December 3—A year after creating chaos by refusing to raise the tax rate by two mills, the council adopts a budget with a five-mill increase, to $53 per $1,000 of assessed valuation. More than half (29.13 mills) will go to the schools, with the city's general fund accounting for twelve mills.[327]

Firemen Fight Festge and Flaten

Madison and its Fire Fighters Local 311 make Wisconsin history this year—the first mass sick-out by firefighters and the first municipal restraining order against their union activity.

Because Madison's base monthly pay of $620 is second lowest only to Green Bay among major Wisconsin cities, the 240-member union is asking for a $110 raise, as city police just received. The city bargaining committee, led by Ald. Milo Flaten, offers $64. Negotiations deadlock in July and stay that way till fall, when union president Captain Edward D. Durkin and his men suspend all nonemergency work—including standard fire inspections, drills, housekeeping, and public information programs.

The slowdown starts on October 24, and three days later it becomes a sick-in; thirty firemen call in sick over the weekend, forcing fire chief Ralph McGraw to close three stations for seven hours and cancel all vacations.[328]

The next weekend, thirty-eight firemen come down with the "Flaten Flu," and Durkin threatens an all-out strike if any fireman is disciplined for sick leave abuse. McGraw declares another "state of emergency," as staffing again dips below the minimum level. The union modifies its demand—$80, with a series of reclassifications being processed by the Personnel Board; the city holds to a $64 monthly raise.[329]

On November 4, Circuit Judge W. L. Jackman issues a restraining order to stop union members from "any mass absenteeism from duty for sickness or other reasons." Jackman's order also prohibits the firemen from "abstaining in whole or in part from the full, faithful and proper performance of their duties," forcing their resumption of all non-emergency duties.[330]

McGraw and Durkin both say the situation is the city's fault. "The city is pushing us toward illegal action, and it's going to be a bloody, violent fight all the way," the union president says. "It is irresponsible of the city to push my men to the striking point," chimes in his chief.[331]

Durkin (Madison Fire Department Chief, 1979–1985) says union members are willing to break the law. "We intend to strike if we don't get our way, despite the injunction," he says. Judge Jackman "can put us in jail right now."[332]

The third weekend, another fifteen firemen claim illness; Festge wants Jackman to cite the union for violating his order, but the judge calls the parties into his chambers and hammers out a deal instead—$70 a month, consideration of the reclassifications, and an increased pension. It's quickly ratified. [333]

Then other city workers, who want another $25 biweekly, also come down with the Flaten Flu when exposed to the city's offer of $15. On November 18, more than two-thirds of Madison's 230 streets, sanitation, garbage, and engineering employees belonging to City Employees Union Local 236 call in sick.[334] Four days later, more than four hundred City Hall and school janitors, most of them members of Employees Union Local 60, do so, too.[335]

On November 26, Festge orders that seventy-three firemen, along with other municipal employees, have their pay docked for improper sick leave.[336] The next day—the day before Thanksgiving—Judge Richard Bardwell orders the city to pay firefighters their full wages, unless it can show individual abuse. It never really tries.[337] Bardwell doesn't provide the same relief for the other employees, who ultimately settle for a $20 biweekly raise, double pay for holidays, and a pension boost.[338]

Aldermen Rohr, Cooper, and Soglin try to reverse Festge's order and reimburse the day's wage to the employees; the day after Christmas, the council rejects their proposal, 13–6.[339]

In Memoriam

Elma Christianson, fifty-five, a former caseworker who became the city's first female welfare director in 1953 and was virtually unchallenged in her administration, dies of a heart attack around January 4, alone at her home at 2205 Rowley Ave. Her body is found on January 10, after concerned neighbors contact police.[340]

William J. P. Aberg, eighty, a pioneering conservationist who worked with Aldo Leopold to create the state Conservation Commission in 1927, where he served from 1939 to 1951, dies on March 18. A founder and director of the National Wildlife Federation, instrumental in the restoration of the Horicon March, Aberg was the man after whom the east side connector highway was named.[341]

F. Edwin Schmitz, seventy-five, a second-generation downtown clothier and civic leader, dies on April 14 following a stroke. Son of the founder of the Hub clothing store and chairman of Madison Bank and Trust, "Uncle Ed" was also the longtime treasurer of the Wisconsin Student Aid Foundation. A semipro baseball pitcher in his youth, he was to receive the Pat O'Dea Award at the Madison Sports Hall of Fame dinner in June.[342]

August is the cruelest month for the city's newspapers and their staffs.

Capital Times city-county reporter Richard Brautigam, fifty-eight, dies in his sleep of a heart attack at his home in Verona on August 20. A native of Racine, he worked for the *Milwaukee Sentinel*, Associated Press, and Wisconsin Republican Party before joining the *Capital Times* in 1963. Brautigam attended the UW's Experimental College under founder Alexander Meiklejohn in the 1930s and served in China during World War II. A member of the Madison Kennel Club, he owned three handsome Airedale terriers, including a recent champion. The council observes a moment of silence and adopts a resolution in his memory.[343]

Wisconsin State Journal art and drama critic Elizabeth "Teto" Gould, sixty-four, 2135 Chamberlain Ave., suffers a fatal heart attack shortly before midnight August 29 at Madison Municipal Airport while awaiting the arrival of her daughter Stephanie. The Madison native graduated from the UW in 1925, received a master's degree from Stanford in 1927, and taught English at East High School before becoming a full-time journalist. Gould sold numerous stories to national magazines and was recently honored by the local Theta Sigma Phi journalism sorority with its coveted "Ladies of the Press Writer's Cup." Her older daughter, Whitney, former columnist for the *Daily Cardinal,* is a reporter for the *Capital Times.*[344]

Adolph C. Bolz, seventy-four, retired senior vice president of Oscar Mayer and Company, dies on November 28 after suffering a heart attack. Bolz was the meatpacking plant's second employee when he arrived in Madison to manage his father-in-law's new facility; under his guidance, it became Madison's largest private employer, with more than four thousand employees on a 112-acre site, and an international reputation. A member of the Downtown Rotary Club and a director of the Madison General Hospital Association, Bolz supported numerous civic and cultural associations, along with his wife, Eugenie Mayer. A native of St. Louis, Bolz served as a flying officer of the Army Air Corps during World War I before coming to Madison in 1919.[345]

State Street, July, 1969. COURTESY OF CAPITAL NEWSPAPERS ARCHIVES, PHOTO BY ROGER L. TURNER

1969

UW

COMMENCEMENT, JUNE 9
- ▸ Baccalaureate: 2,850
- ▸ Master's/PhD: 1100
- ▸ JD/MD: 235[1]

FALL ENROLLMENT
- ▸ Total Students: 35,549

HOMECOMING
- ▸ Show: Bill Cosby, Ramsey Lewis Trio
- ▸ Dance: Freddie and the Freeloaders[2]

NEW BUILDINGS OF NOTE
- ▸ [George L. Mosse] Humanities Building, 455 N. Park St.[3]
- ▸ Meteorology and Space Science, 1225 W. Dayton St.[4]

The Black Strike

The climactic protest of the decade is sparked by a symposium, as the weeklong conference "The Black Revolution: To What Ends?" leads to ten days of disruption, an hour of destruction, and the creation of the Black Studies Department.[5]

"The Black Revolution: To What Ends?" featuring twenty-one nationally renowned guest speakers and forty-three faculty, staff, and students, runs February 3–8. Produced by Union Forum Committee chairs Margery Tabankin and Neil Weisfeld for $8,861, the conference attracts 16,500 attendees and crystallizes the incipient black student revolution at the university. Chancellor Young later learns that he helped underwrite the conference, through a $2,500 contribution his office made to the Afro American and Race Relations Center, which turned it over to the conference.[6]

Among the speakers is sociology professor Nathan Hare, acting chairman of the embryonic and groundbreaking Department of Black Studies at San Francisco State University, active in the bitter three-month-old Black Student Union strike that led to its creation there. On Wednesday, February 5, he tells a standing-room-only Great Hall crowd that "the White university establishment" is destroying black society and culture and that "we may have to cut off the ears of a few college deans." At a panel that night, he tells students they must "do whatever needs to be done [to get the university to] meet your demands." Afterward, Hare meets with Willie Edwards of the Black People's Alliance and other black student leaders and puts black activism at the UW into context with the hard-line crackdown that new SF State president S. I. Hayakawa has begun. "We are on the front lines at SF State and getting our asses kicked," he tells them. "You are on a

The Southeast dorms and lower campus, October 1969. The Humanities Building (1) is open, with the neighboring Elvehjem Art Center [Chazen Museum of Art] (2) to follow next September. Lorenzo's and Paisan's have been razed and excavation has begun for construction of Vilas Communications Hall (3), which is to be completed by the fall of 1972. At the end of North Park Street, construction of Helen C. White Hall (4) is underway, to open in two years. The Old Red Gym (5) remains, both as a gym and fulfilling its armory function by housing ROTC headquarters. Construction has topped out at the Devine family's Roundhouse apartment on Langdon Street (6), but hasn't started on the Memorial Library expansion, leaving the University Book Store, Calvary Lutheran chapel, and the Kollege Klub beer bar undisturbed in the 700 block of State Street (7). UNIVERSITY OF WISCONSIN-MADISON ARCHIVES IMAGE S17015

Black campus leaders, including football player Harvey Clay (left, in sunglasses and beret) and Bernard Forrester (right, with bullhorn), explain the thirteen demands at the start of the Black Strike at the noon rally on Library Mall, February 7.
UNIVERSITY OF WISCONSIN–MADISON ARCHIVES IMAGE S00407, PHOTO BY GARY SCHULZ

radical campus and have a responsibility to your brothers and sisters to take action." Edwards and the others embrace Hare's challenge and start planning a Wisconsin black strike, led by the Wapenduzi Weusi.[7]

A little before noon on Friday, February 7, about ten black students, led by Edwards, present a list of thirteen demands to Vice Chancellor Chandler Young for delivery to Chancellor Edwin Young. They demand, among other things, an "autonomous black studies department controlled and organized by black students and faculty" with a black chairman "approved by black students and faculty"; that "black students have veto power in hiring and firing all administrators and teachers involved in anything relating" to the new black studies department; at least five hundred additional black students be admitted to the university by fall; black student control over the Black Cultural Center; amnesty for all strike participants; and admission of any expelled Oshkosh student to UW–Madison.[8]

That afternoon, as the Reverend Andrew Young, executive director of the Southern Christian Leadership Conference, prepares to speak at the conference on "Where Do We Go From Here?" about three hundred students sweep up Bascom Hill from the noon rally to disrupt classes in seven university buildings. Members of the group, about three-quarters of whom are white, briefly take over numerous classrooms to read and explain the demands; some professors and students are intimidated, but there are no serious incidents or arrests. Swelling to about five hundred, the group marches down to Library Mall banging trash cans and chanting, "On strike, shut it down!" for a rally where black leaders again explain the demands. Then it's back up the hill for another round of classroom disruptions, including Professor Harvey Goldberg's History 474 lecture, followed by a mass meeting of about more than a thousand in the Union Theater, where a black speaker calls for "complete disruption, and if that doesn't work, complete destruction" of the university.[9]

Speaking to an overflow crowd of about thirteen hundred in the Great Hall that evening, the Reverend Jesse Jackson says the thirteen demands "should be followed to the letter. Until I see white America go through the psychological exercise of freeing herself of superior delusions, she can't relate to me. And that's why there is a black revolt here tonight, and why wise white people and black people will support it." Jackson also attacks the UW for purportedly supporting white supremacy, particularly Germanic.[10]

Later, and throughout the weekend, blacks who had previously been marginalized make a concerted and successful effort to reach out to white students in social settings, explaining their demands, person to person, point by point. It works; UW police chief Hanson is impressed by "the very large number of people from our dormitory areas who participated actively, people who never carried a sign before in their lives." "This was perhaps the amazing part of the whole demonstration," he testifies before the Joint Committee in late March. Hanson is also impressed at how successful strike leaders have been: "They created a lot of fuss here and focused a lot of attention on 13 demands." Not all the persuasion is gentle; there are reports of coercive phone calls and some physical intimidation. Some white students also worry about being called racist if they don't support the strike.[11]

On Saturday, a *Daily Cardinal* editorial calls the group's demands for student control over a new department, the cultural center, and other university actions "impossible" to meet, and says the black students "know that they are demanding that an institution destroy itself."[12]

Saturday afternoon, Willie Edwards tells a large Great Hall crowd during a lengthy rally that "the only power we have is to disrupt," and if the thirteen demands are not met, "This university will not function."[13] After the rally, at about 2:30 p.m., approximately six hundred students, chanting "Two, four, six, eight, organize and smash the state" march on the Field House to disrupt the Badger basketball game with Ohio State. Alerted by agents at the rally, the university calls in city police; a contingent of about 150 helmeted police with riot sticks and tear gas arrives barely five minutes before the protesters.

"If they had not arrived at the Field House when they did," Chancellor Young tells the regents the following Friday, "six hundred persons would have poured into that basketball game and there would have been a great deal of violence between spectators and disrupters." As it is, there are scuffles at various Field House gates, and Governor Knowles's black Rambler is vandalized. Four students—one black, three white—are arrested for disorderly conduct and battery to a police officer; most of the eleven thousand basketball fans inside are unaware of the disturbance. Edwards and about two dozen black students have tickets and are inside, but their only disruption is giving the black power salute during the national anthem, and some synchronized seat switching. They leave after halftime to scattered applause and miss the Badgers' upset victory over the Buckeyes.[14]

That night, Chancellor Young issues a statement highlighting the university's initiatives, including "efforts to" recruit minority and faculty, adding one more black staff member to the Student Affairs office, creating the task force to administer the Special Program, and seeking further funding. Young touts "recent changes" in the university's academic program: the first three-credit "Afro-American Culture and Intellectual Tradition" course in the new Afro-American concentration in the American Institutions program, with a series of guest lecturers; a "black literature course taught by a black professor" in the English department; a black history course in the history department; a law school seminar on law and minority groups; a senior course in Contemporary Trends that "has turned to the urban crisis," and Gwendolyn Brooks's creative writing course, which he does not note is only for this semester. "It would be a tragedy if anything were allowed to cloud this progress and threaten the future," he says, warning that anyone who obstructs classes or other university activities is subject to arrest for unlawful assembly; students who do so may also get suspended or expelled. "While peaceful picketing and legal protest must and will be protected on this campus," Young declares, "intentional disruption of classes cannot and will not be tolerated."[15]

The Wisconsin Student Association (WSA) Student Senate votes on Sunday to support the strike, provide bail money for arrestees, and condemn "indiscriminate violence."[16] The WSA releases a report by WSA president David Goldfarb and Black Revolution conference organizer Tabankin (National Student Asssociation president, 1971; VISTA director, 1977–1981) calling the university "a racist institution [whose] only response has been manipulation, avoidance and co-optation." The WSA report concludes with a call for "all students to mobilize in a united front to strike against the racism endemic in this institution."[17] Libby Edwards tells about 150 students at the Green Lantern Eating Cooperative, 604 University Ave., that "disruption will take place but the tactics must remain secret."[18]

The week of February 10 starts peacefully with about fifteen hundred picketing, but not obstructing, major classroom buildings. Classes continue, with strikers entering some classrooms and asking for permission to address the students. Chancellor Young issues another statement, calling for "an atmosphere of reasoned cooperation and mutual concern. No one who talks about shutting down the University can convince me that the welfare and advancement of black people is his foremost concern."[19]

At night, a thousand rally on the mall, then climb the hill to Bascom Hall; amid shouts of "Burn, baby, burn," demonstrators burn an effigy of university administrators in Abraham Lincoln's lap. Then they march to the Capitol, filling nearly three city blocks, their number augmented by many high school students.[20]

After a Tuesday morning mall rally for a thousand, an uptick in intensity—a few hundred protesters walk through buildings chanting, "On strike, shut it down!" They don't attract any adherents and leave when police arrive.[21]

BELOW: Start of the obstruction, Tuesday afternoon, February 11. COURTESY OF CAPITAL NEWSPAPERS ARCHIVES, PHOTO BY RICH FAVERTY

BELOW, RIGHT: The strike pits students against students. COURTESY OF CAPITAL NEWSPAPERS ARCHIVES, PHOTO BY RICH FAVERTY

When officers arrive in force on Tuesday afternoon, protesters "make like steam and vaporize." COURTESY OF CAPITAL NEWSPAPERS ARCHIVES

But a few hours later, around the same time the state Senate is unanimously adopting a resolution denouncing the "wanton destruction, illegal activity and disruption of our universities by revolutionaries and their supporters," black leaders tell a Union Theater rally for one thousand of the new tactic—a "non-penetrable" picket line, people standing in the College of Letters and Science schoolhouse doors to block anyone from getting in. But when police come, to "make like steam and vaporize." And they do. A few fistfights break out between students blockading buildings and those wanting to enter, but the lines hold, and hundreds leave or are turned away. It's the start of the first of the Madison SDS "affinity groups"—semi-autonomous, usually clandestine cells of a handful of radicals committed to group self-defense and often willing to engage in revolutionary vandalism and disruptive confrontation.

Groups in the hundreds have effectively seized control of several university buildings, when close to two hundred city and county officers sweep up the hill. The students blocking building entrances withdraw at their approach. Several hundred occupy Bascom Hall hallways until it is cleared and closed by police about 4:15 p.m. After that, police form a line in front of the building and endure abusive shouts from a mob of two thousand, many of whom pelt them with snowballs as they later retreat.[22]

Wednesday morning, an overflow crowd of fifteen hundred at a Union Theater rally cheer as black leaders urge them to close down the university. Afterward, hit-and-run strikes by strikers escalate; they block and occupy more buildings for more than three hours, even briefly blocking Van Hise, which houses President Harrington's office. There are several minor injuries, most coming when some of the two hundred antistrike "Hayakawas"—named after the strikebreaking president of SF State and including members of the Young Americans for Freedom, Sigma Epsilon Phi fraternity, and some football players—battle blockaders on the line. Three buses are vandalized on their campus routes, and traffic is so badly disrupted that the Madison Bus Company shuts down campus bus service for two hours. Police make several arrests, including freshman football player Harvey Clay.[23]

Former NAACP leader Marshall Colston, now heading a UW–Extension exchange program with historically black colleges in the south, charges that the black students' demands, which he supports, are being downplayed by white radicals who have seized control of the strike.[24] But he's wrong. While white radicals comprise a majority of bodies on the line, they fully support the strike and respect the Wapenduzi Weusi, which maintains tight top-down control. Other black leaders include Willie Edwards's wife, Libby Edwards, Horace Harris, Kenneth Williamson, Bernard Forrester, and John Felder, who came to UW in 1968 under Ruth Doyle's Special Tutorial and Financial Assistance Program (and actually stayed at the Doyle home while his permanent housing was arranged).[25]

With city and county law enforcement unable to maintain this pace or scope of response, Mayor Festge and the university leadership ask Governor Knowles to call out the Wisconsin National Guard, which he does at 3:10 p.m. The first battalion of nine hundred guardsmen begin arriving—in jeeps with machine guns permanently attached—around 9:30 p.m.[26]

On Thursday, February 13, the guardsmen prove a mixed blessing. Deployed in and around the major campus buildings, they keep the buildings open and accessible and exhibit a level of professionalism that impresses both university administrators and strikers. But they also trigger a defensive reaction among students, causing strike participation to grow sharply and prompting an escalation of response. That afternoon, six or seven thousand strikers take to the city streets under the disciplined direction of black marshals with walkie-talkies. The crowd blocks University Avenue four times in two hours, until strikers are removed by police with clubs and guardsmen with fixed bayonets. Police club some students, fire a couple of tear gas cannisters into crowds to clear intersections, and make ten arrests, but there are no major confrontations. At about 6 p.m., Governor Knowles activates another 1,200 guardsmen.[27]

National Guardsmen at parade rest in front of Bascom Hall on February 13. COURTESY OF CAPITAL NEWSPAPERS ARCHIVES, PHOTO BY CARMINE A. THOMPSON

That night, eight to ten thousand students, many with torchlights, march from the library mall to the Square and back. The march is self-policed and orderly, marred only by some racist catcalling by a few onlookers.[28]

After the march, about five hundred go to 6210 Social Sciences to hear SDS cofounder and Chicago Eight defendant Tom Hayden talk about the war, which he says America has lost. His appearance is unrelated to the strike, and except for saying that the activation of the National Guard is "the last trump card of the establishment," he demurs commenting on the action.[29]

On Friday, things are calming down, with only some token picketing of academic buildings and targeted obstruction of University Avenue. The Guard and 230 police from outside agencies are withdrawn from the central campus, but not deactivated. A noon march to the Capitol and back disrupts traffic but is disciplined and peaceful, as is another torchlit march of about a thousand that night.[30]

Meanwhile, at their meeting in Milwaukee, the regents unanimously commend Chancellor Young for his handling of the crisis but demand an investigation into the "Black Revolution" conference; several say it sparked the disruptions.

Nighttime march to the Capitol and back, February 14. COURTESY OF CAPITAL NEWS-PAPERS ARCHIVES

Young tells the regents of the potential for trouble beyond the thirteen demands. "Even if we had no black students on campus," he says, "we would still have difficulties, because there is a determined group of white students who are truly revolutionary and say that this is a corrupt and rotten society, and that it ought to be destroyed."[31]

Saturday, a petition supporting the university administration "in its refusal to surrender to mob pressure and lawless force, in its determination to continue normal educational activities, in its efforts to deal with problems, including those involving the disadvantaged members of society, through rational methods" is signed by 1,372 of the 2,050 faculty members.[32] The campus is quiet; the biggest excitement is at the Camp Randall Memorial Building, where two thousand fans cheer the Wisconsin track team to victory over Michigan State; Coach Charles "Rut" Walker takes no action against the eight black trackmen who boycott the meet.[33]

The strike's momentum begins to wane on Monday, February 17, with numbers down to about seven hundred, but strikers continue to obstruct streets and disrupt classes. Some shout down Professor George Mosse as he attempts to lecture on European cultural history, but Mosse takes a historian's view of the incident and is nonplussed. Late in the day, the Black People's Alliance (BPA), WSA, and Third World Liberation Front issue a statement calling on students to return to class and engage their professors and classmates on the underlying issues.[34]

By Tuesday, BPA leader Willie Edwards tells a small rally of about 150 that the strike is officially suspended, pending Wednesday's special faculty meeting called to consider their demands. "The support we got all last week began to dwindle," he explains. Over the fourteen days of the strike, attendance has been off by about 10 percent; some classes were shut down and some were reduced to half, while the western campus generally had full attendance. That afternoon, about half the guardsmen are sent home, with the rest to follow on Thursday.[35]

In the predawn hours of Wednesday, February 19, arsonists set nine separate fires, which heavily damage the UW Afro American and Race Relations Center, 929 University Ave. The center, on the third floor of an old apartment building, which is also used by the speech department and Institute for Research on Poverty, has been the main meeting place for the strike leaders.[36]

Later that day, faculty vote at a special meeting, 524–518, against recommending that three black students expelled from Oshkosh be immediately admitted to the Madison campus. Harrington also announces that Dr. Samuel Proctor, dean for special projects, "has been called east on an assignment of national import that cannot yet be announced" and is leaving the university.[37]

On Monday, February 24, with neither fanfare nor wide public notice, the Board of Regents' Finance Committee sells the university's 3,300 shares of stock in Chase Manhattan Bank, as demanded last year by the Concerned Black People, University Community Action, and Wisconsin Student Association. The sale is not widely known until May, when announcement of the action causes cancellation of an African Students Union rally to demand that the regents do what they've already done.[38]

Monday afternoon, Governor Warren Knowles tells a press conference that his fellow Republicans controlling the legislature should "not adopt legislation on the basis of prejudice or panic." In the two weeks since the Black Strike started, Assembly Speaker Harold Froelich and others have introduced a raft of bills to punish protesters and cut state support for the university.[39]

"Black studies must be controlled by black people, man, otherwise it's just another exotic course in social hippery," poet and playwright LeRoi Jones says that night, kicking off the WSA Symposium "Juxtaposition: Progress and Despair" before a packed Union Theater. "Unless you know where you come from, you will not know where you are going. That is why nationalists embrace black culture."[40]

Also on Monday night, the Faculty Committee on Studies and Instructions in Race Relations, chaired by Professor Wilson Thiede, recommends establishment of a Black Studies Department, the primary demand of the strike.[41] But because students would not have equal authority with faculty in establishing curriculum, making appointments, and granting tenure, the *Daily Cardinal* denounces the report as an "utterly unacceptable [and] insulting compromise [that] recommends only token efforts and denies even a token student participation."[42]

After several days pass with little progress, the black leaders are frustrated at the lack of action on the Thiede Committee recommendation, as well as the faculty's refusal to admit the Oshkosh students; they call for a resumption of the strike. In a forty-five-minute outburst on Thursday, February 27, about two hundred mostly white militants invade eight campus buildings, doing about $2,000 in damage and setting off a smoke bomb that drives right-wing state senator Gordon Roseleip (R-Darlington) from the stage of a Social Sciences classroom. Chancellor Young calls these deeds "acts of desperation by a small group of militants who have lost most of their following." At about the same time, the State Senate gives final legislative approval to a joint special committee, its members overwhelmingly Republican, to investigate campus disturbances. Black Council leader Horace Hanson later denounces the property damage but says it is "not the place of the Black Council to impose sanctions upon those whose intense reaction to destructive oppression has been destruction."[43]

On March 3, by a vote of 540–414, the faculty endorses the Thiede Committee's recommendation for an autonomous Department of Afro-American Studies within the College of Letters and Science. The proposal still needs approval from the regents and the Coordinating Committee on Higher Education (CCHE), but the target date for implementation is July 1970.[44] Black Council representative John Felder calls the move "a first step," and says black activists "are going to maintain the pressure" for their other twelve demands.[45]

But their pressure only changes so much; on March 14, the regents vote unanimously to refuse early admission to the ninety black students suspended from the State University at Oshkosh.[46]

On April 17, Chancellor Young names political science professor M. Crawford Young (no relation) as the chairman of the Black Studies Steering Committee, which will detail specifics for submission to the regents and CCHE for creation of the Afro-American

Studies department. Professor Young, who is white, is a specialist in African affairs and was the National Student Association overseas representative concentrating on African students in the late fifties.[47]

Black Council chairman Harris assails Chancellor Young for "the racist audacity to appoint a white chairman and white majority" to the Steering Committee and urges all black students "to totally reject any participation" on the committee, which they do.[48] Professor Young remains as chair until the end of the summer, when he steps down, as he had planned, to assume the chairmanship of the political science department.[49]

In September, Chancellor Young appoints a black man, Nolan E. Penn, associate professor of student counseling, as the new chairman of the steering committee. [50] The program sends out 1,400 applications to high school seniors; 285 are returned properly completed, and 210 are accepted, about evenly split between Wisconsin residents and nonresidents.[51]

The Joint Committee to Study Disruptions issues its report on October 14; it denounces UW administrators and calls for enactment of a series of pending bills, including one requiring the UW to contract with the Madison Police Department for police coverage on campus. Among its findings:

- "Certain members of the faculty have used their position in the classroom as a podium to indoctrinate their students with their personal political views and convictions or have failed to meet their classes while participating in 'strikes.' This is wrong and is not in keeping with their professional positions. Such individuals should be subject to discipline. They have not been."
- "The university administration failed almost totally to anticipate the situations that developed. As a result, when they did develop, they responded inadequately. For the money the state is paying these administrators, the state should receive some foresight."
- "The administration acts in times of crisis much like an ostrich—burying its head in the sand—waiting for the crisis to solve itself. The administration has displayed an incompetence to handle these matters properly."
- "The discipline procedures of the university are inadequate. The university has floundered through a maze of inadequate and less than competent disciplinary procedures. . . . The university must assume a responsibility for the conduct of its students on or off campus when such conduct demonstrates a danger or threat to the university community. University discipline is appropriate and necessary for certain conduct of students which affects the university community or the community in which the university is located."[52]

On December 1, the faculty unanimously accept the detailed plans from the College of Letters and Science to establish a Department of Afro-American Studies that would grant BA and BS degrees in the new Afro-American Studies major. Proponents hope the regents and Coordinating Council for Higher Education give final approval for the department to start by next fall.[53]

WHY DON'T WE DO IT IN THE ROAD

SAT MAY 3
4 p.m. until ...

500 Blk Mifflin be there

Roll Your Own Reality
BriNG/Share: Food, Fun Drums, Dogs

OFF the PIG!

I.W.W.C. ⟶   ENERGY-977

Invitation to the Mifflin Street block party. TOM SIMON, INTERNATIONAL WERE WOLF CONSPIRACY, UNIVERSITY OF WISCONSIN-MADISON ARCHIVES S000104

The Mifflin Street Block Party Riots

SDS cofounder Tom Hayden calls the student neighborhood bounded by West Washington Avenue and Dayton, Bedford, and Broom Streets—"Miffland"—one of America's "liberated zones." In this angry year it becomes a war zone, as a spring block party turns into a three-night riot.[54]

It's early May, and unidentified organizers are planning a party in the 500 block of West Mifflin Street. They don't care that they don't have a permit; lots of neighborhoods throw block parties without official sanction. Police had even diverted traffic for an unauthorized block party on West Gilman Street just the week prior.[55]

Most of the hippies and heavies just want to celebrate spring—hang out, dance in the street, smoke some pot (lots, and nary a drop of alcohol). Of course, some wouldn't mind a little confrontation, and they put out a poster designed to affront and mock authority.

It does—especially the department's number-two man, Inspector Herman Thomas. Though relieved of his former duties as movie censor, he's indeed offended by the calls to "roll your own reality," for "armed love," and to "off the pig"; he even thinks people might start to "do it in the road," if he doesn't bust up the party.[56]

For Detective Tom McCarthy, it's personal; two years after his face was broken at the Battle of Dow, he just wants to "bring the war to Mifflin Street."[57]

It's Sergeant Arnie Brager who brings Chief Emery the intelligence on April 29 about a street party on May 3; once Emery learns there's no permit closing the street, he orders twenty night-shift officers to report early on the third and arranges with Sheriff Vernon "Jack" Leslie for one hundred county deputy sheriffs to be on standby. Emery doesn't consult with Mayor William Dyke on the matter.[58]

Organizers set up some speakers on the porch at 512 West Mifflin that Saturday, and by 3:00 p.m., a crowd of a few dozen is grooving to the Janis Joplin record Alison Klairmont, one of the four women living there, is playing. But it's too loud for an elderly woman in the 400 block, who phones the police with a noise complaint; Thomas and two officers respond. Thomas tells Klairmont to turn it down; she hollers at him to get a warrant. He pushes his way through the crowd and pulls the plug himself, before relenting and letting the music stay on at a lower volume.[59]

But as soon as Thomas leaves the house the volume goes back up, the Rolling Stones celebrating the "Street Fighting Man." The group jumps in a flash to more than a hundred, dancers spilling into the street. Officers cite the ban on block parties and push them back on the sidewalk.

Thomas goes back to the station to gather eight more officers—in riot gear. "Stay behind me, men, we're going down there to crack some skulls," he tells them, returning to the scene at about 4:15 p.m. More officers are also on their way.[60]

Calling for a squad car with a loudspeaker, Thomas broadcasts the order to clear the street. The crowd responds with rocks and vulgar catcalls, and someone sticks a roasted pig's head near the car.[61]

Baton-wielding police start pushing into the crowd and making isolated arrests—including Ald. Paul Soglin, for "failing to obey a lawful order," namely driving on the street they're supposedly trying to keep open.[62]

By 5 p.m., there are thirty officers, all but a handful in riot gear, arrayed down the middle of the street, and about five hundred youth on lawns, porches and roofs, a handful hurling rocks and bottles; Thomas later claims they even throw feces.

Ald. Eugene Parks arrives and pleads in vain with Thomas to let the party go on; Parks then gets on the loudspeaker and tells the crowd to cool it while he appeals to Mayor Dyke and Chief Emery. But when Parks returns around six, without being able to contact either, he's booed and jeered, and a smoke bomb is thrown to within a few feet of the squad car. As if by signal, more rocks fly.

"Enough of this nonsense," Thomas declares, and unleashes his officers to disperse the crowd "in whatever manner they saw fit." Shedding the restraint they showed during the campus Black Strike in February, they charge into groups of youths with nightsticks up—and are hit with a hail of rocks and bricks from an affinity group David Williams, a radical freshman from Stoughton who had been active with SDS during the Black Strike, has organized, supplied, and positioned a bit to the west of the co-op; several officers are badly injured. Thomas deploys tear gas, withdraws his men for about an hour, and calls for county and university support; 122 more officers respond.[64]

As his constituents watch in outrage, police pull Ald. Paul Soglin out of his 1959 Triumph convertible and put him into their paddy wagon. Accompanied by attorney Mel Greenberg, Soglin had planned to follow the paddy wagon to the City-County Building to find out who had been arrested; he is soon among their number. Before he's bailed out, jailers cut Soglin's hair. The arresting officer, Sergeant Gordon Hons, center, testifies at Soglin's trial in July that Soglin was alone in the car. "I'm as sure of that fact as I am of any other in the case," he tells the jury.[63] COURTESY OF CAPITAL NEWSPAPERS ARCHIVES

The 500 block of West Mifflin Street, about 5:00 p.m., May 3, shortly before the first non-racist white riot of the decade. COURTESY OF CAPITAL NEWSPAPERS ARCHIVES

For the next several hours, there's pandemonium as autonomous affinity groups engage in hit-and-run battles with police, showering them with bricks, rocks, and bottles, often in coordinated attacks and ambushes. A nearby building demolition provides a ready source for bricks.[65]

County deputies pump out massive amounts of tear gas with their new Smith and Wesson "pepper fogger," spraying gas at a distance of up to two hundred yards; a toxic cloud settles over the three-flats. Sometimes, police fire or hurl tear gas cannisters right inside, including into Professor Harvey Goldberg's apartment at 521 W. Dayton St.[66]

Young Socialist Alliance activists Pat Quinn and Lew Pepper liberate a flatbed truck and block the intersection of West Washington Avenue and North Bassett Street; with mattresses and furniture, it's a barricade reminiscent of the ones radicals used in the Paris riots precisely a year prior. It provides a perfect perch for Williams and a group of about forty to launch volleys of rocks and bricks on approaching police, who are twice driven back until they finally overrun the rampart.[67]

Police draw blood and sometimes their weapons; one officer separated from his group brandishes his revolver at students who briefly have him cornered, another puts his gun to the head of an arrestee. Another officer throws a rock through a window at the Mifflin Co-op.[68]

The crowd blocks Bassett Street with material from a pipe-laying project and sets trash fires. When police vehicles knock the burning barricades down, they're set back up just to be knocked down again.[69]

By the time Soglin returns at about 9 p.m., his ward looks like a war zone, with clouds of tear gas visible from blocks away. When he calls for calm over a squad car loudspeaker, a rock crashes through the windshield, splattering him with glass.[70]

Police make twenty-five arrests, including Dow flag cutter Jonathan Stielstra, and nineteen-year-old John Tuschen (Madison Poet Laureate, 1973), identified as a "poet from

Chicago." Fifteen policemen and thirteen youths are injured; the most serious injury is to a policeman who suffers broken ribs from being hit by a brick.[71]

Chief Emery, who doesn't arrive until 8:30 p.m., later tells a mayoral commission investigating the riot that he "couldn't think of any different tactics to take other than what was being done."[72]

Detective Tom McCarthy thinks it went well. "We went down there and bombed the shit out of them," he says later.[73]

After a brief lull, the chaos resumes and spreads to State Street. An uneasy calm finally comes about 12:30 Sunday morning.

It doesn't last long.[74]

In the early afternoon of Sunday, May 4, several hundred officers from area communities, called in under the mutual aid agreement, muster at the Coliseum as Mifflanders start to gather around the co-op. By 4 p.m., there are about four hundred people milling around; Thomas declares the entire area an unlawful assembly and threatens everyone with arrest. A phalanx of about forty cops with riot gear advances on the crowd, which moves out of the street. Some rocks and bottles fly; police chase suspects, from the street to porches and often into houses, clubbing them when they resist.[75]

Even though the unlawful assembly statute applies only to groups of people and not to geographic areas, Soglin is again arrested on that charge, this time while standing by himself on private property near 113 N. Bassett St. Eugene Parks is arrested nearby shortly afterward, when he protests the apparent beating of a student.[76]

West side alderwoman Alicia Ashman tries to post Soglin's $507 bail, but the jailers won't take her check; she calls fire captain Ed Durkin, president of Firefighters Local 311, who authorizes the use of union funds. He says it's so Soglin can help restore order among his constituents and reduce the incidence of fires, but it's also in appreciation of Soglin's support during the illegal strike Durkin led three months earlier as union president. The gesture further angers both the police department and the Police and Fire Commission.[77]

As the sun sets Sunday night, police don their gas masks, and the trouble resumes in earnest. More trash fires and barricades, more billy clubs, and lots more tear gas.[78]

Mayor Dyke refuses repeated calls to issue a temporary street permit, urging students to party in the parking lot and tennis courts around the southeast dorms instead. If that's not good enough, he says, "It may be necessary for me to invoke the emergency powers of my office" and declare a street-clearing curfew.[79]

Ald. Eugene Parks being arrested Sunday afternoon, May 4, at the intersection of Mifflin and Bassett Streets. The Mifflin Community Co-Op is in the background. COURTESY OF CAPITAL NEWSPAPERS ARCHIVES, PHOTO BY RICH FAVERTY

Again, the chaos spreads far beyond Miffland, with kids and cops engaging in battles throughout downtown. A large crowd gathers at North Frances and State Streets; police and county deputies disperse it with yet more tear gas. There's no visible damage to property before the gas bombs go off, but by dawn Monday, eleven windows on lower State Street are broken.[80]

Soglin's 1968 concern about police not being competent to use riot gear seems sustained when officers leave unguarded a full box of tear gas canisters, which students soon seize and start using.[81]

At about 10 p.m. Sunday night, a group of around a thousand—mainly students but also some faculty, clergy, and professionals—marches to the City-County Building, where an informal meeting of the council is under way; they demand, in vain, to see the mayor. When the group dwindles to about seventy-five, a horde of high school students and other townies attack and beat some of the picketers; sheriff's deputies turn their backs and make no effort to protect the assaulted. "After last night," Sheriff Leslie tells Reverend Ray Gillies, youth pastor of First Congregational Church, "they deserve everything they get."[82]

Police make another fifty-five arrests before the end of the night; University and Madison General Hospitals treat three officers and thirty-five students and bystanders.

On Monday, May 5, more of the same, only more so. In the early evening, Mayor Dyke comes down to ground zero; speaking from the steps of the Mifflin Co-op to a jeering and hostile crowd of close to a thousand, he rejects Soglin's demand for amnesty and a new block party ordinance (see photo on page 397). As he leaves, Dyke tells the people they have half an hour to disperse before police return; they build new barricades instead. Within forty minutes of Dyke's departure, the 225 city and county officers, augmented by two hundred officers from neighboring counties, resume their tear gas offensive, and the third night's riot is on.[83]

The mayor's appearance doesn't calm the situation; the Monday night fight is the worst yet. Tear gas blankets the area, with rocks thrown and trash fires set from the fraternities to the southeast dorms. Police fire tear gas at a group of girls dispensing first aid in front of the Hillel Foundation on Langdon Street and directly into a group of professors on the porch of the University Club; even students studying for finals are forced to evacuate Memorial Library when tear gas blows through the building's open doors. Police finally exhaust their supply of tear gas and try to scatter students by tossing empty soda cans at them.[84]

Students fight back, not just with a barrage of projectiles aimed at vehicles and officers, but by firebombing three city, state, and university offices. At 10 p.m., for the second May in three years, student chaos in the streets shuts down city bus service.[85]

By the time it's all over Tuesday morning, there are shattered storefronts up and down State Street. The four downtown hospitals and two clinics treat eighty-six people for injuries, including eighteen law enforcement officers, thirty-four students, and twelve observers or children. The student senate puts $1,900 into a student bail fund for the hundred or so arrestees, with more money being raised on the streets. The city and county spend $42,448 and $35,000, respectively, for police overtime and other emergency costs.[86]

And Madison has again made its mark, with the nation's first white urban riot of the era that isn't against civil rights. In California, a sibling city's underground press pays respects on its front page; "On Wisconsin!" the *Berkeley Barb* declares.[87]

Tuesday, May 6, starts with a group of about twenty concerned citizens meeting at the First Baptist Church, searching for a way to end the rioting; they send a delegation, led by attorney Shirley S. Abrahamson, Lowell Frautschi, and the Reverend Max Gaebler, to urge Mayor Dyke to withdraw the police while their group ventures into the neighborhood to hear the residents' complaints. Dyke agrees and gives the group a name—the "Committee of Thirty." Its members are chosen mainly by Abrahamson.[88]

> **ROUNDY SAYS**
>
> "If the football team could get a march on like a lot of the students did Sunday night they would go to the Rose Bowl."
> —*Wisconsin State Journal*, May 6

For the next three nights, about a hundred members of the committee, wearing white armbands, conduct extensive interviews, registering widespread complaints about substandard housing and police brutality for a later official inquiry. A small group of militants, including the expelled former SDS leader Robert Zwicker, tries to foment renewed confrontation; Soglin calls them "armchair radicals," and the group shouts them down. But as an uneasy peace returns to the streets, tension racks Tuesday night's council meeting.[89]

First, even though Mayor Dyke praises Soglin for his "desperate and significant attempt" to keep things calm and supports his bid to have a street permit issued for the coming weekend, the council refuses to act on the request. Then an alderman from the far east side presents a petition calling for the "immediate dismissal" of Soglin and Parks from the council "if they are arrested for any violation during any demonstration of any nature." Parks storms out in righteous anger.[90]

On Wednesday, the Inter-Fraternity Council and the Panhellenic Council—the governing bodies for fraternities and sororities—each pledge $1,000 to the Wisconsin Student Association bail fund for students arrested during campus demonstrations.[91]

Several hundred Mifflanders, meeting in the 500 block, vote to demand amnesty for those arrested and to hold another block party on Saturday. They also adopt a resolution "declaring solidarity" with Firefighters Local 311 and apologizing to a fireman who was reportedly hurt during the riots.[92]

After an emotional debate that ends on Friday at about one in the morning, the council rejects, 17–3, Soglin's plea for a four-hour block party permit for Saturday. "These people have showed a lack of respect for anything honest and decent," Ald. Ralph Hornbeck says in explaining his opposition.[93]

Friday afternoon, after Dyke declares he will use "whatever level of law enforcement is required [to] maintain order," Soglin asks fire captain Ed Durkin to come to the neighborhood to try to cool things down. Durkin, whom the Mifflanders like because of his affability, zealous union leadership, and willingness to challenge the police, unexpectedly invites the whole neighborhood to his expansive spread at 5606 Old Middleton Rd., just west of Old Sauk Road. "There are people in Madison willing to help you," he says.[94]

Late that night, Soglin also succeeds in getting Madison realtor Patrick J. Lucey to lease a vacant lot in the 400 block of West Mifflin Street to the Mifflin Street Community Cooperative for a year for $1. "Perhaps this will help relieve some of the pressure building up there," says Lucey, whose gubernatorial campaign brought Senator Edward Kennedy to the Stock Pavilion in 1966.[95]

With two city buses provided without charge by Mayor Dyke, and beer donated by the Mifflin Street Co-op, about four hundred Mifflanders hold a five-hour party and pig roast on Durkin's three and a half acres on Saturday, May 11. Although the weather's wet and unseasonably cold, and many resent not being able to have the party in their own neighborhood, a good time is had by almost all. "I've never had so many squad cars pass by my house looking for trouble," Durkin says. The *New York Times* and other national media take note: "Campus riots in many parts of the country have given some people the idea that there are too many radicals," CBS newsman Murray Fromson reports, "but perhaps in fairness it should be said there are too few Ed Durkins."[96]

A week later, Mayor Dyke appoints a panel of three lawyers—former Supreme Court Chief Justice George Currie, former Justice Emmett Wingert, and attorney Ken Hur—to investigate the riots. Soglin and Parks protest the lack of community representation, but the panel is confirmed and holds six weeks of hearings over the summer. In addition to tense relations with police, tenants repeatedly cite substandard housing conditions as a serious concern.[97]

In early June, Mayor Dyke orders city building inspectors to conduct a comprehensive inspection of the 140 buildings of the four core blocks bounded by West Washington, Dayton, Bedford and Broom. They order corrections for 221 sanitary and building code violations, including fifty-five safety violations, thirty-five electrical violations, sixteen plumbing violations, ninety-six maintenance issues, twenty-six garbage violations, and three cases of rodent infestation.[98] Mayor Dyke admits there is "considerable legitimacy" to tenant complaints.[99]

On June 26, after a three-day trial, a Dane County jury takes less than an hour to find Ald. Parks not guilty of unlawful assembly. Although Parks's successful defense was that he was there in his aldermanic capacity, the council deviates from its normal practice and refuses to pay his $3,359 bill from attorney Richard Cates, who waives it.[100]

Two weeks later, Circuit Judge Richard Bardwell rules that Inspector Thomas incorrectly applied the "unlawful assembly" statute during Sunday's disturbance by designating an area rather than a crowd; he orders the dismissal of charges against four individuals about to go to trial, and district attorney James C. Boll drops charges against the remaining defendants, including Ald. Soglin.[101] But the next day, a Dane County Traffic Court jury convicts Soglin of "failing to obey a lawful police order" for the encounter on Saturday.[102]

The three-man panel appointed by Mayor Dyke issues its report on September 16, essentially blaming both sides and pleasing neither.[103]

The "greatest factor in causing the confrontations and disorders," it finds, was "the underlying antagonism which existed before the incidents" between Mifflanders and the police. The fact that residents were aware that police had allowed the "more conventionally dressed students of the Langdon-Gilman Street area" to have a block party just the week before "added to the prevalent belief of unfair discrimination."[104]

Police chief Emery and Inspector Thomas testified that the lesson they took from the Battle of Dow was the need to respond with overwhelming force at the outset of a disturbance. While finding that police "did not resort to the use of tear gas until they had been pelted with missiles," the commission still implicates the police in the Mifflin riot: "The second additional precipitating factor was the bringing of police attired in riot gear into the Mifflin Street area before there had been any actual violence."[105]

Once the violence began, the report states, "Training proved inadequate in the case of certain few officers, who during the disorders engaged in beatings, improper use of riot sticks and indiscriminate and improper use of tear gas. More and better training in this field is needed."

An offshoot of the Committee of Thirty—"Citizens Concerned for University-Community Issues"—issues its own report, warning that "Madison has cause for concern [over the] serious rift [that] exists" between youths and police.[106]

The mayor's panel also makes a series of recommendations, including assigning officers to the campus area "on the basis of their ability to relate understandingly to students and their problems," providing a "better method of testing [to] detect in advance those officers who are unable properly to react to the stress of a riot situation," employing foot patrols in the neighborhood, and appointing "a panel of experts in the field of public-police relations" to advise the mayor when group activities threaten a breach of the peace.[107]

The five members of the Police and Fire Commission—the statutory body with authority over police appointments and discipline—like that last idea; they name themselves "citizen observers and civilian consultants" to advise the mayor on "future crises and disturbances." "Excellent," says Mayor Dyke.[108]

The day after Christmas, the council refuses to honor about $8,000 in claims against the city, brought under a state law making the city liable for damages in cases of "injury to persons or property by a mob or riot." The largest claims are for damages to properties on State Street, including the University Book Store.[109]

Campus Calendar

January—The university's economic impact to the city is estimated at $300 million, largely due to its $100 million payroll and $22 million in purchases. Staff and faculty own or rent more than 4,600 residences in Madison, and about 21,000 students live off-campus.[110]

January 10—After the *Daily Cardinal* Board of Control declines to appear as requested, the regents vote, 4–3, to cut off the $9,100 annual support the university has been providing to the paper, as punishment for the *Cardinal* not providing a plan on how it will prevent obscenities from being published again. But the regents accede to the strong pleas of the administration and allow the paper to remain on campus, upon payment of market rate rent.[111]

January 10—On the recommendation of Chancellor Young and President Harrington, the regents dismiss Ivan "Ivy" Williamson from the athletic directorship he assumed in November 1955 upon the sudden death of then-director Guy Sundt. Williamson, who came to Wisconsin to coach the football team in 1949, remains a professor of athletics in the School of Education.[112] The athletic department projects a $442,700 deficit this academic year, for a two-year loss of more than $700,000—largely due to the winless football team, whose former coach, assistant athletic director Milt Bruhn, is named interim director until a new one is appointed.[113]

February 23–March 6—The tenth WSA Symposium, "Juxtaposition: Progress and Despair," presents black playwright LeRoi Jones and members of the Black Arts Repertoire Theater, TV newsman Sander Vanocur, ousted University of California president Clark Kerr, radical organizer Saul Alinsky, economist futurist Robert Theobold, and New Journalist Tom Wolfe.[114]

February 28—Elroy "Crazylegs" Hirsch (inductee, College and Professional Football and Wisconsin Athletic Halls of Fame) succumbs to entreaties from most of the state and accepts appointment as athletic director. The Wausau native was a star running back for the Badgers in 1942 and for the University of Michigan in 1943; from 1949 to 1957 he was a star receiver for the National Football League's Los Angeles Rams, replacing Pete Rozelle as the team's general manager in 1960 when Rozelle became commissioner of the NFL. Hirsch vows to turn the dismal football program around and says that coach John Coatta is "not on the spot [or] under an ultimatum." He takes charge at his first athletic board meeting in late March, describing the department offices as "a hovel," the coaches' room as "a mess," and the locker rooms as inferior to "every high school in the state." He's also incredulous at the lack of support personnel: "Doggone it," he exclaims, "if an athletic director of a major university can't have his own secretary, how can he do his job?"[115]

March 5—The Campus Planning Committee approves construction of eight hundred student housing units on the University-owned farm on the southeast corner of Whitney Way and Mineral Point Road. If the proposal is accepted by the Coordinating Committee on Higher Education and the legislature, the first 150 units could be ready by fall of 1971.[116]

March 6—Several state senators demand the firing of American history teaching assistant and *Connections* editor Ann Gordon for bad "character," because the latest issue of *Connections* includes an article by Jim Rowen featuring frequent use of a four-letter obscenity. Only Senator Fred Risser (D-Madison) comes to her defense, noting the need for due process and the lack of any official connection between *Connections* and the university. Gordon continues as editor and TA.[117]

March 7—History professor William Appleman Williams, whose students helped make history by their leadership of the New Left, announces his retirement after twelve years here. The Annapolis graduate and veteran of World War II has been at the University of Oregon in Eugene for much of the past three years and last taught on UW's campus in the spring semester of 1968.[118]

March 14—The regents vote to reduce nonresident freshmen enrollment from the current 30 percent to 25 percent this fall, 20 percent in 1970, and 15 percent in 1971.[119]

April 10—Punishing the university for various student uprisings and offenses, the Legislature's Joint Finance Committee cuts $38 million from the UW budget. Governor Knowles later restores most of the funds.[120]

April 11—Alumni appear as offended as legislators; Wisconsin Alumni Association director Arlie Mucks reports membership has declined from 39,000 to 37,000 since the Dow riot eighteen months prior.[121]

April 20—Troubadour Phil Ochs performs a Stock Pavilion benefit concert for the Community Co-Op.[122]

April 22—The final issue of the first underground newspaper in Wisconsin, *Connections*, is published.[123]

April 30—Athletic director Elroy Hirsch attributes some of the football team's difficulties to student unrest, telling the *Daily Cardinal* he couldn't recruit several top prospects "because their parents didn't want to send their sons into a situation such as we had here."[124]

May 8—Gwendolyn Brooks, the only black poet to win the Pulitzer Prize and this semester's Rennebohm Professor of Creative Writing, gives a reading in Tripp Commons.[125]

May 9—Dolores Huerta, vice president of the United Farmworkers Organizing Committee, speaks in Van Vleck hall on the four-year-old strike and grape boycott.[126]

May 11—The University Community Co-op, 401 W. Gorham St., announces at the "Miffland West" block party at Ed Durkin's spread that it has declared bankruptcy. The co-op, conceived by Robert "Zorba" Paster in the fall of 1967, opened in February 1968; after a promising initial flurry, sales tapered off, and the store began to lose money; it made a slight profit that fall, but its substantial order of textbooks arrived a week late, and the co-op never recovered.[127]

May 11—Folk Arts Society and the Union Music Committee present "From the Delta to Chicago" blues festival, featuring Otis Rush, Big Joe Williams, and more, for two shows at the Union Theater.[128]

June 16—The Steve Miller Band releases the album *Brave New World*, featuring four songs written by Miller and his former UW classmate Ben Sidran, including "Space Cowboy."[129]

June—The Park Street pedestrian bridge by the Memorial Union, little used since its opening in the summer of 1966 and the object of an occasional paint-in, is taken down.[130]

June—Members of the conservative Young Americans for Freedom announce plans for a new weekly campus newspaper, *The Badger Herald*. Editor-to-be Patrick Korten, an officer in the group who was active with the "Hayakawas" during the Black Strike, says the paper "will not print obscenity or any material which is in questionable taste" and will conform its standards to members of the broader Madison community, "not those of a group of way-out ivory towerists high atop Bascom Hill." The *Daily Cardinal* prints about ten thousand copies daily; the new paper will have an initial press run of about that per week.[131]

June 23—The first issue of *Madison Kaleidoscope*, Madison's second underground newspaper, is published. The weekly paper is edited by former *Connections* poetry editor Dave Wagner and affiliated with, but editorially independent of, the paper of the same name started in Milwaukee in 1967. In a letter to former *Connections* subscribers, Wagner says the paper's purpose is "to create a critical consciousness of life and culture in Madison, of the Madison environment, as a step toward building a radical movement to change and control that environment to serve human needs."[132]

Summer—History professor Harvey Goldberg leaves for a year's sabbatical, which he spends at his apartment in Paris.[133]

September 2—University law student David Keene, who founded the campus chapter of the conservative Young Americans for Freedom in 1965, is elected, without opposition, national chairman of the fifty-five-thousand-member group, which he calls "the most important conservative organization" in the country.[134]

September 10—The first issue of the free weekly *Badger Herald* is published. The initial press run is fifteen thousand.[135]

September 25–26—Howlin' Wolf, Richie Havens, and Luther Allison's Blues Nebulae headline the UW Folk-Rock Festival at the Field House and Union Theater, presented by WSA, Folk Arts Society, and Broom Street Theater.[136]

November 9—Beat poet Gary Snyder gives a Sunday night reading in Great Hall.[137]

November 12—Uniformed UW Protection & Security officers start regular patrols through Memorial Union.[138]

November 13—After entertaining thousands at the Dane County Memorial Coliseum on November 13, folksingers Peter, Paul and Mary perform another full set at a crushingly crowded Moratorium Midnight Vigil at University Catholic Center on lower State Street. At both shows, they urge fans to join the Moratorium in Washington that weekend, and many do.[139]

November 14—Fed up with sex, drugs, and protests, the regents reinstate women's hours and raise the minimum age at which students may live in unsupervised housing without parental permission from twenty to twenty-one. Regents president Dr. James T. Nellen calls it "a vote against the permissiveness that is going on in universities." Over the strong opposition of President Harrington and Chancellor Young, the regents vote, 7–3, to give freshmen women under twenty-one a curfew of midnight on weeknights and 2 a.m. on weekends. Cross-gender visitation, in housing units where it is allowed, will be limited to the hours between noon and midnight on Fridays and Saturdays, and between noon and 10:30 p.m. on Sundays. Regent Maurice Pasch, the Madison attorney who is now the sole Democratic appointee on the board, cites "promiscuity and immoral behavior" as grounds for the new restrictions, which take effect next fall. Regents endorsing the new restrictions claim overwhelming support from parents.[140]

November 15–23—Delayed a year by strikes and shortages, the grand opening of the Humanities building is celebrated by four formal dedication programs and a series of recitals and lectures. Due to unfavorable construction bids, the regents eliminated from the massive building several architectural features, including significant amounts of trim and decorative plaster, stone entrances, and a sculpture garden in the interior courtyard.[141]

November 16—President Harrington starts a two-month leave of absence and vacation to India and Egypt, accompanied by his wife, under a so-called "tired president" grant from the Danforth Foundation.[142]

December 2—Acting on the recommendation of athletic director Elroy Hirsch, the Athletic Board declines to renew the contract for football coach John Coatta and his staff. Coatta's teams compiled a record of 3–26–1 in the three years since he replaced the ousted Milt Bruhn, with Camp Randall attendance averaging barely 48,000 per game. Coatta is out immediately, and contracts for his assistants expire June 30, except for Les Ritcherson, who still has a year remaining on his five-year personal services contract with President Harrington.[143]

December 6–7—About seventy women—students, TAs, young professionals, wives, and mothers—attend the Women's Liberation Conference at the University YWCA, 306 N. Brooks St. The workshops include "The Psychology of Women," "Women and Sex," "Family Structure Alternatives," "Women and Racism," "Roles of Women in Other Cultures," "Images of Women in the Mass Media," "Women as Exploited Consumers," "Jobs and Pay Structure for Women," and "Women's Liberation as a Part of Total Change."[144]

December 19—Business professor James Graaskamp, UW PhD 1964, is named the state's Handicapped Person of the Year by the Governor's Committee on Employment of the Handicapped. A quadriplegic, Graaskamp developed polio in 1950 at age seventeen and has been in a wheelchair since. He joined the faculty in 1964 and is an owner of Landmark Research Inc., and a commissioner of the nonprofit Industrial Land Utility Corp.[145]

December 22—John Jardine, top assistant to UCLA coach Tommy Prothro and former star lineman at Purdue, is introduced as the Badgers' new football coach. "I am very optimistic," he says. "I certainly wouldn't be sitting here today if I didn't believe we were going to win."[146]

ROUNDY SAYS

"It was awful sad to read about the death of Ivy Williamson. He was the best football coach Wisconsin had in years he won the games. He was one of the most brilliant students that ever graduated from Michigan."
—*Wisconsin State Journal*, February 21

In Memoriam—UW

Ivan "Ivy" Williamson, fifty-eight, dies February 19 of a head injury suffered falling down the basement stairs of his Maple Bluff home five weeks after being dismissed as athletic director. Captain of the Michigan football team in 1932, Williamson succeeded Harry Stuhldreher as Badger head coach in 1949; his teams went 41–19–4 in seven seasons and won their first Big Ten Championship in forty years, losing the 1953 Rose Bowl to USC 7–0.[147]

Professor G. William Longenecker, sixty-nine, the "father of the Arboretum" and its director for thirty-four years, dies after a long illness on February 25. The arboretum's entire horticultural area was named in his honor upon his retirement in 1967.[148]

Protest

As antiwar protests grow and some activists edge into violence, state and university officials step up their crack-down.

Protest Dateline

February 14—The Wisconsin Supreme Court rejects arguments that the state disorderly conduct statute is unconstitutionally vague and upholds convictions arising from the two Dow demonstrations in 1967.[149]

February 14—Regents vote 8–2 to replace the five-hour mandatory ROTC orientation for freshman with a voluntary summer program, as freshmen activists demanded last fall.[150]

February 26—Dow Chemical Company conducts thirty-six job interviews, with no pickets or protests.[151]

March 4—The state senate, by voice vote, gives final legislative approval to a bill making students convicted of crimes during university disruptions ineligible for state financial aid for two years.[152]

March 6—The regents hold a special meeting to enact an emergency administrative rule prohibiting students suspended or expelled for illegal acts during demonstrations, or nonstudents convicted of such acts, from entering any UW campus for a year. The regents reject the proposal by board vice president James Nellen, team physician for the Green Bay Packers, that all students be fingerprinted.[153]

March 28—James Rowen (Madison Mayor Paul Soglin's administrative assistant, 1973–1978; Milwaukee Mayor John Norquist's chief of staff, 1996–2004) reveals in a *Daily Cardinal* exclusive that the Army Mathematics Research Center (AMRC), located in Sterling Hall, "is providing important research and advice for many Army weapons systems and projects [under a] contact which has brought over $5 million from the Army to the Center since 1956." The AMRC denies Rowen's charge that the work involves the Antiballistic Missile or other missile systems. In November, the faculty's University Committee issues a report concluding that there has been no classified work done for the Defense Department on campus since June 1968. In December, Rowen reveals a number of meetings AMRC director J. Barkley Rosser and other staff had with Army officials, which were omitted from their annual reports.[154]

May 1–2—On the fourth anniversary of the first May 2 demonstration against the war, a group of about forty peace activists read the names of the 37,812 Americans killed in Vietnam in a solemn twenty-four-hour vigil at the State Capitol.[155]

May 6—President Harrington reminds the Joint Committee to Study Disruptions that "we have been willing to use force" to keep the university open, and vows to continue to do so, even against increasing violence and militarism by protesters. He dates the university's assumption about the need for a strong police presence to 11:15 a.m., October 18, 1967: "In October '67, it was our belief—and this was a mistaken belief as it turned out—that the disruptors would accept arrest when we came to arrest them. As it turned out, they would not accept arrest, and since that time we have not anticipated that they would."[156]

May 8—Governor Knowles signs into law three bills designed to curb campus disruptions by restricting access to campus by persons previously convicted of or expelled for disruptive acts, limiting sound amplification equipment, and extending emergency powers to all cities and villages.[157]

June 13—Regents unanimously ban all political groups from participating in the summer orientation program for incoming freshmen on the Madison campus when they learn SDS is scheduled to participate.[158]

July 7—In the first action by a local chapter following the chaotic national SDS conference in Chicago earlier this month, Madison SDS votes 66–35 to stay neutral in the struggle for control between the national office/Revolutionary Youth Movement faction (headed by Mark Rudd, Bernadine Dohrn, Bill Ayers, and others) and the Progressive Labor Party/Worker Student Alliance group from Boston.[159]

Summer—Inspector Thomas, who celebrates the protesters' penchant for calling police "pigs" by naming his undercover agents after breeds of hogs, gets a new recruit—Mark Baganz, a law school student from northern Wisconsin, code-named "Duroc." He's recruited by Detective George Croal, who came to Madison in 1963 on a Woodrow Wilson fellowship to study with history professor George Mosse. That relationship soured, especially when Mosse called him a fascist for supporting Barry Goldwater in 1964.[160] To fend off damage from such police informants and provocateurs, SDS develops a confidential leadership group, the "Mother Jones Revolutionary League."[161]

August 26—There are no uniformed city police at the Memorial Union for former Secretary of State Dean Rusk's evening address to 1,400 attendees of the Graduate School of Banking. So when a group of about 150, led by members of the Young Socialist Alliance, hit Rusk's and others' cars with rocks as he is leaving, pound on citizens' cars, swear at drivers, and partially block traffic on Park Street, there are no arrests.[162] This shows "the fallacy of the theory that dissident groups do not become violent or attack with deadly weapons unless agitated by police," police chief Wilber Emery says, noting that "only when fully-marked police cars and uniformed officers moved into the trouble area did the mob disperse and violence stop."[163] The Joint Committee to Study Disruptions blames the university's "incompetence to handle these matters properly" for the incident.[164]

September 9—Inspector Thomas tells attendees of an interagency meeting at the governor's mansion that police informants have reported rumors that Mifflin Street radicals are gathering machine guns and grenades. The consensus is to expect bloodshed, probably a death, on campus this year.[165]

September 16—Draft resister Ken Vogel, under indictment for refusing induction into the Armed Services, takes sanctuary in the First Congregational Church, 1609 University Ave.[166] Although the US attorney says the warrant on the ex-seminarian from Manitowoc County won't be executed for a week or so, about fifty other young white men join him, vowing to peacefully assist him resist arrest. They all wear name tags that read, "Hello, I'm Ken Vogel." That night, unidentified persons throw rocks at the Naval ROTC armory across the street from the church, shattering several large windows.[167] Vogel and his supporters remain at the church for twelve days; having established that the FBI would respect the church's sanctuary, he moves to Resistance House, 211 Langdon St., where he is arrested on October 3.[168]

September 18—The semester's first "monster meeting" of Madison SDS in Great Hall features a failed attempt to take over the meeting by SDS national secretary Jeff Jones and a half-dozen members of the militant Weatherman faction. Jones berates the crowd with revolutionary rhetoric for about fifteen minutes until most of the eight hundred or so attendees follow Allen Hunter's lead and turn their chairs around to proceed with the real business of the meeting—adoption of the "Three Demands," formulated by the "Woody Guthrie Collective": removal from campus of ROTC, the Army Mathematics Research Center, and the Land Tenure Center.[169]

September 20—The Dane County Board of Supervisors approves a monthlong riot-control training program for three hundred lawmen from twenty county municipalities. The training starts on September 22 at the rifle range in Verona, with "mass events" training at the drill hall in the National Guard armory on Wright Street in Madison.[170] At 2:45 in the morning on September 26, a bomb—between fifteen and twenty sticks of dynamite with a timing device—explodes at the armory, ripping through steel doors and sending the armory door flying forty yards into the drill hall, which is filled with the riot gear being used in the training program. The explosion, which occurs about an hour after a similar explosion damaged the federal building in downtown Milwaukee, does about $15,000 in damage.[171]

October 9—The council adopts, 16–6, Ald. Soglin's resolution endorsing the Moratorium to End the War in Vietnam, the national demonstration and teach-in, "in principle" and welcoming home the men of the 826 Ordinance Company, returning after a year in Vietnam. The resolution asks each citizen to regard the moratorium as "a call to conscience and reflection."[172]

October 15—Moratorium morning starts with a Library Mall rally in a cold drizzle, attracting about three thousand. Among the day's seventy programs and activities are pickets at the ROTC and Army Math Research Center, a draft resistance workshop in Gordon Commons, well-attended lectures and teach-ins, and less well-attended special sermons and programs at five leading religious centers. The events, which include speakers ranging from members of the Young Socialist Alliance to the Inter-Fraternity Council, are coordinated by moratorium committee chair Margery Tabankin.[173]

SDS representatives Bill Kaplan and Marc Levy present the SDS's "Three Demands"—removal of ROTC, the Army Math Research Center, and the Land Tenure Center—to

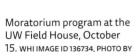

Moratorium program at the UW Field House, October 15. WHI IMAGE ID 136734, PHOTO BY DAVID SANDELL

Chancellor Edwin Young, who rejects the demands, the October 27 deadline for compliance, and the SDS's request to negotiate.[174]

At night, fifteen thousand people fill the Field House for a series of antiwar speeches—it's the building's largest crowd since Senator John Kennedy's campaign appearance in October 1960. Marcella Kink of Middleton moves many in the crowd to tears with her pained and plaintive plea for meaning in the recent death of her son after his helicopter crashed northwest of Saigon. "What did he die for?" she asks, but there is no answer. James Rowen gives a sharp critique of the university itself, as the "fourth branch of the military" for its Army-related research, and calls for a moratorium on such activity.[175]

Afterward, almost the entire crowd marches through the cold rain, singing and chanting, with umbrellas and lit candles, filling State Street with flickering light from mall to square. There are no disturbances, other than some angry drivers honking at being briefly inconvenienced, and the few radicals chanting "Ho Ho Ho Chi Minh, NLF is gonna win!" don't get much traction. At the capitol, all falls to a hush but for the tolling of the bell of Grace Episcopal Church, an ecumenical memorial service for the more than nine hundred Wisconsin servicemen who have died in the war so far. As each name is read, a candle is extinguished. The mournful ceremony ends just before midnight.[176]

October 17—Over the objections of President Harrington and Chancellor Young, the regents further tighten restrictions on the use of sound amplifying equipment, essentially eliminating the chancellor's discretion to grant approval for the use of bullhorns or other devices. The policy allows amplification for "events of an all-campus nature," such as homecoming, but limits sound equipment "for any rallies or meetings sponsored

A peaceful march to end a
war, October 15. WHI IMAGE ID
136733, PHOTO BY DAVID SANDELL

by politically oriented groups [except] in extremely unusual circumstances." When Harrington says political rallies are precisely where sound amplification is appropriate, Regent Gelatt says he's seen bullhorns used on the Madison campus "in much the same fashion as the Hitler movement using the bullhorn in the thirties to whip up the crowd." Afro-American Center director Elrie Chrite and SDS leader Kaplan are among the first to be arrested under the new policy, for using sound equipment at a moratorium rally in November.[177]

November 13–14—The city engages in two "Days of Thought and Quiet" in observance of the Vietnam Moratorium. About fifteen hundred Madisonians fill thirteen chartered buses heading to Washington for Saturday's massive march and rally.[178]

November 14—The Dow Chemical Company announces it has lost the government contract for manufacturing napalm and has ceased its production.[179]

November 18—ROTC reports that freshman enrollment has dropped from 279 last fall to 125 this fall, and that overall enrollment has dropped from 751 in 1968 to 550 in 1969.[180]

November 19—About five hundred SDS supporters stage a quick, orderly march from Bascom Hall to the Army Mathematics Research Center to the Army ROTC building on Linden Drive, across University Avenue to the Air Force ROTC offices in the Mechanical Engineering building and back; their only infraction is some jaywalking.[181]

December 10—Governor Warren Knowles signs into law the seventh antidisruption bill since February's Black Strike, setting a minimum one-semester suspension from university attendance or employment for any person convicted of a crime or misdemeanor arising out of the forceful disruption of classes, the disruption of pedestrian or vehicular traffic, or the seizure of university buildings.[182]

December 12—An SDS action against T-16, the Quonset hut at the corner of Linden and Babcock Drives used for ROTC instruction, leaves four protesters arrested and four campus policemen injured after a free-swinging melee. About two hundred demonstrators then move through campus, smashing windows in the AMRC, Bascom Hall, and the Humanities Building before a vanguard of about two dozen students attack the unguarded Peterson Administration Building, where they throw garbage cans through the large interior plate glass windows and destroy or remove thousands of the hated photo identification cards. The destructive vandalism is attributed to small, autonomous affinity groups, whose ranks have been growing since the Black Strike. The *Daily Cardinal* applauds the objectives and accomplishments of the march but decries that poor execution resulted in the "needless and counterproductive" property destruction.[183]

December 28—At 4:15 a.m., Karl Armstrong breaks three windows in T-16, tosses two gallon jugs filled with gasoline inside, and lights a match. University senior Bryce Larson hears the breaking glass, sees the flickering flames, and calls campus police; the Madison Fire Department is able to save the building, limiting damage to about a thousand dollars. Police track Armstrong's footprints to Tripp Circle but lose the trail and never develop any suspects.[184]

December 31—Armstrong enlists his brother Dwight in a plan to steal a plane from Morey Airfield, where Dwight works, to make a bombing run on the Badger Ordnance Works in Baraboo. About two hours into 1970, Karl drops three makeshift bombs of ammonium nitrate and fuel oil (ANFO); they fall harmlessly into the snow and do not explode. Driving back to Madison, Karl is pulled over by police and given a warning for speeding. It's the start of the "New Year's Gang," which will undertake a series of firebombings and other actions, culminating in the ANFO bombing of Sterling Hall, home of the Army Mathematics Research Center, at 3:42 a.m. on August 24, 1970. The explosion does about $2 million in damage and kills postdoctoral physics researcher Robert Fassnacht, thirty-three, who has no connection to the AMRC.[185]

War Dead/War Hero

Army Specialist 4-C Lyle C. Hansbrough, twenty-five, son of Mrs. Lyle Hansbrough, 4817 Bayfield Ter., and the late Dr. Hansbrough, is killed in action in Gia Dinh Province on March 17. A graduate of West High School and Whitewater State University, he was drafted in February 1968 and had been in country since last July.[186]

Chief Warrant Officer 2 William C. Pierson III, twenty-one, a helicopter copilot with the First Cavalry, 101st Airborne Division, is on an attack run in Quang Nam province when his helicopter is shot down April 13, his eighteenth day in country. His body is never recovered, and he is listed as a prisoner of war until October 1978, when he is declared dead.[187]

Navy Medical Corpsman Gary Johnson, 3725 Hammersley Ave., is killed in a night search-and-destroy mission southeast of Da Nang on April 30, three days before his twenty-second birthday. The 1965 graduate of Central High School and member of Glenwood Moravian Church had been in country for forty-four days.[188]

Army Specialist 5-C James V. Spurley Jr., twenty, 1602 Norman Way, is killed during a rocket and mortar attack on an aircraft landing zone northwest of Saigon on May 11, during the Battle of Hamburger Hill. A 1967 graduate of West High School, he entered the Army's First Air Cavalry in February 1968, arriving in Vietnam that July. A former carrier boy for the *Capital Times,* he attended Dale Heights Presbyterian Church.[189]

Army Private Thomas A. Greisen, twenty, 446 Hilltop Dr., is killed in action June 6. A 1967 graduate of West High School, he worked at the Pure Oil Company at Westgate before entering the Army in May 1968. He was sent to Vietnam that December.[190]

Josephine Brantmeyer, 2426 Commonwealth Ave., learns on July 9 that her son Ricky, an Army First Lieutenant, has been awarded the Bronze Star for heroism in ground combat for "continually exposing himself to hostile fire" while directing artillery to suppress an enemy attack. The West High School graduate, twenty-two, is returning home to enter the University of Wisconsin.[191]

Two-time Purple Heart recipient Marine Corporal Charles R. Le Bosquet, twenty-one, 4409 Cherokee Dr., is killed in action in Quang Nam province August 21. A 1965 graduate of West High School and member of First Baptist Church, he was a platoon radio man with the First Marine Division. He attended UW and enlisted in the Marines in August 1968, arriving in Vietnam this past February.[192]

Army Specialist 4-C Dennis W. Shew, twenty-one, 1101 Mendota St., a 1966 graduate of East High School, is killed in a non-combat vehicle crash on September 11. A native Madisonian and member of St. Paul's Lutheran Church, he entered the Army in March 1968, and was sent to Vietnam a year later.[193]

Civil Rights

The Movement

January 3—Governor Warren Knowles appoints Madison police inspector Herman Thomas to the state Equal Rights Council.[194]

January 10—The regents confirm the appointment of Merritt Norvell, the community services administrator with the city Housing and Community Development department, as vice chancellor for student affairs.[195]

January 20—Ruth B. Doyle resigns as administrator of the Special Program of Tutorial and Financial Assistance she initiated and nurtured, becoming assistant to Vice Chancellor for Student Affairs, Norvell. Black students praise her as "a beautiful person" but insist the program be run by a black director.[196]

March 18—Ald. Alicia Ashman, joined by National Organization of Women co-founder Dr. Kathryn Clarenbach, reports that several city ordinances discriminate against women, from employment to banking. "Even in Madison," she says, "unwed mothers employed by the city are ineligible for maternity benefits." Ashman and Clarenbach propose amending the Equal Opportunities Ordinance to prohibit discrimination on the basis of sex or age; the commission agrees to draft the amendment.[197]

March 28—Black fraternity Kappa Alpha Psi presents Flip Wilson and the Impressions at the Field House in a benefit for the Martin Luther King Scholarship Fund.[198]

April 1—Three white west side teenage boys, ages thirteen to fifteen, apologize to African American music professor James Latimer and his wife for burning a four-foot-high wooden cross on the front lawn of their home at 3922 Hillcrest Dr. a few nights earlier. The boys explain they had "nothing else to do" and had no malicious intent. The Latimers accept their apology. In the immediate aftermath of the cross burning, 230 neighbors sign a petition declaring they are "deeply ashamed [by] such an inhumane act."[199]

May 20—Fred Hampton, the charismatic chairman of the Illinois Black Panther Party, tells an enthusiastic overflow crowd in 6210 Social Sciences that class struggle is a more pressing problem than racism. "We must fight white capitalism not with black capitalism but with black socialism," he says to a standing ovation.[200]

May 20—Bill Russell, player-coach of the Boston Celtics, talks about race relations and politics and answers questions for about two hours in a Panhellenic Council event for nearly two hundred white students at the First Congregational Church. He condemns the US Olympic Committee and its president, Avery Brundage, as racist and celebrates the protest by sprinters Tommie Smith and John Carlos at the Mexico City Olympics last summer: "It's hep what those guys did with the black gloves and all."[201]

August 4—Mary Louise Symon, former chair of the Equal Opportunities Commission (EOC), and others announce the formation of Citizens for Civic Peace, formed to press the Madison Police Department to integrate the force through new recruitment and training policies. "These are not normal times and we cannot rely on normal procedures," says Madison Urban League president Hilton E. Hanna.[202]

August 11—Madison Area Technical College names Richard Harris, director of the South Madison Neighborhood Center, instructor in sociology and director of recruiting and counseling for disadvantaged students.[203]

September 18—Air Force Sergeant Johnny E. Winston, twenty-one, recently returned from Vietnam, is certified by the Police and Fire Commission as the first black member of the 226-member police department. Currently an air policeman at the Tyndall base in Panama City, Florida, Winston enlisted shortly after graduating from high school in South Bend, Indiana. During a two-year posting at Truax Field, he married Mona Adams, 15 Lakeshore Ct.; they have a year-old son, John Jr. Sergeant Winston is scheduled for discharge next June but may be released early to start his new job.[204]

October 24—Sophomore Carolyn Williams of Racine, a member of the social and service sorority Delta Sigma Theta, is named UW's first black homecoming queen.[205]

December 1—Governor Warren Knowles appoints State Department of Local Affairs and Development division administrator Charles Hill as acting secretary of the department, making him the highest-ranking black official in state history. Knowles promises to make the appointment permanent once Hill, who was the Madison Redevelopment

Authority's former community services director, completes the probationary period for his current civil service administrator post.[206]

December 11—The first issue of the first black newspaper at the university, . . . *and Beautiful,* is dedicated to Black Panthers Fred Hampton and Mark Clarke, recently shot to death by Chicago police officers: "Remember December 4, 1969 with anger and determination."[207]

December 30—The Dane County Board's judiciary committee endorses a resolution by Madison supervisors Richard A. Lehmann and James T. Sykes adopting as county policy the recent city ordinance cracking down on private clubs with race-based membership rules. The resolution goes to the County Board, where its chances are uncertain.[208]

Breese Stevens Field—Coda

Kids (white and black) and cops (all white) were both to blame for last August's racial ruckus at Breese Stevens Field, the Equal Opportunities Commission says in a 116-page report to the council with a stark conclusion: "The hatred and resentment which are evident give a warning to Madison. Tension must be alleviated."[209]

"The mistrust and hostility which black youth feel toward the police clearly contributed to the violence of both their verbal and physical behavior" that night, the April report states, while "similar feelings on the part of some police officers toward black youths clearly influenced their behavior and judgment in dealing with the situation." Assigning so many officers to follow the black youth up East Washington Avenue, the report states, "was an overreaction to the actual threat of damage to property and to the size of the group."

"Tensions do indeed exist between the black community and the Police Department," the report states, and can be remedied "only by changing attitudes and behavior of citizens of both races, by eliminating institutional practices of discrimination which perpetuate the blacks' resentment and feeling of second-class citizenship."

The commission offers several recommendations, including making recruitment of "a significant number" of black officers "a high and urgent priority" for the still all-white department, appointing "at least one experienced black officer at a status level," upgrading and centralizing community relations programs, delegating major recruitment responsibilities to the personnel department, and establishing a community complaint procedure separate from formal misconduct complaints.

The EOC insists the report is not "anti-police," but the Police and Fire Commission (PFC) bristles at the charge that it has refused to hire qualified black applicants. And it challenges the EOC's underlying assessment, claiming "belief, innuendo and feeling were used as a substitute for fact in a great many instances."[210]

Tensions do exist between police and black residents who have "attained professional status as well as juveniles who have had frequent contacts with the police," the PFC acknowledges, but "a sound, amenable relationship exists between police and the older, established and law-abiding black citizens."[211]

On August 14—just over a year since the Breese Stevens incident—the council adopts a compromise resolution, which endorses much of the EOC's analysis but none of its specific recommendations. The resolution, drafted by Mayor Dyke and approved 18–2, does state that "although there is some difference of opinion as to the extent of tension, there is agreement that significant tension does exist between the black community and the police."

EOC director Reverend James C. Wright celebrates the near-unanimous adoption of the resolution as "a step in the right direction."[212]

Banning Club Bias Redux

Three years after the council approved the Equal Opportunities Commission's recommendation that the city stop granting liquor licenses to private organizations with discriminatory membership policies "at some future date" after 1969, the EOC on March 18 opens an inquiry to see if any of Madison's fourteen private clubs with liquor licenses have national charters limiting membership to white males. The same three clubs that did in 1966—the Eagles, Elks, and Moose—still do.[213]

At least Madison Elks Lodge 410 is trying to change; in late March, more than 250 members vote almost unanimously for a resolution calling on its national Grand Lodge to eliminate the "white males" provision. The Grand Lodge refuses to do so.[214]

In mid-May, the EOC reaffirms its long-held position that the council should "deny any and all privileges granted by the city to those organizations which discriminate against others because of race, creed, color, national origin or ancestry." And it adds two new standards—that elected and appointed city officials "should not belong to private clubs which discriminate in the selection of their membership," and that no city functions or meetings may "use the facilities" of such clubs, including for retirement or office parties.[215]

The next week, the council sends the matter back to the EOC, "suggesting" that it provide a five-year grace period.[216] But the whites-only clubs have already had three years to eliminate the discriminatory provisions, the commission notes the next afternoon, offering June 1970 as the deadline for compliance.[217]

One of the aldermen on the commission, Robert Dries, says the commission shouldn't make "a crusade" of the issue.

On June 10, a past state officer of the Loyal Order of Moose gives an emphatic but counterproductive defense of the club's whites-only provision, which he ends by inviting to the club "those of you who are qualified to go," namely persons "of Caucasian blood" who are not married to a person of another race. African Americans Ald. Eugene Parks, sitting directly in front of Moose attorney Willis Donley, and EOC executive director Reverend James Wright, who is sitting a few rows back, are not amused.[218]

On June 24, after approving liquor license renewals for the three clubs with race-based membership, the Committee of the Whole votes 17–4 to recommend adoption of the EOC package. But it also votes 12–10 to delay implementation of the license ban until

1971, which would be five years after the council said it opposed such licenses and would stop issuing them.

"It's the classic example of the liberalism that supports racial equality, but not enough to do something definite, today," says Ald. Parks.[219]

As with every civil rights initiative this decade, council opposition is led by south side Ald. Harold "Babe" Rohr, who insists the three clubs "probably do more for minority groups than the minority groups do for themselves," and suggests the ordinance is tantamount to "calling thousands of good Christian people racists." Mayor Dyke disagrees, calling the vote setting a deadline "absolutely appropriate."[220]

Two nights later, the full council formally adopts the full EOC package, including restrictions on city employees or appointees belonging to or scheduling city meetings at clubs with discriminatory provisions. It's a voice vote, without recorded opposition.[221]

That August, the Eagle national convention votes by about 4–1 to retain the "whites-only" provision.[222]

Schools

GRADUATION, JUNE 5
- ▸ West: 506
- ▸ East: 492
- ▸ La Follette: 412
- ▸ Memorial: 386
- ▸ Central-University: 186[223]

FALL ENROLLMENT
- ▸ Total Students: 34,281[224]

Dress and Grooming Code

About 150 of West High's 1,510 students stage a sit-in near the school's Ash Street entrance for about two hours on January 28 supporting the demands of the Concerned Students of West High School, which include abolishing the dress and grooming code, letting girls wear slacks to class, reestablishing the open lunch hour, allowing distribution of the student-controlled *Free Press,* creating a student smoking lounge, hiring more minority teachers, and not providing any information to the Selective Service System. West High principal David A. Spencer says the *Free Press* is unnecessary because the school publishes the *West High Times* and "we do not censor it." A month later, however, Spencer prevents distribution of an issue of the *West High Times* because he thinks its coverage of the sit-in is "an editorial disguised as a news story."[225]

On February 20, Spencer agrees to let girls wear slacks and says an open lunch will start after Easter vacation, provided students keep the cafeteria "immaculate" until then.

Girls at James Madison Memorial High School can already wear slacks, with parental permission, but not girls at any other school in Madison; girls at La Follette High School can wear slacks over their clothes to get to school in the winter, but not in class.[226]

In March, federal judge James E. Doyle strikes down a Williams Bay High School dress code; that's when the debate gets personal, after La Follette High School assistant principal Donald Wendt asks if he could suspend a girl for wearing slacks, which she would be able to do at West.

"Yes, and we would back you," board member Albert McGinnis replies.

"But I think I remember a quote from Mrs. Doyle that she didn't feel the board could do this," Wendt replies.

"She lives with Judge Doyle, remember," McGinnis snaps back.[227]

On May 5, as the worst night of the Mifflin riot rages all around the school administration building on Bedford Street, the board gives up its nine-month struggle to write specific dress and grooming guidelines, repeals its earlier mandate for "all boys to be clean shaven," and delegates to building principals the authority to make "reasonable rules of conduct."

The new rules, which shall be "as nearly as is practical uniform" through the system, "shall prohibit conduct which disrupts, hinders or interferes with the education of other students, and conduct which endangers the health, safety or welfare of students, faculty and staff. The board will support with all its resources the action of any teacher, custodian, supervisor or administrator which is within the scope necessary to prevent disruption of any function of the school system. In considering the expulsion of any student, the board shall consider, along with the facts of the case, the reasonableness of the rule violated. The burden of proof of the reasonableness of the rule rests with the student."

Principals will continue to have authority to suspend, with expulsions coming to the board. "Why the hell did we get into this," McGinnis wonders.[228]

Race and Classrooms

Black students at Central-University High School fear that they will lose a sense of racial solidarity and identity when the school closes this June and they are dispersed among other city schools, according to a study by the Equal Opportunities Commission and the Pupil Services Division of the Madison Public Schools. "There was a consensus that the closing of the school would force them to scatter and become a less powerful group," the study team reports. Black students are said to seek "equal rights and opportunities [but not] total assimilation in the name of integration," while white students "unconsciously tried to strip the Negro of his identity and heritage by denying any differences in socio-cultural backgrounds."[229]

In the spring semester, thirteen of the system's fifty-six schools have no black pupils; there are 544 black pupils in the other forty-three.[230] For fall, school officials announce the hiring of six new black teachers, to join the twelve returning black teachers (the thirteenth will be on a year's maternity leave). Although the district takes four recruiting trips to historically black colleges in six southern states, all but one of the new hires are from the Midwest.[231] A course in black history, a two-semester elective open to juniors and seniors previously offered only at Central High School, becomes available in all high schools.[232]

In late November, the East Senior High Student Senate votes against participating in the Elks Club scholarship contest until the white male clause is stricken from the club's national charter. "We can't morally cooperate," student president Dix Bruce says of the decision to forfeit the chance to compete for $2,250 in scholarships. The West High Senate quickly follows suit.[233]

School Days

January 1—As the tax rate for the school system jumps from $18.06 per $1,000 in full value to $19.30, Madison falls from lowest to second-lowest rate in the county, behind the Village of DeForest, at $18.24.[234]

April 1—Attorney and sports referee Eugene S. Calhoun and insurance supervisor Douglas M. Onsager, both products of the Madison school system, are elected to the board, succeeding president Ray F. Sennett and Arthur "Dynie" Mansfield, who declined to seek reelection after twenty-three and twelve years, respectively. Sennett, chairman of Security State Bank and Randall State Bank, says the "press of banking duties" is too great for him to continue on the board; Mansfield will be retiring next year as the UW baseball coach and says it "would not be fair" to seek another term. Their departure will mark the complete turnover of the board in five years—the greatest change in the shortest amount of time since the 1920s. Sennett and Mansfield are given a standing ovation at the close of their last meeting on June 16.[235]

June 5—The final bell tolls for Central-University High at its hundredth—and last—graduation. Valedictorian Karen Bergstedt calls on her 185 classmates in dark blue caps and gowns to remember their "fierce pride" in going to what she says is the "smallest but very best high school in the city." Her comments fit the official class motto: "There'll be no tears, for these were happy years." The last diploma goes to Joseph W. Vultaggio, chosen by lot for the bittersweet honor. The choir sings "Blessing, Glory and Wisdom" by Bach, the Rogers and Hammerstein classic from *Carousel* "You'll Never Walk Alone," and the school song—"Hail, Central High, Grand Old School." School board president Ray Sennett, Madison High class of 1922—the last class before the school became Central High—closes by paraphrasing William Seward's comment on the death of Abraham Lincoln: "From this day forward, Central-University High School belongs to the ages."[236] Of Central's remaining students, 227 will go to West High, 67 to East, 58 to Madison Memorial, and 19 to La Follette. More of Central's teachers will transfer to West than any other school, as well.[237]

July 7—In keeping with its practice of having its most senior member serve as president, the board names Ruth B. Doyle, elected in 1964, its first woman leader. She calls for more citizen involvement and the development of a long-range plan for the entire educational program.[238]

Board of Education,
December 15. WHI IMAGE ID
136736, PHOTO BY DAVID SANDELL

September 2—Full middle schools—sixth, seventh, and eighth grades—are established at Schenk and La Follette Schools, with La Follette High School adding ninth-graders to become a four-year high school.[239]

October 15—All four Madison high schools host programs about the war in Vietnam, but do not close for the moratorium, and its organizers don't try to get pupils to boycott classes. School board rules permit calling off classes only for appearances by the president or presidential candidates.[240]

November 3—The school board unanimously approves the 1970 contract with Madison Teachers Inc., raising teachers' starting pay $450 to $7,250.[241]

December 1—Furious over another drastic council cut to its budget (this time for $522,000) and its "dismal" relationship with the "yahoos" running City Hall, the school board votes, 6–1, to pursue becoming a fiscally independent unified school district. The board, still smarting at being represented by city attorney Edwin Conrad—whose opinions always seem to favor the city—also votes to seek its own counsel.[242]

December 10—West High School principal David A. Spencer suspends a student for the unauthorized distribution of a recent issue of the *Daily Cardinal,* which contained an article on growing radicalism at the school.[243]

December 15—Close to five hundred people pack a school board meeting to protest the potential midyear closing of Lakewood and Badger Schools, which the board has proposed as a way to deal with the council-imposed budget cuts.[244] The board relents, eliminating instead summer music, library, and academic programs, raising textbook fees, limiting bus transportation of parochial school students, and making other cuts.[245]

School officials increase their criticism of Dyke and the other "financial wizards" in City Hall for their "strange" priorities.[246]

In Memoriam—Schools

Dr. Ray Huegel, 1829 Van Hise Ave., former president of the Board of Education, dies on September 3 at age seventy-eight after a long illness. A Madison native, Huegel served on the school board from 1934 to 1968 and headed the building committee for fifteen years; the "school in the round" on Post Road is named in his honor. Winner of six varsity letters at Marquette University, Huegel also officiated Big Ten Conference football games for twenty-three years, including working a Rose Bowl; a former coach at Central High School, he was instrumental in developing the recreation program in the public schools. Huegel also practiced as a dentist from 1912 to 1966, served on the Madison Board of Health for five years, and was a past president of the Wisconsin Dental Society.[247]

Law and Disorder

January 9—Six months after Mayor Otto Festge proposed tightening the city's gun registration ordinance, the council extends to private citizens the requirement already borne by businesses—to notify the police within twenty-four hours, even on weekends and holidays, of the sale or donation of a firearm, listing its make, model, and serial number. Ald. Rohr's second piece of gun registration legislation, the ordinance is adopted 18–4. Strongly supported by police chief Wilbur Emery, the ordinance also raises the minimum fine for failure to register from $10 to $250, the maximum from $100 to $500.[248]

January 9—The council votes 17–5 (Ashman, Burke, Flaten, Soglin, and Wheeler) to empower the mayor to "impose a curfew on all or any part of the city" in the event of "an actual or imminent emergency," requiring all persons in the area to leave, closing any street or business, and calling on "regular or auxiliary law enforcement agencies and organizations" to keep the peace. Prior to the council's action, Milwaukee was the only Wisconsin city to have provisions for a curfew.[249]

January 10—"We are in a period of unlawful conduct bordering on outright rebellion and anarchy," Chief Emery tells the thirty-two police cadets graduating from the fourteen-week training school academy, and the courts are "building legal curtains around the criminal while restricting the police officer."[250]

January 29—Legislative Council staff attorney James R. Klauser issues a forty-five-page report recommending that the Madison Police Department be given control of the university campus because university police are incapable of dealing with increased campus disorder, drug traffic, and violent crime.[251]

February—Owners and patrons of Madison discotheques are outraged by the new "entertainment guidelines" Mayor Otto Festge issues, limiting how much skin the go-go girls can show and how they can shake it. See-through tops with pasties and low-riding panties are out; instead, women must wear a top "of non-transparent material" that "must encircle the body, so that the areola of the breast(s) are completely covered," and a bottom that "must completely cover the mons pubis and the cleavage of the buttocks." The guidelines also allow for some "sensual elements," but caution that "these should not become so blatant that they completely overshadow all other elements of the dancing, or become the dominant interest of the spectators." Dancers must also "remain on their feet during their act" and not include "movements in a prone or semi-prone position." The guidelines have an impact. "Business has dropped off [and] a lot of our customers are complaining," says Al Reichenberger, coproprietor with his brother Tom of the Dangle Lounge, as he leads a protest march of go-go girls in bikinis and winter coats around the Square two weeks later. "Some of these guidelines are pretty ridiculous."[252]

March 10—The FBI releases statistics showing that all crimes except auto theft have increased in Madison from 1967 to 1968.

	1967	1968
Auto theft	516	424
Rape	20	27
Robbery	36	51
Aggravated assault	9	17
Burglary/Breaking & entering	794	1,057
Larceny >$50	1,118	1,206[253]

March 26—Police chief Emery complains to a joint legislative committee about "a most disturbing lack of enforcement and initiative" from the university in curbing campus drug traffic, which he says has forced him to assign drug investigators to campus without being asked. He strongly endorses legislation to have Madison take over law enforcement on campus, which passes the Assembly and is set for Senate consideration in January 1970.[254]

November 25—The council enacts a new obscenity law that city attorney Edwin Conrad says will require stores to keep adult magazines in an area where persons under seventeen can't enter, and would outlaw the topless dancing now featured in several city nightspots. Conrad recently dropped several prosecutions of stores and nightclubs because he felt the old ordinance was unconstitutionally vague. Reverend Richard Pritchard proposes a city commission, patterned on the Equal Opportunities Commission, to review questionable material and "help keep people away from temptation." Second Ward alderman Gordon Harmon speaks emotionally against referral for further consideration: "Would you want your daughter to dance naked before these people? That's what's going to happen" without immediate adoption, he warns.[255]

December 18—Quirky attorney Edward Ben Elson, twenty-eight, declares his candidacy for Dane County district attorney at the Wilson Hotel while wearing a modish grey Edwardian suit and maroon shirt, befitting the part owner of the No Hassel head shop and clothing store, 813 University Ave. Convicted in June of violating the state law requiring motorcyclists to wear helmets, Elson vows to not enforce that and other "bad laws," such as those against marijuana and cohabitation; he warns that it may even become a crime someday not to wear a seat belt. Despite his weak showing in the spring mayoral election, and calling himself "mad as the hatter," Elson says he's "dead serious" and will campaign vigorously as the only candidate of the American Transcendental Party.[256]

Auditorium

The year opens with the hope that construction can soon start on phase one of the grand Monona Basin plan, the "great circular drum" auditorium. But hope soon starts to fade, and then vanishes for good.[257]

On January 15, architect William Wesley Peters tells the Auditorium Committee that he's had to eliminate elevators from the seven-story building for economic reasons and cut parking for the twenty-three-hundred-seat auditorium from 775 spaces to 361 to facilitate traffic movement. The performing arts palace will also lack a sound system; Peters says traveling shows provide their own light and sound, and he suggests a portable system be purchased for use during conventions.[258]

Two weeks later, Mayor Otto Festge insinuates that traffic engineer John Bunch is trying to sabotage the Monona Basin Project by issuing a misleading report falsely claiming the auditorium would illegally extend past the authorized dockline. "I question the motive in releasing this report," Festge tells the Auditorium Committee. "There are forces that apparently want to stop this work."

On February 11, the council votes, 14–6, to approve final plans and specifications for the auditorium and to put the project out to bid. "We are at a crossroads," lame duck mayor Festge tells the council; if this project doesn't proceed, he says, "I predict it will be twenty or thirty years before the idea of an auditorium can be brought up again." As it did in 1961, the council sets an unrealistically early deadline—March 20—for potential bidders. After a late change in the specifications, the deadline is pushed back to April 1—local election day, as it was in 1961.[259]

As in 1961, general contractors show limited interest in bidding on the project, with only two firms prequalified to bid. Most probably don't bother because they believe the $5.2 million budget is not adequate—but some are certainly discouraged from bidding by an organized campaign to sabotage the process conducted by former mayor Henry Reynolds, Ald. Babe Rohr, and city building inspector Raymond Burt. "In all the work we've done across the country," Peters tells the Auditorium Committee, "we've never experienced the lack of co-ordination of civic spirit, the petty jealousies, the mean sniping that has occurred here in Madison."[260]

As in 1961, bids come in over budget; exactly how much is unclear when they're opened on April 1, but it appears to be at least $1.5 million.[261] The Monona Basin Foundation starts a fund-raising campaign to cover the difference, but after a strong start—thanks to a $25,000 pledge from the Evjue Foundation, the charitable arm of the *Capital Times*—the drive falters and fails.[262]

On the last night of the Festge administration, April 14–15, the council tries to direct Peters to rebid the project but does not authorize any additional funds. "This action tonight was the most irresponsible act I ever heard of," Peters says, refusing to hollow out his golden drum any further.[263]

In his inaugural address on April 15, Mayor Dyke leaves little hope that building a civic auditorium will be a high priority for his administration. "The division, the preoccupation, and frustration which has for so long been a part of the auditorium fight must be placed behind us," he tells the council. "It will not and cannot be continued. This is no time to ask the people of Madison for more money."[264]

"The auditorium is not the prime responsibility of my administration," Dyke reiterates on July 16 for the Madison Civic Music Association, which would have been one of the primary groups to use the auditorium. "We need a new dump as much as we need an auditorium." Dyke, the strongest supporter of a Law Park site during the 1965 mayoral campaign, declares that site now out of the question; he floats instead the idea of a cultural facility as part of a "high class park and amusement center" at Olin Park, modeled on the Tivoli Gardens of Copenhagen.[265]

The council, discovering to its surprise that Dyke has not yet appointed new members to the Auditorium Committee, directs him on August 18 to do so immediately, so that the committee can report back within sixty days on whether the city should hold a new referendum. Dyke does not make his appointments until April 1970.[266]

In Memoriam—Auditorium

The decade ends with the deaths of two stellar citizens who fought each other for years over Frank Lloyd Wright and the Monona Terrace.

Economics professor emeritus Harold M. Groves, seventy-two—a founder of the modern cooperative movement, the intellectual and political father of Wisconsin's first-in-the-nation unemployment compensation act and the homestead tax credit for the elderly, and an important supporter of Frank Lloyd Wright—passes away in his sleep on December 2 at the family home, 1418 Drake St. One of six children of a Lodi farm couple, Groves earned three degrees at Wisconsin; he received his doctorate in 1927 under the legendary professor John R. Commons, and later held the endowed chair named in his honor. Groves served in the Assembly and Senate in the early 1930s as a Progressive Republican, and also as state tax commissioner. Groves was the chief faculty sponsor and patron of the interracial, interreligious women's cooperative Groves House, which opened at 150 Langdon St. in 1943, with the Green Lantern Eating Co-op in the basement. A friend of Wright's since the 1930s, Groves and his wife, Helen, helped the architect build the Unitarian Meeting House and were leaders of Citizens for Monona Terrace; Groves served six years on the city's Auditorium Committee until he was replaced by the anti–Monona Terrace mayor Henry Reynolds in 1961. He ran for the Common Council in 1963, losing to veteran incumbent Harrison Garner.[267]

Joseph W. "Bud" Jackson, ninety, indefatigable advocate for Madison improvements and implacable foe of Frank Lloyd Wright and Monona Terrace, dies on May 23 at Colonial Manor nursing home after a long illness. Known as Colonel Jackson for his World War I service organizing the Army's last mounted cavalry unit under General Pershing, Jackson was business manager for the medical clinic founded by his father, a Civil War surgeon; he left the Jackson Clinic in 1937 to found and lead the Madison and Wisconsin Foundation, forerunner to the Madison Chamber of Commerce, until 1952. A devoted follower of urban planner and landscape architect John Nolen, Jackson helped secure private funds for the University Arboretum, the Madison School Forest, and eighteen city parks, as well as public funds for such projects as the Municipal Airport, Veterans Administration Hospital, City-County Building, Methodist Hospital, and Beltline Highway.[268]

Miscellanea

January 15–16—Morris Edelson presents Julian Beck and Judith Molina and their Living Theatre in a two-night engagement for capacity crowds of five hundred at the First Unitarian Society in Shorewood Hills. Opening night, an intense and often discomforting performance of Berthold Brecht's *The Antigone of Sophocles*. At the following night's performance of their notorious *Paradise Now*, the integrated cast, in loincloths and brief halters, is upstaged at one point by two women and five men from the audience who disrobe entirely, while others swear, argue, spit, and form a pile of nude and nearly nude bodies. The shows had to move from Turner Hall when city building inspectors ruled the building, used primarily for gymnastics and other physical education, needed a theater permit, which it did not have.[269]

January 19–February 23—The Madison Art Center presents an exhibition of sixty-seven paintings, drawings, and lithographs by American regional realist painter John Steuart Curry, including the large *Wisconsin Landscape*, on special loan from the Metropolitan Museum in New York. Curry, the university's first artist in residence, died here in 1946, during the tenth year of his residency.[270]

March 27—Madison Area Technical College calls off classes so students can celebrate the announcement by the North Central Association of Colleges and Secondary Schools that it has granted the college full accreditation, allowing students to receive work study grants and transfer credits to UW and the state universities.[271]

April 1—Voters continue the Common Council turnover they began in 1968, ousting four incumbents and electing eight new aldermen, including Eugene Parks, twenty-one, the first African American elected in the city's 113-year history. Parks, associate editor of the *Madison Sun*, runs in the nonpartisan election with the support of the Wisconsin

Alliance Party and defeats, by better than 4–1, incumbent alderman George F. Jacobs, law partner of mayor-elect Dyke, in the campus-area Fifth Ward.[272] Two-term alderman James T. Crary, the deputy sheriff who fought the Equal Opportunities Commission while a member, is beaten by union leader and telephone repairman Roger W. Staven. Insurance agent Richard J. Landgraf ousts the two-term incumbent alderman James T. Devine Jr. in the near west Thirteenth Ward.[273]

The election results in a council with only three of its twenty-two members having served more than one term in office.[274] Parks is removed from office in early August when he moves to the wrong side of North Murray Street and out of the district; he reestablishes district residency at the university YMCA, 306 N. Brooks St., and is unanimously appointed to his former seat on August 26. Even though he was elected to a two-year term in April, he'll have to run again in 1970, since he's now serving by appointment.[275]

May 9—Seven months after his updated version of *Peter Pan* closed Screw Theater on campus, Stuart Gordon directs the inaugural effort of the new community-based Broom Street Theater. It's another provocative production—a modernized version of *Lysistrata*, Aristophanes's classic Greek drama about women withholding sex until their warrior husbands and lovers end the long and bloody Peloponnesian War. Gordon spends two months getting a proper permit and submits his script to city attorney Edwin Conrad, but police chief Wilbur Emery still has his doubts; he sends two detectives and three policewomen to view the bare-bones opening-night production above a paint store at 152 W. Johnson St. There are several complaints to the mayor's office about the scantily clad women bumping and grinding, and some very ribald jokes, but Conrad lets the play go on. The production, which earns good reviews for its twelve performances over three weekends, is Gordon's only one with Broom Street Theater before he and wife, Carolyn, are ousted by the actors; they found Chicago's Organic Theater Company in the fall. Gordon is later succeeded as Broom Street Theater artistic director by Joel Gersmann.[276]

July 4—Disappointing many but surprising few, Bob Dylan does not appear as advertised to play a free show at the People's Park, 434 W. Mifflin St.[277]

October 5—About eight thousand junior and senior high schoolers walk thirty-two miles in Madison's second Walk for Development, raising about $100,000 for food development projects in Sunflower County, Mississippi, and Chad, Africa.[278]

November 6—Mayor William Dyke proposes a budget that would lay off seventy city employees (including twenty-four firemen), close fire station No. 4 at the corner of Randall and West Dayton Streets, prohibit snow removal outside the normal forty-hour work week, eliminate lifeguards at city beaches, delay the start of the State Street Mall, adopt a $9 auto registration fee, and double the $3 hotel room tax in order to hold the city's share of the current fifty-three-mill rate at 11.96 mills.[279]

November 13—The council abolishes the Committee of the Whole. Starting in December, the council will hold public hearings, consider noncontroversial items on the second and fourth Thursdays of the month, and consider new business and controversial items on the preceding Tuesdays. But observers worry that increased personal tension among alderpersons, the council's relative inexperience, and the desire of new alderpersons to debate at greater length than their predecessors will minimize the hoped-for efficiencies from the new system.[280]

November 26—Prohibition-era bootlegger Jennie Justo Bramhall closes her supper club, Justo's Club, 3005 University Ave., after almost thirty-six years; she and husband, Art, a former infielder for the Philadelphia Phillies, sell the building to Leonard "Smoky" Schmock and his wife, Janet, owner-operators of Smoky's Club, which currently occupies Justo's first building at 2925 University Ave., slated for razing during the University Avenue expansion.[281]

December 9—The Zoning Board of Appeals grants the request by Madison Neighborhood Center director Chester Zmudzinski for a variance to construct a Marquette community center on a portion of the Marquette School property, funded by a $100,000 donation from the Rennebohm Foundation.[282]

December 12—The council adopts, 13–9, a 1970 budget that adds $178,200 to support Madison residents whose welfare grants were reduced by state cuts, doubles the hotel room tax, rejects the wheel tax, adds a $30 ambulance fee, maintains Fire Station No. 4, and limits, but doesn't eliminate, lifeguards and overtime snow removal.[283]

The Mifflin Street Community Co-op

The Mifflin Street Community Cooperative opens January 13 at 32 N. Bassett St., with first-day receipts of $130. Initially, the co-op is run by volunteers; to underscore community ownership, the cash register is periodically turned around for members to ring themselves out. In March, with sales averaging $700 weekly, full-time staff start to receive a $42 weekly salary, and a bail fund—the Electric Tetradactyl Transit Authority—is created and funded. In April, at the spring general membership meeting, members elect the co-op's first board of directors, including Bill Winfield, Peter Wright, and Dorothy Feely.[284]

As the sense of community intensifies after the block party riot in May, the co-op assumes an even greater role as a center of the growing counterculture. By summer, with five hundred members, the co-op sells more Alpo dog food than any store in the state, and more Coca-Cola than any store in Madison.[285] On September 5, the co-op announces it will give a 6 percent discount to all welfare and pension recipients and provide transportation to the store on Saturday and weekday evenings.[286]

In the fall, after the staff (including Annie Habel, Bobby Golden, Frank Burnham, and Paul Nichols) and volunteers win a power struggle with the board, the bylaws are rewritten to declare that the co-op "exists to embody a belief in community self-determination, and to encourage struggles in our community and elsewhere which we understand to further these goals. We define community self-determination in opposition to the dominant trends in all communities by which control is increasingly concentrated outside the community and operated for profits which are not used for the betterment of that community. Our assets, as people and money, are committed to this struggle by any means necessary." And the community responds; after a diminutive eleven-year-old drug abuser who ran away from Mendota State Hospital steals $967 in cash and checks on October 21,

Mayor Dyke waits to speak to a large and hostile crowd at the Mifflin Street Community Cooperative, 32 N. Bassett St., May 5. The building still shows signs of its former identity as a White Front grocery.
WHI IMAGE ID 136737, PHOTO BY DAVID SANDELL

a collection brings in $950 in donations.[287] Checks totaling $437 are recovered a week later, leaving the co-op better off—financially, at least—after the robbery than before.[288] But tensions persist between some members of the co-op community and the remaining nonstudent residents of the neighborhood, and some staff-volunteer conflicts remain unresolved.

The Madison Tenant Union

After a summer of grassroots recruitment, the Madison Tenant Union (MTU) draws 250 people to its organizational meeting in Tripp Commons on September 23. Copresident Phil Ball (Madison Mayor Paul Soglin's committee coordinator, ca. 1973–1979) says rent strikes, boycotts, and other forms of "legal harassment" are possible weapons against certain landlords. "They'll know that we are after them, and I doubt they'll be able to stop us," Ball says.[289]

MTU claims its first small victory in late October, when developer James T. Devine Sr. agrees to negotiate regarding his round thirteen-story building under construction at 610–630 Langdon St.[290] Acting under a state law allowing tenants to withhold rent in the case of substandard housing, the MTU on December 10 starts "limited" rent strikes against Devine for his property at 625 Mendota Ct., as well as landlord Philip Engen, depositing rent checks in a Canadian bank pending repairs. Ball, among those withholding his own $100 rent, also announces MTU has successfully resolved 45 of 115 complaints against various landlords.[291]

MTU notches its first real win when Engen agrees on December 17 to make the repairs tenants demanded at 435 W. Dayton St. The union, which now has about seven hundred members in three "locals," continues the rent strike against Devine, but says talks with Miffland-area landlord William T. Bandy are productive and a rent strike against him is "not going to happen."[292]

Race for Mayor

The campaign year starts on January 4, when conservative Republican attorney William Dyke, who lost to Mayor Otto Festge by sixty-two votes two years ago, declares his candidacy; two days later, Festge surprises city hall insiders by announcing he's stepping down after two terms. Festge says he made the decision three days prior. Liberal Democratic attorney Robert "Toby" Reynolds, who didn't seek reelection to the council in 1968, is his heir apparent.[293]

Adapting Festge's 1965 campaign against what Festge called the "Reynolds-Hall administration," Dyke attacks the Festge-Reynolds team: "This city deserves change, and you can't tell one of these Bobbsey Twins from the other."[294] Reynolds celebrates his relationship with Festge, as well as his leadership of Senator Eugene McCarthy's 1968 Wisconsin primary campaign.[295]

Dyke cruises to an easy primary victory on March 4, with more than 56 percent in the six-candidate race, beating Reynolds by two to one and carrying thirty-seven of the city's forty-one wards. UW–Extension curriculum analyst Adam Schesch, twenty-six, backed in the nonpartisan race by the new leftist Wisconsin Alliance Party, carries four student wards, finishing a distant third. Unconventional attorney Edward Ben Elson finishes a very weak fourth, followed by two other fringe candidates.[296]

The clearest policy difference in the campaign is in transportation. Dyke, a former aide to GOP lieutenant governor Jack Olsen and onetime city attorney in Jefferson, Wisconsin, wants "a major form of [limited access] highway connector from the east side through the center of the city" and says mass transit systems "haven't worked," either financially or programmatically. Reynolds, former head of the trust department at Security State Bank and senior warden and lay reader at St. Andrew's Episcopal Church, is "totally opposed to freeways" and says the city "must buy the Madison Bus Company and must do it at once" as the first stage to a comprehensive mass transit system.[297]

Although Reynolds rejected an endorsement from the Federation of Labor's Committee on Political Education in 1964 because it supported aldermen who opposed the fair housing ordinance, he accepts it this time. The *Capital Times, Union Labor News,* and the minority-focused *Madison Sun* all endorse Reynolds. Former mayor Reynolds is so sure his former supporters in the Citizens for Better Government committee will endorse

Dyke he places the newspaper ad touting the endorsement before the endorsement meeting and vote.[298]

Both candidates say the city is in bad fiscal shape. Dyke blames Festge for "the most expensive" administration in city history; Reynolds blames the legislature for statutory constraints and inadequate state revenue.

Dyke, a former radio and television announcer, campaigns on holding the line on city spending and working with the private sector to generate economic development, and not on law and order or cultural issues.[299] Appointed to the Madison Housing Authority by conservative mayor Henry Reynolds, Toby Reynolds wants more scattered-site low- and moderate-income housing.[300]

Harkening back to Mayor Henry Reynolds's go-slow policy on annexations, Dyke proposes a "good neighbor policy of cooperation" with surrounding towns and villages, and a "metropolitan approach toward mutual problems and interests." Reynolds says he'll "declare war" on the suburbs and continue the Festge/Nestingen policy of aggressive annexations.[301]

Reynolds, who championed the fair housing code in 1964, attacks the lack of diversity in city appointments. "Citizen participation is too white, too college educated, too West Side," he says, vowing to appoint minorities and students.[302]

As the campaign winds down, Reynolds narrows the primary gap—until a chaotic council meeting four nights before the election and the illegal, 52-hour firefighter strike that follows. Dyke ultimately rides high taxes, campus disturbances, and the election-eve firemen's strike to a 52 to 48 percent victory, 22,237–20,162.[303]

Dyke's appointments set the tone for his administration. He starts by not reappointing Reynolds to another term on the Madison Housing Authority, then he covers that act of apparent disrespect with the politically brilliant appointment of Richard Harris, the African American director of the South Madison Neighborhood Center, to replace him. Dyke reappoints former GOP county chairman Stuart Becker to the Police and Fire Commission, along with Ellsworth Swenson, the alderman Paul Soglin unseated in 1968, and puts liberal Republican feminist Betty (Mrs. William Bradford) Smith, chair of the Governor's Commission on the Status of Women, on the Madison Redevelopment Authority. There's wholesale housecleaning at the Equal Opportunities Commission as Dyke declines to reappoint chair Mary Louise Symon and four other members. And he limits aldermen Soglin and Parks to single appointments that they didn't request, on the Board of Health and Family Services Agency, respectively.[304]

Dyke focuses in his inaugural address on city finances, vowing to "halt the march up the tax mountain" and bring economic development to the abandoned Truax Air Field. He decries "the harm we do daily to our air, water and land" and calls for adoption and enforcement of a "code of environmental control." And while his campaign largely steered clear of hot-button social issues, he declares he will "not reward public tantrums with participation in government."[305]

Festge's disappointing spring continues when the Alliance of Cities, which he founded and served as president, rejects his bid to become its full-time executive director.[306] He takes a job selling insurance instead, later serving sixteen years as home secretary to US Representative Robert W. Kastenmeier (D-Watertown).[307]

Highways and Transportation

NEW ROADS

▸ Campus Drive opens November 26.

January—City planners propose eliminating nonemergency vehicles on State Street in the four blocks from Gilman to Park Streets and turning the area into a full pedestrian mall with plantings and benches. For the remaining four blocks up to the Square, they propose eliminating parking, reducing traffic to one lane each way, and extending the sidewalks. Chancellor Young calls the idea "exciting and viable," but many merchants worry that they will be put out of business before the new stalls open at the expanded Lake Street parking ramp.[308]

Principal planner John Urich explains that such malls have increased sales in sixteen of the seventeen cities he's studied, but owners in the 500 and 600 blocks harden their opposition over the summer.[309] Merchants in the upper stretch support the project, so the Board of Public Works budgets $300,000 for phase one in that area.[310] The proposal gets a major boost with council approval in September of a zoning change allowing the University Book Store—which will be forced to vacate its current location for the expansion of the Memorial Library—and Calvary Lutheran Chapel to build on the southwest corner of State and Lake Streets. As a condition of approval, the bookstore is required to support the mall project. "If we get the bookstore [relocation], I think we'll get the mall," Ald. Paul Soglin says. Also forced to relocate prior to the library's construction in 1973—the Kollege Klub beer bar and grill, which moves to Lake Street.[311]

November 8—Flirting with disaster, the city and the Madison Bus Company wait until the last minute to agree to extend the subsidy and set an April 30, 1970, deadline for the city to buy the company for the price agreed upon a year ago. Mayor Dyke, who campaigned against municipal ownership and fought for a three-year extension of the subsidy through the summer and fall, thinks the $910,000 price is too high but reluctantly goes along with the council's 17–2 vote. Now the city just has to negotiate an agreement protecting the Teamsters' wages and pensions, and certify to the federal Department of Labor that it has done so. That will prove easier said than done.[312]

November 26—Campus Drive opens, diverting about fifteen thousand cars a day from University Avenue by providing nonstop driving from Babcock Drive to Farley Avenue and University Bay Drive. The $4.5 million project, phase two of the expansion adopted in 1961, was funded at the referendum in 1966 and begun in 1967. The third and final phase will start next year—six lanes out to the Blackhawk Drive overpass just west of Segoe Road.[313]

The congestion and conflicts between pedestrians and vehicles that planners hope to eliminate by making the last four blocks of lower State Street a pedestrian mall. WHI IMAGE ID 137180, PHOTO BY DAVID SANDELL

December—As the decade ends, the council approves the Marquette Neighborhood Association's plan to use traffic management to save its quality of life. "We're not going to lie down and get paved over," says association officer David Mollenhoff. By banning left turns from Atwood Avenue to Lakeland or Oakridge Avenues and putting a cul-de-sac at the west end of Jenifer Street, the city removes about seven thousand cars a day from Spaight and Rutledge Streets. Parking restrictions will allow for two full lanes on Atwood Avenue and Winnebago Street inbound in the morning and two lanes outbound at night.[314]

December—The city ends the decade with 490.38 miles of paved streets and highways—182 more miles than at its start.[315]

Wrong-Way Is the Wrong Play

Circuit Judge W. L. Jackman rules on March 18 that the city acted illegally in creating the "wrong-way" bus lane on University Avenue for the exclusive use of the Madison Bus Company and dismisses the ticket attorney Ken Hur got in January 1967 for driving there. The city doesn't appeal but continues to enforce the ban on private use of the bus lane.[316]

It's one of the few policies of Mayor Otto Festge's that Mayor William Dyke continues, much to the disapproval of Circuit Judge Richard Bardwell. "Either the city is going to follow the law or subject itself to some severe financial penalties," including for false arrest, Bardwell says when he hears the appeal of another driver, ticketed in May. "The city arrests students in disorderly conduct cases," he notes. "How does it expect the students to obey the law when it fails to do so itself?"[317]

When Bardwell formally dismisses the ticket, the city has to choose between repealing the ordinance or appealing the decision. After a resolution to abandon the bus lane fails in mid-December, 9–11, city attorney Edwin Conrad takes the case to the state Supreme Court.

"The question is not whether I have been flouting the law, but rather what is the law?" he says. "Like the famous Diogenes, I am still seeking the truth with lantern in hand, though I may appear to be blind."[318]

A decision is expected sometime in 1970.

Planning and Development/Urban Renewal

GENERAL STATISTICS
▸ Population: 171,485[319]
▸ Area: 48.54 square miles (end-of-year total)[320]

Business Wire

January 22—The Madison Redevelopment Authority approves the sale of the final Triangle parcels to Fred Mohs and Associates for $542,845 (to build 350 apartment units) and to David and James Carley's Public Facilities Associates for $335,516 (to build 250 units and a shopping center at the corner of Park and Regent Streets). Neither development takes place.[321]

March 3—First National Bank officials announce plans to raze and replace their forty-seven-year-old building at the corner of South Pinckney Street and East Washington Avenue and construct a nine-story, multimillion-dollar banking complex.[322]

March 14—Parks superintendent James Marshall, sixty-four, retires after forty-two years with the city—thirty-two as superintendent. There were 350 acres of city parkland when Marshall became city forester in 1927; there are now more than 3,000 acres in the system, including the 27 acres on the western shore of Lake Mendota named in his honor in 1961. Marshall is succeeded by his former assistant, Forrest W. Bradley.[323]

April 21—Developer and former Democratic lieutenant governor Patrick J. Lucey unveils "Wexford Village," a planned unit development involving a site of more than a square mile from north of Mineral Point Road up into Middleton, and from Gammon Road to just east of the Beltline. Lucey, a likely candidate for governor in 1970, anticipates at least a ten-year build-out of the 683-acre project, which will include single-family homes and apartments, a shopping center, a church complex, offices, a nursing home, and 192 acres of permanent open space. City planners support the project, which is larger than the entire University Hill Farms development.[324]

June 11—Site preparation begins on the hundred acres at Mineral Point and Gammon Roads for the $10 million West Towne Shopping Center, set to open next fall. The initial construction of the Jacobs, Visconti and Jacobs development will have seven hundred thousand square feet and three major department stores—H. C. Prange Company, Sears, and J. C. Penney.[325]

July 3—Development plans for the 600–900 blocks of University Avenue are formalized with the signing of contracts between the Madison Redevelopment Authority (MRA) and the University of Wisconsin, between the MRA and the Lake Park Corporation, and between the university and the corporation. Under the once-controversial plan, the university will construct a $9.4 million communication arts building in the 800 block, where demolition is currently under way; a pharmacy school and parking ramp in the 900 block, retaining the Rennebohm's drugstore and First National Bank currently there; and a classroom building in the 700 block. The corporation, comprising the area's property owners, will build an enclosed mall shopping center in the rest of the 700 block and a combination motel and apartment building in the 600 block, with ground-floor retail. Sol Levin, director of the MRA and of the Housing and Development Department, calls the project a "landmark." Among the venerable businesses about to be razed are Paisan's Restaurant, which has been at 821 University Ave. for seventeen years, and Lorenzo's Restaurant, which has been at 813 University Ave. for twenty-six years.[326]

November 2—The Sears, Roebuck and Company on East Washington Avenue is among the company stores nationwide to start a two-month test of opening on Sundays. Stores will open at noon, allowing employees to attend church, and close at 5 p.m.[327]

December 2—The Plan Commission hears a debate over a proposed massive urban renewal project for the Mifflin-Bassett neighborhood that would focus on high-rise condominium units for adults employed downtown. Area alderman Paul Soglin challenges planner John Urich's priorities, advocating the rehabilitation of existing housing stock through renovation and cooperatives rather than new construction.[328]

Mapleside

Abel and Pamela Dunning were the first white settlers to plant crops in Dane County; a delegate to the constitutional convention of 1846, Abel built their Greek Revival farmhouse out in the Town of Madison in 1853. With buff sandstone, eighteen inches thick, from the quarry just across University Avenue and massive beams up to thirty-three feet long, the home became known as Mapleside. Basement tunnels were said to date from Mapleside's days as a stop on the Underground Railroad. It was later given the address 3535 University Ave.[329]

In 1962, after it had been through a number of uses, including as a tearoom and hotel in the 1920s, the house became vacant and remained that way until Professor William G. Reddan and his wife rented it from its owner, local developer Daniel Neviaser, in 1964.[330]

But now Neviaser wants to put up a filling station and restaurant on the site, and plans to raze the historic structure in July.[331] In March, he offers to donate Mapleside to the Taychopera Foundation, the group of local historic preservationists that formed last April, for the foundation to remove. He suggests it could be moved "just a few feet to the

Mapleside, ca. 1965, after years of abuse and neglect.
WHI IMAGE ID 39822

west," for about $70,000. Taychopera wants a site in the Arboretum, but is not able to acquire one, putting Mapleside's future in jeopardy.[332]

When Neviaser's plan becomes public in late spring, preservationists mobilize to save the house. On June 13, Mayor Dyke forwards to the Plan Department the three dozen postcards he's received protesting the demolition, asking if it's possible to create a "historic site zoning category" to save the building. After city attorney Edwin Conrad issues an opinion that "aesthetics are a proper subject of the police power" of a city, Dyke says he'll propose "four or five city ordinances"—possibly a comprehensive preservation plan with historic districts, tax incentives, and amendments—to the building and zoning codes. Early aldermanic support comes from R. Whelan Burke, Fourth Ward, and Gordon Harmon, Second Ward, who lives with his wife, Dolly, in the stunning stone Gothic Revival house Mayor William T. Leitch built at 752 E. Gorham St. in 1857. A recent survey of 130 homes on Mansion Hill and in Tenney Lapham by students of urban and regional planning professor Leo Jakobson identified twelve buildings they deem "musts" for preservation, with many others that should also be protected through such an ordinance.[333]

In October, Neviaser sells the Mapleside property to the Burger King company for $150,000; the foundation still seeks to save it.

At a meeting in Mayor Dyke's office on November 28, Burger King district manager James Herbst agrees to delay demolition for a month and offers the building to Taychopera if it can raise the money to move it within that time. Or he'll sell it on site for the $150,000 he paid. Herbst later drops the price for the building and land to $100,000, with an early January deadline.

In December, the newly formed Friends of Mapleside hold an auction and sale at the First Unitarian Society with donated works from about a dozen Madison artists, including Aaron Bohrod, Lee Weiss, and Warrington Colescott. It doesn't raise enough, and by the end of the year, Taychopera has raised less than $5,000.[334]

To the dismay of local and national preservationists, Mapleside is set to be razed on Saturday, February 14, 1970—a heartbreaking way to mark the first Valentine's Day of the seventies.[335]

View to the east in the summer of 1969. UNIVERSITY OF WISCONSIN-MADISON ARCHIVES S17020

MADISON CITY LIMITS

JANUARY 1960
29.2 SQUARE MILES

LAKE MENDOTA

MIDDLETON

SHOREWOOD

UNIVERSITY AVE.

UNIVERSITY AVE.

W. BELTLINE HWY.

GAMMON RD.

OLD SAUK RD.

MINERAL POINT RD.

TOKAY BLVD.

WHITNEY WAY

SCHROEDER RD.

HAMMERSLEY RD.

RAYMOND RD.

PRAIRIE RD.

MEADOWOOD DR.

VERONA RD.

SEMINOLE HWY.

LAKE WINGRA

FITCHBURG

WHEELER RD.

HWY. CV

SHERMAN AVE.

HWY. 151

INTERSTATE HWY.

LIEN RD.

MAPLE
BLUFF

HWY. 30

HWY. T

HWY. 51

MILWAUKEE ST.

ACEWOOD BLVD.

COTTAGE GROVE RD.

BUCKEYE RD.

LAKE MONONA

MONONA DR.

SPANEM AVE.

HWY. 51

MONONA

PFLAUM RD.

FEMRITE DR.

WINGRA CR.

JOHN NOLEN DR.

YAHARA R.

BROADWAY RD.

BELTLINE HWY.

PARK ST.

RIMROCK RD.

MARSH RD.

HWY. 14

MOORLAND RD.

McCOY RD.

SIGGLEKOW RD.

McFARLAND

LAKE WAUBESA

MADISON CITY LIMITS

DECEMBER 1969

48.5 SQUARE MILES

LAKE MENDOTA

MIDDLETON

UNIVERSITY AVE.

SHOREWOOD

UNIVERSITY AVE.

W. BELTLINE HWY.

GAMMON RD.

OLD SAUK RD.

MINERAL POINT RD.

LAKE WINGRA

SCHROEDER RD.

HAMMERSLEY RD.

SEMINOLE HWY.

RAYMOND RD.

MEADOWOOD DR.

VERONA RD.

PUTNAM RD.

FISH HATCHERY

HWY.

FITCHBURG

Acknowledgments

I had as much fun researching this book as I did writing it. I especially enjoyed the fact that so many resources were the work of friends, starting with the latest, *The Capital Times: A Proudly Radical Newspaper's Century-Long Fight for Justice and for Peace* by Dave Zweifel and John Nichols. I lost track of how many times I watched Glenn Silber and Barry Brown's *The War at Home* and read their full interview transcripts, gaining a greater understanding of several seminal events in the student protest movement with each viewing/reading. As he has done on so many subjects, David Maraniss wrote the definitive account of the protest against the Dow Chemical Company in *They Marched into Sunlight: War and Peace, Vietnam and America, October 1967*. It was a huge benefit to have David's narrative, but a daunting challenge to write in his shadow. The first-person accounts in Paul Buhle's *History and the New Left: Madison, Wisconsin 1950–1970* are a wonderful resource. Matt Levin's *Cold War University: Madison and the New Left in the Sixties* is an important new contribution to the literature. David Mollenhoff and Mary Jane Hamilton's *Frank Lloyd Wright's Monona Terrace: The Enduring Power of a Civic Vision* is an extraordinary book cataloguing the longest-running civic issue of the twentieth century. Doug Moe absolutely owns both the Charlie Mohr and Otis Redding stories (*Lords of the Ring* and various magazine articles, respectively). While I knew neither E. David Cronon nor John W. Jenkins, I know that their final work together, *The University of Wisconsin: Renewal to Revolution*, is the gold standard for histories of the university, as is Jim Feldman's *The Buildings of the University of Wisconsin*.

I am also obviously indebted to the reporters, photographers, editors, and publishers of the day, several of whom I worked with or against when I was a reporter for the *Capital Times* and *Madison Press Connection*; without their efforts, this book could not have been written. The sixties were a great time for Madison newspapers—they were fat with advertising and filled with long, accurate, and informative stories and series (despite their occasional biases on Monona Terrace, the Causeway, and mayors). Those who seek to write today's history fifty years from now will stand in awe and envy of my digital clipping files. I got a special kick out of using articles by Dave Zweifel, who in 1975 started my Madison life by hiring me to be the *Capital Times*'s Washington correspondent when I was only twenty-one.

It is an embarrassment of research riches to have the Madison Public Library, the Wisconsin Historical Society Archives and Library, and the University of Wisconsin–Madison Archives and Memorial Library all in my hometown. For making my time there so productive and pleasant, I give deep thanks to all their personnel and a warm goodbye to two who retired during this project: University Archives director David Null and Wisconsin Historical Society Archives visual material curator Andy Kraushaar. Thanks to Madison Public Library director Greg Mickells and library foundation director Jenni Collins for enabling me to conduct my foundational research. Additional University Archives thanks to Troy Reeves, who heads the outstanding Oral History program; digital and media archivist Catherine Phan; and student assistant Sarah Cooper. Additional Wisconsin Historical Society Archives thanks to director of public services and reference Lisa Saywell, reference archivist Lee Grady, and all the archivists, technicians, and assistants on the fourth floor.

Thanks to Dennis McCormick, digital archive director at Capital Newspapers, and digital media specialist Chris Lay for providing many vital images. And I was lucky that *Isthmus* illustrator David Michael Miller was available to create maps and annotate photographs.

Thanks to many people I've never met—members of the Facebook groups "If You Grew Up in Madison, Wisconsin, You Remember . . . ," "Historic Madison WI Photo Group," and "University of Wisconsin–Madison Friends," who shared first-person accounts and provided crowd-sourced fact-checking on a wide variety of topics. I also greatly appreciate everyone who responded to direct inquiries, by either phone or email.

Of course, thanks to everyone at the Wisconsin Historical Society Press, especially former director Kathy Borkowski and her successor and former editor-in-chief Kate Thompson; developmental editor Elizabeth Wyckoff; copyeditor Barb Walsh; image researcher John Nondorf; and production editor Elizabeth Boone. They are the ones who made this a book.

Notwithstanding the efforts of those noted above, errors of fact or interpretation herein are mine alone.

Finally, my deepest thanks to all who have helped make my life in Madison so full of fulfilling engagement. But for the sky, there have been no fences facin'.

Notes

Abbreviations used in notes: *BH, Badger Herald; CT, Capital Times; DC, Daily Cardinal; WSJ, Wisconsin State Journal;* WHSA, Wisconsin Historical Society Archives. All interviews and email and Facebook exchanges are to/with the author unless otherwise noted.

Introduction

1. Stuart Levitan, "The Second Time as Farce," *Boston Phoenix,* December 5, 1978.

2. City of Madison Department of Planning, Community Development and Economic Development; Wright's Madison City Directory 1960 (Milwaukee, WI: Wright Directory Co., 1960), x–xviii.

3. Richard Brautigam, "Plan Group Opposes Manchester Skywalk," *CT,* January 26, 1965.

4. Mrs. Ethel Brown, "Committee of the Whole Procedure," *The Municipality* 60, no. 3 (March 1965): 59.

5. "School Board Approves Advance Notice on Agendas of Meetings," *WSJ,* September 14, 1964; Brautigam, "Vote 'Accessible' City Unit Meetings," *CT,* October 27, 1965; Matt Pommer, "Says School Board Must Obey City Rule," *CT,* November 11, 1965; CC minutes, October 28, 1965.

6. "School Enrollments Will Continue to Rise in '60s," *CT,* January 12, 1960.

7. "City's Child Population Rises 2,746, with Most of Gain in School Ages," *CT,* August 9, 1960.

8. Pommer, "An Era Ends on Madison School Board," *CT,* January 27, 1969.

1960

1. David V. Mollenhoff and Mary Jane Hamilton, *Frank Lloyd Wright's Monona Terrace: The Enduring Power of a Civic Vision* (Madison: University of Wisconsin Press, 1999), 91–151.

2. Mollenhoff and Hamilton, *Monona Terrace,* 151–157.

3. Mollenhoff and Hamilton, *Monona Terrace,* 122, 128, 130, 131.

4. Mollenhoff and Hamilton, *Monona Terrace,* 102–103, 142, 152, 161, 173; "Alderman Rohr Defends His Auditorium Position," *CT,* February 20, 1960; editorial, "Ald. Rohr Ducks Questions on His Auditorium Proposal," *CT,* February 22, 1960; "A Letter from Ald. Rohr," *CT,* March 22, 1960; "Know Your Madisonian—Marshall E. Browne Sr.," *WSJ,* April 2, 1961.

5. Herbert Marcus, "Foe of Terrace Loses Suit," *CT,* January 21, 1960; editorial, "Monona Terrace Obstructionists Lose Another Spite Case," *CT,* January 21, 1960.

6. Mack Hoffman, "Authorize Wright Payment," *CT,* February 12, 1960; "Terrace Hall Can Easily Seat 5,000, Architect Reports," *CT,* April 4, 1960; "Jackson Appeals Terrace Suit to Supreme Court," *CT,* September 2, 1960.

7. Stanley Williams, "Times Preview of Terrace Plans Arouses Auditorium Unit's Ire," *WSJ,* April 5, 1960; Marcus, "Order Working Plans for Monona Terrace," *CT,* June 23, 1960; "Terrace Plans Detailed Here," *WSJ,* July 9, 1960; "Terrace Plan to Be Complete Dec. 31," *CT,* September 28, 1960; Marcus, "Engineers OK Terrace Site," *CT,* September 29, 1960; Williams, "Terrace Site Found to Be Feasible," *WSJ,* September 30, 1960.

8. Williams, "Rohr Will Ask New Terrace Vote," *WSJ,* February 25, 1960; editorial, "Ald. Rohr Plays a Cynical Game with Auditorium Issue," *CT,* February 27, 1960; "Council Rejects New Terrace Referendum," *WSJ,* March 11, 1960; Hoffman, "Terrace Foes Beaten, 13-6," *CT,* March 11, 1960; editorial, "Again, It's City Hall's Move," *WSJ,* March 14, 1960; "Mayor to Call Session for Auditorium's Users," *WSJ,* March 15, 1960.

9. John Creighton, "Terrace Foes Form Own Group to Seek New Site Referendum," *WSJ,* May 25, 1960; Marcus, "Terrace Foes' Rally Attracts Only 70 as 'Crusade' for Referendum Is Launched," *CT,* May 25, 1960; "Auditorium Group Appoints Advisors; Seeks Referendum," *WSJ,* July 17, 1960; David Gordon, "Anti-Terrace Suit Appealed," *WSJ,* September 2, 1960; "Jackson Appeals Terrace Suit to Supreme Court," *CT,* September 2, 1960; "Terrace Foes File 5,000 Names," *CT,* September 17, 1960; Marcus, "Foes of Terrace Not in Agreement on Any Substitute," *CT,* September 21, 1960.

10. Williams, "Council Refuses a New Vote on Monona Terrace," *WSJ,* October 12, 1960; Hoffman, "Terrace Foes Lose Battle," *CT,* October 12, 1960; CC minutes, October 13, 1960; editorial, "A Council Afraid of the People," *WSJ,* October 13, 1960; editorial, "Who Was Deprived of a Right to Vote?" *CT,* October 13, 1960; "Terrace Opponents to Keep Up Battle against Project," *CT,* October 13, 1960; Hoffman, "Council Affirms Refusal to Bow to Terrace Foes," *CT,* October 14, 1960.

11. Marcus, "Anti-Terrace Suit Appeal Is Argued," *CT,* December 2, 1960; "Terrace Site Foes Set Court Referendum Bid," *WSJ,* December 18, 1960; Richard Bradee, "To Fight New Terrace Suit," *CT,* December 20, 1960; "Terrace Site Foes Set New Referendum Bid," *WSJ,* December 21, 1960; "Foes of Terrace Win Show-Cause Hearing," *WSJ,* December 22, 1960; "Five Aldermen Will Not Defend Anti-Terrace Suit," *CT,* December 23, 1960.

12. "Monona Terrace Meets Key Points Listed by Experts," *CT,* December 14, 1960; Bradee, "Terrace Site Test Pile Quickly Finds

Firm Foundation," *CT*, December 22, 1960; "Monona Terrace Tests Are 'Very Favorable,'" *CT*, December 30, 1960; Williams, "Final Monona Terrace Plans Ready by Jan. 20," *WSJ*, December 31, 1960; Mollenhoff and Hamilton, *Monona Terrace,* 157–159.

13. "Population Up 15% in Final Census Tab," *WSJ*, December 3, 1960; "The Black Book," (Madison Branch NAACP, 1970), 6; Matthew Levin, *Cold War University* (Madison: University of Wisconsin Press, 2013), 54–59.

14. NAACP, *Negro Housing in Madison* (Madison: The Branch, 1959).

15. Madison Redevelopment Authority, *Triangle Urban Renewal Area, Estimated Housing Resources,* Dane Series 326, box 1, folder 8, WHSA.

16. Naomi Lede, *Madison's Negro Population*, Community Welfare Council of Madison/National Urban League (1966).

17. "Truax Housing Aide Agrees to Scrap 'Segregation' Lists," *WSJ*, January 4, 1960.

18. "Students to Picket in Bias Protest at 11," *DC*, February 27, 1960; Matt Levin interviews with Franklynn Peterson (December 19, 2005), Saul Landau (December 12, 2005) and Paul Breines (December 8, 2000); Walter P. Klein, "'Studies on the Left' Called Important Academic Outlet," *DC*, December 15, 1960; James Weinstein, "Studies on the Left," in *History and the New Left: Madison, Wisconsin, 1950–1970*, edited by Paul Buhle (Philadelphia: Temple University Press, 1990), 113–117; Paul Breines, email, April 20 and September 26, 2017; Franklynn Peterson email, September 10, 2017; Gary Weissman email, September 15, 2017.

19. Bradee, "Students Picket Woolworth Store to Protest Southern Segregation," *CT*, February 27, 1960; Kim Willenson, "Students Here Picket Stores, Cite South," *WSJ*, February 28, 1960; Hoffman, "Pickets Are Commended by NAACP," *CT*, March 1, 1960; "Odell A. 'Tally' Taliaferro," *WSJ*, May 9, 1999.

20. "Student Picketing Creates Controversy," *DC*, March 1, 1960.

21. "Saturday Picketing Continues," *DC*, July 12, 1960; "Taliaferro Re-Elected By NAACP," *CT*, December 13, 1960.

22. John Patrick Hunter, "Students Plan March to Back Negroes," *CT*, March 1, 1960; "Anti-Bias Marchers Map Plans," *DC*, March 2, 1960.

23. "'U' Hints Action on Demonstration," *DC*, March 2, 1960; Willenson, "U.S. Deplores Students' 'Protest' March," *WSJ*, March 2, 1960; Hunter, "Elvehjem, Luberg Fail to Halt Demonstration Plans," *CT*, March 2, 1960.

24. "Many Faculty Give Protest Solid Support," *DC*, March 2, 1960.

25. Willenson, "U.W. March Shifts to Rally," *WSJ*, March 3, 1960; "Rally Set for Mall at 2:30," *DC*, March 3, 1960; Mary Lee Gruber, "Student Senate Backs Movement," *DC*, March 3, 1960; John Kellogg, "Cowan Explains Aims of Demonstration," *DC*, March 3, 1960; editorial, "The March," *DC*, March 3, 1960; "Fight Bias at Home, Nelson Asks," *CT*, March 3, 1960; Levin, *Cold War University,* 113.

26. "Fight Bias at Home, Nelson Asks," *CT*, March 3, 1960; "Mall Demonstration," *DC*, March 4, 1960; Hunter, "500 Attend Campus Protest over Negro Mistreatment," *CT*, March 4, 1960; Willenson, "500 at U.W. Rap Race Bias," *WSJ*, March 4, 1960; "U.W. Students Hold Orderly Protest Rally," *WSJ*, March 4, 1960; BOR minutes, March 12, 1960; "Regents Praise Elvehjem on Handling of Protest," *WSJ*, March 13, 1960.

27. "50 Students Picket City Chain Stores," *WSJ*, May 1, 1960; "Luberg Backs Pickets' Methods," *WSJ*, May 2, 1960; "Luberg Still Opposed to Madison Store Picketing," *CT*, May 2, 1960; "No Approval of Picketing, Luberg Says," *WSJ*, May 3, 1960; "Saturday Picketing Continues," *DC*, July 12, 1960.

28. "Students Picket, Plan More," *DC*, May 3, 1960; "Visit to 'U' by Tennesseans: Generally Seen 'Good Step,'" *DC*, May 3, 1960; "Pickets Vote to Maintain Ad Hoc Role," *DC*, May 4, 1960; Harriet Tanzman, "Civil Rights and History," in Buhle, ed., *History and the New Left,* 143; Gary Weissman email, September 15, 2017.

29. Kathleen McGinley, "Senate Defeats March Bill," *DC*, May 11, 1960; "New Group Backs Civil Rights March," *DC*, May 12, 1960; "March Nears, Police Prepare," *DC*, May 13, 1960; editorial, "Voluntary," *DC*, May 13, 1960; "New Student Group to Stage March Backing Civil Rights," *WSJ*, May 13, 1960; "U.W. Rally to Hail Civil Rights," *WSJ*, May 17, 1960; Avi Bass, "600 Attend Civil Rights Rally," *DC*, May 18, 1960; McGinley and Dan Drosdoff, "Nelson, Elvehjem, Nash Praise Rights Rally," *DC*, May 18, 1960; "Walk Marks Supreme Court Decision," *DC*, May 18, 1960; Samuel C. Reynolds, "U.W. Students Protest Discrimination," *WSJ*, May 18, 1960; "350 Students in Rights Parade; Praised by Nelson, Evehjem," *CT*, May 18, 1960.

30. Editorial, "Handled Well," *DC*, July 29, 1960; "Probe Ban of Negroes by Tavern," *CT*, July 29, 1960; Williams, "City Rights Unit Hits Tavern in Bias Report," *WSJ*, August 9, 1960; "Students Buy Their Own Bar," *WSJ*, September 25, 1960.

31. Bonnie Ryan, "'Satchel' Paige Stars at Prep Cage Fete," *CT*, March 30, 1960; Reynolds, "Jackie Robinson Raps Ike, Kennedy on Rights Stand," *WSJ*, April 1, 1960; Hoffman, "Ex-Baseball Star Praises Both Humphrey and Nixon," *CT*, April 1, 1960; "Jackie Robinson Campaigns Here for Humphrey," *CT*, April 1, 1960; David R. Obey, *Raising Hell for Justice: The Washington Battles of a Heartland Progressive* (Madison: University of Wisconsin Press, 2007), 37–38.

32. "Du Bois, NAACP Founder, to Lecture on Socialism, American Negro Tonight," *DC*, April 9, 1960; Bass, "Du Bois Cites 'Red' Strides," *DC*, April 12, 1960; Gruber, "Sit-In Leader Cites Scope of Movement," *DC*, April 26, 1960; "Liberties Union Hears Anti-Segregation Leader," *CT*, April 26, 1960; Peterson, *Whitey Joins the Revolution,* 57–58; Franklynn Peterson interview with Matt Levin, 2005.

33. Stuart D. Levitan, *Madison: The Illustrated Sesquicentennial History, Vol. 1* (Madison: University of Wisconsin Press, 2006), 220–225.

34. "Official Visits City Brittingham Redevelop Site," *WSJ*, August 28, 1957; Williams, "U.S. Funds Set for City Redevelopment Work," *WSJ*, January 3, 1958; "Redevelopments Halt on U.S. Agency Order," *WSJ*, February 20, 1958; Williams, "Redevelopment Authority Voted," *WSJ*, July 11, 1958; Hank Feuerzeig, "MRA Was Given Unanimous OK When Established," *CT*, March 18, 1964; Feuerzeig, "Renewal Areas Once Held Many Poor Buildings," *CT*, March 20, 1964; Florence Zmudzinski, "Leaving Greenbush," *Historic Madison: A Journal of the Four Lakes Region* 20 (2005): 46–49.

35. June Dieckmann, "Redevelopment Law Void, Judge Decides," *WSJ*, February 26, 1959; *Redevelopment Authority of the City of Madison v. Joseph and Catherine Canepa*, 7 Wis. 2nd 643 (1959); "4 of 6 Constitutional Amendments Voted In," *WSJ*, April 5, 1961.

36. John Newhouse, "Triangle Area Cost Split Told," *WSJ*, October 26, 1958; "Appraisals Near on Triangle Site," *CT*, December 4, 1959; "Federal OK Is Granted to Triangle," *CT*, December 24, 1959.

37. John Addington, "Bonds Voted for Triangle," *WSJ*, November 5, 1958; Madison Redevelopment Authority (Wis.): Urban Renewal Project Records, 1954–1975; Triangle Urban Renewal Project, box 4, folder 9, Carson to Rupnow, November 25, 1958, WHSA.

38. Madison Redevelopment Authority (Wis.): Urban Renewal Project Records, 1954 – 1975; Triangle Urban Renewal Project, box 4, folder 9, Schaller to Nestingen, June 8, 1959, WHSA.

39. Madison Redevelopment Authority (Wis.): Urban Renewal Project Records, 1954–1975; Triangle Urban Renewal Project, box 1, folder 6, "Eligibility and Relocation Report, Triangle Renewal Area," August 29, 1958; "Triangle Urban Renewal Project Area Eligibility and Relocation Report, November 1959," WHSA.

40. Madison Redevelopment Authority (Wis.): Urban Renewal Project Records, 1954–1975; Triangle Urban Renewal Project, box 1, folder 1, "Triangle Redevelopment & You," WHSA.

41. Madison Redevelopment Authority, "Eligibility and Relocation Report," 5.

42. Madison Redevelopment Authority (Wis.): Urban Renewal Project Records, 1954–1975; Triangle Urban Renewal Project, box 1, folder 3; "Federal OK Is Granted to Triangle," *CT*, December 24, 1959.

43. MRA minutes, April 7, 1960; Williams, "$32 Million Renewal Plans Offered," *WSJ*, April 8, 1960.

44. Triangle Urban Renewal Area, *Application for Loan and Grant,* Final Project Report, "Estimates of Housing Needs and Resources," May 1960, City of Madison Planning Department, Dane Series 236, box 1, folder 8, WHSA; MRA Minutes, May 5, 1960; "Renewal Area Loan Move Okd," *WSJ*, May 6, 1960.

45. Dane Series 236, box 1, folder 8, WHSA.

46. "Set Hearing Thursday on Triangle," *CT*, June 11, 1960; Williams, "Triangle Project Hearing Set," *WSJ*, June 14, 1960; Mayor Ivan Nestingen Public Statement, June 16, 1960; Gordon, "Triangle Plans Draw Crowd," *WSJ*, June 17, 1960; "300 at Hearing on Triangle Plans," *CT*, June 17, 1960; "Housing OKd for Triangle," *WSJ*, June 21, 1960.

47. "Renewal Area Prices Are Set," *WSJ*, April 22, 1960; "City Makes Progress on Brittingham Project," *WSJ*, June 18, 1960.

48. MRA Minutes, July 7, 1960; "Contract for a Social Worker in Triangle Area Is Approved," *WSJ*, July 8, 1960; MRA Minutes, August 4, 1960; MRA Minutes, September 1, 1960.

49. Madison Redevelopment Authority (Wis.): Urban Renewal Project Records, 1954–1975, Triangle Urban Renewal Project, box 4, folder 9, McCollum to Nestingen, October 20 and October 27, 1960, WHSA.

50. MRA Minutes, November 23, 1960.

51. MRA Minutes, November 3, 1960; Williams, "147–158 Housing Units for Brittingham Backed," *WSJ*, November 4, 1960; "Apartment Plan Voted in Project," *CT*, November 4, 1960; "City Renewal Housing Plan Meets Opposition," *WSJ*, November 18, 1960; MRA Minutes, December 1, 1960; Williams, "MRA Disfavors Public Housing at Brittingham," *WSJ*, December 2, 1960; Willenson, "Public Housing Urged in Triangle Area Now," *WSJ*, December 15, 1960; "Shift Plans for Public House Unit," *CT*, December 15, 1960.

52. Williams, "Federal Unit OKs Plans for Brittingham Project," *WSJ*, December 30, 1960.

53. Elliott Maraniss, "Refusal to Transfer License Shakes His Faith in City," *CT*, July 23, 1960; Richard Harris, *Growing Up Black in South Madison: Economic Disenfranchisement of Black Madison* (Madison: RoyTek, 2012), 80–89.

54. "Renewal Plan Gets Approval," *WSJ*, April 5, 1960; Hoffman, "Negro's Tavern Move Is Blocked in Bitter Debate," *CT*, July 15, 1960; "Transfer of Licari Bar OK'd Despite Nearness to School," *CT*, April 25, 1961.

55. "Brittingham Bar Bids Made," *WSJ*, June 25, 1960; "Madison (Wis)—Mayor's Commission on Human Rights," *Minutes Covering the Meetings which Dealt with the Implied Race Prejudice Encountered in the Attempt to Relocate Trotter's Tavern, and the Commission's Report on the Trotter Case, 1960,* WI-M 1 MAY R1.2:T 3/1960, at 13, Wisconsin Historical Society Library.

56. Marcus, "Proposed Transfer of Displaced Bar Will Be Opposed," *CT*, July 12, 1960; Hoffman, "Tavern Move Voted Down; Racial Prejudice Charged," *CT*, July 13, 1960; Williams, "City Council Kills Tavern Move; Blocks Prejudice Charge Probe," *WSJ*, July 15, 1960; Hoffman, "Negro's Tavern Move Is Blocked in Bitter Debate," *CT*, July 15, 1960.

57. "Rights Body Sets Tavern Case Probe," *CT*, July 16, 1960; Williams, "Probe of 'Racial Bias' Voted," *WSJ*, July 26, 1960; Marcus, "City Rights Group to Study Tavern Prejudice Charge," *CT*, July 26, 1960; Hunter, "Rights Group Sets Ground Rules on Trotter Inquiry," *CT*, July 29, 1960.

58. Robert Bouzek, "Rohr Admits Leading Tavern Move, Unit Says," *WSJ*, August 17, 1960; "Anti-Trotter Drive Admitted by Rohr," *CT*, August 17, 1960.

59. Gordon, "Trotter Case Is Buried as Council Hails Itself," *WSJ*, August 26, 1960; "Report on Trotter Case Prejudice Quietly Put on File," *CT*, August 26, 1960.

60. Williams, "City Council Kills Tavern Move; Blocks Prejudice Charge Probe," *WSJ*, July 15, 1960; Hoffman, "Negro's Tavern Move Is Blocked in Bitter Debate," *CT*, July 15, 1960.

61. "Blocked Tavern Move Seen Periling Renewal," *WSJ*, July 29, 1960; "MRA to Check Federal Unit on Tavern Issue," *CT*, August 5, 1960.

62. MRA minutes, October 6, 1960; "Renewal Timetable Adopted," *CT*, October 8, 1960; MRA Minutes, December 1, 1960; MRA Minutes, December 14, 1960.

63. Hoffman, "Tavern Site Deadlock Reported," *CT*, December 21, 1960.

64. Triangle Urban Renewal Area, *Application*, "Size and Income Characteristics of Families to Be Displaced from Project Area Wis. R-2, R-223(2)," May 1960, Dane Series 236, box 1, folder 8, WHSA.

65. Hunter, "2,500 Are Given Degrees at U.W. Commencement," *CT*, June 6, 1960.

66. "U.W. 5th in Full-Time Enrollment," *CT*, December 5, 1960.

67. Kurt Brokaw, "Homecoming Show 'Woeful Fiasco,'" *DC*, November 5, 1960; Hunter, "Homecoming Show Is Disappointment," November 5, 1960.

68. Henry J. McCormick, "Badgers' Dream Shattered, 44-8," *WSJ*, January 2, 1960; John Talbot, "200 Fans Give Cheer for Returning Badgers," *WSJ*, January 4, 1960; Mark Wyman, "Faculty Still Backs No Rose Bowl Pact," *DC*, February 2, 1960; editorial, "U. of W. Faculty Acts Wisely in Vote Against the Rose Bowl," *CT*, February 6, 1960; "Rose Bowl Participation OKd," *DC*, May 21, 1960; editorial, "The Hysteria of Post-Season Football Bowl Games," *CT*, December 15, 1960.

69. Wyman, "Voluntary ROTC Approved," *DC*, January 5, 1960; Hunter, "Regents OK Voluntary ROTC," *CT*, February 20, 1960; Jon Stillman, "ROTC Course Is Voluntary for Two-Year Trial Period," *Daily Cardinal 1960 New Student Issue*; Karl Gutnkecht, "Voluntary ROTC 'Is Assured,'" *DC*, October 25, 1960.

70. Dan Webster, "About 5,600 Spectators Drawn by Symposium," *DC*, February 23, 1960; "The Challenge of the Sixties," *Wisconsin Alumnus* 61, no. 13 (May 1960): 10–17.

71. Alexius Baas, "Holbrook's Twain Is Living Being," *CT*, March 18, 1960.

72. Reynolds, "Morse's Blasts at Both Parties Enlivens Mock Convention at U.W.," *WSJ*, March 19, 1960; Kay Pofahl, "Mock Democrats Choose Stevenson," *DC*, March 22, 1960; Hoffman, "Stevenson Draws Overflow Crowd in Kennedy Plea," *CT*, October 11, 1960.

73. Hunter, "Friedrick Named U. Regent," *CT*, March 25, 1960; "Portrait of a Regent," *Wisconsin Alumnus* 61, no. 14 (June 1960): 16–18.

74. Pofahl, "New Poetry Discussed by R.P. Warren," *DC*, April 8, 1960.

75. "Spring Is Here at Last; Mil Ball Makes It Official," *DC*, April 8, 1960; "Blackwell Elected Mil King," *DC*, April 9, 1960; "Anti-Mil Ball Skit Readied for Tonight," *DC*, April 9, 1960; Saul Landau in Buhle, ed., *History and the New Left*, 111; Lee Baxandall, "New York Meets Oshkosh," in Buhle, ed., *History and the New Left*, 132; Roz Bacandall, in Buhle, ed., *History and the New Left*, 138–139.

76. "Elm Drive Halls Combine Beauty with Function," *DC*, April 7, 1960; David Bednarek, "500 Attend U.W.'s Dedication of Dormitories, Elm Drive Halls," *WSJ*, April 11, 1960; "500 Attend Dedication of U.W.'s New Elm Drive Halls," *CT*, April 11, 1960; Feldman, *Buildings of the University*, 307–308.

77. "Garvey Wins, Results Split," *DC*, April 13, 1960; Dave Zweifel, "Ed Garvey, Labor Lawyer and Progressive Firebrand, Has Died," *CT*, February 22, 2017.

78. "Faculty Oks Apartment Parties," *DC*, May 10, 1960; Reynolds, "New Social Rules, ROTC Trial Voted by Faculty," *WSJ*, May 10, 1960; "Apartment Rule Details Not Set," *DC*, May 12, 1960; *Wisconsin Alumnus* 61, no. 14 (June 1960): 31–32.

79. "Dale Hackbart Voted 'Athlete of Year' at 'U,'" *DC*, May 17, 1960; "Packers in 'Pitch' for Hackbart," *CT*, June 7, 1960; Lew Cornelius, "Hackbart, Mueller Signed by Pirates," *CT*, June 8, 1960; Steven D. Schmitt, *A History of Badger Baseball: The Rise and Fall of America's Pastime at the University of Wisconsin* (Madison: University of Wisconsin Press, 2017), 105–109.

80. "Jazz Pianist Jamal to Play at Union," *DC*, May 12, 1960.

81. "Begin Clearing Johnson St. Site for Chemistry Building," *CT*, July 6, 1960; "Razing Begins on Site for New Chemistry Building," *DC*, July 7, 1960; Jim Feldman, *The Buildings of the University of Wisconsin* (Madison, WI: University Archives, 1997), 314.

82. BOR Minutes, July 8, 1960; "Plan for 10-Year Dorm Expansion Recommended," *CT*, July 8, 1960; Reynolds, "Critical Co-Ed Housing Picture Spurs U.W. Housing Demands," *WSJ*, July 9, 1960; "Regents Start Taking Long Look at Future Development for U.W.," *WSJ*, July 9, 1960; "Advance Plan for Student Housing," *CT*, July 23, 1960; "Coed Housing Called 'Critical,'" *DC*, July 12, 1960; BOR Minutes, September 10, 1960; Hunter, "O.K. Dorms South of U. Ave.," *CT*, September 10, 1960; "U. Dorm Project Will Take $70,000 from City in Taxes," *CT*, September 12, 1960; "Fall

Sorority Rush Ends with Pledging of More Than Four Hundred Students," *DC*, September 29, 1960; "364 Pledge UW Fraternities," *CT*, October 1, 1960; Newhouse, "U.W. Acts for Dormitory Site," *WSJ*, November 12, 1960; Barry Teicher and John W. Jenkins, *A History of Housing at the University of Wisconsin–Madison* (Madison: University of Wisconsin Press, 2006), 73–79; Feldman, *Buildings,* 362–365.

83. Hunter, "Brubeck Enchants with 'Bracketed Rhythm,'" *CT*, October 1, 1960; Alice Siegel, "Miss Makeba—'Exciting, Sincere,'" *DC*, October 1, 1960; "Dave Brubeck, Miriam Makeba to Appear in Fall Jazz Festival," *DC*, May 19, 1960.

84. "City Stays Calm During Blackout," *WSJ*, October 4, 1960; "Can't Study, So Students Hold Rally on Langdon St.," *WSJ*, October 4, 1960; "Crowds Form as All Lights Go Out," *DC*, October 4, 1960; "City Blacked Out by Short Circuit in Power Plant," *CT*, October 4, 1960.

85. "Socialists Face Possible 'U' Action on Tito, Mr. K Bids," *DC*, October 1, 1960; editorial, "Is One Warranted?" *DC*, October 4, 1960; "Socialist Club Is Reprimanded," *DC*, October 5, 1960; Ron Radosh email to author, May 27, 2017.

86. "French Literature Expert Lecturing," *DC*, October 12, 1960; Bob Jacobson, "Love of Camus Universal—Critic," *DC*, October 18, 1960.

87. "Travanti to Play Manager in 'Our Town' Production," *DC*, October 5, 1960; Jacobson, "Overall Excellence Marks Players' 'Our Town'—Critic," *DC*, October 19, 1960; Bill Doudna, "Players' 'Our Town' Generally Excellent," *CT*, October 19, 1960; http://www.thorntonwilder.com/about-wilder/biography/.

88. Dan Drosdoff, "Cuban Revolution Defended," *DC*, November 1, 1960; Hunter, "7 Students Who Went to Cuba Unanimous in Praise of Castro," *CT*, January 10, 1961; Saul Landau, "From the Labor Youth League to the Cuban Revolution," in Buhle, ed., *History and the New Left,* 107–112.

89. "Nixon Coming; Elvehjem Acts," *DC*, November 5, 1960; "U.W. Attitude on Nixon Visit Raises Eyebrows," *CT*, November 5, 1960; Aldric Revell, "Nixon Heard by 5,000 Here," *CT*, November 7, 1960; Llewellyn G. Roberts, "10,000 Give Nixons Lift Here," *WSJ*, November 8, 1960; Bruce Thorp and Avi Baas, "Students Meet Nixon at Truax," *DC*, November 8, 1960.

90. Drosdoff, "Luberg Explains Risks in Joining Political Groups," *DC*, December 8, 1960; Hunter, "CIA Here: U. Clean, Union Muddy," *CT*, March 9, 1967; Neil Eisenberg, "Student Asks Check on Luberg-CIA Link," *DC*, April 12, 1967.

91. BOR Minutes, December 9, 1960; "Out-of-State Student Admissions Tightened," *WSJ*, December 10, 1960; "Regents Pass Rule Making Non-State Entrance Tougher," *DC*, December 15, 1960; Reynolds, "U.W. Study Reports What Students Spend," *WSJ*, December 3, 1961.

92. "Charlie Mohr Named on Boxing All-America Squad," *DC*, April 5, 1960; Bonnie Ryan, "Charlie Nothing but Best," *CT*,

April 18, 1960; Doug Moe, *Lords of the Ring* (Madison: University of Wisconsin Press, 2004), 3–22, 209–232.

93. McCormick, "Five Wisconsin Boxers Win, Six Fight in Tonight's NCAA Finals," *WSJ*, April 9, 1960; "UW Boxer Mohr Battles for Life," *WSJ*, April 11, 1960; Louis John Haugh, "Mohr Continues Fight for Life," *DC*, April 12, 1960; Dr. Manucher Javid interview, August 2, 2016.

94. "Boxer Mohr, 22, Loses Life Fight," *WSJ*, April 18, 1960; "Charles Mohr Succumbs to Injury Sustained in NCAA Boxing Bout," *CT*, April 18, 1960.

95. Maraniss, "Mohr Had Been Patient Twice of Psychiatry Wards," *CT*, April 19, 1960.

96. Editorial, "Decide on Reason," *DC*, April 26, 1960; Reynolds, "Overwhelming Vote by Faculty Knocks Out Intercollegiate Boxing Program at Wisconsin," *WSJ*, May 10, 1960; "Great Sports Chapter Ends," *WSJ*, May 10, 1960; Bruce Thorp, "'U' Drops Interschool Boxing," *DC*, May 10, 1960; Maraniss, "End U.W. Intercollegiate Boxing," *CT*, May 10, 1960; David Fellman, interviewed by Donna Hartshorne, 1982, OH #0220, digital audio file, University Archives and Records Management Services, Madison, Wisconsin; Jim Doherty, "Requiem for a Middleweight," https://www.smithsonianmag.com/issue/april-2000/; Scott Tinley, "The Tragic Story of Charlie Mohr," *Sports Illustrated,* April 16, 2010, https://www.si.com/more-sports/2010/04/16/mohr.

97. Editorial, "Irresponsible," *DC*, May 11, 1960.

98. Moe, "50 Years Ago, UW Athlete's Death Ended College Boxing," *WSJ*, April 10, 2010; College Boxer, "NCAA and NCBA Champion Boxing Teams," *Intercollegiate Boxing,* January 10, 2011, https://www.intercollegiateboxing.com/2011/01/ncaa-and-ncba-champion-boxing-teams/.

99. "Tom Brittingham of U.W. Fame Dies," *CT*, April 17, 1960; Bradee, "100 Hear Dr. Fred Pay Last Tribute to Brittingham," *CT*, April 23, 1960; "Tom Brittingham Funeral Is Set Here Wednesday," *CT*, April 18, 1960; *Wisconsin Alumnus* 61, no. 14 (June 1960): 12–15.

100. "E. E. Witte, 'Father of Social Security,' Dies Here at Age 73," *WSJ*, May 21, 1960; "Prof. Witte, Famed Economist, 73, Dies," *CT*, May 21, 1960; David B. Johnson, "The 'Government Man': Edwin E. Witte and the University of Wisconsin," *Wisconsin Magazine of History* 82, no. 1 (Autumn 1998): 32–51.

101. "Central High School Awards Diplomas to 155," *CT*, June 17, 1960; "379 Get Diplomas at East, 414 at West," *CT*, June 17, 1960.

102. "School Enrollment Reaches 21,174," *CT*, September 17, 1960.

103. "New City School Is Dedicated," *CT*, November 28, 1960.

104. Reynolds, "Salaries of City Teachers to Rise Minimum of $240 Yearly in Fall," *WSJ*, January 19, 1960; Reynolds, "City Raises the Ante to Get Better Teachers," *WSJ*, February 1, 1960; Hoffman, "Cut Budget for Schools $170,115," *CT*, December 6, 1960.

105. "City School Board Men Win Easily," *CT*, April 6, 1960.

106. Reynolds, "Dire Effects Seen if School Bond Vote Fails," *WSJ*, April 3, 1960; "School Bonds Win 5 to 1 Victory," *CT*, April 6, 1960; "School, Renewal Bond Issues Are Authorized," *WSJ*, April 29, 1960.

107. Reynolds, "Question of Hiring Negro Teachers Stays Unresolved," *WSJ*, May 5, 1960; Levitan, *Madison*, 220.

108. Reynolds, "Mitby, Green Bay, Offered Post as Vocational School Director," *WSJ*, May 7, 1960; Marcus, "Mitby Takes Over Vocational Post," *CT*, July 1, 1960.

109. "250 Attend Dedication Ceremony at New Samuel Gompers School," *WSJ*, November 28, 1960.

110. "Weatherly Hurt Slightly as Truck Hits Squad Car," *WSJ*, January 9, 1959; Dieckmann, "Ousted Weatherly to Appeal Firing," *WSJ*, April 14, 1959; "'Patrol Captain' Emery Takes Over Police Chief's Post Today," *WSJ*, November 2, 1959; Paul Soglin email, February 28, 2017.

111. Robert G. Trautman, "7 Months of Chief Emery—Police Morale Is Gaining," *CT*, June 18, 1960; Newhouse, "Chief Emery Due Back to Tangle with New Set of Traffic Problems," *WSJ*, October 30, 1960; "Police Chief Wilbur Emery," *WSJ*, December 18, 1960; Gordon, "Emery Acclaims FBI Academy," *WSJ*, December 18, 1960.

112. John Aehl, "As City Grows, So Does Crime," *WSJ*, January 12, 1961.

113. Steven E. Hopkins, "Browne Heads City Police-Fire Group," *WSJ*, May 12, 1960; "Browne to Head Police, Fire Group," *CT*, May 12, 1960; Williams, "Doyle, Adlai's No. 1 Backer, Waits for Spotlight to Turn," *WSJ*, July 6, 1960; "Know Your Madisonian—Marshall E. Browne, Sr.," *WSJ*, April 2, 1961; "Know Your Madisonian—Attorney James E. Doyle," *WSJ*, August 13, 1961.

114. "Madison Policeman, Named in Woman's Complaint, Fired," *WSJ*, July 14, 1960; "Emery and Two Aides Are Sued," *CT*, October 15, 1960.

115. "Asst. Fire Chief Durkin May Be Forced to Retire," *CT*, August 11, 1960; "Board Halts Retirement of Durkin," *CT*, August 18, 1960; "Mayor Calls Meeting on Durkin Next Wednesday," *CT*, August 25, 1960; Marcus, "Durkin Wins Fire Job Fight," *CT*, August 31, 1960; James Oset, "Determination Is Mark of Durkin," *WSJ*, October 30, 1968.

116. "Weatherly Is Awarded $1,850," *WSJ*, November 10, 1960; "City Sues Weatherly For Auto," *CT*, December 2, 1960; Roberts, "Commission Upholds Award to Weatherly," *WSJ*, December 14, 1960; Gordon, "Council Votes Appeal of Award to Weatherly," *WSJ*, December 21, 1960.

117. "Dr. J. S. Supernaw Found Dead; Officials Investigate Six Shots," *WSJ*, March 3, 1960; "Dr. J. S. Supernaw Found Dead of Bullet Wounds in His Office," *CT*, March 3, 1960.

118. Dieckmann, "Young Hayes Is Charged with Two Murder Counts," *WSJ*, March 14, 1960; "Hayes Youth in Insanity Plea after Double Slaying," *CT*, March 14, 1960; Trautman, "Hayes Murder Trial Opens: 2 Teen-Agers Tell of Party," *CT*, September 20, 1960; Dieckmann, "Insanity Plea Wins Acquittal For Hayes," *WSJ*, September 23, 1960; Trautman, "Hayes Not Guilty, Goes to Hospital," *CT*, September 23, 1960.

119. Dieckmann, "Judge Bloodgood Takes Own Life in Hospital," *WSJ*, July 8, 1960; Hopkins, "His Death Shocks Judge's Colleagues," *WSJ*, July 8, 1960; "Bloodgood Takes Own Life," *CT*, July 8, 1960; Dieckmann, "Friends Pay Tribute to Judge Bloodgood," *WSJ*, July 12, 1960; Facebook exchange with Susan Bloodgood, November 22, 2017.

120. "Beltline Interchange to Open Soon," *CT*, July 16, 1960.

121. "Segoe Rd.–University Ave. Intersection Open," *WSJ*, July 18, 1960.

122. Harry Johnson, "No Bands Play when Trains End Their Run," *CT*, January 6, 1960.

123. Hoffman, *CT*, "Council Buries Municipal Bus Plan," *CT*, January 29, 1960.

124. Williams, "Council Opposes W. Mifflin St. Extension for Badger Bus Line," *WSJ*, April 13, 1960.

125. Marcus, "City, UW in $7 Million Road Pact," *CT*, April 28, 1960; Williams, "University Ave. Plans Backed," *WSJ*, April 29, 1960.

126. Williams, "Madison Voters Face 2 Big-Money Questions," *WSJ*, November 6, 1960; Williams, "Two City Bond Issues Pass by Better than 3-1 Margin," *WSJ*, November 9, 1960.

127. "Dimensions and Dividends," City of Madison Planning Department, March 1965.

128. City of Madison Department of Planning, Community Development and Economic Development.

129. "City's Population At 126,000," *CT*, March 7, 1960.

130. "State Street Businessmen Organize New Group," *CT*, January 8, 1960.

131. "Proposed Annexation to City Shown," *WSJ*, February 20, 1960; Williams, "Area Annexed as 22nd Ward," *WSJ*, June 10, 1960; "Large Grove Area Annexation Voted," *CT*, June 10, 1960; John Creighton, "Maher Area Annexing Voted," *WSJ*, July 22, 1960; Creighton, "The Zeier Annexation: Its Issues Explained," *WSJ*, July 25, 1960; Williams, "City Valuation Is $460 Million," *WSJ*, November 1, 1960; Bradee, "City Wins $4.8 Million Annexation," *CT*, November 29, 1960; Williams, "Beltline Annexation Is Upheld," *WSJ*, November 30, 1960; Williams, "Madison Gains Room to Grow from Aggressive Annexations," *WSJ*, December 5, 1960; "'Tank Farm' Annex Invalid," *WSJ*, December 9, 1960.

132. William Riermerman, "8,000 Persons Get ESBMA's Festival Off to Good Start," *WSJ*, June 30, 1960; "100,000 Expected for ESBMA's 6-Day Festival," *CT*, June 30, 1960.

133. "Labor in Madison Boosts Pay Level Past Milwaukee's," *CT*, September 5, 1960.

134. "Grant's to Close Store on Square," *CT*, December 29, 1960.

135. "Merchants Say City Can Support Downtown and Suburban Shops," *WSJ*, January 12, 1960.

136. "New Shopping Center Slated for East Side," *WSJ*, March 13, 1960.

137. Creighton, "Throngs of Customers Give the New Westgate Shopping Center a Promising Opening," *WSJ*, March 25, 1960; "Wards-Westgate to Open at 10 A.M. on Thursday," *CT*, July 26, 1960; "Manchester's at Westgate Has Opening Ceremony," *CT*, November 3, 1960.

138. "Ground Is Broken for North Gate," *CT*, June 7, 1960.

139. "State-Business Issue Argued in Hilldale Shop Center Suit," *WSJ*, November 2, 1960; "High Court Backs Hilldale," *CT*, December 2, 1960; Maraniss, "Will Rennebohm Have a Store in Hilldale? Nobody Is Talking," *CT*, December 14, 1960; "The Hill Farms Story," *Wisconsin Alumnus* 62, no. 9 (January 1961): 13–21; James Rowen, "Elite Cashes In at Hilldale," *DC*, March 14, 1969; E. David Cronon and John W. Jenkins, *The University of Wisconsin: A History, 1945–1971: Renewal to Revolution, Volume IV* (Madison: University of Wisconsin Press, 1999), 253–255.

140. "PTA Ends Sponsored Films," *WSJ*, January 8, 1960.

141. Reynolds, "1,410 Tour Sequoya Library," *WSJ*, April 4, 1960.

142. Williams, "City 'Beer Pack' Curb Rejected," *WSJ*, April 27, 1960; Hoffman, "Off-Premises Beer Curb Is Rejected," *CT*, April 27, 1960.

143. "Concerts Set for Square on Mondays," *WSJ*, June 11, 1960.

144. "Historic Vilas House and Hanks Home Up for Sale," *CT*, March 9, 1960; "Bare Plan to Buy Vilas Property for Housing for Aged," *CT*, November 28, 1960; "Trustees Discuss Financing Plan of Apartment Project for Aged," *WSJ*, December 18, 1960; "Building Height Unknown, but Zone Exemption OK'd," *CT*, December 19, 1960; "Senior Citizens Apartment Price Hiked to $35,900," *CT*, December 27, 1960; "Trustees Studying Name for Apartments on Vilas Property," *CT*, December 31, 1960.

145. Marcia Crowley, "Winkie Needs New Home at Vilas Zoo," *WSJ*, April 27, 1960; "Your Young, Old Friends Worry Over the Housing Plight, Winkie," *WSJ*, April 29, 1960; "City's Largest Citizen Moves," *CT*, June 28, 1960.

146. "City Has 'Worst Flood,'" *WSJ*, July 3, 1960; "City Cleans Up after $500,000 Storm," *CT*, July 4, 1960.

147. Bednarek, "Vilas Park Display Is Biggest Ever," *WSJ*, July 4, 1960.

148. "4th Dutch Elm Case Discovered," *WSJ*, July 8, 1960.

149. Williams, "$40,000 Fog Idea Rejected," *WSJ*, June 25, 1960; "DDT (for Drat Them) Given Mosquitoes in Nine Areas," *WSJ*, July 28, 1960.

150. "36 Monkeys Flee Vilas Zoo; May Get Tree-Top Washout," *CT*, August 5, 1960; Crowley, "Still Free, 2 Monkeys Defy Capture Attempts," *WSJ*, November 26, 1960; "Last of Zoo Monkeys Is Caught," *CT*, December 5, 1960.

151. "Council Supports Door-to-Door Plan," *CT*, September 5, 1960; Williams, "Council Orders Voter Registering Campaign," *WSJ*, September 9, 1960; "50,962 Voters Register in City," *WSJ*, September 10, 1960; Williams, "Voter Drive Stirs Up Political Row," *WSJ*, September 24, 1960.

152. Willenson, "City's Voters Line Up to Cast Record Ballots," *WSJ*, November 9, 1960.

153. "Officials to Dedicate Atomic Fallout Shelter Here Today," *WSJ*, November 18, 1960.

154. "Kennedy Will Launch State Tour Here Today," *WSJ*, February 16, 1960; Revell, "Kennedy Pledges a Constructive State Campaign," *CT*, February 16, 1960; William C. Robbins, "Vigorous Kennedy Seeks Hands—and Votes—at a Personal Level," *WSJ*, February 17, 1960; "Seeks Votes, Not Delegates," *DC*, February 17, 1960; Richard Arnesen interview, March 20, 2017; Dave Zweifel and John Nichols, *The Capital Times* (Madison: Wisconsin Historical Society Press, 2017), 173–177.

155. Revell, "Crowd of 1,000 Greets Kennedys at Reception Here," *CT*, February 25, 1960; Maraniss, "3 Kennedy Sisters Campaign Here," *CT*, March 2, 1960; "200 Students See Kennedy Press Talk," *DC*, March 10, 1960; Louis John Haugh, "Kennedy—U.S. Prestige 'Not Better,'" *DC*, March 15, 1960; Robbins, "Kennedy Reception, Talk Draws Crowds," *WSJ*, March 17, 1960; "Kennedy Stops In at 'Dames' Show," *DC*, March 17, 1960; Bruce, "Kennedy Asks Stronger Role by President in Main Issues," *DC*, March 26, 1960; Hunter, "Overflow Crowd Hears Kennedy Hit Administration," *CT*, March 26, 1960.

156. Maraniss, "Kennedy Margin Is 100,000," *CT*, April 6, 1960.

157. "Nixon, Kuehn Take Mock Vote," *DC*, October 2, 1960.

158. Williams, "Nestingen Also Scores with Kennedy's Victory," *WSJ*, July 15, 1960; "Wisconsin Goes to Nixon by 50,000," *CT*, November 9, 1960; "Mayor Won't Accept U.S. Job Elsewhere," *WSJ*, November 11, 1960.

159. Revell, "15,000 Cheer Kennedy Here," *CT*, October 24, 1960; "As Madison Throngs Cheered Kennedy," *CT*, October 24, 1960; Roberts, "Kennedy Hits 'Rigid' Nixon," *WSJ*, October 24, 1960; Bass, "Kennedy Hits U.S. Role," *DC*, October 25, 1960.

1961

1. "Play-by-Play of Seven Years's Terrace War," *WSJ*, March 2, 1961; Mollenhoff and Hamilton, *Monona Terrace,* 160–162.

2. Aldric Revell, "Terrace Wins In High Court; Jackson's Suit Thrown Out," *CT*, January 10, 1961.

3. Herbert Marcus, "Final Terrace Plans Backed by Committee," *CT*, January 26, 1961.

4. John Newhouse, "Terrace Plans Finally OKd," *WSJ*, January 31, 1961; "Mayor Says Farewell to Council," *WSJ*, January 31, 1961; Mack Hoffman, "Council Approves Call for Bids on Monona Terrace," *CT*, January 31, 1961.

5. "Two Large Firms Unable to Bid on Auditorium," *WSJ*, February 15, 1961; "Five Qualified for Terrace Bid; Findorff's Out," *WSJ*, February 28, 1961; David Gordon, "Terrace 'Extras' to Cost Millions," *WSJ*, March 3, 1961.

6. "Terrace Foes Lose Action to Force Vote on Abandoning Site," *CT*, February 24, 1961; editorial, "Obstructionists Lose Another Court Test on Terrace Site," *CT*, February 24, 1961.

7. "Bird's Eye View of Wilson Street Entrance to Monona Terrace," *CT*, February 14, 1961; "Pageantry of the Old Shown in New Terrace Project Drawing," *WSJ*, February 15, 1961.

8. Marcus, "Terrace Bids $9.6 Million; Perini Company Is Lowest," *CT*, March 7, 1961; "Minimum Terrace Total Placed at $13 Million," *WSJ*, March 8, 1961; editorial, "Madison's Moment of Truth," *WSJ*, March 8, 1961; editorial, "Mayoralty Election Again Shows Majority for Monona Terrace," *CT*, March 8, 1961.

9. Stanley Williams, "Bids on Terrace Rejected," *WSJ*, March 10, 1961; "Council Keeps Terrace Chances Alive," *CT*, March 10, 1961.

10. "Terrace Aid Pledged by Mrs. Guggenheim," *CT*, March 16, 1961; "Announce Plans to 'Save the Terrace,'" *CT*, March 18, 1961; "Group Again Requests Referendum on Terrace," *WSJ*, March 21, 1961; "Vote on Terrace Bonds Rejected," *WSJ*, March 22, 1961; Williams, "Prof. Graves to Direct Save-Terrace Campaign," *WSJ*, March 23, 1961; Hoffman, "Terrace Foes' Bond Maneuver Killed by Council," *CT*, March 24, 1961; Marcus, "Terrace 'Hidden Costs' Disproved," *CT*, March 24, 1961.

11. "Reynolds Bares Auditorium Plan," *WSJ*, March 12, 1961; editorial, "Flim-Flam Headlines about Reynolds' Auditorium Plans," *CT*, March 14, 1961; Williams, "Reynolds Offers Auditorium Sites," *WSJ*, March 26, 1961; Gordon, "City Elects Reynolds By 2,600-Vote Edge," *WSJ*, April 5, 1961.

12. Gordon, "Reynolds Hints No Big Changes in City Policy," *WSJ*, April 15, 1961; Marcus, "Reynolds to Oust Three Citizens on Auditorium Body," *CT*, April 15, 1961; William Riemerman, "City Auditorium Tops Reynolds' First Plans," *WSJ*, April 19, 1961; "Foes of Terrace Are Appointed to Auditorium Group," *CT*, April 19, 1961; editorial, "Top Priority for the Auditorium," *WSJ*, April 19, 1961; Gordon, "Auditorium Unit Seeks Wright Contract's End," *WSJ*, April 27, 1961.

13. "Reynolds for Conklin Center Site," *CT*, May 20, 1961; Riemerman, "Plan Unit Eyes 5 Auditorium Sites," *WSJ*, July 13, 1961; "Mayor's Waterworks Site to Cost $1 Million," *CT*, July 13, 1961; editorial, "A Peak at Pig-in-Poke Auditorium," *CT*, July 13, 1961; "Reynolds' Site for Auditorium Is Rated Last," *CT*, November 9, 1961.

14. Riemerman, "Wright Contract Write-Off Asked," *WSJ*,
June 15, 1961; Marcus, "City Asked to Break Wright Pact," *CT*, June 15, 1961; Gordon, "Move to End Wright Contract Up Tonight," *WSJ*, June 19, 1961; editorial, "Looks Like Obstructionists Buried Terrace Prematurely," *CT*, June 21, 1961; "Auditorium Possible in 3 Years, City Told," *WSJ*, August 5, 1961.

15. Gordon, "Council Split on Wright Contract Issue," *WSJ*, July 26, 1961; Marcus, "Balk at Move to End Terrace Contract," *CT*, July 26, 1961; Hoffman, "Council Keeps Terrace Contract Alive," *CT*, August 11, 1961; Gordon, "Vote on Terrace Contract Shows that Issue Is Fluid," *WSJ*, August 14, 1961; "Termination Clause Missing in Wright Group's Contract," *WSJ*, November 17, 1961.

16. "Peters Cuts Terrace Price to $9 Million," *WSJ*, September 11, 1961; Marcus, "Peters Says Terrace Costs Can Be Cut," *CT*, September 12, 1961; editorial, "Mayor Shrugs Off Terrace Facts in Shocking Manner," *CT*, September 12, 1961; Marcus, "Terrace Referendum Test Thursday," *CT*, September 13, 1961.

17. "Mansfield Opposes Community Center in Terrace Auditorium," *WSJ*, March 27, 1961; "School Board Swaps Ideas," *WSJ*, July 16, 1961; Falk, "Re-Evaluation of Board of Education Long Range Community Center Program," August 10, 1961; editorial, "New Pieces in the Terrace Jigsaw," *WSJ*, July 21, 1961; Samuel C. Reynolds, "Education Board Views Alter City Planning," *WSJ*, September 24, 1961.

18. Riemerman, "Veto Threat Halts Terrace Vote Plan," *WSJ*, September 15, 1961; Marcus, "Mayor Bars Terrace Poll," *CT*, September 15, 1961; editorial, "Veto Threat by Reynolds Shows Terrace Foes' Fears," *CT*, September 15, 1961; Riemerman, "Extra Cost Listed for Terrace's Site," *WSJ*, September 21, 1961.

19. Gordon, "Auditorium Unit Asks Referendum Rejection," *WSJ*, October 10, 1961; Gordon, "Terrace Referendum OKd," *WSJ*, October 11, 1961; Gordon, "Terrace 'Citizens' Will Not Provide Vote Funds," *WSJ*, October 11, 1961; Marcus, "Vote Terrace Referendum," *CT*, October 11, 1961; "Won't Volunteer Terrace Poll Fund," *CT*, October 12, 1961; Newhouse, "$5 Million Referendum Figure $3 Million Low," *WSJ*, October 15, 1961.

20. "Reynolds Vetoes Vote on Terrace Fund Hike," *WSJ*, October 22, 1961; Gordon, "Monona Terrace Shows Its Paralytic Power," *WSJ*, October 22, 1961.

21. Marcus, "Wright Pact Saved Again," *CT*, November 10, 1961; "Reynolds Renews Drive to End Wright Contract," *WSJ*, November 11, 1961; editorial, "Tide Turns in the Terrace Battle," *WSJ*, November 13, 1961.

22. "Auditorium Unit to Seek New Council," *WSJ*, October 22, 1961.

23. Marcus, "Seek Terrace Arbitration," *CT*, November 15, 1961; editorial, "A Break in the Terrace Impasse," *WSJ*, November 16, 1961; editorial, "Let's Look at the Record," *WSJ*, November 21, 1961; Gordon, "City Council to Oppose Wright Group's Demand for Arbitration," *WSJ*, November 22, 1961; Marcus, "Council Votes to Seek Court Test of Terrace Pact," *CT*, November 22, 1961.

24. BOR minutes, April 7, 1961; John Patrick Hunter, "Regents Accept Bequest to Aid Protestants Only," *CT*, April 7, 1961.

25. Editorial, "Discrimination In U.W. Bequests Sanctioned by Regents," *CT*, April 12, 1961.

26. Kim Willenson, "U.S. Must Abolish Its Racism, Southern Negro Leader Asserts," *WSJ*, May 11, 1961.

27. BOR minutes, September 15, 1961; "Regents Told UW Can't Terminate Race-Faith Trusts," *CT*, September 15, 1961; "Regents Will Discuss Question of Bequests," *WSJ*, September 16, 1961.

28. BOR minutes, October 20, 1961; "Regents Stiffen Stand on 'Restrictive' Gifts," *WSJ*, October 21, 1961; "U.W. Moves to Stop Prejudicial Grants," *CT*, October 21, 1961; BOR minutes, November 17, 1961; "Phi Delts Out; Regents Hear Rights Policy," *DC*, November 18, 1961.

29. Faculty Document no. 1497, 1960–1961 Annual Report of the Committee on Human Rights.

30. "Rally at Union Will Mark Integration Anniversary," *WSJ*, May 16, 1961; Fred Todd, "Integration Rally Hears Call for Student Support," *DC*, May 18, 1961; Marshall Brickman email, May 26, 2017.

31. Rich Wilson, "Another Rally and March Planned Today by Council," *DC*, June 22, 1961; editorial, "Ineffectual," *DC*, June 22, 1961; Rich Wilson and Cecil Conrad, "Freedom Rides Supported at Rally, March Thursday," *DC*, June 23, 1961; "Student March Here Protests Rider's Jailing," *WSJ*, June 24, 1961; CORE, "The Freedom Rides," http://www.core-online.org/History/freedom%20rides.htm.

32. "'Freedom Rider' to Speak to Council," *DC*, September 13, 1961; "Freedom Rider Describes Journey," *DC*, September 14, 1961; Paul Breines, "The Mosse Milieu," in Buhle, ed., *History and the New Left*, 246–251; Paul Breines email, November 29, 2017.

33. Civil Rights Digital Library. http://crdl.usg.edu/export/html/mus/sovcomph/crdl_mus_sovcomph_2-55-6-69-1-1-1.html.

34. "Council Fights 'Bias' Eviction," *DC*, September 12, 1961; Gordon, "City Rights Unit Finds Race Bias against U.W. Instructor," *WSJ*, September 15, 1961.

35. Hunter, "Majority at Hearing Support Rights Law without Penalty," *CT*, March 4, 1952; "Rights Group Prepares to Help on Relocation," *WSJ*, July 26, 1961; Ruth Doyle, "A Conversation with John McGrath," *Historic Madison: A Journal of the Four Lakes Region* 93 (2003): 23.

36. Bruce Thorp, "Sigma Chi Extension Voted," *DC*, March 8, 1960; Hunter, "Sigma Chi Gets Year's Extension," *CT*, March 8, 1960; "Sigma Chi Reveals Secret Document," *DC*, March 9, 1960; "Sigma Chi Clause Extension Meets NAACP Disapproval," *DC*, February 23, 1960; U.W. (Madison) Faculty Document 1497, "1960-61 Annual Report of the Committee on Human Rights, October 2, 1961.

37. Bob Karlman, "'U' Bias Film Stirs Dispute," *DC*, March 20, 1962.

38. Patricia Lange, "Farmer Speaks, Cites CORE Gift as Largest," *DC*, October 17, 1961.

39. Karl Gutknecht, "Phi Delts Face Suspension; Case before SLIC Thursday," *DC*, September 19, 1961; "SLIC Asks Year's Extension in Phi Delt Clause Question," *DC*, September 20, 1961; Tom Peterson, "Fraternities Back Phi Delt Request," *DC*, September 23, 1961; "Faculty Delays Phi Delt Vote," *DC*, October 3, 1961; "SLIC Reaffirms Report Asking Phi Delt Extension," *DC*, October 25, 1961.

40. Editorial, "New Field," *DC*, November 4, 1961; Gutknecht, "Phi Delta Theta Banned," *DC*, November 7, 1961; editorial, "Faltering," *DC*, November 7, 1961.

41. Gordon, "MHA Endorses 150 Units at Triangle," *WSJ*, January 24, 1961.

42. Harold E. Entwistle, "MHA Housing Plan, City Manager Defeated," *CT*, November 8, 1950; Williams, "Contrasts in Truax Housing," *WSJ*, January 8, 1961.

43. Williams, "Will Redevelopments Create New Problems?" *WSJ*, January 29, 1961.

44. Williams, "Brittingham Plan Given Approval," *WSJ*, January 27, 1961.

45. Williams, "Triangle 'Delay' Draws Fire," *WSJ*, February 3, 1961.

46. MRA Minutes, February 2, 1961; "Brittingham Site Put on Sale," *WSJ*, February 4, 1961.

47. "Rohr Tries to Bar Sale of Church to Negro Group," *CT*, April 12, 1961; "Negro Parish to Buy Church on South Side," *WSJ*, April 13, 1961.

48. "Group Demands Ald. Rohr Quit Post on MRA," *CT*, April 15, 1961; "NAACP Asks Renewal Unit to Remove Rohr," *WSJ*, April 26, 1961; "Reynolds Tells NAACP 'to Turn the Other Cheek,'" *CT*, April 27, 1961; "Mayor Rejects Unitarian Plea to Oust Rohr," *WSJ*, June 10, 1961.

49. "Firm's Plans for Redevelopment Residences," *CT*, April 7, 1960; MRA minutes, May 4, 1961; Gordon, "Renewal Site Bids of $162,000 OKd," *WSJ*, May 5, 1961.

50. "Need on Housing Spurs Hot Debate," *WSJ*, May 9, 1961; Marcus, "Units Clash Over Sites for Housing," *CT*, May 9, 1961.

51. "Public Housing Door Is Left Open," *WSJ*, May 12, 1961; "Renewal Projects Face Contest," *WSJ*, May 13, 1961.

52. Gordon, "Public Housing Asked for Brittingham Area," *WSJ*, May 16, 1961; Gordon, "Public Housing Pleas Rejected," *WSJ*, May 24, 1961; Hoffman, "Public Housing in Brittingham Area Defeated," *CT*, May 24, 1961.

53. Editorial, "Is Housing Problem to Be Settled by Real Estate People?" *CT*, May 24, 1961.

54. "MHA Drops Aberg Ave. Public Housing Plans," *WSJ*, December 1, 1961; "Plan Group Approves 3 Public Housing Sites," *WSJ*, December 12, 1961.

55. Gordon, "Agreement Made on Public Housing," *WSJ,* May 26, 1961; Hoffman, "City Announces 'Compromise' on Public Housing," *CT,* May 26, 1961; "'Triangle' People Get Housing Aid," *WSJ,* May 29, 1961.

56. Editorial, "Get the Facts on Resettlement," *WSJ,* May 25, 1961.

57. MRA minutes, September 27, 1961; "Renewal Apartment Plan OK'd," *CT,* September 28, 1961.

58. "Public Housing Plans Win Council's Backing, 17 to 2," *CT,* July 26, 1961."

59. "65 Families Out at Truax," *WSJ,* May 30, 1961; "Triangle Funds Plea Wins Preliminary OK," *WSJ,* June 27, 1961.

60. "MHA Rejects Plea for Truax Airmen," *WSJ,* June 5, 1961.

61. "Triangle Funds Plea Wins Preliminary OK," *WSJ,* June 27, 1961; "Group Asks for Restudy on Triangle," *WSJ,* July 21, 1961.

62. MRA Minutes, August 17, 1961; Gordon, "Triangle Project's Plans OK'd, Despite Opposition from MGE," *WSJ,* August 23, 1961; Marcus, "Triangle Project Nears Final OK," *CT,* August 23, 1961; "Meter Cab Rate Boost Asked in Council Plea," *WSJ,* August 24, 1961; "Triangle Plan Gets Final OK," *CT,* August 25, 1961.

63. MRA Minutes, September 14, 1961; "Apartments at Brittingham to be Named Sampson Plaza," September 15, 1961; "Renewal Apartment Plan OK'd," *CT,* September 29, 1961.

64. Richard Bradee, "Ask Realtors to Shun Artificial Negro Barriers," *CT,* September 22, 1961.

65. MRA minutes, November 9, 1961; Stanley Shivers to MRA, November 30, 1961; George Vukelich, "We Were Called Darkies," *Isthmus,* March 9, 1984, 22.

66. MRA minutes, November 9, 1961.

67. "Redevelopment Authority Takes on Relocation Job," *WSJ,* October 15, 1961; "Field Office Set to Aid Triangle Renewal Project," *WSJ,* December 2, 1961.

68. MRA minutes, December 14, 1961; "OK Final Plan for New Links," *CT,* December 16, 1961; MHA minutes, December 21, 1961; "Levin to Accept City Position with New Housing-Renewal Unit," *WSJ,* December 23, 1961; MRA minutes, December 27, 1961.

69. "Rent Ultimatum to Trotter Tavern," *CT,* February 1, 1961; "'Harassment' Charged in City's Rental Action against Trotter," *WSJ,* February 7, 1961.

70. "Trotter Finds Site on Beld St. for Relocation of His Tavern," *CT,* March 23, 1961; Hoffman, "Reynolds Promises to Veto Zoning for Trotter's Bar," *CT,* April 24, 1961; Gordon, "Rezoning for Trotter Tavern Move Refused," *WSJ,* April 25, 1961.

71. Hoffman, "Transfer of Licari Bar Gets Final OK," *CT,* April 28, 1961.

72. Gordon, "Council Again Rejects Relocation for Trotter," *WSJ,* May 12, 1961.

73. "Maloney Dismisses Suit by MRA to Evict Trotter on Rent Basis," *WSJ,* May 27, 1961.

74. MRA minutes, June 1, 1961; "Pasch Named U.W. Regent," *CT,* June 2, 1961; Marcus, "MRA Decides to Seek Immediate Trotter Eviction," *CT,* June 2, 1961; "Trotters Ordered Evicted from Project Site Aug. 1," *CT,* June 9, 1961.

75. "Trotter Submits 3rd Request for New Tavern Site," *CT,* June 20, 1961; "Rohr Says He Will Not Oppose Trotter Tavern on Beld St. Site," *CT,* July 8, 1961.

76. "Trotter Tavern's Beld St. Transfer Voted by Council," *CT,* July 12, 1961.

77. Willenson, "Spectators 'Explode' at Trotters' Transfer," *WSJ,* July 14, 1961; "Trotter Transfer Stirs Council Uproar," *CT,* July 14, 1961.

78. "Trotter Tavern Transfer Signed," *WSJ,* July 21, 1961; "Wilkie Denies Trotter's Move to Avoid Eviction," *WSJ,* July 29, 1961.

79. "MRA Agreement to Let Trotter Stay Till Dec. 1," *WSJ,* August 1, 1961.

80. "Trotter Given Building Permit for New Tavern," *WSJ,* September 30, 1961.

81. "Mayor Still Has No Official Word on U.S. Position," *WSJ,* January 13, 1961.

82. "Nestingen Puts His Nomination Papers into Circulation," *CT,* January 13, 1961.

83. Williams, "Nestingen Named as Top Cabinet Aide," *WSJ,* January 27, 1961.

84. "Know Your Madisonian—Robert Nuckles," *WSJ,* November 27, 1960; "Federal Post to Nestingen," *CT,* January 13, 1961; Williams, "Reynolds Makes Race for Mayor," *WSJ,* January 28, 1961; Williams, "Hanson Elected Interim Mayor on Unanimous Vote of Council," *WSJ,* February 4, 1961; "Bus Fare Boost Recalls Reynolds' Role on Board," *CT,* March 22, 1961; "Campaign for Mayor Sharpest in Long Time," *WSJ,* April 2, 1961.

85. Hoffman, "Reynolds Says He Won't Campaign on Anti-Center Plank," *CT,* January 28, 1961; "Reynolds Stresses Four Issues as He Announces His Platform," *WSJ,* February 5, 1961; "Reynolds 'Quits' Foes of Terrace," *CT,* February 8, 1961; "Reynolds Urges Fast Go-Ahead on Monona Bay Causeway Work," *WSJ,* March 15, 1961; "Nuckles Charges Reynolds Is Playing Politics with Causeway," *CT,* March 15, 1961; "Reynolds Hits Nuckles, Times, for Bypassing Mayor, Council," *WSJ,* March 25, 1961; Gordon, "Annex Policy, Tavern Site Stir New Debate," *WSJ,* March 28, 1961; "Nuckles and Reynolds Give Views on Campaign," *CT,* April 1, 1961; "Mayor Candidates List Their Goals," *WSJ,* April 2, 1961.

86. "Does Reynolds Live in City? Westport 'Cottage' Is Cited," *CT,* February 1, 1961; "Young Adults for Reynolds Committee," *WSJ,* March 28, 1961; https://www.reynoldstransfer.com/; "Reynolds Costs Top Nuckles' by $1,929," *WSJ,* April 12, 1961.

87. Gordon, "City Elects Reynolds by 2,600-Vote Edge," *WSJ,* April 5, 1961; Marcus, "Stay-Homes Elect Reynolds," *CT,* April 5,

1961; "Nuckles Takes Engineer Post with Oscar Mayer Co.," *CT*, May 9, 1961.

88. Editorial, "Madison Picks Henry Reynolds," *WSJ*, April 5, 1961; editorial, "Madison Looks Backward—Backward to Cowbarn," *CT*, April 5, 1961.

89. "Reynolds Sworn, Sets Eight Goals," *CT*, April 18, 1961; "Reynolds Leaves Bus Firm Board," *CT*, April 20, 1961.

90. "Mayor-Elect Reynolds Will Skip Naming an Assistant for While," *WSJ*, April 11, 1961; Marcus, "Name Mrs. Brown Council President," *CT*, April 18, 1961; "Foes of Terrace Are Appointed to Auditorium Group," *CT*, April 18, 1961; "Reynolds Withdraws 3 of His Choices as Opposition Rises," *WSJ*, April 19, 1961.

91. "Reynolds Vetoes Council Move to Hike Own Pay," *CT*, June 29, 1961.

92. Riemerman, "Council Rejects Conrad for City Attorney," *WSJ*, July 28, 1961.

93. Marcus, "Reynolds Rebuffed Again on Conrad's Nomination," *CT*, August 25, 1961; "Heassler Gets Council's Approval as City Attorney," *CT*, September 15, 1961; "Conrad to Start Next Week as Assistant City Attorney," *CT*, October 21, 1961.

94. Hoffman, "Liquor-Bowling Plan Is Defeated," *CT*, January 11, 1961.

95. "City Backs Bond Issue for Library," *WSJ*, April 5, 1961; Williams, "Three Aldermen Lose Seats on City Council," *WSJ*, April 5, 1961.

96. "Mrs. Harry Hamilton Named 'Citizen of Year' by Guild," *CT*, April 8, 1961.

97. Marcus, "Name Mrs. Brown Council President," *CT*, April 18, 1961.

98. Frank Custer, "David Lease, 12, Hawthorne School, Is Mibs Champ," *CT*, May 6, 1961.

99. "Shelter Builders Told Madison Is Nuclear Target Ringed by Others," *WSJ*, September 1, 1961; "Building Permits Needed for City Fallout Shelters," *WSJ*, September 27, 1961; David Bednarek, "5,000 Families Have A-Shelters," *WSJ*, October 2, 1961; "Profs Attack Shelter Plan as 'Tragic,'" *DC*, December 14, 1961.

100. Custer, "Sam Liberace Is Quietly Proud of Success of Son 'Walter,'" *CT*, September 28, 1961; Custer, "Liberace Plays Good, Solid Piano," *CT*, September 28, 1961.

101. "City, Area Troops Depart," *CT*, October 24, 1961; James D. Selk, "Hurry Back!" *WSJ*, October 25, 1961; Hunter, "Madison Area Soldiers Reach Dakotas," *CT*, October 25, 1961.

102. "Capitol Park Nativity Scene to Stress Meaning of Season," *WSJ*, November 29, 1961.

103. Bednarek, "More VD Cases Reported in City," *WSJ*, October 26, 1961; Newhouse, "Madison Hospital Use Lags; Lacks Facilities," *WSJ*, October 28, 1961.

104. Bednarek, "City Movie Ad Policy Wins City Praise," *WSJ*, October 30, 1961.

105. Irvin H. Kreisman, "Madison Swastikas Bring Grim

Reminder to Horror Survivor," *CT*, November 1, 1961; Sidney Iwanter Facebook exchange, December 1, 2017.

106. "Motorists Warned: Spraying for Dutch Elm Disease Slated," *WSJ*, November 7, 1961.

107. Robert G. Trautman, "6-Hour Blaze on State St.," *CT*, December 13, 1961; Newhouse, "$500,000 Blaze Wrecks Huge Section on State St.," *WSJ*, December 14, 1961; "Students Routed in Blaze," *DC*, December 14, 1961; "Parking Facilities Eyed at State St. Fire Scene," *WSJ*, December 15, 1961.

108. Hunter, "Guard Freedom, U.W. Grads Told," *CT*, June 5, 1961.

109. "State Record Set by Student Total," *CT*, October 17, 1961.

110. Advertisement, *DC*, October 27, 1961.

111. "Lowell Hall, $2½ Million Co-ed Dorm, Opens," *CT*, June 17, 1961.

112. Madison City Directory 1962 (St. Paul, MN: Wright Directory Co., 1962).

113. Anthony Scaduto, *Bob Dylan: An Intimate Biography* (New York: Grosset & Dunlap, 1971), 49–51; Nadine Goff, "Ginsberg's Death Brings Back Memories of Madison's Pad," *WSJ*, April 13, 1997; Ronald Radosh, *Commies: A Journey through the Old Left, the New Left and the Leftover Left* (San Francisco: Encounter Books, 2001), 76–78; Clinton Heylin, *Bob Dylan: Behind the Shades Revisited* (New York: William Morrow/HarperCollins, 2001), 54–59; David Hadju, *Positively 4th Street: The Lives and Times of Joan Baez, Bob Dylan, Mimi Baez Farina, and Richard Farina* (New York: North Point Press, 2001), 71; Lawrence J. Epstein, *Political Folk Music in America from Its Origins to Bob Dylan* (Jefferson, NC: McFarland & Co., 2010), 145–147; Dean Robbins, "Dylan Slept Here," *Wisconsin Life*, February 27, 2013, https://www.wisconsinlife.org/story/dylan-slept-here; Ann Lauterbach email, April 14, 2017, and January 4, 2018; Jennifer Warren email, April 26, 2017, and January 5, 2018; Paul Breines email, April 20, 2017, May 26, 2017, and January 4, 2018; Ron Radosh email, May 25–26, 2017, and January 4, 2018; Radosh and Marshall Brickman email, May 26–27, 2017; Marshall Brickman email, January 4, 2018; and Fred Ciporen email, January 4, 2018.

114. "Symposium Tickets Ready Next Thursday," *DC*, January 25, 1961.

115. Hunter, "Miss De Mille Hits at State Unions," *CT*, February 16, 1961.

116. Marilyn Shapiro, "New Yorker, Typical Out-of-State Stereotype Seen as Sophisticated, Intellectual, In-Bred," *DC*, March 2, 1961.

117. "Von Braun 'U' Speech Cancelled; Forced by Russian Success," *DC*, April 18, 1961.

118. Shapiro, "Right, Left Debate Cuba As Garvey Quells Chaos," *DC*, April 22, 1961; Reynolds, "Castro Rally at U.W. Backfires," *WSJ*, April 22, 1961; "Pro-Castro Rally Turns Into

Loud Anti-Fidel Demonstration," *CT*, April 22, 1961; Peterson, "SLIC Keeps Rally Policy; Phi Kappa Action Off," *DC*, December 6, 1961; Ron Radosh email, May 30, 2017; LeRoy Luberg, interviewed by Donna Hartshorne, 1975, OH #0066, digital audio file, University Archives and Records Management Services, Madison, Wisconsin.

119. Todd, "Lerner 'U' Lecture Gets Legion Protest," *DC*, May 2. 1961.

120. "Miss Thielman, Travanti Lead in 'Cat' Production," *DC*, January 9, 1961; "Academic Honors For 'Cat' Lead," *CT*, March 18, 1961; Kurt Brokaw, "'Cat on a Hot Tin Roof' is 'Magnificent Theater' – Critic," *DC*, March 22, 1961; Alexius Baas, "'Cat On A Hot Tin Roof' Well Performed By Players," *CT*, March 22, 1961; https://www.wisconsinhistory.org/Records/Article/CS2673.

121. "Pat Richter Outstanding Athlete In First Annual Cardinal Poll," *DC*, May 23, 1961; "VanderKelen Lost to Badger Football Team," *WSJ*, June 22, 1961; "Jim Bakken Ties Field Goal Recod," *DC*, October 13, 1961; John Bubolz, "Richter Wins S-I Magazine Lineman Award," *DC*, November 15, 1961; "Richter Named UPI All-American," *WSJ*, December 7, 1961; "Richter Voted on AP Second All-America," *CT*, December 8, 1961.

122. "Pasch Named U.W. Regent," *CT*, June 2, 1961; "Atty. Pasch Named U.W. Regent," *WSJ*, June 3, 1961; William C. Robbins, "Hill Farms Plan, Hilldale Cited in Praise for Regent Rennebohm," *WSJ*, June 3, 1961; Llewellyn G. Roberts, "Democrats Win Surprise Fight," *WSJ*, June 9, 1961.

123. Hunter, "Guard Freedom, U.W. Grads Told," *CT*, June 5, 1961.

124. Tom Olson, "Problem of Disarmament Discussed by Kissinger," *DC*, July 19, 1961.

125. Willenson, "Wisconsin Man to Head NSA; Liberals, Moderates Elected," *WSJ*, August 31, 1961; "Garvey Picked NSA President, Vows 'Change, Not Destruction,'" *DC*, September 12, 1961.

126. Ron Leys, "Students Organize Local ADA Chapter," *DC*, September 15, 1961.

127. "Fraternities Pledge 330 in Fall Rush," *DC*, September 26, 1961.

128. Michael Comer, "Wisconsin Swings Peterson 'Brilliant,'" *DC*, October 7, 1961.

129. Hunter, "Robert Frost Is Given Ovation at Union Recital of His Poems," *CT*, October 17, 1961.

130. Sandra Wojcik, "Dyke Sees Walker Censure Result of Power Change," *DC*, November 1, 1961; Eric Pace, "Gen. Edwin Walker, 83, Is Dead; Promoted Rightist Causes in 60's," *New York Times*, November 2, 1993.

131. Editorial, "Whose Fault?" *DC*, October 3, 1961; A. Lee Beier, "2,000 Welcome Badger 'Heroes,'" *WSJ*, November 26, 1961.

132. Bednarek, "2,000 Youths Storm U.W. Co-Ed Dorms," *WSJ*, October 9, 1961; "Dismiss Charges Against 2 in Riot," *CT*,

October 9, 1961; "Judge Drops Charges against 2 in Riots," *WSJ*, October 10, 1961; "'Riot' Students Face Stern Action," *WSJ*, October 10, 1961; Colin McCamy, "'Riot' Gets Over-Blown Press," *DC*, October 10, 1961; "Rioters to Appear Before Conduct Committee—Luberg," *DC*, October 11, 1961; John Kellogg, "Girl Claims Role in 'Riot,'" *DC*, October 12, 1961; "5 Students Disciplined For 'Riot' Involvement," *DC*, October 25, 1961.

133. Feldman, *Buildings*, 314, 318, 322; Kathleen McGinley, "Students Like Low Rent; Owners Fear Profit Loss," *DC*, January 12, 1961; "See Progress on $14 Million in U. Buildings in 1961," *WSJ*, January 17, 1961.

134. "Dormitory Plan Approved," *WSJ*, February 7, 1961; BOR minutes, February 11, 1961; "New Dorm Land Purchase, Loans Ordered," *WSJ*, February 12, 1961; BOR minutes, September 18, 1961; "Complete Purchase of Land for New Dormitory Units," *CT*, September 16, 1961.

135. BOR minutes, May 12, 1961; "Dormitory Space Assured for State Students at U.W.," *WSJ*, February 28, 1961; Feldman, *Buildings*, 363.

136. BOR minutes, May 12, 1961; "U.W. Urges Big Urban Plan," *CT*, May 12, 1961; "Regents Approve Joint UW-City Renewal Plan," *WSJ*, May 13, 1961; "Regents Invite City of Madison to Join in Renewal Program," *DC*, May 13, 1961; "U. Renewal Plan Given Backing," *CT*, July 28, 1961.

137. "Teamster Fund Is Helping Finance Langdon St. Dorm," *CT*, April 8, 1960; "U.W. Asks Rooms for Men Students," *WSJ*, September 6, 1961; Lynne Abraham, "Lowell Hall, Luxury Dorm, Has Pool, Air Conditioning," *DC*, November 19, 1960.

138. BOR minutes, December 8, 1961; "Approve Union, Center Expansion, Alumni House," *CT*, December 8, 1961; Abraham, "Dream Campus Planned," *DC*, December 9, 1961; "A Symbol of the University," *Wisconsin Alumnus* 63, no. 9 (January 1962): 10–12.

139. Marcia Crowley, "West Graduates Face Major Issues Proudly," Reynolds, "Do Your Own Thinking, East Seniors Urged," Alan Cleveland, "Central's Class Hears of Future Challenges," all *WSJ*, June 17, 1961.

140. "City School Enrollments at 24,337," *CT*, September 16, 1961.

141. "4,500 Enrolled in Parochial Schools," *CT*, September 7, 1961.

142. "City School Pupils to Find Building Changes This Fall," *WSJ*, August 12, 1961; Reynolds, "Madison Schools Plan New Looks for the Fall," *WSJ*, August 13, 1961.

143. "School Census Report Is Guide to Future," *WSJ*, August 13, 1961.

144. Reynolds, "Allis, Glendale Schools Join City; List Problems," *WSJ*, July 3, 1961; Gordon, "School Annexings Add $1.5 Million to City Debt," *WSJ*, September 22, 1961.

145. Falk, "City's School Board Will Face Teaching, Classroom

Problems," *CT*, January 18, 1961; Reynolds, "$9.5 Million School Bond Vote Planned," *WSJ*, May 16, 1961.

146. "City School Officials Ask Civil Defense Directions," *WSJ*, October 17, 1961.

147. "Seniors at Wis. High Balk at DAR Contest," *CT*, January 28, 1961.

148. Reynolds, "West, East Students Force Police to Act," *WSJ*, March 31, 1961.

149. Reynolds, "Madison Pupils Ranked Above National Norm," *WSJ*, May 14, 1961.

150. John Shivers, "The Natural," *Isthmus*, June 29–July 5, 1990, 1; "We Celebrate Roots," *Umoja*, April 1992; Judy Martin Facebook message, September 10, 2017.

151. "City School Officials Ask Civil Defense Directions," *WSJ*, October 17, 1961.

152. Reynolds, "First Plans for New High School in 22nd Ward Approved by Board," *WSJ*, November 7, 1961.

153. "Midsummer Night Here Is No Dream," *WSJ*, August 13, 1961; "We Lack Manpower to Correct Loitering Abuses, Chief Claims," *WSJ*, August 14, 1961; editorial, "Restore Night Order Downtown," *WSJ*, August 14, 1961; "Of 178 City Policemen, 32 Kept on Duties Inside Headquarters," *WSJ*, August 15, 1961; "Mayor Gives Chief Go-Ahead on Plan to Stop Hoodlumism," *WSJ*, August 18, 1961; "Police Help Quiet State Street, Square," *WSJ*, August 20, 1961.

154. Sanford Moss, "Halloween Tricks Keep Police Busy," *WSJ*, November 1, 1961; "Police Defend Clamp on Youths," *WSJ*, November 3, 1961.

155. "New Try for Beer, Liquor Permits Due," *CT*, November 10, 1961.

156. Trautman, "2 Officers Cover for Dem Solons in Beer-Can Case," *CT*, November 8, 1961; "Police Refuse to Release Text of Beer Can Reports," *CT*, November 16, 1961.

157. Selk, "2 Slaying Suspects Fail in Try for Jailbreak Here," *WSJ*, December 27, 1961; "Jailer Relates Fight with Pair," *WSJ*, December 27, 1961.

158. "Dimensions and Dividends," *City of Madison Planning Department*, March 1965.

159. Madison Department of Planning, Community Development and Economic Development.

160. James Scotton, "Low Unemployment Rate Here in Contrast with Other Cities," *WSJ*, March 12, 1961; "Owner-Occupied Housing Up Here," *WSJ*, July 15, 1961; "Employment Here on a Par with 1960's Figures," *CT*, December 21, 1961; Levitan, *Sesquicentennial History*, 230; Marcus, "City's Valuation Up $29 Million Above '60 Level," *CT*, November 1, 1961; "Assessment Cuts Voted for Buildings on Square," *WSJ*, May 8, 1961.

161. Kreisman, "$3.5 Million, Eight-Story Building for Park Hotel Site," *CT*, April 12, 1961; "Work on Park Motor Hotel Starts Sept. 1," *WSJ*, August 1, 1961.

162. Gordon, "Commission Names City Park for Supt. Marshall," *WSJ*, January 5, 1961.

163. "Two Frautschi Sons Named New Democrat Co. Officers," *WSJ*, January 7, 1961.

164. "Mohs Purchases Kennedy Manor," *WSJ*, March 3, 1961.

165. Kreisman, "New Park Hotel's Details Are Told," *CT*, May 9, 1961; Roberts, "Park Motor Hotel Planned," *WSJ*, May 10, 1961.

166. "Findorff Firm Buys Vilas Land," *CT*, May 26, 1961.

167. Willenson, "Agreement Ends Electric Strike," *WSJ*, June 28, 1961.

168. Marcus, "148-Unit Project for Apartments Given Approval," *CT*, November 21, 1961.

169. Reynolds, "City Picked for First U.S. Open Space Grant," *WSJ*, December 13, 1961.

170. Newhouse, "Happy Throng Takes I-Road," *WSJ*, October 7, 1961.

171. "Vilas Traffic Reversal Sought," *WSJ*, June 8, 1961; "Traffic Flow in Vilas Park Is Reversed," *CT*, June 9, 1961; "You Drive 'the Other Way' in Vilas Park Now," *WSJ*, June 10, 1961.

172. "4 Beltline Crossings to Get Traffic Lights," *WSJ*, February 7, 1961; "Traffic Signals Ready at Key Beltline Corners," *WSJ*, June 27, 1961.

173. "State Street Is Suffering from Congestion and Poor Esthetics," *CT*, July 15, 1961.

174. "$25 Monthly City Pay Raise Asked," *WSJ*, September 15, 1961.

175. Willenson, "Monona Causeway Urgent," *WSJ*, March 26, 1961; Marcus, "See City Reaching a Population of 170,000 by 1968," *CT*, April 19, 1961; editorial, "Now Mayor Reynolds Says Trucker Reynolds Isn't Interested," *CT*, October 26, 1961; "Monroe St. Library Unit Approved," *CT*, October 11, 1961; Marcus, "Midvale Truck Route Approved by Council, 14-6," *CT*, October 27, 1961; "Mayor in Clash on School Law," *CT*, October 27, 1961.

176. "City Officials Vote to Install Car Seat Belts," *WSJ*, November 23, 1961.

177. "Fred Meyer Kills Himself," *CT*, May 9, 1961; June Dieckmann, "Upset, Fred Meyer Ends His Life," *WSJ*, May 10, 1961; "Consolidation of Lay, Frito Firms Planned," *WSJ*, August 11, 1961.

178. "Brokers Suspend Gill's License," *CT*, November 10, 1961; "Charles H. Gill Found Dead in Car; Despondency Blamed," *WSJ*, November 23, 1961; "Charles H. Gill Is Suicide; Business Tangles Blamed," *CT*, November 23, 1961.

179. "Harry L. French, 74, Dies; Civic and Business Leader," *CT*, February 2, 1961; John W. Jenkins and Eric D. Olmanson, *A Centennial History of the Rotary Club of Madison 1913–2013* (Madison, WI: Rotary Club of Madison, 2014), 163–165.

180. "Know Your Madisonian—William E. Walker," *WSJ*, April 10, 1960; "William E. Walker 64, President of WISM, Dies," *CT*, September 15, 1961.

181. Dieckmann, "Mike Malloy, Coroner, Dies," *WSJ*, November 29, 1961; Reynolds, "Michael Malloy, Before Death, OKd Sale of Land to School Forest," *WSJ*, December 4, 1961.

182. "Melvin Diemer, Pioneer Photographer, Dies at 74," *CT*, November 30, 1961.

1962

1. Robert Meloon, "Terrace Suit Shocks Judge," *CT*, January 15, 1962; editorial, "Judge Bardwell Expresses the Sentiments of the Community," *CT*, January 15, 1962.

2. "Group Will Seek Referendum on Terminating Terrace Plans," *WSJ*, January 30, 1962; "Terrace Foes Ask April 3 Vote on Cancelling Project," *CT*, January 30, 1962.

3. Herbert Marcus, "Referendum on Terrace Plans Has Council Majority," *CT*, February 7, 1962.

4. Bob Jacobson, "Philadelphia Orchestra Offers Magnificent Finale to Season," *DC*, May 11, 1962; Alexius Baas, "Over 3,000 Hear a Notable Concert," *CT*, May 11, 1962; Feldman, Jim, *The Buildings of the University of Wisconsin* (Madison, WI: University Archives, 1997), 115–116; Karen Johnson Kretchmann Facebook comment, January 2, 2018.

5. David Gordon, "3 Terrace Ballot Proposals Given," *WSJ*, February 9, 1962; Marcus, "Receive Proposals for Referendum on Terrace Plan," *CT*, February 9, 1962; Gordon, "Wording on Terrace Ballot to Be Argued," *WSJ*, February 20, 1962; editorial, "Let the Council Majority Explain," *WSJ*, February 20, 1962; Gordon, "Terrace Supporters' Ballot Plan Favored," *WSJ*, February 21, 1962; "Council Approves Terrace Vote Plan; Veto Almost Sure," *CT*, February 21, 1962.

6. "New Go-Around Slated Tonight on Auditorium," *WSJ*, February 22, 1962; editorial, "A Shortage of Honest Men," *WSJ*, February 22, 1962; "Terrace Referendum Test Tonight," *CT*, February 22, 1962.

7. Gordon, "Terrace Foes Win Vote Test," *WSJ*, February 23, 1962; Marcus, "Bow to Mayor on Terrace," *CT*, February 23, 1962; editorial, "Obstructionists Ask Madison to Buy Pig-in-the-Poke," *CT*, February 23, 1962; editorial, "Better, But Still No Price Tag," *WSJ*, February 27, 1962; "Sox Pro-Terrace Aldermen Explain Referendum Vote," *CT*, March 3, 1962.

8. John Newhouse, "Terrace Backers Cover Failures," *WSJ*, March 4, 1962; "Terrace Bond Proposal Faces a Speedy Defeat," *WSJ*, March 6, 1962; William Riemerman, "Proposal for Terrace Bond Issue Shelved," *WSJ*, March 7, 1962; Marcus, "Terrace Bond Vote Proposal Killed," *CT*, March 7, 1962.

9. Gordon, "Voters Kill Terrace Plan," *WSJ*, April 4, 1962; John T. Aehl, "3 Pro-Terrace Aldermen Lose," *WSJ*, April 4, 1962; "Terrace Defeated by 2,687," *CT*, April 4, 1962; "Three Aldermen Are Unseated," *CT*, April 4, 1962.

10. Editorial, "Madison Is Still in the Cow Barn Era after 50 Years of Effort," *CT*, April 10, 1962.

11. Gordon, "Auditorium Unit Meeting Set," *WSJ*, April 5, 1962; Gordon, "Unit Asks City Council to End Wright Contract," *WSJ*, April 7, 1962; Marcus, "City Moves to End Terrace Contract," *CT*, April 7, 1962; "Wright Attorneys Ask Arbitration in Fees Dispute," *CT*, April 9,1962.

12. "Conrad Will Be Named Acting City Attorney," *WSJ*, April 3, 1962; "No Action Taken on Terrace Pact," *CT*, April 10, 1962; Gordon, "Action on Wright Contract Put Off," *WSJ*, April 11, 1962; Gordon, "Full Study Set on Wright Pact," *WSJ*, April 13, 1962; Marcus, "Postpone Terrace Contract Action," *CT*, April 13, 1962; "City Challenges Wright Group," *WSJ*, April 17, 1962.

13. "'Stacks' Auditorium Group," *CT*, April 17, 1962; Gordon, "Last Terrace Backer Out," *WSJ*, April 18, 1962; Marcus, "'Packing' of Auditorium Unit Is Shock," *CT*, April 18, 1962.

14. Editorial, "A Dictator Takes Over in Madison's City Hall," *CT*, April 18, 1962.

15. Gordon, "20-1 Vote Ends Wright Pact," *WSJ*, May 9, 1962; Marcus, "Vote Terrace Contract Break," *CT*, May 9, 1962; Aehl, "City Council Officially Ends Wright Contract," *WSJ*, May 11, 1962; "City Council Votes 16-3 to Break Wright Contract," *CT*, May 11, 1962.

16. "Ask Segoe for Advice on Downtown," *WSJ*, July 6, 1960; Marcus, "Mayor Wants Consultant to Help Pick Auditorium Site," *CT*, May 14, 1962; Gordon, "Auditorium Aid Asked," *WSJ*, May 17, 1962; Marcus, "Auditorium Unit Decides to Ask Segoe's Advice," *CT*, May 17, 1962; Gordon, "Auditorium Unit Plans Segoe Visit," *WSJ*, May 26, 1962; Marcus, "Auditorium Unit Approves Hiring Segoe, Consultants," *CT*, May 26, 1962.

17. "Segoe Sends Aide to City Meeting," *CT*, May 31, 1962; "Wright's Plans Become Primer," *WSJ*, June 2, 1962; Marcus, "Spell Out Auditorium Functions: Segoe Aide," *CT*, June 6, 1962.

18. Aehl, "Multiple Uses Urged for Auditorium Here," *WSJ*, June 8, 1962; Marcus, "Two Auditorium Experts Support Multi-Use Facility," *CT*, June 8, 1962; "Segoe, Chief Aide Will Discuss Auditorium Plans with Officials," *WSJ*, July 3, 1962; Marcus, "Propose Arena Auditorium," *CT*, July 5, 1962.

19. Gordon, "Segoe Suggests Downtown Site," *WSJ*, July 6, 1962.

20. Aehl, "Segoe's Pick: Conklin Area," *WSJ*, August 3, 1962; "Conklin Area Best: Segoe," *CT*, August 3, 1962.

21. "With One Reservation, Mayor's Satisfied with Segoe Choice," *WSJ*, August 4, 1962; Marcus, "Segoe's Site Cost Gives Pause to Auditorium Unit," *CT*, August 9, 1962; editorial, "Progress on an Auditorium Site," *WSJ*, August 13, 1962.

22. Michael Kirkhorn, "Comparison of Terrace Plan, Segoe Site Urged by Potter," *CT*, August 18, 1962; Aehl, "Free Choice on Auditorium Site Is Set," *WSJ*, August 22, 1962; "Auditorium Committee Backs Some Site in Conklin Park Area," *CT*, August 23,

1962; Gordon, "Auditorium Unit Favors Conklin Area," August 23, 1962; Aehl, "Auditorium Site Left in a Limbo by Council Vote," *WSJ*, September 14, 1962; Marcus, "Block Conklin Auditorium Plan," *CT*, September 14, 1962.

23. "Committee Picks Segoe Site Area," *WSJ*, October 4, 1962; Marcus, "Auditorium Unit Urges Reduced Conklin Area Site," *CT*, October 4, 1962.

24. Gordon, "Conklin Site Given Final Approval," *WSJ*, October 26, 1962; Marcus, "Council Stamps 'Tentative' OK on Site at Conklin," *CT*, October 26, 1962.

25. Marcus, "Upholds Terrace Contract," *CT*, November 15, 1962; "Arbitration of Wright Pact Is Upheld," *WSJ*, November 16, 1962; Marcus, "Council Approves Appeal of Terrace Arbitration Ruling," *CT*, November 21, 1962; Aehl, "Wright Contract Ruling Appealed," *WSJ*, November 21, 1962; "Decision of Arbitration on Wright Fee Is Appealed," *WSJ*, December 5, 1962.

26. Marcus, "Pick Shaw Auditorium Architect," *CT*, December 4, 1962; Aehl, "Auditorium Issue Delayed to Dec. 27," *WSJ*, December 14, 1962; "Court Action Halts in Wright Fee Case," *WSJ*, December 22, 1962; Marcus, "Council Tie Vote Bars Auditorium Architect Switch," *CT*, December 28, 1962.

27. "Razing Starts Triangle Project," *CT*, January 18, 1962; "MRA Purchases 11 More Parcels in Triangle Area," *WSJ*, February 6, 1962; "14 More Triangle Area Properties Sold to MRA," *WSJ*, May 2, 1962; "Condemnation Set for Triangle Area," *WSJ*, June 8, 1962; "MRA Gets 7 Options in Triangle," *WSJ*, June 18, 1962; MRA minutes, December 13, 1962.

28. MRA minutes, January 11, 1962; "Refusal to Negotiate Will Bring Condemnation Moves in Triangle," *WSJ*, January 12, 1962; "New Approach Urged for Work in Triangle," *WSJ*, March 9, 1962; "Nearly 50% in Triangle Relocated, MRA Notes," *WSJ*, September 16, 1962; MRA minutes, October 12, 1962.

29. "Urban Renewal Efforts Now at Critical Stage," *CT*, November 17, 1962; Gordon, "Triangle Negroes All But Homeless," *WSJ*, November 19, 1962.

30. "Strict Housing Code Would Make MRA's Director Happy to Retire," *WSJ*, June 8, 1962; "End to Truax Barracks Housing Urged," *WSJ*, July 19, 1962; Florence Zmudzinski, "Leaving Greenbush," *Historic Madison: A Journal of the Four Lakes Region* 20 (2005): 63, n. 26.

31. "Triangle Grant Is $2.7 Million," *CT*, January 4, 1962; Gordon, "Triangle Project Grant Approved," *WSJ*, January 5, 1962.

32. "MRA Approves Merger with MHA," *WSJ*, January 25, 1962; "MHA-MRA Merger Move May Face Snag over Salary," *CT*, February 8, 1962; MRA minutes, February 8, 1962; "Pay Issue Snags Merger of City Renewal Units," *WSJ*, February 9, 1962; "Plan Expert's Resignation Seen Killing MHA-MRA Merger Plan," *WSJ*, February 13, 1962.

33. "Trotter's Old Tavern Finally Yields to Wrecker," *WSJ*, February 8, 1962; MRA minutes, June 14, 1962.

34. MRA Minutes, March 8, 1962; "New Approach Urged for Work in Triangle," *WSJ*, March 9, 1962; "Piecemeal Plan Urged in Triangle," *CT*, March 10, 1962; editorial, "Why Destroy Usable Houses?" *WSJ*, May 23, 1962.

35. MRA Minutes, January 11, 1962; Florence Zmudzinski Oral History, 1984, Historic Madison, Inc.

36. Marcus, "Public Housing Wins Council Test," *CT*, May 9, 1962; "Public Housing Project Given Council Approval," *WSJ*, May 9, 1962; "$2,147,176 U.S. Loan for City Housing Project Ok'd," *CT*, June 8, 1962; "Site for City Housing Purchased," *CT*, October 13, 1962.

37. Harold E. Entwistle, "MHA Housing Plan, City Manager Defeated," *CT*, November 8, 1950.

38. "75 Applied for Housing Last Month, MHA Reports," *CT*, January 15, 1962; MRA minutes, June 14, 1962; "Public Housing Needed in City, MHA Director Tells Citizen Unit," *WSJ*, October 13, 1962.

39. Newhouse, "'Where Do We Go': Worried Residents of Triangle Ask," *WSJ*, April 12, 1962; MRA minutes, June 14, 1962.

40. MRA minutes, May 24, 1962; "Greater Renewal Agreements Come Up Tonight," *WSJ*, May 24, 1962; Marcus, "Council Fails to Back Pact for U.W. Area Development," *CT*, May 25, 1962; "Urban Renewal Plan for South Side," *WSJ*, June 11, 1962; "South Side Renewal Plans Gets 1st OK," *WSJ*, June 13, 1962; "South Madison Public Housing Study Eyed Next," *CT*, June 1, 1962; Marcus, "University-City Study of Urban Renewal Is OK'd," *CT*, June 29, 1962; "Urban Renewal Plan Fund Okd," *WSJ*, December 13, 1962.

41. MRA minutes, July 19, 1962; "Sampson Plaza Apartment Plans Win MRA's Approval," *WSJ*, July 19, 1962; "Brittingham Apartment Plans Given Final OK," *CT*, July 20, 1962; Zmudzinski, "Leaving Greenbush," 46–63.

42. "Report of the Madison City Redevelopment Authority, 1962 (Zmudzinski)," WI-M 1, RED.1/6: T/7, 1962, Wisconsin Historical Society Library.

43. "Urban Renewal Efforts Now at Critical Stage," *CT*, November 17, 1962; Gordon, "Triangle Negroes All But Homeless," *WSJ*, November 19, 1962.

44. MRA minutes, September 13, 1962; "Neighborhood Unit's Relocation Okd," *WSJ*, September 14, 1962.

45. Gordon, "Resettling Difficulty Spurs Talk of Public Housing Here," *WSJ*, November 1, 1962.

46. MRA minutes, November 8, 1962; Gordon, "Relocation Critique Stirs Up Fuss," *WSJ*, November 16, 1962; Gordon, "More, Fast Relocation Housing Urged in Report," *WSJ*, December 2, 1962; Dave Prosten, "'Triangle' Relocation May Be Finished by Next October," *DC*, December 6, 1962.

47. Editorial, "Triangle Relocation Is in Trouble," *WSJ*, November 16, 1962.

48. MRA minutes, November 21, 1962; Gordon, "City Lease Plan Seeks to Aid in Relocations," *WSJ*, November 22, 1962; Gordon, "Leases Housing Program Backed," *WSJ*, November 29, 1962.

49. Gordon, "MHA Stays Cool to Leasing Plan," *WSJ*, November 30, 1962; Marcus, "Relocation Lease Plan Gets Cool Reception from MHA," *CT*, November 30, 1962.

50. MRA minutes, December 13, 1962; "MRA Approves Three Rental Leases," *WSJ*, December 14, 1962.

51. Gordon, "Test of Leased Housing Plan Pushed," *WSJ*, December 28, 1962; "Leased Housing Vote Falls Short," *CT*, December 28, 1962.

52. "New Rights Ordinance Proposed for Madison," *WSJ*, February 27, 1962; "Tougher Rights Ordinance Drawn Up by NAACP Here," *CT*, February 27, 1962; "Public Meetings Are Planned to Help Get Housing Rights," *WSJ*, March 15, 1962; George McCormick, "Rights Unit Shares Stories of Housing Prejudice," *CT*, October 11, 1962.

53. Gordon, "Last Terrace Backer Out," *WSJ*, April 18, 1962.

54. Elliott Maraniss, "Community Chest Halts Madison Club Dues of Director," *CT*, May 24, 1962; "Stop Paying Director's Club Dues, Chest Group Is Urged," *WSJ*, May 25, 1962.

55. "Need for City Urban League to Be Discussed," *WSJ*, August 11, 1962; Kirkhorn, "Urban League Needed in Madison, Group Told," *CT*, August 15, 1962.

56. "Marshall Colston Elected to Head Local NAACP Unit," *CT*, December 29, 1962.

57. "Rohr Seeking Fourth Term as Alderman," *CT*, January 23, 1962; "Marfyak Attacks Rohr's Votes for More Taverns," *CT*, February 28, 1962; "Marfyak Asserts Rorh Is Displaying '1st Class Bigotry,'" *CT*, March 1, 1962; "Fourteenth Ward Citizens Group Attacks Rohr for Racism," *CT*, March 3, 1962; Marcus, "Ald. Rohr Refuses to Attack Race Rumors about Marfyak," *CT*, March 21, 1962.

58. Gordon, "Marfyak Shocked by Rohr's Charge," *WSJ*, March 2, 1962.

59. "Fourteenth Ward Racial Lies Assailed," *WSJ*, March 21, 1962.

60. Stephen Maersch, "Rohr, Marfyak Clash on Race Issues at Rally," *CT*, March 29, 1962; "Rohr and Marfyak Again Clash over Race Issue in Fourteenth Ward," *WSJ*, March 30, 1962.

61. Editorial, "Ald. Rohr Launches an Appeal to Race Hate and Suspicion," *CT*, March 2, 1962; editorial, "What Are Democrats and Labor Going to Do about Rohr," *CT*, March 22, 1962.

62. "Wilkie Denies Backing Rohr for Re-Election," *CT*, March 31, 1962; "Wilkie Denies Backing Rohr," *WSJ*, April 2, 1962.

63. "Three Aldermen Are Unseated," *CT*, April 4, 1962.

64. Editorial, "We Can Do without the Marchers," *WSJ*, April 27, 1962.

65. BOR minutes, January 5, 1962; Samuel C. Reynolds, "'Discriminatory' Gifts Prohibited by Regents," *WSJ*, January 6, 1962; Bob Karlman, "Regent Vote Eliminates Scholarship Bias Clauses," *DC*, January 5, 1962; John Patrick Hunter, "Regents Set Ban on Bias Gifts to U.W.," *CT*, January 6, 1962; Reynolds, "U.W. Anti-Bias Moves Leave a Big Question," *WSJ*, January 21, 1962.

66. "Quits U.W.; Claims Bias Film Banned," *CT*, March 19, 1962.

67. Karlman, "'U' Bias Film Stirs Dispute," *DC*, March 20, 1962; Hunter, "NAACP Pickets U.W. Buildings," *CT*, March 20, 1962; Karlman, "Campus Picketed in Bias Film Row," *DC*, March 21, 1962; Levitan, *Sesquicentennial History*, 245.

68. Karlman, "NAACP Meets With 'U'; Film Fight Still Unsettled," *DC*, March 22, 1962; Hunter, "U. of W. Officials Back Ban on Movie," *CT*, March 22, 1962.

69. "Elvehjem Rejects Powell Film Bid," *DC*, March 17, 1962; "Rep. Powell Will Receive 'Typescript' of Bias Film," *WSJ*, March 27, 1962.

70. "Senate Backs University on Discrimination Film," *DC*, March 28, 1962.

71. Steve Sobota, "ADA Calls for Film Release; Backs NAACP in Dispute," *DC*, March 23, 1962; "State Civil Liberties Union Backs University's Film Ban," *CT*, March 23, 1962; editorial, "Lesson for U.W. and NAACP in Current Film Controversy," *CT*, March 23, 1962; "ACLU Position on Movie Backed," *CT*, March 28, 1962; "Bias Film Ban Stirs ACLU Meeting," *CT*, March 29, 1962.

72. Allen Stagl, "Bias Film Producer Declares Non-Candid Methods Better," *DC*, May 3, 1962; Daphne E. Barbee-Wooten, ed., *Justice for All: Selected Writings of Lloyd A. Barbee* (Madison: Wisconsin Historical Society Press, 2017), 10–11, 245–250; Hunter, "Pasch Requests Bias Film Screening for U. Regents," *CT*, March 28, 1962; "Pasch Asks Airing of Housing Film," *DC*, March 29, 1962; John Gruber, "Rights Council Delays Action on Bias Film," *DC*, March 29, 1962; "UW Regents Will See Bias Film Typescript," *WSJ*, March 29, 1962.

73. BOR minutes, April 6, 1962; "Reports UW Sealed Film in Archives," *CT*, April 6, 1962; Karlman, "'U' Bias Film Typescript Is Released," *DC*, April 7, 1962; "Regents Express Backing of UW Stand on Bias Film," *WSJ*, April 7, 1962.

74. "King Will Speak at Union on Future of Integration," *DC*, March 21, 1962; Robert E. Bouzek, "Race Barriers Yielding, Dr. King Says," *WSJ*, March 31, 1962; Gruber, "King Says Non-Violence Key to Civil Rights Gain," *DC*, March 31, 1962; "Rev. King Lashes Churches," *CT*, March 31, 1962.

75. Stagl, "Malcolm X Asks Race Separation," *DC*, April 3, 1962; editorial, "A Bitter Dose," *DC*, April 4, 1962.

76. James Livingston, "Vanishing Act," *The Nation*, November 3, 2014; Jerry Gafio Watts, *Harold Cruse's The Crisis of the Negro Intellectual Reconsidered* (New York: Psychology Press, 2004), 26; Madison City Directory 1962; Ron Radosh, "Remembering an Evening with Malcolm X, and Some Thoughts on the New

Manning Marable Biography," *PJ Media*, April 4, 2011, https://pjmedia.com/ronradosh/2011/4/4/remembering-an-evening-with-malcom-x-and-some-thoughts-on-the-new-manning-marable-biography/2/; Fred Ciporen email, August 27, 2017.

77. "Committee Urging Greek Autonomy," *DC*, September 22, 1962; "Greeks in Protest March Today," *DC*, October 4, 1962.

78. "Beloit Sorority Unit Faces Ouster for Pledging Madison Negro Girl," *WSJ*, April 30, 1962; "DG National Denies Bias," *DC*, May 11, 1962; Hunter, "Beloit Sorority Suspended; U.W. May Close Unit," *CT*, July 12, 1962; "Beloit DG Unit Suspended; Jeopardizes Local Chapter," *DC*, July 13, 1962; Jeff Greenfield, "Rights Committee Asks DG Ban," *DC*, September 21, 1962; "Delta Gamma Attacks Rights Group Report," *DC*, September 22, 1962; Sharon Coady, "Pickets Protest Fraternity Bias," *WSJ*, September 23, 1962; Reynolds, "Sorority Ban Raises 'Unfair Play' Charge," *WSJ*, September 23, 1962; Reynolds, "SLIC Asks for Month's Delay in Faculty Action on Sorority," *WSJ*, September 26, 1962; Karlman, "Senate Asks Faculty Vote Delay," *DC*, September 27, 1962; "Expect Faculty to Delay Action on Sorority Ban," *CT*, September 27, 1962; John Stocking, "An Analysis of Greek Discrimination," *DC*, October 12, 1962.

79. Karlman, "Greeks Hold Silent March," *DC*, October 5, 1962; LeRoy Luberg, interviewed by Donna Hartshorne, 1975, OH #0066, digital audio file, University Archives and Records Management Services, Madison, Wisconsin.

80. Editorial, "Private Matter," *DC*, May 2, 1962; editorial, "Unwise," *DC*, October 5, 1962; editorial, "A Contrast," *DC*, October 6, 1962; editorial, "As We Said," *DC*, October 10, 1962; Jeff Greenfield email, April 23, 2014.

81. Gruber, "Silent Moment Marks Meredith Rights Rally," *DC*, October 6, 1962.

82. Karlman, "Faculty Passes DG Stay," *DC*, December 4, 1962; editorial, "Happy Ending to a Sad Affair," *DC*, December 5, 1962; BOR minutes, December 7, 1962; Reynolds, "Regents Criticize Faculty Delta Gamma Decision," *WSJ*, December 8, 1962; Lynne Abraham, "Regents Doubt National's No-Bias Pledge Sincerity," *DC*, December 8, 1962.

83. "Greeks Offer Rewritten Autonomy Rule Today," *DC*, October 16, 1962; "U. Tightens Fraternity Bias Rules," *CT*, November 16, 1962; BOR minutes, December 7, 1962.

84. "Phi Delta Theta Quits National," *DC*, September 18, 1962; "UW's Phi Delta Theta Unit Quits National Fraternity," *WSJ*, September 18, 1962.

85. "566 City Students Due to Get U.W. Degrees," *WSJ*, June 3, 1962; Hunter, "Proud Relatives See over 2,500 Get U.W. Degrees," *CT*, June 4, 1962; *Wisconsin Alumnus* 63, no. 15 (July 1962): 12–13.

86. "Ella Fitzgerald to Be at Homecoming," *CT*, September 26, 1962; "Fitzgerald, Miller Orchestra Highlight 1962 Homecoming Show, November 9," *DC*, September 26, 1962.

87. Feldman, *Buildings*, 313, 318, 321.

88. John Kellogg, "SLIC Passes Coed Living in Undergraduate Apts.," *DC*, January 4, 1962.

89. "U. Students Need Trains, Dean Tells ICC Hearing," *CT*, January 15, 1962.

90. "Symposium Opens Monday," *DC*, February 3, 1962.

91. "Greenfield, Loeb Named to Fill Cardinal Positions," *DC*, February 6, 1962; "Greenfield Is Daily Cardinal Chief Editor," *CT*, February 6, 1962.

92. "Novelist Bellow Speaks Tonight," *DC*, March 2, 1962; Maxine Sidran, "Author Bellow Traces Paths of Moralism In U.S. Writers," *DC*, March 3, 1962; Ben Sidran, *A Life in the Music* (New York: Taylor, 2003), 40.

93. "SPAD Plans Demonstration to Protest Test Resumption," *DC*, March 23, 1962.

94. Bob Booker, "Wisconsin Shatters Ohio State's Streak in Blazing 86-67 Romp," *WSJ*, March 4, 1962.

95. Elizabeth Gould, "Singer's Most, Man, Isn't Quite Enough," *WSJ*, March 17, 1962; Hunter, "Singer Captivates With Folk Songs," *CT*, March 17, 1962; Jacobson, "Theodore Bikel's Folk Singing Makes Evening a Sprightly One," *DC*, April 13, 1962; Gruber, "Modern Folk Trio Captivating," *DC*, December 2, 1962; Serene Wise, "Top Flight Group Disappointing," *DC*, September 22, 1962; Gould, "The Weavers Weave a Spell with Songs," *WSJ*, September 22, 1962; Jacobson, "Folk Songstress Odetta Has Warmth, Originality," *DC*, February 13, 1962; Dan Kalb, "Fuller, Elliott Spark 'Real' Folksing Night," *DC*, May 9, 1962; Ben Sidran, "Trio's Performance Dynamic," *DC*, October 6, 1962.

96. Gruber, "Socialist Club Mulls Stand on South Viet Nam Crisis," *DC*, March 17, 1962.

97. Bill Wineke, "Sex Seminar Hears Boyes [*sic*] Speak on Contraceptives," *DC*, March 28, 1962; "500 U. Students Hear Talk on Sex," *CT*, March 28, 1962.

98. Baas, "Isaac Stern in Powerful Recital," *CT*, April 2, 1962; Jacobson, "Audiences Acclaim Isaac Stern; Master Violinist Proves Genius," *DC*, April 3, 1962.

99. "Ellington to Play at Mil-Ball," *DC*, April 5, 1962.

100. Editorial, "Our Right to Know," *DC*, April 11, 1962.

101. BOR minutes, May 3, 1962, Exhibit E, 2; "Board of Visitors Criticizes Daily Cardinal's 'Low Taste,'" *WSJ*, May 4, 1962.

102. Stagl, "Buckley Hits at Liberal Pacifism," *DC*, April 17, 1962.

103. Hunter, "Overflow Throng of 1,800 Gives Hall Polite Hearing," *CT*, May 8, 1962; James D. Selk, "Quiet Crowd Hears Top U.S. Red Spout Off Here," *WSJ*, May 8, 1962.

104. BOR minutes, May 4, 1962; "Regents Raise no Objection to Campus Talk by Commie," *CT*, May 4, 1962; Greenfield, "A John Birch Leader Speaks," *DC*, May 15, 1962; Gruber, "Communism Denies U.S. Heritage, Manion Says," *DC*, May 15, 1962; Maersch, "Small, Skeptical U. Crowd Hears Birch Society Leader," *CT*, May 15, 1962.

105. Stagl, "Clark Views Constitution as 'A Living Document,'" *DC*, May 19, 1962.

106. "Jobs Are Plentiful For '62 Graduates," *CT*, March 7, 1962.

107. Ben Sidran, "Folk Genius Makeba is 'U' Success," *DC*, October 28, 1962; Gould, "Miriam Makeba's Velvety Voice Brings Africa to Union Theater," *WSJ*, October 30, 1962.

108. "U. Would Accept Rose Bowl Bid," *CT*, November 19, 1962; BOR minutes, December 7, 1962; Hunter, "Bowl Games 'Unfortunate,'" *CT*, December 7, 1962; Karlman, "President Hits 'Emphasis' but Favors This Bowl Trip," *DC*, December 8, 1962.

109. Tom Butler, "Wisconsin Trips Minnesota, 14-9, Takes Big Ten Title to Rose Bowl," *WSJ*, November 25, 1962; A. Lee Beier, "California, Here We Come!" *WSJ*, November 25, 1962.

110. Coady, "Off Field, Richter Still Shows Finesse," *WSJ*, November 24, 1962; "Badgers Second by UPI; Richter Is All-American," *DC*, November 28, 1962; "Badgers Second in UPI; Washington Picks Richter," *DC*, December 4, 1962; "Richter All-American on AP, UPI," *DC*, December 6, 1962; Roger Cantwell, "Richter Unanimous All-American," *WSJ*, December 7, 1962; Vince Sweeney, *Always a Badger: The Pat Richter Story* (Black Earth, WI: Trails Books, 2005), 38; Don Kopriva and Jim Mott, *On Wisconsin! The History of Badger Athletics* (Champaign, IL: Sports Publishing, 2001), 107.

111. Nina Simpkins, "AWS Passes New Hours Plan," *DC*, December 7, 1962; editorial, "Distorted," *DC*, April 5, 1962.

112. Editorial, "Let's Make This Bowl Trip the Last One," *DC*, December 12, 1962.

113. Prosten, "Anti-HUAC Club Faces Near-Violent Hostility," *DC*, December 18, 1962.

114. "Form University Ave. Development Group," *CT*, December 20, 1962; "New Group Formed to Assist University Ave. Development,' *WSJ*, December 21, 1962.

115. "U.W. Purges 25 for 'Panty' Raids," *WSJ*, May 21, 1952; "Students Stage Near-Riot Here," *WSJ*, October 13, 1962; "Arrest 15 In U.W. 'Riot,'" *CT*, October 13, 1962; "13 Arrested, 7 Injured in Campus Area Riot," *WSJ*, October 14, 1962; A. Lee Beaer, "47 Arrested in Riots at UW," October 15, 1962; "20 U.W. Rioters Face Trial," *CT*, October 15, 1962; "15 Pay in Court for Riots at UW," *WSJ*, October 16, 1962; June Dieckmann, "UW Drops 20 Held in Riots," *WSJ*, October 16, 1962; Mike Gremaud, "'U' Re-Instates 15 Rioters," *DC*, October 17, 1962; Janie Donahoe, "Two Students Freed in First 'U' Riot Trials," *DC*, November 16, 1962; Wineke, "Eleven 'Rioters' Cleared; One Case Still Pending," *DC*, December 6, 1962; Dieckmann, "Not 'Offside,' Students Told," *WSJ*, December 6, 1962.

116. "Death of President Elvehjem Stuns University and Community," *Wisconsin Alumnus* 64, no. 1 (October 1962): 9–12.

117. E. David Cronon and John W. Jenkins, *The University of Wisconsin: A History, 1945–1971* (Madison: University of Wisconsin Press, 1999), 109–127; "Harrington Quits 'U'; Talent Exodus Feared," *DC*, May 12, 1962.

118. "Elvehjem Dies," *DC*, July 27, 1962, Extra; Hunter, "U. Pres. Elvehjem, 61, Dies Soon after Heart Attack," *CT*, July 27, 1962; "Heart Attack Ends Career of UW's Conrad Elvehjem," *WSJ*, July 28, 1962; "The Man that Was Elvehjem," *DC*, July 31, 1962; "Rites Today for Elvehjem," *DC*, July 31, 1962; BOR minutes, Special Meeting, July 31, 1962.

119. Hunter, "Hint Harrington to Head U.," *CT*, July 28, 1962; "Harrington Arrives from Japan," *WSJ*, July 30, 1962; "Harrington Is Acting President," *DC*, July 31, 1962; Hunter, "Pick Harrington to Head U.," *CT*, August, 1962; Hunter, "Elect Harrington Formally Monday," *CT*, August 2, 1962; Hunter, "Regents Formally Elect Harrington U.W. President," *CT*, August 6, 1962; BOR minutes, August 6, 1962; "Regents Make It Official—Harrington New President," *DC*, August 7, 1962; Roberts, "UW Serves All, Harrington Vows," *WSJ*, August 7, 1962; "A Positive Force," *Wisconsin Alumnus* 64, no. 1 (October 1962): 13–15; Cronon and Jenkins, *The University of Wisconsin*, 163–178.

120. Hunter, "Harrington to Be Inaugurated Today," *CT*, October 20, 1962; editorial, "Pres. Harrington of Wisconsin: The Challenge to Him and to Us," *CT*, October 20, 1962; Reynolds, "New President of UW Pledges Aid for Cities," *WSJ*, October 21, 1962; Raymond Moucha, "UW Inaugurates Harrington Era," *WSJ*, October 21, 1962; "The University and the State," *Wisconsin Alumnus* 64, no. 2 (November 1962): 13–16.

121. "Ex-Dean Sellery Dies on Birthday," *WSJ*, January 22, 1962; "Ex-Dean George Sellery Dies on His 90th Birthday," *CT*, January 22, 1962; editorial, "The University Will Long Carry the Stamp of Dean Sellery," *CT*, January 22, 1962.

122. "Carson Gulley, Well-Known Madison Chef, Dies at 65," *CT*, November 3, 1962; "Nationally Famous City Chef Carson Gulley Dies at Age 65," *WSJ*, November 4, 1962; http:// recollectionwisconsin.org/carson-gulley-madisons-first -celebrity-chef; Scott Seyforth, "The Life and Times of Carson Gulley," *Wisconsin Magazine of History* 99, no. 4 (Summer 2016): 2–15.

123. "Madison High Schools to Graduate 1,085," *WSJ*, June 10, 1962; "409 Get Diplomas at West High, 226 at Central; East High Has 423 Graduating Seniors," *CT*, June 15, 1962.

124. "Year of Records, Problems Facing Schools," *CT*, September 1, 1962.

125. Irvin Kreisman, "Honor to 'Old Bob' Universally Praised," *CT*, January 19, 1962; "Facts of School Bond Issue," *WSJ*, March 4, 1962; Kreisman, "Falk Sees Double Shifts If Bond Issue Defeated," *CT*, March 10, 1962; "Questions on School Bond Answered," *WSJ*, April 1, 1962; "Site of La Follette High and Area It Will Serve," *CT*, July 7, 1962.

126. Editorial, "Council Should Ask Questions about $9½ Million Bond Issue," *CT*, January 25, 1962; "Falk Says School Bonds Aren't Tied to Terrace Issue," *CT*, January 26, 1962; editorial, "Is Huge School Bond Issue to Scare Voters from Auditorium?" *CT*,

January 31, 1962; "Terrace Backers Call for Support of School Bonds," *CT*, February 14, 1962; editorial, "Why We Need the $9.5 Million Now," *WSJ*, March 15, 1962; Reynolds, "Here's Why City Needs $9.5 Million for Schools," *WSJ*, March 16, 1962.

127. "3 On School Board Seek Re-Election," *CT*, January 3, 1962; Reynolds, "School Board Race Unusual for City," *WSJ*, March 4, 1962; editorial, "A Chance to Add New Vigor and Ideas to the School Board," *CT*, March 22, 1962; Reynolds, "Incumbents Stay on School Board," *WSJ*, April 4, 1962.

128. "School Bond Issue Backed by 4-1 Edge," *WSJ*, April 4, 1962; "School Bonds Win, 4 to 1," *CT*, April 4, 1962; Kirkhorn, "Board Says Central High Is Needed 10 More Years," *CT*, July 10, 1962.

129. Helena White and WORT News Department, "Madison's First African-American Teacher," https://www.wortfm.org /madisons-first-african-american-teacher/; Geraldine Bernard interview, September 12, 2017; "Bias in Schools? No and Yes," *WSJ*, August 15, 1963; "We Celebrate Roots," *Umoja*, April 1992.

130. "Ease Policy on Couples in Teaching," *CT*, January 3, 1962.

131. Reynolds, "School Superintendent Needed," *WSJ*, April 1, 1962; Reynolds, "School Board Will Act on Successor to Falk," *WSJ*, May 8, 1962; editorial, "School Board to Pick a New Superintendent in Secret," *CT*, May 9, 1962; Reynolds, "Gilberts New School Chief," *WSJ*, May 15, 1962; "Oconomowoc Man Named to Head Madison Schools," *CT*, May 15, 1962.

132. Reynolds, "School District Deadline Passes," *WSJ*, July 1, 1962; Gordon, "City Reaffirms Strong Stand on School Area's Annexation," *WSJ*, July 13, 1962; Marcus, "$1 Million Debt Added by School Annexations," *CT*, December 3, 1962; "City's School Census Tops 51,000," *WSJ*, August 7, 1962; "School-Age Population Jumps 5,350 in Year," *CT*, August 7, 1962; "Year of Records, Problems Facing Schools," *CT*, September 1, 1962; "Teachers Meet In-Coming Chief," *CT*, September 8, 1962.

133. Reynolds, "City Board Oks Merger of Schools," *WSJ*, November 20, 1962; "Approve Merger of Central and Wisconsin High," *CT*, November 20, 1962; Reynolds, "Wisconsin High-Central Merger Is Okd," *WSJ*, December 8, 1962.

134. "Board Names New School in Honor of Dr. Elvehjem," *CT*, August 7, 1962; David Bednarek, "Conrad A. Elvehjem School Is Dedicated Here," *WSJ*, December 12, 1962.

135. "Reynolds, Parents, Others, Tell School Needs," *WSJ*, December 18, 1962; Marcus, "Argue How to Cut School Budget," *CT*, December 18, 1962.

136. McCormick, "Falk Has Kept City's Schools Apace with Changing World," *CT*, December 26, 1962.

137. "Dimensions and Dividends," City of Madison Planning Department, March 1965, 1.

138. City of Madison Department of Planning, Community Development and Economic Development.

139. "Jobs in Madison Show a Sizeable Increase This Year," *CT*, June 26, 1962.

140. "City's Value Goes over Half Billion," *CT*, August 29, 1962; "Square, State St. Land Values Down $1 Million for This Year," *WSJ*, September 21, 1962; Maraniss, "Hill Farms Office to Hurt Downtown Rental Properties," *CT*, January 13, 1962.

141. "CC Backs Closing of Non-Essential Stores," *WSJ*, June 22, 1962; "Madison C.C. to Oppose 'Unneeded' Sunday Sales," *CT*, June 22, 1962.

142. Aehl, "Teamster Strike Here to Curb Construction," *WSJ*, April 12, 1962; "Strike May Be Costly to UW Project," *CT*, April 12, 1962; "Strike Seen Damaging to State, UW Projects," *WSJ*, April 14, 1962; Selk, "Strike Halts Big Building Works," *WSJ*, April 20, 1962; "State and U.W. Losses in Strike Spelled Out," *CT*, April 27, 1962; Richard Bradee, "Feinsinger Reports Progress in Teamster Strike Talks," *CT*, April 28; Selk, "City Teamster Strike Is Just about Settled," *WSJ*, May 3, 1962; "Teamster Pact Hammered Out," *CT*, May 3, 1962; Selk, "City Strike Settlement Collapses as Teamsters Union Rejects Offer," *WSJ*, May 4, 1962; "Suit Snags Teamster Pack OK," *CT*, May 4, 1962; Selk, "Teamster Strike Ends Here," *WSJ*, May 5, 1962; "Firm Drops Suit, Strike Settled," *CT*, May 5, 1962; "Strike Tightens Building Schedule," *WSJ*, May 5, 1962.

143. "Era of History Passes as Synagogue Closes," *WSJ*, April 30, 1962; Carol Goodwin Goroff, Iza Goroff, Catherine Tripalin Murray, *The Spirit of Greenbush* (Madison: Greenbush Memorial, 2000), 14–15; Frank Custer, "City's First Synagogue, Recently Dentists' Office, Is Sold Again," *CT*, July 11, 1962; Levitan, *Sesquicentennial History*, 57.

144. "Library Board Approves W. Mifflin Site Appraisal," *CT*, January 4, 1962; Aehl, "Mifflin Site Approved for New Public Library," *WSJ*, April 27, 1962; "Library Site Approved," *CT*, April 27, 1962; Aehl, "City Buys Parcel for Library Site," *WSJ*, July 27, 1962; "City to Get Final Site for Library," *WSJ*, October 13, 1962.

145. Reynolds, "1,000 Visit New Monroe Street Branch Library's Open House," *WSJ*, May 28, 1962.

146. "Co-Op Apartments Set Here," *WSJ*, May 6, 1962; "Vilas Towers Clears 2nd Hurdle," *WSJ*, November 11, 1962; "Start $1 Million Apartment Project on Far East Side," *CT*, November 26, 1962.

147. Gordon, "Council Annexes 29 Suburban Parcels," *WSJ*, September 14, 1962; Marcus, "29 Suburban Areas Annexed under New State School Law," *CT*, September 14, 1962; Aehl, "Villages Boil over City's Secret Annexing Move," *WSJ*, September 15, 1962; "Reynolds Doubts Right Procedure Used in Surprise Annexations," *CT*, September 15, 1962; Gordon, "City 'Stands Pat' on Big Annexing," *WSJ*, September 16, 1962; Sanford Moss, "'Surprise' Mayor's Fault, Alderman Says," *WSJ*, September 17, 1962; Gordon, "Mayor Hints OK for Some Annexations," *WSJ*, September 19, 1962; Gordon, "Mayor Lets 29 Annexes Pass," *WSJ*, September 20, 1962; "Mayor Lets Annexations Become Law—Unsigned," *CT*,

September 20, 1962; "Annexed Areas' Value Placed at $5½ Million," *WSJ*, September 22, 1962; "Court Tests of City's Annexations Now Loom," *WSJ*, November 22, 1962.

148. "Hilldale Buzzing for Big Opening," *WSJ*, October 14, 1962; Newhouse, "Foresight Builds Hilldale," *WSJ*, October 25, 1962; "Giant Hilldale Opening," *WSJ/CT*, October 25, 1962; Harva Hachten, "Hilldale Shopping Center to Open Officially Today," *WSJ*, October 25, 1962; Havens Wilber, "Hilldale Is Opened; Thousands Pour In," *CT*, October 25, 1962; James Rowen, "Hilldale: Bonus for University, Inc.," *DC*, March 13, 1969.

149. "Gorham St. Extension Is Opened," *CT*, September 28, 1962.

150. "New I-Road Will Open Friday," *WSJ*, November 1, 1962.

151. Levitan, *Sesquicentennial History*, 241; Mollenhoff and Hamilton, *Monona Terrace*, 176–177.

152. Zweifel and Nichols, *The Capital Times*, 131–133.

153. Editorial, "The Pell-Mell Rush to Get the Causeway Underway," *CT*, July 19, 1962.

154. Gordon, "$900,000 Price Placed on First Causeway Job," *WSJ*, April 12, 1962.

155. Editorial, "Action—at Last—on the Causeway," *WSJ*, March 12, 1962.

156. "Tentative O.K. for Causeway," *CT*, April 20, 1962; Newhouse, "First Fill Placed for Monona Causeway," *WSJ*, May 1, 1962.

157. Editorial, "What's the Mayor Up to with His Fanfare about Causeway?" *CT*, May 2, 1962; editorial, "The Mayor's Curious Stampede to Put the Causeway Over," *CT*, May 21, 1962; editorial, "Reason for Causeway Pause," *CT*, June 7, 1962.

158. Newhouse, "First Fill Placed for Monona Causeway," *WSJ*, May 1, 1962; editorial, "What's the Mayor Up to with His Fanfare about Causeway?" *CT*, May 2, 1962; "PSC Asked to Hold Public Hearing on Causeway Plan," *CT*, May 8, 1962; Citizens Advisory Committee Minutes, May 16, 1962; Aehl, "Citizens Advisory Committee Supports Causeway," *WSJ*, May 17, 1962; Marcus, "Admits Causeway Will Require Appropriation," *CT*, May 25, 1962; Marcus, "Causeway Push Tied to Plan for Auditorium at Olin Park," *CT*, May 31, 1962; Aehl, "Causeway Won't Harm Water Flow, Expert Says," *WSJ*, June 5, 1962; Marcus, "Admits Causeway Will Reduce Waterway 98%," *CT*, June 5, 1962; Gordon, "Causeway's Cost Put at $2.2 Million," *WSJ*, July 17, 1962; "Sees $2 Million Causeway," *CT*, July 17, 1962; Gordon, "Foes Attack Monona Causeway Project," *WSJ*, July 18, 1962; Marcus, "Warn Causeway Will Destroy Monona Bay," *CT*, October 1, 1962; Zweifel and Nichols, *The Capital Times*, 131–133.

159. Custer, "Italian Co-Op, Born of Grim Need, Marks Happy 50th Jubilee," *CT*, January 24, 1962.

160. "Library Board Oks Appraisal of Site," *WSJ*, February 14, 1962.

161. "Capital Times Rejects Ad for Orpheum Theater Film," *CT*, February 2, 1962.

162. Marcus, "Council Passes Work Relief Plan," *CT*, April 10, 1962; Aehl, "Council Group Backs Work-Relief Program," *WSJ*, April 11, 1962; "Work-Relief Program for City Given Final Council Approval," *WSJ*, April 13, 1962.

163. Owen Coyle, "City's Official Flag Has Been Hanging Forgotten and Upside Down Since '62," *CT*, August 2, 1965.

164. Citizens Advisory Committee minutes, May 2, 1962; Aehl, "Truax to Get Nuclear Weapons Soon," *WSJ*, May 3, 1962.

165. "Thousands To See Ceremonies Here," *CT*, May 28, 1962; Custer, "15,000 See Memorial Parade; More Than 60 Units Take Part," *CT*, May 30, 1962; Selk, "20,000 Jam Square for Parade," *WSJ*, May 31, 1962.

166. "Historic Cathedral Mass to Mark Bishop's Golden Jubilee Today," *WSJ*, June 25, 1962; "Overflow Crowd at Cathedral as Bishop Marks 50th Jubilee," *CT*, June 25, 1962.

167. "Weatherly Shot To Death," *CT*, July 25, 1962; "Mrs. Weatherly Charged With Ex-Chief's Murder" *WSJ*, July 26, 1962; Robert Meloon, "Ten Stormy Years In Madison Highlighted Weatherly's Career," *CT*, July 26, 1962; "Weatherly's Wife Free, Reports Say," *WSJ*, September 20, 1962; "Grand Jury Frees Mrs. Weatherly," *CT*, September 20, 1962.

168. Aehl, "Duszynski Gets Works Chief Job," *WSJ*, August 24, 1962; Marcus, "E. J. Duszynski Confirmed as City's Works Director," *CT*, August 24, 1962.

169. "Library to Use Western Union Boys to Collect Overdue Books," *WSJ*, September 12, 1962.

170. Gould, "Papa Hambone's a Novelist," *WSJ*, October 7, 1962.

171. Aehl, "Larger Areas' Battle on Elm Disease Hailed," *WSJ*, October 27, 1962.

172. Gruber, "Cuba Stirs Riots and Pickets," *DC*, October 26, 1962; Beier, "200 March to Protest, Back Cuba Actions Here," *WSJ*, October 27, 1962; Dave Zweifel, "200 Join Peace March on Square," *CT*, October 27, 1962; "Blockade Rally Triggers Rows," *DC*, October 30, 1962.

173. "Ms. Braxton, Well-Known Social Worker, Succumbs," *CT*, March 26, 1962; "Miss Gay Braxton, Organizer of Neighborhood House, Dies," *WSJ*, March 26, 1962; Levitan, *Sesquicentennial History*, 224.

174. "Broadfoot, State's Chief Justice, Dies," *WSJ*, May 19, 1962; "Chief Justice Broadfoot Dies," *CT*, May 19, 1962; "Say Doyle Rejects High Court Offer," *CT*, May 22, 1962; "Risser Seeks Election to Fourth Assembly Term," *CT*, May 22, 1962; Bradee, "Court Post to Sen. Wilkie," *CT*, May 25, 1962; "Fred A. Risser Expected to Run for Wilkie's Seat," *CT*, May 25, 1962; "Nelson Appoints Horace Wilkie to State Supreme Court Vacancy," *WSJ*, May 26, 1962; Reynolds, "Dane County Democrats Capture All but One Legislative Seat," *WSJ*, November 7, 1962; "Risser In; No Dane Co. Party Shifts," *CT*, November 7, 1962.

175. "Former Judge Ole A. Stolen Dies in His California

Home," *CT*, August 17, 1962; editorial, "Ole Stolen Was a Great Servant of the Community," *CT*, August 18, 1962; Levitan, *Sesquicentennial History*, 222.

176. "City Atty. Heassler Killed in Car Crash," *WSJ*, May 31, 1962.

1963

1. Ruth Doyle, "A Conversation with Betty MacDonald," *Historic Madison: A Journal of the Four Lake Region* 18 (2003): 3–17; Doyle, "A Conversation with John McGrath," *Historic Madison: A Journal of the Four Lake Region* 18 (2003): 18–37; Doyle, "A Conversation with Rev. James Wright," *Historic Madison: A Journal of the Four Lake Region* 18 (2003): 38–53.

2. MRA, Triangle Urban Renewal Area, Estimated Housing Resources; "Racial Fear Blocks Sale of House," *WSJ*, August 6, 1963.

3. "Rights Group Seeks Legal Ruling on Bias Ban Plan," *CT*, January 16, 1963; "Civil Rights Groups Seek Stringent Anti-Bias Action," *DC*, January 17, 1963; David Gordon, "Madison Gains under Human Rights Group," *WSJ*, January 20, 1963; "Pritchard in Plea for Negro Rights," *CT*, February 12, 1963; Gordon, "Fair Housing Bill Backed by Mayor's Rights Group," *WSJ*, March 26, 1963; "Ask Local Housing Bias Ban," *CT*, May 14, 1963; "Fair Housing Group to Meet at St. Martin's," *WSJ*, September 13, 1963; "Madison Group on Fair Housing Seeks Members," *CT*, September 13, 1963.

4. Herbert Marcus, "Council Kills Human Rights Ordinance by 14 to 5 Vote," *CT*, March 14, 1952; "City's Human Rights Group Gets Started," *WSJ*, September 10, 1954; "Know Your Madisonian—Betty MacDonald," *WSJ*, August 25, 1974; Doyle, "Conversation with Betty MacDonald," 5; Doyle, "A Conversation with John McGrath," 23–26; Doyle, "Conversation with Rev. James Wright," 41–43.

5. George McCormick, "Candidates Debate Housing Bias Issue," *CT*, March 26, 1963.

6. "Fair Housing Law for City Planned," *WSJ*, June 22, 1963; "Start Fair Housing Ordinance for City," *CT*, June 22, 1963; Marcus, "NAACP Hits City's Delay in Acting on Anti-Bias Plan," *CT*, June 24, 1963; Michael Kirkhorn, "Realtors and Chamber Duck Queries on Bias," *CT*, June 28, 1963; "New Discrimination Study Urged," *WSJ*, June 29, 1963; "City Rights Unit Asked," *WSJ*, July 6, 1963.

7. Gordon, "City to Consider Rights Law," *WSJ*, July 10, 1963; "Mayor, NAACP Officials Discuss City Anti-Bias Law," *CT*, July 10, 1963; McCormick, "Colston Says NAACP Discards Moderation," *CT*, July 10, 1963.

8. Roger Gribble, "Leaders of NAACP, Realtors Disagree Over Housing Bias," *WSJ*, July 25,1963; "City, Scoon at Odds On City Discrimination," *DC*, July 25, 1963.

9. Gordon, "'Unrest' Case Possible, City Rights Group Told,' *WSJ*, July 25, 1963; editorial, "Civil Rights: Everyone's Concern," *WSJ*, August 1, 1963; Kirkhorn, "How Long Will Madison Negroes Feel Heel of Bias?" *CT*, August 6, 1963; "Realtors Take New Look at Housing," *WSJ*, August 9, 1963.

10. "Meet NAACP Leader in City," *WSJ*, July 30, 1963; Kirkhorn, "Colston Aiming City NAACP Drive at Monied Society," *CT*, August 9, 1963; "Colston Gets State Welfare Dept. Post," *CT*, August 31, 1963; "City's Candid Look at Bias Is Hailed," *WSJ*, November 16, 1963; "Know Your Madisonian—Marshall Colston," *WSJ*, October 3, 1965; John Newhouse, "Most Everybody Cares Now," *WSJ*, August 10, 1968.

11. "Two Rights Laws on Books; Housing Bias Ban Planned," *WSJ*, August 20, 1963; Kirkhorn, "Fair Housing Groups Plan Ordinance Drive," *CT*, September 17, 1963; Edwin Conrad to Mayor's Commission on Human Rights, October 3, 1963, *Records, Madison Equal Opportunities Commission*, C2014/044, box 8, WHSA; "Fair Housing Law Is Planned," *WSJ*, October 4, 1963; Hank Feuerzeig, "Conrad Blames Fight on Rights Ordinance to 'Medieval' Views," *CT*, December 9, 1963; Shirley S. Abrahamson emails, April 26 and April 30, 2017.

12. "Rev. Pritchard Emphasizes Anti-Bias Steps of Church," *CT*, October 7, 1963; "First Methodist Church Supports Fair Housing," *CT*, October 15, 1963; "League of Women Voters Backs Open Housing Policy," *CT*, October 29, 1963; Gribble, "Aid on Anti-Bias Law, Church Groups Urged," *WSJ*, November 12, 1963; Richard Brautigam, "250 at Meeting Vow to Support City Ban Upon Discrimination," *CT*, November 14, 1963; "Group Will Urge Passage of City Fair Housing Law," *WSJ*, November 16, 1963; "WSA Promotes Madison Anti-Bias Ordinance; Urges Action," *DC*, December 7, 1963; "Bishops, 29 Priests Support Rights Law," *CT*, December 10, 1963; Doyle, "Conversation with Betty MacDonald," 5–11; Doyle, "Conversation with John McGrath," 26–33.

13. Madison Citizens for Fair Housing, *CT*, October 26, 1963; "Foes of Fair Housing in Anonymous Drive," *CT*, November 16, 1963.

14. Feuerzeig, "Will Widen City Rights Ordinances," *CT*, October 15, 1963; Feuerzeig, "Sweeping Anti-Bias Ordinance Is Drafted," *CT*, November 4, 1963; Gordon, "Proposed Rights Law to Cover Five Areas," *WSJ*, November 5, 1963.

15. Feuerzeig, "City Bias Ban Proposal Ready to Go to Council," *CT*, November 20, 1963.

16. Samuel C. Reynolds, "Assembly Defeats 3 Civil Rights Bills," *WSJ*, November 8, 1963.

17. Feuerzeig, "City Bias Ban Proposal Ready to Go to Council," *CT*, November 20, 1963; Brautigam, 'Equal Chance' Ordinance Gets Commission Approval," *CT*, November 21, 1963; Gordon, "Proposed Rights Law Backed," *WSJ*, November 21, 1963.

18. Editorial, "Equal Opportunities Now," *WSJ*, December 9, 1963.

19. Charles Hippenmeyer, "Ad of Realtors Draws Fire of 2 Church Leaders," *CT*, December 4, 1963; Feuerzeig, "Mayor Asks Citizens to Back Equal Rights Ordinance Proposal," *CT*, December 5, 1963; Kirkhorn, "Colston Says Realtors' Ad 'Confuses' and 'Divides,'" *CT*, December 6, 1963; Brautigam, "Panelists Praise Mayor's Rights Ordinance Support," *CT*, December 6, 1963; "Honor Mayor for Rights Stand," *CT*, December 9, 1963.

20. Feuerzeig, "Ald. Kopp Predicts Defeat of Opportunity Ordinance," *CT*, December 6, 1963; Feuerzeig, "Ald. Rohr Sees No Problem, to Vote against Rights Law," *CT*, December 7, 1963; Feuerzeig, "Chances Doubtful for Anti-Bias Ordinance," *CT*, December 10, 1963; Harvey Shapiro, "Fair Housing Bill Faces Council Today," *DC*, December 10, 1963.

21. Brautigam, "Jam-Packed Rights Debate Is Vigorous But Orderly," *CT*, December 11, 1963; Doyle, "Conversation with Betty MacDonald," 12–17; Doyle, "Conversation with John McGrath," 26–35.

22. "Know Your Madisonian—Patrick J. Lucey," *WSJ*, September 1, 1963; "City Realtors to Study Open Housing; Indicates Coolness to Ordinance," *CT*, October 22, 1963; Havens Wilber, "Local Realtors Urged to Draft Anti-Bias Policy," *CT*, October 24, 1963; Kirkhorn, "Realtors Not Consulted on Bias Ads," *CT*, December 7, 1963; "Fair Housing Unit Answers Realtors," *CT*, December 9, 1963; "Realtors' Role in Bias Hit by NAACP Official," *CT*, December 10, 1963; John T. Aehl, "Debate on Rights Draws Big Crowd," *WSJ*, December 11, 1963.

23. Advertisement, "Human Rights and the Realtor," *WSJ*, December 2, 1963; "Anti-Ordinance Spending $1,182," *CT*, December 9, 1963.

24. Brautigam, "Reject City Action on Housing Rights," *CT*, December 11, 1963.

25. Gordon, "Keep Housing Section of Rights Bill Dies," *WSJ*, December 11, 1963; Aehl, "Debate on Rights Draws Big Crowd," *WSJ*, December 11, 1963; Stu Chapman, "Housing Decision Postponed," *DC*, December 11, 1963; Brautigam, "Rejects City Action on Housing Rights," *CT*, December 11, 1963; Aehl, "CORE Bias-Testing Procedure Questioned at Council Hearing," *WSJ*, December 12, 1963.

26. Marcus, "Council Kills Ordinance for Human Rights," *CT*, March 14, 1952.

27. Feuerzeig, "Rights Backers Hunt for Key 'Swing' Vote," *CT*, December 11, 1963; editorial, "The Council Agrees that 'The World Is Built on Prejudice,'" *CT*, December 11, 1963; editorial, "Will Madison Labor Back Rohr's Stand on Human Rights?" *CT*, December 12, 1963; editorial, "One Vote Could Remove Smear of Prejudice from Madison," *CT*, December 12, 1963.

28. William Bradford Smith, interviewed by Lorraine Orchard, 1989, Historic Madison, Inc. Oral History Project; Gordon,

"More Support Hinted on Rights Law Tonight," *WSJ*, December 12, 1963; Feuerzeig, "Housing Rights Compromise to Be Introduced," *CT*, December 12, 1963; "Final Rights Vote Due Today," *DC*, December 12, 1963; Gordon, "More Support Hinted on Rights Law Tonight," *WSJ*, December 12, 1963.

29. "Rapid-Fire Action on New Law Has City Hall Picking Up Pieces," *WSJ*, December 13, 1963; Doyle, "Conversation with John McGrath," 37.

30. Gordon, "Amended Rights Law OKd," *WSJ*, December 13, 1963; "Amended Fair Housing Rule Passes," *DC*, December 13, 1963; Brautigam, "Amended Housing Bias Ban Approved," *CT*, December 13, 1963.

31. Feuerzeig, "40% of City Dwelling Units under Equality Ordinance," *CT*, December 13, 1963.

32. Feuerzeig, "City Rights Leaders Are 'Disappointed,'" *CT*, December 13, 1963; Gordon, "Clarification Is Asked on New City Rights Law," *WSJ*, December 14, 1963; editorial, "An Important Step Forward in the Fight against Bigotry," *CT*, December 13, 1963; editorial, "A Small Step Forward," *DC*, December 14, 1963; editorial, "Liberals Desert Civil Rights," *WSJ*, December 18, 1963.

33. Doyle, "Conversation with John McGrath," 37; Betty MacDonald interview, September 27, 2017.

34. "Mrs. Abrahamson Partner in La Follette Law Firm," *CT*, July 5, 1963.

35. Doyle, "Conversation with John McGrath," 37; Brautigam, "Local Labor for 'Rights,' but Not Here," *CT*, December 17, 1963; editorial, "The Sad Hypocrisy of Labor on Equal Opportunity Law," *CT*, December 18, 1962.

36. "Equal Rights Unit Named; Council Confirms Choices, *WSJ*, December 27, 1963.

37. "C.C. Board Backs Equal Job Chances," *CT*, July 2, 1963; Kirkhorn, "Madison Stores May Be Picketed in Job Bias Drive," *CT*, July 3, 1963; "City Rights Unit Asked," *WSJ*, July 6, 1963; Kirkhorn, "Madison Negroes Make Minor Dents in Local Job Bias," *CT*, August 7, 1963; Jeff Smoller, "Negroes Ask Jobs, Not Love," *DC*, October 26, 1963.

38. "Survey Reveals Job Bias in Madison Restaurants," *CT*, July 6, 1963; Kirkhorn, "No Negro Trade Apprentices Here," *CT*, June 26, 1963; James D. Selk, "Firms Deny Discrimination," *WSJ*, November 22, 1963; Kirkhorn, "47 Negroes Employed by 9 Big Firms Here," *CT*, November 29, 1963.

39. "UW Slap at State's Righters Rejected," *WSJ*, March 5, 1963; "Also Rejects 'Nullification' Sports Plan," *DC*, March 5, 1963.

40. Editorial, "Crossroads in Rights March," *WSJ*, August 1, 1963; Kirkhorn, "Madison People to Join Washington Rights March," *CT*, August 13, 1963; "35 from Madison in Civil Rights Bus Trip," *CT*, August 24, 1963; "38 Leave for Rights March; Two Thirds of Group White," *CT*, August 27, 1963; "38 Leave City to

Join March on Washington," *WSJ*, August 28, 1963; John Patrick Hunter, "Colston Praises March on Capital for Its Unity, Size," *CT*, August 29, 1963; Hunter, "'We Shall Overcome,' Chant Weary, but Happy Marchers," *CT*, August 30, 1963; "Madison's Marchers Welcomed upon Return," *WSJ*, August 30, 1963.

41. "NAACP Tells CC: End Job Bias," *CT*, June 15, 1963.

42. BOR minutes, August 2, 1963; Hunter, "University Plans Civil Rights Study," *CT*, August 3, 1963.

43. Kirkhorn, "Negroes Consider Education as Key to Their Future," *CT*, August 10, 1963; "Bias in Schools? No and Yes," *WSJ*, August 15, 1963.

44. Sharon Coady, "Negro Youth Discovers People Listen to Him," *WSJ*, October 20, 1963.

45. "Birmingham Sympathy March Slated Sunday," *CT*, September 20, 1963; "Sunday March Set for Bomb Victims," *DC*, September 21, 1963; William E. Hauda, "Rights March Here Disrupted," *WSJ*, September 23, 1963; "Nazi Symbol at Local Ceremony," *CT*, September 23, 1963; John Gruber, "700 Rally for Alabama Victims," *DC*, September 24, 1963; "Reierson Will Get Jury Trial," *CT*, September 28, 1963.

46. Irvin Kreisman, "Donald Murphy Appointed Assistant District Attorney," *CT*, September 24, 1963.

47. "'U' Bias Film Debuts Monday," *DC*, October 26, 1963; "Film on Bias in Housing to Have Premiere Monday," *CT*, October 26, 1963; Selk, "UW Housing Bias Films Attracts 600," *WSJ*, October 29, 1963; Lynne Abraham, "Housing Bias Film Lacks Suspense; Panel Stars," *DC*, October 29, 1963; Brautigam, "UW Film on Housing Bias Stirs Audience Questions," *CT*, October 29, 1963; editorial, "The Bias Film Case," *DC*, October 30, 1963.

48. "SNCC Leader Pledges Peaceful Upset of Bias," *DC*, November 12, 1963.

49. Student Organization Registration file, University Archives; Selk, "CORE Plans Drive against Bias," *WSJ*, November 20, 1963.

50. "CORE to Organize University Group," *DC*, April 3, 1963; Phyllis Berman, "Farmer Outlines Racial Conflicts," *DC*, November 20, 1963; Selk, "CORE Plans Drive Against Bias," *WSJ*, November 20, 1963; Student Organization Registration files, University Archives.

51. Gordon, "Urban Renewal in City Hailed," *WSJ*, January 25, 1963; "Housing for Elderly Started," *WSJ*, May 26, 1963; MRA minutes, June 11, 1963; "85% of Triangle Land Acquired," *WSJ*, June 12, 1963; "Preliminary Study Work Begun for Marquette Area Renewal," *WSJ*, November 11, 1963; "Turf's Too Tough at MHA Ground Ceremony," *WSJ*, December 20, 1963; "Work Starts on Four Public Housing Sites," *WSJ*, December 20, 1963; "Break Ground for Public Housing," *CT*, December 20, 1963; MRA minutes, November 12, 1963.

52. Editorial, "City Housing Squabble Must End," *WSJ*, January 4, 1963.

53. "MHA Declines to Act on Plan for Rental of Public Housing," *WSJ*, March 22, 1963; MRA Minutes, June 25, 1963.

54. CC minutes, May 23, 1963; "Triangle Building Plan Approved," *WSJ*, May 24, 1963; Marcus, "Council Backs Remap Under 22-Ward Plan," *CT*, May 24, 1963; MRA minutes, June 11, 1963.

55. MRA minutes, June 11, 1963; "85% of Triangle Land Acquired," *WSJ*, June 12, 1963; MRA minutes, June 25, 1963.

56. "Public Housing Project's Costs Cut by MHA Changes," *WSJ*, November 12, 1963.

57. MRA minutes, December 10, 1963; "Vilas Towers Given Tentative Approval for Site in Triangle," *WSJ*, November 13, 1963; "MRA to Bail Out Vilas Towers, Inc.," *CT*, December 11, 1963.

58. "Mayor Hits McGinnis for Renewal Problem," *WSJ*, March 13, 1963; Marcus, "Mayor Says McGinnis 'Bungled' on Renewal," *CT*, March 13, 1963.

59. MRA minutes, March 14, 1963; "MRA Members Assail Mayor," *WSJ*, March 15, 1963; "MRA Members Lash Mayor; See Criticism as 'Political,'" *CT*, March 15, 1963.]

60. Marcus, "McGinnis Quits MRA Job," *CT*, April 8, 1963; Gordon, "McGinnis Leaves MRA with a Blast at Mayor," *WSJ*, April 9, 1963; editorial, "McGinnis' Resignation from MRA Provides an Opportunity," *CT*, April 10, 1963.

61. Marcus, "Rohr Follows McGinnis out of Post with MRA," *CT*, April 9, 1963; "Ald. Rohr Also Leaves MRA; Urges End to Renewal Study," *WSJ*, April 10, 1963.

62. "Falk Named to MRA; Forster on Police Unit," *WSJ*, April 17, 1963; MRA minutes, April 18, 1963; Gordon, "Falk Elected New Chairman of MRA," *WSJ*, April 19, 1963; "Falk Elected Chairman of Redevelopment Authority," *CT*, April 19, 1963.

63. MRA minutes, May 24, 1962; "U.W.-City Planning Study Set," *WSJ*, June 29, 1962.

64. Marcus, "Detail $13.8 Million U. Renewal Project," *CT*, February 4, 1963; "Move for UW Renewal Area Study Prepared," *WSJ*, February 5, 1963; Gordon, "Urban Renewal Merits, Drawbacks Discussed," *WSJ*, February 14, 1963; Marcus, "McGinnis Backs Study of U.W. Area Renewal," *CT*, February 22, 1963; Aehl, "Urban Renewal Involves 14,000," *WSJ*, March 3, 1963.

65. Bob Karlman, "City Council Hears 'U' Urban Renewal Plan," *DC*, February 27, 1963; Marcus, "U. Area Renewal Plan Snarled in Council Row," *CT*, February 27, 1963; CC minutes, February 28, 1963; Aehl, "UW Area Renewal Study Is Approved," *WSJ*, March 1, 1963; Marcus, "Council Approves Federal Aid for U.W. Area Study," *CT*, March 1, 1963; Karlman, "Urban Renewal: A New University Area Study," *DC*, March 2, 1963; Robert Franzmann, "UW Renewal Area Explanation Eases Fears of Neighborhood," *WSJ*, March 7, 1963; McCormick, "150 Hear MRA, U.W. Tell Urban Renewal Objectives, *CT*, March 7, 1963; "McGinnis Hits 'U'-City Urban Renewal Plan," *DC*, March 16, 1963.

66. Gordon, "Group Set to Fight Renewal Area Study," *WSJ*, March 19, 1963; McCormick, "Stormy Meeting Hears Attacks on UW Renewal Study," *CT*, March 19, 1963.

67. "Mayor Pushed UW Renewal Fund Plea," *CT*, April 1, 1963; "Citizen Unit Renewal Circular 'Not True,' Ald. Elder Asserts," *WSJ*, April 5, 1963; "Asserts Ald. Elder Spoke Up Too Late," *CT*, April 5, 1963; "Rupnow Hits Campaign Charges," *WSJ*, April 6, 1963; "'Watchdog' Committee Defends 'Pink Sheets,'" *WSJ*, April 8, 1963.

68. Gordon, "Mayor Reynolds Wins," *WSJ*, April 3, 1963; Aehl, "Six New Aldermen Elected; 4 Ousted," *WSJ*, April 3, 1963; "Mayor in Close Victory," *CT*, April 3, 1963; "Four Aldermen Defeated in Big Council Shake-Up," *CT*, April 3, 1963.

69. Marcus, "Rohr Follows McGinnis out of Post with MRA," *CT*, April 9, 1963; "Ald. Rohr Also Leaves MRA; Urges End to Renewal Study," *WSJ*, April 10, 1963; "Renewal Area Survey Fund Backed by Mayor," *WSJ*, April 20, 1963.

70. Gordon, "Bid for Renewal Study Fund Rescinded," *WSJ*, April 24, 1963; Marcus, "Council Vote Backs Halting U.W. Area Renewal Study," *CT*, April 24, 1963.

71. CC minutes, April 25, 1963; Gordon, "Renewal Area Study Revived," *WSJ*, April 26, 1963; "City Council Reverses Decision to Ask Urban Renewal Funds," *DC*, April 26, 1963; Marcus, "One-Vote Council Margin Saves UW Area Study Plan," *CT*, April 26, 1963; Gribble, "OK Is Seen on Funds for UW Renewal Study," *WSJ*, November 22, 1963.

72. "Residents in Campus Area Plan Anti-Renewal Drive," *CT*, August 8, 1963; "UW Area Group Fights Renewal," *WSJ*, August 9, 1963; Kirkhorn, "Group Plans Drive against MRA Plans for U.W. Area," *CT*, August 23, 1963; Kirkhorn, "Ex-Triangle Residents Hit MRA," August 26, 1963; William Witt, "Referendum on Urban Renewal Plans Pushed," *WSJ*, September 18, 1963.

73. "Council Considers East Side Area Renewal Study," *WSJ*, September 23, 1963; "Group Raps Plan on Renewal Study," *WSJ*, September 24, 1963; Feuerzeig, "Council Vote Slaps Foes of Renewal, *CT*, September 25, 1963; CC minutes, September 26, 1963; Aehl, "Urban Renewal Study Is OKd for Marquette School's Area," *WSJ*, September 27, 1963; "Council Oks Marquette Area Redevelopment Study," *CT*, September 27, 1963; "East Side Renewal Report Due Nov. 21," *WSJ*, October 9, 1963; Brautigam, "300 Hear Attacks on MRA Renewal Record," *CT*, October 17, 1963; Gribble, "Urban Renewal, MRA Draws Fire at Home Owners Group Session," *WSJ*, October 17, 1963; "Preliminary Study Work Begun for Marquette Area Renewal," *WSJ*, November 11, 1963.

74. Gordon, "East Side Block Action Delayed," *WSJ*, November 29, 1963; "3 Alternatives Suggested for East Side Improvement," *WSJ*, December 4, 1963; "Renewal Foes Issue New Blast," *CT*, December 7, 1963; MRA Minutes, December 10, 1963; "Council Receives Proposals for Aiding Marquette Area," *WSJ*, December 14, 1963; Feuerzeig, "Asks 'Moderate' Plan for Marquette Section," *CT*, December 17, 1963; CC minutes, December 26, 1963; Aehl, "'Moderate' Approach on Renewal Supported," *WSJ*, December 27, 1963; "Form Marquette Renewal Plan Group," *CT*, December 27, 1963.

75. Helen Matheson, "Urban Renewal Wins Favor," *WSJ*, November 3, 1963.

76. Richard W. Vesey, "Part of Old Madison Dies with St. Joseph's," *WSJ*, August 25, 1963; Goroff, et al, *The Spirit of Greenbush*, 11; Matheson, "Urban Renewal Wins Favor," *WSJ*, November 3, 1963.

77. "MRA Official Says Realtors Gave Little Help in Relocations Here," *WSJ*, December 12, 1963.

78. Hauda, "UW Sociologist Raps Report on Relocation," *WSJ*, January 18, 1964; "Methods of MRA Are Hit," *CT*, January 18, 1964; "Relocation Report's Critic Apologizes to MRA Director," *WSJ*, January 25, 1964.

79. MRA minutes, January 11, 1963; "MRA Sets Ban on Bias in South Side Project," *WSJ*, January 12, 1963; MRA minutes, March 14, 1963.

80. MRA minutes, November 12, 1963; "Open Housing List Rejected," *WSJ*, November 13, 1963; "MRA to Continue White-Only Listing," *CT*, November 13, 1963.

81. "Ald. McCormick Pressed to Run in Mayor Race," *CT*, September 28, 1962; "Atty. Albert J. McGinnis Is Candidate for Mayor," *CT*, November 10, 1962; "McGinnis Announces Candidacy for Mayor," *WSJ*, November 11, 1962; "City Ring Has 2, Awaits More Hats," *WSJ*, December 10, 1962; "Ex-Ald. Hutchison Weighs Entry in Race for Mayor," *WSJ*, December 19, 1962; "Bert Hutchison Takes out Papers for Mayor's Race," *CT*, December 19, 1962; "Otto Festge Is Seriously Considering Mayor's Race," December 28, 1962; Gordon, "With Carley Out, Festge Seen Entering Mayor Race," *WSJ*, December 29, 1962; Kreisman, "Festge Will Not Seek Mayor Post in April," *CT*, January 14, 1963.

82. "McGinnis Says Mayor Has Fiscally 'Mismanaged' City," *CT*, January 29, 1963; "McGinnis Still Pounds at City Finance Issue," *CT*, January 31, 1963; Marcus, "McGinnis Says Mayor Ignored Water Survey," *CT*, February 1, 1963; editorial, "McGinnis Wants 'Instant' Spending," *WSJ*, February 1, 1963; "McGinnis Says Conklin Park Site Unsuitable for City's Auditorium," *WSJ*, February 4, 1963; Marcus, "McGinnis Raps 'Lump' Street Bond Vote Plan," *CT*, February 6, 1963; Elliott Maraniss, "McGinnis Backs Monona Terrace as 'Good' Location," *CT*, February 8, 1963; Marcus, "Put Madison's Interests Above Surburbs: McGinnis," *CT*, February 11, 1963; editorial, "Wrong Step on Referendum," *WSJ*, February 12, 1963; "McGinnis Cites Boost in City Property Taxes," *CT*, February 21, 1963; Marcus, "McGinnis Backs Study of U.W. Area Renewal," *CT*, February 22, 1963; Marcus, "McGinnis Attacks 'Packing' of Bond Issues on Ballot," *CT*, March 8, 1963; "McGinnis Hits Mayor on Tax 'Half-Truths,'" *CT*, March 16, 1963;

"McGinnis Refutes Mayor's Claim of Curb on Mill Rate," *CT,* March 28, 1963.

83. Ron McCrea email, January 3, 2017.

84. "Mayor Says City Finances Are in Sound Condition," *CT,* February 28, 1963; "Mayor Criticizes McGinnis on Three Issues in Campaign," *WSJ,* March 19, 1963; "Mayor Hits McGinnis on City School Issue," *WSJ,* March 28, 1963; "Mayor Deplores McGinnis' Use of Word 'Smear,'" *WSJ,* March 29, 1963.

85. Editorial, "Some Things to Consider about Voting Bonds for Causeway," *CT,* February 26, 1963; editorial, "Monona Bay Causeway Is Now within Grasp," *WSJ,* March 1, 1963; "Reynolds Defends Causeway," *CT,* March 9, 1963; editorial, "Causeway: Reynolds vs. McGinnis," *WSJ,* March 12, 1963; editorial, "McGinnis Weak on Causeway," *WSJ,* March 19, 1963; editorial, "A Mayor from Madison for Madison—Albert J. McGinnis," *CT,* March 19, 1963.

86. Marcus, "Mayor Says McGinnis 'Bungled' on Renewal," *CT,* March 12, 1963; "Mayor Hits McGinnis for Renewal Problem," *WSJ,* March 13, 1963; editorial, "McGinnis Bungles Public Housing," *WSJ,* March 13, 1963; Marcus, "Reynolds Smears McGinnis in Letter to City Teachers," *CT,* March 25, 1963; Gordon, "Reynolds, McGinnis Vie to End," *WSJ,* March 31, 1963.

87. Gordon, "Mayor Reynolds Wins," *WSJ,* April 3, 1963; "Mayor in Close Victory," *CT,* April 3, 1963.

88. "All Five Bond Issues Given City Support," *WSJ,* April 3, 1963; "Vote $8 Million City Debt," *CT,* April 3, 1963.

89. Aehl, "Six New Aldermen Elected; Four Ousted," *WSJ,* April 3, 1963; "Four Aldermen Defeated in Big Council Shake-Up," *CT,* April 3, 1963.

90. Marcus, "Kopp New Council Head," *CT,* April 16, 1963; Gordon, "Kopp Defeats Davidson for Council Presidency," *WSJ,* April 17, 1963.

91. Hunter, "2,700 Get Degrees at Commencement," June 10, 1963.

92. "Over 2,700 Receive Degrees at 110th Commencement," *Wisconsin Alumnus* 64, no. 10 (July 1963): 6.

93. "UW Acts to Limit Out-of-State Students," *WSJ,* April 22, 1963.

94. Ben Sidran, "Stage Show Just Misses them Mark," *DC,* November 9, 1963.

95. "Slate Van Vleck Open House on Saturday," *CT,* May 6, 1963; Feldman, *Buildings,* 324–326.

96. Marcia Crowley, "UW Dorm Greets Men, Women," *WSJ,* September 11, 1963; Feldman, *Buildings,* 362–365.

97. BOR minutes, January 11, 1963; David Bednarek, "Harrington Pledges Help of UW in Industrial Research Facilities," *WSJ,* January 12, 1963; Hunter, "U. Balks at Research Park Idea," *CT,* January 12, 1963.

98. "U.W. Police Force Gets First Woman Investigator," *CT,* January 24, 1963.

99. Maxine Sheets, "Cunningham Concert Artistic Display of Free Movement," *DC,* February 19, 1963.

100. "Statistical Information about American Casualties in the Vietnam War," https://www.archives.gov/research/military/vietnam-war/casualty-statistics.html.

101. "Five Bands to Entertain at Military Ball," *DC,* February 19, 1963; Photo, *Daily Cardinal,* March 6, 1963.

102. A. Lee Beier, "Poet Auden's 'Lecture' Wins Approval of Student Audience," *WSJ,* March 11, 1963; Jeff Smoller, "Tension, Originality Are Poet's Problems: Auden," *DC,* March 12, 1963.

103. Witt, "Badgers Get Heroes Welcome," *WSJ,* January 4, 1963; "The Badgers' Glorious Defeat," *Wisconsin Alumnus* 64, no. 4 (January 1963): 12–15.

104. Walter Sheppard, "Segovia Thrills Audience with Tone and Technique," *DC,* March 27, 1963; McCormick, "Segovia's Music Awes Audience," *CT,* March 27, 1963.

105. Harva Hachten, "Women Credited at Their Day," *WSJ,* April 24, 1963; "Wisconsin Women Enjoy Their Special Day," *Wisconsin Alumnus* 64, no. 9 (June 1963): 4.

106. Bednarek, "Later Hours for UW Coeds Are Approved," *WSJ,* April 26, 1963; Bill Wineke, "SLIC OK's New Women's Hours," *DC,* April 26, 1963; "Women Student Hours Liberalized by SLIC," *Wisconsin Alumnus* 64, no. 9 (June 1963): 8; "New Hours for Women," *Wisconsin Alumnus* 65, no. 5 (February 1964): 12–13.

107. Coady, "Margaret Mead Assails Early Marriages," *WSJ,* April 29, 1963.

108. Dave Prosten, "Change Arms Race into Economic Race: Reuther," *DC,* May 3, 1963.

109. "Ferlinghetti Delights Crowd, Reads 'Controversial' Work," *DC,* May 3, 1963.

110. Advertisement, *DC,* May 17, 1963; Sidran, *A Life in the Music,* 35–42.

111. "Faculty Makes ROTC Optional," *DC,* May 8, 1963; "ROTC Becomes Voluntary on a Permanent Basis," *Wisconsin Alumnus* 64, no. 9 (June 1963): 9.

112. "Good Memories, Future Hopes Mark University Swingout Event," *WSJ,* May 20, 1963.

113. Wineke, "SLIC Allows Senior Apartments," *DC,* May 22, 1963.

114. "Richter to Be Honored at Founder's Day," *WSJ,* May 14, 1963; Jay Poster, "A Tribute to Pat Richter," *DC,* May 23, 1963; Monte McCormick, "Richter Signs Redskins Contract," *WSJ,* May 30, 1963; Lew Cornelius, "Richter Signs Pro Grid Contract With Redskins," *CT,* May 30, 1963; Vince Sweeney, *Always a Badger: The Pat Richter Story* (Black Earth, WI: Trails Books, 2005), 9–51; Steven D. Schmitt, *A History of Badger Baseball: The Rise and Fall of America's Pastime at the University of Wisconsin* (Madison: University of Wisconsin Press, 2017), 109–110.

115. "Beer Parties Rescued, Smut Prove Approved," *WSJ,* August 3, 1963.

116. "Students Plan Hiroshima Bomb Demonstration," *DC*, August 6, 1963.

117. "Goldberg, French History Specialist, to Return to U.," *CT*, August 19, 1963; Ron McCrea and Dave Wagner, "Harvey Goldberg," in Buhle, ed., *History and the New Left*, 241–245.

118. "Hayden to Give Critique of U.S. Liberalism," *DC*, September 28, 1963.

119. John Efferding, "Campus Groups Protest U.S. Action in Vietnam," *DC*, October 18, 1963; "Students Protest Viet Nam Policy," *WSJ*, October 19, 1963; "350 Gather for Viet Nam Rally," *DC*, October 19, 1963; "Statistical Information about American Casualties in the Vietnam War," https://www.archives.gov /research/military/vietnam-war/casualty-statistics.html.

120. "Dr. Rosser Is Appointed Math Research Center Head," *CT*, December 23, 1963; https://en.wikipedia.org/wiki/J._Barkley _Rosser.

121. "Madison High Schools Mark Graduation," *WSJ*, June 15, 1963; "475 Are Graduated at West, 213 at Central; 408 Get Diplomas at East High Ceremony," *CT*, June 15, 1963.

122. "City Schools Enroll 28,969," *WSJ*, September 14, 1963.

123. "La Follette School Dedicated to Memory of State's Greatest Son," *CT*, October 12, 1963.

124. "Hailed at His School, Falk Credits Others," *WSJ*, November 20, 1963.

125. "Robert D. Gilberts Takes Over as Superintendent of Schools," *WSJ*, January 3, 1963.

126. Bednarek, "Lincoln School to Be Closed in Fall," *WSJ*, March 5, 1963; Sanford Moss, "Lincoln Parents Ask Board to Reconsider Closing Plan," *WSJ*, March 13, 1963; "Lincoln School's Closing Reviewed," *WSJ*, April 16, 1963; "Lincoln School to Get New Chance," *CT*, April 17, 1963; "Lincoln School Closing Upheld," *WSJ*, May 7, 1963; "Reaffirm Closing of Lincoln School," *CT*, May 7, 1963; "Lincoln School Is Eyed for Art Association Use," *CT*, May 16, 1963.

127. Bednarek, "Site for New West Side High Is Recommended," *WSJ*, March 7, 1963; "Eye Site for 5th City High," *CT*, March 7, 1963; Bednarek, "$9.2 Million Is Sought to Build New Schools," *WSJ*, August 2, 1963; Bednarek, "South Side Junior High Plans Given Go-Ahead," *WSJ*, September 4, 1963; "Back Junior High on Burr Oaks Site," *CT*, September 4, 1963.

128. Bednarek, "Board Extends Quitting Time for City's Pregnant Teachers," *WSJ*, May 21, 1963.

129. June Dieckmann, "Young Vandals Damage Schools at Record Rate, Lack Respect," *WSJ*, August 26, 1963.

130. Bednarek, "Cuba Traveler's Talk Is Opposed," *WSJ*, October 22, 1963; "Board Takes Yes-and-No Stand on Speech on Cuba," *CT*, October 22, 1963; "Board's Refusal to Permit Talk Is 'Appalling' to Cuba Visitor," *DC*, October 24, 1963; Efferding, "Board Will Probably Let Visitor to Cuba Speak," *DC*, October 25, 1963; John Coatsworth interview, July 18, 2017.

131. "School Board Bars Cuba Talk," *DC*, November 5, 1963; "School Board Rejects New Plea for Speech on Cuba," *CT*, November 5, 1963.

132. Bednarek, "Vocational School's 50 Years Old," *WSJ*, March 10, 1963; "50 Years of Continuous Growth in Education," Madison Vocational Technical and Adult Schools, WI-M 1 VOC.2:E5/1963.

133. "La Follette Family in School Dedication," *CT*, October 2, 1963; "La Follette School Dedicated to Memory of State's Greatest Son," *CT*, October 12, 1963; Coady, "La Follette School Dedicated," *WSJ*, October 14, 1963.

134. George McCormick, "New School to Be Named for Falk," *CT*, July 1, 1963; "Falk School Dedication Slated, *CT*, November 16, 1963; Bednarek, "Hailed at His School, Falk Credits Others," *WSJ*, November 20, 1963.

135. Kirkhorn, "Police Censor Orders Scene Cut from Film," *CT*, January 7, 1963; editorial, "Is Inspector Thomas to Tell Madison What It Can Know?" *CT*, January 8, 1963; "Thomas' Censorship Disturbs Liberties Unit," *CT*, January 9, 1963; "Thomas Tells Events in Film Cutting Incident," *CT*, January 10, 1963; "Citizen Group to Get Movie Censorship Task," *WSJ*, January 11, 1963; "Says Faculty Censored Art Exhibited at U.W.," *CT*, January 11, 1963; "Love Scene Reinstated in 'Phaedra,'" *DC*, January 11, 1963; editorial, "The Absurdities of Censorship Can Come to Madison, Too," *CT*, January 12, 1963; editorial, "Censorship Not a Police Task," *WSJ*, January 14, 1963; "Group on Cultural Freedom Asks Review, Not Censorship," *CT*, January 16, 1963; "No City Censorship Board, Conrad Advises," *WSJ*, March 11, 1963; "Mayor's Censorship Plans Invalid, City Counsel Says," *CT*, March 11, 1963.

136. "Raid 'Bongo Party' at Church," *CT*, May 11, 1963; "21 Face Charges for 'Bongo Party,'" *WSJ*, May 12, 1963; "Bongo Drum, Devotees Deny Disorderly Counts," *WSJ*, May 14, 1963; John Gruber, "'Bongo' Case Set for June 19," *DC*, May 14, 1963; Gruber, "'Bongo' Students Hit Police for Misconduct," *DC*, May 15, 1963; "'Bongo' Students Can't Enroll Until Court Decision Is Made," *DC*, May 17, 1963; "Senate Urges No 'U' 'Bongo' Action," *DC*, May 22, 1963; Dieckmann, "Drums Parade Silently as Bongo Trial Starts," *WSJ*, June 20, 1963; Kreisman, "Judge's Gavel Sets the Beat at Bongo Party Trial of 19," *CT*, June 20, 1963; Kreisman, "Defense Subpoena's Sheriff's Dog as Bongo Party Trial Beats Along," *CT*, June 21, 1963; Kreisman, "Bongo Trial Ends on Apology Notes," *CT*, June 22, 1963; editorial, "Suitable Action on Bongo Case," *WSJ*, June 22, 1963; "Bongo Students Dismissed by Letters of Apology," *DC*, June 25, 1963; Ben Sidran email, May 3, 2017.

137. Dieckmann, "Dragnet on Square Eluded by Gunman," *WSJ*, October 29, 1963.

138. Dieckmann, "Gun Kills UW Student in Suite at Edgewater," *WSJ*, December 17, 1963; Gruber, "Former 'U' Student

Found Slain," *DC*, December 17, 1963; "Fatal Edgewater Shooting Reveals Dope Probe Here," *CT*, December 17, 1963; Dieckmann, "UW Area Dope Ring Bared," *WSJ*, December 18, 1963; Gruber, "Police Chief Reveals Narcotics Probe," *DC*, December 18, 1963; "UW Admits Narcotic Problem," *CT*, December 18, 1963; Dieckmann, "UW Co-ed Link to Campus Area Dope Ring Eyed," *WSJ*, December 19, 1963; "'U' Assists City Dope Probe," *DC*, December 19, 1963; "Secrecy Lid Clamped on Probe of Dope Ring," *WSJ*, December 20, 1963; "Dope Probe to Continue over Holiday," *DC*, December 20, 1963; "Accidental Death Reveals Dope Probe," *Wisconsin Alumnus* 65, no. 4 (January 1964): 5.

139. "Bruns Garage Mechanics Walk Out in Wildcat Strike," *CT*, May 24, 1963; Selk, "Non-Striking Garage Workers Tell of Threats at WERB Hearing," *WSJ*, June 29, 1963; "Students Aid Striking VW Mechanics," *DC*, July 11, 1963; "MFL Attacks Hiring Out of Off-Duty Police in Strikes," *CT*, July 16, 1963; "Ban Off-Duty City Police Guards at Bruns Garage," *CT*, July 18, 1963; Kirkhorn, "Bruns Strikers Run Their Own Garage," *CT*, October 2, 1963; Selk, "Six of 11 Strikers Go Back to Work at Bruns," *WSJ*, December 10, 1963; C. Clark Kissinger, "Students Get Back into Labor (on the Ground Floor)," SDS Collection, Series 2B, box 15, WHSA; Kirkpatrick Sale, *SDS* (New York: Random House, 1973), 126–128, 663–664; C. Clark Kissinger email, April 16, 2017.

140. Gordon, "Anti-Secrecy Law Set as City Policy," *WSJ*, March 15, 1963; Marcus, "Council Votes Tough Ban on City Board Secrecy," *CT*, March 15, 1963.

141. Witt, "McGraw Named New Fire Chief," *WSJ*, March 17, 1963; "Fire-Police Unit Elects New Chief at Secret Meet," *CT*, March 18, 1963.

142. Gordon, "'No-Work, No-Relief' Policy Is Formalized," *WSJ*, May 15, 1963.

143. "Shelters' CD Supplies Arrive," *WSJ*, May 21, 1963.

144. "It's James Madison Park Now," *WSJ*, June 6, 1963; "Conklin Recreation Area Now James Madison Park," *CT*, June 6, 1963; Levitan, *Sesquicentennial History,* 95.

145. "Record 388 Dutch Elm Cases Confirmed This Year," *WSJ*, October 1, 1963; "Dutch Elm Spray Work Will Start," *WSJ*, October 24, 1963; "Dutch Elm Spray Work to Expand," *WSJ*, October 26, 1963.

146. Aldric Revell, "Approve Monona Causeway," *CT*, January 4, 1963; editorial, "PSC Again Fails to Protect Public Interest in Lake Monona," *CT*, January 5, 1963; "PSC Gives Green Light to Causeway," *WSJ*, January 5, 1963; editorial, "Causeway Approval Is Good News," *WSJ*, January 7, 1963; "All Five Bond Issues Given City Support," *WSJ*, April 3, 1963.

147. "Dump Rubble in Monona," *CT*, January 9, 1963; editorial, "The Mayor Wastes No Time," *CT*, January 10, 1963; "PSC Denies Rehearing on Monona Causeway," *CT*, February 12, 1963; Aehl, "Split Vote Is Planned on Causeway Bonds," *WSJ*, February 13, 1963; Marcus, "Plan Separate Causeway Bond Vote," *CT*,

February 13, 1963; Newhouse, "Causeway Raises Questions," *WSJ*, February 17, 1963; editorial, "Some Things to Consider about Voting Bonds for Causeway," *CT*, February 26, 1963; "Causeway Vital to City, CC Says," *WSJ*, February 26, 1963; Marcus, "Causeway Cost Estimates 'Far Too Low,' Is Charge," *CT*, February 26, 1963; Gordon, "Referendum on Causeway Approved," *WSJ*, February 27, 1963; Marcus, "Causeway Bonds Put on Ballot," *CT*, February 27, 1963; editorial, "Monona Bay Causeway Is Now Within Grasp," *WSJ*, March 1, 1963; Gordon, "Causeway, Street Bonds Ballot OKd," *WSJ*, March 1, 1963; Gordon, "Causeway's Costs So Far: $28,095," *WSJ*, March 27, 1963; Marcus, "Mayor's Firm Owns Land Near Causeway," *CT*, March 29, 1963.

148. Aehl, "City Causeway, Airport Action Set," *WSJ*, April 12, 1963; "Bellevue Ct. Area Razing Is Seen in Causeway Plan," *CT*, April 22, 1963; CC minutes, May 23, 1963; Gordon, "Council Authorizes Fill for Monona Causeway," *WSJ*, May 24, 1963; Gribble, "Flad Firm Draws Plans for Causeway," *WSJ*, June 14, 1963; Gordon, "Causeway Faces Aid Fund Delay," *WSJ*, July 16, 1963; "Causeway Faces Long Wait for Aid," *CT*, July 16, 1963; editorial, "Madison Pays Price for Its Thoughtless Rush on Causeway," *CT*, July 17, 1963; "Mayor Hits C-T Editorials, Defends Causeway Policy," *CT*, July 18, 1963; "Causeway Needed, Mayor Points Out," *WSJ*, July 19, 1963; editorial, "The Costly Delay of Causeway," *WSJ*, July 22, 1963; Marcus, "Don't Use Mayor's Rubble for Causeway, City Told," *CT*, August 2, 1963; "Engineers Oppose Rubble Fill for Use in Causeway Project," *WSJ*, August 3, 1963; "Report on Causeway Awaits Traffic Study," *WSJ*, September 12, 1963; "Four-Lane Causeway Placed at $896,000," *WSJ*, November 6, 1963; editorial, "Causeway: Cause for Smiles," *WSJ*, November 8, 1963; "First Relocation Okd for Causeway Plan," *WSJ*, December 20, 1963; "Action on Acquiring 11 Causeway Sites Delayed," *WSJ*, December 28, 1963.

149. "Ceremony Opens Library Project," *WSJ*, October 29, 1963; Feuerzeig, "Plan Twin-Tower State St. Dorm," *CT*, June 22, 1963; Selk, "Building Surge Pushes City Upward, Outward," *WSJ*, August 11, 1963; "Anchor Bank Rises Rapidly," *WSJ*, September 11, 1963; "City Council Authorizes Loan for Lake St. Ramp," *WSJ*, May 25, 1963; "Lake Street Parking Ramp Work Will Start Monday," *CT*, September 28, 1964.

150. "580-Unit Living Complex Rises," *WSJ*, December 12, 1963.

151. "Park Inn Opens in May," *WSJ*, March 10, 1963; Newhouse, "Park Motor Inn Opens Today," *WSJ*, May 2, 1963; Coady, "Hustle at Hostelry Greets Park Guests," *WSJ*, May 3, 1963.

152. Gordon, "Buy Hanks-Vilas Site, Special Unit Urges City," *WSJ*, May 2, 1963; "Parks Commission Gets Vilas-Hanks Site Proposal," *CT*, May 2, 1963; Newhouse, "Findorff Firm Sells Hanks-Vilas Property," *WSJ*, May 5, 1963; Marcus, "Criticize Hanks-Vilas Property Sale to Firm," *CT*, May 6, 1963; Maraniss, "Firm Begins to Raze Historic Vilas Manse," *CT*, May 23, 1963;

"Vilas Mansion Turns to Rubble as Wrecking Crews End an Era," *WSJ*, May 24, 1963.

153. *Madison v. Frank Lloyd Wright Foundation*, 20 Wis. 2d 361 (1963); "Auditorium Issues Up Tonight," *CT*, January 8, 1963; Gordon, "Auditorium Question Delayed by 'Shortage,'" *WSJ*, January 9, 1963; Marcus, "Auditorium Issue Is Delayed Again by Absenteeism," *CT*, January 9, 1963; "McGinnis Says Conklin Park Site Unsuitable for City's Auditorium," *WSJ*, February 4, 1963; Gordon, "OK on Architect May Await Spring Election," *WSJ*, February 13, 1963; Marcus, "Council Reaffirms Decision Blocking Hiring of Architect," *CT*, February 15, 1963; "High Court Hears of Terrace Again," *WSJ*, June 5, 1963; Marcus, "Wright-City Pact Valid," *CT*, June 28, 1963; "Wright Pact Ruling Hailed by Attorney," *CT*, June 28, 1963; "Wright Pact with City Valid, High Court Says," *WSJ*, June 29, 1963; Gordon, "New Look at Auditorium Is Hinted," *WSJ*, July 18, 1963; editorial, "A Fresh Look at the Auditorium," *WSJ*, July 25, 1963; editorial, "And Now—a New 'Question'—Do We Need an Auditorium?" *CT*, July 26, 1963; "Rehearing Sought in Wright Dispute," *WSJ*, July 27, 1963; Feuerzeig, "Mayor Says City Needs Auditorium Despite Coliseum," *CT*, September 24, 1963; editorial, "County Coliseum Is Intended to Kill City Auditorium," *CT*, September 27, 1963; "City Denied Terrace Fee Rehearing," *CT*, October 1, 1963; Gordon, "Talks Set on Auditorium," *WSJ*, October 9, 1963; Brautigam, "Wright Auditorium 'Alive,'" *CT*, October 9, 1963; editorial, "Auditorium Door Not Closed," *WSJ*, October 10, 1963; Feuerzeig, "Wright-Type Auditorium Chances Appear Brighter," *CT*, October 16, 1963.

154. "New Christ Presbyterian Church Dedicated," *WSJ*, June 10, 1963; Frank Custer, "A Church Goes Down—and 2 Women Weep," *CT*, August 12, 1963.

155. "Built By Findorff—1923," *WSJ*, December 29, 1923; Brautigam, "Revised Library Bidding Indicates $1,466,937 Cost," *CT*, October 18, 1963; "Ceremony Opens Library Project," *WSJ*, October 29, 1963; George Austin email, September 27, 2017.

156. Feuerzeig, "Cherokee Issue Heads Rough Council Agenda," *CT*, November 14, 1963; Gordon, "Cherokee Lands' Condemning OKd," *WSJ*, November 15, 1963; Brautigam, "Condemnation of Cherokee Ok'd; Mayor Breaks Tie," *CT*, November 15, 1963.

157. "Apartments Near Completion," *CT*, April 12, 1963; "Plan Big East Side Apartment Project," *CT*, July 29, 1963; Gordon, "Strong Opposition Hits Union's Apartment Plan," *WSJ*, September 10, 1963; "Federation Apartment Plan Fought," *CT*, September 10, 1963; "Northport Housing Explained," *WSJ*, September 15, 1963; Gordon, "Zoning Plea Rejected for Union Apartments," *WSJ*, September 24, 1963; "Apartment Project Is Set Back," *CT*, September 25, 1963; Gordon, "Union Apartment Zone OKd," *WSJ*, September 27, 1963; Earl Hutchison, "Council Approves Rezoning for North Side Apartments," *CT*, September 27, 1963; CC Minutes, October 10, 1963; Gordon, "Northport Housing Zoning

Approved," *WSJ*, October 11, 1963; Brautigam, "Northport Dr. Housing Survives Opponents' Final Council Attack," *CT*, October 11, 1963; Feuerzeig, "New Move to Block Apartments," *CT*, November 4, 1963; "Writ to Block Housing Asked," *WSJ*, November 5, 1963; "Northport Drive Housing Is Injunction Suit Target," *CT*, November 5, 1963.

158. "Kennedy's Attend Luncheon: Dedication of J.P. Kennedy Jr. New Memorial Laboratories," *DC*, November 20, 1963; Owen Coyle, "JFK's Relatives Attend Kennedy Lab Dedication," *CT*, November 20, 1963; Marion Withington and Lynne Abraham, "Ted Kennedy Helps Honor Late Brother," *DC*, November 21, 1963; "Kennedy's Fast Pace Here Recalls Political Campaign," *WSJ*, November 21, 1963; Coyle, "Kennedy Kin Ducks Politics in Dedicating Retardation Lab," *CT*, November 21, 1963; "Waisman, Head of Kennedy Laboratories, Heads Battle against Mental Retardation," *DC*, November 21, 1963; "UW Researchers Probe Mental Retardation," *Wisconsin Alumnus* 65, no. 5 (February 1964): 17.

159. "JFK Slain," *CT*, November 22, 1963; "Faces of a Campus in Mourning," *DC*, November 23, 1963; "State Capitol Shows City's Sense of Loss," *WSJ*, November 23, 1963; "Sorrow Spreads over Whole City," *WSJ*, November 23, 1963; Tom Butler, "Wisconsin-Minnesota Grid Game Postponed," *WSJ*, November 23, 1963; "All Wisconsin Schools Will Close for Funeral," *WSJ*, November 23, 1963; "News of Death Spreads Grief over UW Campus," *WSJ*, November 23, 1963; Ward Remington, "To Traveling Fans, It's Blurred Report," *WSJ*, November 23, 1963; Avi Bass, "A President on Campus," *DC*, November 23, 1963; Maraniss, "JFK Began Trek to Martyrdom in Wisconsin, His 'Second Home,'" *CT*, November 23, 1963; "JFK's Death Halts Classes, Football Game," *DC*, November 23, 1963; Elizabeth Ewen, "A Way of Seeing," in Buhle, ed., *History and the New Left*, 150; Whitney Gould, Tim Holmes, Bruce Koepcke email/telephone interviews, 2013.

160. "City Joins U.S. Today in Tribute to Kennedy," *WSJ*, November 25, 1963; "Clergymen Find Lessons in JFK's Tragic Death," *WSJ*, November 25, 1963; Wineke, "Madison Prays for JFK, World," *WSJ*, November 25, 1963; "Harrington, Friedrick to Lead Official State Program at UW," *WSJ*, November 25, 1963; "800 in Tribute to Kennedy at Cathedral Mass Here," *CT*, November 25, 1963; "Clergymen Warn Madison of Reaping Seeds of Hate," *CT*, November 25, 1963; "'Will We Go Forward?' Asks Harrington at U. Tribute," *CT*, November 25, 1963; Matheson, "Packed Cathedral Honors President," *WSJ*, November 26, 1963; Bednarek, "10,000 Pay Tribute at UW Event," *WSJ*, November 26, 1963; Llewellyn G. Roberts, "Activity Ceases Here on Day of Mourning," *WSJ*, November 26, 1963; "Fr. Schmitz, Native of City, Assists at Mass for Kennedy," *WSJ*, November 26, 1963; "10,000 Honor Kennedy Here," *DC*, November 26, 1963; Gruber, "A Silent Sorrow on Bascom Hill," *DC*, November 26, 1963; Paul Schweizer, "Kennedy Tributes Cite Friendship with Youth," *DC*, November 26, 1963; "A Mourning Campus Curtails Its Activities," *DC*,

November 26, 1963; Reynolds, "UW Hush Tells Feelings," *WSJ*, November 26, 1963; "Students Watch TV Silently," *WSJ*, November 26, 1963; "Crime Just About Ceases Here during the Funeral," *WSJ*, November 26, 1963.

161. "Reierson Ordered to Waupon for a Mental Examination," *DC*, November 27, 1963.

162. "Parole Is Revoked for Owen Reierson," *WSJ*, February 7, 1964; "Reierson's Parole Ended; To Go Back to California," *CT*, February 8, 1964; "The Wrong Guy in the Wrong Place," *Berkeley Barb*, September 6–12, 1974; Stu Levitan, "Madison Remembers JFK," *Isthmus*, November 14, 2013.

1964

1. MRA minutes, January 7, 1964, and January 14, 1964; CAC minutes, January 8, 1964; Hank Feuerzeig, "MRA Reports It Saves Money in Buying Land," *CT*, January 7, 1964.

2. MRA minutes, January 7, 1964; "Price Cut for Neighborhood House Site," *WSJ*, January 8, 1964; Richard Brautigam, "Cut Neighborhood House Land Price," *CT*, January 8, 1964; "MRA Gets Apology of Mayor in Letter Row," *CT*, January 15, 1964; "Medical Center's Offer for Site in Triangle Is Rejected by MRA," *WSJ*, April 24, 1964; "Glidden Building Inches Home," *WSJ*, April 5, 1965.

3. MRA minutes, February 25, 1964; "Number of MRA-Displaced on Relief Will Be Studied," *WSJ*, February 26, 1964.

4. "Referendum on Calling Halt to Urban Renewal Proposed," *WSJ*, January 23, 1964; Feuerzeig, "Renewal Foes Open Drive to End MRA, Its Program," *CT*, January 23, 1964; "Anti-Renewal Group Tries for November Referendum," *CT*, February 11, 1964; John T. Aehl, "Public 'Doesn't Understand' Redevelopment, MRA Says," *WSJ*, February 12, 1964; Feuerzeig, "Renewal Foes to Take Fight to Council Meet," *CT*, February 13, 1964; William Witt, "Renewal Foes Plan Drive for Referendum on April 7," *WSJ*, February 21, 1964; Feuerzeig, "Key Role in Fight on Renewal Held by Home Owners," *CT*, March 19, 1964.

5. David Bednarek, "Bigger and Better UW Predicted," *WSJ*, January 20, 1964.

6. MRA, February 20, 1964; David Gordon, "Urban Renewal Foes Claim 8,108 Signers," *WSJ*, February 26, 1964; "Petitions to End MRA Are Filed," *CT*, February 26, 1964.

7. Editorial, "Don't Rush Urban Renewal Vote," *WSJ*, February 27, 1964; editorial, "Thoughtful Renewal Discussion Needed; Not Haste and Emotion," *CT*, February 27, 1964; "Urban Renewal Best in Fall, Mayor Declares," *WSJ*, February 27, 1964; Gordon, "Apr. 7 Vote Set on Killing MRA," *WSJ*, February 28, 1964; "Move to End MRA Goes to Voters in April Election," *CT*, February 28, 1964; Gordon, "Questions Raised on Renewal Vote," *WSJ*, March 2, 1964;

Gordon, "Apr. 7 Vote on MRA Upheld," *WSJ*, March 3, 1964; Brautigam, "Rules April Renewal Vote Legal," *CT*, March 4, 1964.

8. Feuerzeig, "Referendum Imperils Triangle Financing," *CT*, March 5, 1964; "Anti-Renewal Referendum Seen as 'Purely Advisory,'" *CT*, March 7, 1964; Feuerzeig, "Vote on Urban Renewal Will Be Mandatory, View," *CT*, March 9, 1964; MRA minutes, March 10, 1964; Brautigam, "Conrad Tells MRA to Hire Own Lawyer on April Vote," *CT*, March 11, 1964; "MRA Hires Attorney to Aid on Question of Referendum," *WSJ*, March 14, 1964; Brautigam, "MRA Counsel Considers Referendum Court Test," *CT*, March 14, 1964; Feuerzeig, "Federal Men Not Sure of Renewal Poll Effect," *CT*, April 2, 1964.

9. Bednarek, "Official Says MRA Has UW's Support," *CT*, March 11, 1964; "Women Voters Ask 'No' Vote on Ending Renewal," *CT*, March 27, 1964; "Mayor, Harrington Back Urban Renewal," *WSJ*, April 3, 1964; John Newhouse, "Williamson St. Fights MRA, Urban Renewal," *WSJ*, April 3, 1964; "Written Pledges by MRA Decried," *WSJ*, April 4, 1964; "Falk, MRA Chief, Urges 'NO' Vote on Tuesday," *WSJ*, April 6, 1964; "The University and MRA," *DC*, April 7, 1964.

10. MRA, March 3, 1964; Brautigam, "MRA Plans Push for Referendum," *CT*, March 4, 1964; Brautigam, "Mayor's Group to Fight for Renewal," *CT*, March 5, 1964; editorial, "The Urban Renewal Referendum," *WSJ*, March 11, 1964; Feuerzeig, "Urban Renewal—It Started as a Housing Program," *CT*, March 16, 1964; CAC minutes, March 18, 1964; Feuerzeig, "MRA Was Given Unanimous OK When Established," *CT*, March 18, 1964; Feuerzeig, "Renewal Area Once Held Many Poor Buildings," *CT*, March 20, 1964; Feuerzeig, "Relocation: City's Crucial Problem," *CT*, March 22, 1964; Feuerzeig, "'Low' Prices Are Cause of Many Renewal Squawks," *CT*, March 24, 1964; CAC minutes, March 25, 1964; Gordon and Richard Gribble, "Urban Renewal: Pro and Con; Citizens Unit Quizzes Foe; MRA Lambasted at Meeting," *WSJ*, March 26, 1964; Newhouse, "MRA Gives South Side Chance to Better Itself," *WSJ*, March 29, 1964; editorial, "Let MRA Put It in Writing," *WSJ*, March 30, 1964; editorial, "'No' Vote on MRA Referendum," *WSJ*, April 3, 1964; editorial, "Vote 'No' on Urban Renewal Referendum Next Tuesday," *CT*, April 3, 1964; "Madison Voters Face Crucial Issue on MRA Issue," *WSJ*, April 5, 1964; Newhouse, "With or Without MRA, Renewal Must Continue," *WSJ*, April 5, 1964.

11. CAC minutes, March 25, 1964; "Triangle Site to Be Reserved for Moderate Income Housing," *WSJ*, March 26, 1964; "Moderate Income Housing Is Voted," *WSJ*, March 28, 1964; Gordon, "Non-Profit Housing Project Planned," *WSJ*, April 1, 1964; "Triangle Housing Plan Told," *CT*, April 1, 1964; "Mrs. Remeika Attacks Plan for Housing in Triangle," *CT*, April 2, 1964; "Non-Profit Housing Plan for Triangle Criticized," *WSJ*, April 6, 1964; "Housing Project's Backers Insure Non-Profit Condition," *WSJ*, May 26, 1964.

12. "MRA's Urban Renewal Setup Wins by a Razor-Thin Margin," *WSJ*, April 8, 1964; Feuerzeig, "MRA Weathers Foes' Ballot Test by Only 367 Votes," *CT*, April 8, 1964.

13. Feuerzeig, "Carnes and Elder Are Out of Council," *CT*, April 8, 1964.

14. Editorial, "Beneficial MRA Debate," *WSJ*, April 10, 1964; CAC minutes, April 15, 1964; Brautigam, "Consider Individuals First in Future Renewal Plans," *CT*, April 16, 1964.

15. "Regents' OK Sought for Big U. Ave. Business Plan," *CT*, January 8, 1964; BOR minutes, March 6,1964, and April 10, 1964; "University Park Corp. Gets Go-Ahead," *WSJ*, April 11, 1964; John Patrick Hunter, "Regents Approve Private University Ave. Project," *CT*, April 11, 1964; "Pressure's on UW for Land," *WSJ*, August 30, 1964; BOR minutes, November 13, 1964; "UW to Seek Approval of University Ave. Plan," *WSJ*, November 14, 1964; "University Ave. Property Owners Complain of Lack of Information," *WSJ*, November 14, 1964; "Regents Split on Dummy Land Deal," *CT*, November 14, 1964.

16. Frank Custer, "Since 1916 Neighborhood House Has Met Changing Needs of Growing City," *CT*, January 20, 1964; "City Landmark is Demolished," *CT*, September 26, 1964.

17. MRA minutes, July 21, 1964; "Fund for UW Renewal Project Wins Approval," *WSJ*, July 22, 1964; "U.W.-MRA Pact Given 'Legal' OK," *CT*, August 21,1964; MRA minutes, September 8, 1964; "Status on Renewal Projects Outlined," *WSJ*, September 9, 1964; Aehl, "Contract Is Received on UW Renewal Study," *WSJ*, October 21, 1964; Brautigam, "City-U.W. Renewal Study Given Federal Approval," *CT*, October 21, 1964; MRA minutes, Special Meeting, November 19, 1964; Aehl, "Urban Renewal Study in UW Area Supported," *WSJ*, November 21, 1964.

18. Owen Coyle, "Council Blocks Nuckles in MRA Post," *CT*, April 21, 1964; Gordon, "Mayor's Choices for MRA Held Up," *WSJ*, April 22, 1964; "Mayor Seeks Clarification of MRA Board Expansion," *CT*, April 22, 1964; Coyle, "To Rename Nuckles to MRA," *CT*, April 23, 1964.

19. Brautigam, "Mayor Takes Second Defeat on MRA Posts," *CT*, May 15, 1964; Feuerzeig, "Nemec Quits Post on MRA, Citing Press of Work," *CT*, June 30, 1964.

20. Feuerzeig, "Two Chosen for Vacancies on MRA," *CT*, July 9, 1964; "Appointees on MRA Rejected," *CT*, July 10, 1964; Feuerzeig, "Mayor Finally Able to Fill One MRA Vacancy," *CT*, July 25, 1964.

21. Gribble, "'Anti-Renewal' Attitude Shown in Rejection of MRA Appointee," *WSJ*, October 9, 1964; Brautigam, "Ald. Reynolds Again Fails to Win MRA Confirmation," *CT*, October 9, 1964.

22. "Espeseth, Realtors' Head, Elected Chairman of MHA," *WSJ*, April 29, 1964; Aehl, "Housing Survey Given a Push," *WSJ*, May 12, 1964.

23. "Some Low-Cost Housing to Be Ready by Jan. 1," *WSJ*, December 15, 1964.

24. CAC minutes, September 9, 1964; "'Humanness' Sought in Urban Renewal," *WSJ*, September 10, 1964; CAC minutes, October 7, 1964; Coyle, "Levin Is Named Aide to Mayor on Renewal," *CT*, November 2, 1964.

25. Coyle, "MRA Head Owns Land in Renewal Study Area," *CT*, November 9, 1964; "MRA Will Weigh Rupnow's Holding," *WSJ*, November 10, 1964.

26. Coyle, "Rupnow's Resignation from MRA Demanded," *CT*, November 10, 1964; Aehl, "Urban Renewal Program Faces Attack," *WSJ*, November 12, 1964; MRA minutes, November 13, 1964.

27. MRA minutes, November 10, 1964; Aehl, "MRA Raps Rupnow for His Land Deal," *WSJ*, November 11, 1964; Brautigam, "MRA Censures Rupnow's Land Conflict," *CT*, November 11, 1964.

28. "Driving after License Loss, Callsen, MHA's Chief, Jailed," *WSJ*, November 13, 1964; Coyle, "Traffic Charge Jails MHA Director Callsen," *CT*, November 13, 1964; Brautigam, "Callsen Free; May Accept Demotion," *CT*, November 14, 1964; "Buenzli Gives Callsen 75-Day Jail Term," *WSJ*, December 16, 1964.

29. MRA minutes, November 13, 1964; Brautigam, "Rupnow Offers to Resign from MRA," *CT*, November 13, 1964; Aehl, "Rupnow Out; Sol Levin Is Acting MRA Director," *WSJ*, November 14, 1964; Coyle, "Rupnow Out; Levin Acting MRA Chief," *CT*, November 14, 1964; editorial, "MRA and MHA Need Overhaul," *WSJ*, November 17, 1964.

30. Reynolds, "84-Unit Apartment Co-Op for Elderly Planned Here," *WSJ*, March 6, 1960; "First Housing Co-Op for Elderly Will Go Up Near Madison Soon," *CT*, December 12, 1960; "Co-op for Elderly Returned to FHA," *CT*, August 17, 1964; Aehl, "Romnes Named MHA's Director," *WSJ*, November 18, 1964; Coyle, "Romnes Appointed Director of MHA," *CT*, November 18, 1964.

31. Robert A. Davis, "'Folk-Poet' Scores When Anger's Lost," *WSJ*, November 20, 1964; John Gruber, "Bob Dylan—a Cry against Social Evil," *DC*, November 20, 1964; Harrand, "Bob Dylan Songs Don't Entertain," *CT*, November 20, 1964; Joe Harrand, "Lombardo Fans Love 'The Sweetest Music,'" *CT*, November 24, 1964; Thomas Starkweather Facebook exchange, January 3, 2018.

32. MRA minutes, November 19, 1964; Brautigam, "MRA and Foes Line Up for New Renewal War," *CT*, November 20, 1964; "Council Again Faces Urban Renewal Issue," *WSJ*, November 24, 1964; Aehl, "Further Renewal Jobs Halted for Year," *WSJ*, November 25, 1964; Brautigam, "1-Year Delay of Renewal Plans Voted," *CT*, November 25, 1964; Coyle, "Mayor Considers Veto of Council's Renewal Freeze," *CT*, November 25, 1964; "Mayor May Veto Renewal Freeze," *WSJ*, November 26, 1964; editorial, "Veto of Urban Renewal Action," *WSJ*, November 30, 1964.

33. MRA minutes, November 30, 1964; Aehl, "Mayor to Veto Freeze on Urban Renewal Job," *WSJ*, December 1, 1964; Coyle, "Renewal Foes Prepare New Referendum Try," *CT*, December 1, 1964; CAC minutes, December 2, 1964; Brautigam, "Group Urges

Veto of Freeze on MRA," *CT*, December 3, 1964; Aehl, "Council Will Get Two Vetoes," *WSJ*, December 4, 1964.

34. "Harrington Wants to Work with City on UW Expansion," *CT*, December 2, 1964.

35. "Urban Renewal Freeze, Alcoholism Fund Vetoed," *CT*, December 5, 1964; Brautigam, "Renewal Foes Urge Overriding of Veto," *CT*, December 7, 1964; editorial, "Sustain the UW Study Veto," *WSJ*, December 9, 1964; "Let Renewal Study in UW Area Continue, Falk Urges Council," *WSJ*, December 10, 1964; editorial, "Mayor's Veto of MRA Freeze Should Be Sustained," *CT*, December 10, 1964; Aehl, "City Urban Renewal Saved Till March," *WSJ*, December 11, 1964; Brautigam, "Mayor Wins Reprieve for U.W. Area Renewal Study," *CT*, December 11, 1964.

36. Aehl, "Special Unit to Study UW Renewal Area Plan," *WSJ*, December 18, 1964; "Referendum on Renewal Seems Sure," *WSJ*, December 11, 1964; Aehl, "First Urban Renewal Hearing Set for Jan. 5," *WSJ*, December 29, 1964; Brautigam, "Ground Rules Set Up for Renewal Hearing," *CT*, December 29, 1964; "Six Nights Reserved for Renewal Hearings," *WSJ*, December 30, 1964.

37. Gribble, "University Ave. Group Asks Renewal," *WSJ*, December 22, 1964.

38. Gordon, "Equal Opportunities Group Is Organized," *WSJ*, January 14, 1964; Brautigam, "City Opportunities Group Formally Organized," *CT*, January 14, 1964; "Equal Opportunity Group Will Emphasize Education," *CT*, January 27, 1964; Sharon Coady, "New Rights Group Will Keep Procedure Simple, Flexible," *WSJ*, February 4, 1964; Brautigam, "Opportunities Unit Votes Its Rules of Procedure," *CT*, February 4, 1964; Feuerzeig, "Mayor Will Name Rohr to Opportunity Group," *CT*, May 14, 1964; Gordon, "Ald. Rohr Given an Opportunity to Help Equal Opportunity Unit," *WSJ*, May 15, 1964

39. EOC minutes, February 18, 1964; Records of the Madison Equal Opportunities Commission, C2014/044, box 6, WHSA; "Widespread Housing Discrimination Here Exposed in U. Survey," *CT*, January 11, 1964; Harrand, "Opportunities Group Dismisses Complaint," *CT*, February 19, 1964.

40. Hunter, "Firms, State Hit on Job Bias," *CT*, February 13, 1964; Hunter, "Why Industrial Commission Is Leading Fight on Bias," *CT*, February 24, 1964.

41. Hunter, "Why Industrial Commission Is Leading Fight on Bias," *CT*, February 24, 1964; "CORE Demonstrator's Bail Forfeited Despite Protest," *CT*, March 23, 1964; Gruber, "Strikes at Hiring Discrimination," *DC*, March 24, 1964; "Sit-In Defendant Forfeits $55 Bail," *WSJ*, March 26, 1964; EOC minutes, March 30, 1964; "CORE Pickets Sears Again to Protest Hiring Practices," *DC*, April 14, 1964; Elizabeth Ewen in Buhle, ed., *History and the New Left*, 150; Levin, *Cold War University*, 132.

42. "NAACP Denies Part in Picketing of Sears," *WSJ*, March 23, 1964; editorial, "Picketing at Sears-Roebuck," *WSJ*, March 27, 1964.

43. "A Hearing Open to the Public, of the CORE-Sears Fair Employment Dispute Held Before the Equal Opportunities Commission," April 6, 1964, Records of the Madison Equal Opportunities Commission, C2014/044, WHSA; Brautigam, "Opportunities Group Airs Sears-CORE Case," *CT*, April 7, 1964; Sue Reeve, "Equal Opportunity Group to Give Future Decision," *DC*, April 7, 1964; "Hiring 'Bias' Charge Studied," *WSJ*, April 7, 1964; EOC minutes, April 14, 1964; Gordon, "Rights Unit Dismisses Bias in Hiring Charge," *WSJ*, April 15, 1964; Gene Wells, "Sears, CORE Near Accord on Prejudice," *DC*, April 15, 1964.

44. "City Rights Rally Will Be Held Today," *WSJ*, April 25, 1964; Hunter, "Negro Leader Sees Civil Disobedience Possibility," *CT*, April 25, 1964; Davis, "Rally Wants Rights Bill Passed," *WSJ*, April 26, 1964; Lowell Bergman and Sue Reeve, "Shuttlesworth Rally Sparks Rights Drive," *DC*, April 28, 1964.

45. "Ald. Rohr in Bid for Re-Election," *WSJ*, January 4, 1964; "Race Issue Raised in Fourteenth; 3 Candidates Trade Insults," *WSJ*, February 26, 1964; Brautigam, "Ald. Rohr Hits Clergy for Aiding Rights Law," *CT*, March 24, 1964.

46. Brautigam, "Rohr Again Raises 'Anti-White' Issue in Fourteenth Ward Row," *CT*, February 25, 1964.

47. "Rohr Blocks Four Democrat Officials," *WSJ*, February 14, 1964; Feuerzeig, "Voids Naming of Rohr Group to Election Posts," *CT*, February 14, 1964; Feuerzeig, "Angry Rohr Cries Anti-White Bias in Poll Switch," *CT*, February 15, 1964; Gordon, "Selection of Rohr's Poll Officials Ruled Invalid," *WSJ*, February 15, 1964; "Rohr Is Defeated in Ward Fight on Election Board," *CT*, February 28, 1964; "Rohr Bid Blocked in Poll Aide Test," *WSJ*, February 28, 1964; "Roberts, Rohr Trade More Charges in Fourteenth Ward Race," *WSJ*, April 4, 1964; "Ban on New Rights Unit's Use of Hidden Cameras Is Proposed," *WSJ*, April 10, 1964.

48. Brautigam, "Council Supports Ban on 'Bugging,' Hidden Cameras," *CT*, May 13, 1964.

49. William Brissee, "Gov. Wallace Given Good Reception Here," *WSJ*, April 3, 1964.

50. Brautigam, "MFL Backs Rohr, Refuses to Support Rights Ordinance," *CT*, February 18, 1964; "Teachers' Local Won't Back Equality Opponents," *CT*, February 19, 1964; Harrand, "COPE Endorses 2 Foes of Opportunities Ordinance," *CT*, February 21, 1964.

51. Brautigam, "Council Candidate Rebukes COPE on Civil Rights Issue," *CT*, February 22, 1964; "Robert L. Reynolds Skips COPE Backing," *WSJ*, February 22, 1964.

52. Gordon, "3 Candidates Challenge COPE over Rights Issue," *WSJ*, March 20, 1964.

53. Feuerzeig, "Carnes and Elder Are Out of Council," *CT*, April 8, 1964.

54. Gordon, "U.S. Negroes at UW Total under 100 Now," *WSJ*, June 5, 1964; Hunter, "Only 21 Wisconsin Negroes Enrolled at University," *CT*, June 5, 1964.

55. Lynne Abraham, "Boycotter Faces Jail Term, Fine," *DC*, February 27, 1964; Abraham, "'U' Rights Leader Will Serve Prison Sentence in Louisiana," *DC*, February 28, 1964; "U.W. Student Must Serve Rights Protest Jail Term," *CT*, February 28, 1964; Abraham, "'U' Campus Rallies to Aid Diamond," *DC*, February 29, 1964; "Diamond Is Jail Bound; $258 Raised," *DC*, March 3, 1964.

56. Editorial, "Rights Committee Proposal," *DC*, April 15, 1964; "Strengthening of Fraternity Anti-Bias Policy to Be Eyed," *WSJ*, April 17, 1964; Bednarek, "UW Greek Alumni Hit Rights Group Proposals," *WSJ*, May 4, 1964; "Faculty Approval Given Rights Plan," *WSJ*, May 5, 1964; Harvey Shapiro, "Rights Proposal Has Faculty OK," *DC*, May 5, 1964; "Faculty Votes 2 Measures on Bias in Campus Groups," *CT*, May 5, 1964; BOR minutes, May 8, 1964; Shapiro, "'U' Regents Support Fraternity Human Rights Independence," *DC*, May 9, 1964; "Stronger Anti-Bias Policy for Fraternities Approved," *WSJ*, May 9, 1964.

57. Hunter, "CORE Disrupts Assembly Session," *CT*, April 28, 1964; editorial, "Hard Road for Civil Rights," *WSJ*, April 29, 1964; "CORE Plans Rights Rally," *WSJ*, June 5, 1964; Evan Stark email, June 27, 2017; Mark Ford, "A Strong Song Tows Us—the Life of Basil Bunting by Richard Burton—Review," *The Guardian*, November 29, 2013; Amy Petulla, *The Corpsewood Manor Murders of North Georgia* (Charleston, SC: Arcadia, 2016), 24.

58. John Michael, "Prof. Commands I-F: 'Adjust to Freedom,'" *DC*, October 14, 1964; "Fraternity Group Oks Anti-Discrimination," *WSJ*, October 15, 1964; Michael, "I-F Refuses Certificates 2a, 2b," *DC*, October 15, 1964.

59. Paul Schweizer, "Greek Nationals May Fight 'Local Autonomy' Policies," *DC*, January 11, 1964; Schweizer, "Greek Alumni Join to Save System," *DC*, January 15, 1964; Hunter, "UW Fraternity Alumni Attack Rights 'Club,'" *CT*, January 16, 1964; "I-F Autonomy Bid Ok'd," *DC*, March 4, 1964; *Human Rights Committee Annual Report, 1964–1965*, May 3, 1965, UW–Madison Campus Faculty Meeting, Series 5/2/15, box 1, University Archives.

60. Dave Wolf, "'I'm Scared as Hell, But I'm Going,'" *DC*, June 25, 1964; "Missing Rights Aide Once at UW," *WSJ*, June 25, 1964; Gruber, "Government Intervention Urged by Speakers at Rights Rally," *DC*, June 30, 1964; "Slain Rights Worker Was U.W. Student During 1961," *CT*, August 5, 1964; Michael Edmonds, ed., *Risking Everything: A Freedom Summer Reader*, (Madison: Wisconsin Historical Society Press, 2014), xiv; Louis Lomax, "Road to Mississippi," in *Risking Everything*, 91–95; Doug Moe, "Madison Is Home to Civil Rights History," https://www.channel3000 .com/madison-magazine/opinion/doug-moe/madison-is -home-to-civil-rights-history/155611495; Valerie Johnson, "Michael Edmonds: Bold (Not To Say Crazy)," https://president .rotarymadison.org/tag/civil-rights-documents-from-the-1960s/.

61. Harrand, "U. Students Busy Raising Bail for Rights Workers," *CT*, July 9, 1964; Feuerzeig, "Rights Fund 'Tag Day' Is Rejected by Council," *CT*, July 10, 1964; editorial, "City Council Backs Away from Civil Rights Solicitation," *CT*, July 10, 1964; "Veterans Tag Day Approved; Ban on Rights Unit Recalled," *WSJ*, July 22, 1964; "Rights Group Plans Square Fund Drive," *CT*, July 30, 1964; "Mississippi Fund Drive Here Disappointing," *CT*, August 5, 1964.

62. Mark Lipschutz, "Freedom Fast's Goals Exceeded," *DC*, November 17, 1964; "8,000 at U.W. Pledged to Join in 'Freedom Fast,'" *CT*, November 18, 1964; editorial, "Public Should Join in U.W. Students' Splendid Gesture," *CT*, November 18, 1964; Edwin S. Kohn, "'Fast for Freedom' Will Probably Pass Its Goal," *DC*, November 20, 1964.

63. Feuerzeig, "City Gets Wright Offer," *CT*, January 20, 1964.

64. Brautigam, "City in Own Fee Offer," *CT*, January 24, 1964.

65. Gordon, "Arbitration Seen on Wright Issue," *WSJ*, January 25, 1964; Feuerzeig, "Refuse Terrace Fee Bid," *CT*, January 28, 1964.

66. Brautigam, "City in Own Fee Offer," *CT*, January 24, 1964.

67. "Wright Foundation Formally Rejects $135,000 City Offer," *WSJ*, February 11, 1964; Brautigam, "Mayor Halts Move to Settle Fee Fight," *CT*, February 14, 1964.

68. Gordon, "Bid to Redesign Terrace Made," *WSJ*, February 18, 1964; Feuerzeig, "Reject Terrace Redesign," *CT*, February 18, 1964; Gordon, "Mayor Opposes Latest Offer by Wright Group," *WSJ*, February 19, 1964.

69. Feuerzeig, "Wright Group Asks Immediate Settlement," *CT*, February 25, 1964.

70. Aehl, "Arbitration Set on Wright Fee Issue," *WSJ*, February 28, 1964; Brautigam, "Mayor Blocks Wright Accord," *CT*, February 28, 1964; Feuerzeig, "Nothing Due Wright, Mayor Will Maintain," *CT*, February 28, 1964; editorial, "Madison Is to Stay in Cow Barn Era in Cultural Life," *CT*, February 28, 1964; "Lawyer Issue Up Tonight," *CT*, March 25, 1964; Aehl, "Council Hires Cushman to Settle Wright Claim," *WSJ*, March 27, 1964; Brautigam, "Council Hires Eastern Lawyer," *CT*, March 27, 1964.

71. Feuerzeig, "Terrace Arbitration Set," *CT*, July 1, 1964; "Terrace Arbitration Talks Set September 15," *WSJ*, July 3, 1964; Feuerzeig, "Stafford Named Terrace Arbitrator," *CT*, July 5, 1964; Feuerzeig, "Choice of Third Arbitrator Nears in Terrace Dispute," *CT*, August 14, 1964; Feuerzeig, "How Much Is Philadelphia Lawyer Costing Madison," *CT*, August 12, 1964; Feuerzeig, "City Counterclaims in Terrace Arbitration," *CT*, September 17, 1964.

72. Hunter, "3,100 Receive U. Degrees," *CT*, June 8, 1964.

73. *The State of Wisconsin Blue Book 1970* (Madison: State of Wisconsin, 1970), 631.

74. Harrand, "9,000 Hail Belafonte's Magnetic Performance," *CT*, October 31, 1964.

75. Steven Barney, "New Lab Houses 'U' Primate Study," *DC*, April 28, 1964; "UW Dedicates Primate Center," *WSJ*, April 28, 1964; Elliott Maraniss, "New Building Dedicated for McArdle Laboratory," *CT*, October 17, 1964; "Unprecedented Building

Program Is Pressed with Top Speed at U.W.," *WSJ,* January 5, 1965; Feldman, *Buildings,* 264, 336, 339, 344, 351, 354, 361, 364, 368.

76. BOR minutes, February 7, 1964; Bednarek, "UW to Limit Its Enrollment Here," *WSJ,* February 8, 1964; Schweizer, "Regents View Enrollment Increase," *DC,* February 8, 1964.

77. BOR minutes, January 10, 1964; Abraham, "Increased Housing Construction Slated," *DC,* January 11, 1964; "New Dormitory, Parking Studies Revealed," *Wisconsin Alumnus* 65, no. 5 (February 1964): 24–25.

78. BOR minutes, May 8, 1964; Hunter, "Married Students' Project Ok'd for Reider [*sic*] Farm Area," *CT,* May 8, 1964; "$20 Million Building Plans for UW Listed," *WSJ,* May 9, 1964.

79. Feldman, *Buildings,* 336.

80. Marcus, "U.W. Not Trying to Hurt Westgate, Rennebohm Says," *CT,* July 29, 1961; "Map Shows How U.W. Farm Bars Whitney Way Route," *CT,* August 5, 1961; "Temporary Whitney Extension OKd," *WSJ,* August 26, 1964; Faculty Document 53, "The Problem of a Second Campus in Madison," March 7, 1966, Madison Campus Faculty Meeting, Series 5/2/15, box 1, University Archives.

81. BOR minutes, September 25, 1964; "U.W. Eyes New College on W. Side or Truax," *CT,* December 3, 1964.

82. BOR minutes, January 10, 1964.

83. BOR minutes, April 10, 1964.

84. Shapiro, "'U' Planner Prepares Report on Campus Cars," *DC,* January 9, 1964; BOR minutes, January 10, 1964; "Regents Eye Move to Curb Traffic on Local Campus," *CT,* January 11, 1964.

85. Schweiser, "Faculty Ok's Senior-21 Apartment Ruling," *DC,* January 7, 1964.

86. BOR minutes, January 10, 1964; "Illinois Prof Named 'U' Campus Provost," *DC,* January 11, 1964; Charles Martin, "Meet the New Provost: Robben Fleming," *DC,* February 11, 1964; "Robben Fleming Named Provost at Madison," *Wisconsin Alumnus* 65, no. 5 (February 1964): 5; Robben W. Fleming, *Tempests into Rainbows: Managing Turbulence* (Ann Arbor: University of Michigan Press, 1996), 129 et. seq.; Cronon and Jenkins, *The University of Wisconsin,* 183 et. seq.

87. "Communist Will Balance Symposium Speaker List," *DC,* January 15, 1964; "Senator Nelson to Keynote Symposium 1964," *DC,* February 4, 1964; "Podium Set for Symposium '64," *DC,* February 15, 1964; Jeff Smoller, "Gaylord Nelson Stresses Need for Dissension in College Life," *DC,* February 18, 1964; "Wallace Handles Heckling Crowd," *WSJ,* February 19, 1964; Jim Nathan, "Macdonald Castigates Mass Culture," *DC,* February 20, 1964; Phyllis Berman, "Lomax Hits White Hypocrisy," *DC,* February 26, 1964; *Wisconsin Alumnus* 65, no. 7 (April 1964): 11–14.

88. Student Organization Registration File, University Archives; "New 'Left Liberal' Club Starts Here," *DC,* February 11, 1964; Pam McAllister, "SDS Seeks 'A Society of Freedom,'" *DC,* October 14, 1964; C. Clark Kissinger email to author, April 16, 2017.

89. "Visiting Rusk Will Face Asia Policy Protesters," *CT,* March 4, 1964; "Dean Rusk, Wallace Visit Madison," *DC,* March 6, 1964; Harrand, "Rusk Defends World Aid as Boost to U.S. Industry," *CT,* March 7, 1964; Gribble, "Viet Nam Seen 'Settling Down,'" *WSJ,* March 7, 1964; Gribble, "Dean Rusk Hits Aid Plan Foes," *WSJ,* March 7, 1964; Maraniss, "Angry Dems Plan Fight," *CT,* March 7, 1964; "Student Group Organized for Anti-Wallace Struggle," *DC,* March 19, 1964.

90. "Bo Diddley Headlines Mil Ball," *DC,* March 6, 1964; Ben Sidran, "Carawan Underlines 'Protest' Songs with Own Experience," *DC,* April 18, 1964; Shapiro, "Anti-Mil Ball Tonight; Jug Band Performs," *DC,* April 18, 1964; "Anti-Military Ball: Pacifist's Revenge," *DC,* April 21, 1964.

91. "Dick Gregory Keynotes SNCC 'Rights' Week," *DC,* April 8, 1964; "Gregory Plus Freedom Singers Equals Great Show Coming Up," *DC,* April 28, 1964; Randy Lee, "SNCC Starts Drive for Gregory Show," *DC,* May 6, 1964; "Gregory Performs in Music Hall Tonight," *DC,* May 9, 1964; Maxine Sidran, "Dick Gregory Speaks of Whites and Negroes," *DC,* May 12, 1964.

92. "Forms Unit on Status of Women," *CT,* May 16, 1964; "Know Your Madisonian: Mrs. Kathryn Clarenbach," *WSJ,* December 18, 1964.

93. Murray Olderman, "Biggest Bonus of All Beckoning Reichardt, Claim," *CT,* June 23, 1964; "Reichardt to Sign Angels' Pact Today," *CT,* June 24, 1964; Charles Maher, "Reichardt's Bonus Set at $175,000," *CT,* June 25, 1964; "Reichardt Signs Angels Contract," *WSJ,* June 25, 1964; Dave Wolf, "Reichardt Signs with Angels," *DC,* June 25, 1964; Wolf, "Rick Reichardt—Pride and Determination," *DC,* July 2, 1964; Wolf, "Reichardt Named Player of the Year," *DC,* July 10, 1964; Jim Hawkins, "The Summer of a Badger Bonus Baby," *DC,* September 16, 1964; Edwin Shrake, "The Richest Bonus Baby Ever," *Sports Illustrated,* July 6, 1964, https://www.si.com/vault/1964/07/06/607968/the-richest -bonus-baby-ever.

94. Susan Detering, "Friedan Asserts Women Must Escape 'The Feminine Mystique,'" *DC,* July 24, 1964.

95. "Ellison Will Read Here," *WSJ,* September 20, 1964; "Ellison Speaks to Literary Committee," *DC,* September 24, 1964; Judy Blackstone, "Novel Is Symbolic, Ellison Tells Lyceum," *DC,* September 25, 1964.

96. Carmen Elsner, "'Dynamo with Violin,' Isaac Stern Adds to Madison Stature at UW," *WSJ,* November 23, 1964; Kaaren Plant, "Stern Masters Violin, Audience," *DC,* November 24, 1964; Collis H. Davis, Jr., "CARavan Program Proves Enjoyable," *DC,* November 19, 1964; Jane K. Zucker, "Flatt and Scruggs Sing 'Bluegrass,'" *DC,* October 2, 1964; Harrand, "Country Music Comes to Union, Wows Crowd," *CT,* October 3, 1964; "Noted India Musician Will Present Concert," *WSJ,* October 28, 1964; Zucker, "India's Famous Sitarist to Give Concert Here," *DC,* October 28, 1964; Liz Kantor, "Van Ronk's Blues Move His Audience," *DC,* November 3, 1964.

97. Brautigam, "U. Faculty Group Hits Widening of Viet War," *CT*, December 14, 1964.

98. David Boroff, "Status Seeking in Academe," *Saturday Review*, December 19, 1964, 46; "Rathskeller Praised as Most Celebrated Academic Hangout," *DC*, January 27, 1965.

99. BOR minutes, March 6, 1964.

100. BOR minutes, March 6, 1964; Hunter, "Harrington Calls for 12,500 Added Camp Randall Seats," *CT*, March 6, 1964; Mike Hirsley, "'U' OK's Stadium Expansion," *DC*, March 7, 1964; "More Seats, New Press Box for Stadium," *Wisconsin Alumnus* 65, no. 8 (May 1964), 25–26; BOR minutes, September 25, 1964; "Regents Authorize Plan for Stadium," *CT*, September 26, 1964; https://en.wikipedia.org/wiki/List_of_Wisconsin_Badgers_football_seasons.

101. BOR minutes, August 14, 1964; Hunter, "U. Skyscrapers Set Here," *CT*, August 14, 1964; Bednarek, "$37 Million UW Building Plans OKd by Regents," *WSJ*, August 15, 1964; BOR minutes, September 25, 1964; "$10 Million Classroom Building OKd," *WSJ*, September 26, 1964; "More Buildings—and More on the Way," *Wisconsin Alumnus* 66, no. 1 (October 1964): 22–24; "South Lower Campus Project Approved," *WSJ*, December 8, 1964; "Final Land Purchases for Lower Campus Approved," *CT*, December 11, 1964; Feldman, *Buildings*, 382–385, 396–399.

102. Rich Cassell, "Knowles Warns of Budget Cuts," *DC*, December 11, 1964; editorial, "The 'U's Future and Mr. Knowles," *DC*, December 12, 1964; Hunter, "U. Regents Are Bitter at Knowles," *CT*, December 12, 1964.

103. "UW Has a 'Snow Ball,'" *WSJ*, March 9, 1964; "The Great Snow Fight," *DC*, March 10, 1964.

104. "Albert Gallistel, UW Builder for 75 Years, Dies at Age 75," *WSJ*, January 2, 1964; "Albert F. Gallistel, 75, Dies; Headed U. Campus Planning," *CT*, January 2, 1964.

105. Wolf, "'I'm Scared as Hell, But I'm Going,'" *DC*, June 25, 1964; "U. Student Writes Tribute to Missing Rights Campaigner," *CT*, June 27, 1964; "Slain Rights Worker Was U.W. Student During 1961," *CT*, August 5, 1964; https://andrewgoodman.org/who-we-are/about-andy/; Peter Ames Carlin, *Homeward Bound: The Life of Paul Simon* (New York: Henry Holt, 2016), 103.

106. "1,300 to Get Diplomas Friday," *WSJ*, June 7, 1964; "Graduates Urged 'To Learn, to Love, to Be Strong,'" *CT*, June 12, 1964; "West Graduates Told Enthusiasm Makes Life Good," *CT*, June 12, 1964; William R. Wineke, "Another Historic Event Marked at Central High," *WSJ*, June 13, 1964; "Use Optimism of Graduation Day to Meet Life," *CT*, June 12, 1964; Coady, "East High Reminded: Keep Sense of Humor," *WSJ*, June 13, 1964.

107. "30,242 Enrolled in Public Schools," *WSJ*, September 15, 1964.

108. "Catholic Schools Enroll 5,200," *WSJ*, September 24, 1964.

109. "Formal Policy Adopted for Pupils' Homework," *WSJ*, January 7, 1964; Harrand, "Madison Pupils' IQ Put at 14 Points Above Average," *CT*, February 4, 1964.

110. June Dieckmann, "Schools Enforce Social Behavior," *WSJ*, February 14, 1964; "Vandals Wreck 7 East High Rooms," *WSJ*, October 30, 1964; "Vandals Cause $1,700 Damage at West High," *CT*, October 31, 1964.

111. "Mrs. Doyle in School Board Race," *CT*, January 16, 1964; "Mrs. Doyle Criticizes School Board Process," *CT*, March 11, 1964; "Mrs. Doyle Offers Program to Help Board-Public Ties," *WSJ*, March 27, 1964; "School Board Race Lively One," *WSJ*, April 5, 1964; Bednarek, "Mrs. Doyle and Glenn Stephens Win Positions on School Board," *WSJ*, April 8, 1964; editorial, "Board of Education's Agenda," *WSJ*, September 14, 1964; "School Board Approves Advance Notice on Agendas of Meetings," *WSJ*, September 22, 1964; Brautigam, "School Board to Publicize Agenda of Its Meetings," *CT*, September 22, 1964.

112. James D. Selk, "City Teachers Pick MEA to Be Bargaining Agent," *WSJ*, June 5, 1964.

113. Bednarek, "Raises Set for Beginning Teachers," *WSJ*, August 4, 1964; Harrand, "Teachers' Raises Get Board's OK," *CT*, August 4, 1964; editorial, "City Improves Teacher Pay," *WSJ*, August 11, 1964.

114. Matt Pommer, "Male Teachers Turn Down Contracts; Crisis Looms," *CT*, September 28, 1964.

115. Bednarek, "New West High Chief Makes Some Changes," *WSJ*, July 26, 1964; Brautigam, "New West High Principal Doesn't Expect Upheaval," *CT*, September 2, 1964; Pommer, "West High Delays Plan to 'Close' Lunch Hour," *CT*, October 29, 1964; Pommer, "West High May Start 'Closed' Lunch in '65," *CT*, November 18, 1964; "Know Your Madisonian—Douglas S. Ritchie," *WSJ*, November 28, 1965.

116. Brautigam, "School Board to Receive Report on Minority Study," *CT*, October 3, 1964; "Human Relations Guide OKd," *WSJ*, October 6, 1964; Brautigam, "Board Approves Guide on Human Relations Study," *CT*, October 6, 1964; Pommer, "City Rights Group Raps 'Snub' in School Guide," *CT*, November 21, 1964.

117. "New High School Site Annexed," *WSJ*, May 29, 1964; Bednarek, "Additions to Two City High Schools Approved," *WSJ*, June 2, 1964; Bednarek, "Vocational Board Eyes Central," *WSJ*, June 12, 1964; "Vocational Board Won't Get Central High, Board Asserts," *WSJ*, June 16, 1964; Brautigam, "Future of Central High Is Problem, City Is Told," *CT*, August 18, 1964.

118. Bednarek, "School Population 'Slows' Here," *WSJ*, September 9, 1964; Pommer, "Male Teachers Turn Down Contracts; Crisis Looms," *CT*, September 28, 1964; Pommer, "City to Lose 800 Pupils, Aid," *CT*, November 20, 1964; Pommer, "Burr Oaks Enrollment Estimates Are Down 19%," *CT*, December 3, 1964.

119. "'Kennedy' Name Urged for School," *CT*, July 30, 1964.

120. Havens Wilber, "Madison in 'Golden' Era," *CT*, January 3, 1965.

121. Newhouse, "Downtown Project Set," *WSJ*, April 5, 1964; "Bartell, Brooks Sell Baron's Store to Manchester's," *CT*, April 7, 1965.

122. "Gerald Bartell," Wisconsin Broadcasting Museum, http://www.wisconsinbroadcastingmuseum.org/hall-of-fame /gerald-bartell/; Stuart Brooks email, June 19, 2017.

123. Havens Wilber, "Store Tells 'Shoppers Bridge' Plan," *CT*, May 8, 1964; Brautigam, "Governor Asks Delay on Manchester's Walk Plan," *CT*, May 12, 1964; Newhouse, "Governor Stalls Skywalk Drive," *WSJ*, May 17, 1964; editorial, "City Policy on 'Skywalk' Plan," *WSJ*, May 20, 1964; "Manchester Presents His Plea for Overhead," *CT*, May 21, 1964; "Design for Manchester's Walkway Is Revised," *CT*, May 21, 1964; Maraniss, "Skywalk Design Changed in Move to Woo Governor," *CT*, May 21, 1964; "New Skywalk Design Proposed," *WSJ*, May 22, 1964; Gordon, "City Policy Proposed on Handling Skywalks," *WSJ*, May 23, 1964; "Six UW Artists Support Skywalk Plan," *WSJ*, May 22, 1964.

124. Aldric Revell, "Governor Backs Skyway," *CT*, May 25, 1964; "State Won't Oppose Skywalk," *WSJ*, May 26, 1964.

125. Editorial, "Chance to Be Heard on Skyways," *WSJ*, May 25, 1964; Gordon, "Plan Unit Approves Skywalk Principle," *WSJ*, May 26, 1964; Brautigam, "1st Victory for Skywalk," *CT*, May 26, 1964; editorial, "The Governor's Curious Stand on Skywalk Proposal," *CT*, May 26, 1964.

126. Gordon, "City Council Defeats Skywalk Proposal," *WSJ*, May 29, 1964; Gordon, "Skywalk Defeat Spurs Move for a City Policy," *WSJ*, May 29, 1964; Brautigam, "Skywalk Plan Defeated," *CT*, May 29, 1964; editorial, "Council Skyway Vote Reflects Sentiment of Madison People," *CT*, May 29, 1964; Feuerzeig, "Skywalk Called Key to Downtown Project," *CT*, June 1, 1964; Gordon, "Skywalk Project Termed Vital," *WSJ*, June 2, 1964.

127. Gordon, "Council Will View Policy on Skywalks," *WSJ*, June 13, 1964; editorial, "City Needs Skywalk Policy," *WSJ*, June 23, 1964; editorial, "Serious Deliberations Needed on Skyway Policy for City," *CT*, June 23, 1964; Gribble, "Skywalk Principle Gets Council OK," *WSJ*, June 25, 1964; Brautigam, "Campaign for Skywalks Is Slowed," *CT*, June 26, 1964; Gordon, "Plan Group Puts Off Action on Skywalks," *WSJ*, July 7, 1964; editorial, "Mayor Reynolds' Wise Decision on Skywalk Policy Question," *CT*, July 7, 1964; Feuerzeig, "City-State Committee in Clash on Skywalks," *CT*, September 1, 1964; Feuerzeig, "City-State Unit Finally Puts Skywalk Policy into Words," *CT*, September 23, 1964.

128. Aehl, "Council Clears Way for Skywalk Project," *WSJ*, October 6, 1964; Feuerzeig, "Skywalk Policy Given Plan Group Approval," *CT*, October 6, 1964; Feuerzeig, "Manchester Revives Skywalk Campaign," *CT*, October 21, 1964.

129. "Skywalk Unit Sees Design, Sets Meeting," *CT*, November 21, 1964; "Special Unit Eyes Skywalk Plan," *WSJ*, November 24, 1964.

130. "Edgewater Hotel Buys Part of Hanks Property," *WSJ*, January 6, 1964; Newhouse, "Guardian Life Starts Building," *WSJ*, February 7, 1964.

131. Wilber, "Bare Big U. Ave. Project," *CT*, April 24, 1964; "Bartell-Brooks Plan New 10-Story Holiday Inn on State St. Location," *WSJ*, April 25, 1964.

132. "Hill Farms State Office Building Dedicated," *WSJ*, July 21, 1964.

133. Feuerzeig, "Annexation Package Deal Goes to Council Tonight," *CT*, September 10, 1964; Aehl, "City Annexes Eagle Heights," *WSJ*, September 11, 1964; Brautigam, "City Pact with Towns Ends Disputes on Annexations," *CT*, September 11, 1964.

134. Aehl, "New 'Family' Zone Law Backed," *WSJ*, October 20, 1964; John Powell, "City Council Shelves 'Family' Housing Bill," *DC*, October 23, 1964; Aehl, "Council Kills Change in 'Family' Zone Law," *WSJ*, October 23, 1964; Brautigam, "Student Rent Curb Is Killed," *CT*, October 23, 1964.

135. "Hilldale Shopping Center Marks 2nd Anniversary," *Hilldale Section*, October 21–22, 1964; "Value of Center Set at $12 million," *Hilldale Section*, October 21–22, 1964.

136. Maraniss, "Truax Air Base to Close," *CT*, November 19, 1964; Newhouse, "Truax Will Be Stripped of All Defenses By '68," *WSJ*, November 20, 1964; "$20 Million Sum Flies Away," *WSJ*, November 20, 1964; "Zeidler Views Closing as Opportunity for City," *WSJ*, November 20, 1964; Wineke, "Truax Linked to Madison: An 'Adopted Relative,'" *WSJ*, November 20, 1964; Maraniss, "Madison Seeks Methods to Offset Loss of Truax," *CT*, November 20, 1964.

137. Brautigam, "Atwood Improvement Pushed by Plan Bureau," *CT*, November 28, 1964.

138. "City Will Buy Land for West Side Park," *WSJ*, December 22, 1964.

139. Dieckmann, "Retaliation Gang Fight Averted Here after Tip," *WSJ*, February 7, 1964; Dieckmann, "Verona School Restricts 15 Youths for Gang Fight Role," *WSJ*, February 11, 1964; Dieckmann, "Guilty Youths Face Curbs; Parents Rapped for Laxity," *WSJ*, February 12, 1964.

140. Newhouse, "Youthful Smoking Increases in City," *WSJ*, January 1, 1964; "UW Man Shows Smoke-Cancer Link," *WSJ*, February 6, 1964; Aehl, "Youthful Smokers Face Up to $20 Fines Here," *WSJ*, March 25, 1964; "Young Smokers Given Reprieve," *WSJ*, March 27, 1964; Gordon, "City Cigarette Ban Place on Youths under Age 16," *WSJ*, April 24, 1964.

141. Harrand, "South Siders Air Pleas for Better Bus Service," *CT*, February 8, 1964; "City-Owned Bus Plan Study Asked by Kopp," *CT*, February 14, 1964; Revell, "Madison Bus Co. Agrees to Burr Oaks Extension," *CT*, February 19, 1964; Llewellyn G. Roberts, "Extension of Bus Line Expected in Burr Oaks," *WSJ*, February 20, 1964.

142. Newhouse, "'Outer Circle' Due for Square," *WSJ*, April 12, 1964; Aehl, "Traffic Group Supports 'Outer Circle' Proposal,"

WSJ, April 17, 1964; "New 'Outer Loop' Traffic Plan Set," *WSJ*, May 13, 1964; "New 'Outer Loop' Traffic Plan OKd," *WSJ*, May 16, 1964; "Capitol Square Traffic Proposal Moves Forward," *WSJ*, June 24, 1964; "Council Backs Off Skywalk Principle," *WSJ*, June 26, 1964; Newhouse, "'Outer Circle' Gains Popularity," *WSJ*, November 29, 1964.

143. Gordon, "Plan Group Approves Freeway for Beltline," *WSJ*, June 9, 1964; Brautigam, "Plan Group Backs Project for Freeway on Beltline," *CT*, June 10, 1964.

144. "Mayor Undecided on Ambulance Plan," *WSJ*, September 11, 1964.

145. Aehl, "City's Voters Approve 3 Bond Issues," *WSJ*, November 4, 1964.

146. Coyle, "State Approves Causeway Plans," *CT*, November 5, 1964; "PSC Grants Dredging Permit for Causeway," *WSJ*, November 6, 1964.

147. CAC minutes, December 2, 1964; Aehl, "University Ave. Work Given State Go-Ahead," *WSJ*, December 3, 1964; Brautigam, "University Ave. Plan Given Go-Ahead," *CT*, December 3, 1964; Revell, "Knowles Is Unhappy about University Ave. Complaints," *CT*, December 4, 1964.

148. "Bike Ban in Rush Hours Eyed," *WSJ*, December 18, 1964.

149. "State St. Is Placed on List of Scenic Wisconsin Roads," *WSJ*, December 31, 1964.

150. "Praise Bethel's Courage in Expanding Building," *CT*, February 3, 1964.

151. "Artist Lee Weiss Receives Honors in New York Show," *CT*, February 19, 1964.

152. "Eugene Parks Is Oratorical Contest Winner," *CT*, March 9, 1964.

153. Brautigam, "Park Commission Extends Dog Ban to Seven Areas," *CT*, April 2, 1964.

154. "Viet Nam Protest to Be Held on Square," *CT*, May 1, 1964; "U.S. Role in Vietnam Protested Today," *DC*, May 2, 1964; Jean Sue Johnson, "May 2 Committee Pickets for Peace," *DC*, May 6, 1964; Harriet Tanzman, *Civil Rights and History*, in Buhle, ed., *History and the New Left*, 148; Levin, *Cold War University*, 123.

155. "Silver Jubilee for Beth El Temple," *CT*, May 21, 1964; Gribble, "Beth El Reveals Building Project," *CT*, May 27, 1964.

156. Robin Rafeld, "Manchester's Breaks the Breast Barrier," *DC*, July 14, 1964; Feuerzeig, "Topless Bathing Suits Returned by Manchester," *CT*, July 14, 1964.

157. "Elm Disease Appears to Be Under Control," *WSJ*, July 14, 1964.

158. Coady, "Art Foundation Pledge Spurs Center Campaign," *WSJ*, February 26, 1964; Brautigam, "Lincoln School Art Use Backed," *CT*, May 13, 1964; "Art Center's Season Set," *WSJ*, September 13, 1964; Witt, "Lincoln School Becomes Gallery," *WSJ*, September 17, 1964; "Banner Display Feature of Art Center Tour," *CT*, September 22, 1964; "Madison Art Center Moves to Old School," *WSJ*, October 1, 1964.

159. Revell and Hunter, "Barry Here, Rips Court," *CT*, September 24, 1964; Roberts, "10,000 Hear Barry Blast Power Grab, Court 'Laws,'" *WSJ*, September 25, 1964; Roberts, "Heckling Quiets as Goldwater Speaks," *WSJ*, September 25, 1964; Stu Chapman, "Barry Gets Cheers, Jeers," *DC*, September 25, 1964.

160. Lea Andresen, "French Festival? La, La, the Greatest," *WSJ*, September 27, 1964; Andresen, "Chic Imports Bring New Style Outlooks," *WSJ*, September 27, 1964; Elsner, "Sedate Square Kicks Up Its Heels and Goes French," *WSJ*, September 27, 1964; "Madison Will Have Its Own Left Bank," *WSJ*, September 27, 1964; "Festival de France," *WSJ*, September 27, 1964.

161. "Ald. Garner to End Long Council Service," *WSJ*, December 3, 1964; Newhouse, "Ald. Garner Bids Adieu," *WSJ*, April 16, 1965.

162. Roberts, "Thomas E. Coleman, Leader in GOP, Dies," *WSJ*, February 5, 1964; editorial, "Thomas E. Coleman," *WSJ*, February 5, 1964; Revell, "Thomas Coleman, Longtime Leader in GOP, Is Dead," *CT*, February 5, 1964; Roberts, "Dignitaries from Home and Afar Attend Thomas Coleman Funeral," *WSJ*, February 7, 1964; "Reed Coleman Heads Madison Kipp," *WSJ*, March 22, 1964; Maraniss, "Reed Coleman Will Keep Madison-Kipp Right Here," *CT*, March 23, 1964.

163. "Dr. Arnold S. Jackson, 71, Retired Clinic Director, Dies," *WSJ*, August 31, 1964; "Dr. A.S. Jackson Is Dead at Age 71," *CT*, August 31, 1964.

164. "Mrs. Edward Samp, Former School Board Member, Dies," *WSJ*, December 24, 1964.

165. "Angus McVicar, 60, Dies; Ex-Photographer for C-T," *CT*, May 9, 1964; "Richard Vesey, State Journal Photographer, Reporter, Dies," *WSJ*, December 30, 1964.

1965

1. "Crew Starts Madison Hotel Wrecking," *WSJ*, June 26, 1965.

2. "University Survey Shows Students for Viet Policy," *DC*, July 19, 1966.

3. Matt Fox, "As the Draft Increases, Teens May Get Called," *DC*, August 6, 1965.

4. Gil Lamont, "March on Capitol Protests Bombings in Viet Nam War," *DC*, February 10, 1965; William Witt, "'Anti-War' Rally Draws 200," *WSJ*, February 10, 1965; "UW Group Raps Demonstration," *WSJ*, February 10, 1965; John Patrick Hunter, "'War' Protest Here Attended by 300," *CT*, February 10, 1965; editorial, "Pacification and Apology," *DC*, February 13, 1965; John Coatsworth email, July 17, 2017.

5. Edwin S. Kohn, "Police Admit Demonstration Dossier," *DC*, February 24, 1965; Dave Zweifel, "Police Keep Film Files on Rally Participants," *CT*, February 24, 1965; Kohn, "Police Film Revelation Draws 'U,' City Reaction," *DC*, February 25, 1965; June Dieckmann, "Photos of Crowds Defended by Chief," *WSJ*, February 25, 1965; Owen Coyle, "Police Face Query on Demonstration Films," *CT*, February 25, 1965; Richard Brautigam, "Block Discussion of Police Protest Films," *CT*, February 26, 1965; editorial, "Demonstration File: Not Even Living," *DC*, February 26, 1965; Brautigam, "Aldermen Defend Police against Photo Protests," *CT*, March 25, 1965.

6. Zweifel, "300 Join Peace Picketing Here," *CT*, February 13, 1965; "Students Rap Viet Policy, Hold Capitol Rally," *WSJ*, February 14, 1965; Stuart Ewen, "The Intellectual New Left," in Buhle, ed., *History and the New Left*, 181; John Coatsworth interview with Matt Levin, November 22, 2000; Stu Ewen email, May 13, 2017; Evan Stark email, June 27, 2017; John Coatsworth interview, July 17, 2017.

7. Student Organizations Registration File, University Archives; John Powell, "Protest Committee Asks Local Support," *DC*, February 19, 1965; Zweifel, "Viet Nam War Opponents Explain Set-Up, Beliefs," *CT*, February 22, 1965; Todd Gitlin, *The Sixties: Years of Hope, Days of Rage* (New York: Random House, 2013), 112.

8. Powell, "YAF Ratifies Political Bills," *DC*, March 12, 1965; Student Organizations Registration File, University Archives.

9. Matt Pommer, "'Teach-In' Protest Set on Viet Nam," *CT*, March 25, 1965; John Gruber, "Faculty-Student Group Maps Challenges to U.S. Viet Policy," *DC*, March 30, 1965; Gruber, "Anti-Viet War 'Teach-In' Set for Social Science Today," *DC*, April 1, 1965; Raymond Mouch, "10-Hour UW 'Teach-In' Gives Viet War an 'F,'" *WSJ*, April 2, 1965; Gruber, "'Teach-In' Fills Social Science," *DC*, April 2, 1965; "1,000 Attend Viet Nam Protest While Pro-War Group Is Formed," *CT*, April 2, 1965; Cliff Behnke, "Week Long Anti-War Protest Climaxed by Friday Noon Rally," *DC*, April 3, 1965; "Says Viet Nam Ceasefire Is 'Must' within 30 Days," *CT*, April 3, 1965; "Of 'Teach-Ins' and Petitions," *Wisconsin Alumnus* 6, no. 8 (May 1965): 16–17; William Sewell, interviewed by Laura Smail, 1977, OH #0101, digital audio file, University Archives and Records Management Services, Madison, Wisconsin; David Maraniss, *They Marched into Sunlight: War and Peace, Vietnam and America, October 1967* (New York:Simon & Schuster, 2003), 121–122.

10. Cliff Behnke and Jean Sue Johnson, "Placards Are Sole Response of 'U' Students: Chapelle," *DC*, April 2, 1965; Johnson, "Student Petition Supports American Viet Nam Policy," *DC*, April 3, 1965; "Pro-Viet Nam War Unit Being Formed at U.W.," *CT*, April 3, 1965; Norm Lenburg, "'U' Campus Leaders Support U.S. Presence in Viet Nam," *DC*, April 4, 1965; "UW Petition Supporting U.S. Policy in Viet Set," *WSJ*, April 5, 1965; "Seek 5,000 Signers Backing U.S. Policy in Viet Nam," *CT*, April 5, 1965; "6,000 Sign Viet Nam Support," *CT*, April 16, 1965.

11. Eric Newhouse, "Anti-War Group Votes 'No Civil Disobedience,'" *DC*, October 8, 1965; Newhouse, "'U' Now Focal Point of Renewed Anti-War Protest," *DC*, October 12, 1965; Newhouse, "Rebellious Career Illustrates Merging Protest Movements," *DC*, October 12, 1965; "Anti-Viet War Unit Here Plans 'Citizen Arrest,'" *CT*, October 13, 1965; William R. Wineke, "Peace Groups Go on Different Paths," *WSJ*, October 15, 1965.

12. Robert A. Davis, "Mitchell Trio Lures Crowd to UW Group's Viet Protest," *WSJ*, October 16, 1965; "End Viet Nam War Protest Countered by 'Ram Day,'" *DC*, October 16, 1965; Don Fitzgibbons, "Students Hear Protest on War," *DC*, October 19, 1965.

13. "End Viet Nam War Protest Countered by 'Ram Day,'" *DC*, October 16, 1965; Zweifel, "Nab 11 in Truax Sitdown," *CT*, October 16, 1965; Lenburg, "Picket Arrest Plot Foiled; Police Ticket 11 Viet War Demonstrators," *WSJ*, October 17, 1965; Dieckmann, "Judge to Study Cases of 5 Viet Protesters," *WSJ*, November 10, 1965; Dieckmann, "Viet Protesters Close Their Defense," *WSJ*, November 11, 1965; Richard Scher, "Truax Defendants Present Their Case," *DC*, November 12, 1965; Johnson, "Truax Demonstrators Fine, Plan to Appeal Conviction," *DC*, November 16, 1965; Dieckmann, "5 Viet Protesters Are Found Guilty," *WSJ*, November 16, 1965.

14. Editorial, "The Protesters: Bigots and Martyrs," *DC*, October 19, 1965; editorial, "Deplorable Protest Movement," *WSJ*, October 18, 1965; "Harrington Defends Free Speech over Viet," *WSJ*, November 13, 1965; editorial, "No Savio Needed Here," *DC*, November 18, 1965.

15. "Alumni President Raps Demonstrations at U.W.," *CT*, May 5, 1965; Robert R. Spitzer, "Put the Emphasis on UW's Greatness," *WSJ*, May 7, 1965.

16. Neal Ulevich, "600 Hear Three on Viet Nam," *DC*, May 7, 1965; Steven Barney, "Hostile Students at UW Delay Viet Policy Talks," *WSJ*, May 7, 1965; "Hostile Students Harass Three Experts on Viet Nam," *CT*, May 7, 1965.

17. Editorial, "Demonstrators Hurt Academic Freedom," *DC*, May 7, 1965; editorial, "Childish Exhibition of Students Interferes with Free Speech," *CT*, May 8, 1965; editorial, "The Right to Act Foolishly," *WSJ*, May 10, 1965.

18. Powell, "Harriman: Viet Guerillas Hanoi-Supplied, Directed," *DC*, May 14, 1965; Davis, "Polite Applause, Some Hisses Greet Harriman," *WSJ*, May 14, 1965; Barney, "Foe of Viet Policy Says City Needn't Fret over UW Rifts," *CT*, May 21, 1965; Evan Stark email, June 27, 2017.

19. Powell, "YAF Plans Right's First Demonstration," *DC*, July 2, 1965; Powell, "YAF Capitol Protest Supports Taft-Hartley," *DC*, July 8, 1965; Powell, "YAF Plans Taft-Hartley Debate, Denies Ties with Radical Right," *DC*, July 14, 1965.

20. Charles M. Martin, "Internal Security Committee Invites 'U' Students to DC," *DC*, July 27, 1965.

21. Matt Fox, "Draft Hike Affects Campus," *DC*, July 30, 1965.

22. Coyle, "Block Viet Hearing Here," *CT*, July 19, 1965; Zweifel, "Plea for Capitol Hearing Stalled," *CT*, July 20, 1965; Zweifel, "Set Viet Hearing in Federal Building," *CT*, July 21, 1965; editorial, "Viet Hearings Will Go On, but What of Free Speech Issue?" *CT*, July 22, 1965; "Viet Hearing Is Shifted to 1st Methodist Church," *WSJ*, July 29, 1965; Coyle, "Viet Nam Hearings Here Are Switched, Extended a Day," *CT*, July 29, 1965; editorial, "Kastenmeier Recruits Witnesses," *WSJ*, July 30, 1965; Coyle, "Air Viet War Views Here," *CT*, July 30, 1965; David Bednarek, "Left to Right, All Are Orderly at Viet Hearing," *WSJ*, July 31, 1965; Coyle, "Most Speakers at Viet Nam Hearing Back Negotiations," *CT*, July 31, 1965; Witt, "Few Back Viet Policy," *WSJ*, August 1, 1965; Robert W. Kastenmeier, *Vietnam Hearings: Voices from the Grass Roots* (Waterloo, WI: Artcraft Press, 1965); Zweifel and Nichols, *Capital Times*, 184–186.

23. "Foes of Viet War to Set Up National Office in Madison," *CT*, August 18, 1965; Fox, "Anti-War Group Opens National Office Here," *DC*, September 14, 1965; Harvey Breuscher, "UW Grad Coordinates Protest in U.S.," *WSJ*, October 17, 1965; "Why Peace Group Selected Madison as Headquarters," *CT*, October 20, 1965; Frank Emspak email, May 20, 2017.

24. Hunter, "Humphrey Wins Cheers of NSA Despite Picketing," *CT*, August 24, 1965.

25. "Council, Union Oppose Campus Protest on Viet," *WSJ*, October 29, 1965; "City Council States Citizens Abhor Protests," *DC*, October 29, 1965.

26. Lenburg, "Protesters Told Their Actions May Backfire," *WSJ*, November 1, 1965; "War Foes Causing Neo-McCarthyism," *CT*, November 1, 1965.

27. BOR minutes, November 12, 1965; Pommer, "U. Free Speech to Stay, Harrington Tells Board," *CT*, November 13, 1965.

28. "Young Adults Back U.S. Policy in Viet," *WSJ*, July 16, 1966; "University Survey Shows Students for Viet Policy," *DC*, July 19, 1966.

29. Dana Hesse and Marsha Cutting, "Referendum—No in Small Turnout," *DC*, November 24, 1965; Hesse, "SRP Takes Most Seats; but Vote Turnout Is Poor," *DC*, November 25, 1965.

30. "Eggs Greet Viet War Foes; Paper 'Coffin' Kicked In," *CT*, November 29, 1965.

31. Powell, "Busload Leaves for Selma," *DC*, March 16, 1965; "UW Group Leaves to Join Freedom Rally in Alabama," *CT*, March 16, 1965.

32. Newhouse, "Buses Head for Capitol," *DC*, March 17, 1965; Newhouse, "Students Picket White House," *DC*, March 18, 1965; Newhouse, "'U' Students Continue D.C. Vigil; 20 Head Homeward," *DC*, March 19, 1968; Newhouse, "D.C. Buses Arrive Today," *DC*, March 20, 1965.

33. Rich Scher, "Medicine to Montgomery," *DC*, March 17, 1965; "U.W. Rights Group at White House," *CT*, March 17, 1965.

34. "Alabama-Bound Trip to Resume," *WSJ*, March 18, 1965.

35. "Madison's 'Freedom Flyers' in Alabama," *CT*, March 18, 1965; "Freedom Fliers Given Active Roles in Alabama," *CT*, March 19, 1965; Gail Bensinger, "20 Return from Montgomery," *DC*, March 20, 1965; Davis, "34 Madison Residents, Students Return from Montgomery Trip," *WSJ*, March 28, 1965; Janet M. Schlatter, "4 Madison Women Look Back on the March to Montgomery," *CT*, May 26, 1965.

36. Bensinger, "88 Arrested in Montgomery," *DC*, March 19, 1965; Dave Wolf, "Taut Montgomery Greets Contingent," *DC*, March 19, 1965; Wolf, "Alabama: 'You Don't Call Cops,'" *DC*, March 23, 1965; Allison Handschel, *It Doesn't End With Us: The Story of the Daily Cardinal* (Westminster, MD: Heritage Books, 2007), 51–52, 57–59.

37. EOC Minutes, January 19, 1965; Davis, "City Rights Unit Settles Complaints," *WSJ*, January 20, 1965.

38. "2 to Close Youth Series at Church," *CT*, February 26, 1965.

39. EOC minutes, April 27, 1965; "City's Equal Opportunity Law Helps Disperse Negro Population," *WSJ*, July 1, 1965; Pommer, "Major Integration Gains Are Scored in Madison," *CT*, October 11, 1965.

40. Wineke, "600 Hold Vigil at State Capitol," *WSJ*, March 15, 1965; "He Leads Congregation in Prayer, Protest," *WSJ*, March 15, 1965; Hunter, "800 Honor Fallen Rights Figure Here," *CT*, March 15, 1965; "1,000 Gather at Capitol for Selma Prayer Vigil," *DC*, March 16, 1965.

41. "Mayor Calls Opportunity Law His Term's Top Accomplishment," *WSJ*, April 4, 1965.

42. "St. Paul A.M.E. Sets Last Service in Its Old Church," *CT*, August 27, 1965.

43. Leslie Simon, "'Fast for Freedom' in '65 Will Aid War on Negro Poverty," *DC*, November 9, 1965; Dale Shanley, "Fast Expects $3500 from Meal Refunds," *DC*, November 19, 1965.

44. Ruth B. Doyle, "Profile of the Negro Student, University of Wisconsin, 1964–1965," May 13, 1965, SC 2232 MAD 4 /14/SC 2232, WHSA; Pommer, "Only 118 U.S. Negroes Are Students at U.W.," *CT*, May 22, 1965.

45. Advertisement, *DC*, November 18, 1965.

46. Neal Ulevich, "CORE Leader Views 'Caste,'" *DC*, May 6, 1965.

47. Bednarek, "Rights Activists Explained: They're Against All Violence," *WSJ*, November 3, 1965; Fox, "John Lewis Condemns Government System," *DC*, November 3, 1965.

48. Nicholls, "Dr. King Proposes Public Works Plan," *WSJ*, November 23, 1965; Johnson, "More Federal Action Is Needed in Civil Rights Field, Says King," *DC*, November 24, 1965; Hunter, "King Says Negroes Now Emphasize Poverty War," *CT*, November 24, 1965.

49. Llewellyn G. Roberts, "Madison Club Battles Bias," *WSJ*, November 13, 1965.

50. "Harrington Quits Madison Club as Jews Are Barred," *CT*, October 12, 1965; "Harrington Note Tells Reason He Left Madison Club," *CT*, October 23, 1965.

51. Zweifel, "Madison Club Directors Stay Silent on Bias Report," *CT*, October 13, 1965.

52. "Municipal Affairs," *WSJ*, October 13, 1965; editorial, "'U' Bookstore Trustees Evade Discrimination Issue Again," *DC*, October 21, 1965.

53. "Jewish Council Hails Public Indignation over Club Bias," *WSJ*, November 12, 1965.

54. Coyle, "Exclusion Imperils Club Liquor Permit," *CT*, October 13, 1965; Coyle, "No Ordinance Ban on License Bias," *CT*, October 14, 1965; Coyle, "Ordinance Is Drawn Banning City Permits for Discrimination," *CT*, October 22, 1965; John T. Aehl, "Banning of Any Club License for 'Biased' Clubs Proposed," *WSJ*, October 23, 1965.

55. Aehl, "Club Discrimination to Mean License Ban," *WSJ*, October 27, 1965; Aehl, "Council Sets Anti-Bias Policy,' *WSJ*, October 29, 1965; Brautigam, "Council Passes Licensee Bias Ban," *CT*, October 29, 1965.

56. Newhouse, "Bookstore Board Might Leave Club," *DC*, October 20, 1965; "Knowles to Urge Changes at Club," *WSJ*, November 6, 1965; "Petition in Madison Club Seeks to Reverse Ban," *CT*, November 6, 1965; Nicholls, "Club Bias Vote Reversal Asked," *WSJ*, November 9, 1965; Wineke, "Rights Unit to Study Bias in Private Clubs," *WSJ*, November 9, 1965.

57. "Bias in Bylaws Denied," *WSJ*, October 27, 1965

58. "Justice Gordon, Atty. Sinykin Accept Madison Club's New Bid," *WSJ*, November 17, 1965.

59. Raymond Moucha, "Bias Study Group to Seek Solution," *WSJ*, November 18, 1965; EOC minutes, December 14, 1965; Davis, "Rights Group Praises Bias Erasure at Club," *WSJ*, December 15, 1965.

60. Aehl, "George Hall Enters Race for Mayor," *WSJ*, December 10, 1964; Coyle, "Mayor Says 'No,' Will Back Hall," *CT*, December 12, 1964; Coyle, "Festge Runs for Mayor," *CT*, December 12, 1964; Otto Festge Oral History, interviewed by Ruth Doyle, 1989, Historic Madison, Inc.; Wineke, "Former Mayor Festge Dies at 86; He Was Madison's Mayor for Two Terms," *WSJ*, November 6, 2007.

61. Aehl, "Hall: 'He's Good Clerk;' Festge: 'Hospital Chief,'" *WSJ*, March 17, 1965; Aehl, "Pressure Felt, Two Candidates for Mayor Trade Few Hard Jabs," *WSJ*, March 31, 1965.

62. Coyle, "Dyke Indicates Favor for Monona Terrace," *CT*, January 21, 1965; "Hall Ends Silence, Raps Terrace Auditorium Site," *CT*, February 8, 1965; editorial, "Festge's Stuck with Terrace," *WSJ*, February 23, 1965; Coyle, "Hall Favors Expressway through Site of Terrace," *CT*, March 13, 1965; Brautigam, "Major Rivals Say That Terrace Site Is Principal Issue," *CT*, March 17, 1965.

63. "Festge Cites Lack of Land for Crosstown Expressway," *CT*, March 22, 1965; "Bus Service in Madison," *WSJ*, March 30, 1965.

64. Witt, "Mayor Candidates Oppose Skywalks," *WSJ*, March 26, 1965; Brautigam, "Metropolitan Problems Take Spotlight at Forum," *CT*, March 30; Coyle, "Auditorium, Road Plan Pace Candidates' Jabs," *CT*, April 1, 1965.

65. "Hall Stresses Planning for New City Hospital," *WSJ*, March 14, 1965; "Festge Presses Action on East Side Hospital," *WSJ*, March 28, 1965.

66. "Festge Pledges Himself to City Beautification Program," *CT*, April 1, 1965.

67. "Hall Says City, County Health Agency Needed," *WSJ*, March 29, 1965.

68. "Dane GOP Chairman Is Helping Campaign of Hall for Mayor," *CT*, January 14, 1965; "Doyle Cites Festge's Work as Important Background," *CT*, March 29, 1965.

69. "11 City Labor Leaders Support Hall for Mayor," *WSJ*, January 17, 1965; Witt, "COPE Endorses Hall, Festge," *WSJ*, February 19, 1965; Coyle, "Terrace Dominates COPE Candidate Forum," *CT*, February 19, 1965; editorial, "How Long Will Madison Let Ald. Rohr Dictate Its Politics," *CT*, February 19, 1965; Brautigam, "COPE Continues Dual OK for Festge, Hall," *CT*, March 23, 1965.

70. Brautigam, "Hall Maps Anti-C-T Campaign; Hits Festge 'Machine' and Hart," *CT*, January 11, 1965; Brautigam, "Mayor Hits C-T as Council 'Dictator'" *CT*, March 26, 1965; editorial, "Festge Can Get Madison Moving Again," *CT*, March 30, 1965; editorial, "George Hall: The Man for the Mayor's Job," *WSJ*, April 5, 1965.

71. Aehl, "Festge Wins Mayor Race by 8,000 Votes," *WSJ*, April 7, 1965; Coyle, "Festge in Landslide Win," *CT*, April 7, 1965.

72. Otto Festge, "Mayor's Annual Message," April 20, 1965, Wisconsin Historical Society Library, WI-M 1 MAY 50.1:1965/4/20; Coyle, "Council Urged: Shun Battles over Personnel," *CT*, April 20, 1965; Aehl, "Festge Asks 'Metro' Planning," *WSJ*, April 21, 1965.

73. Mollenhoff and Hamilton, *Monona Terrace*, 165–167.

74. Brautigam, "Mayor Rivals Say That Terrace Site Is Principal Issue," *CT*, March 17, 1965.

75. Aehl, "Business Leaders Back Terrace Site," *WSJ*, February 13, 1965; editorial, "Business Leaders Move to Revitalize Downtown," *CT*, February 13, 1965; "A Cultural Center in the Center of Madison," *WSJ*, February 14, 1965; Zweifel, "Metzner Hits Out at Manchester," *CT*, February 19, 1965.

76. Coyle and Brautigam, "Seek Terrace Fee Truce," *CT*, February 13, 1965; "Mayor Reynolds Hits Terrace Endorsement," *WSJ*, February 14, 1965; Coyle, "Mayor Refuses to OK Delay in Arbitration," *CT*, February 23, 1965; Aehl, "Council Moves to Build Its Auditorium Account," *WSJ*, March 12, 1965.

77. "Joseph W. Jackson Revives Attack on Wright's Patriotism," *CT*, March 24, 1965; "Hall and Festge Deplore Jackson Attack on Wright," *CT*, March 24, 1965.

78. Festge, "Mayor's Annual Message," April 20, 1965, Wisconsin Historical Society Library, WI-M 1 MAY 50.1:1965/4/20; Coyle, "End Arbitration: Festge," *CT*, April 20, 1965; editorial, "Mayor's First Talk to City," *WSJ*, April 22, 1965; Coyle, "Move to Halt Cushman," *CT*, April 22, 1965; Aehl, "Arbitration Is Stayed for Wright 'Settlement,'" *WSJ*, April 23, 1965; Brautigam, "Wright Talks to Reopen," *CT*, April 23, 1965; editorial, "The New Auditorium Picture," *WSJ*, April 26, 1965.

79. Aehl, "New Terrace Group Asks Reynolds View," *WSJ*, April 30, 1965; "Arbitrate, Terrace Unit Urged," *WSJ*, May 14, 1965.

80. Coyle, "Wright Group Ready for Meeting with City," *CT*, June 8, 1965; Brautigam, "Mayor Sees Wright Pact," *CT*, June 9, 1965.

81. Aehl, "Settlement of Terrace Dispute Sought Today," *WSJ*, June 10, 1965; Coyle, "Accord Seen in Terrace Fee Fight," *CT*, June 10, 1965; "Feinsinger's Choice Follows Long Session," *WSJ*, June 11, 1965.

82. Aehl, "Wright Issue Over; City Pays $150,000," *WSJ*, June 11, 1965; Brautigam, "City Settles Wright Fee," *CT*, June 11, 1965; Coyle, "14 Hours of Talks Precede Fee Accord," *CT*, June 11, 1965; Aehl, "Fee Settlement Means New Auditorium Start," *WSJ*, June 12, 1965.

83. Editorial, "Festge Delivers on Promise to End Costly Arbitration," *CT*, June 11, 1965; editorial, "Monona Terrace Fee Dispute," *WSJ*, June 14, 1965.

84. Mollenhoff and Hamilton, *Monona Terrace*, 294, 172.

85. Roger Gribble, "Auditorium Committee Is Selected by Mayor," *WSJ*, June 23, 1965; Brautigam, "Mayor Asks Fresh Auditorium Start," *CT*, June 23, 1965; Gribble, "Auditorium Unit of 12 Confirmed," *WSJ*, June 25, 1965; Brautigam, "Terrace Enemies Are Balked Again," *CT*, June 25, 1965; Brautigam, "Back Theater Guild Use of Auditorium," *CT*, August 3, 1965; Aehl, "Theater Guild Plans Backed," *WSJ*, August 5, 1965.

86. Coyle, "State Solons Cool to Jackson's Bid to Curb Terrace," *CT*, June 16, 1965; Robert Meloon, "Jackson Terrace Block Advanced," *CT*, June 23, 1965; Meloon, "Kill Terrace Foe's Move," *CT*, October 12, 1965.

87. Aehl, "Auditorium-Theater Urged," *WSJ*, October 14, 1965; Coyle, "Auditorium and Theater Set as Basic Center Needs," *CT*, October 14, 1965; Coyle, "Monona Terrace Area Included in New Site," *CT*, November 17, 1965; Aehl, "Auditorium Unit Trims Site Choices to Three," *WSJ*, November 18, 1965; Coyle, "Auditorium Sites Are Cut to Three," *CT*, November 18, 1965.

88. Coyle, "Foes of Terrace Would Rather Fight than Build," *CT*, November 30, 1965; Frank Custer, "Obstructionists Once More Move to Block Auditorium," *CT*, November 30, 1965.

89. Aehl, "Auditorium's Nearer, Mayor Claims," *WSJ*, December 23, 1965; Brautigam, "Foe Fails to Slow Auditorium Talks," *CT*, December 23, 1965.

90. John Newhouse, "Madison Public Housing Opens," *WSJ*, January 4, 1965.

91. "Housing Project Officially Named after Gay Braxton," *WSJ*, June 25, 1965.

92. Aehl, "Tenants Hail Triangle Housing," *WSJ*, February 3, 1965; Zweifel, "Elderly Like Their Housing Project," *CT*, February 24, 1965; MRA minutes, June 2, 1965; Coyle, "37-Year-Old Grapevine in Triangle Saved," *CT*, June 22, 1965; Coyle, "Sentiment Glows at Dedication of Triangle Housing," *CT*, June 24, 1965; Goroff, et al, *The Spirit of Greenbush*, 19.

93. "Glidden Building Inches Home," *WSJ*, April 5, 1965; "New Neighborhood House Is Discovering a New Job," *WSJ*, June 28, 1965; Helen Matheson, "Neighborhood House Event's Today," *WSJ*, October 31, 1965; Edward Nichols, "200 Attend Dedication at Neighborhood House," *WSJ*, November 1, 1965.

94. Brautigam, "Renewal Gripe Sessions Started by Council Group," *CT*, January 6, 1965; "Human Problems in Renewal Cited," *WSJ*, January 7, 1965.

95. Coyle, "Renewal Boosts Taxes Fivefold," *CT*, June 29, 1965.

96. MRA minutes, June 2, 1965; "MRA Acts to Sell Triangle Section for a Shop Center," *WSJ*, June 3, 1965; "Triangle Plans New Site Sale," *WSJ*, August 16, 1965; MRA minutes, November 17, 1965; "Design Competition Planned for Shop Center in Triangle," *WSJ*, November 18, 1965; "Apartments Sought in Triangle," *WSJ*, November 18, 1965.

97. "Work on W. Washington Walkway Will Wind Up in 2 Weeks," *WSJ*, November 13, 1965.

98. Brautigam, "MRA Starts Third South Madison Try for Rehabilitation," *CT*, February 17, 1965; "South Side Renewal to Get $41,000 Study," *WSJ*, April 2, 1965; "Survey on South Madison's Urban Renewal Project Set," *WSJ*, June 16, 1965.

99. "Sol Levin Named Director of MRA," *WSJ*, April 14, 1965.

100. Aehl, "Chunks of UW Renewal Study Area Sliced Off," *WSJ*, February 11, 1965; "Proposed and Amended Area for UW Urban Renewal Study," *WSJ*, February 23, 1965; editorial, "Renewal Study Pared Too Far," *WSJ*, February 24, 1965; Aehl, "Smaller Neighborhood Renewal Plan Wins Council's Approval," *WSJ*, February 26, 1965; Brautigam, "Renewal Feuding Is Ended," *CT*, February 26, 1965; Brautigam, "Moderate Income Housing for Triangle Supported," *CT*, September 1, 1965; BOR minutes, December 10, 1965; "Jurisdiction Set on Renewal Study," *WSJ*, December 10, 1965; "U.W. Co-operation in Renewal Plan Is Voted," *CT*, December 10, 1965; "New Renewal Unit Starts on Study," *WSJ*, December 15, 1965.

101. BOR minutes, January 8, 1965; Bednarek, "UW Regents Reject City Groups' Pleas on Beach, Renewal Plans," *WSJ*, January 9, 1965; Lee Linton, "Murray Mall Project: Progress through

Pain," *DC,* March 4, 1965; editorial, "MRA vs. the Monolith," *DC,* March 6, 1965.

102. Aehl, "MRA Supports Urban Renewal Project for University Ave.," *WSJ,* January 20, 1965; Brautigam, "MRA Backs Plans on University Ave.," *CT,* January 20, 1965; Gribble, "Study of University Ave. Renewal Project Wins Approval," *WSJ,* January 29, 1965.

103. Coyle, "City Challenges U.W. University Ave. Plans," *CT,* April 29, 1965; Scher, "Council Halts Building Plans," *DC,* May 12, 1965; Brautigam, "Construction Ban Backed in U. Ave. Project Blocks," *CT,* May 12, 1965; Aehl, "Planned Renewal Area 'Protected,'" *WSJ,* May 12, 1965; Coyle, "U.W. Agrees to Meet City on Renewal Snarl," *CT,* May 17, 1965; Coyle, "Regent President Hits Merchants on U. Ave.," *CT,* May 18, 1965; "'U' to Meet with City on Block Development," *DC,* May 18, 1965; Aehl, "MRA to Push Mall Solution," *WSJ,* May 19, 1965; Brautigam, "MRA Wants State Building Unit to Join in UW Talks," *CT,* May 19, 1965; editorial, "University Ave. Development," *WSJ,* May 25, 1965.

104. "'U' City Still Deadlocked on Murray Mall Project," *DC,* June 25, 1965; "City Set to Nudge Regents on Avenue Renewal Projects," *WSJ,* August 11, 1965; Brautigam, "City Gets U.W. Offer to Join in 4-Block Renewal Project," *CT,* August 13, 1965.

105. "City Set to Nudge Regents on Avenue Renewal Project," *WSJ,* August 11, 1965; "Owners OK 'Look' at Renewal Plan," *WSJ,* August 13, 1965; Brautigam, "City Gets U.W. Offer to Join in 4-Block Renewal Project," *CT,* August 13, 1965.

106. Aehl, "Council Oks Expanded Avenue Renewal Study," *WSJ,* August 19, 1965; BOR minutes, August 20, 1965; "UW Regents Join City Renewal Plea," *WSJ,* August 21, 1965; Coyle, "U. Ave. Project Will Cost $2 Million More," *CT,* September 21, 1965.

107. National Academy of Arbitrators, Presidential Interviews, http://www.naarb.org/interviews/RobbenFleming.PDF.

108. "Poverty Pocket Found in South Side Survey," *WSJ,* November 19, 1965; Coyle, "'Pocket of Poverty' in South Madison Is Discovered in Survey," *CT,* November 19, 1965.

109. "Madison and the University: A Survey," *Wisconsin Alumnus* 67, no. 3 (December 1965): 7.

110. Johnson, "Crowd Tolerates Vaudeville, but There Was Still Hope," *DC,* October 23, 1965.

111. Feldman, *Buildings,* 334, 364.

112. Sharon Coady, "Reston Questions Goal of Fighting in Viet Nam," *WSJ,* February 15, 1965; Stu Chapman, "New Perspective Needed," *DC,* February 16, 1965; Joe Harrand, "Norman Thomas Cheered as He Asks Viet Nam Peace," *CT,* February 24, 1965.

113. Tibor Zana, "American Ballet: Exciting, Ambitious," *DC,* February 25, 1965.

114. "Seeger Will Attend Reception Thursday," *DC,* March 3, 1965; Davis, "Pete Seeger Infects Crowd with His Art," *WSJ,*

March 5, 1965; Hunter, "Pete Seeger Has His Audience Joining Him in Songs of Protest," *CT,* March 5, 1965.

115. "'U' Has New Police Chief," *DC,* March 26, 1965; Maraniss, *They Marched into Sunlight,* 181–184.

116. Editorial, "Madison Lives Up to Its 'Cow Barn Culture' Reputation," *CT,* March 29, 1965; "Marian Anderson Given Standing Ovation; Spirituals Are Favorites," *CT,* March 29, 1965; Carmen Elsner, "Marian Anderson Displays Greatness," *WSJ,* March 29, 1965; Karen Plant, "Marian Anderson Concert: 'Long Remembered Evening,'" *DC,* March 31, 1965; Mollenhoff and Hamilton, *Monona Terrace,* 170.

117. "Count Basie Headlines Mil Ball—Timeout '65," *DC,* March 19, 1965.

118. Advertisement, *DC,* February 18, 1965.

119. Powell, "Buckley: America's Liberal Ideals Rigid," *DC,* April 29, 1965.

120. BOR minutes, January 8, 1965; *Wisconsin Alumnus* 66, no. 5 (February 1965): 7; Maraniss, *They Marched into Sunlight,* 134–136.

121. Hunter, "Doom of 'Old Red Gym' Is Sealed by Building Group," *CT,* August 25, 1965.

122. Edward Nicholls, "To Fredric March, UW's Even Better," *WSJ,* September 4, 1965; "Fredric March Likes City Despite 45-Year Changes," *CT,* September 4, 1965; Levitan, *Sesquicentennial History,* 220; Bednarek, "UW Frats Boom Despite Trend," *WSJ,* October 17, 1965.

123. Hunter, "Bob Hope Draws Laughter, Cheers at the Fieldhouse," *CT,* October 23, 1965; Norman Lenburg, "Hope Hoists Homecoming Hearts," *CT,* October 24, 1965.

124. "Vice-President of UW Dies," *WSJ,* October 24, 1965; "Memorial Rites Today for Alfred W. Peterson," *CT,* January 25, 1965; BOR minutes, November 12, 1965; BOR minutes, June 14, 1968.

125. Hunter, "Halt Viet Bombing, McGovern Urges in Visit to U.W.," *CT,* November 8, 1965; Powell, "McGovern Calls for 'New Asian Policy,'" *DC,* November 9, 1965.

126. Collis H. Davis Jr., "Noted Jazz Musician Will Give Concert Here," *DC,* November 2, 1965; Collis H. Davis Jr., "Monday's Concert by Roland Kirk Proves to Be a Musical Success," *DC,* November 10, 1965.

127. Newhouse, "Opposition Doubts SRP Poster Claims," *DC,* November 17, 1965; Paul Soglin, "WSA Candidates' Election Statements," *DC,* November 23, 1965.

128. Pommer and Hunter, "Board Asks Bruhn Firing," *CT,* December 8, 1965; Tony Dombrow, "Bruhn Remains Calm Amid Shakeup Rumors," *DC,* December 8, 1965; editorial, "Bruhn Should Be Judged on His Whole Record," *CT,* December 9, 1965; Hunter, "Reveal 2nd Secret Meeting on Bruhn," *CT,* December 9, 1965; Pommer, "Compromise on Bruhn Is Possible," *CT,* December 10, 1965; BOR minutes, December 10, 1965; Pommer,

"Harrington Stand Saves Bruhn's Job," *CT*, December 11, 1965; Bednarek, "Bruhn to Remain Football Coach," *WSJ*, December 11, 1965; Newhouse, "Regents Vote to Keep Bruhn," *DC*, December 11, 1965.

129. Powell, "Res Hall Adopts Policy Eliminating Old Dress," *DC*, April 9, 1965.

130. "New Women's Hours Passed!" *DC*, October 5, 1965; Terri Zuehlke, "New Procedure for Dorm Hours," *DC*, November 12, 1965.

131. "Regents Regulate Campus Traffic," *DC*, New Student Edition, 1965.

132. Stuart Ewen in Buhle, ed., *History and the New Left*, 181; Stu Ewen email, January 29, 2017; Soglin, OH #0102, interviewed by Laura Smail, 1977, University Archives and Records Management Services, Madison, Wisconsin.

133. "'Quixote' to Go on Sale Wednesday," *DC*, December 9, 1965; Soglin OH #0102; Morris Edelson email, February 6, 2017.

134. Richard Goldstein, "They Call It Pot," *CT*, November 30, 1965; Dennis Sandage, "These Are Drugs Students Use," *CT*, December 9, 1968; confidential emails and crowd-sourced interviews through social media.

135. Allison Hantschel, *It Doesn't End with Us: The Story of the Daily Cardinal* (Westminster, MD: Heritage Books, 2007), 53–57.

136. Hunter, "Sen. Leonard Asks Probe of Editor of DC," *CT*, January 30, 1965; Roberts, "Sen. Leonard Asks Regent Probe of Cardinal Editor, Policy," *WSJ*, January 31, 1965; "Cardinal Controversy Grows," *WSJ*, February 1, 1965; Harvey Shapiro, "Cardinal Controversy Grows," *DC*, February 2, 1965; Revell, "2nd Solon Hits U. Paper," *CT*, February 4, 1965; Roberts, "Sen. Roseleip Blasts Cardinal; Wants Lawmakers to Get It Free," *WSJ*, February 5, 1965; Lenburg, "Gordon Roseleip Makes Verbal Attack on DC and Managing Editor," *DC*, February 5, 1965.

137. "University GOP Blasts Charges by Leonard," *DC*, February 2, 1965; editorial, "No Probe of DC," *WSJ*, February 1, 1965; editorial, "Leonard Proves That McCarthyism Is Still Alive," *CT*, February 1, 1965; Hunter, "University Y-GOP Attacks Sen. Leonard on Cardinal," *CT*, February 2, 1965; Stu Chapman, "'U' Profs Defend Cardinal; Paper Not 'Left-Wing': Mosse," *DC*, February 2, 1965; Dale Bartley, "I-F Supports Cardinal; Delays New Pledge Plan," *DC*, February 3, 1965; Don Fitzgibbons, "Y-Dems Support Cardinal, Editor," *DC*, February 3, 1965.

138. BOR minutes, February 5, 1965; Hunter, "Regents Rebuff Leonard," *CT*, February 5, 1965; Bednarek, "Regents Reject Demand for Probe of Cardinal," *WSJ*, February 6, 1965; Hunter, "Cardinal Editors Certain Right Along That Regents Would Back Paper," *CT*, February 6, 1965; editorial, "No Witch-Hunting in State," *WSJ*, February 8, 1965; "Cardinal, Free Opinion Backed by Harrington," *WSJ*, March 11, 1965; "The Cardinal Controversy," *Wisconsin Alumnus* 66, no. 6 (March 1965): 16–17.

139. Editorial, "A Respectful but Firm Affirmation," *DC*, February 6, 1965.

140. Revell, "Governor Supports Regents on Cardinal," *CT*, February 12, 1965; "Gov. Backs Regents on Probe Rejection," *DC*, February 13, 1965; "Knowles Defends Cardinal Freedom," *WSJ*, February 13, 1965; editorial, "Knowles' Actions Commendable on Cardinal, Building Group," *CT*, February 13, 1965; Witt, "Faculty, Staff Answer Questions about Cardinal," *WSJ*, February 14, 1965.

141. Bednarek, "High Schools Graduate Record 1,850," *WSJ*, May 29, 1965; "1,850 in City High Schools Graduate Friday at 10 A.M.," *CT*, June 16, 1965; "West Graduates Told to Continue Educating Selves," *CT*, June 18, 1965; Kay Witt, "Keep on Learning, First La Follette Grads Told," *WSJ*, June 19, 1965; William Witt, "East Graduates Warned of 'Elastic Conscience,'" *WSJ*, June 19, 1965; Lenburg, "Central Grads Given Recipe for Success," *WSJ*, June 19, 1965.

142. "Schools List Total of Nearly 32,000," *WSJ*, September 18, 1965.

143. Bednarek, "Classes Come to Order Nicely," *WSJ*, September 9, 1965.

144. Pommer, "Downtown School Crisis: What Statistics Mean," *CT*, February 26, 1965; Pommer, "Chart Shows Escalating Downtown School Crisis," *CT*, March 8, 1965; Pommer, "Central High Report Has Gloomy Outlook," *CT*, September 8, 1965; Levitan, *Sesquicentennial History*, 150.

145. Hunter, "School Space Crisis Bigger Than Expected," *CT*, January 23, 1965.

146. Pommer, "Central High Parents Seek to Save School," *CT*, October 2, 1965; "Parents Will Fight Closing of Central," *WSJ*, November 2, 1968; Frank Custer, "Says School Chiefs Try to 'Gag' Central PTA," *CT*, November 16, 1965; Pommer, "Problems in Closing Central: What Happens to South Side?" *CT*, November 29, 1965; Brautigam, "NAACP Will Watch Central High Moves," *CT*, November 30, 1965.

147. "Lincoln Junior High Almost Ready for Pupils," *CT*, August 17, 1965; Robert A. Davis, "Parents Protest Violence at School," *WSJ*, October 1, 1965; "School Officials Decry Protests," *WSJ*, October 1, 1965; Pommer, "Principal Backed by Neighborhood House Members," *CT*, October 1, 1965; Dale Wirsing, "Is There 'Terror' in Lincoln School?" *CT*, October 1; 1965; Brautigam, "More Counseling Funds Asked for Lincoln School," *CT*, October 19, 1965; Pommer, "Modify Study Program at Lincoln Junior High," *CT*, October 11, 1965; Wirsing, "Lincoln School to Modify 'Modular' Study Program," *CT*, October 12, 1965; "Help Sought for Lincoln School," *WSJ*, October 19, 1965; Brautigam, "More Counseling Funds Asked for Lincoln School," *CT*, October 19, 1965.

148. Naomi W. Lede, "Madison's Negro Population," Urban League of St. Louis, April 1965, citing Cora E. Bagley, "Some Factors Affecting Academic Achievement among Negro High

School Students," UW–Madison unpublished master's thesis, 1965; "New School Pay Schedule Helps to Attract Teachers," *WSJ*, April 21, 1965; Pommer, "Schools Seek More Negroes as Teachers," *CT*, September 23, 1965.

149. Irvin Kreisman, "Gilberts Plugs for Bonds, Says All Area Will Benefit," *CT*, April 3, 1965; "$6.4 Million School Bond Issue OKd," *WSJ*, April 7, 1965; editorial, "Keep a Good City School Board," *WSJ*, March 31, 1965; editorial, "Chance for Fresh, New View on School Board," *CT*, April 1, 1965; Pommer, "Prof. MacDonald, McGinnis Capture 2 School Posts," *CT*, April 7, 1965.

150. Pommer, "W. High to Hold Pupils for Lunch Starting in Fall," *CT*, June 29, 1965; Bednarek, "West High 'Eat In' to Stay," *WSJ*, October 31, 1965.

151. "Pupils to Carry Lists of Shelter," *WSJ*, September 21, 1965.

152. "May Cancel Two Bus Runs Due to Student Rowdyism," *CT*, December 7, 1965.

153. Editorial, "Does Madison Need Group to Second Guess School Board?" *CT*, December 17, 1965; "School Board Will Hear 'Advisory' Group Plan," *CT*, December 18, 1965; Brautigam, "School Board Cold to 'Advisory' Plan," *CT*, December 21, 1965.

154. "It's Lincoln Junior High School," *WSJ*, May 18, 1965; Brautigam, "Lincoln Name Is Given to New School on South Side," *CT*, May 18, 1965.

155. "Kennedy, Madison, Leopold or Muir?" *WSJ*, June 19, 1965; Brautigam, "Board, by Secret Vote, Names New School 'Madison,'" *CT*, June 22, 1965.

156. Brautigam, "15 Aldermen Call for High School Renaming," *CT*, July 2, 1965; editorial, "This Is Still Pressure from the Council on School Board," *CT*, July 3, 1965.

157. Bednarek, "It's Madison High, School Board Says," *WSJ*, July 7, 1965; Pommer, "Tie Blocks Reconsideration of New High School's Name," *CT*, July 9, 1965.

158. Bednarek, "Christmas Modified in Schools," *WSJ*, December 19, 1965.

159. "School Board Head G.W. Stephens Dies," *WSJ*, August 1, 1965; editorial, "Glenn Stephens—Distinguished Lawyer and Citizen," *CT*, August 2, 1965; editorial, "Madison Schools Lose a Friend," *WSJ*, August 2, 1965; Coyle, "Cates on School Board," *CT*, August 24, 1965; editorial, "Cates Named to School Board," *WSJ*, August 25, 1965; "Know Your Madisonian—Attorney Richard L. Cates," *WSJ*, November 13, 1966.

160. "Herbert Schmiege Dead at Age 67," *CT*, May 20, 1965; "Herbert Schmiege, Member of School Board, 67, Dies," *WSJ*, May 21, 1965.

161. CAC minutes, March 3, 1965; Aehl, "Mayor Slaps Council for 'Political' Motives," *WSJ*, March 4, 1965; "Mayor Takes Whack at Council's 'Politics,'" *CT*, March 4, 1965.

162. "Good Friday Time Off Plea Is Rejected by Council," *CT*, March 26, 1965; "Municipal Union Rakes Ald. Smith on Holiday Charge," *CT*, April 1, 1965.

163. Louise C. Marston, "She's Prejudiced—Over Losses," *WSJ*, March 31, 1965; Jo Banko, "Viet Nam Is Dickey Chapelle's Topic at 35th Annual Matrix Table," *CT*, March 31, 1965.

164. Kenneth Scheibel, "Delay in Naming Judge Embarrasses Wisconsin," *WSJ*, March 21, 1965; "James Doyle Named to U.S. Judgeship," *WSJ*, April 30, 1965; Meloon, "Hail Choice of Doyle for Judgeship," *CT*, April 30, 1965; editorial, "At Long Last, It's Doyle," *WSJ*, April 30, 1965; editorial, "Doyle Appointment Ends Bitter Feud in Democratic Party," *CT*, April 30, 1965; Meloon, "Senate Confirms Doyle," *CT*, May 21, 1965; James D. Selk, "Doyle Takes Post in Federal Court," *WSJ*, June 23, 1965.

165. Coyle, "13 Aldermen to Offer Strikebreaker Ban," *CT*, May 12, 1965; Aehl, "Strikebreakers' Use Here Will Be Barred," *WSJ*, May 26, 1965; "Mayor Signs Strikebreaker Ban," *CT*, June 11, 1965.

166. Brautigam, "Move to Regulate Local Discotheque," *CT*, August 11, 1965; Coyle, "Don't Go-Go Too Far, City Guidelines Urge," *CT*, August 27, 1965; Gribble, "Tip for Go-Go Waitresses: Dress!" *WSJ*, August 28, 1965.

167. Brautigam, "Vote 'Accessible' City Unit Meetings," *CT*, October 27, 1965; Pommer, "Says School Board Must Obey City Rule," *CT*, November 11, 1965; CC minutes, October 28, 1965.

168. Robert Davis, "Tracy Does Very Well Indeed," *WSJ*, November 14, 1965; Tracy Nelson Messenger exchange, May 13, 2017.

169. Brautigam, "Don't Bar Ladies from Bar," *CT*, January 13, 1965; "Women Belong Only in Front of Bars, City Council Feels," *WSJ*, January 15, 1965; "License No Bar to Ladies," *CT*, January 15, 1965.

170. Robert A. Davis, "Women Can Be Bartenders If Qualified, City Decides," *WSJ*, November 10, 1965; "Bartender License Okd for Women," *WSJ*, November 12, 1965.

171. Editorial, "City Hall Is Responsible for Turning State St. to Skid Row," *CT*, September 2, 1965; editorial, "Will Council Approve More State St. Taverns?" *CT*, September 17, 1965; "Tavern Fighting Erupts on State St.-U. Ave. 'Front,'" *CT*, September 21, 1965.

172. Aehl, "19 More Policemen Sought," *WSJ*, September 9, 1965.

173. Newhouse, "State Street Acts to Bar 'Skid Row,'" *WSJ*, September 2, 1965; Brautigam, "State St. Clean-Up Drive Demanded," *CT*, September 2, 1965; Dieckmann, "Chief Pledges to Help in State St. 'Cleanup,'" *WSJ*, September 3, 1965; editorial, "State St. 'Clean-Up' Action," *WSJ*, September 3, 1965; Maraniss, "Friday Evening on State St. Belies 'Skid Row' Talk," *CT*, September 11, 1965; Robert Franzmann, "Returning Students Make State St. Hum Again," *WSJ*, September 12, 1965; Powell, "State Street a Skid Row?" *DC*, September 14, 1965; Powell, "Bar Owners Back Proposal for Improving State Street," *DC*, September 15, 1965.

174. Coyle, "3 New State St. Places Seeking Tavern Licenses," *CT*, September 16, 1965; Coyle, "Festge Vows He Will Veto New State St. Beer Permits," *CT*, September 20, 1965; Newhouse, "Campus Beer Bar Applications Fail," *DC*, November 10, 1965; Brautigam, "State St. Beer Drive Blocked," *CT*, November 10, 1965.

175. Coyle, "Ethics Code Drafted for City's Employees," *CT*, March 6, 1965; Brautigam, "Alderman Back Hearing on Ethics Code Proposal," *CT*, March 24, 1965.

176. "Four Aldermen Hold Mustang Posts," *WSJ*, July 1, 1965.

177. "Alderman-Mustang Officials Claim No Conflict or Profit," *WSJ*, July 2, 1965; editorial, "Aldermen Hold Public Trust," *WSJ*, July 6, 1965; "Mustang Issue Spurs Plea for 'Guidelines' to Council," *WSJ*, July 7, 1965.

178. Don Lindstrom, "Olshanski Resigns, Novell Coach of Mustang Grid Club," *WSJ*, August 28, 1965.

179. "Dimensions and Dividends," City of Madison Planning Department, March 1965, 1.

180. City of Madison Department of Planning, Community Development and Economic Development.

181. Coyle, "Committee Rejects Manchester Skywalk," *CT*, January 6, 1965.

182. Aehl, "Plan Group Opposes Manchester Skywalk," *WSJ*, January 26, 1965; Aehl, "Manchester Skywalk Proposal Gets Delay," *WSJ*, January 29, 1965.

183. "Mrs. Manchester Buys Parking Lot," *CT*, June 10, 1965.

184. Aehl, "City to Get Nearly 450 Acres in Cherokee Site," *WSJ*, January 15, 1965; "Sign Cherokee Park Pact, City Council Tells Mayor," *WSJ*, January 29, 1965.

185. Selk, "Allied to File Bankruptcy Plea," *WSJ*, January 19, 1965.

186. Aehl, "East Side Hospital Site Will Be Bought," *WSJ*, January 27, 1965.

187. Brautigam, "Alderman Approve Study of Maple Bluff Park Site," *CT*, February 12, 1965.

188. "Begin Five Homes in Meadwood-East Plat," *CT*, May 18, 1965.

189. "New Development Puts City Half-Mile to West," *WSJ*, June 26, 1965.

190. Bednarek, "New Library Gets Nods of Approval," *WSJ*, June 24, 1965.

191. "Crew Starts Madison Hotel Wrecking," *WSJ*, June 26, 1965.

192. Havens Wilber, "Joblessness Here Is 1.6%; Far Below National Average," *CT*, October 27, 1965.

193. "New Interchange to Open Today," *WSJ*, November 3, 1965.

194. "1st Leg of Improved Packers Ave. Stretch Opens," *WSJ*, December 3, 1965.

195. Levitan, *Sesquicentennial History*, 134–135; John Newhouse, "Express Bus to Start Monday," *WSJ*, February 21, 1965;

John Newhouse, "Riders, Drivers Hail Success of Madison's Express Bus Test," *WSJ*, March 28, 1965.

196. Wineke, "Madison Jet Service Launched," *WSJ*, May 24, 1965.

197. Maraniss, "N.W. Depot Sale Is Near," *CT*, June 14, 1965; Wilbur, "CNW to Stop Using Its Old Depot Monday," *CT*, June 16, 1965.

198. Aehl, "State St., Square Ban on Bicycles Proposed," *WSJ*, November 19, 1965; Alan Rubin, "State Street Bicycle Ban Is Condemned by Senate," *DC*, December 15, 1965; Rubin, "Festge Hears Bike Pleas," *DC*, December 17, 1965.

199. Coyle, "Fill Trouble May Push Causeway Completion beyond 1967 Target," *CT*, December 20, 1965; "Year's Delay Possible for Monona Causeway," *WSJ*, December 21, 1965.

200. Franzmann, "City Policeman Beaten, Kicked," *WSJ*, March 20, 1965; "Officer Injured in State St. Melee," *CT*, March 20, 1965; Franzmann, "Four More Jailed in Police Beatings," *WSJ*, March 21, 1965; Dieckmann, "Three Men Enter Innocent Pleas to Charge of Beating Policeman," *WSJ*, March 23, 1965; editorial, "Is State St. to Be Unsafe Even for Madison Police?" *CT*, March 23, 1965.

201. Franzmann, "Badge Saves Detective's Life in City Shooting," *WSJ*, April 5, 1965; Dieckmann, "'Badge-Shot' Captive Charged," *WSJ*, April 6, 1965; "Chief Limits Newsmen in Police Station Area," *WSJ*, October 21, 1965.

202. Dieckmann, "Two-Man Police Cars to Return to Madison after 15-Year Gap," *WSJ*, June 24, 1965.

203. Coyle, "Police Bid to Ban 'Playboy' Rejected Here," *CT*, October 18, 1965.

204. "Oscar G. Mayer, Firm's Chairman, Dead at 76," *CT*, March 5, 1965; editorial, "Oscar G. Mayer: A Great Life," *WSJ*, March 8, 1965; "Oscar G. Mayer, 76, Packing Firm Board Chairman, Dies in Illinois," *WSJ*, March 6, 1965; Levitan, *Sesquicentennial History*, 201.

205. "William J. Meuer Dies; Founded Photoart House," *CT*, April 8, 1965; "William J. Meuer, 79, Founder of Photo Art House, Inc., Dies," *WSJ*, April 9, 1965.

206. "Dudley Montgomery, 82, Dies Here on Tuesday," *CT*, October 27, 1965.

207. "J. Jesse Hyman, Emporium Co. President, Civic Leader, Dies," *WSJ*, December 10, 1965; "J. Jesse Hyman, 79, Dies; President of Emporium," *CT*, December 10, 1965.

208. "Versace's Goal: To Become Priest," *WSJ*, September 28, 1965; Rudy Pelecky, "Capt. Versace Mass Held; Desire to Serve Stressed," *CT*, September 30, 1965; "Humbert Roque Versace," The Virtual Wall ® Vietnam Veterans Memorial, www.virtualwall .org/dv/VersaceHR01a.htm.

209. "Son of Madison Woman Dies in Viet Nam Action," *CT*, October 5, 1965; "Roscoe Ammerman," The Virtual Wall® Vietnam Veterans Memorial, www.virtualwall.org/da /AmmermanRx01a.htm.

210. "Cong Blast Kills War Reporter, Photographer Dickey Chapelle," *WSJ*, November 4, 1965; Custer, "Dickey Chapelle, War Reporter, Is Killed by Viet Nam Booby Trap," *CT*, November 4, 1965; Moucha, "Memorial to Honor Dickey Chapelle," *WSJ*, November 5, 1965; "Dickey Chapelle Fund to Aid S. Vietnamese," *WSJ*, November 29, 1965; John Garofolo, *Dickey Chapelle under Fire* (Madison: Wisconsin Historical Society Press, 2015).

1966

1. Dave Zweifel, "How Draft Will Affect U.W. Students," *CT*, January 4, 1966.

2. Zweifel, "Madison Boys Flock to Enlist; Waiting Lists Are Reported," *CT*, March 1, 1966; "Army Says Students May Not Be Drafted," *DC*, March 16, 1966; John Strumretter, "How Viet Nam Draft Affects Students," *CT*, August 10, 1966.

3. "Draft Boards Won't Get Private Information from University without Student's Consent," *DC*, March 29, 1966; "Student Must O.K. Release of Standing to Draft Board," *CT*, April 12, 1966.

4. Faculty Document 74, May 23, 1966.

5. John Vaughan, "SDS to Protest at Draft Exam," *DC*, May 5, 1966; "2 Groups to Picket Draft Delay Test," *CT*, May 11, 1966; Marsha Cutting, "SDS Plans Exam Picket and Rally," *DC*, May 11, 1966; "Report and Recommendations on the University and Selective Service," June 10, 1966, Chancellor Robben Fleming papers, Series 4/19/1 box 44; "The Anatomy of a Protest," *Wisconsin Alumnus* 67, no. 8 (June–July 1966): 5–11, 28; Levin, *Cold War University,* 3–7; Maraniss, *They Marched into Sunlight,* 103–106; Cronon and Jenkins, *The University of Wisconsin,* 454–458.

6. "Report and Recommendations," exhibit I.

7. Dale Wirsig, "2,300 in UW Draft Test," *CT*, May 14, 1966; "Pickets Protest Draft at UW," *CT*, May 14, 1966; "Student Group Asks 'U' Stop Aiding Draft," *DC*, May 14, 1966.

8. "Report and Recommendations," Exhibit III; Martin Tandler email, July 12, 2017.

9. "250 U.W. Students Begin Sit-In against Draft Test," *CT*, May 16, 1966; Henry W. Haslach interview, box 4, folder 15, Glenn Silber/*The War at Home* papers, M93-235, WHSA; Henry W. Haslach OH# 0047, interviewed by Laura Smail, digital audio file, University Archives and Records Management Services, Madison, Wisconsin; Soglin OH# 0102; Martin Tandler email, July 12, 2017; Haslach email, July 15, 2017.

10. Feldman, *Buildings,* 399.

11. Margery Tabankin interview, *War at Home* papers, box 4, folder 28, WHSA.

12. David Bednarek, "Sit-In by UW Students Protests Draft 'Tie-In,'" *WSJ*, May 17, 1966; Bednarek, "Sit-In Continues; Blockade's Out," *WSJ*, May 18, 1966.

13. "Report and Recommendations," Exhibit V; Matt Fox, "Students Continue Draft Sit-In; Fleming Cites Group's Conduct," *DC*, May 18, 1966.

14. John Patrick Hunter, "Clash Avoided at U.W. Draft Sit-In," *CT*, May 17, 1966; "Draft Policy Causes Protest," *DC*, May 17, 1966; Fox, "Faculty to Decide Student Demands," *DC*, May 17, 1966; Christy Sinks, "Student Reactions Differ over Handling of Draft," *DC*, May 17, 1966; "Why Are They Sitting In? Students Tell Why," *CT*, May 17, 1966; "Hell No, We Won't Go! A History of the Movement in Madison, Part II," *TakeOver* 4, no. 13 (October 23–November 4, 1974): 12–13; Ralph Hanson interview, *War at Home* papers, box 4, folder 14, WHSA; Ken Mate, *War at Home* papers, box 4, folder 17, WHSA.

15. "Report and Recommendations," 3; "University Survey Shows Students for Viet Policy," *DC*, July 19, 1966.

16. Mate, *War at Home* papers, box 4, folder 17, WHSA; Lowell Bergmann email, July 19, 2017; Stark, "In Exile," in Buhle, ed., *History and the New Left,* 174–175.

17. "Report and Recommendations," exhibit VI.

18. Gregory Graze, "Senate Exacts SSS Resolution," *DC*, May 18, 1966.

19. John Kitchen, "Student Groups Voice Opinions on the Draft," *DC*, May 19, 1966; Faculty Document 74, UW–Madison Campus Faculty Meeting, Series 5/2/15, box 1, University Archives, 74, May 23, 1966.

20. Vaughan, "US Officials Defend Policy in Viet Nam," *DC*, May 18, 1966; Wirsig, "Students Break Up State Dept. Meet," *CT*, May 18, 1966; Richard Gribble, "Students Jam Up Policy Talks," *WSJ*, May 18, 1966; Paul Soglin interview, *War at Home* papers, box 4, folder 26, WHSA.

21. "Report and Recommendations," exhibit VII.

22. "Report and Recommendations," exhibit VIII.

23. Richard Scher, "Draft Demands Heard; Faculty Meeting Called," *DC*, May 19, 1966; "Sit-In Continues," *DC*, May 19, 1966.

24. Paul Soglin to Fred Harrington, May 19, 1966, Harrington to Soglin, May 20, 1966, Harrington Papers, University Archives; Maraniss, *They Marched into Sunlight,* 105–106.

25. Matt Pommer, "U.W. Sit-In Force Cut to Token Group," *CT*, May 19, 1966; "Sit-In Reduced to Token Force," *DC*, May 20, 1966; Pommer, "Student Sit-In Is Ended," *CT*, May 20, 1966; "No More Sit-Ins: Fleming," *CT*, May 23, 1966; Harvey Shapiro, "Protest Demonstration on Draft May Provoke State Legislature," *DC*, May 24, 1966.

26. "1,700 Men Students Take Selective Service Deferment Tests at U. Today," *CT*, May 21, 1966.

27. Minutes, Special Faculty Meeting, UW–Madison, May 23, 1966.

28. "Protesters Pick Stark, Zweifel to Give Case," *DC*, May 21, 1966; Faculty Documents 74–76, May 23, 1966.

29. Faculty Document 79, May 23, 1966.

30. Faculty Document 80, May 23, 1966.

31. Faculty Document 77, May 23, 1966.

32. Faculty Document 78, May 23, 1966; Richard Scher, "Profs. Pass Resolution," *DC*, May 24, 1966; Brautigam, "UW Faculty in Compromise on Draft Stand But Pleases No One," *CT*, May 24, 1966.

33. Faculty Document 78, May 23, 1966.

34. Vaughn, "'Total Defeat,' Committee Says," *DC*, May 24, 1966; Mate, *War at Home* papers, box 4, folder 17, WHSA.

35. Bednarek, "Students Defy Ban on Further Sit-Ins," *WSJ*, May 24, 1966.

36. "Renewed Demonstrations Follow Faculty Proposals," *DC*, May 24, 1966; Zweifel, "Defiant Sit-In Is Ended," *CT*, May 24, 1966; Bednarek, "UW Sit-In Protesters Become Stand-By Group," *WSJ*, May 25, 1966; Gene Wells, "CUD Gets Tentative Approval by WSA," *DC*, July 22, 1966.

37. BOR minutes, June 10, 1966.

38. BOR minutes, June 10, 1966; Pommer, "UW Praises Protesters; Pictures in Press Hit," *CT*, June 10, 1966; "'Beatnik' Pictures of Sit-in Criticized," *WSJ*, June 11, 1966.

39. Dolly Katz, "Sit-Ins Draw 'U' Together," *DC*, September 28, 1966; Steven Barney, "Professor Hails 'Unifying' Factor of UW Sit-In Protesting the Draft," *WSJ*, September 28, 1966.

40. "200 Climax Peace Walk," *CT*, February 5, 1966.

41. Scher, "Aptheker Compares Viet Policy to Hitlerism," *DC*, March 25, 1966; Barney, "Red Speaker Rips U.S. Viet Policy," *WSJ*, March 25, 1966.

42. Cutting, "'Town Meeting' on Viet Issue," *DC*, March 29, 1966; Andy Piascik, "Forever Young: Staughton Lynd," November 16, 2013, https://zinnedproject.org/2013/11/forever-young-staughton-lynd/.

43. Cutting, "Bunche Speaks on UN," *DC*, April 1, 1966.

44. Ruth Ann Wenslaff, "Viet War Protesters Will Hold July 4 Fast," *DC*, July 1, 1966; "Police Cite Non-Existent Ordinance, Force Peace Pickets from Vilas Park," *CT*, July 5, 1966; "Police Bar Pamphleteering by Anti-War Group in Park," *DC*, July 7, 1966; Robben Fleming to Otto Festge, July 19, 1966, Fleming Papers, University Archives; Roger Gribble, "Ban on Literature Sale in Park Eyed," *WSJ*, August 10, 1966; Brautigam, "Free Speech Row Goes On as Festge Defends Police," *CT*, August 10, 1966; "Police Action Draws Protest by Fleming," *WSJ*, August 10, 1966; "Police Park Action OKd by Mayor," *WSJ*, August 11, 1966; Gene Wells, "City Council to Draft Ban on Sale of Literature," *DC*, August 11, 1966; "City Liberty Unit Assails Park Ban," *WSJ*, August 12, 1966.

45. Brautigam, "Ald. Smith Regrets . . . He's Tied Up in Viet," *CT*, July 15, 1966; Hunter, "Ald. Smith Posed as 'Newsman' During Eight-Day Viet Nam Trip," *CT*, July 26, 1966; "Portage Paper Calls Smith Trip 'Trick,' 'Gimmick,'" *CT*, July 30, 1966; Pommer, "Kastenmeier's Margin Near 20,000," *CT*, November 9, 1966.

46. "Council Sets Nov. 8 School Bond Date," *CT*, October 14, 1966.

47. June Dieckmann, "5 War Protesters Arrested Near Polls," *WSJ*, November 9, 1966; "Protester Pays Poll Picketing Fine," *CT*, November 9, 1966; Willa Rosenblatt, "SDS Helps War Pickets," *DC*, November 10, 1966; Phyllis Rausen, "CEWVN Decides To Assist Anti-War Demonstrators," *DC*, November 11, 1966; "Four Viet Protesters Fine for Campaigning Near Polls," *WSJ*, November 17, 1967; *1979–1980 Blue Book* (Madison: Department of Administration, 1979), 490; "Lea Zeldin," Cress Funeral Home, http://www.cressfuneralservice.com/obituary/32203/Lea-Zeldin/, April 2, 2009.

48. Katz, "Students Demand Referenda," *DC*, December 3, 1966; "Campus Action Group Sets Mass Meeting," *CT*, December 5, 1966; Paul Soglin email, July 16, 1966; Fred Ciporen email, August 27, 2017.

49. "West High Students Form Viet War Discussion Group," *CT*, December 17, 1966.

50. "The Senator and the Hecklers," *Wisconsin Alumnus* 68, no. 3 (December 1966): 6–7; Levin, *Cold War University*, 138–139; Cronon and Jenkins, *The University of Wisconsin*, 458; Michael Meeropol and Gerald Markowitz, "Neighborhood Politics," in Buhle, ed., *History and the New Left*, 213–214.

51. "Teddy Kennedy to Stump for Lucey Here on Oct. 27," *CT*, October 15, 1966; Rita Braver, "CEWVN Apologizes for Being 'Ineffective,'" *DC*, November 1, 1966; Evan Stark interview, the *War at Home* papers, box 4, folder 27, WHSA; Evan Stark email, July 17, 2017.

52. Stark interview, *War at Home* papers, box 4, folder 27, WHSA; Stark email, July 14, 2017.

53. James D. Selk, "Heckled Kennedy Loses No Cool," *WSJ*, October 28, 1966; Hunter, "Kennedy Talk Disrupted by Small Heckler Group," *CT*, October 28, 1966; Graze, "Lash Kennedy," *DC*, October 28, 1966; George H. Armor, "Admirers, Hecklers Keep Kennedy Busy," *Milwaukee Journal*, October 28, 1966; Zweifel and Nichols, *Capital Times*, 187–190.

54. Faculty Document 96, November 7, 1966, 7.

55. BOR minutes, November 4, 1966; Clifford C. Behnke, "Reaction to UW Heckler's Antics Keeps Growing," *WSJ*, October 28, 1966; Brautigam, "Council Votes Apology to Ted Kennedy," *CT*, October 28, 1966; "Fleming Raps Viet Protesters," *DC*, October 28, 1966; Faculty Document 96, 2.

56. Faculty Document 96, 4; "Future UW Hecklers May Face Discipline," *WSJ*, October 29, 1966; Faculty Document 96, 5, October 30, 1966; "Heckling Spurs Request by UW Group for Rules," *WSJ*, October 30, 1966; William Mullen, "UW Hecklers Isolated Selves, Professor Says," *WSJ*, October 31, 1966; Pommer, "Faculty Maps 'Right to Listen' Policy," *CT*, October 31, 1966.

57. Richard Levine, Robert Cohen, and David Lehman, "One

Step Backward, Two Steps Forward," October 30, 1966, CEWV Papers, box 2, folder 1, WSHA.

58. "Why We Confronted Senator Kennedy," CEWV Papers, box 2, folder 1, WHSA; "CEWVN's Position on Kennedy," *DC*, November 2, 1966; Rita Braver, "CEWVN Apologizes for Being 'Ineffective,'" *DC*, November 1, 1966; "Anti-Viet Nam War Leaders Retain Control of Unit," *WSJ*, November 1, 1966; Evan Stark email, July 17, 2017.

59. John Reed, "Committee Probes Actions of CEWVN," *DC*, November 3, 1966; Faculty Document 96, 8; Graze, "WSA Calls CEWVN Status 'Provisional,'" *DC*, November 4, 1966; Samuel Adams, "No Censure for 'Heckler' Unit at UW," *WSJ*, November 4, 1966.

60. Faculty Document 96, 8; Stark email, July 14, 2017.

61. BOR minutes, November 4, 1966; Pommer, "'Over-Reaction' to UW Heckling Is Opposed," *CT*, November 4, 1966; Sinks, "Regents Criticize Kennedy Hecklers," *DC*, November 5, 1966.

62. Faculty Document 96, 1–2, 1966; Gribble, "UW to Take No Further Action against Hecklers, Fleming Says," *WSJ*, November 30, 1966.

63. Robert Sullivan, "Hecklers Labeled Free Speech Peril," *CT*, November 30, 1966; Raymond Moucha, "Hecklers Termed Peril to UW Policy," *WSJ*, November 29, 1966; Braver, "Fleming Says Disorders May Bring Loss of Liberty," *DC*, November 30, 1966; "Faculty Adopts New Speaker Policy Rules," *Wisconsin Alumnus* 68, no. 4 (January 1967): 22–23.

64. Gribble, "New Policy Will Protect Speaker from Hecklers at UW Facilities," *WSJ*, November 17, 1966; Sinks, "Speaker, Listener Rights Reaffirmed by 'U' Faculty," *DC*, December 13, 1966; Behnke, "UW Faculty Approves Anti-Heckling Rules," *WSJ*, December 13, 1966; "Faculty Adopts New Speaker Policy Rules," *Wisconsin Alumnus* 68, no. 4 (January 1967): 22–23.

65. Editorial, "Vocal Minority Disgraced the 'U,'" *DC*, October 28, 1966; editorial, "Speech Safeguards Insured by Faculty," *DC*, December 13, 1966.

66. CEWV Papers, box 2, folder 1, WHSA.

67. "Viet Nam War Victims' Burial in Forest Hill OKd," *WSJ*, February 9, 1966; "Cpl. Dowling's Funeral Set for Friday," *CT*, February 9, 1966; "Jean Pierre Dowling," The Virtual Wall® Vietnam Veterans Memorial, www.virtualwall.org/dd /DowlingJP01a.htm.

68. "Sgt. Neubauer Is Killed by Viet Nam Booby Trap," *CT*, February 8, 1966; "James R. Neubauer," The Virtual Wall® Vietnam Veterans Memorial, www.virtualwall.org/dn /NeubauerJR01a.htm.

69. "Madison Marine Receives Viet Nam Combat Medal," *CT*, April 4, 1966; Jeffrey Fields Facebook exchange, January 2, 2018.

70. "City Marine M.J. Banovez Killed in Viet," *CT*, July 19, 1966; "Services for Cpl. Banovez Scheduled for Monday Here," *CT*,

August 4, 1966; Facebook message from Fred Haltvick; "Michael Joseph Banovez, Jr," The Virtual Wall® Vietnam Veterans Memorial, www.virtualwall.org/db/BanovezMJ01a.htm.

71. "Madison Marine Killed by Accident in Da Nang Area," *CT*, September 20, 1966; "Donald Glen Dingeldein," The Virtual Wall® Vietnam Veterans Memorial, www.virtualwall.org/dd /DingeldeinDG01a.htm.

72. Pommer, "Build Auditorium, Knowles Tells City," *CT*, January 26, 1966.

73. Owen Coyle, "Back Site on Wilson St.," *CT*, January 28, 1966; "How Plan Unit Rated 3 Sites for Auditorium," *CT*, January 29, 1966.

74. John T. Aehl, "All Auditorium Sites Rejected by Committee," *WSJ*, March 16, 1966; Coyle, "Auditorium Unit Ducks Selection of Center's Site," *CT*, March 16, 1966; Coyle, "Confusion, Tempers Blamed for Fizzle in Auditorium Meeting," *CT*, March 16, 1966.

75. Editorial, "Madison Auditorium Committee Gives City a Big Fat Zero," *CT*, March 16, 1966.

76. Coyle, "Include Part of Terrace: Festge," *CT*, April 7, 1966; Coyle, "With Council Having Last Word, Terrace Site Is Still Alive," *CT*, April 7, 1966; Aehl, "Auditorium Site at Olin Is Urged," *WSJ*, April 8, 1966.

77. Coyle, "Move to Split Center Facilities," *CT*, April 8, 1966.

78. Coyle, "Spell Out Terms: Peters," *CT*, April 8, 1966.

79. Brautigam, "Don't Sacrifice Downtown: Peters," *CT*, April 9, 1966.

80. Aehl, "Potter Proposes Civic Center along Lake Monona Shoreline," *WSJ*, April 10, 1966; editorial, "The Opportunity to End Futile Fighting over Auditorium," *WSJ*, April 12, 1966.

81. Aehl, "Oks Olin Site, Plus a Center for Law Park," *WSJ*, April 14, 1966; Coyle, "Terrace Civic Center OK'd," *CT*, April 14, 1966; editorial, "Madison's Dream of Greatness in Hands of Council," *CT*, April 14, 1966; Coyle, "OK Peters Negotiations," *CT*, April 15, 1966.

82. Aehl, "City Plan Unit Rejects Olin as Auditorium Site," *WSJ*, May 9, 1966; Brautigam, "Plan Unit Rejects Split-Site Proposal," *CT*, May 10, 1966.

83. Editorial, "No, Mayor Festge, We Won't Go Along on Auditorium Deal," *CT*, May 10, 1966; Aehl, "Olin Auditorium Site Picked," *WSJ*, May 13, 1966; Brautigam, "Festge Scuttles Terrace," *CT*, May 13, 1966; editorial, "Mayor Could Have Cast Vote to Keep Promise," *CT*, May 13, 1966; editorial, "An Auditorium in City's Future," *WSJ*, May 16, 1966; editorial, "Festge Is State Journal Hero: What of People Who Elected Him?" *CT*, May 16, 1966.

84. Coyle, "Peters Asks City to Restudy Plan for Split Center," *CT*, June 1, 1966; "Text of Peters Letter to Mayor on 2-Site Center," *CT*, June 4, 1966.

85. Zweifel, "Peters Says Mayor Seeks Foundation's 'Political' Aid," *CT*, June 7, 1966.

86. Coyle, "Peters Lashes 2-Site Center Idea," *CT*, June 11, 1966.

87. Aehl, "Peters Points Talks toward Law Park," *WSJ*, June 11, 1966.

88. Coyle, "No Further Talk: Peters," *CT*, June 14, 1966; Aehl, "City Unit Nearly Breaks with Peters," *WSJ*, June 17, 1966; Coyle, "City Keeps Peters Talks Alive," *CT*, June 17, 1966.

89. Coyle, "Mayor Claims Accord with Peters on Talks," *CT*, June 20, 1966; Brautigam, "Peters Postpones His Trip to Europe to Study Action," *CT*, June 24, 1966; Aehl, "Mayor, Architect Plan More Talks," *WSJ*, June 25, 1966.

90. Aehl, "Council Action Leaves Auditorium Site 'Open,'" *WSJ*, July 15, 1966; Brautigam, "City Will Deal with Peters on Monona Basin Plan," *CT*, July 15, 1966.

91. Coyle, "Wright Contract Proposal Asks Total Contract Cost of $9 Million," *CT*, September 20, 1966; "Hot Words Fly over Closed Session," *WSJ*, September 22, 1966; Aehl, "It's a 'Giveaway,' Angry Forster Claims, Quitting Auditorium Unit," *WSJ*, September 27, 1966; Coyle, "Forster Thinks Better of His Auditorium 'Walkout,'" *CT*, September 27, 1966.

92. Coyle, "Wright Contract Is OK'd by Aldermen, 15-7," *CT*, October 14, 1966; Aehl, "Wright Contract Faces Lawsuit," *WSJ*, October 14, 1966.

93. Brautigam, "Plan New Wright Suit," *CT*, November 5, 1966; Coyle, "Smiles All Around as City Signs Wright Contract," *CT*, November 7, 1966; Aehl, "Wright Contract OKd; Legal Challenge Eyed," *WSJ*, November 8, 1966; Zwefiel, "Metzner Files Suit to Stop Auditorium Plans," *CT*, November 29, 1966.

94. EOC minutes, March 15, 1966; Wirsig, "'Renter's Market' Aids Fight on Housing Bias," *CT*, March 16, 1966; Coyle, "Sees Madison as Sold on Bias Curbs," *CT*, June 14, 1966.

95. Frank Custer, "He's Out to Prove Need for Newspaper for Negroes Here," *CT*, January 31, 1966; "Madison Paper for Negroes Is Planned," *CT*, May 3, 1966.

96. "Guild Names Rev. Wright as 'Citizen of the Year,'" *CT*, May 14, 1966.

97. "City Realtors Fight Fair Housing," *CT*, May 31, 1966.

98. Ellen Chesler, "Lives Well Lived: Kathryn F. Clarenbach; NOW, Then," *New York Times*, January 1, 1995; Kathryn Clarenbach, 1987, OH# 0466, digital audio file, University Archives and Records Management Services, Madison, Wisconsin.

99. "Harris Is Named Director," *CT*, May 4, 1966; Pommer, "'Rights Hostility a Good Sign,'" *CT*, August 26, 1966; Richard Harris, *Growing Up in South Madison: Economic Disenfranchisement of Black Madison,* (Madison: Roy Tek, 2012), 35.

100. Community Relations Service, U.S. Conference of Mayors, "Enlarging Equal Opportunity in Madison (1965), Pam 322, WHS Library; Coyle, "Find Bias in Jobs, Housing Here," *CT*, April 12, 1966; "Action Urged on Bias, Poverty," *WSJ*, April 13, 1966.

101. Naomi W. Lede, "Madison's Negro Population," Urban League of St. Louis, Inc., April, 1966; Pommer, "Welfare Unit Asks Forming of Madison Urban League," *CT*, May 13, 1966.

102. "Red Feather Officials Explain Rejection of Urban League Unit," *WSJ*, December 22, 1966; Zweifel, "Community Chest Isn't Telling Whole Story on Urban League Refusal," *CT*, December 22, 1966.

103. EOC minutes, September 22, 1966; Aehl, "Racial Bias Still Found in City," *WSJ*, September 30, 1966.

104. Coyle, "Club Bias Ban Proposed as Licensing Condition," *CT*, June 14, 1966; EOC minutes, June 16, 1966; "Rights Group Urges Clubs to Ban 'Invidious' Bias," *WSJ*, June 17, 1966; Brautigam, "Council Approves Action on Club Bias," *CT*, June 25, 1966; "Colston Calls Club Incident Key Point in Relations Here," *CT*, August 31, 1966.

105. Zweifel, "At Least 3 Judges Here in 'White-Only' Organizations," *CT*, August 25, 1966.

106. Robert A. Davis, "First City Bartender Licenses for Women Given Approval," *WSJ*, February 9, 1966; Brautigam, "Council Advances Bartender Permits for Five Women," *CT*, February 9, 1966; Brautigam, "Council Votes 5 Women's Permits as Bartenders," *CT*, February 11, 1966.

107. William T. Evjue, *A Fighting Editor* (Madison: Wells Printing Company, 1968), 257–273; editorial, "Why Rush Women Bartenders? Why Not a Test Case?" *CT*, February 11, 1966.

108. "Woman Bartender Argument Revived," *WSJ*, July 12, 1966.

109. "3 City Officials to Face Court over Woman Bartenders Dispute," *WSJ*, August 26, 1966; John Strumreiter, "Sachtjen Throws Out Lady Bartender License Order," *CT*, August 30, 1966; Dennis Cassano, "City Wins 1 Test over a Barmaid," *WSJ*, August 31, 1966.

110. "City Policies on Women Bartenders Held Biased," *WSJ*, August 4, 1966; "Find Bias against Lady Bartender," *CT*, September 21, 1966.

111. "Woman Bartender Ban Is Defeated," *WSJ*, September 9, 1966; "City Will Appeal Bias Finding over Barmaid," *WSJ*, September 23, 1966; "Woman Bartender Case Delayed," *WSJ*, October 6, 1966.

112. Cassano, "Judge Ponders State Role in Woman Bartender Case," *WSJ*, December 29, 1966.

113. "Bardwell Questions State Sex Bias Ban Issue," *CT*, December 29, 1966.

114. Aehl, "City Votes Bar Dances," *WSJ*, December 7, 1966; "It's All Set for Dancing in Taverns," *WSJ*, December 9, 1966; Davis, "37 New Dance Places Ready," *WSJ*, December 23, 1966.

115. Bonnie Ryan, "Negro Accepts UW Coach Job," *CT*, February 14, 1966; Ritcherson, Lewis H., OH #1227, Interviewed by Greg Bond & Troy Reeves, May & June 2012.

116. Vaughn, "'Murders Are Same in Viet Nam, South,'" *DC*, May 6, 1966.

117. Annual Report, Special Program of Tutorial and Financial Assistance, University of Wisconsin Division of Student Affairs, November 1968, 2.

118. "Evers to Discus Goal Achievement," *DC*, September 20, 1966; Peter Abbott, "Evers Demands Whites Uproot Their Own Bias," *DC*, September 22, 1966.

119. John Koch, "'Black Power—Sense of History,'" *DC*, November 15, 1966; "'Concerned Negro Students' Group Organized At U.W.," *CT*, November 28, 1966; "Constitution," Office of Student Organization Activities, December 14, 1966.

120. MHA Relieves Callsen of Assistant Director Duties," *CT*, February 15, 1966.

121. "Kopp Named to City Plan Group," *WSJ*, April 20, 1966.

122. MRA minutes, May 18, 1966.

123. "MRA Picks Norvell for Relocation Post," *CT*, June 9, 1966; Merritt Norvel Facebook exchange, August 23, 2017.

124. MRA minutes, February 16, 1966; Aehl, "Awaiting U.S. Aid, MRA Lines Up Avenue Project," *WSJ*, February 17, 1966.

125. "Start on Medical Center at Triangle," *WSJ*, May 7, 1965; "Medical Center Dominates Triangle," *WSJ*, March 15, 1966; Goroff, et al, *The Spirit of Greenbush*, 16; Libby Schwartz Facebook message, December 16, 2017; Steve Schwartz Facebook message, December 16, 2017.

126. MRA minutes, August 26, 1966; "Research Site Sale Approved By MRA," *CT*, August 27, 1966.

127. "MRA Seeks Proposals for Use of Triangle Area," *CT*, August 29, 1966.

128. MRA minutes, November 16, 1966; "MRA Authorizes Director to Deal on Triangle Site," *WSJ*, November 18, 1966.

129. Coyle, "Sampson Plaza Requests Extension to Offset Losses," *CT*, November 15, 1966; MRA minutes, November 16, 1966; "Expansion Sought for Sampson Plaza," *WSJ*, November 16, 1966; MRA minutes, December 14, 1966.

130. Aehl, "Awaiting U.S. Aid, MRA Lines Up Avenue Project," *WSJ*, February 17, 1966; Coyle, "U. Ave. Plan Grant OK'd," *CT*, March 21, 1966; Aehl, "U. Ave. Renewal Study OKd," *WSJ*, March 21, 1966; John Powell, "'U' Ave. Renewal Gets Funds," *DC*, March 21, 1966.

131. BOR minutes, October 7, 1966; Scher, "Board Outlines University Ave. Redevelopment," *DC*, October 8, 1966; Gribble, "Regents Agree 'in Principle' to University Ave. Renewal," *WSJ*, October 8, 1966; Pommer, "U.W., Merchants End Dispute over University Ave.," *CT*, October 8, 1966; "Renewal Project Work Can Start Next Year," *CT*, October 8, 1966.

132. Brautigam, "Public Housing Plea Approved by Council," *CT*, May 27, 1966.

133. Brautigam, "Madison Housing Unit Vacancy Rises," *CT*, August 16, 1966.

134. "MHA Votes Housing Units for Elderly," *WSJ*, August 16, 1966; "130 Units for Elderly Advanced," *CT*, August 16, 1966.

135. Pommer, "D-Day Has Special Meaning as 3,600 Get U. Diplomas," *CT*, June 6, 1966.

136. "U.W. Enrollment Here Is 30,287," *CT*, September 10, 1966.

137. "Shondells to Shine," *DC*, October 27, 1966; Robert Joslyn, "Homecoming Show Goes Off with 'Big Band' for 8,000," *WSJ*, November 6, 1966.

138. Feldman, *Buildings of the University*, 384, 377, 387; "Stadium Gaps to Be Filled Soon," *CT*, August 12, 1966.

139. "'U' Symposium to Start Sunday," *DC*, February 11, 1966.

140. "U. to Name Building for Gulley," *CT*, February 11, 1966; Feldman, *Buildings*, 195.

141. Morley Beloytte, "Coltrane Proves Vexing," *DC*, March 1, 1966.

142. BOR minutes, March 4, 1966.

143. "Dickey, Writer-in-Residence, Wins National Book Award," *DC*, March 17, 1966; "Dickey to Conduct Workshop on Poetry," *DC*, March 23, 1966; "Dueling Banjos," Wikipedia, https://en.wikipedia.org/wiki/Dueling_Banjos; Dave Rattay Facebook exchange, May 26, 2017.

144. "Bob Johnson Is New Puck Coach," *DC*, April 2, 1966; "Johnson Aims to Keep UW Hockey Moving Up," *WSJ*, April 3, 1966.

145. Donna Stein, "Dave Brubeck Quartet Plays to Capacity Crowd at UW," *CT*, May 2, 1966.

146. John Michael, "University Dedicates Dormitory Complex," *WSJ*, May 9, 1966.

147. *CT*, May 11, 1966.

148. Wirsig, "Superlative Is Word for Ella's Songs," *CT*, May 16, 1966.

149. "Social Diseases No Problem to University: McMaster," *DC*, February 1m 1967.

150. Dieckmann, "Police Find Dope and Nab 3 Students," *WSJ*, August 13, 1966.

151. Joe Lagodney, "Enforcement Grows with Campus Drug Use," *DC*, March 12, 1968.

152. Edith Frank, "10,000 Big Wheels on Campus," *CT*, September 10, 1966; Duane Freitag, "UW Students Won't Cross Bridge When Coming to It," *WSJ*, September 17, 1966; Jim Carlson, "Madison Police to Enforce Use of Pedestrian Bridge," *DC*, December 2, 1966; Brautigam, "Move to Force Overpass Use," *CT*, December 2, 1966; John Newhouse, "UW Students to Take High Road," *WSJ*, December 3, 1966.

153. LeRoy Shorey, "Union Committee Brings Film Directors to Madison," *DC*, September 28, 1966.

154. Wells, "CUD, Quixote May Bring Mime Theater Show to U," *DC*, July 21, 1966; Gary Rettgen, "Banned in Denver, Mime Troupe Acts Here Tonight," *CT*, September 30, 1966; Behnke, "Troupe's Four-Letter Word Show at UW Raises Funds and Eyebrows," *WSJ*, October 1, 1966; Robert Sullivan, "'Civil Rights in

a Cracker Barrel' Shows Where It's at, Obscenity and All," *CT*, October 1, 1966; Karen Malpede, "Minstrel Show Mimics Negro," *DC*, October 6, 1966; Morris Edelson email, June 13, 2017.

155. "377 University Men Pledge 30 Fraternities," *CT*, October 8, 1966.

156. Adams, "Peace Move Termed No Issue in Ghetto," *WSJ*, October 14, 1966; "'Black Power' Needn't Be Negative," *CT*, October 14, 1966.

157. Keith Clifford, "Attorney Defends Role of Protesters in Society," *DC*, November 15, 1966.

158. Elizabeth Gould, "When Martha Graham Dances, Audience Does, Too, in Spirit," *WSJ*, November 17, 1966; Hunter, "Graham Group Peerless in Modern Dance World," *CT*, November 17, 1966.

159. Tom Butler, "Milt Bruhn Quits Job as UW Football Coach," *WSJ*, November 18, 1966; Ryan, "Milt Bruhn Didn't Quit; Was Fired by Harrington," *CT*, November 18, 1966; editorial, "Milton Bruhn Learns about the Inflexible Rule of Winning," *CT*, November 18, 1966; Behnke, "Bruhn Comes Out a Winner," *WSJ*, November 20, 1966; Mike Goldman, "Coatta Grabs Top Spot," *DC*, December 10, 1966; David Maraniss interview, 2017.

160. Faculty Document 53, "The Problem of a Second Campus in Madison," March 7, 1966, Madison Campus Faculty Meeting, Series 5/2/15 box 1; Bednarek, "Second UW Campus Plan Gets Backing," *WSJ*, February 17, 1966; Eric Newhouse, "Fleming Outlines New Campus Idea," *DC*, February 17, 1966.

161. Pommer, "2nd Campus Idea Draws Hot Attack from Legislators," *CT*, February 17, 1966; "Second Campus Proposal Rebuffed by Legislators," *Wisconsin Alumnus* 67, no. 6 (March 1966): 16.

162. Faculty Document 61, April 4, 1966; Gribble, "2nd Campus Issue Here Delayed," *WSJ*, September 16, 1966.

163. "Develop Your Talents, East High Grads Told," *CT*, June 17, 1966; "Central-University Grads Told: Improve Your Skills," *CT*, June 17, 1966; "283 Graduate at La Follette, 657 at West," *CT*, June 17, 1966.

164. Pommer, "Public School Enrollment Reaches 32,768 Pupils," *CT*, September 19, 1966.

165. Gribble, "City Schools Open Tuesday," *WSJ*, September 5, 1966.

166. Custer, "3 Cheers for the Orange and Black," *CT*, February 8, 1966; Levitan, *Sesquicentennial History*, 150.

167. Bednarek, "Central-University High Will Close in June, 1969," *WSJ*, February 8, 1966; Brautigam, "Board Votes, 6-1, to Close Central," *CT*, February 8, 1966.

168. "Mansfield's Motion Draws Uneasy Second," *CT*, February 8, 1966.

169. Pommer, "Pfefferle Says Central Decision Was 'Railroaded,'" *CT*, February 8, 1966.

170. Wirsig, "Challengers Rap 'Rubber-Stamping' by School Board," *CT*, February 18, 1966; Pommer, "Incumbents Win School Board Seats," *CT*, April 6, 1966; Aehl, "City Bond Issues Win Approval," *WSJ*, April 6, 1966.

171. Pommer, "U.W. to Accept City Vocational School Credits at 'Full Value,'" *CT*, September 19, 1966.

172. Brautigam, "Pupils Get Bus but No Lunches," *CT*, January 25, 1966; Coyle, "City and Gilberts Head for Showdown on Buses," *CT*, February 2, 1966; Brautigam, "Franklin Busing Request Withdrawn," *CT*, February 8, 1966.

173. "Morals Trial of Ex-Lapham Principal Goes to Jury," *CT*, March 1, 1966; "Acquitted Principal Resigns," *CT*, March 3, 1966.

174. Pommer, "Schools' Photo Request Labeled Discrimination," *CT*, March 4, 1966; Pommer, "Drop Photos, AG Tells Schools," *CT*, March 7, 1966; "School Board Quits Asking Teacher Applicant Photos," *WSJ*, March 8, 1966; Brautigam, "City Schools End Use of Photos in Hiring Teachers," *CT*, March 8, 1966; Irna Moore, "Can't Use Photos on Teacher Job Forms, Fagan Tells Schools," *CT*, June 18, 1966.

175. Bednarek, "3 School Names Voted by Board," *WSJ*, June 21, 1966; Brautigam, "Vote to Name 3 Schools 'Kennedy,' 'Huegel,' 'Muir,'" *CT*, June 21, 1966; Bednarek, "Three New Schools Are Named; Pupil Transport Plan Approved," *WSJ*, July 12, 1966.

176. Brautigam, "Council Sets Nov. 8 School Bond Date," *CT*, October 14, 1966.

177. "Slingshots Used to Break 14 Lapham School Windows," *CT*, October 19, 1966.

178. "School Bond Issue Wins by 2-1 Margin," *WSJ*, November 9, 1966.

179. Brautigam, "School Board Approves Project for $500,000 Football Stadium," *CT*, December 6, 1966.

180. Bednarek, "Worst Teacher Shortage Seen," *WSJ*, August 6, 1966; Pommer, "Schools Desperately Need Substitutes," *CT*, August 16, 1966; Pommer, "City Pupil Census: School by School," *CT*, August 19, 1966; Pommer, "School Taxes Here Highest in State," *CT*, September 2, 1966; Pommer, "$22 Million School Budget," *CT*, September 5, 1966.

181. "Dimensions & Dividends," Madison City Planning Department, April 1, 1968.

182. City of Madison Department of Planning, Community Development and Economic Department.

183. Aehl, "Wording of New Zoning Law Finally Is Accepted," *WSJ*, January 14, 1966; Brautigam, "New Zoning Map OK'd by Council," *CT*, June 24, 1966.

184. "Mayer Co. Names Beach President," *CT*, February 8, 1966.

185. Coyle, "Merchants Spark Bid to Bar Baldwin St. Closing for Gisholt," *CT*, February 23, 1966; editorial, "Off on Wrong Foot, Gisholt Changes Tactics and Gains," *CT*, February 25, 1966; Aehl, "Council Vacates Block for Gisholt Expansion," *WSJ*, February 26, 1966; "S. Baldwin to Be Closed to Traffic at 6 p.m. Friday," *CT*, October 15, 1966.

186. Zweifel, "3 High Rises Urged for Turville Point," *CT*, June 6, 1966; Brautigam, "OK Bid for Federal Turville Pt. Funds," *CT*, September 7, 1966; Brautigam, "Turville Point Condemnation Backed," *CT*, September 21, 1966; Coyle, "U.S. Aids City Park Plan," *CT*, December 21, 1966.

187. Havens Wilber, "Housing Starts Here Show 50% Slump," *CT*, November 3, 1966.

188. "Park Plaza Center's Opening Is Boost to South Side," *WSJ*, August 23, 1966.

189. Coyle, "City's Largest Real Estate Development on Sale Today," *CT*, September 14, 1966; Aehl, "Cherokee Is a Happy Compromise," *WSJ*, September 18, 1966.

190. Aehl, "City Holds Own in Elm Attack," *WSJ*, September 18, 1966.

191. "Grand Opening," *WSJ*, October 16, 1966; "Emporium on the Square: From the Old to the New," *WSJ*, October 23, 1966.

192. "New Library Expects 10,000 Users," *WSJ*, March 3, 1966; "New Pinney Branch Library Gets Ready," *WSJ*, November 17, 1966; "Workers Will Tear Down Old Madison Library Today," *WSJ*, June 28, 1966; Levitan, *Sesquicentennial History*, 150.

193. Ann Waidelich email, January 26, 2017.

194. Irvin Kreisman, "Once-Flourishing Atwood Ave. Now Shows Distress Signs in Windows," *CT*, March 28, 1966; Kreisman, "Parking Woes Dominate Atwood Avenue's Decline," *CT*, March 29, 1966; Kreisman, "Atwood Ave. Businessmen Fear Bulldozer Project," *CT*, March 31, 1966; "Economic and Market Analysis: Atwood Business District, Prepared for Madison Plan Commission by Real Estate Research Corporation, September 1966; Aehl, "Shopping Center Urged to Revive Atwood Ave.," *WSJ*, November 1, 1966.

195. "An Analysis and Proposal of the Atwood Business District," City Planning Department, October 1964; Brautigam, "Atwood Improvement Pushed by Plan Bureau," *CT*, November 28, 1964.

196. "Cycle, Scooter Parking Banned on State Street," *DC*, April 29, 1966; Brautigam, "Warn Parking Ban Will Ruin State St.," *CT*, August 23, 1966; Davis, "Parking Issues Action Delayed," *WSJ*, August 24, 1966; "Hold Off on Parking Ban," *CT*, August 24, 1966.

197. Coyle, "Causeway Price Tag Doubled to $2 Million," *CT*, February 18, 1966; "Causeway Dredged by July?" *WSJ*, May 2, 1966; "People Plague Causeway Work," *WSJ*, July 2, 1966; Zweifel, "Says Causeway Is 'Coming Along,'" *CT*, July 25, 1966.

198. Newhouse, "Madison Bus Bounces Back," *WSJ*, January 2, 1966; "New Express Bus Route Ready to Start Tuesday," *CT*, September 3, 1966.

199. "New Johnson Stretch to Open Today for Cars One-Way East," *WSJ*, November 4, 1966; Aehl, "At First, It's Street of Sorrows," *WSJ*, November 5, 1966; editorial, "Johnson St.—a Blessing?" *WSJ*, November 10, 1966.

200. Aehl, "University Ave.'s One-Way Plan Set," *WSJ*, November 17, 1966; "University Ave. Goes West, Young Man," *WSJ*, November 19, 1966; "New Expressway Brings Problems," *WSJ*, November 26, 1966.

201. "Dedication of Terminal Set Tuesday," *WSJ*, December 9, 1966; Aehl, "New Terminal Gets Off to a Good Flying Start," *WSJ*, December 14, 1966; Coyle, "They're Off at New Airport," *CT*, December 15, 1966.

202. "Downtown Freeway Urged to Aid Traffic," *WSJ*, December 15, 1966.

203. Gribble, "Zoo Elephant Winkie Grabs, Kills Girl, 3," *WSJ*, June 29, 1966; "City to Block Area under Gate Where Tot Entered Winkie's Cage," *WSJ*, June 30, 1966; James Maraniss, "Child Zoo Visitors Think Winkie Should Be Punished," *CT*, June 30, 1966; Zweifel, "Zoo Begins Blocking Gate Opening at Winkie's Cage," *CT*, July 1,1966; "A Parting Gift to Madison," *CT*, August 17, 1966; "Zoo Trades Winkie to Farm in West," *CT*, October 14, 1966; Coyle, "With a Few Tugs and Heaves, Winkie Yields Her Home to Youngster," *CT*, October 28, 1966; Larry Avila, "Just Ask Us," *WSJ*, May 22, 2017; Becky Harth Landes, Facebook exchange, May 27, 2017.

204. Brautigam, "Suggests Athenian Oath as Guide for Ethics Code," *CT*, February 17, 1966; Aehl, "Committee Proposes Council Code of Ethics," *WSJ*, March 27, 1966; Coyle, "City Ethics Proposal Up for Final Review," *CT*, June 16, 1966; Brautigam, "City Ethics Code Is Aired; Some Changes Suggested," *CT*, July 1, 1966; Aehl, "Code of Ethics Adopted for All in City Employ," *WSJ*, September 9, 1966; Brautigam, "Council Approves Ethics Code," *CT*, September 9, 1966.

205. Franzmann, "Defective Wiring Is Blamed for $250,000 State St. Fire," *WSJ*, January 10, 1966; Zweifel, "Greater Love Has No Man," *CT*, January 11, 1966; Dieckmann, "Young, Old Pay Last Tribute to Fireman Who Lost His Life," *WSJ*, January 12, 1966; Tianna Parkinson Facebook exchange, June 7, 2017; Christine Parkinson interview, June 8, 2017.

206. "Ralph A. Hult, 75, Pioneer City Chevrolet Dealer, Dies in Florida," *WSJ*, February 21, 1966; editorial, "Ralph Hult—Last Member of Pioneer Business Family," *CT*, February 23, 1966.

1967

1. "Resistance and Revolution: The Anti-Vietnam War Movement at the University of Michigan, 1965–1972," University of Michigan, http://michiganintheworld.history.lsa.umich.edu/antivietnamwar/exhibits/show/exhibit/military_and_the_university/dow_chemical

2. "Students Challenge Administration in Vietnam War Protest," *Wisconsin Alumnus* 68, no. 6 (March, 1967): 18–20; *Scotton*

Report on the Anti-Dow Protests, December 1967, 8–10, Chancellor William Sewell papers, series 4/20/1, box 21, University Archives; Maraniss, *They Marched into Sunlight*, 106–109.

3. Mike Burns, "SDS to Block Chemical Co. Interviewing," *DC*, February 16, 1967; "UW Groups Will Picket Dow Men," *CT*, February 20, 1967; Burns, "SDS Shifts Strategy for Dow Protest," *DC*, February 21, 1967.

4. Matt Pommer, "Two Arrested in UW Sit-In," *CT*, February 21, 1967; Pat McCall, "SDS 'Disruptive' Sit-In," *DC*, February 22, 1967; Lynne Ellestad, "Protesters Debate, Plan Bascom Talks," *DC*, February 22, 1967; Lucy Cooper, "Three Students Arrested for Disorderly Conduct," *DC*, February 22, 1967.

5. Levitan, *Sesquicentennial History*, 42; Clifford C. Behnke, "'Anti-Dow' Protesters Plan New Sit-In at UW," *WSJ*, February 22, 1967; editorial, "SDS: Obstruction of a Right," *DC*, February 22, 1967.

6. Peter Abbot and Lucy Cooper, "Arrest Sixteen; 'Brutality' Alleged," *DC*, February 23, 1967.

7. "Fleming Besieged in Bascom; Way Blocked by 300," *DC*, February 23, 1967; Behnke, "UW Officials Blockaded," *WSJ*, February 23, 1967.

8. Pa McCall and Irv White, "Chancellor Pays Bail," *DC*, February 23, 1967; "Trial Set for U. Protesters," *CT*, February 23, 1967; June Dieckmann, "Fleming Provides Bail for Students," *WSJ*, February 23, 1967; Fleming, *Tempests into Rainbows*, 150–152; Haslach OH #0047; Fred Harvey Harrington, interviewed by Tom Bates, 1988, OH #0135, digital audio file, University Archives and Records Management Services, Madison, Wisconsin; Edwin Young, interviewed by Tom Bates, 1987, OH #0117, digital audio file, University Archives and Records Management Services, Madison, Wisconsin; Ralph Hanson, interviewed by Tom Bates, 1987, OH #0117, digital audio file, University Archives and Records Management Services, Madison, Wisconsin.

9. Steve Shulruff, "Draft Resistors Union Organizes; Establishes Policies for Future," *DC*, April 6, 1967; Joseph McBride, "Draft Resistance Union: Freedom from Fear," *DC*, October 13, 1967; Jim Rowen interview, *War at Home* papers, box 4, folder 25, WHSA; James E. Rowen, interviewed by Laura Smail, 1978, OH #0137, interviewed by Tom Bates, 1987, OH #0117, digital audio file, University Archives and Records Management Services, Madison, Wisconsin.

10. Minutes, Special Meeting of the University of Wisconsin (Madison Campus) Faculty, February 23, 1967, UW Faculty Meetings, series 5/2/2/1, box 10; Pommer, "Says U. May Need 'Additional Forces,'" *CT*, February 24, 1967; Behnke, "Extra Police Need Eyed for UW Rifts," *WSJ*, February 24, 1967.

11. Owen Coyle, "City Council Moves to Probe U. Pickets," *CT*, February 24, 1967; Robert A. Davis, "Aldermen Slap UW Protesters," *WSJ*, February 24, 1967; Behnke, "Who Are Leaders of Sit-Ins at UW?" *WSJ*, March 2, 1967.

12. Editorial, "SDS Protesters Negate Own Cause," *DC*, February 24, 1967; "Daily Cardinal 'Appalled' by Tactics of Protesters," *CT*, February 24, 1967.

13. Frank Ryan, "Governor Pledges Order for Campus," *WSJ*, February 25, 1967.

14. Raymond Moucha, "Anti-Protest Rally Applauds Fleming," *WSJ*, February 25, 1967; "'No Berkeley Wanted Here,'" *DC*, February 28, 1967.

15. John C. Sammis, "Anti-War Protest 'Invades' 1st Congregational Church," *CT*, February 27, 1967.

16. Pommer, "Aftermath of a Strange Protest," *CT*, February 27, 1967; James R. Polk, "Protesters at UW May Affect Budget, Finance Chiefs Say," *WSJ*, February 28, 1967; Marv Levy, "State Asks Harrington about University Policy," *DC*, March 1, 1967.

17. Gregory Graze, "SDS Loses Registration," *DC*, March 3, 1967; Roger Gribble, "UW Protest Group Banned," *WSJ*, March 3, 1967; "U. Anti-War Group Call Ban 'Childish,'" *CT*, March 3, 1967; Harold Froelich–Fred Harvery Harrington correspondence, March 3–4, 1967, Chancellor Robben Fleming papers, series 4/19/1, box 57, University Archives; Haslach OH #0047; Paul Soglin interview, 2017.

18. Minutes, University of Wisconsin (Madison Campus) Faculty Meeting, March 6, 1967, UW Faculty Meetings, series 5/2/2/1, box 10, University Archives.

19. Minutes, Special Meeting of the University of Wisconsin (Madison Campus), March 8, 1967, UW Faculty Meetings, Series 5/2/2/1, box 10, University Archives; Pommer, "UW Faculty Rejects Ban on War Firms," *CT*, March 9, 1967; William Sewell, OH #0101; Maraniss, *They Marched into Sunlight*, 137.

20. BOR Minutes March 10, 1967.

21. Duane Freitag, "2 UW Protesters Are Found Guilty," *WSJ*, September 28, 1967.

22. Peter Abbott, "CIA Funds Support NSA, 'Ramparts' Story Says," *DC*, February 15, 1967; Sol Stern, "NSA and the CIA," *Ramparts Magazine*, March 1967, 29–39; Karen M. Paget, *Patriotic Betrayal* (New Haven: Yale University Press, 2015), 253.

23. "Referendum Tallies Shown," *DC*, April 5, 1967.

24. Neil Eisenberg, "CIA Protest Finds Unity," *DC*, April 11, 1967; "Peaceful Demonstrators Circle Law Building," *DC*, April 12, 1967; Sinks, "No Trouble Expected; Police Held in Reserve," *DC*, April 12, 1967; "CIA Demonstrations Continue—No Incidents," *DC*, April 13, 1967; Gene Wells, "Former SDS President Describes Job Interview," *DC*, April 14, 1967; Marty Tandler interview.

25. Hunter, "100 Well-Wishers Hail Mrs. Boardman," *CT*, May 1, 1967; "Says N. Vietnam Fights for Freedom," *CT*, May 3, 1967; Dieckmann, "Ired over Bid to Mrs. Boardman, Leslie and Wife Quit Democrats," *WSJ*, May 4, 1967; Betty Boardman interview, *War at Home* papers, box 4, folder 11, WHSA.

26. Rich Wener and John Koch, "WSA: No Class Rank for SSS," *DC*, May 17, 1967.

27. Christy Sinks, "Bridge Paint-In Halted; Eight Students Arrested," *DC*, July 18, 1967.

28. Matt Fox, "Spock Attacks Viet War Policy," *DC*, November 8, 1967; "Group Seeks Vote Here on Viet War," *WSJ*, November 22, 1967.

29. Peter Greenberg and William Thedinga, "Five Hundred Walk Out of U Forum," *DC*, November 14, 1967; Soglin OH #0102; Sewell OH #0101; Paul Soglin email, October 11, 2017.

30. "SDS to Obstruct CIA Interviews," *CT*, November 7, 1967; Caroline Orzac, "Y-Dems Protest Coming of CIA," *DC*, November 15, 1967; Gribble, "CIA, Air Force Cancel Campus Job Interviews," *WSJ*, November 18, 1967; Pommer, "CIA Talks Set Off Campus," *CT*, November 18, 1967; Graze and Bill Hoel, "CIA to Interview, But Not on Campus," *DC*, November 18, 1967; "CIA Visit Here Is Off Till February," *CT*, November 25, 1967.

31. Frank Custer, "Complete U. Interviews," *CT*, November 20, 1967; Fox, "Protesters Picketing Interviews Greeted by 300 Riot Policemen," *DC*, November 21, 1967.

32. Gay Leslie, "100 Women March to Protest Draft," *WSJ*, November 5, 1967.

33. James D. Selk, "McCarthy Hailed by Campus Crowd," *WSJ*, December 9, 1967; John Patrick Hunter, "McCarthy Cheered at UW; Keeps Up Attack on War," *CT*, December 9, 1967; Stuart D. Levitan, "Midge Miller, Insider and Agitator, Dies at 86," *Isthmus*, April 17, 2009.

34. "Peace Referendum Petitions Ready for Filing," *CT*, December 22, 1967.

35. Bill Hoel, "CEWV Plans for March on Dow," *DC*, October 13, 1967; "'Stop Draft Week' Begins," *WSJ*, October 17, 1967.

36. "Prof. William Sewell to Succeed Fleming as Chancellor," *Wisconsin Alumnus* 68, no. 9 (June 1967): 16.

37. "Day of Obstruction," *Wisconsin Alumnus* 69, no. 2 (November 1967): 4–9; "Special Issue: The Great Dow War," *Connections* 2, no. 3 (November 1–14, 1967); "History of the Movement in Madison," *TakeOver* 4, no. 15 (November 20–December 4, 1974), 10–11; *War at Home,* chap. 5; Herman Thomas interview, *War at Home* papers, box 4, folder 29, WHSA; Harrington OH #0135; Paul Soglin with Stuart Levitan, "Soglin Remembers Dow," *CT*, October 18–19, 1997; Maraniss, *They Marched into Sunlight,* 233–243, 316–329, 348–399; 446–454, 460–466, 475–478; "Two Days in October," PBS, www.pbs.org/wgbh/americanexperience/films/two-days-in-october/#part01.

38. Soglin, "Hi There, Badger!" *DC*, September 28, 1967; Faculty Document 122.

39. *Scotton Report on the Anti-Dow Protests,* Exhibit D, 2–4; James Oset, "UW Protest-Turned-Riot Didn't 'Just Happen,'" *WSJ*, October 23, 1967; Stark, "In Exile," in Buhle, ed., *History and the New Left,* 176.

40. BOR minutes, October 13, 1967; Sandy Boehm and Steve Shulruff, "Harrington and Sewell Tell Regents That U Will Act Before Courts Do," *DC*, October 14, 1967; Carol Welch, "U Promises Crack-down on Dow Co. Obstructors," *DC*, October 12, 1967; Gribble, "New Chancellor Gets Firm," *WSJ*, October 16, 1967; editorial, "UW Warning against Disruptive Protesting," *WSJ*, October 17, 1967.

41. "The Dow Protest: A Narrative," *Connections* 2, no. 3 (November 1–14): 1967.

42. Joel Brenner, "Kauffman Facing Legality Question," *DC*, October 17, 1967.

43. Shelley Marder, "Dow Protest Starts Today," *DC*, October 17, 1967.

44. Special Assignment Officer's Report, Madison Police Department, October 16, 1967.

45. Hanson OH# 0671, University Archives; Ralph Hanson interview, *War at Home* papers, box 4, folder 14, WHSA.

46. Editorial, "Big Deal," *DC*, October 17, 1967.

47. Pommer, "Picketing of Dow Starts Peacefully," *CT*, October 17, 1967; Sally Platkin, "Recruiting at Commerce Meets Quiet Opposition," *DC*, October 18, 1967.

48. "Mime Troupe: Slaughtering Sacred Cows," *DC*, September 23, 1967.

49. Larry Cohen, "S.F. Mime Troup Here, Watering All the Flower Children with Gestures," *DC*, October 19, 1967.

50. Scotton Report, 23, Exhibit G.

51. Peter Coyote, *Sleeping Where I Fall* (Washington, DC: Counterpoint, 1998), 57–60.

52. Joel Skornicka interview, August 29, 2017.

53. Fred Harrington testimony, *Joint Committee to Study Disruptions at the University of Wisconsin,* May 6, 1969; Joseph F. Kauffman, interviewed by Laura Smail, 1977, OH #0060, Fred Harvey Harrington interviewed by Tom Bates, 1987, OH #0117, digital audio file, University Archives and Records Management Services, Madison, Wisconsin.

54. Maraniss, *They Marched into Sunlight,* 361.

55. Statement by Chancellor William H. Sewell to a Special Meeting of the University of Wisconsin Madisno Campus Faculty, October 19, 1967, UW Faculty Meetings, series 5/2/2/1, box 10, University Archives; Scotton Report, 29; Sewell OH #0101; Kauffman OH #0060.

56. Sewell OH #0101; Stark, "In Exile," in Buhle, ed., *History and the New Left,* 176.

57. Sewell OH #0101.

58. Maraniss, *They Marched into Sunlight,* 368.

59. *Scotton Report,* 29–30.

60. Maraniss, *They Marched into Sunlight,* 368–370.

61. *Scotton Report,* 31.

62. Custer, "Emery Says He Didn't Order Use of Riot Clubs," *CT*, October 19, 1967.

63. Jim Rowen interview, *War at Home* papers, box 4, folder

25, WHSA; John Gruber, "After a Warning, the Clubs Swing," *WSJ*, October 19, 1967.

64. Custer, "Excitement, Fear, Drama—Then Stark Terror," *CT*, October 19, 1967; Maraniss, *They Marched into Sunlight*, 369–379.

65. Hunter, "'How Did They Ever Let Things Get to This?'— Chief Emery," *CT*, October 19, 1967.

66. Maraniss, *They Marched into Sunlight*, 370.

67. Maraniss, *They Marched into Sunlight*, 388–389.

68. Pommer, "City Police Battle 200 U. Protesters," *CT*, October 18, 1967; Dieckmann, "76 Hurt in UW Rioting; Campus Strike Results," *WSJ*, October 19, 1967.

69. "So Proudly It Falls," *WSJ*, October 19, 1967.

70. Selk, "Guard Won't Be Called to Campus Melee—Yet," *WSJ*, October 19, 1967; Sewell OH#0101.

71. Sewell OH# 0101.

72. Paul Soglin interview, *War at Home* papers, box 4, folder 26, WHSA; Soglin with Levitan, "Soglin Remembers Dow."

73. Dieckmann, "Chief Looks Back on 'Fight for Life,'" *WSJ*, October 20, 1967; "Hurt in U.W. Riots: 48 Students, 18 Policemen, Six Non-Students," *WSJ*, October 21, 1967.

74. Stark, "In Exile," in Buhle, ed., *History and the New Left*, 177; Evan Stark email, July 27, 2017.

75. "Mayor Praises Police for UW Riot Conduct," *WSJ*, October 25, 1967.

76. Herman Thomas interview, *War at Home* papers, box 4, folder 29, WHSA; Harrington OH #0135.

77. Maraniss, *They Marched into Sunlight*, 453–454.

78. Gribble, "UW to Charge Riot Leaders," *WSJ*, October 19, 1967.

79. Robert Meloon, "Legislators Demand Stiff Penalties for Protesters," *CT*, October 19, 1967; Meloon, "Senate Orders UW Fact-Finding," *CT*, October 20, 1967.

80. Maraniss, *They Marched nto Sunlight*, 475.

81. Editorial, "The Spectacle of Violence," *CT*, October 19, 1967.

82. Robert Gabriner, "The Capital Times Confounded," *Connections* 2, no. 4 (November 27–December 11, 1967), 2.

83. Oset, "Students, Faculty Vote Strike Today," *WSJ*, October 19, 1967.

84. Pommer, "Riot Leaders Suspended; Some Face Civil Unrest," *CT*, October 19, 1967; Whitney Gould, "Why They Are Striking," *CT*, October 20, 1967; Pommer, "Suspension Ends for 7 Demonstraters," *CT*, February 5, 1968.

85. Stevie Twin and David Jacobs, "TAA Condemns Riot Police Role, Student Suspensions," *DC*, October 21, 1967; BOR minutes, November 17, 1967; Pommer, "One Vote Margin on Regents Stops Mass U.W. Firing," *CT*, November 18, 1967; "Protest Activity Shifts to the Courts Following Oct. 18 Disruption," *Wisconsin Alumnus* 69, no. 3 (December, 1967); Maraniss, *They Marched into Sunlight*, 423.

86. Pommer, "UW Campus Strike Move Fizzles," *CT*, October 19, 1967; Pommer, "UW Campus Near Normal Despite Some Picketing," *CT*, October 20, 1967.

87. "The Dow Protest: A Narrative," *Connections* 2, no. 3 (November 1–14, 1967), 7.

88. Sewell, Statement to a Special Meeting of the University of Wisconsin Faculty, October 19, 1967, series 5/2/2/1, box 10, University Archives; Minutes, Special Meeting of the University of Wisconsin (Madison Campus) Faculty, October 19, 1967, series 5/2/2/1, box 10, University Archives; Chancellor William H. Sewell papes, series 4/20/1, box 20, University Archives; Gribble, "Faculty Backs Sewell's Handling of UW Riots," *WSJ*, October 20, 1967; Pommer, "Dow Talk Cutoff Backed," *CT*, October 20, 1967; Sewell OH #0101.

89. Pommer, "UW Faculty Badly Split on Violence," *CT*, October 20, 1967.

90. Maraniss, *They Marched into Sunlight*, 436–440.

91. March for the Rights of Students & Their Protection," *War at Home* papers, WHSA; John Keefe, "UW Protesters Plan 'Funeral' Walk Here," *WSJ*, October 21, 1967; Caroline Orzac, "Students to Stage Silent March on Sidewalks to Capitol and City Jail," *DC*, October 21, 1967.

92. Paul Soglin email; Frank Emspak email, July 28, 2017.

93. Kendrick, "2,000 Students in State Street March," *CT*, October 21, 1967; Marvin Levy, "1,700 Protest Police on Campus," *WSJ*, October 22, 1967.

94. Levy, "University Students Call Recess to Class Boycott," *WSJ*, October 23, 1967; John Keefe, "UW's Moderates Drop Out of Movement," *WSJ*, October 24, 1967; Soglin OH #0102.

95. Zweifel, "Homecoming Color Brought Home to Randall," *CT*, October 28, 1967; John E. Mollwitz, "Shivering Crowd Greets Lynda," *WSJ*, October 29, 1967.

96. BOR minutes, November 17, 1967; Gribble, "Firm Regent Stand Seen on Obstructors," *WSJ*, November 17, 1967.

97. Pommer, "Shouts, Whistles, Cowbells Mark U Discipline Hearing," *CT*, November 28, 1967; Pommer, "Disorder Stalls U Hearing," *CT*, November 29, 1967.

98. Pommer, "Disorder Stalls U. Hearing," *CT*, November 29, 1967; Pommer, "Expulsion Protest Rally Fizzles on U.W. Campus," *CT*, December 1, 1967.

99. Advertisement, *DC*, December 6, 1967.

100. "Cohen to Leave, Wed State Girl," *WSJ*, December 16, 1967.

101. Dennis Cassano, "Five UW Protesters Convicted, One Freed," *WSJ*, December 16, 1967.

102. "Capt. Charles Thoma, 30, Killed in Action in War," *CT*, January 14, 1967; www.virtualwall.org/dt/ThomaCJ01a.htm; Maraniss, *They Marched into Sunlight*, 448–449.

103. "Army Private Thomas Matush Killed in Viet," *CT*, January 17, 1967; "Thomas Erwin Matush," The Virtual Wall®

Vietnam Veterans Memorial, www.virtualwall.org/dm /MatushTE01a.htm.

104. "Former Madison Resident Dies in Vietnam War," *CT,* April 19, 1967; "James Richard Clifcorn," The Virtual Wall® Vietnam Veterans Memorial, www.virtualwall.org/dc /ClifcornJR01a.htm.

105. "Madison GI Dies in Viet Ambush," *WSJ,* April 28, 1967; "Leonard Dean Thompson," The Virtual Wall® Vietnam Veterans Memorial, www.virtualwall.org/dt/ThompsonLD01a.htm.

106. "Cpl. G.W. Stoflet Dies of Wounds Suffered in Viet," *CT,* June 30, 1967; "Gordon Wayne Stoflet," The Virtual Wall® Vietnam Veterans Memorial, www.virtualwall.org/ds /StofletGW01a.htm.

107. "Ex-Madisonian Killed in Viet Nam," *WSJ,* August 11, 1967; "Vernon Gene Stich," The Virtual Wall® Vietnam Veterans Memorial, www.virtualwall.org/ds/StichVG01a.htm.

108. "City Man Is Killed on Extra Viet Duty," *WSJ,* August 29, 1967; "Mark Willard Neumann," The Virtual Wall® Vietnam Veterans Memorial, www.virtualwall.org/dn /NeumannMW01a.htm.

109. "Madison Navy Corpsman Is Killed in Vietnam," *CT,* September 16, 1967; "Ronald Richard Reinke," The Virtual Wall® Vietnam Veterans Memorial, www.virtualwall.org/dr /ReinkeRR01a.htm.

110. "Madison Soldier, R.P. Caspersen, Killed in Vietnam," *WSJ,* November 18, 1967; "Robert P Caspersen, II," The Virtual Wall® Vietnam Veterans Memorial, www.virtualwall.org/dc /CaspersenRP01a.htm.

111. "Marine Cpl. James Plecity Killed in War in Vietnam," *CT,* December 9, 1967; Jim Bisbee Facebook message, May 29, 2017; "James Donn Plecity," The Virtual Wall® Vietnam Veterans Memorial, www.virtualwall.org/dp/PlecityJD01a.htm.

112. Dennis Cassano, "Judge Denies City's Motion to Dismiss Auditorium Case," *WSJ,* July 30, 1967; Coyle, "Puts UW Project Fees at 8 Per Cent of Cost," *CT,* August 22, 1967; Cassano, "Trial over Wright Pact Ends," *WSJ,* August 25, 1967; Melloon, "City's Wright Contract Ruled Legal by Wilkie," *CT,* September 12, 1967; Cassano, "Wright Pact Valid, Judge Rules," *WSJ,* September 13, 1967.

113. Aehl, "Peters Asks Downtown Site for an Auditorium," *WSJ,* September 28, 1967; "Peters Lists Area's Facilities," *WSJ,* September 28, 1967; Brautigam, "Peters Shows City First Design for Monona Basin," *CT,* September 28, 1967.

114. Zweifel, "Monona Plans Revealed," *CT,* December 6, 1967; Aehl, "Auditorium Urged for Law Park Site," *WSJ,* December 7, 1967; Mollenhoff and Hamilton, *Monona Terrace,* 175–181.

115. Mollenhoff and Hamilton, *Monona Terrace,* 178.

116. Zweifel, "Long-Time Foes Hit Monona Plan," *CT,* December 7, 1967.

117. Zweifel, "Mayor Sees Monona Plan as Key to City's Greatness," *CT,* December 6, 1967; editorial, "A Practical Proposal to Lift Madison Above Mediocrity," *CT,* December 7, 1967; editorial, "Full Circle on City Auditorium," *WSJ,* December 7, 1967; "Milestone in Madison," *Architectural Forum* 127 (November 1967): 130–131; *Progressive Architecture* 49 (May 1968): 66–67.

118. "What of Wright Plan Costs?" *WSJ,* December 7, 1967.

119. Aehl, "New Auditorium Session Is Set," *WSJ,* December 15, 1967.

120. Feuerzeig, "40% of City Dwelling Units under Equality Ordinance," *CT,* December 13, 1963.

121. EOC minutes, March 14, 1967, August 22, 1967.

122. Aehl, "Full Open Housing Law Proposed Here," *WSJ,* September 6, 1967; Zweifel, "Full Open Housing May Have 'Good Chance,'" *CT,* September 6, 1967.

123. EOC minutes, September 5, 1967.

124. CAC minutes, September 19, 1967; Gruber, "Open Housing Given Backing," *WSJ,* September 20, 1967.

125. Pommer, "UW Professor's Son Told to Leave U.S.," *CT,* February 21, 1967; Joel Brenner, "Negro Prof Victim of Firebomb Attack at Madison Home," *DC,* September 26, 1967.

126. "Rights Chairman Is Taken Ill," *CT,* September 26, 1967.

127. Brautigam, "Vote Wider Open Housing," *CT,* September 27, 1967; Aehl, "City Housing Made More Open," *WSJ,* September 27, 1967; Brautigam, "Religious, Civic Leaders Plead for Open Housing," *CT,* September 27, 1967.

128. Aehl, "Open Housing Passes, Liability Fear Noted," *WSJ,* September 29, 1967.

129. EOC minutes, December 19, 1967; Aehl, "Race Bias Found in City," *WSJ,* December 20, 1967.

130. Brautigam, "Wider Open Housing Survives Two Attacks, Passed by Council," *CT,* September 29, 1967.

131. "Rights Unit Head to Leave Shortly," *WSJ,* September 15, 1967; EOC minutes, October 17, 1967; "Mrs. Symon Stays as Acting Head of Rights Group," *WSJ,* October 18, 1967; "Rev. James Wright to Be Honored," *WSJ,* November 4, 1967.

132. Peter Bunn to Willie Edwards, February 20, 1967, Student Organizations, University Archives; Cornelius K. Gilbert, "Their Time and Their Legacy: African American Activism in the Black Campus Movement at the University of Wisconsin–Madison and Its Enduring Impulse," unpublished dissertation, 2011, 110.

133. Gould, "Community Chest OK's Urban League's Entry," *CT,* March 28, 1967.

134. EOC minutes, July 18, 1967; Brautigam, "City Equal Opportunity Group Reports on 'Good Year,'" *CT,* July 19, 1967.

135. EOC minutes, August 22, 1967.

136. EOC minutes, November 14, 1967, December 19, 1967; Aehl, "Pupils' Race Identity Here to Face Challenge," *WSJ,* December 21, 1967; WSJ 12.21.67; Ray Spangenberg, Diane Moser, Douglas Long, *African Americans in Science, Math and Invention,* (New York: Infobase Publishing, 2014), 34–35.

137. Report and Recommendations, Madison Equal Opportunities Commission, Dec. 1967; Aehl, "Rights Unit List 18 Racial Conflict Cases," *WSJ*, March 29, 1968.

138. Aehl, "Marquette, South Side Residents to Be Heard," *WSJ*, August 1, 1967; Brautigam, "Marquette Area Racial Efforts Assured of Support," *CT*, August 3, 1967; Brautigam, "Negroes Complain of City Landlord's 'Solid Front,'" *CT*, August 4, 1967.

139. John Stumreiter, "Madison Police Recruit Ad Pledges No Race or Creed Discrimination," *CT*, August 12, 1967.

140. Coyle, "Rumors of Madison Riot Prove False, Police Say," *CT*, August 5, 1967; Coyle, "Negroes Expect No Violence Here," *CT*, August 7, 1967.

141. Linda Dean to A. Roy Anderson, December 6, 1967, *Records, Equal Opportunities Commission of Madison, Wisconsin*, box 6, folder 1, WHSA; EOC minutes, December 19, 1967; Aehl, "Race Bias Found in City," *WSJ*, December 20, 1967.

142. "Dyke Beats Deadline, Files To Oppose Festge," *WSJ*, February 1, 1967.

143. "'Fiscal Restraint' Proposed by Dyke," *WSJ*, March 8, 1967; Aehl, "Mayoral Race Based on Leadership, Taxed," *WSJ*, April 2, 1967.

144. "County GOP Backs Dyke for Mayor," *CT*, March 31, 1967; Moucha, "Dyke Plea Fails, COPE OKs Festge," *WSJ*, February 17, 1967.

145. Coyle, "Festge vs. Dyke: Are There Any Issues?" *CT*, February 25, 1967; Aehl, "Dyke, Festge 'Attack, Defend,'" *WSJ*, March 11, 1967

146. Aehl, "Festge Barely Wins by 75-Vote Margin," *WSJ*, April 5, 1967; Coyle, "Festge's Win Is Affirmed," *CT*, April 15, 1967.

147. Coyle, "Mayor Vows Effort To Hold Tax Line," *CT*, April 18, 1967.

148. Coyle, "Forster, Smith Off Auditorium Group," *CT*, April 18, 1967.

149. Otto Festge, "Mayor's Annual Message, April 18, 1967," WI-M 1 MAY 50.1:1967/4/18, Wisconsin Historical Society Library.

150. Zweifel, "City Left without Budget as Car Tax Fails," *CT*, December 29, 1967.

151. Gribble, "Teacher Protest Fails, Board OKs Budget," *WSJ*, October 3, 1967; Zweifel, "Budget Slash Will Pinch Schools," *CT*, November 8, 1967; Aehl, "$48 Tax Rate Proposed by Board," *WSJ*, November 9, 1967; Gribble, "$500,000 Budget Slash Angers School Officials," *WSJ*, November 10, 1967; Pommer, "Schools, City Remain Deadlocked on Budget," *CT*, November 16, 1967.

152. Brautigam, "$9 Tax on Cars Asked for City," *CT*, November 18, 1967; Zweifel, "See Wheel Tax Passage; Road Club Raps Proposal," *CT*, November 20, 1967; Gribble, "Crowd Backs School Budget," *WSJ*, November 21, 1967.

153. Aehl, "$9 City Car Tax Voted," *WSJ*, November 21, 1967.

154. Aehl, "New Vehicle Tax Stalls in Legal Traffic Snarl,"

WSJ, November 24, 1967; Zweifel, "Auto Tax Is Void, La Follette Tells City," *CT*, November 30, 1967.

155. Aehl, "Budget Remains 'Up in Air' Here," *WSJ*, December 2, 1967.

156. Aehl, "Homeowners Stymied on Early Tax Payment," *WSJ*, December 9, 1967.

157. Brautigam, "Council Fails to Unsnarl City's '68 Budget Tangle," *CT*, December 8, 1967.

158. Aehl, "City's Car Tax Ready to Roll," *WSJ*, December 13, 1967; Brautigam, "Tax Bills to Go Out as If Car Levy OK," *CT*, December 13, 1967.

159. Zweifel, "City Left without Budget as Car Tax Fails," *CT*, December 29, 1967; Aehl, "How Now, Budgetless City?" *WSJ*, December 30, 1967.

160. "Most UW Grads Are From Wisconsin," *CT*, June 3, 1967

161. Gary Rettgen, "Nancy Wows Homecoming Crowd," *CT*, October 28, 1967; "Homecoming Dance," *DC*, October 26, 1967.

162. Feldman, *Buildings*, 382–385; 347; 369–370.

163. Wright's Madison City Directory 1967 (St. Paul: Wright Directory Co., 1967).

164. "The Day the Buses Stopped Running," *Wisconsin Alumnus* 68, no. 9 (June 1967): 6–8; "A History of the Movement in Madison: Bus Lane," *TakeOver* 4, no. 14 (November 6–20, 1974), 12.

165. Custer, "Beauty Loses Leg in U. Ave. Mishap," *CT*, March 2, 1967.

166. BOR minutes, April 7, 1967; "Regents Support Plan to Remove Bus Lane," *CT*, April 8, 1967; Stanley Williams, "University Ave. Plans Backed," *WSJ*, April 29, 1960; Jim Carlson, "Bus Lane Rift Hits Regents; Protest Hinted," *DC*, May 6, 1967; "Regents Again Ask City for Bus Lane Removal," *WSJ*, May 6, 1967.

167. Robben Fleming to Michael D. Fullwood, May 15, 1967, Fleming Papers, University Archives; "Fleming Tells Students: No Bus Lane Show," *WSJ*, May 16, 1967.

168. Carlson, "Protesters on Bikes to Strike at 'Wrong-Way' Bus Lane," *DC*, May 17, 1967; Coyle, "'Lawful' Bus Lane Protest Is Still On," *CT*, May 16, 1967; editorial, "The Bus Lane," *DC*, May 17, 1967.

169. Coyle, "Ordinance Would Block Bus Lane Protest Action," *CT*, May 9, 1967; Brautigam, "Bus Protest Penalty Is Defeated," *CT*, May 12, 1967; Aehl, "Leave Bus Lane Alone, City Warns Students," *WSJ*, May 12, 1967.

170. Carlson, "Thirteen Jailed in Bus Protest; Police Quell Bus Protest by Students," *DC*, May 18, 1967; Dieckmann and Richard W. Jaeger, "25 UW Students Arrested for Protest on Bus Lane; 3,000 Turn Out, No One Injured," *WSJ*, May 18, 1967; Coyle, "Anti-Bus Students, Police in Skirmish," *CT*, May 18, 1967; "9 Students Pay $13 Each as Loiterers," *WSJ*, May 26, 1967.

171. Robert Franzmann, "Spirited Students Take Over Avenue," *WSJ*, May 18, 1967.

172. Aehl, "Bus Lane Should Stay, City Unit Says," *WSJ*, May 19, 1967; Carlson, "Group Asks Changes—But Not for Buses," *DC*, May 19, 1967.

173. "Police, Students Stage a Standoff," *WSJ*, May 19, 1967; "Rioting Students Invade Downtown," *CT*, May 19, 1967.

174. Zweifel, "Bus Drivers Won't Make Campus Runs," *CT*, May 19, 1967; Dieckmann, "Protected City Buses Resume Runs Today," *WSJ*, May 20, 1967.

175. "Council Resolutions Show Aldermen's Anger at U.W.," *CT*, May 24, 1967; Aehl, "City Asks $2,717 in Protester Costs," *WSJ*, May 26, 1967.

176. Hunter, "Assembly Reacts Angrily to Protests," *CT*, May 26, 1967.

177. BOR minutes, June 9, 1967; "Harrington Defends UW Handling of Protesters," *WSJ*, June 10, 1967.

178. Coyle, "Fleming Declares U.W. Won't 'Crack Heads,'" *CT*, May 20, 1967.

179. Brautigam, "Aldermen Reject Change in Bus Lane," *CT*, May 24, 1967; Aehl, "Bus Lane to Stay, City Council Decides," *WSJ*, May 24, 1967; Brautigam, "Council Reaffirms Decision On Wrong-Way Bus Lane," *CT*, May 26, 1967; "New Stop-Go Lights on U. Ave. Readied," *WSJ*, June 14, 1967.

180. "Lawyer Given Ticket for Driving Bus Lane," *WSJ*, June 14, 1967; James Maraniss, "Hur Pleads Not Guilty On Bus Lane Charge; Gets Different Judge," *CT*, June 19, 1967.

181. Dieckmann, "Taxis Will Use Bus Lane," *WSJ*, June 21, 1967.

182. Abbott, "Carmichael Attacks 'White Supremacy,'" *DC*, February 7, 1967.

183. "Soglin Resigns, Calls for Unity of Student Factions," *DC*, February 7, 1967; "A History of the Movement in Madison: UCA, *TakeOver* 4, no. 14 (November 6–20, 1974): 12.

184. "WSA Symposium: Facts, Faces," *DC*, February 1, 1967; Graze, "Dr. Masters Dispels Sex 'Myths'; Physical 'Nitty Gritty' Detailed," *DC*, February 14, 1967; Moucha, "Asking for Questions on Sex, One Must Have the Answers," *WSJ*, February 14, 1967; Sinks, "'Turn On, Tune In, Drop Out,'" *DC*, February 15, 1967; Ellestad, "Bishop Pike, Accused Heretic, Raps Church as Behind Times," *DC*, February 17, 1967; Rita Braver, "Kissinger Sees Increased Chance of Negotiation of Vietnam War," *DC*, February 18, 1967; BOR minutes, March 10, 1967.

185. "Monroe Plays Bluegrass Tune," *DC*, February 11, 1967.

186. Editorial, "Legalize Pot," *DC*, February 17, 1967; "Daily Cardinal Backs Marijuana," *DC*, February 17, 1967.

187. Rich Wener, "SDS, 'Quixote,' to Share Sponsorship of 'MacBird,'" *DC*, February 17, 1967; Irv White, "Police Face 'Mac-Bird,'" *DC*, February 18, 1967; "Controversial 'MacBird' Premiers Here—Almost," *DC*, February 22, 1967; Larry Cohen, "'Mac-Bird!'": Blitzkrieg Attack, Fusing Blows in Total Theater," *DC*, March 3, 1967; Morris Edelson email, February 8, 2017.

188. *Connections* 1, no. 1 (March 1–14, 1967); Braver, "Printers Kill Job," *DC*, March 7, 1967; Gould, "'Connections' Cuts Loose," *CT*, March 8, 1967; *Connections,* Microfilm P77-5438 at the Wisconsin Historical Society; Connections (Madison, WI: Connections, 1967–1969) online facsimile at www.wisconsinhistory.org /turningpoints/search.asp?id=1800; Stuart Ewen in Buhle, ed., *History and the New Left,* 181–182; Stu Ewen email, January 29, 2017.

189. Steve Cony, "Smokey Robinson Swings," *DC*, March 14, 1967.

190. Len Shapiro, "Cagers Choose Franklin as Most Valuable Player," *DC*, March 14, 1967.

191. Robert Sullivan, "'Thundering, Crashing, Wailing' from Band," *CT*, March 18, 1967; "The Fantastic Butterfield Blues Band," *DC*, May 12, 1967; Advertisement, *DC*, October 4, 1967.

192. Jeanette Lee and Maxine Woodford, "Bloomfield Advises Others—Be Honest, Lose Hang Ups," *DC*, October 28, 1967.

193. Sullivan, "'The Animals' Are Loud—But Not Very Good," *CT*, March 9, 1967.

194. Marv Levy, "Froelich Attacks 'U' for Decline of Morals," *DC*, March 23, 1967.

195. "Fleming Offered President Post at Minnesota," *WSJ*, March 19, 1967; Gribble, "Michigan U. Post Hinted for Fleming," *WSJ*, March 28, 1967; Pommer, "Fleming Is Chosen as Michigan U. President," *CT*, March 28, 1967; Fleming, *Tempests into Rainbows,* 155–161.

196. "Dizzy Gillespie Quintet Here April 2 for Concerts at Union," *CT*, March 3, 1967.

197. Gribble, "Opposite Sex Visits, Door Ajar, Supported," *WSJ*, February 9, 1967; "Faculty Asks Beer Change," *DC*, April 3, 1967.

198. "Ball to Feature Band, Skits," *DC*, April 5, 1967.

199. Mark Goldblatt, "Ginsberg, Fugs, Be-In; Truly Unique Weekend With Love," *DC*, May 16, 1967; Morris Edelson email, February 6, 2017.

200. Mark Menachem, "A Chat with Fitzgerald & Henderson," *DC*, June 27, 1967; Mary Silas, "Ella's Performance Electrifies Audience," *DC*, June 27, 1967.

201. BOR minutes, July 7, 1967; Sinks, "Regent Board Ups Harrington's Pay," *DC*, July 11, 1967.

202. Joe Lagodney, "Enforcement Grows with Campus Drug Use," *DC*, March 12, 1968.

203. BOR minutes, September 15, 1967; Pat McCall, "Regents Okay 5% Beer at U," *DC*, September 19, 1967; Margery Tabankin, "Strong Beer Starts Nov. 1," *DC*, September 30, 1967.

204. Bob Beecher, "Decline in Rushing, Frats' Faults Discussed," *DC*, October 4, 1967.

205. Julie Kennedy, "Black Sorority Stresses Service and Unity; Repudiates Typical Greek Social Stereotype," *DC*, October 8, 1968.

206. "Parks to Lead UN, Washington YMCA Seminar," *WSJ*, October 27, 1967.

207. "American Ballet Performs Tonight," *DC*, November 8, 1967.

208. "Music of India" advertisement, *DC*, October 20, 1967.

209. Tom Klein, "Co-op Ends Drive for Members; Goal Passed," *DC*, December 14, 1967.

210. Gribble, "William Sewall [*sic*] Named New Chancellor at UW," *WSJ*, June 10, 1967; Keefe, "New UW Chancellor Steps into 'Hot Spot' Position," *WSJ*, June 11, 1967; "Prof. William Sewell to Succeed Fleming as Chancellor," *Wisconsin Alumnus* 68, no. 9 (June 1967): 16; Maraniss, *They Marched into Sunlight*, 119–126.

211. Soglin, "The Fire Burns," *DC*, June 23, 1967; Sewell OH #0101.

212. Schulruff, "Preview: Chancellor Sewell," *DC*, July 13, 1967; "Interview with Chancellor Sewell," *DC*, July 20, 1967; Peter Greenberg, "The Man or the Job—Which Controls?" *DC*, November 22, 1967; Sewell OH #0101.

213. Sewell OH #0101; Harrington OH #0135.

214. Melissa Evans, "Armory Site Up for Clubbing," *DC*, January 10, 1967.

215. BOR minutes, January 13, 1967.

216. Pommer, "Old Red Gym to Be Razed This Summer," *CT*, January 13, 1967.

217. John Powell, "They Still Argue: Gym or Faculty Lounging?" *DC*, February 1, 1967; editorial, "Save the Red Gym," *DC*, February 1, 1967; Stevie Twin, "SSO Loves Gym," *DC*, February 2, 1967; Bart Howard, "I-F Votes to Save Gym," *DC*, February 2, 1967; editorial, "Old Red Gym to Stay—Maybe," *DC*, February 11, 1967.

218. BOR minutes, February 10, 1967; Pommer, "'Old Red Gym' Not Dead Yet; Regents May Save It," *CT*, February 10, 1967.

219. BOR minutes, February 10, 1967; "Regents Warned on Opposition to Razing UW's Old Red Gym," *WSJ*, February 10, 1967; City of Madison Landmarks Commission Nomination Form, http://www.cityofmadison.com/planning/landmark/nominations/169_716LangdonStreet.pdf.

220. Levitan, *Sesquicentennial History*, 129.

221. "Lower Campus Recommendations Outlined," *CT*, May 3, 1967; BOR minutes, May 5, 1967.

222. BOR minutes, May 5, 1967, exhibit F; Pommer, "Question Razing of 'Old Red Gym,'" *CT*, May 5, 1967.

223. "Helen C. White, UW's Honored English Teacher, Author, Dies," *WSJ*, June 8, 1967; "Prof. Helen C. White, Noted U.W. English Scholar, Dies," *CT*, June 8, 1967.

224. "Prof. Harry Steenbock, 81, Finder of Vitamin D, Dies," *CT*, December 26, 1967; "UW Scientist Prof. Steenbock, Discoverer of Vitamin D, Dies," *WSJ*, December 26, 1967; editorial, "Prof. Harry Steenbock," *WSJ*, December 27, 1967.

225. "West Seniors Asked to Listen, Get Involved," "Accept Challenges of the World, East High School Seniors Urged," "La Follette Graduates Reminded to Find Strengths in Their Doubts," "Central Grads Told to Keep Learning," all *CT*, June 9, 1967.

226. Pommer, "School Budgets Will Be Steeper," *CT*, September 21, 1967.

227. "Strike to Delay School, Street Projects in City," *WSJ*, May 3, 1967; "May Rent Church Space," *CT*, May 31, 1967; Irna Moore, "All Schools but One to Be Opened on Sept. 5," *CT*, August 16, 1967; Gribble, "Bus Strike Cost to Schools Cited," *WSJ*, November 7, 1967; "New Muir School's Opening Now Postponed Till Jan. 2," *WSJ*, November 29, 1967; Brautigam, "After 4 Delays, Muir Opens Jan. 29," *CT*, December 19, 1967.

228. Pommer, "City's School Aids per Pupil Prove County's Lowest," *CT*, October 16, 1968.

229. Brautigam, "Approve Payment Plan for School Damages," *CT*, May 16, 1967.

230. Gribble, "Teachers and Board OK Pay, Negotiation," *WSJ*, January 10, 1967; Brautigam, "Finds Madison Is Handicapped in Hiring Teachers," *CT*, April 4, 1967; Pommer, "School Budgets Will Be Steeper," *CT*, September 21, 1967.

231. Brautigam, "Memorial High Stadium OK'd at $408,265," *CT*, January 10, 1967.

232. "Two New Schools Yearly, Double Present Rate, Seen," *WSJ*, January 27, 1967; Coyle, "Festge Won't Back School Unit Idea," *CT*, April 24, 1967; Aehl, "City Keeps Reins on School Budget," *WSJ*, April 26, 1967.

233. Pommer, "West High Student Senate Opposes Forced Pledge," *CT*, February 17, 1967.

234. Pommer, "City Schools' Pupil Services Division Rated in Top 20," *CT*, February 21, 1967.

235. Pommer, "No Beard, La Follette High Tells Student Teacher," *CT*, March 16, 1967; "Verona Accepts Bearded Teacher Madison Barred," *CT*, March 24, 1967.

236. "School Vandalism Damage Grows," *WSJ*, March 29, 1967.

237. "Ruth Doyle, Marcus, Win School Posts," *CT*, April 5, 1967.

238. Pommer, "School Chief May Quit City," *CT*, April 17, 1967; Gribble, "Gilberts Is Expected to Accept Offer to Head Schools in Denver," *WSJ*, April 18, 1967; "Gilberts Accepts Denver Offer," *CT*, April 21, 1967; Gribble, "Ritchie Is Named City School Chief," *WSJ*, July 6, 1967; Pommer, "School Board, by 4-3 Vote, Names Ritchie Superintendent," *CT*, July 6, 1967.

239. Brautigam, "City Wants Teachers from Many Races," *CT*, August 8, 1967; Pommer, "Schools Have 13 Negro Teachers, 512 Negro Pupils," *CT*, December 18, 1967.

240. Pommer, "Arrest Teachers for War Protest," *CT*, August 31, 1967.

241. "Pupil-Teacher Ratio Improves Here," *CT*, August 7, 1967; "The Mini-Crisis in City Schools," *WSJ*, March 25, 1968.

242. "Ritchie Calls for Action against 'Pupil Arrogance,'" *CT*, November 8, 1967.

243. Gribble, "Schools May Still Cut City Hall Ties," *WSJ*, December 4, 1967; Brautigam, "School Board Oks Study of Unified District," *CT*, December 5, 1967.

244. Brautigam, "Vocational Board Sets Academic Freedom Policy," *CT*, June 13, 1967.

245. "Ask New Name for City's Vocational-Technical School," *CT*, February 20, 1967; Gribble, "Madison Vocation Board Holds Last Session; Gilberts Praised," *WSJ*, June 13, 1967; Gribble, "Vocational Board Votes Control of Central High," *WSJ*, May 9, 1967; "Students Endorse Changing of Name," *WSJ*, November 16, 1967.

246. "Police Union Local Here Is Disbanded," *WSJ*, May 12, 1967.

247. Brautigam, "Commission Head Asks Support for Police, Firemen," *CT*, May 18, 1967.

248. "Police Station's Plaque Honors Bruce Weatherly," *WSJ*, September 20, 1967.

249. Kreisman, "Officer Uses New Chemical to Subdue Resisting Pair," *CT*, November 23, 1967; Joshua Greene, "WCLU Asks Festge-Police MACE Policy," *DC*, December 2, 1967; "Festge Backs Policemen in Use of Chemical Mace," *CT*, December 6, 1967; "Mayor Approves Police Use of Mace to Curb Violators," *WSJ*, December 6, 1967.

250. Kreisman, "Theft in Ginger's Dressing Room," *CT*, December 7, 1967.

251. "Set $2 Million for Housing Unit Here," *CT*, February 21, 1967; Coyle, "Triangle Renewal Revision Approved," *CT*, July 31, 1967.

252. MRA minutes, August 15, 1967; Raymond Merle, "U.S. Aide Opposes High Rises in Triangle," *WSJ*, August 15, 1967; Coyle, "Set Appraisal Rules for Triangle," *CT*, August 15, 1967; "Triangle Land Use Left Up to Builders," *WSJ*, August 16, 1967; "MRA Votes Flexible Plan for Triangle Apartments," *CT*, August 16, 1967.

253. MRA minutes, October 12, 1967; Aehl, "Sale of Fifth Triangle Site to Davis-Duehr Clinic Is OKd," *WSJ*, October 13, 1967.

254. "1st Urban Renewal Project Winds Up," *WSJ*, April 14, 1967.

255. "Housing 'Mix' for Elderly Eyed," *WSJ*, January 10, 1967; Coyle, "City Loses Grants for Renewal Projects," *CT*, June 22, 1967; MRA minutes, July 6, 1967; Coyle, "MRA Approves Speed-Up for South Madison Project," *CT*, July 7, 1967; "MRA Told Funds Will Be Available," *CT*, July 24, 1967; MRA minutes, August 9, 1967; "MRA OKs South Madison Project," *CT*, August 10, 1967; "South Side Project Receives Go-Ahead," *WSJ*, October 4, 1967; Zweifel, "MRA to Buy 16 Properties in South Project Location," *CT*, November 7, 1967.

256. Coyle, "City Loses Grants for Renewal Projects," *CT*, June 22, 1967; MRA minutes, July 6, 1967.

257. Coyle, "GNRP Plan Grant Given Federal OK," *CT*, August 29, 1967.

258. Zweifel, "MRA Completes Plan for UW Area Renewal," *CT*, August 30, 1967.

259. "Dimensions & Dividends," Madison City Planning Department, Information Series no. 17, April 1968.

260. Madison Department of Planning, Community Development and Economic Development.

261. Zweifel, "Plumbers on Strike Here," *CT*, April 1, 1967; "6 Unions in City Building Trades Council on Strike," *CT*, April 3, 1967; John E. Mollwitz, "Strike Will Halt Building in City, County Today," *WSJ*, April 3, 1967; "Strike Halts Big Work on Big UW Project," *WSJ*, April 8, 1967; Zweifel, "The Inside Story of Building Strike," *CT*, April 18, 1967.

262. Zweifel, "Striking Sheetmetal Union, Contractors Settle Dispute," *CT*, June 1, 1967; "Pay Raise Ends Plumbers Strike," *WSJ*, June 7, 1967; "Long Strike in Building Work Ends," *WSJ*, June 8, 1967.

263. Coyle, "Madison Building Still Plods Along 30% Below 1965," *CT*, February 15, 1968.

264. "5,000 New Jobs in Area during Year," *WSJ*, January 19, 1968.

265. "Physical Development Plan, Atwood Business District," Midwest Planning And Research, Inc., April 1967.

266. Coyle, "Urban Renewal Program for Atwood Ave. Offered," *CT*, May 8, 1967; Aehl, "Private Effort Held Atwood Ave. Key," *WSJ*, May 9, 1967.

267. Brautigam, "Penney's Shopping Center Gets OK," *CT*, June 23, 1967; "Penney Shop Center Plans a New Concept," *WSJ*, July 11, 1967; "Penny's Center Given Boost," *WSJ*, July 18, 1967; "Penny Co. Completes Purchase," *WSJ*, August 10, 1967.

268. "American Family Mutual to Join City," *WSJ*, May 16, 1967; Aehl, "East Side Hospital Location Annexed," *WSJ*, November 10, 1967; Merle, "City Annexing Action Termed 'Railroading,'" *WSJ*, September 15, 1967.

269. Coyle, "Square 'Shopping Center' Proposed for Mifflin St.," *CT*, September 25, 1967.

270. Merle, "State St. Hotel Planned," *WSJ*, July 20, 1967.

271. "$411,628 Grant Aids Park Plan," *WSJ*, April 14, 1967.

272. Aehl, "Turville Point Bought by City for $895,000," *WSJ*, August 11, 1967; Zweifel, "Turville Point Is Added to City's Parks for $895,000," *CT*, September 1, 1967.

273. Gribble, "Architect Discusses Coliseum; Building Facts Listed," *WSJ*, March 14, 1967; Davis, "Coliseum Will 'Swing' after Easter Dedication," *WSJ*, February 4, 1967; Davis, "It Took Just Five Tranquil Years," *WSJ*, March 26, 1967; William Mullen, "4,000 Help Dedicate Coliseum," *WSJ*, March 27, 1967.

274. Custer, "Reindahl Park, Dedicated Today, Honors Bachelor Who Liked Kids," *CT*, September 13, 1967.

275. Donald K. Davies, "Eastwood to Become 'The Cinema'

with New Looks, New Policy," *WSJ*, October 1, 1967; Rettgen, "New Theater Puts New Life into Atwood Business Area," *CT*, December 20, 1967.

276. "Council Sets Ban on Cycle Parking," *WSJ*, January 27, 1967.

277. Brautigam, "Free Monday Night Shoppers From Parking Meter Fees," *CT*, March 24, 1967.

278. Merle, "No 'Conflict of Interest' Seen for Straub on City Traffic Unit," *WSJ*, May 9, 1967.

279. Newhouse, "Monona Causeway Opens Wednesday," November 19, 1967; "Monona Causeway Gets a Workout," *CT*, November 23, 1967.

280. "City Bus Workers Pick Teamsters," *WSJ*, May 10, 1967; Merle, "Bus Drivers Strike; Better Seek a Ride," *WSJ*, September 20, 1967; Zweifel, "Expect Long Bus Strike," *CT*, September 20, 1967.

281. "Downtown Retail Suffers as Bus Strike Lasts," *CT*, September 27, 1967; Merle, "Bus Strike Hurts Sales for Downtown's Stores," *WSJ*, September 28, 1967.

282. Coyle, "Mayor Gloomy on Chances for Bus Strike Settlement," *CT*, October 1, 1967; Zweifel, "Feinsinger Takes Role in Bus Strike," *CT*, October 4, 1967; Zweifel, "Feinsinger Sets Talks; Hopes He'll Achieve Bus Pact by Midnight," *CT*, October 5, 1967.

283. Merle, "All Day Talks Set in City Bus Strike," *WSJ*, October 6, 1967; "Feinsinger Sure Bus Strike Near End," *CT*, October 6, 1967; Zweifel, "Hopes That Bus Strike End Is Near Dimming, but Meetings Continue," *CT*, October 7, 1967.

284. "Bus Union Accepts Points, Raps Firm," *WSJ*, October 14, 1967; Coyle, "City Told Law Gives It Bus Vote 'Flexibility,'" *CT*, October 14, 1967.

285. Merle, "Bus Firm Weighs Dissolution," *WSJ*, October 19, 1967; Coyle, "Bus Firm to Dissolve, Stockholder City Told; Call Council Meeting," *CT*, October 19, 1967.

286. Merle, "Bus Settlement Fails; Bleak Future Forecast," *WSJ*, October 27, 1967; Coyle, "Seek Bus Lease or Sale," *CT*, October 27, 1967; "Methods Sought to Resume Buses," *WSJ*, October 28, 1967; Merle, "Mayor Sees Hopes for Renewed Talks," *WSJ*, November 1, 1967.

287. Zweifel, "Bus Co. Spurned Merchants' Aid," *CT*, November 2, 1967.

288. Aehl, "Mayor Blasts Bus Firm's 'Obstinacy,'" *WSJ*, November 3, 1967; Zweifel, "Mayor Rips Firm; Cites Monopoly," *CT*, November 3, 1967.

289. "PSC to Hear Views Today on Bus Issue," *WSJ*, November 10, 1967; Zweifel, "Mayor Says Bus Pact May Be Imminent," *CT*, November 10, 1967; Gould, "Angry Audience Rips Bus Firm," *CT*, November 10, 1967.

290. Zweifel, "Bus Settlement Reached; Service Awaits Payment," *CT*, November 11, 1967; Merle, "City Buses May Be Back on Runs Soon," *WSJ*, November 11, 1967; Merle, "Bus Company, Union Sign Pact," *WSJ*, November 12, 1967.

291. Levy, "$65,000 Drive for Bus Firm Given Impetus," *WSJ*, November 13, 1967; Zweifel, "Small Gifts Begin Coming In to Make Up Bus Fund," *CT*, November 13, 1967; Zweifel, "Bus Firm 'Subsidy' Just Dribbles In," *CT*, November 14, 1967; editorial, "Confusion Compounded over the $65,000 Bus Question," *CT*, November 14, 1967; Merle, "Questions Rise Faster Than Special Bus Fund," *WSJ*, November 14, 1967; "City, Bus Firm Try to Stir Up Fund Donations," *CT*, November 15, 1967; editorial, "Bus Strike Picture Is Bleak," *WSJ*, November 16, 1967; Merle, "Mayor Hopes Bus Runs to Return Thanksgiving," *WSJ*, November 16, 1967; "Feinsinger Prods C.C. on Bus Fund," *CT*, November 16, 1967.

292. "25-Cent Bus Fare Approved by PSC," *CT*, November 20, 1967; Merle, "City Buses Resume Runs; Adult Fares Up 5 Cents," *WSJ*, November 21, 1967; Zweifel, "Bus Service Resumption Catches Users by Surprise," *CT*, November 21, 1967; Brautigam, "Outside Firm Will Advise City on Future of Buses," *CT*, November 22, 1967.

293. Zweifel, "Straub Says Bus Company Is 'Libel, Slander' Victim," *CT*, December 13, 1967.

294. "Judge Voids State Agency Order in Case of Barmaid," *WSJ*, January 21, 1967.

295. "For Three Hours Today, World's Christians Pause to Remember," *WSJ*, March 24, 1967; "Good Friday Draws Protesters," *WSJ*, March 25, 1967.

296. Richard W. Jaeger, "For Bishop O'Donnell, a Goodbye in Chicago, Welcome in Madison," *WSJ*, April 25, 1967; Coyle, "Bishop Pledges Program Rooted in Vatican Council," *CT*, April 25, 1967.

297. "Fireworks Are Out at Vilas Park Site," *CT*, April 22, 1967.

298. Keefe, "Madison Says 'Hello' to Lady Bird, Freeman," *WSJ*, September 24, 1967.

299. Rosemary Kendrick, "25 Vets for Peace Join in Ceremony Honoring the Dead," *CT*, November 11, 1967.

300. Louise Marston, "Jimmy Demetral—a Giver—Receives Well-Earned Salute," *WSJ*, November 12, 1967.

301. Hunter, "Nixon in Madison; Is Running Hard," *CT*, November 17, 1967; Selk, "Still a 'Hawk,' Nixon Asks Revised Viet Bid," *WSJ*, November 18, 1967.

302. Havens Wilber, "Camp Indianola Closes after 62 Years of Service," *CT*, December 13, 1967; Levitan, "Lowell Frautschi sets the record straight on Orson Welles' Time in Madison," *Isthmus*, August 8, 2013.

303. Duane Freitag, "DDT Spraying by Copter Proposed," *WSJ*, October 5, 1967; Brautigam, "Parks Unit Backs 'Copter DDT Plan," *CT*, October 5, 1967; Brautigam, "Split Board Backs DDT Spraying," *CT*, October 24, 1967.

304. Brautigam, "11-10 Split Blocks Council Decision on DDT Elm Spray," *CT*, October 25, 1967; Aehl, "DDT Spray Divides

Council," *WSJ*, October 25, 1967; Brautigam, "Council Rejects DDT Use on City Trees," *CT*, October 27, 1967.

305. "Thomas R. Hefty, Ex-President of First National Bank, Dies at 81," *WSJ*, January 19, 1967.

306. "Floyd McBurney Jr., New D.A., 29, Dies," *WSJ*, February 21, 1967; editorial, "The Life of Floyd (Mike) McBurney," *WSJ*, February 22, 1967; "McBurney Inspiration to All Hailed at Funeral Service," *WSJ*, February 24, 1967; Georgie Stebnitz email, January 27, 2017.

307. "Herman Loftsgordon, 84, Civic, Banking Leader, Dies," *CT*, September 14, 1967; "Herman Loftsgordon, Anchor Bank Chairman, Dies at 84," *WSJ*, September 15, 1967; editorial, "Madison Has Lost a Leader in Death of Herman Loftsgordon," *CT*, September 15, 1967; Levitan, *Sesquicentennial History*, 232.

308. "Milton B. Findorff Dies; Chairman of Building Firm," *CT*, September 19, 1967; "Milton B. Findorff, 73, Builder Who Helped City Grow, Dies," *WSJ*, September 20, 1967; "Who We Are," Findorff, https://findorff.com/who-we-are/

309. "Leo T. Kehl, Longtime Local Dance Instructor, Is Dead," *CT*, October 19, 1967.

310. "General Phone Board Chairman Thomas H. Moran Dies in Fall," *WSJ*, October 24, 1967.

311. Ken Adamany interview, October 13, 2017.

312. Mark Ribowsky, *Dreams to Remember: Otis Redding, Stax Records and the Transformation of Southern Soul* (New York: Liveright, 2015), 263; "Find Plane in Lake Silt," *CT*, December 11, 1967.

313. Ribowsky, *Dreams*, 263–264.

314. Robert Gordon, *Respect Yourself: Stax Records and the Soul Explosion* (New York: Bloomsbury, 2013), 166; Doug Moe, "Soul Finale," *Isthmus* 42, no. 19 (December 7, 2017): 13–16.

315. Levy, "Monona Residents Watch in Disbelief," *WSJ*, December 11, 1967.

316. "Redding Plane Didn't Sound Trouble Call," *WSJ*, December 11, 1967.

317. Moe, "45 Years Later, Questions Still Remain over Otis Redding's Plane Crash," *WSJ*, December 10, 2012.

318. "Body of Last Plane Crash Victim Found," *WSJ*, December 21, 1967; Jonathan Gould, *Otis Redding: An Unfinished Life* (New York: Crown Architype, 2017), 437.

319. Gruber, "They Came to Listen—They Heard," *WSJ*, December 11, 1967; Adamany interview, 2017; David Maraniss Facebook message, June 4, 2017.

320. Adamany interview, 2017; *The East Sider*, "Small Planes Don't Kill People," http://willystreetblog.com/wp/2012/12/14/small-planes-dont-kill-people/.

321. Ribowsky, *Dreams*, 260–261.

322. (Sittin' On) The Dock of the Bay," Wikipedia, https://en.wikipedia.org/wiki/(Sittin%27_On)_The_Dock_of_the_Bay#Universal_success.

323. Otis Redding: The NTSB Report," The Death of Rock: The Archive, http://www.angelfire.com/music5/archives/OtisNTSB.html.

1968

1. Steve Reiner, "U Blacks, Sewell, Spar on Service," *DC*, April 6, 1968.

2. Owen Coyle and Whitney Gould, "Black Students Say Non-Violence Died With King," *CT*, April 5, 1968.

3. Rob Gordon, "Thousands Line Bascom to Mourn Death of King," *DC*, April 6, 1968.

4. Dennis Cassano, "Somber UW March Tells Reaction Here," *WSJ*, April 6, 1968.

5. Sewell OH #0101.

6. Sewell OH #0101.

7. Marvin Levy, "2,500 Silently Trek for King," *WSJ*, April 8, 1968; "Schools Told to Use Own Judgment on King Funeral," *CT*, April 8, 1968.

8. Equal Opportunities Commission, "Report to the Common Council as Directed by Resolution no. 18,140, August 22, 1968," April 24, 1969.

9. Robert Pfefferkorn, "Youth, Alderman Tell EOC of Disturbance," *WSJ*, September 24, 1968; Dennis Sandage, "EOC Hears of Breese Stevens Incident," *CT*, September 24, 1968; Pfefferkorn, "Racial Tensions Are Told," *WSJ*, September 26, 1968.

10. Jim Cowan, "Officer Denies Tension before Stevens Dance," *CT*, October 3, 1968.

11. Pfefferkorn, "Police Tell EOC Arrests Justified," *WSJ*, October 10, 1968.

12. Eugene Williams interview, August 1, 2017.

13. Rosemary Kendrick, "Breese Stevens Dance Clash Brings Warning from Equality Unit Chief," *CT*, August 5, 1968.

14. EOC minutes, August 13, 1968; Kendrick, "Disagreement on Police Race Bias Marks Hearing," *CT*, August 7, 1968; William Luellen, "Rev. Wright Is Commended for His Emergency Actions," *WSJ*, August 14, 1968.

15. Dave Zweifel, "Breese Dance Probe Delayed until After Council Is Consulted," *CT*, August 14, 1968.

16. Kendrick, "Leading Negro Citizens Hit Police on Racism," *CT*, August 14, 1968.

17. Irv Kreisman, "Madison Police Angrily Deny Claims of Racial Prejudice," *CT*, August 15, 1968.

18. George Mitchell, "State Official, Other Negroes, Accuse Police of 'Racism,'" *WSJ*, August 15, 1968.

19. Editorial, "Bigotry in Police Department Brings Inevitable Trouble," *CT*, April 15, 1968.

20. Zweifel, "Alderman May Try to Kill Special Quiz of Breese

Stevens Fight," *CT*, August 20, 1968; Zweifel, "Council Delays Police Racism Inquiry," *CT*, August 21, 1968.

21. EOC minutes, August 22, 1968.

22. Zweifel, "Council Lets Equality Unit Study Police Racism Issue," *CT*, August 23, 1968; Raymond Merle, "EOC Will Conduct a Probe of Racism," *WSJ*, August 23, 1968.

23. Sandage, "Chief's Report Sets Stage for Hearing," *CT*, September 14, 1968; John M. Keefe, "Madison Police Deny Fracas Misdeeds," *WSJ*, September 15, 1968.

24. Sandage, "Contradicts Police on Dance Arrests," *CT*, September 26, 1968.

25. Keefe, "'Blown-Up' Incident Responsible for Added Tensions, Chief Says," *WSJ*, September 18, 1968.

26. Sandage, "EOC Probe Hears Bias Charges," *CT*, September 20, 1968; Keefe, "Bigotry Is Here, EOC Told," *WSJ*, September 20, 1968.

27. Sandage, "Police Leader Shuns EOC Inquiry," *CT*, September 17, 1968.

28. Sandage, "Alderman Moves to End Equal Opportunities Group," *CT*, November 11, 1968.

29. Cowan, "EOC Backed Almost Unanimously," *CT*, November 13, 1968.

30. *Report,* Equal Opportunities Commission, "Report to the Common Council as Directed by Resolution no. 18,140, August 22, 1968," April 24, 1969. 93–94.

31. David Charlton, "Vast Racial Bias in City Charged," *WSJ*, January 29, 1968.

32. Coyle, "Minorities Slow to Apply for Vacant City Positions," *CT*, January 30, 1968; John T. Aehl, "City Gains Negro Families," *WSJ*, April 9, 1968.

33. John Gruber, "It's No Joke, Gregory Warns," *WSJ*, February 17, 1968.

34. Aehl, "Rights Unit Lists 18 Racial Conflict Cases," *WSJ*, March 29, 1968.

35. "For the First Time, Negro Seeks Seat on City Council," *WSJ*, March 27, 1968; Aehl, "Voters Dump Four City Councilmen," *WSJ*, April 3, 1968.

36. Kreisman, "Madison Police Angrily Deny Claims of Racial Prejudice," *CT*, August 15, 1968.

37. "Job Opportunity Draws Crowd," *WSJ*, April 18, 1968.

38. "ESBMA Ends Teen Dances after Fight," *WSJ*, May 8, 1968.

39. EOC minutes, April 22, 1968; "Hire Minority Groups, City Employers Urged," *WSJ*, May 22, 1968.

40. "113 City Employers Pledge Non-Discrimination," *CT*, September 25, 1968.

41. "Program Tells Story of Madison's Subtle Race Bias," *CT*, May 27, 1968.

42. "Urban League Head Can't Find Housing," *WSJ*, September 10, 1968; Nelson Cummings interview, 2017.

43. Gary Rettgen, "Police Study Reports of Negro-White Upsets Here," *CT*, September 23, 1968.

44. "One Youth Given Term for His Part in Cross-Burning," *WSJ*, December 10, 1968.

45. EOC minutes, January 16, 1968.

46. Aehl, "Full-Time Rights Unit Director Backed," *WSJ*, March 20, 1968.

47. Aehl, "Rights Unit Director Approved by Council," *WSJ*, April 12, 1968; EOC minutes, April 22, 1968.

48. "James C. Wright Named Executive Director of EOC," *CT*, May 18, 1968.

49. Gould, "Crowd Cheers Ali, Not His Message," *CT*, April 27, 1968; Lawrence Stein, "Muhammad Ali Calls for Creation of Black State," *DC*, April 27, 1968; Merle, "Pugilist Poet Preacher Muhammad Has Stage," *WSJ*, April 27, 1968.

50. Special Assignment Officer's Report, Madison Police Department, April 26, 1968.

51. Monica Deignan, "YMCA Project TEACH Hits Racism in Wisconsin Area," *DC*, April 26, 1968.

52. Rena Steinzor, "Students Pose Plans to Pres. Harrington," *DC*, May 4, 1968.

53. "Sewell Names Faculty Unit on Race Relations," *CT*, May 17, 1968.

54. BOR minutes, May 17, 1968; Matt Pommer, "Regents Back U.W. Plan to Assist Disadvantaged," *CT*, May 17, 1968.

55. Roger A. Gribble, "No Sale, Regents Reply to Protest," *WSJ*, May 18, 1968; Jay Wind, "Board Keeps Chase Stock; Lifts Living Regulations," *DC*, May 18, 1968.

56. BOR minutes, May 17, 1968; Pommer, "UW Students Hold Seven-Hour Sit-In," *CT*, May 18, 1968; Hugh Cox, "350 Ask Stock Sale; Take Administration Building," *DC*, May 18, 1968.

57. Richard Brautigam, "Fire Bomb Sets South Hall Blaze, U. Records Damaged," *CT*, May 18, 1968; "UW Officials Deplore Bombing," *WSJ*, May 19, 1968.

58. "UW Protesters Rally Today," *WSJ*, May 20, 1968; David Greiling and Mike Gondek, "Student Protesters Polarize as Tactics Become Confused," *DC*, May 21, 1968; "Protester Cohen Returns for Rally," *WSJ*, May 21, 1968.

59. Pommer, "U.W. Meets Some Demands of Blacks," *CT*, May 20, 1968; Gruber, "Regents Spurn Protesters' Bid," *WSJ*, May 21, 1968.

60. BOR minutes, June 14, 1968; "Negro Educator Joins UW Administration," *Wisconsin Alumnus* 69, no. 9 (June 1968): 6.

61. "New Center to Encourage Afro-American Programs," *DC*, November 8, 1968.

62. "Greeks Plan First Black Homecoming," *DC*, October 31, 1968.

63. Annual Report, Special Program of Tutorial and Financial Assistance, Division of Student Affairs, November 1968, Chancellor Edwin Young papers, University Archives; Wind, "Aid to

Disadvantaged Students Increases, Doyle Program Shows Major Development," *DC*, November 7, 1968.

64. Gribble, "Blacks' Advisor Warns on Racial Gulf at UW," *WSJ*, November 14, 1968.

65. Robert H. Atwell to Edwin Young, November 14, 1968; Young Papers, series 4/20/1, University Archives.

66. Annual Report, Special Program of Tutorial and Financial Assistance, Division of Student Affairs, November 1968, Special note, Chancellor Edwin Young papers, University Archives; "UW Students Seek Black Curriculum," *CT*, November 16, 1968.

67. "Black Nonstudent Arrested in Rathskeller Altercation," *DC*, November 19, 1968.

68. Steven Reiner, "Food Boycott Closes Union Rath," *DC*, November 20, 1968; Allen Swerdlowe, "Students Boycott; Union Takes Loss," *DC*, November 21, 1968.

69. "Boycott Continues at UW Union; Food Sales Down," *CT*, November 21, 1968; R. Lovelace, "Food Service Discontinued in Union; Rath, Cafeteria Take Third Day Loss," *DC*, November 22, 1968; Ted Crabb email, October 31, 2017.

70. Minutes, Special Meeting, Special Scholarship Advisory Committee, November 20, 1968; Edwin Young papers, UA; Gilbert, "Their Time & Their Legacy," 148–149.

71. "Oshkosh Rampage Jails 100," *WSJ*, November 22, 1968; Graze, "Black Students Expelled at Oshkosh after Protest," *DC*, November 23, 1968; Michael David Rosen, OH #1383, digital audio file, University Archives and Records Management Services, Madison, Wisconsin; Jeffrey Schachner, OH #1384, digital audio file, University Archives and Records Management Services, Madison, Wisconsin; Schachner email, October 31, 2017.

72. Annual Report, Special Program of Tutorial and Financial Assistance, Division of Student Affairs, November 1968, Special Note.

73. Testimony, H. Edwin Young, *Joint Committee to Study Disruptions at the University of Wisconsin*, April 30, 1969, series 1810 MAD 2M/23/D5, WHSA.

74. Gene Wells, "Blacks Stop Classes, Traffic," *DC*, November 26, 1968; Gilbert, "Their Time & Their Legacy," 122–124.

75. Archibald O. Haller to Edwin Young, December 9, 1968; Edwin Young papers, University Archives; minutes, Special Scholarship Advisory Committee, Special Meeting, November 22, 1968, "Proposal to the University of Wisconsin from the Black People's Alliance"; "Black Students Submit Demands," *DC*, November 26, 1968.

76. Ron Legro, "Black Students Confuse Library," *DC*, November 27, 1968; Gribble, "UW Permits Blacks to Make Up Exams," *WSJ*, November 27, 1968.

77. Ruth B. Doyle, interviewed by Joyce Erdman, 1991, OH #0216, digital audio file, University Archives and Records Management Services, Madison, Wisconsin; *Annual Report*, special note.

78. George Koconis, "Proctor Panel Backs Black Demands," *DC*, October 3, 1968; Pommer, "More Black Students, Staff Urged by U.W. Committee," *CT*, December 3, 1968.

79. Ruth Doyle to Chancellor Young, November 16, 1968, Edwin Young papers, University Archives.

80. Glenn Miller, "UW to Hear Black Grievances," *WSJ*, November 28, 1968.

81. Patricia Rogeberg Facebook message, October 22, 2017; David Maraniss interview, August 2017.

82. Miller, "UW to Hear Black Grievances," *WSJ*, November 28, 1968.

83. "Football Problems Alone Led to Boycott of Banquet," *CT*, November 27, 1968; Tom Butler, "Boycott Is Directed at Coaches," *WSJ*, November 28, 1968.

84. Bob Greene, "Race Problem Hurt Badger Grid Team," *CT*, November 27, 1968.

85. Barry Tempkin, "Black Gridders Speak to Board," *DC*, December 4, 1968; Tempkin, "Board Discloses Grid Complaints," *DC*, December 5, 1968.

86. Miller, "Coatta, Whites Defend Coaches," *WSJ*, December 5, 1968.

87. "Felker Resigns as U.W. Football Aide," *WSJ*, December 6, 1968; Pommer, "5-Year Pledge to Ritcherson Told," *CT*, December 6, 1968; "Felker Levels Blast," *DC*, December 7, 1968; Steve Klein and Barry Temkin, "Felker Resignation Adds Fuel to Fire," *DC*, December 7, 1968.

88. BOR minutes, December 6, 1968; Miller, "Coatta Stays, Regents Pledge Aide," *WSJ*, December 7, 1968; Pommer, "Coatta Will Stay; Aides in Jeopardy," *CT*, December 7, 1968; Pommer, "UW Athletics Cash Crisis Is Told Regents," *CT*, December 6, 1968.

89. "Cohen Volunteers for His Jail Term," *WSJ*, January 6, 1968; Sewell OH #0101.

90. Stuart Warren, "SDS Threatens to Protest Return of Dow Recruiters," *DC*, February 9, 1968.

91. Pommer, "Sewell Delays Dow, Service Interviews," *CT*, February 12, 1968.

92. BOR minutes, February 16, 1968; Gribble, "UW Regents Criticize Sewell for Delaying Dow Interviews," *WSJ*, February 16, 1968; Kendrick, "Dow Visit Delay Draws Regents' Fire," *CT*, February 17, 1968.

93. "UW Student, 25, Guilty of Disorderly Conduct," *WSJ*, February 17, 1968.

94. Gruber, "UW Group Wants Dow Interviews," *WSJ*, February 28, 1968.

95. "Stark Charged on Dow Protest; Case Postponed," *WSJ*, March 6, 1968; Harold Sours, "Evan Stark: Alive and Well at Minn.," *DC*, October 18, 1968; Evan Stark email, August 21, 2017.

96. J. Jacob Wind, "Sewell Reschedules Chemical Interviews," *DC*, March 16, 1968; Pommer, "Dow Talks End with Only Minor

Trouble," *CT*, March 30, 1968; Steinzor, "Relative Peace Greets Dow's Return," *DC*, April 2, 1968; Pommer, "Handful Protest Peacefully as Navy, Marines Recruit," *CT*, April 11, 1968; Sewell OH #0101.

97. Pommer, "Anti-Dow Demonstration Winds Up Peacefully at U," *CT*, November 8, 1968; Steve Twin, "Dow Protesters Seek Neutral U," *DC*, November 8, 1968.

98. Brautigam, "War Issue on City Ballot," *CT*, January 27, 1968.

99. Zweifel, "Anti-War Vote Is Loser by 7,000 Margin," *CT*, April 3, 1968; "In Loss, Viet Foe Still Sees Victory," *WSJ*, April 4, 1968.

100. Cox, "Soglin Wins Ward Eight," *DC*, April 3, 1968.

101. Pommer, "Freshman Group to Try ROTC Challenge," *CT*, September 12, 1968; Kendrick, "Academic Year's First Demonstration Proves to Be Spirited but Peaceful," *CT*, September 14, 1968.

102. Steinzor, "Freshmen Continue Disruption of ROTC," *DC*, September 17, 1968; Monica Deignan, "Senate Bill Passed to End ROTC Requirement," *DC*, September 20, 1968.

103. Steinzor, "Women Students Disrupt ROTC Meeting," *DC*, September 24, 1968.

104. Kendrick, "Women Invade Protest Movement against ROTC," *CT*, September 20, 1968.

105. "End Nearly All Grad Student Deferments," *CT*, February 16, 1968.

106. Pommer, "U. Group Split 8-6 on Wartime Job Interviews," *CT*, March 5, 1968.

107. Rettgen, "Booing Shortens U. Speech by Freeman," *CT*, March 22, 1968; Sewell OH #0101.

108. John Patrick Hunter, "With Rocky Out of Race, Nixon Shifts Strategy," *CT*, March 22, 1968; "COPE Rejects All 'Doves' in City Council Races," *CT*, March 22, 1968.

109. Pommer, "Only Handful at UW Join Nationwide War Protest," *CT*, April 26, 1968.

110. Merle, "Pugilist Poet Preacher Muhammad Has Stage," *WSJ*, April 27, 1968.

111. Mike Gondek, "Student Strike Ends after Quiet Protest," *DC*, April 27, 1968.

112. John E. Mollwitz, "Peace March Is Picnic-Like," *WSJ*, April 28, 1968.

113. Hunter, "300 War Foes Here Splatter Gen. Hershey Car with Eggs," *CT*, May 15, 1968; James D. Selk, "UW Protesters Fling Eggs at Hershey Car," *WSJ*, May 16, 1968; Cassano, "Hershey Handles Protest in Stride," *WSJ*, May 16, 1968; editorial, "Egg-Pelting Was Disgraceful," *WSJ*, May 16, 1968; editorial, "The Deplorable Aspects of the Anti-Hershey Protest," *CT*, May 16, 1968.

114. "UW's Protesters Lose in High Court," *WSJ*, Mary 21, 1968; "Anti-War Group Fined," *WSJ*, May 29, 1968.

115. Pommer, "War Foes Stage Silent Protest at U.W. Exercises," *CT*, June 10, 1968.

116. Gondek, "Tactic Change Seen in Merger of WDRU-SDS," *DC*, September 19, 1968; Pommer, "SDS, Draft Resisters on Campus Merge," *CT*, September 19, 1968.

117. Julie Kennedy, "Justice Thurgood Marshall Speaks Here; Applauded, Heckled by 1,000 in Union," *DC*, September 24, 1968.

118. Rettgen, "Set Fire at State Draft Office Here," *CT*, October 1, 1968.

119. Steinzor, "Freshmen Veto Mandatory ROTC," *DC*, October 8, 1968

120. CAC minutes, September 9, 1968; Holly Dunlop, "New Parade Ordinance Suggested to Council," *WSJ*, September 10, 1968; Steinzor, "City Council Rules Curbs on Parades," *DC*, September 27, 1968; Steinzor, "Parade Permit Granted; Mayor Reverses Police," *DC*, October 9, 1968; "War Protesters Plan Camp Randall March," *WSJ*, October 11,1968; Gondek, "3000 Hear Ex-GI's Hit Vietnam War," *DC*, October 15, 1968.

121. Christy Sinks, "UW Faculty OKs Orderly Protest Rule," *WSJ*, February 4, 1968.

122. BOR minutes, April 19, 1968.

123. BOR minutes, July 19, 1968; Pommer, "Tough Discipline Code Set for U.W.," July 19, 1968.

124. BOR minutes, September 6, 1968; Pommer, "Non-Student Class Ban Gets Unanimous Regent OK," *CT*, September 6, 1968.

125. Hunter, "Knowles Echoes Rightist Attacks on U.W. Chiefs," *CT*, October 16, 1968; Selk, "Knowles Asks Firmer UW Discipline," *WSJ*, October 17, 1968; John Wyngaard, "Knowles Reflects Mood over UW," *WSJ*, October 27, 1968.

126. Stephen Koehl, "Chancellor Vows Action against Obstruction," *WSJ*, November 3, 1968.

127. Gondek, "Students Overflow Theater, Vote Down Building Coup," *DC*, November 6, 1968.

128. Kreisman, "Doyle Curbs U.W. Misconduct Rule," *CT*, December 14, 1968.

129. "Funeral Rights Friday for Edgar Gerlach, Viet Victim," *CT*, February 7, 1968; "Paul Edgar Gerlach," The Virtual Wall® Vietnam Veterans Memorial, www.virtualwall.org/dg /GerlachPE01a.htm.

130. "Bruce Knox Is Viet Victim at Age 20," *CT*, March 11, 1968; "Medals Awarded to Parents of Bruce Knox, Viet Victim," *CT*, September 17, 1968; "Bruce Neal Knox," The Virtual Wall® Vietnam Veterans Memorial, www.virtualwall.org/dk /KnoxBN01a.htm.

131. "Thomas Blaha, 19, City Marine, Killed in Vietnam," *CT*, February 16, 1968; "Thomas John Blaha," The Virtual Wall® Vietnam Veterans Memorial, www.virtualwall.org/db /BlahaTJ01a.htm.

132. "Lawrence Herfel Killed in Vietnam," *CT*, February 26, 1968; "Laurence John Herfel," The Virtual Wall® Vietnam Veterans Memorial, www.virtualwall.org/dh/HerfelLJ01a.htm.

133. "Pfc. Meysembourg Killed in Action," *WSJ*, March 18, 1968; Michael Meysembourg interview, October 17, 2017.

134. "Sp. 4 Mazursky Rites Tuesday," *WSJ*, May 13, 1968; "Bernard Richard Mazursky," The Virtual Wall® Vietnam Veterans Memorial, www.virtualwall.org/dm/MazurskyBR01a.htm; Beverly Mazursky Claudy Facebook message, June 28, 1968.

135. "Draft Aide's Son Killed in Vietnam," *CT*, August 12, 1968; "James Alexander Leahy," The Virtual Wall® Vietnam Veterans Memorial, www.virtualwall.org/dl/LeahyJA01a.htm.

136. "Harry B. Hambleton III Dies of War Combat Injuries," *CT*, September 23, 1968; "Harry B. Hambleton, III," The Virtual Wall ® Vietnam Veterans Memorial, www.virtualwall.org/dh/HambletonHB01a.htm.

137. "City Family's Christmas: Father Is Killed in Vietnam," *CT*, December 20, 1968; "Dan Michael Bennett," The Virtual Wall ® Vietnam Veterans Memorial, www.virtualwall.org/db/BennettDM01a.htm; Dan Michael Bennett Jr. email, October 11, 2017.

138. Coyle, "Metzner Not Appealing Monona Suit," *CT*, January 10, 1968.

139. "Ex-Mayors Rip Monona Plan," *WSJ*, January 19, 1968.

140. Coyle, "Law Park Site Gets Auditorium Unit OK," *CT*, February 15, 1968; Brautigam, "Council OKs Law Park Site; Asks 1st Auditorium Plan," *CT*, February 23, 1968; Aehl, "The Anatomy of an Auditorium," *WSJ*, February 26, 1968.

141. "Auditorium Plans Sent to Council," *CT*, August 7, 1968; Brautigam, "Auditorium Schematic Plan Approved," *WSJ*, August 9, 1968.

142. Brautigam, "Plan Unit OK's Designs of Auditorium, Monona Basin," *CT*, August 5, 1968.

143. Gould, "A Stunning, Circular Wright Structure Will Join Lake and Landscape," *CT*, September 9, 1968; Merle, "Peters Says $5.3 Million Can Build City Auditorium," *WSJ*, September 10, 1968; Mollenhoff and Hamilton, *Monona Terrace*, 181.

144. Merle, "City Takes Auditorium Another Step," *WSJ*, September 13, 1968.

145. "3,790 to Get Degrees at U. Commencement," *CT*, May 10, 1968.

146. "UW Classes Begin with Increased Enrollments," *WSJ*, September 16, 1968.

147. "Dances Highlight 1968 Homecoming Festivities," *DC*, November 1, 1968.

148. *Wisconsin Alumnus* 69, no. 9 (June 1968): 8–13.

149. Bill Hoel, "Pass-Fail, Doors, Bill Cosby Here?" *DC*, January 5, 1968.

150. Jeannette Lee and Maxine Woodford, "Former U Student Back, at the Factory," *DC*, January 12, 1968.

151. Pommer, "Sewell 'Distressed' by Community Hostility to Students, University," *CT*, January 24, 1968.

152. "Kauffman Leaving UW to Take Rhode Island Post," *CT*, February 1, 1968; Sewell OH #0101; Pommer, "Regents OK Post of Vice-Chancellor," *CT*, April 19, 1968.

153. "A Full House of Critics Listed for U. Symposium," *CT*, January 27, 1968.

154. Jerry Liska, "Franklin Unanimous Big 10 Pick," *CT*, March 6, 1968; "Franklin Is Big Ten Rebounding King," *DC*, March 26, 1968; Bonnie Ryan, "Joe Franklin: The Fire Burned Inside," *CT*, March 11, 1968.

155. Levy, "Survival Chances Slim, Joan Baez Says," *WSJ*, March 10, 1968; "Joan Baez Captivates Young, Old," *CT*, March 11, 1968.

156. Gribble, "H. Edwin Young Will Return to Campus as Vice President," *WSJ*, March 16, 1968; Sewell OH #0101.

157. Gribble, "Faculty Lifts Rules on UW Co-eds' Hours," *WSJ*, April 2, 1968; Susan Fondiler, "Faculty Votes to Abolish Hours," *DC*, April 2, 1968.

158. "'Pot' and 'Pill' Legalization Favored in Campus Voting," *CT*, April 5, 1968.

159. BOR minutes, exhibit F, April 19, 1968; "Co-ed Hours, Student Disciplining Deferred," *WSJ*, April 20, 1968.

160. Reiner, "Conference on Afro-American Culture," *DC*, May 3, 1968; David Greiling and Ira Zarov, "Madison Afro-American Arts Conference Discusses US and African Black Art," *DC*, May 7, 1968.

161. "Magic Sam's Last Stand," *DC*, May 10, 1968.

162. BOR minutes, May 17, 1968; Pommer, "End of Co-ed Curfew Approved by Regents," *CT*, May 17, 1968.

163. "City Girl Appears in Hippie Film 'Revolution,'" *CT*, May 17, 1968; Gould, "Hippie 'Revolution' Repulses," *WSJ*, May 17, 1968; Tracy Nelson Facebook Messenger exchange, October 17, 2017.

164. "Lightnin' Hopkins," *DC*, May 21, 1968.

165. "Few Students Really Protest," *WSJ*, October 7, 1969.

166. Hunter, "'Lindsay for President,' Shouted Here," *CT*, July 13, 1968.

167. Rob Gordon, "Goldberg's History Course Questioned by Class," *DC*, September 19, 1968.

168. Bury St. Edmund, "B.B. King: The Blues," *DC*, September 21, 1968.

169. John W. English, "Belafonte Charms His Audience but Gospel Singers Turn 'Em On," *WSJ*, September 28, 1968.

170. Keefe, "McCarthy Vows to Keep 'Dream,'" *WSJ*, October 21, 1968.

171. Kendrick, "Gregory Pushes for Write-in Vote," *CT*, October 23, 1968; Gondek, "Gregory Sees '68 Election as Death of 2-Party System," *DC*, October 23, 1968; Gay Leslie, "Gregory Shows His Independence Here," *WSJ*, October 23, 1968.

172. Peter Greenberg, "Cleaver Cancels Speech; May Speak Here in Nov.," *DC*, October 24, 1968.

173. "Madison's First Blues Festival," *DC*, October 25, 1968.

174. St. Edmund, "Full Fish and Quicksilver," *DC*, November 9, 1968.

175. "Campus," *DC*, November 1, 1968.

176. Deignan, "Freedom Not End in Itself, Black Milw. Alderman Says," *DC*, November 13, 1968.

177. Lynne Ellestad, "A Beautiful Tenseness Marks Lloyd Quartet," *WSJ*, November 18, 1968.

178. Carmen Elsner, "Violinst Pinchas Zuckerman, 20, Could Become New Isaac Stern," *WSJ*, November 23, 1968.

179. Stein, "Moynihan: Internal Political Violence Threatens Freedom," *DC*, December 10, 1968.

180. Pommer, "Name Robert Knight U. Basketball Coach," *CT*, April 24, 1968; Glenn Miller, "Bob Knight of Army Named Wisconsin Basketball Coach," *WSJ*, April 25, 1968; Bonnie Ryan, "Powless Is Cage Coach as Knight Rejects Bid," *CT*, April 27, 1968; Brautigam, "Remington Denies Alibis for Knight," *CT*, April 27, 1968; BOR minutes, May 17, 1968, Exhibit H.

181. "Chancellor Sewell Resigns after Disquieting Year," *Wisconsin Alumnus* 69, no. 9 (June 1968): 5; Pommer, "Courage Marked Sewell's Term," *CT*, July 1, 1968; Harrington OH #0135; Editorial, "Bill Sewell—The Victim of the Irrational Right and Left," *CT*, July 2, 1968; Brautigam, "Protest Problems Plagued Sewell Era," *CT*, June 29, 1968; Cronon and Jenkins, *The University of Wisconsin*, 468.

182. Pommer, "Young Chosen U. Chancellor," *CT*, September 13, 1968.

183. Harrington OH #0135; Sewell OH #0101.

184. Harrington OH #0135; "Young Wants to Be Chancellor, Not Policeman," *WSJ*, September 14, 1968.

185. Joe Lagodney, "Use of Illegal Drugs on Campus Goes Sky-High," *DC*, March 13, 1968; Pommer, "UW Will Cooperate to Halt Drug Use," *CT*, October 4, 1968.

186. Dieckmann, "Crackdown Started on City Drug Traffic," *WSJ*, October 1, 1968; "City Drive on Drug Users and Sales Has Nabbed 26," *WSJ*, October 16, 1968.

187. Dieckmann, "First 6 Face Judge in Drug Crackdown," *WSJ*, October 2, 1968.

188. Sandage, "Festge Lauds Cops on Drug Raid; Hits U.," *CT*, October 2, 1968.

189. Peter Abbott, "State Drug Prober Boasts Aim Is 'Direct Attack' at U," *DC*, October 4, 1968.

190. "FBI Men Criticize Police Drug Tales," *CT*, October 4, 1968.

191. BOR minutes, October 4, 1968; Gribble, "Move to Reinstate Co-ed Hours Defeated by UW Regents 7-2," *WSJ*, October 5, 1968.

192. Richard W. Jaeger, "Teen Drug Use Here Appears to Be on Rise," *WSJ*, October 5, 1968.

193. Sandage, "Don't Fuss about Legality in Drug Cases, DA Says," *CT*, October 11, 1968; Zweifel, "Drug Prosecution Row Splits District Attorney and Aide," *CT*, October 12, 1968.

194. "Froelich Fears UW 'Destruction,'" *WSJ*, October 12, 1968; Pommer, "Drugs Not Dorm Problem, Harrington Tells Knowles," *CT*, October 24, 1968.

195. Mitchell, "Madison Drug Problem Labeled 'Out of Control,'" *WSJ*, October 17, 1968; editorial, "You Bet Our Drug Problem Is 'Completely Out of Control,'" *CT*, October 18, 1968.

196. BOR minutes, December 6, 1968; Pommer, "Non-Student Use of Union Being Cut, Chancellor Says," *CT*, December 7, 1968.

197. BOR minutes, November 1, 1968; Pommer, "Regents Threaten Action against the Daily Cardinal," *CT*, November 1, 1968.

198. Peter Greenberg and Tim Greene, "Regents Charge Cardinal with Obscene Language," *DC*, November 2, 1968.

199. Editorial, "Up against the Wal, Re...ts," *DC*, November 5, 1968; Pommer, "Cardinal Defies Regents with 4-Letter Literature," *CT*, November 5, 1968.

200. Len Fleischer, "Regent Answers Cardinal, Threatens to Expel Editors," *DC*, November 7, 1968.

201. BOR minutes, December 6, 1968; Pommer, "Regents Study Ban on Daily Cardinal Use of Campus Facilities," *CT*, December 7, 1968.

202. Greenberg, "Dean Young Selected as V-Chancellor; Regents Call Cardinal Reply 'Retaliatory,'" *DC*, December 7, 1968; Hantschel, *It Doesn't End With Us*, 61–64.

203. Doug Moe, "Peter Pan, Michael Douglas and Murder," *WSJ*, June 9, 2014; Stuart Gordon email, July 7, 2017.

204. Lagodney, "Legal Scare Drops Curtain on 'Peter Pan,'" *DC*, September 25, 1968; Roy Chustek, "'Peter Pan' Lives On; Controversial Play Will Be Seen by DA," *DC*, September 26, 1968.

205. "Conrad Says Madison Not Ready for Nudes on Stage," *CT*, October 1, 1968.

206. James Oset, "'Pan' Ruled Obscene; Show Staged Anyway," *WSJ*, October 2, 1968.

207. Steve Twin and Roy Chustek, "'Peter Pan' Performed Twice Despite DA's Threat to Prosecute," *DC*, October 2, 1968; Stuart Gordon email, July 7, 2017.

208. "Murder is Everywhere: Ten Renowned Crime Writers Blog from Different Corners of the World," Murder is Everywhere Blog, http://murderiseverywhere.blogspot.com/2013/07/felony-nudity-peter-pan.html#comment-form.

209. Robert Skloot, "A Play of Lost Childhood," *DC*, October 3, 1968.

210. Frank Ryan, "Complaint Signed against Producer of Nude 'Pan,'" *CT*, October 5, 1968.

211. BOR minutes, October 4, 1968; Pommer, "No Nudes Good News for U.," *CT*, October 4, 1968.

212. "'Pan' Producer Is Charged in Court," *WSJ*, October 8, 1968.

213. "Janesville Co-ed Accused of Being 'Peter Pan' Nude," *CT*, October 12, 1968.

214. Jaeger, "'Peter Pan' Pair Face Same Charge," *WSJ*, November 20, 1968; Kreisman, "'Peter Pan' Charge Is Dropped by Boll," *CT*, December 3, 1968.

215. Gordon, "Remembering My Father-in-Law," *Talkhouse*, May 2, 2016.

216. "Kenneth Greenquist Dies; U.W. Regents' President," *CT*, April 5, 1968; "Kenneth L. Greenquist, 58, UW Regent President, Dies," *WSJ*, April 6, 1968; BOR minutes, April 19, 1968; Pommer, Charge GOP 'Takeover' of UW Regent Control," *CT*, April 19, 1968; Pommer, "The New Board of Regents: How Far Right Will It Go?" *CT*, April 29, 1968.

217. "Prof. Rudolph Langer Dies; World Mathematics Leader," *CT*, March 12, 1968.

218. "Ex-Gov. Rennebohm Dies," *CT*, October 15, 1968; "Oscar Rennebohm, 79, State, Civic Leader, Dies," *WSJ*, October 16, 1968; "Oscar Rennebohm: 1889-1968," *Wisconsin Alumnus* 70, no. 2 (November 1968): 31.

219. "Character Counts, Richter Tells East Grads," "West Grads Told to Relate to Our Turbulent Society," "Call for Faith at La Follette," "DeZonia Urges Grads to Preserve Freedoms," "Individual Answers Urged by Central High Seniors," all *CT*, June 5, 1968.

220. Gribble, "34,000 Attend Madison Schools," *WSJ*, September 21, 1968.

221. Gribble, "$3 Million in New Schools Open in Fall," *WSJ*, June 29, 1968.

222. William Luellen, "School Bells Ring Out on Tuesday," *WSJ*, September 1, 1968.

223. Pommer, "2.3% in Schools from Minorities," *CT*, October 8, 1968.

224. Kreisman, "Judge Forbids Suspension of Mustached Pupil," *CT*, January 2, 1968.

225. "All Quiet at West High; No 'Connections' in Sight," *CT*, January 16, 1968.

226. Pommer, "Technical College Name Is Official," *CT*, January 23, 1968.

227. Pommer," John Muir School Opening Delayed," *CT*, December 18, 1967.

228. Gribble, "Proposed Student Code Is Criticized at Hearing," *WSJ*, February 6, 1968.

229. Editorial, "School Board Ignores PTA in Adopting Conduct Code," *CT*, February 27, 1968; "Shaving Rule Splits School Board," *CT*, January 12, 1968; Gribble, "Board Adopts New School Code," *WSJ*, February 27, 1968; Gribble, "School Grooming Code to Get Review," *WSJ*, August 13, 1968.

230. Mitchell, "Fewer Pupils Mean Trouble at Longfellow, Board Told," *WSJ*, April 2, 1968.

231. Pommer, "Yelinek, DeZonia Join School Board," *CT*, April 3, 1968.

232. "Schools Told to Use Own Judgment on King Funeral," *CT*, April 8, 1968.

233. Gribble, "Better Negro History Promised in Schools," *WSJ*, May 21, 1968.

234. Pommer, "Massive Rights Education Urged on School Board," *CT*, May 22, 1968.

235. CAC minutes, June 10, 1968; "SDS Is Pictured as Trying for High School Rebellion," *WSJ*, June 11, 1968; "High School Group Denies Tie with SDS," *CT*, June 11, 1968; Jonathan Lipp email, October 20, 2017.

236. Pommer, "City Schools Unable to Attract Negro Teachers," *CT*, June 17, 1968; Brautigam, "School Board, NAACP Near Agreement," *CT*, July 9, 1968.

237. "City Teacher Unit Names Secretary," *WSJ*, May 31, 1968.

238. Gribble, "Rights Backers Ask School Aide," *WSJ*, August 10, 1968; Brautigam, "School Board OKs Relations Director," *CT*, August 13, 1968.

239. Pommer, "City Schools Face Critical Need for Substitute Teachers," *CT*, August 16, 1968.

240. "Ritchie Cites Top Problems: Activism and Building Needs," *WSJ*, August 19, 1968.

241. "MHA Will Reserve Units for Migrants," *WSJ*, January 9, 1968.

242. "Triangle Area Apartments Get U.S. Go-Ahead," *WSJ*, February 3, 1968.

243. "Norvell Named MRA Community Services Officer," *CT*, February 6, 1968; "Ex-Gridder Tapped for UW Staff Post," *WSJ*, December 21, 1968; Merritt Norvell Facebook exchange, August 23, 2017.

244. Aehl, "South Side Plans Given a Big Boost," *WSJ*, April 19, 1968; Merle, "Renewal Tag Jolts City," *WSJ*, May 15, 1968; Merle, "Urban Renewal Funds Available," *WSJ*, May 16, 1968; MRA minutes, June 19, 1968; Merle, "South Madison Renewal Project Moving," *WSJ*, July 29, 1968; MRA minutes, December 4, 1968.

245. Merle, "U Ave. Renewal Gets U.S. Aid," *WSJ*, August 28, 1968; MRA minutes, August 29, 1968.

246. Sandage, "MRA to Weigh Two Plans to Finish Triangle Project," *CT*, October 29, 1968; Sandage, "Builders Argue on Triangle Redevelopment," *CT*, November 7, 1968; MRA minutes, November 19, 1968; John Mollwitz, "Triangle Area Developing Set," *WSJ*, November 20, 1968.

247. Cowan, "MHA OK's $2.5 Million in Low Rent Housing Bonds," *CT*, December 10, 1968.

248. Coyle, "Levin to Act as MHA Chief," *CT*, April 17, 1968; MRA minutes, September 18, 1968; "Joint Department Urged by MHA, MRA," *WSJ*, September 19, 1968; "Council OKs New Parade Regulations," *WSJ*, September 27, 1968.

249. "Lombardi to Join Carley's Housing Development Firm," *CT*, May 8, 1968; Gould, "Richmond Hill Delights New Tenants," *CT*, June 19, 1968; "Housing Project for Elderly Here Honors Bjarne Romnes," *WSJ*, November 19, 1968.

250. Brautigam. "Crime Rate in City Shows Sharp Rise," *CT*, July 18, 1968.

251. Gould, "Shoplifting: Why Has It Soared?" *CT*, January 17, 1968.

252. Dennis Reis, "U Defense Groups to Patrol Campus," *WSJ*, May 23, 1968; Zweifel, "Need Answers to Beatings, Solgin Asserts," *CT*, May 24, 1968.

253. "Man Fined $207 for Role in Mustache-Shaving Case," *WSJ*, April 25, 1968; "Gets Probation in Mustache Shaving Case," *CT*, May 23, 1968.

254. Aehl, "Police Policy Draws Raps," *WSJ*, March 27, 1968.

255. "Emery Has Mild Coronary Attack," *WSJ*, October 17, 1968.

256. Zweifel, "Festge to Seek Ordinance for Registration of Guns," *CT*, June 5, 1968.

257. James Marannis, "Mayor Registers Guns as Example," *CT*, June 19, 1968; Merle, "Mayor Registers Guns with Police," *WSJ*, June 20, 1968.

258. Merle, "City Council Turns Down Gun Register," *WSJ*, June 26, 1968.

259. Brautigam, "New Life Is Given to City Gun Control," *CT*, June 28, 1968; Luellen, "Gun Control Study Starts with Others," *WSJ*, September 5, 1968; Mitchell, "Mild City Gun Control Change Proposed," *WSJ*, October 3, 1968.

260. Cowan, "City Gun Plan Will Be Redrawn," *CT*, October 11, 1968.

261. Coyle, "Stop Using Mace Now, Conrad Warns Police," *CT*, May 8, 1968; Dieckmann, "Officials Decide Today on Use of Mace in City," *WSJ*, May 9, 1968.

262. Coyle, "Use of Mace Is Halted by Madison Police Force," *CT*, May 9, 1968.

263. Dieckmann, "Mayor Halts Use of Mace Pending Study of Effects," *WSJ*, May 10, 1968.

264. "Police Group Asks Festge to Allow Mace Use Again," *CT*, June 29, 1968.

265. Dieckmann, "Conditional Mace OKd," *WSJ*, October 26, 1968.

266. Sandage, "Council Passes Ordinance on Mace; Gets Proposal for Curfew Powers," *CT*, November 15, 1968.

267. Zweifel, "Soglin Questions 'Pass' Vote for Police Riot Funds," *CT*, July 12, 1968.

268. Cassano, "Court Writ Sought to Block Riot Gear," *WSJ*, July 23, 1968.

269. "One Anti-Riot Curb Vote Is Criticized," *WSJ*, July 17, 1968.

270. Zweifel, "City Atty. Doubts Soglin's Case, but Will Study Plea," *CT*, July 15, 1968; Zweifel, "Challenge to Riot Fund Can't Stand, Says Conrad," *CT*, July 17, 1968; "More Riot Control Gear OKd; No New Police Policy Is Seen," *WSJ*, July 20, 1968.

271. Cassano, "Court Writ Sought to Block Riot Gear," *WSJ*, July 23, 1968.

272. Cassano, "New Vote Set on Riot Gear," *WSJ*, July 25, 1968.

273. EOC Minutes, July 26, 1968.

274. Pfefferkorn, "Riot Control Gear Approved on New 17-3 Vote of Council," *WSJ*, August 9, 1968; Brautigam, "'Funny Thing' Is Staged by Riot Gear 'Supporters,'" *CT*, August 9, 1968.

275. "A Happy Life Ends for Well-Liked Girl," *WSJ*, May 28, 1968.

276. Zweifel, "Co-Ed Stabbed 14 Times," *CT*, May 27, 1968.

277. Dieckmann, "No Suspects, Motive Seen in UW Slaying," *WSJ*, May 28, 1968.

278. Kreisman, "Ex-U.W. Surgeon Sought for Quiz in Co-Ed Slaying," *CT*, September 17, 1968; Michael Arntfield, *Mad City: The True Story of the Campus Murders That America Forgot* (New York: Little A, 2017).

279. "Dimensions & Dividends: City Development: City Development 1968," Madison City Planning Department, March 1969.

280. City of Madison Department of Planning, Community Development and Economic Development.

281. Zweifel, "Public Employment Makes Madison an 'Uncommon Market,'" *CT*, January 19, 1968.

282. Zweifel, "No Talks at Ray-O-Vac," *CT*, May 16, 1968.

283. "UAW Strike against Ray-O-Vac Settled; Machinists Remain Out," *WSJ*, September 20, 1968.

284. Zweifel, "Labor Relations Upheaval Here," *CT*, July 2, 1968.

285. Rudy Pelecky, "Gisholt Pact Grants 67-Cent Raises," *CT*, September 28, 1968.

286. Mollwitz, "Economy Unaffected by City Strikes," *WSJ*, September 1, 1968.

287. John Newhouse, "Homeowners Balk at Selling Land to City," *WSJ*, August 12, 1968.

288. Zweifel, "Park Purchase Pressure Angers 13 Homeowners," *CT*, August 13, 1968.

289. Oset, "Gorham St. Residents Fight Condemnation," *WSJ*, October 16, 1968.

290. Cowan, "Council Rejects Gorham Street Condemnations for Park Expansion," *CT*, December 11, 1968.

291. Mollwitz, "City Given 52-Acre Southwest Side Park," *WSJ*, October 2, 1968.

292. Havens Wilber, "2 New Shop Centers Set," *CT*, September 25, 1968.

293. "Rev. DeVore to Head Neighborhood Center," *CT*, July 3; "Neighbor Center Opens on Jenifer St.," *WSJ*, September 27, 1968.

294. Steinzor, "City Council Passes Jenifer St. Rezoning," *DC*, October 24, 1968; "211 Sign Petition Protesting Luxury Apartment Rezoning," *CT*, October 31, 1968; Kendrick, "Zone Board Denies Church Use to Neighborhood Center," *CT*, July 9, 1968.

295. "Jenifer Rezone Plan Is Vetoed," *WSJ*, November 8, 1968.

296. Merle, "Parking Proposed Under Bascom Hill," *WSJ*, January 12, 1968.

297. Newhouse, "UW Traffic Headache Up for Decision," *WSJ*, February 19, 1968; Pommer, "Try to Foist $23.6 Million Expressway on City, U.W.," *CT*, June 27, 1968; Zweifel, "City Officials Dislike U.W. By-Pass Plan," *CT*, June 28, 1968.

298. Brautigam, "Festge Hits By-Pass Expressway," *CT*, July 2, 1968; "Expressway Bypassing UW Seen Unacceptable to City," *CT*, September 11, 1968.

299. Sandage, "City, Campus Units Agree Reluctantly on University Ave.," *CT*, September 12, 1968.

300. Zweifel, "Bus Consultant Gives City a Gloomy Report on Company Future," *CT*, January 17, 1968; Aehl, "Disaster Seen for City Bus Firm," *WSJ*, January 18, 1968; Newhouse, "Buses on the Skids," *WSJ*, March 8, 1968.

301. Merle, "Bus Fund Is Withheld as Mayor Awaits Data," *WSJ*, February 2, 1968; Merle, "Buses Can Stop, Mayor Warned," *WSJ*, February 6, 1968; "Bus Drivers to Stay on Job Despite City-Firm Dispute," *CT*, February 10, 1968; "Bus Firm's Debt Put at $110,000," *WSJ*, February 16, 1968.

302. Mitchell, "Bus Ownership Issue Up to Voters," *WSJ*, February 21, 1968; "Two Bus Questions Go on City Ballot," *WSJ*, February 23, 1968.

303. Coyle, "Festge Planning to Dump Top Brass of Madison Bus Company," *CT*, March 11, 1968; Aehl, "Bus Company Files to Quit Its Service," *WSJ*, March 12, 1968.

304. Coyle, "OK City Operation of Bus Company," *CT*, April 3, 1968.

305. Keefe, "Bus Firm's Head Sees No Profitable Future," *WSJ*, April 10, 1968

306. Merle, "Bus Firm's Offer: $910,000 Plus," *WSJ*, May 22, 1968; Coyle, "City to Subsidize Buses Under Pact," *CT*, May 22, 1968; Merle, "Bus Subsidy Share Agreement Reached," *WSJ*, August 17, 1968.

307. Zweifel, "Bus Stockholders Approve City Sale," *CT*, June 4, 1968; Merle, "Bus Deal Formally OKd," *WSJ*, June 14, 1968.

308. Zweifel, "Added Express Bus Routes Will Speed Downtown Trips," *CT*, August 30, 1968; "Bus Company Hopeful after October Profit," *WSJ*, November 21, 1968.

309. Gould, "Festge Vetoes Council's Vote That Killed Budget," *CT*, January 2, 1968; Brautigam, "Aldermen in Shouting Match over Budget Cuts, Auto Tax," *CT*, January 3, 1968; Aehl, "City Has Budget, but No Auto Tax," *WSJ*, January 12, 1968.

310. st. edmund, "Hendrix Alive at Factory," *DC*, March 1, 1968; Maxine Woodford and Jeannette Lee, "Jimi Hendrix—Bold as Love," *DC*, March 5, 1968; "An Open Letter to the Stalwart Patrons of the Jimi Hendrix Show," *DC*, March 6, 1968; http://crosstowntorrents.org/showthread.php?4436-1968-02-27-The-Factory-Madison-Wisconsin-USA&s=fd7c4c20ce608493708ce3 6e2a291d00; Ken Adamany email, October 31, 2017; Adamany interview, January 16, 2018.

311. "MHA, City Manager Lose," *WSJ*, November 8, 1950; "City to Fight Bus Stoppage," *WSJ*, March 15, 1968.

312. Kendrick, "It's Happening Here Tonight," *CT*, March 25, 1968; Selk, "15,000 Jam Coliseum to Cheer McCarthy," *WSJ*, March 26, 1968; Hunter, "18,000 Hail McCarthy Here," *CT*, March 26, 1968; Brautigam, "Size of Crowd Tells a Story of Its Own," *CT*, March 26, 1968; "Running McCarthy Headquarters 'Wild' but Rewarding," *CT*, April 10, 1968.

313. Ken Adamany email, January 19, 2018.

314. "WKOW Inaugurates the NOW Sound," *WSJ*, April 3, 1968.

315. Aehl, "Voters Dump Four City Councilmen," *WSJ*, April 3, 1968; "Voters Percentage Sets a City Record," *WSJ*, April 3, 1968; Gould, "Mrs. Ashman: Brimming with Ideas and Verve," Coyle, "Soglin Hopes to Cool Ward Fears," Zweifel, "Wheeler, Upset Victor, Sees Bigger Battles Ahead," all *CT*, April 3, 1968.

316. Coyle, "OK City Operation of Bus Company," *CT*, April 3, 1968.

317. Levy, "Belmont Hotel Bows as Founder Relaxes," *WSJ*, April 12, 1968; "YWCA Beats Deadline," *WSJ*, May 16, 1968.

318. "Some Stores Plan to Remain Open on Good Friday," *WSJ*, April 12, 1968.

319. "Taychopera Group Files State Papers," *CT*, April 17, 1968; "Taychopera Has Election," *WSJ*, May 7, 1968; Taychopera Foundation Records, Mss 371, box 1, WHSA.

320. Brautigam, "Council OKs Political Activity Rights for City Employees," *CT*, June 28, 1968; Brautigam, "Political Activity Vetoes Upheld," *CT*, July 12, 1968; Brautigam, "OK Politicking by City Employees," *CT*, August 7, 1968.

321. Advertisement, *DC*, July 2, 1968; https://www.thoughtco.com/the-first-mcdonalds-1779332.

322. William Hess, "New Fire Buildings Near Completion," *WSJ*, July 29, 1968; "New No. 1 Fire Station Opens for Business," *WSJ*, August 28, 1968.

323. Brautigam, "Minority Finally Prevails as Presbytery Fires Pritchard," *CT*, March 13, 1968; Brautigam, "Pritchard Accepts Church's Call," *CT*, June 3, 1968; "Heritage Installs Rev. Pritchard," *WSJ*, September 9, 1968.

324. Mark B. Rohrer, "A History of Glen & Ann's," *Madison Kaleidoscope* 1, no. 10, December 25, 1969.

325. Michael Bodden, "A History of the Mifflin Street Co-Op," *Waxing America*, www.waxingamerica.com/2006/05/history_of_the_.html.

326. Dieckmann, "Leslie Wins Sheriff Contest," *WSJ*, November 6, 1968; "Eugene Parks' Vote Total Put at 7,939 in Canvass," *CT*, November 13, 1968.

327. Merle, "We'll Pay $53 Realty Tax," *WSJ*, December 4, 1968.

328. Mitchell, "3 Fire Stations Closed as Men Call in Sick," *WSJ*, October 28, 1968; Sandage, "Round-Clock Talks Urged by Mayor," *CT*, October 28, 1968.

329. Dieckmann, "Firemen Getting 'Sicker,'" *WSJ*, November 2, 1968; Zweifel, "Emergency Council Meet Called in Firemen Crisis," *CT*, November 2, 1968; Mitchell, "Council OKs Writ to Halt Fire Strike," *WSJ*, November 3, 1968; Mitchell, "Curbs on Fire Sick Rate Eyed," *WSJ*, November 4, 1968.

330. Sandage, "Writs Served on All Firemen," *CT*, November 4, 1968.

331. "City's Fact-Finding Procedure Is Rejected by Firemen's Union," *WSJ*, November 5, 1968.

332. Sandage, "Firemen Bargain Again," *CT*, November 7, 1968.

333. Mitchell, "'Sick Call-Ins' Seen," *WSJ*, November 9, 1968; Cowan, "City, Fire Union Reach Pay Pact," *CT*, November 9, 1968.

334. Sandage, "154 City Workers Stay Home 'Sick,'" *CT*, November 18, 1968.

335. Sandage and Pommer, "200 City Workers Stay Off Jobs," *CT*, November 21, 1968.

336. Merle, "City Will Dock 'Sick-Ins' Pay," *WSJ*, November 27, 1968.

337. Dieckmann, "Firemen Will Get Full Pay; Writ Bars 'Sick-In' Docking," *WSJ*, November 28, 1968.

338. Cowan, "$20 Offer Voted to 2 City Unions," *CT*, December 4, 1968; Merle, "City and Local 60 Sign Pact," *WSJ*, December 14, 1968; Merle, "Local 236 Accepts Wage Offer of City," *WSJ*, December 20, 1968.

339. Mitchell, "Council Kills Move to Pay Deductions on 'Sick-Ins,'" *WSJ*, December 27, 1968.

340. "Elma A. Christianson, City's Welfare Chief, Dies at Home," *WSJ*, January 11, 1968.

341. "Aberg, Conservation Pioneer, Dies," *WSJ*, March 19, 1968.

342. "F. Edwin Schmitz, 75, Dies; Was Noted City Businessman," *CT*, April 15, 1968.

343. "Richard Brautigam, C-T Reporter, Dies in His Sleep," *CT*, August 21, 1968.

344. James Maraniss, "Mrs. Elizabeth Gould Dies; Won Praise for Her Writing," *CT*, August 30, 1968; Whitney Gould email to author, October 17, 2017.

345. "Adolph C. Bolz, 74, Dies; Built Up Mayer Plant Here," *CT*, November 29, 1968.

1969

1. Matt Pommer, "4200 Will Receive U.W. Degrees," *CT*, June 9, 1969.

2. "Enrollments Top UW Estimates by 412," *CT*, October 4, 1969; *DC*, October 21, 1969.

3. Feldman, *Buildings,* 399; Whitney Gould, "Humanities Building: A Marriage of the Esthetic and the Functional," *CT*, November 17, 1969.

4. Feldman, *Buildings,* 395.

5. Monica Deignan, "Strike Climaxes History of Black Demands," *DC*, February 13, 1969; "Unhappy First for Wisconsin," *Wisconsin Alumnus* 70, no. 5 (March 1969): 5; Margery Tabankin interview, *War at Home* papers, box 4, folder 28, WHSA; "Chronology of Activity Regarding Black Students," series 4/21/1, box 20, University Archives; Gilbert, "Their Time & Their Legacy."

6. Frank A. Aukofer, *Milwaukee Journal,* February 10, 1969; Arthur Hove, "Report on the Conference 'The Black Revolution: To What Ends?'" Edwin Young papers, University Archives; Edwin Young testimony, *Joint Committee to Study Disruptions,* April 30, 1969.

7. Roger A. Gribble, "Blacks Meeting Averts Threat to Block Exits," *WSJ*, February 6, 1969; Gould, "Educational System Called Irrelevant to Black Needs," *CT*, February 6, 1969; Gilbert, "Their Time & Their Legacy," 122–123; Rosen OH #1383; Rosen email, October 26, 2017; Schachner OH #1384.

8. Pommer, "UW Black Students Serve 13 Demands," *CT*, February 7, 1969; Editorial, "Revolution, and Then . . . ," *DC*, February 8, 1969; "We Demand," *Connections* 3, no. 7 (February 25–March 11, 1969), 1; Young OH #0117.

9. Gary Rettgen, "Blacks' Strike Call Disrupts U. Classes," *CT*, February 8, 1969; George Mitchell, "Group at UW Disrupts Classes to Aid Blacks," *WSJ*, February 8, 1969; "Blacks Demand Reform, Students Stop Classes," *DC*, February 8, 1969; "The Strike Begins," *Connections* 3, no. 6 (February 5–20, 1969), supplement.

10. James Oset, "UW Black Students Backed," *WSJ*, February 8, 1969; Jim Cowan, "Black Conference Closes with Cry: Learn to Produce," *CT*, February 8, 1969.

11. Wahid and Liberty Rashad (Willie and Libby Edwards), *War at Home* papers, box 4, folder 22, WHSA; Ralph Hanson testimony, *Joint Committee to Study Disruptions,* March 28, 1969; Gilbert, "Their Time & Their Legacy," 118–119.

12. Editorial, "Revolution, and Then . . . ," *DC*, February 8, 1969.

13. "Black Threatens Shutdown of UW," *WSJ*, February 9, 1969.

14. Aukofer, "UW Students Storm Game; 4 Arrested," *Milwaukee Journal,* February 9, 1969; BOR minutes, February 14, 1969; Ralph Hanson testimony, *Joint Committee,* March 28, 1969.

15. Statement by Madison Campus Chancellor Edwin Young," February 8, 1969, Edwin Young papers, University Archives.

16. Joan Rimalover and Monica Deignan, "WSA Student Senate Passes Resolution Supporting Strike," *DC*, February 11, 1969.

17. Margery Tabankin and David Goldfarb, "A History of Participation by Black Students in the University Structure," Edwin Young papers, University Archives; Deignan, "Strike Climaxes History of Black Demands," *DC*, February 14, 1969.

18. "Class Disruption, Boycott Set to Support UW Blacks," *WSJ*, February 10, 1969; "The Panthers of Wrath Are Wiser Than the Horses of Instruction," *Connections* 3, no. 7 (February 21–March 16, 1969), 9.

19. Pommer, "1,000 Picket UW Peaceably," *CT*, February 10, 1969.

20. Mike Gondek and Len Fleische, "Students Strike Class, March," *DC*, February 11, 1969; Mitchell, "Peaceful Pickets Tell Blacks' Story," *WSJ*, February 11, 1969; Robert Pfefferkorn, "Group Again Marches and Plans a New Rally," *WSJ*, February 11, 1969; Wilbur Emery testimony, *Joint Committee*, March 28, 1969.

21. Pommer, "Police on Campus, but Leave Quickly," *CT*, February 11, 1969; Dave Zweifel, "Solons Vow U Budget Cut," *CT*, February 11, 1969.

22. Pommer, "Police on Campus, but Leave Quickly," *CT*, February 11, 1969; Emery testimony, *Joint Committee*, March 28, 1969; "History of the Movement in Madison, Part V: Black Strike," *TakeOver* 5, no. 1 (January 8–22, 1975), 8–9; Gribble, "Police Halt Grab of U.W. Buildings," *WSJ*, February 12, 1969; Mitchell, "UW Blacks Seek White Protest Allies," *WSJ*, February 12, 1969; "Police Shut Bascom while 1200 Picket," *DC*, February 12, 1969.

23. Pommer, "Hit-Run Blockades Are Begun at U.W.," *CT*, February 12, 1969; Pommer, "Three More Student Strikers Arrested," *CT*, February 13, 1969; Emery testimony, *Joint Committee*, March 28, 1969; "Bus Firms Halts Campus Service," *WSJ*, February 13, 1969; Gribble, "Hit-Run at UW Foil Police," *WSJ*, February 13, 1969; Mitchell, "Rival Emotions Spur UW Fights," *WSJ*, February 13, 1969.

24. "Colston Says UW Blacks No Longer Control UW Protest," *CT*, February 13, 1969.

25. Liberty Rashad (Libby Edwards) interview, *War at Home* papers, box 4, folder 22, WHSA; Rosen OH #1383; Schachner OH #1384; Michael David Rosen email, December 31, 2017; Gilbert, "Their Time & Their Legacy," 34–35, 106, 129.

26. James D. Selk, "Guard Called In to Aid Campus Control," *WSJ*, February 13, 1969.

27. Pommer and John Patrick Hunter, "Troops, Cops Use Tear Gas to Rout U. Avenue Blockers," *CT*, February 13, 1969; 'Strike Goes On, More Guard Coming," *DC*, February 14, 1969; Gribble, "UW Strikers Clash with Troops, Police," *WSJ*, February 14, 1969; Gilbert, "Their Time & Their Legacy," 49–50; Schachner OH #1384; Edwin Young testimony, *Joint Committee*, April 30, 1969.

28. James Oset and Victor Yehling, "Mass March Backs UW Blacks' Stand," *WSJ*, February 14, 1969; Mitchell, "UW Protesters Show Discipline," *WSJ*, February 14, 1969.

29. Rich Wener and Peter Greenberg, "Hayden's Speech Follows Parade," *DC*, February 14, 1969; "SDS Leader Tells UW Students America Has Lost the Viet War," *CT*, February 14, 1969; Jeffrey Schachner email, October 31, 2017.

30. Gould, "U.W. Blacks Vow Not to Quit until Their Demands Are Met," *CT*, February 14, 1969; Gribble, "Troops, Police Quit Campus," *WSJ*, February 15, 1969; Mitchell, "Disciplined Group Continues March," *WSJ*, February 15, 1969; "Guard Withdraws; 800 Disrupt Traffic, Violence Averted," *DC*, February 15, 1969; Mike Frost and Len Fleischer, "Fifth Day Torch March to Capitol Sees Police Clubbings, Arrests," *DC*, February 15, 1969.

31. BOR minutes, February 14, 1969; Pommer, "U.W. Regents Back Young; Seek Report on Symposium," *CT*, February 14, 1969.

32. Pommer, "1,372 on Faculty Support Actions of Administration," *CT*, February 15, 1969.

33. John E. Mollwitz, "Silence Reigns on UW Campus," *WSJ*, February 16, 1969.

34. Donald Janson, "U. of Wisconsin Campus Quiet; Governor Lunches with Guard," *New York Times*, February 17, 1969; Wener, "End of Disruption Urged by Blacks as Strike Fades," *DC*, February 18, 1969; George L. Mosse, interviewed by Laura Smail, 1982, OH #0227, digital audio file, University Archives and Records Management Services, Madison, Wisconsin.

35. Ron Legro, "Strike Called Off until Thurs.," *DC*, February 19, 1969; Gribble, "Strike Halt Calms UW Campus," *WSJ*, February 19, 1969; Ralph Hanson testimony, *Joint Committee*, March 28, 1969.

36. June Dieckmann, "Arson Blamed in UW Blaze," *WSJ*, February 20; Greenberg, "Arson Destroys Race Center," *DC*, February 20, 1969.

37. Judy Shockley and Rena Steinzor, "Narrow Vote Follows Heated Deliberation," *DC*, February 20, 1969; "Proctor Leaving UW for New Job," *WSJ*, February 21, 1969.

38. BOR Business and Finance Committee minutes, February 24, 1969; "UW Sells Its Stock in Chase; Protest Dropped," *WSJ*, May 10, 1969.

39. Selk, "Keep Cool, Knowles Urges Critics of UW," *WSJ*, February 25, 1969.

40. Gay Leslie, "UW Blacks Told to Acquire Skills," *WSJ*, February 25, 1969.

41. Pfefferkorn, "Black Studies Unit to Be Urged," *WSJ*, February 25, 1969.

42. Editorial, "Expected," *DC*, February 27, 1969.

43. Greenberg, "Blacks Organize to Resume Strike at Noon Today," *DC*, February 27, 1969; Richard W. Jaeger, "Protesters Leave a Destructive Path," *WSJ*, February 28, 1969; Franklin Berkowitz, "Strikers Interrupt Roseleip Appearance," *DC*, February 28, 1969; Selk, "Legislative Probe of Campuses Set," *WSJ*, February 28, 1969; Gould, "Campus Is Quiet; Rally Fizzles Out," *CT*, February 28, 1969; Gould, "'Like Theater of Absurd,'"

CT, February 28, 1969; "Black Council Hits Damage to Property," *CT*, March 4, 1969.

44. University of Wisconsin (Madison Campus) Faculty Document 260, March 3, 1969, University Archives; Wener, "Faculty Endorses Black Studies Dept.," *DC*, March 4, 1969.

45. Pfefferkorn, "UW Black Studies Unit Viewed as a 'First Step,'" *WSJ*, March 5, 1969.

46. BOR minutes, March 14, 1969.

47. Shockley, "Faculty Committee Will Develop Black Studies," *DC*, April 17, 1969; James Rowen, "Black Studies Chairman Linked to CIA Positions," *DC*, August 5, 1969; Karen M. Paget, *Patriotic Betrayal* (New Haven: Yale University Press, 2015), 169.

48. Horace T. Harris, "Black Studies?" *DC*, April 24, 1969.

49. "Black Studies Committee to Get New Chairman Soon," *WSJ*, August 7, 1969.

50. Leo Burt, "Prof. Nolan Penn Appointed Chairman of Afro Studies," *DC*, September 17, 1969.

51. Charlotte Robinson, "Special Plan for Getting Blacks to U. Nears Goal," *CT*, September 2, 1969.

52. *Report of the Joint Committee to Study Disruptions at the University of Wisconsin*, October 14, 1969.

53. Burt, "Black Studies Major Includes Three Areas," *DC*, December 2, 1969.

54. Kendall Hale, "Radical Passions," iUniverse, 2008; Rena Steinzor, Len Fleischer, and Peter Greenberg, "Block Party Turns to Chaos as Police Use Gas, Clubs," *DC*, special edition, May 5, 1969; Inspector Herman J. Thomas, "Officer's Report—Case 536-336, Riotous Disturbance," Madison Police Department, May 3, 1969; *Report of the Mayor's Commission on the Mifflin Street Disorders*, September 16, 1969, HV7595 M3 E3 1969, University of Wisconsin Law Library.

55. *Report of the Mayor's Commission*, appendix; Howard N. Fox, "Gilman St.: The Other Dance," *DC*, May 7, 1969.

56. Paul Soglin interview, 2016.

57. Clara Bingham, *Witness to the Revolution: Radicals, Resisters, Vets, Hippies, and the Year America Lost Its Mind and Found Its Soul* (New York: Random House, 2016), 49.

58. *Report of the Mayor's Commission*, 2–3.

59. Rosemary Kendrick, "Mifflin Testimony in Sharp Relief," *CT*, June 17, 1969; Kendrick, "Dyke Contradicted by Mifflin Witness," *CT*, June 18, 1969; Ronee Epstein Bergmann and Barbara Rochwerger Haynes, Facebook exchanges, October 2017; Alison Klairmont Lingo email, December 31, 2017, January 1, 2018.

60. *Report of the Mayor's Commission*, 4; Paul Soglin interview, April 2016.

61. *Report of the Mayor's Commission*, 4.

62. Jon Wegge, "Police, Students Clash in Raid on Block Party," *WSJ*, May 4, 1969; "Students vs. Police: Clash of Cultures? Generation Gap?" *CT*, May 5, 1969.

63. Jim Hougan, "Mittelstadt's Crack about Soglin's Hair Angers Atty. Cates," *CT*, July 10, 1969; Paul Soglin interview, *War at Home* papers, box 4, folder 26, WHSA.

64. Kendrick, "Mifflin Testimony in Sharp Relief," *CT*, June 17, 1969; *Report of the Mayor's Commission*, 5; David Williams email, January 2, 2018.

65. Dennis Sandage, "Dyke Considering Curew Tonight," *CT*, February 5, 1969; Thomas Report no. 536, 336.

66. Steve Kravit, "Faculty Is Shocked by Actions of Police," *DC*, May 10, 1969.

67. David Williams emails to author, November 5, 2017, January 15, 2018.

68. Sandage, "Dyke Considering Curfew Tonight," *CT*, May 5, 1969; *Report, Appendix*.

69. *Report of the Mayor's Commission*, 6.

70. Soglin interview, *War at Home* papers, WHSA; *Report of the Mayor's Commission*, 6.

71. "Police Arrest over 80," *WSJ*, May 5, 1969; Kendrick, "18 Policemen, 48 Others Treated at City Hospitals," *CT*, May 5, 1969.

72. Clifford S. Behnke, "Emery Defends Mifflin St. Action," *WSJ*, June 24, 1969.

73. Bingham, *Witness to the Revolution*, 49.

74. "Chronology of a Riot," *DC*, special edition, May 5, 1969.

75. Stefan Koehl and Jon Wegge, "Dyke Delays Action in Renewed Clashes," *WSJ*, May 5, 1969.

76. "Police Arrest over 80," *WSJ*, May 5, 1969; "Students vs. Police: Clash of Cultures? Generation Gap?" *CT*, May 5, 1969; Paul Soglin interview, *War at Home* papers, box 4, folder 26, WHSA; Paul Soglin email, December 23, 2017.

77. "Durkin Tells Why Firemen Bailed Out Soglin," *CT*, May 5, 1969; John Aehl, "Police-Fire Group Raps Soglin Bail," *WSJ*, May 6, 1969; Sandage, "Soglin Bail Detours Talk on Fire Strike," *CT*, May 6, 1969; Edward D. Durkin interviewed by Ruth B. Doyle, History Madison , Inc. Oral History Project, November 16, 1989; Ed Durkin interview, May 17, 2016.

78. "Melee Extends into State St.," *WSJ*, May 5, 1969.

79. Koehl and Wegge, "Dyke Delays Action In Renewed Clashes," *WSJ*, May 5, 1969

80. Sandage, "Dyke Considering Curfew Tonight," *CT*, May 5, 1969.

81. *Report of the Mayor's Commission*, 8.

82. William R. Wineke, "Mayor Eyed 'Pullout,' Mifflin Probers Hear," *WSJ*, July 9, 1969; *Report of the Mayor's Commission*, 9; Kendrick, "18 Policemen, 48 Others Treated at City Hospitals," *CT*, May 5, 1969; Frank Custer, "First of 80 Melee Cases Nets Fine," *CT*, May 5, 1969.

83. Rena Steinzor, Peter Greenberg, Debbie Soglin, Mike Frost, and Amy Tankoos, "Riot into Third Day," *DC*, May 6, 1969; George Mitchell and Jon Wegge, "UW Fight Erupts Anew," *WSJ*, May 6, 1969; Custer, "Dyke Offers to Meet with Student

Representatives," *CT*, May 6, 1969; editorial, "Mayor Dyke Gets Rebuff in Effort to Get Dialogue," *CT*, May 6, 1969.

84. Mitchell and Wegge, "UW Fight Erupts Anew"; Steve Kravit, "Faculty Is Shocked by Actions of Police," *DC*, May 10, 1969; Koehl, "Innocent Student Hit, Chief Hanson Declares," *WSJ*, July 8, 1969; Wineke, "Mifflin Case Probe Closes," *WSJ*, July 18, 1969.

85. "Disruption Halts City Bus Service," *WSJ*, May 6, 1969; Hunter, "Youths, Police Stage 3rd Night of Clashes," *CT*, May 6, 1969.

86. Custer, "86 Protest Arrests Are Handled by Five Judges," *CT*, May 6, 1969; *Report of the Mayor's Commission*, 13–14.

87. "On Wisconsin!" *Berkeley Barb* 8, no. 19 (May 9–15), 1969.

88. Oset, "Talks Ease Tension in Mifflin Section," *WSJ*, May 7, 1969; Custer, "Mifflin Peace Talks Halt Street Battles," *CT*, May 7, 1969; Steinzor, "The Final Lesson Mifflin and Bassett," *DC*, May 8, 1969.

89. Wener, "Area Crowd Talks with City Group," *DC*, May 7, 1969.

90. Maureen Santini, "Council Stalls on Street Permit, Parks Walks Out of Tense City Meeting," *DC*, May 7, 1969; Sandage, "Walk-Out, Tears Mark Council Row over Street Issue," *CT*, May 7, 1969.

91. "Fraternity Council Aids Bail Fund," *WSJ*, May 8, 1969.

92. Wener, "Mifflin Residents Demand Amnesty for All Arrested," *DC*, May 8, 1969.

93. Steinzor and Santini, "Aldermen Reveal City's Hostility," *DC*, May 8, 1969; Aehl and Mitchell, "City Blocks Block Party," *WSJ*, May 9, 1969; Santini, "Council Refuses Block Party," *DC*, May 9, 1969.

94. "Dyke States Official Position," *DC*, May 10, 1969; Steinzor, "Mifflin Community Invited to 'Bust' Saturday: Durkin," *DC*, May 10, 1969; Ed Durkin and Paul Soglin interviews, 2016.

95. Kendrick, "Lucey to Give Lease at $1 a Year for Mifflin Street Community Park," *CT*, May 10, 1969.

96. Koehl, "Residents of Mifflin Area Do Their Thing at Durkin's," *WSJ*, May 11, 1969; Bernard L. Collier, "A Party in Madison: Peace Breaks Out," *New York Times*, May 11, 1969; Michael Mally, "Mifflin St. 'Moves' to Middleton Rd.," *DC*, May 13, 1969.

97. Zweifel, "Three Lawyers to Probe Mifflin St. Incidents," *CT*, May 19, 1969; Gould, "Mifflin Witnesses Tell Grim Stories," *CT*, May 23, 1969.

98. "City Lists 231 Code Violations in Mifflin Area," *WSJ*, June 6, 1969.

99. "Dyke Says Mifflin-Bassett Housing Protests Are Justified," *CT*, June 5, 1969.

100. Kreisman, "Jury Clears Ald. Parks of 'Unlawful Assembly,'" *CT*, June 26, 1969; Kendrick, "Parks Files $3,359 Claim with City for Legal Fees," *CT*, September 10, 1969; "Ald. Parks Refused Fee for Defense," *WSJ*, November 14, 1969.

101. Kreisman, "Voids Mifflin St. 'Assembly' Cases," *CT*, July 9, 1969.

102. Pfefferkorn, "Jury Finds Ald. Soglin Guilty," *WSJ*, July 11, 1969.

103. *Report of the Mayor's Commission*; Mitchell, "Mifflin Report Urges Careful Police Choice," *WSJ*, September 21, 1969; "Mifflin Report Is Coolly Received," *CT*, September 22, 1969; Denise Simon, "Mifflin Report Gets Mixed Response," *DC*, September 23, 1969.

104. *Report of the Mayor's Commission*, 14–15.

105. *Report of the Mayor's Commission*, 15.

106. *Report of the Mayor's Commission*, appendix, 3–4.

107. *Report of the Mayor's Commission*, 17–19.

108. Dieckmann, "P-F Commission Names Itself to Observe Police Relations," *WSJ*, October 16, 1969.

109. Tom Foley, "City Refusing to Pay Mifflin Riot Claims," *CT*, December 26, 1969.

110. Jack Burke, "UW's Economic Contribution to City Worth $300 Million," *WSJ*, January 17, 1969.

111. BOR minutes, January 10, 1969; Pommer, "Regents Stop Aid to Cardinal," *CT*, January 10, 1969; Gene Wells, "Cardinal Rent Demanded by Four-Three Vote," *DC*, January 11, 1969.

112. BOR minutes, January 10, 1969; Glenn Miller, "Ivy Williamson Out as Athletic Chief," *WSJ*, January 11, 1969.

113. "Williamson, Bruhn Badger Era Ended," *CT*, January 11, 1969.

114. Greenberg, "WSA Sympsoium: Progress, Despair," *DC*, January 11, 1969.

115. "Hirsch Accepts Badger Athletic Director Post," *CT*, March 1, 1969; Miller, "Crazylegs Starts Kicking," *WSJ*, March 21, 1969; "Way to Go, Crazylegs!" *Wisconsin Alumnus* 70, no. 5 (March 1969).

116. "New Students Housing Setup Planned at UW," *WSJ*, March 6, 1969.

117. Rowen, "Fuck Study," *Connections* 3, no. 6 (February 5–20, 1969), 11; Bill Knee, "Senator Denounces Connections' Editor," *DC*, March 7, 1969; Ann Gordon email, August 15, 2017.

118. Alan Swerdlowe and Amy Tankoos, "History Faculty Loses Williams," *DC*, March 8, 1969; Paul Buhle and Edward Rice-Maximin, *William Appleman Williams* (New York: Routledge, 1995), 160–177.

119. BOR minutes, March 14, 1969; Len Fleischer and Gene Wells, "Regents Cut Nonstate Quota," *DC*, March 15, 1969.

120. John Keefe, "$38 Million Hacked from Budget for UW," *WSJ*, April 11, 1969.

121. Arthur L. Srb, "U. Alumni Group Member Loss Told," *CT*, April 12, 1969.

122. Advertisement, *DC*, April 16, 1969.

123. *Connections* 3, no. 9 (April 22–May 6, 1969).

124. "An Interview with Elroy Hirsch," *DC*, April 30, 1969.

125. "Gwendolyn Brooks to Give Poetry Reading Tonite," *DC*, May 8, 1969.

126. "Talk on Grape Boycott," *DC*, May 8, 1969.

127. 'Community Coop Goes Under," *DC*, May 16, 1969.

128. *DC*, May 7, 1969.

129. Sidran, *A Life in The Music*, 78–79; John Morthland, *Rolling Stone*, July 26, 1969.

130. Allen Swerdlowe, "Park Street Pedestrian Bridge Comes Down," *DC*, June 24, 1969.

131. Shockley, "Badger Herald Weekly to Rival Cardinal," *DC*, June 24, 1969.

132. *Madison Kaleidoscope* 1, no. 1 (June 23–July 6, 1969); Shockley, "Out of the Basement: Madison Kaleidoscope," *DC*, July 2, 1969.

133. University of Wisconsin 1969–1970 Madison Student & Staff Telephone Directory, 100.

134. "Law Student Heads Nat'l YAF Conservative Group," *BH*, September 10, 1969.

135. *BH*, September 10, 1969.

136. Paul Novak, "Blues at the Union," *DC*, September 30, 1969.

137. David Douglas, "The Crazy Man Comes Back," *DC*, November 8, 1969.

138. "Cops Prowl Rathskeller," *DC*, November 13, 1969.

139. Lynne Rasmussen, "Peter, Paul, Mary Sing, with Message," *WSJ*, November 14, 1969; *DC*, November 15, 1969; Donna Vukelich-Selva and Ira Mintz Facebook messages, August 27, 2017.

140. BOR minutes, November 14, 1969; Wells, "Regents Reinstate Hours," *DC*, November 15, 1969; Santini, "Double Standard for Sexes Reopened by Regent Action," *DC*, November 14, 1969.

141. "U.W. Music Faculty Will Dedicate New Facilities," *CT*, October 22, 1969; Feldman, *Buildings*, 398.

142. "Harrington Starts Leave and Vacation," *CT*, November 17, 1969.

143. Harry Temkin, "Coatta Denied New Contract," *DC*, December 3, 1969; https://www.sports-reference.com/cfb/schools/wisconsin/

144. "University YWCA Sets Conference for Women's Liberation for Dec. 6-7," *BH*, December 5, 1969; "YWCA Women's Liberation Conference: 'Breaking Down the Female Stereotypes," *BH*, December 12, 1969.

145. "James A. Graaskamp Is Handicapped Person for '70," *CT*, December 19, 1969.

146. Miller, "Jardine Named UW's New Coach," *WSJ*, December 23, 1969.

147. Tom Butler, "Former Sports Chief Ivan Williamson Dies," *WSJ*, February 20, 1969; *DC*, January 11, 1969.

148. "Prof. G.W. Longenecker, 69, 'Father of Arboretum,' Dies," *CT*, February 26, 1969.

149. Robert Meloon, "High Court Upholds Dow Riot Penalties," *CT*, February 14, 1969.

150. BOR minutes, February 14, 1969; Pommer, "Compulsory Orientation for ROTC Dropped," *CT*, February 14, 1969.

151. Pommer, "Dow Interviews 36 Students Here without Incident," *CT*, February 26, 1969.

152. Selk, "Ban on Disrupter Aid Passed," *WSJ*, March 5, 1969.

153. BOR minutes, March 6, 1969; Pommer, "Nellen Wants All Students at University Fingerprinted," *CT*, March 6, 1969.

154. Rowen, "U Research Aids ABM, Army Munitions," *DC*, March 28, 1969; Steve Krave and Harry Pinkus, "Research Center Denies Charge of Army Missile Connection," *DC*, March 29, 1969; "No Classified Defense Research on Campus," *WSJ*, November 13, 1969; Rowen, "Rosser's Activities Omitted in Report," *DC*, December 9, 1969; Howard Halperin, David Siff, James Rowen, Ed Zeidman, "The Case against the Army Math Research Center," (Madison SDS, UW Moratorium Committee, New University Conference, October 1969), series 7/50, folder 1, Army Mathematics Research Center file, University Archives; Jim Rowen interview, *War at Home* papers, box 4, folder 25, WHSA; Edwin Young interview, *War at Home* papers, box 4, folder 32, WHSA.

155. Allen Swerdlowe, "List of Vietnam Dead Read at Capitol March," *DC*, May 2, 1969.

156. Fred Harvey Harrington testimony, *Joint Committee*, May 6, 1969.

157. "Bill Curbing Campus Rights Are Signed," *WSJ*, May 9, 1969.

158. BOR minutes, June 13, 1969; Pommer, "SDS Issue Causes Ban on Freshman Political Visits," *CT*, June 14, 1969.

159. Jim Hougan, "SDS Here Disaffiliates from National Group," *CT*, July 9, 1969.

160. "Wanted, Dead or Alive," *TakeOver* 4, no. 1 (January 17–30, 1974), 8–9; Herman Thomas interview, *War at Home* papers, WHSA; George Croal, interviewed by Troy Reeves and Mike Lawler, 2011, OH #1138, digital audio file, University Archives and Records Management Services, Madison, Wisconsin; Tom Bates, *Rads* (New York: HarperPerennial, 1992), 132.

161. Rowen OH #0137; Levin, *Cold War University*, 170.

162. Clifford C. Behnke and Barbara Heffling, "UW Protesters Pelt Rusk Car," *WSJ*, August 27, 1969.

163. Dieckmann, "Emery Vows Firm Hand in Disorders," *WSJ*, September 1, 1969.

164. Joint Committee to Study Disorders, Report, October 14, 1969.

165. Bates, *Rads*, 132–133.

166. David Fine, "Protesters Await FBI in Sanctuary," *DC*, September 17, 1969.

167. Jim Hougan and Whitney Gould, "Young Draft Resister Takes Sanctuary in Church Here," *CT*, September 17, 1969.

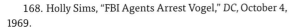

168. Holly Sims, "FBI Agents Arrest Vogel," *DC*, October 4, 1969.

169. Alan Emmerman, "SDS National HQ Routs U SDS Meet," *DC*, September 19, 1969; "Ultra-Militants Split SDS Meeting at UW," *WSJ*, September 19, 1969; Bates, *Rads*, 136–138; Max Elbaum and Harvey Pekar, "Turn Your Chairs Around," in *Students for a Democratic Society: A Graphic Novel*, edited by Paul Buhle (New York: Hill and Wang, 2008), 177–180; Jeffrey Schachner email, November 11, 2017.

170. Tim Greene and Judy Kannel, "County Board Hassles, Passes Riot Training Bill," *DC*, September 23, 1969.

171. Custer, "Mysterious Blast Rips Armory Here," *CT*, September 26, 1969.

172. Kendrick, "Council Backs Moratorium," *CT*, October 10, 1969.

173. George Bogdanich, "Moratorium Blooms at WSA Office, with Barefoot Girls, Rainbow Paper," *DC*, October 11, 1969; Behnke, "Moratorium's Smorgasbord," *WSJ*, October 14, 1969; "Moratorium Events to Take Many Aspects," *CT*, October 14, 1969; Steve Vetzner, "U Anti-War Protests Date Back to 1965," *DC*, October 14, 1969; Gould, "War Foes Here Rap Policies," *CT*, October 15, 1969; "Jam-Packed Teach-Ins Mark Protest Here," *CT*, October 15, 1969.

174. "SDS Gives 'Ultimatum' to End 3 U. Operations," *CT*, October 15, 1969; "Young Refuses to Negotiate SDS Ultimatum," *DC*, October 16, 1969; David Fine, "Demand Limit Past; SDS Plots Course," *DC*, October 28, 1969; Edwin Young interview, *War at Home* papers, WHSA.

175. Bogdanich and Santini, "15,000 Attend Moratorium Day Fieldhouse Rally," *DC*, October 16, 1969; Bogdanich, "Protest Rally Draws 3,000; Outline Morning Activities," *DC*, October 16, 1969; Gould, "Middleton Mother, Who Lost Son in Viet, Stirs Rally," *CT*, October 16, 1969; "Rowen Elucidates U-Military Cooperation," *DC*, October 23, 1969; James Rowen and Margery Tabankin interviews, *War at Home* papers, WHSA.

176. Kendrick, "15,000 Here Rally, March against War," *CT*, October 16, 1969; Gould, "Peace Group Keeps Full Control," *CT*, October 16, 1969.

177. BOR minutes, October 17, 1969; Wells, "Regents Limit Sound Equipment," *DC*, October 18, 1969; Bogdanich, "3 at Rally Arrested," *DC*, November 14, 1969.

178. "1,500 Madisonians to Leave for Washington," *CT*, November 14, 1969.

179. "Dow No Longer Making Napalm," *WSJ*, November 15, 1969.

180. "ROTC Roll Drops," *DC*, November 19, 1969.

181. Elaine Cohen, "SDS Sponsored March Hits U Research, ROTC," *DC*, November 20, 1969.

182. Neil Dunlop, "Knowles OK's Hard Anti-Disruption Law," *DC*, December 17, 1969.

183. Burt, "SDS Hits ROTC, Destroys ID Cards," *DC*, December 13, 1969; editorial, "Comments on Friday," *DC*, December 13, 1969; Hougan, "U.W. Melee Leaves 4 Hurt, 4 Jailed," *CT*, December 13, 1969; Bates, *Rads*, 143–147.

184. Dave Wagner, "Saves U. Building in Fire-Bombing," *CT*, December 29, 1969; Bates, *Rads*, 154–155; Dave Wagner email, November 6, 2017.

185. Greenberg, "Arsonists Warn More Bombs in Near Future," *DC*, January 6, 1970; *Kaleidoscope* 1, no. 11 (January 14, 1970); Bates, *Rads*, 156–166; *The War at Home*.

186. "Lyle Hansbrough Killed in Action in Vietnam War," *CT*, March 19, 1969; "Lyle Cleveland Hansbrough," The Virtual Wall® Vietnam Veterans Memorial, www.virtualwall.org/dh /HansbroughLC01a.htm.

187. "William Cooper Pierson, III," The Virtual Wall® Vietnam Veterans Memorial , www.virtualwall.org/dp /PiersonWC01a.htm.

188. "Seaman Gary Johnson Dies in Vietnam Action," *WSJ*, May 3, 1969; Holly Dunlop, "City Woman Spends Mother's Day Mourning Loss of Corpsman Son," *WSJ*, May 12, 1969; "Gary Alan Johnson," The Virtual Wall® Vietnam Veterans Memorial, www.virtualwall.org/dj/JohnsonGA01a.htm.

189. "James Spurley, 20, Killed in Vietnam; Ex-CT Carrier," *CT*, May 19, 1969; "James Virgil Spurley, Jr," The Virtual Wall® Vietnam Veterans Memorial, www.virtualwall.org/ds /SpurleyJV01a.htm.

190. "Thomas Griesen Killed in Viet; W. High Grad," *WSJ*, June 7, 1969; "Thomas Andrew Greisen," The Virtual Wall® Vietnam Veterans Memorial, www.virtualwall.org/dg /GreisenTA01a.htm.

191. "Lt. Brantmeyer Awarded Bronze Star for Heroism," *CT*, July 10, 1969.

192. "Cpl. C. R. LeBosquet, 21, Killed in Vietnam Action," *WSJ*, August 28, 1969; "Charles Richard Le Bosquet," The Virtual Wall® Vietnam Veterans Memorial, www.virtualwall.org/dl /LebosquetCR01a.htm.

193. "Dennis W. Shew, Madison, Is Killed in Vietnam War," *CT*, September 16, 1969; "Dennis Wayne Shew," The Virtual Wall® Vietnam Veterans Memorial, www.virtualwall.org/ds /ShewDW01a.htm.

194. "Thomas Named to State Rights Unit," *CT*, January 3, 1969.

195. "Merritt Norvell Is Named to Student Affairs Post," *DC*, January 11, 1969.

196. Ruth Doyle, "Memo to Students," January 23, 1969; Greenberg, "Mrs. Doyle Quits Minorities Program," *DC*, February 4, 1969; editorial, "Doyle Case: A Microcosm," *DC*, February 5, 1969; Robert Maynard, "Mrs. Doyle: Ironic Victim of Her Own Faith in Integration," *CT*, February 17, 1969.

197. EOC minutes, March 18, 1969; Peter Otto, "City Private Club Investigation Set," *WSJ*, March 19, 1969.

198. "Flip Wilson Booked for UW's King Fund," *WSJ*, March 7, 1969.

199. Custer, "3 Boys Voluntarily Offer Apology for Cross-Burning," *CT*, April 2, 1969; John Newhouse, "Behind Burning Cross: Forgiveness," *WSJ*, April 3, 1969.

200. Leslie, "Panther Chief Hails Revolt and Socialism," *WSJ*, May 21, 1969; Tim Greene, "Panther Head Favors Violent Class Struggle," *DC*, May 21, 1969.

201. Steve Klein, "Russell Praises Youth, Knocks Wilt," *WSJ*, May 21, 1969.

202. Wineke, "New Citizens Group to Push for Integrated Police Force," *WSJ*, August 5, 1969.

203. "Harris Named MATC Instructor, Counselor," *CT*, August 12, 1969.

204. Dieckmann, "1st Negro Certified to City Police Force," *WSJ*, September 19, 1969.

205. "Carolyn Williams Is Crowned First Black Homecoming Queen," *BH*, October 31, 1969; Kaylee Waxman, "Homecoming Queen Says Crown Was 'Unity Thing,'" *DC*, November 6, 1969.

206. John Keefe, "Hill Appointed Acting Secretary of State Local Affairs Department," *WSJ*, December 2, 1969.

207. Burt, "Afro Center Debuts Monthly Magazine," *DC*, December 9, 1969; "The Black Student at the University of Wisconsin—Madison," Edwin Young papers, University Archives.

208. Joseph McBride, "'Bias' Club Bans Urged for County," *WSJ*, December 31, 1969.

209. "Report to the Common Council as Directed by Resolution 18,140, August 22, 1968," Madison Equal Opportunities Commission, April 24, 1969, HV7936 P8 M33 1968, University of Wisconsin Law Library; Kendrick, "EOC Report Warns City to Heal Police-Black Hatreds," *CT*, April 24, 1969; Pfefferkorn, "Police-Black 'Tension' Cited," *WSJ*, April 25, 1969.

210. Kendrick, "Chief Opposes Council Adoption of EOC Police Recommendations," *CT*, August 13, 1969.

211. Mitchell, "City Council Authority over Police Questioned," *WSJ*, August 13, 1969.

212. Kendrick, "EOC Report Action Put Up to Officials," *CT*, August 15, 1969.

213. EOC minutes, March 18, 1969; Cowan, "14 Private Clubs in City Face Probe on Bias Clauses," *CT*, March 19, 1969.

214. Kreisman, "Madison Elks Lodge Asks End of Anti-Negro Clause," *CT*, March 27, 1969.

215. EOC minutes, May 13, 1969; Otto, "Council Referral of Report Irritates Members of EOC," *WSJ*, May 14, 1969.

216. Oset, "Licensees' 'Bias' Attacked by EOC," *WSJ*, May 23, 1969.

217. EOC minutes, May 24, 1969.

218. Oset, "Private Club Bar Ban Sparks Talk," *WSJ*, June 11, 1969.

219. Kendrick, "Vote 1971 Deadline on Club Race Bars," *CT*, June 25, 1969.

220. Barbara Heffling, "City Sets '71 Deadline on White Club Licenses," *WSJ*, June 25, 1969.

221. Kendrick, "Vote Bar License Ban on Whites-Only Clubs," *CT*, June 27, 1969.

222. "Eagles Vote to Keep Club All White," *CT*, August 4, 1969.

223. "Grad Orators Hit Social and School Flaws," *CT*, June 5, 1969; Holly Dunlop, "Hail, Central—and Farewell," *WSJ*, June 6, 1969.

224. "Public School Enrollment Will Hit Predicted 34,281" *CT*, September 6, 1969.

225. Gould, "West High Students Stage Sit-In Demanding Change," *CT*, January 28, 1969; "West High Times Stopped; Officials Object to Story," *WSJ*, February 28, 1969.

226. Pommer, "West High Approves Girls Wearing Slacks to Classes," *CT*, February 20, 1969.

227. William Luellen, "Grooming Guidelines to Be Set," *WSJ*, March 12, 1969.

228. Luellen, "Proposals Drawn for School Code," *WSJ*, March 15, 1969; Pommer, "Board of Education Drops School Dress-Grooming Guidelines," *CT*, May 6, 1969.

229. Gould, "Central's Black Students Uneasy at Dispersal," *CT*, April 2, 1969.

230. Cowan, "School Candidates Talk with NAACP," *CT*, February 27, 1969.

231. Pommer, "Schools Here Add 6 Black Teachers," *CT*, May 27, 1969.

232. Pommer, "Black History, Vocational Offerings, Are Biggest High School Changes," *CT*, August 28, 1969.

233. Patrick McGilligan, "Madison East Votes Boycott of Elk's Scholarship Contest," *DC*, December 3, 1969.

234. Pommer, "Madison Is Second Lowest in County School Taxes," *CT*, January 7, 1969.

235. Pommer, "An Era Ends on Madison School Board," *CT*, January 27, 1969; Luellen, "Calhoun, Onsager Win Race," *WSJ*, April 2, 1969; "Sennett, Mansfield End Era on Board," *CT*, June 17, 1969.

236. Dunlop, "The Auld Lang Syne's Out," *WSJ*, June 4, 1969; Dunlop, "'Hail Central'—and Farewell," *WSJ*, June 6, 1969; "Last Tribute to Central: 'Smallest but Best,'" *CT*, June 6, 1969.

237. Gribble, "On Last School Turn, Central Finishes Fast," *WSJ*, May 17, 1969.

238. Kendrick, "Mrs. Doyle Heads School Board," *CT*, July 8, 1969.

239. Pommer, "Black History, Vocational Offerings, Are Biggest High School Changes," *CT*, August 28, 1969.

240. "City's High Schools, UW, Plan Vietnam Programs Oct. 15," *CT*, October 9, 1969; Gribble, "Despite Moratorium, Classes Go on Today," *WSJ*, October 15, 1969.

241. "Teachers' Pact Wins Approval," *WSJ*, November 4, 1969.

242. Gribble, "Ired over School Budget Cut, Ritchie to Delay Wielding Ax," *WSJ*, November 26, 1969; Kendrick, "Angry School Board Starts Move to 'Go It Alone,'" *CT*, December 2, 1969.

243. Elaine Cohen, "West High Student Suspended for Distribution of 'The Cardinal,'" *DC*, December 11, 1969.

244. McGilligan, "School Board Budget Cuts Pack 500 into Auditorium," *DC*, December 16, 1969.

245. Pommer, "Lakewood, Badger School to Stay Open," *CT*, December 18, 1969.

246. Pommer, "Angry School Officials Hit Mayor, Council on Funding," *CT*, December 18, 1969.

247. "Dr. Ray Huegel, 78, Education, Sports, Recreation Leader, Dies," *WSJ*, September 4, 1969.

248. Cowan, "Registration of Gun Sales or Gifts Voted by Council," *CT*, January 10, 1969.

249. "'Emergency' Curfew Powers Given Mayor," *WSJ*, January 10, 1969.

250. "Emery Blasts Courts, Hits 'Public Apathy' about Crime," *CT*, January 11, 1969.

251. "City Policing Eyed for Campus," *WSJ*, January 30, 1969.

252. Cowan and Sandage, "Will 'Guidelines' Compel City 'Go-Gos' to Go Away?" *CT*, February 18, 1969; "Excerpts from Guidelines for Discotheques in City," *CT*, February 18, 1969; "Go-Go Girls Demonstrate against Mayor's Guidelines," *CT*, March 1, 1969.

253. "Crime Increases Reported for City," *WSJ*, March 11, 1969.

254. Wilber Emery testimony, *Joint Committee*, March 26, 1969; "Emery Raps UW Stand on Drugs," *WSJ*, March 27, 1969; Selk, "Campus Police Force's Future to Be Decided," *WSJ*, December 31, 1969.

255. Wineke, "Council OKs New Obscenity Laws," *WSJ*, November 26, 1969.

256. Pfefferkorn, "Elson Guilty in Helmet Test Case," *WSJ*, June 10, 1969; Hougan, "Elson Enters DA Race; Wouldn't Enforce 'Bad Laws,'" *CT*, December 18, 1969; Mitchell, "Wilson Hotel Basks in Elson's Limelight," *WSJ*, December 19, 1969.

257. Zweifel, "Dream of City Auditorium May Come True at Last in '69," *CT*, January 17, 1969.

258. Raymond Merle, "Auditorium Parking Cut," *WSJ*, January 16, 1969; Merle, "Action on Auditorium Delayed," *WSJ*, January 21, 1969.

259. Cowan, "Auditorium Plan OK'd for Bidding," *CT*, February 12, 1969; Cowan, "Auditorium Bid Opening Delayed to April 1; Some Material Late," *CT*, March 14, 1969.

260. Merle, "Two Firms OKd to Submit Bids on Auditorium," *WSJ*, March 22, 1969; Zweifel, "Peters Will See Auditorium Through," *CT*, April 4, 1969; Zweifel, "Peters Says Foes of Auditorium Scared Off Prospective Bidders," *CT*, April 4, 1969; Mollenhoff and Hamilton, *Monona Terrace*, 297, n41.

261. Merle, "Auditorium Bids Top Estimates," *WSJ*, April 2, 1969; Zweifel, "Auditorium Bids Near Target; Tally 'Alternate' Figures," *CT*, April 2, 1969; Merle, "Auditorium Cost Put at $1.5 Million More," *WSJ*, April 11, 1969.

262. Gould, "Auditorium Gifts Pass $80,000 Mark," *CT*, April 14, 1969.

263. Cowan, "Council Approves Auditorium Rebids," *CT*, April 15, 1969.

264. "Dyke to Start Talks on Auditorium Cuts," *WSJ*, April 16, 1969.

265. Tom Foley, "Dyke Abandoning Downtown Site," *CT*, July 17, 1969.

266. Zweifel, "No Auditorium Committee, City Finds," *CT*, August 19, 1969; Foley, "Aldermen Turn Back Two Dyke Choices," *CT*, April 22, 1970.

267. "Memorial Rites Set for Harold Groves," *CT*, December 3, 1969; editorial, "Harold Groves—the Epitome of the Wisconsin Idea," *CT*, December 3, 1969; Mollenhoff and Hamilton, *Monona Terrace*, 128.

268. "J.W. Jackson, City Beautifier, Dies at Age 90," *WSJ*, May 23, 1969; Mollenhoff and Hamilton, *Monona Terrace*, 32.

269. Gould, "Why Was Theater Troupe Barred?" *CT*, January 16, 1969; Cowan, "Brecht Play Is Well Done, but Over-Long," *CT*, January 16, 1969; Anson Rabinbach, "The Living Theater: False Forms of Liberation in a Frank Lloyd Wright Church," *Connections* 3, no. 6, February 5–20, 1969; "Inspired by Show, Viewers Get Down to Naked Truth," *CT*, January 18, 1969; Bruce Weber, "Judith Malina, Founder of the Living Theater, Dies at 88," *New York Times*, April 10, 2015.

270. "Center Assembles John Steuart Curry Art Exhibition," *WSJ*, January 8, 1969; "Surprise Painting Joins Curry Exhibit at Art Center," *WSJ*, January 26, 1969.

271. *CT*, March 27, 1969.

272. Aehl, "First Negro Wins City Council Seat," *WSJ*, April 2, 1969.

273. "Foe Accuses Ald. Devine of Conflict," *CT*, January 23, 1969.

274. Sandage, "City Council Gets Eight New Members," *CT*, April 2, 1969.

275. "Parks Re-Instated to 5th Ward Seat," *CT*, August 27, 1969.

276. John W. English, "'Lysistrata'—Bold, Innovative," *WSJ*, May 10, 1969; Howard Gellman, "'Lysistrata,' A 'Broom St.' First," *DC*, May 14, 1969; Gondek, "Broom St. Theatre: Cooperative of the Arts," *DC*, 1969 Fall Registration issue; Stuart Gordon email, August 20, 2017.

277. Hougan, "Mifflin Hails Dylan Non-Arrival," *CT*, July 5, 1969.

278. Sara Sharpe, "Youthful Army Trudges with Enthusiasm for Cause," *WSJ*, October 6, 1969.

279. Mitchell, "Mayor Offers Austere Budget," *WSJ*, November 7, 1969; Foley, "Can Dyke Decree a Legal Limit to the Snow?" *CT*, November 7, 1969.

280. Mitchell, "City Council Takes Steps toward Efficiency," *WSJ*, November 16, 1969.

281. Dieckmann, "Justo's Club Long Era to End," *WSJ*, November 4, 1969.

282. Foley, "Marquette Neighborhood Center Plan Revealed by Plea for Zone Variance," *CT*, December 9, 1969.

283. "What Levy Means," *WSJ*, December 13, 1969; Mitchell, "Budget Adopted: Tax Rises $3.36," *WSJ*, December 13, 1969.

284. Michael Bodden, "A History of the Mifflin Street Co-Op," *Waxing America,* www.waxingamerica.com/2006/05/history_of_the_.html.

285. Gloria B. Anderson, "Co-op Grocery on Mifflin: Marx with Cash Register," *CT*, July 8, 1969.

286. Hougan, "Mifflin Street Co-op Grocery to Aid Welfare Recipients," *CT*, September 5, 1969.

287. "Young Drug User Admits Theft at Mifflin Co-op," *CT*, November 4, 1969.

288. Tim Baxter, "Mifflin Coop Recovers Stolen Checks," *DC*, October 28, 1969.

289. Patricia Simms, "Tenant Union Seeks Shift of Power from Landlords," *WSJ*, September 24, 1969.

290. Hougan, "Tenants Union Says Builder of High-Rise Will Negotiate," *CT*, October 25, 1969.

291. "The Madison Tenant Union," *DC*, November 9, 1969; David Fine and Steve Vetzner, "MTU Withholds Rent from Two Landlords," *DC*, December 11, 1969.

292. "Tenant Union Claims Victory in a Week-Long 'Rent Strike,'" *WSJ*, December 18, 1969.

293. "Dyke to Run for Mayor; Lost by 64 Votes in '67," *WSJ*, January 5, 1969; Dennis Sandage, "Festge Says He Won't Run for Mayor Again," *CT*, January 6, 1969.

294. Sandage, "Dyke for Freeways, Reynolds for Mass Transit," *CT*, March 11, 1969.

295. Sandage, "Festge Record Is Issue at Mayoralty Debate," *CT*, February 6, 1969.

296. Merle, "Dyke Tops Mayor's Field," *WSJ*, March 5, 1969.

297. Sandage, "Dyke for Freeways, Reynolds for Mass Transit," *CT*, March 11, 1969.

298. "Labor Paper, Madison Sun Back Reynolds for Mayor," *CT*, March 27, 1969; Otto, "Citizens' Committee Backs Dyke for Mayor," *WSJ*, March 26, 1969; "Clarenbach Notes 'Foresight' of Good Citizens Group," *CT*, March 29, 1969.

299. Sandage, "Dyke Making His 3rd Try; Sees Spending as Top Issue," *CT*, March 3, 1969.

300. Sandage, "Reynolds Offers Most Experience," *CT*, March 3, 1969.

301. Sandage, "Reynolds Rips Dyke on Suburbs, Freeway," *CT*, March 21, 1969; Sandage, "Festge Hits Dyke's Pitch To Suburbs," *CT*, March 27, 1969

302. Dunlop, "Fiscal Policies Spur Candidates' Debate," *WSJ*, March 11, 1969.

303. Mitchell, "City Elects Dyke by Strong Margin," *WSJ*, April 2, 1969; Sandage, "West Side Gives Dyke His Victory," *CT*, April 2, 1969.

304. Sandage, "Dyke Lists New Appointments," *CT*, April 15, 1969.

305. William Dyke, Mayor's Annual Message, April 15, 1969, WI-M 1 Mun 47 1:1969, Wisconsin Historical Society Library; Merle, "Mayor Sets Priorities to Meet Needs of City," *WSJ*, April 16, 1969.

306. "City Group Ditches Festge's Job Bid," *CT*, April 11, 1969.

307. "Festge Takes Insurance Sales Post," *CT*, April 17, 1969; Bill Lueders, "In Memoriam, 2007," *Isthmus,* December 28, 2007.

308. "State Street: The Next Few Years," City Planning Department, January 1969; Denise Simon, "Merchants Cool to State St. Plan," *DC*, February 12, 1969.

309. Foley, "No Mall, State St. Merchants Say," *CT*, June 25, 1969.

310. "Board Urges Mall on Upper State St.," *WSJ*, July 3, 1969.

311. Foley, "Say Zoning Change Would Advance State Street Mall," *CT*, September 9, 1969; Santini, "U Bookstore Move Seen to Aid State Street Mall," *DC*, September 20, 1969; McGilligan, "Public Favors State St. Mall," *DC*, October 15, 1969; Feldman, *Buildings,* 274.

312. Sandage, "Dyke for Freeways, Reynolds for Mass Transit," *CT*, March 11, 1969; Sandage, "Dyke Is Standing Still on U.S. Bus Aid Requirement," *CT*, April 30, 1969; Sandage, "Bus Commission Gets Tirade as Dyke Insults Chairman," *CT*, May 2, 1969; Jan Gams, "Mayor Blamed in Bus 'Hang-up,'" *WSJ*, July 31, 1969; Kendrick, "City Facing Another Bus Crisis," *CT*, August 19, 1969; Foley, "Dyke Secrecy in Bus Negotiations Raising Questions from Critics," *CT*, August 26, 1969; Foley, "U.S. Clears Way for Bus Purchase by City," *CT*, November 3, 1969; Kendrick, "Council Moves to Keep Buses Rolling," *CT*, November 7, 1969; Mitchell, "Bus Firm Approves City Purchase Bid," *WSJ*, November 9, 1969.

313. "Expressway Section Opens Today," *WSJ*, November 26, 1969.

314. Foley, "Marquette Residents Ask Through Traffic Removal," *CT*, September 19, 1969; "Changes in East Side Traffic Flow," *CT*, December 9, 1969.

315. "Dimensions & Dividends: City Development 1968," Madison City Planning Department, March 1970.

316. Kreisman, "Exclusive Bus Lane Is Ruled Illegal," *CT*, March 18, 1969; Aehl, "Better Not Drive Bus Lane," *WSJ*, September 23, 1969.

317. Kreisman, "Bardwell Rips 'Flouting of Law' by City on Bus Lane," *CT*, October 21, 1969.

318. Kendrick, "Council Stands By 'Wrong' Lane," *CT*, December 17, 1969; "Appeal on Bus Lane Critical, Conrad Says," *WSJ*, December 29, 1969.

319. "Dimensions & Dividends: City Development 1969," Madison City Planning Department, March 1970.

320. Madison Department of Planning, Community Development and Economic Development.

321. MRA minutes, January 22, 1969; "MRA OKs Land Sale Split to Mohs, Carley Groups," *CT*, January 23, 1969; Fred Mohs interview, June 21, 2017.

322. Havens Wilber, "Entirely New 1st National Square Building Planned," *CT*, March 4, 1969.

323. Merle, "Parks Chief Marshall to Retire; F.W. Bradley Named Successor," *WSJ*, January 3, 1969.

324. Sandage, "Lucey to Develop 683-Acre Self-Contained Community," *CT*, April 17, 1969.

325. Merle, "Developers Start Site Grading for West Towne Shop Center," *WSJ*, June 12, 1969.

326. "UW Area Renewal Contracts Signed," *CT*, July 4, 1969.

327. "Sears on E. Washington Ave. Will Test Sunday Openings," *CT*, October 4, 1969.

328. Steve Twin, "Renewal: Problems Beget Problems," *DC*, December 3, 1969; Sandage, "Watch Out Students: They're Gonna Get Your Ghetto (and Make a Profit Too)," *Kaleidoscope* 1, no. 10 (December 1969).

329. Custer, "'Mapleside,' an Architectural, Historic Beauty, Due to Be Torn Down Soon," *CT*, June 2, 1969; Patricia Simms, "Mapleside Gets a Face-Lifting," *WSJ*, December 5, 1969.

330. Joseph McBride, "Youth, Food Chain Don't Know What to Do with Historic House," *WSJ*, November 22, 1969.

331. Zweifel, "Residents Ask Dyke to Save Historic 'Mapleside' Home," *CT*, June 13, 1969.

332. Simms, "Mapleside Friends Granted Month Delay on Demolition," *WSJ*, November 29, 1969; Taychopera Foundation Records, Mss 371, box 2, folder 6, WHSA.

333. "Plans Underway to Save City's Historic Buildings," *CT*, August 27, 1969; Gould, "Mapleside: Profit or Bad Planning?" *CT*, December 31, 1969.

334. "Madison Area Artists Offer Works for Mapleside Sale," *CT*, December 10, 1969; Gould, "Mapleside: Sign of Battle of Values," *CT*, December 30, 1969.

335. Gould, "After 117 Years, Mapleside Yields to Wrecking Crew," *CT*, February 16, 1970; Ada Louise Huxtable, "Pow! Goodby History, Hello Hamburger," *New York Times*, March 21, 1971.

Index

Page numbers in *italics* refer to illustrations.

Aberg, William J. P., 351
Abraham Lincoln Junior High School, 196
Abrahamson, Shirley S., 103, 106, 107, *107*, 369
Ackerman, Adolph J., 203
Ad Hoc Committee Against Extremism, 165
Ad Hoc Committee for Peace in Viet Nam, 169–170
Ad Hoc Committee for Student Choice, 213
Ad Hoc Committee for Thinking, 193
Ad Hoc Committee to Protest Dow Chemical, 254
Adamany, Ken, 153, 297, 299
Adas Jeshurun Synagogue, 72, 73, 93
Adolfson, L. H., 41
affirmative action, 230, 312
African Americans, x, 51, 176; aldermen, 306, 394–395; black
    nationalism, 79, 308, 318; demographics, 4–5, 17; election
    officials, 144; employment, 107, 142–143, 306, 383; and police,
    270–271, 303–304, 306, 308, 312, 383, 384–385; report on,
    226–228; students, 108, 196, 285, 333–334, 387; teachers, 25,
    51, 60, 91, 108, 196, 227, 285, 335–336, 387–388; at UW, 145,
    178, 230, 309–314
African Methodist Episcopal Church, 73
African Students Union, 361
Afro American and Race Relations Center, 310, 354, 361
Agudas Achim Synagogue, 93
alcohol, 9, 61, 329; drinking age, 121; licenses, 16–17; sales, 30,
    46, 50, 280
Ali, Muhammad, 308, *308*, 318
All-University ROTC Policy Committee, 319
Alliance of Cities, 271, 399
Allied Development Corporation, 129, 203
Altemus, Ida B., 38
Altwell, Robert H., 310–311
Amato, Salvatore (Mrs.), 186
American Federation of State, County and Municipal Employees,
    63, 93, 131, 199
American Indians, x, 30, 311, 326, 333
Americans for Democratic Action, 56, 79, 82, 122
Ammerman, Roscoe, 207
AMRC, 122, 376, 378, 380, 381
Amund Reindahl Park, 292, 344
Anchor Savings and Loan, 129, *130*, 168
. . . and Beautiful (newspaper), 384
Anderson, Norman C., 111, 135, 139
Anderson, Ralph, 139

annexations, xi, 29, *29*, 49, 60, 89, 94, 117, 157, 161, 182, 203,
    291, 399
Anthony Grignano Company, 292
Arasmith, Lester, 172
Armstrong, Dwight, 381
Armstrong, Karl, 381
Army Mathematics Research Center (AMRC), 122, 376, 378,
    380, 381
Arringon, Ray, 313
Ashman, Alicia, 341–342, 348, 367, 382, 390
Associated Women Students, 85, 120, 170
Athenean Society, 120
Atwood (neighborhood), 241–242, 290–291
Atwood building, 168
auditorium, 1–3, 35–38, 49–50, 67–71, 90, 129, 147–149, 183–185,
    222–225, 266–267, 271, 272, 322–323, 392–394; cost, 1, 36,
    37, 38, 70, 147–149, 184, 225, 266, 267, 392–393; renderings,
    2, *36*, *267*, *322*; sites, 1, 2–3, 35, 37, 62, 70–71, *71*, 96, 117, 128,
    148, 181, 183, 185, 222–225, 266, *266*, 322, 393
Auditorium Committee, x, xi, 2, 35, 36, 37, 38, 50, 69, 70–71,
    183, 184, 223–225, 266, 272, 322, 392, 393

Bacon Building, 204
Badger Herald (newspaper), 373–374
Badger Ordnance Works, 381
Baganz, Mark, 377
Bakken, Jim, 55, 56
Ball, Phil, 397
Bandy, William T., 398
Bank of Madison, *xiv*
Banovez, Michael Joseph, 222
Barbash, Jack, 153
Barbee, Lloyd, 5, 8, *8*, 16, 41, 76, 78, 101, 143
Bardwell, R. W., 25
Bardwell, Richard W., 67, 71, 129, 137, 147, 230, 295, 334, 340,
    350, 370, 401–402
Bareis, A. W., 32, 96, 105
Baron's (department store), *130*, 158, 203
Baron's (shoe store) *130*
Bartell, Gerald, 158, 159, 183
Bartell, Joyce, *199*
Bascom Hill, *xii*, 22, *133*, 214, *302*, *315*, 345
Bashford Methodist Church, 295
Bass, Clifford, 72
Baxandall, Lee, 21
Bayview Foundation, 231, 287–288, 336–337
Beach, P. Goff, Jr., 239
Beck, Anatole, 253
Becker, Richard, 280
Becker, Stuart, 287, 304, 399

Behrnd, George, 32, 98, 128, 165, 240
Belmont Hotel, 348
Beltline, 27, 63, 64, 163
Bennett, Dan Michael, 321
Bensinger, Gail, 177, 192
bequests: discrimination, 38–40, 77
Bergman, Lowell, 210, 214, 216, 217
Bergstedt, Karen, 388
Bernard, Geraldine, 91
Bersaglieri Fraternal Organization, 73
Beth Israel Center, 93
Bethel Lutheran Church, 129, 164
Bjarne Romnes Apartments, 338
black nationalism, 79, 308, 318
Black People's Alliance (BPA), 269, 311, 312, 354, 361. *See also*
    Concerned Black People (CBP); Concerned Negro Students
Black Revolution conference, 353–355, 360
Black Strike, *ii*, 312, 353–363, *357, 358, 359, 360*, 380
Blaha, Thomas J., 320
Blied building, 168
Blight Elimination and Slum Clearance Act, 11
Bloodgood, Joseph W., 27
Blooming Grove (town), x, 29, 60, 89
Blum, Andre, 272
Bluteau's Market, 161
Board of Education, x, xi–xii, 37, 60, *90*, 91, 197–198, 200, 238,
    290, 334, *389*; elections, 25, 156, 196, 285, 286, 335, 388
Board of Estimates, x, 272, 286, 296, 307
Board of Public Welfare, 97, 127
Board of Public Works, 71, 129, 138, 159, 400
Boardman, Betty, 315, 349
Boettcher, Orris C., 334
Bohrod, Aaron, 158, 165, 203, 405
Bolden, Thomas, 104, 109
Boll, James C., 234, 285, 329, 331–332, 370
Bollig, Melvin, 244
Bolz, Adolph C., 207, 351
bond issues, xi, 11, 25, 28, 51, 60, 69, 89–90, 117, 118, 128, 163,
    196, 237, 238, 267, 338, 346
Borgwardt, Robert, 302
Bowers, John Z., 87
Bowman, Duane, 180
BPA, 269, 311, 312, 354, 361
Bradley, Forrest W., 402
Brager, Arnie, 364
Bramhall, Art, 396
Bramhall, Jennie Justo, 396
Brantmeyer, Josephine, 382
Brantmeyer, Ricky, 382
Brasci, Giorgio, 186

Brasci, Josephine, 186
Brautigam, Richard, 351
Braxton, Gay, 99, 138, 186
Bree, Germaine, 22, 170, 220
Breese Stevens Field incident, 303–305, 384–385
Breines, Paul, 40, *40*, 53, 193
Brickman, Marshall, 21, 40, 53
Brickson, Marv, 25, 145, 286
Brittingham urban renewal project, 10, *10*, 13, 15, 16–17, 42–43,
    45, 47–48, 72, 73, 109–110, 136, 137, 187, 205, 232, 288
Brittingham, Thomas E., Jr., 24
Brittingham Park, 43, 114
Broadfoot, Grover L., 99
Brodie, Abner, 78
Brooks, Gwendolyn, 356, 373
Brooks, Robert, 158, 159
Broom Street Theater, 374, 395
Brown, Ethel L., 51, 105, 145, 348
Brown v. Board of Education, 8, 40
Browne, Marshall, 2–3, 26, 185, 241
Bruce, Dix, 388
Bruhn, Milt, 56, 192–193, 235, 313, 372, 375
Buenzli, William, 86, 125, 133, 143, 172, 229
Bunch, John, 27, 163, 234–235, 392
Burke, R. Whelan, 344, 390, 404
Burnham, Frank, 396
Burt, Raymond F., 51, 392
Bus Utility Commission, 346
Buslee, Henry, 50
Byrne, William D., 109, 229

CAC. *See* Citizens Advisory Committee (CAC)
Calhoun, Eugene S., 388
Calloway, Nathaniel O., 270, 304
Callsen, Robert, 44, 45, 47, 74, 140, 231
Calneck, Terrence, 311
Calvary Methodist Church, 73
Camp Indianola, 296
Camp Randall, *149*, 154, 193, 235
Campus Area Improvement Association, 201
Campus Drive, 28, 400
Candlin, Paul, 237
Capital Community Citizens, 284
Capital Times (newspaper), 78, 99, 105, 279; advertising, 97, *97*,
    103, *104*; and athletics, 20, 23, 192–193, 327; and auditorium,
    68, 69, 90, 96, 128, 148, 184, 223, 224, 267, 393; and civil
    rights, 38, 180, 229, 304; and demonstrations, 174, 261; and
    elections, 32, 49, 50, 77, 117, 145, 182, 398; and urban renewal,
    45, 136–137, 139
Capitol Pavilion, 158–160, 203

Capitol Square, *xiv*, 30, 62, *62*, *66*, 92, 97, *100*, 132, 147, 158–160, 163, 164, 165–166, *165*, *168*, 204, 205, 206, 222, 240, 291; demonstrations, 99, 108, 144, 164, 391
Capitol Theater, *xiv*, *66*
Caputo, Carlo, 14
Carley, David, 337, 338, 402
Carley, James, 338, 402
Carnes, Wilbur R., 70, 137
Carr, David, 170–171
Caruso, Robert, 111
Cashin & Associates, 73
Casperson, Robert P., II, 265
Cates, Richard, 198, 238, 285, 370
Catholic Information Center, *161*
CBP, 254, 255, 269, 301, 309–310, 361
CDA, 172, 217–218, 248, 250–251, 319
censorship, 52, 83, 97, 125, 206, 279, 330–332, 334, 371, 372, 386, 389, 391, 395
Central High School, *xiv*, 24, 59, 89, 90–91, *100*, 122, 123–124, *130*, 157, *159*, 195–196, 236–237, 270
Central-University High School, 91, 156, 182, 195, 236, 283, 285, 286, 303, 333, 386, 387, 388
Cerniglia, Joseph C. "Buffo," 202, 206
CEWV/CEWVN, 169–171, 172, 173, 175, 192, 210, 216, 217, 218–221, 252, 254, 319
Chadbourne Hall (dorm), *82*
Chalet Gardens housing project, 93, 140, 338
Chamberlain, Clyde, 299
Chandler's (shoe store), *130*
Chaney, James, 147
Chapelle, Dickey, 171, *199*, 207
Charles Elver Park, 344
Charmany farm, 151, *151*, 161, 235
Chase Manhattan Bank, 309–310, 361
Cheech, Ottilia, 344
Cheney, Dick, 262
Cheney, Lynn, 262
Cherokee Marsh, 117, 130, 202, 203, 240
Christ Presbyterian Church, *100*, 130, *130*, 159, *168*
Christianson, Elma, 127, 350–351
Chrite, Elrie, 380
Cinema Theater, 292, *292*
Ciporen, Fred, 53, 79, 214, 218
Citizens Advisory Committee (CAC), xi, 73, 75, 97, 137, 139, *199*, 268, 335
Citizens Committee for the Teaching of Negro History in Madison Schools, 335, 336
Citizens Committee to Eliminate Civil Defense, 128
Citizens Concerned for University-Community Issues, 371
Citizens for Better Government, 113, 118, 398

Citizens for Civic Peace, 383
Citizens for Monona Terrace, 38, 67, 96, 394
Citizens in Support of the United States Soldiers in Viet Nam, 175
Citizens' Realistic Auditorium Association (CRAA), 3, *3*, 35, 38, 49, 67, 185
Citizen's Watchdog Committee, 112–114
City Council. *See* Common Council
City Employees Union, 350
City-University Coordinating Committee, 205, 234–235
civil defense, 32, 51, 127–128, *128*, 197
civil rights, 4–9, 17–18, 25, 38–42, 43, 60, 76–81, 101–109, 141–147, 176–181, 182, 225–230, 268–271, 301–314, 326, 335–336, 353–363, 382–386. *See also* discrimination
Clarenbach, Henry, 153
Clarenbach, Kathryn F., 153, *199*, 226, 382
Clark, Kenneth K., 43, 159–160, 185, 224, 344
Clay, Harvey, *355*, 358
Cleland, W. Wallace, 345
Clifcorn, James, 265
Clodius, Robert, 151, 233, 281
Coatsworth, John, 123–124, 164, 170, 174, 214, 248, 254
Coatta, John, 235, 313–314, 372, 375
Cohen, Bob, 172, 211, 218, 220, 247, 248, 252, 254, 255, 257, 262, 263–264, *264*, 275, 276, 310, 314, 318
Coleman, J. Reed, 166
Coleman, Thomas, 166
Colescott, Warrington, 158, 405
Collins, Charles, 46
Colston, Marshall, 6, 76, 102, 103, *103*, 106, 107, 108, 143, 157, 228, 231, 358
Commercial State Bank, *xiv*, *130*
Committee for Direct Action to End the War in Viet Nam (CDA), 172, 217–218, 248, 250–251, 319
Committee for Student Rights (CSR), 262, 263
Committee of Thirty, 369, 371
Committee on the University and the Draft (CUD), 210, 211, 215, 216
Committee to Defend Individual Rights, 253
Committee to End the War in Viet Nam (CEWV/CEWVN), 169–171, 172, 173, 175, 192, 210, 216, 217, 218–221, 252, 254, 319
Committee to Save the Bus Lane for Bicycles, 275
Committee to Support the People of South Viet Nam, 171, 173, 175, 207
Common Council, x, xi, 32, 49, 144, 147, 217, 294, 391; acquisition of land, 94, 161, 162, 203, 240; and alcohol sales, 30, 50, 201; and appointees, 98, 148, 238; and auditorium, 2, 3, 35, 36–38, 67–71, 148, 184, 223–225, 322, 323, 392–393; black members, 306, 394–395; and budgets, xi, 25, 272–274, 347, 349, 389, 396; and city employees, 199, 348, 349–350; and civil rights, 101–107, 131, 180, 268–269, 304–305, 307, 385–386;

Common Council (*continued*)

Committee of the Whole, xi, 44–45, 48, 68, *102*, 104, 113, 163, 268–269, 296, 340, 385–386, 395; and curfew, 390; and DDT, 296; and demonstrations, 175, 220, 250, 275, 277–278, 369, 371, 378; ethics code, 202, 244; and facility names, 157–158, 198, 245; and gun control, 61, 340, 390; and library, 93; and licenses, 16–17, 47, 48, 103, 180, 200, 201, 228–230, 244, 295, 385–386; open meetings, 127, 200; pay raise, 50; and planning, 159–160; and police department, 341–342; and smoking, 162–163; and strikes, 199, 349–350; and transportation, 27–28, 64, 128, 163, 242, 275, 292, 346, 400, 401, 402; and urban renewal, 11, 42, 44–46, 58, 73, 111, 112, 113–114, 137, 138–139, 140, 186, 188, 189, 240, 288, 338; and Vietnam, 315–316; and welfare, 96–97, 396; women members, 51, 348; zoning, 42, 161, 203, 239, 344–345, 400

Community Action Commission, 337

Community Welfare Council, 337

Concerned Black People (CBP), 254, 255, 269, 301, 309–310, 361. *See also* Black People's Alliance (BPA)

Concerned Negro Students, 230, 269

Concerned Students of West High School, 386

Congress of Racial Equality (CORE), 40, 42, 104, 105, 109, 141, 142–143, 145, *146*, 153, 172

Conklin Park, 37, 70, 71, 117, 128, 197–198

Connections (newspaper), 253, 261, 279, 334, 335, 372, 373, 374

Connell, John, 202

Conners, Randolph, 148, 184

Conrad, Edwin S. 50, 69, 74, 97, *97*, 98, 103, 125, 136, 139–140, 144, 147, 148, 164–165, 200, 202, 206, 273, 331, 340, 341, 389, 391, 395, 402, 404

Conrad A. Elvehjem Elementary School, 91

Consigny, Thomas, 244, 268

Contemporary Affairs Forum, 122

conventions, 70, 129, 222; facilities, 185, 224, 266, 322, 392

Cooper, Leo, 105, 113, *114*, 138, 139–140, 200, 350

Corcoran, Robert, *97*, 347

CORE. *See* Congress of Racial Equality (CORE)

Corwin, Ron, 42

Coughlin, Joseph Leo "Roundy." *See* "Roundy Says"

Council of Federated Organizations, 147

Covenant Presbyterian Church, 295

Cowan, Judy, 5, 8

Cowan, Linda, 192

Coyle, Owen, 139

Coyote, Peter, 256

CRAA, 3, *3*, 35, 38, 49, 67, 185

Crabb, Ted, 311

Crary, David, 303

Crary, James T., 268, 269, 304, 305, 307, 316, 395

crime, 9–10, 22, 27, 61, 125–127, 162–163, 203, 205–206, 238, 271, 276, 287, 307, 338–342, 390–392; armed robbery, 206; arson, 268, 309, *310*, 317, 319, 361; battery, 311, 356; cruising, 61; disorderly conduct, 56–57, 85–86, 108–109, 125, 132, 143, 170, 201, 247, 264, 303, 307, 311, 314, 315, 318, 356, 376; drugs, 126, 193–194, 234, 278, 280, 328–329, 334, 338, 391; loitering, 60, 61, 172; murder, 98, 99, 147, 338, 342; shoplifting, 60, 339; statistics, 26, 132, 339, 391; theft, 287, 339; vandalism, 52, 61, 123, 156, 238, 242, 253, 270, 284, 285, 356, 358, 377, 378, 381. *See also* riots; terrorism

Criter, Ken, 313

Croal, George, 377

Cruse, Harold, 79

CSR, 262, 263

Cuba, 21, 22, 54, 99, 123–124

CUD, 210, 211, 215, 216

Cumbler, John, 211, 250

Cummings, Nelson, 307

curfews: city, 367, 390; university, 20, 85, 120, 193, 324, 325, 329, 374

Currie, George, 370

Curti, Merle, 170

Cushman, Edward, 148, 184

Custer, Frank, 348

Cutlip, Scott, 175

Daily Cardinal (newspaper), 22, 54, 82, 87, 192, 281, 347, 374, 376; advertising, 248, 250; and athletics, 24, 55, 85; and campus life, 85; and civil rights, 40, 109, 362; and demonstrations, 8, 40, 80, 171, 172, 174, 177, 221, 250, 255, 264, 356, 381; and drugs, 278, 328; opinions of, 83, 194–195, 251, 279, 330, 371, 389; and Vietnam, 83

Daley, Edward, 126

Dane County: Alcoholic Referral Center, 329; Board of Supervisors, 378, 384; Memorial Coliseum, 291–292; Mental Health Center, 186; Sheriff's Department, 125, 259, 318, 340, 349, 364, 366, 368; Traffic Department, 340

Davenport, Stanley, 328–329

David, Robin, 217, 219, *219*, 220

Davidson, Bruce, 106

Davis, Ron, 256, 262

Day, Roland, 44, 45, 75, 186

DDT, 32, 52, 128, 296

Deadman, C. A. "Doc," 95

DeBardeleben, Arthur, 108, 151, 154, 194, 221, 277, 332

DeBoer, Fritz, 53

Demetral, Jimmy, 295

demonstrations, 165, 391, 395; antidraft, 209–216, *212*, *213*, *214*, *215*, 253, 318; antiwar, 121, 122, *122*, 164, 169–175, *171*, *173*, 210, 211, *212*, 216–221, 247–264, *249*, *258*, *259*, *260*, 295, 315, 316–319, 320, 325, 376, 378–380, *379*, *380*; boycotts, 143, 311,

313, 316, 318, 361; bus lane, 275–278, *276, 277*; civil rights, 5–8, *6, 7,* 40, 42, 78, 80–81, *80,* 108–109, *108,* 142–144, *143,* 145, *145,* 146, *146,* 147, 153, 176, 177–178, *177, 300,* 301–302, 309–310, 311–312, 318, 325, 353–363; Cuba, 54, 99; disruptions, 54, *55,* 85, 108–109, 142–143, 146, *146,* 155, 172, 173, 175, 211–212, 218–221, 248, 255–261, *258,* 275–278, *277,* 311–312, 316, 317, 319, 320, 326, 328, 355–363, *357, 358, 359, 360,* 376, 377; fasts, 147, 178, 217; public relations, 6, 8, 77, 172–173, *174,* 175, 214, 220–221, 277, 318, 320, 323–324, 373; regulations, 220, 221, 250, 251, 254, 256, 262–263, 312, 319–320, 376, 379–380; shop-ins, 142–143; sit-ins, 5, 6, 9, 210–216, *212,* 248, 249, 250, 252, 255–261, *258, 259, 260,* 309, 311–312, 319, 320, 386; strikes, 262–263, 312, 318, 353–363, *357, 358, 359, 360;* teach-ins, 170–171, *171*

Dennis, Elizabeth "Liz," 143, 170

Dennis, Gene, Jr., 194

Devine, James T., Jr., 395

Devine, James T., Sr., 397–398

DeVore, David G., 344

DeZonia, Robert, 335

Diamond, Dion, 145

Dickert, Chris, 298

Dickert, H. R. (Mrs.), 298

Dickey, James, 233–234

Diemer, Melvin, 65

Dingeldein, Donald, 222

discotheques, 199, 390–391

discrimination, 43, 226–228, 270, 306, 307, 313–314; age, 383; bequests, 38–40, 77; education, 196, 227, 387; employment, 5, 25, 103, 107, 108, 142, 177, 228, 238, 271, 295, 306–307, 317, 382–383; foreign students, 142; housing, 4–5, 14, 17–18, 39, 40–41, 44, 46, 72, 74, 75, 76, 78–79, 89, 101–107, 109, 115–116, 141–142, 144, 177, 178, 182, 189, 225–226, 228, 268–269, 307; licenses, 16–17, 200, 228; private clubs, 76, 179–181, 228–229, 384, 385–386; against women, 50, 77, 200, 226, 229–230, 295, 317, 382–383. *See also* Equal Opportunities Ordinance

Dodge, William, 294–295

Dolbeare, Kenneth, 253

Donley, Willis, 385

Dow Chemical Company, 247–252, 254–264, 314–315, 320, 376, 380

Dowling, Jean Pierre, 221

Doyle, James E., Jr., *200*

Doyle, James E., Sr., 26, 78, 99, 182, 199, *200,* 285, 320, 387

Doyle, Ruth B., 76, 156, 178, 198, 199, 200, *200,* 230, 285, 310, 311–313, 334, 359, 382, 387, 388

draft, 169, 174, 175, 209–216, 248–250, 252, 253, 314, 317, 318, 378

Dries, Robert, 385

Dunning, Abel, 403

Dunning, Pamela, 403

Durkin, Edward D., 26, 197, *245,* 349–350, 367, 369–370

Durkin, Edward P., 26

Duszynski, Edwin J., 98

Dutch elm disease, 32, 52, 98, 128, 165, 240, 296, 345

Dyke, William, 56, *397,* 404; and auditorium, 181, 393; and budgets, 395; and civil rights, 386; mayoral elections, 181, 271–272, 398–399; and police department, 364, 385; and public schools, 390; and riots, 365, 367–371; and transportation, 400, 401

Dylan, Bob, 53–54, 140, 395

Eagle Heights (neighborhood), 94, 161

Eagles Club, 228–229, 385, 386

East High School, 24, 59, 60, 89, 122, 123, 156, 195, 236, 270, 283, 333, 386, 388

East Side Businessmen's Association (ESBMA), 290–291, 306; festival, 29

East Side News (newspaper), 241

Eastman, Gerald, 271

Eckloff, Carl, 107

Edelson, Betsy, 193

Edelson, Morris, 193, 394

Edgerton, Russell, 217

Edgewater Hotel, 31, 160

education. *See* Madison Public Schools; University of Wisconsin

Edwards, Conan, 335

Edwards, Liberty, 312, 357, 359

Edwards, Willie, 230, 269, 309, 312, 354–363

Eisenscher, Michael, 194

Elder, George, 105, 114, 127, 137, 163

Elder, Joseph, 170

elections, 99, 217; council, 51, 69, 113, 118, 137, 144–145, 306, 316, 317, 348, 394–395; county, 349; gubernatorial, 155, 333; mayoral, 1, 36, 48–50, 101, 111–112, 113, 117–118, 149, 181–183, 271–272, 398–399; presidential, 8–9, 20, 22, 32–33, 153, 165, 166, 253, 315, 316, 317, 320, 325–326, 347; registration, 32, 33, 96; school board, 25, 156, 196, 285, 335, 388

Elks Club, 228–229, 385, 388

Ella's Delicatessen, *161*

Elm Drive Dorms, 21

Elson, Edward Ben, 248, 392, 398

Elvehjem, Conrad, 6, 7, 8, 22, *55,* 77, 78, 86–87

Elvehjem, Constance, 87, 91

Elvehjem, Robert, 87

Elvehjem Art Center, 121, 191, 290, *354*

Elver, Charles, 344

Emery, Wilbur H. "Bill,": administration, 61, 125, 127, 206, 305, 339, 340–342, 348; and alcohol sales, 30; appointed, 25–26; and bicycles, 164, 205; and censorship, 125, 199, 331–332, 395; and civil rights, 200, 229, 305; and demonstrations, 172, 174, 257–261, 305, 319, 367, 371, 377; and gun control, 390;

Emery, Wilbur H. "Bill" (*continued*)
  health issues, 339; and high school students, 60, 61, 162–163; and intelligence gathering, 170, 364, 395; and UW students, 57, 61, 211, 234, 391
eminent domain, 10–11, 240, 343
employment: discrimination, 5, 25, 76, 103, 107, 108, 142, 177, 228, 238, 271, 317, 382; Plans for Progress Alliance, 306–307; statistics, 5, 28, 29, 62, 92, 94, 107, 142, 204, 207, 290, 306, 342–343
Emporium (department store), 204, 240
Emspak, Frank, 172, 175, 210, 263
Engen, Philip, 397–398
EOC. *See* Equal Opportunities Commission (EOC)
Equal Opportunities Commission (EOC), 103, 107, 141–142, *141*, 143, 180–181, 227, 268, 270–271, 304–305, 307, 336, 399; reports, 176, 177, 225–226, 228, 269, 270, 271, 306, 384–385, 387
Equal Opportunities Ordinance, 76, 101–107, 116, 131, 133, 157, 180, 182, 200, 268–269, 305, 383
Erickson, John, 327
ESBMA, 290–291, 306; festival, 29
Espeseth, Earl A., 104, 139, *186*
Ethics Board, 244
Evjue, William T., 1, 32, 69, 97, 229
Evjue Foundation, 393
Ewen, Stuart, 170, 172, 193, 248, 253, 257, 279

F. W. Woolworth Company, 5–6, *6*, 7, *130*
fair housing ordinance, 41, 101–107, 268–269. *See also* Equal Opportunities Ordinance
Falk, Philip, xii, 25, 37, 59, 60, 89, 90–91, *90*, 112, 124, 231, 285
fallout shelters, 32, 51, 127–128, *128*, 197
Fassnacht, Robert, 381
Fast for Freedom, 147, 178
Faulkner, Austin "Augie," 126, 160
Feely, Dorothy, 396
Feinsinger, Nathan S., 92, 184, 293–295, 326
Felder, John, 359, 362
Felker, Gene, 314
Fellman, David, 24, 221
Ferris, Collins, 137, 179–180, 228
Festge, Otto, 187, 204, 229, 302, 338; appointments, 198, 238; and auditorium, 183–185, 223–225, 267, 272, 322, 392; and budgets, 273, 347; and civil rights, 269, 304–305, 306–307; and demonstrations, 359; and discotheques, 199, 390–391; and fire department, 350; and gun control, 339–340, 390; mayoral elections, 117, 149, 181–183, 271–272, 398–400; and police department, 217, 261, 271, 287, 319, 328, 340–341; and taxes, 285–285; and transportation, 205, 243, 275, 277–278, 293–295, 346, 401; and urban renewal, *186*, 231, 239, 288, 292, *292*, 343–344; vetoes, 345, 347, 348

Festival de France, 165–166, *165*, *166*
Fey, Betty, 335
Fey, Ruth Sharon, 229, 295
Field House, *33*, 68, 379, *379*
Fields, Jeffrey M., 222
Findorff, Milton, 85, 297
Finman, Ted, 263
Fire Fighters Local 311, 349–350, 369
fires, 52, 245; arson, 100, 268, 309, *310*, 317, 319, 361
First Church of Christ Scientist, *130*
First Development Corporation, 43, 44, 109, 288
First Methodist Church, *100*, *130*, 295
First National Bank, *66*, *100*
First Unitarian Society, 43
Fishel, Leslie H., Jr., 76, 336, 348
Fitchburg (town), 161
Fladen, Jerry, 292
Flaten, Milo, 182, 185, 217, 273, 349–350, 390
Fleming, Robben W., 87, 152, 176, 189, 193, 211, 213–214, *215*, 216, 217, 220, 221, 232, 235–236, 248, 250, *251*, 253, 254, 275, 278, 279, 282
Folk Arts Society, 325, 326, 373, 374
Forbes, S. A., 76
Forrester, Bernard, *355*, 359
Forster, George, 137, 185, 225, 272, 322
Foundations for Friendship Inc., 337
Foust, Leonard, 51, 68, 69
Fox, John, 202, 240
Fox, Ron, 198
Frank Lloyd Wright Foundation, 35, 36, 37, 38, 67, 69, 71, 129, 147–148, 181, 183–184, 223–225, 266, 322
Franklin, Callie, 305
Franklin, Joe, 279, 324
fraternities: black, 280, 310, 383; civil rights, 8, 41, 42, 54, 80–81, *80*, 146–147; statistics, 21, 56, 191, 235, 280; and Vietnam, 171
Frautschi, John Jones, 63
Frautschi, Lowell, 137, 369
Frautschi, W. Jerome, 63
Frautschi, Walter A., 63, 65
Fred Mohs and Associates, 337, 402
Free Press (newspaper), 386
Freedman, Ralph, 243–244
Freedman, Ruth Ellen, 243–244
Freedom Riders, 40, 42, 145
French, Harry L. 65
Friedlander, Daniel B., 169, 170
Friedrick, Jacob, 20
Friends of Mapleside, 405
Friends of South Madison, 337

Friends of the Student Non-Violent Coordinating Committee (FSNCC), 109, 147, 176, 190
Friends of the Urban League, 76, 228, 269
Fritz, Herbert, 158, 338
Froelich, Harold, 251, 279, 329, 362
FSNCC, 109, 147, 176, 190
Fuelleman, Gertrude Casey, 51
Fuerst, John, 318

Gabriner, Bob, 193, 256, 279
Gabriner, Vicki, 256, 259, *260*
Gaebler, Max, 7–8, 78, 178, 332, 369
Galbraith, James, 203
Gallistel, Albert F., 37, 155
Gangstad, Eugene, 47, 73, 114
Garner, Harrison, 37, 105, 158, 161, 166, 394
Gartzke, Paul, 287–288
Garvey, Ed, 7, 21, 54, 56, 252
Gates of Heaven Synagogue, 93
Gay Braxton Apartments, 185, *186*, *288*
Gay building, *xiv*, *66*
Gehner, Arnold, 140
Gelatt, Charles, 154, 330, 380
General Neighborhood Renewal Program (GNRP), 57–58, 74, 112–113, 136, 137, 139–141, 187–188, 289; map, *113*
Genna, Joseph, 17
Genna, Paul, 111
Gerlach, Edgar, 320
Gersmann, Joel, 395
Gerth, Hans, 212
Gervasi, Maria, 186
Gibson, Ann, 56
Gilbert, Olin E., 45
Gilberts, Robert D., 91, 123, 124, 156, 196, 197, 237, 238, 284, 285
Gill, Charles H., 65
Gill, George, 316
Gill, Marcella, 65
Gillies, Ray, 368
Ginsberg, Paul, 193
Gisholt Machine Company, 239, 343
Glass, Sidney, 301
GNRP. *See* General Neighborhood Renewal Program (GNRP)
Goff, Nadine, 163
Goldberg, Harvey, 122, 132, 212, 215, 220, 221, 326, 355, 366, 374
Golden, Bobby, 396
Goldfarb, David, 357
Goldwater, Barry, 165, 166
Goodland, Walter, 333
Goodman, Andrew, 147, 155
Gordon, Ann, 372

Gordon, Carolyn, 395
Gordon, Myron, 179, 181
Gordon, Stuart, 330–332, 395
Gordon Commons, 234
Gorton, Richard, 197
Gothard, William, *141*
Gould, Elizabeth "Teto," 351
Goulette, James, 141, 188–189, 337
Governor's Commission on Human Rights, 38, 51
Governor's Commission on the Status of Women, 153
Graaskamp, James, 297, 375
Grace Episcopal Church, *xiv*, *66*
Grand, Stanley I., 143, 172
Grant's (department store), 6, 7, 29
Graze, Gregory, 330
Greenberg, Mel, 365
Greenbush (neighborhood), 10, 110; demographics, 4; history, 9–10; maps, *9*, *12*; urban renewal, 9–18, 72, 110
Greenfield, Jeff, 80, 82
Greenquist, Kenneth L., 194, 216, 221, 332
Greenside, Mark, 285
Greenwald, James, 215
Gregory, Dick, 306, 326
Greisen, Thomas A., 382
Griggs, Mary Lee, 99, *186*
Groves, Harold, 1, 37, 38, 96, 393–394
Groves, Helen, 1, 393
Gruber, John, 194–195
Guiles, Roger, 311
Gulley, Beatrice, 89
Gulley, Carson, 88–89, 233
Gumptow, Roy, 292
gun control, 61, 339–340, 342, 390

Haas, Franz G., 328, 349
Habel, Annie, 396
Haberman, Frederick, 313
Hackbart, Dale, 21, 121
Hall, Franklin, 43, 96–97, 109
Hall, George, 149, 181, 183, 195
Halle, Vern, 46
Haller, Archibald, 312
Halvorsen, D. L., 88
Hamann, Albert, 32, 119
Hambleton, Harry B., III, 321
Hamilton, Harry, 80, 101, *102*
Hamilton, Patricia, 80
Hamilton, Velma, 51, 80, 108
Hammer, Joseph, 302
Hanisch, Stuart, 41, 76, 78–79, 116

Hanks, Lucien, 31, 63, 85

Hanks, Mary Esther Vilas (Lucien), 31

Hanks, Sybil, 31, 63

Hanna, Hilton E., 383

Hansbrough, Lyle C., 381

Hanson, George (Mrs.), 164

Hanson, Harold, 3, 49, 322

Hanson, Horace, 362

Hanson, Ralph E., 190, 212, 248, 255, 256–258, 312, 329, 355–356

Hanson, Russell, 27

Hare, Nathan, 354–355

Harmon, Gordon, 391, 404

Harrington, Fred Harvey, 78, 195, 280, 375; appointed, 86–88, 87; and athletics, 84, 132, 193, 314, 372; and building program, 150–151, 154, 235–236; and city-university relations, 329; and civil rights, 77, 78, 81, 120, 179–181, 309, 310, 374; and demonstrations, 175, 210–211, 213–216, 214, 215, 220, 248, 251, 254, 314, 377, 379–380; personnel decisions, 152, 324, 327–328, 361, 372; and research, 118, 131; and urban renewal, 112, 136, 140, 188, 281–282

Harris, Horace, 359, 363

Harris, Richard, 226, 383, 399

Harry S. Manchester's Inc., xiv, 66, 100, 158, 159, 164–165

Hart, William Osborne, 90, 170, 202

Hartwich, Kenneth, 123

Haslach, Hank, 211, 247, 248, 251, 252, 314

Hawley, Clifford, 195, 335

Hawley, Jim, 170, 172, 174, 210, 210

Hayakawas, 358, 373

Hayes, Harold, 27

Hayes, Jon "Mickey," 27

Health Department, 32

Heassler, Alton, 38, 50, 67, 69, 98, 99

Hefty, Thomas R., 296

Helen C. White Hall, 354

Hellman, Hal F., 126

Hendershot, William "Curly," 254

Herbst, James, 404

Herfel, Andrew S., 244

Herfel, Lawrence J., 321

Herod, Ralph, 15

Hershey, Lewis B., 174, 209, 281, 317, 318

Hershleder, Stanley, 201

Hickory Hill Park, 162

High School Students for Social Justice, 335

High School Voice (newspaper), 335

Hill, Charles, 289, 306, 337, 383

Hill, Edwin, Jr., 306

Hill Farms development, 30, 62, 332, 402

Hill Farms State Office Building, 92, 161

Hilldale Shopping Center, 30, 62, 92, 94, 151, 161, 332

Hill's (department store), xiv

Hirsch, Elroy "Crazylegs," 372, 373, 375

historic preservation, 348; Mapleside, 403–405; North Hall, 234

History Students Association, 326

Hobbins, Joseph, 167

Hoel, Eldon, 136, 273, 349

Hole, Francis D., 170, 341

Holiday Inn, 161

Hollandale, Walter, 251

Holmes, George, 132

Holy Redeemer Catholic Church, xiv, 66

Hornbeck, Ralph, 305, 369

hospitals, 15, 49, 52, 72, 92, 182, 203, 231, 271, 291

Hotel Loraine, xiv, 3, 132

housing, 30, 129, 227–228, 240, 370; discrimination, 4–5, 14, 17–18, 39, 40–41, 44, 46, 72, 74, 75, 76, 78–79, 89, 101–107, 109, 115–116, 141–142, 144, 177, 178, 182, 189, 225–226, 228, 268–269, 307; elderly, 31, 42, 45, 63, 73, 93, 110, 111, 129, 186, 232, 288, 338; integration, 39–40, 63, 93, 101, 131; leased, 75, 110; low-income, 9, 42, 45, 50, 74, 110, 111, 136, 137, 139, 232, 287, 338, 399; Madison Tenant Union, 397–398; public, 13, 15–16, 42–45, 47, 73–75, 110, 111, 139, 178, 185, 186, 232, 288, 289, 336, 338; relocation, 13–15, 18, 40–41, 42–45, 46, 58, 72, 74–75, 101, 110, 111, 115–116, 337; subsidies, 11, 14, 42, 44; veterans, 45, 74

Housing and Community Development Department, 338, 403

Hovde, Donald, 112, 113, 136

Hub (men's clothier), 130

Huegel, Ray W., 90, 124, 196, 197, 238, 283, 335, 390

Hult, Ralph A., 245

human rights ordinance. See Equal Opportunities Ordinance

Humphrey, Hubert, 8–9, 32, 175

Hunter, Allen, 378

Hunter, John Patrick, 215

Hur, Ken, 278, 370, 401

Hurst, Frances, 51

Hutchinson, Bert, 37, 44

Hyman, J. Jesse, 207

Icke, George, 180, 348

Iltis, Hugh, 197

income, 4–5, 17, 29, 62, 92, 186, 189, 226, 343

Independent Awake America Committee, 99

Independent Housing Association, 325

Inter-Fraternity Council, 6, 81, 147, 170, 194, 212, 369, 378

International Brotherhood of Electrical Workers, 63

International Days of Protest, 172–173, 175, 210, 216–217

International Students Against War, Racism and the Draft, 308, 318

Irwin, Kenneth, 301
Isaksen, Leon, 141
Italian Workmen's Club, 73, 96
Iwanter, Selig, 52

J. H. Findorff and Son Inc., 58, 63, 129
Jackman, W. L., 264, 350, 401
Jackman building, *xiv*
Jackson, Arnold S., 166–167
Jackson, James, 166–167
Jackson, Joseph W. "Bud," 1, 2, 35, 70, 71, 128, 183–184, 185, 197–198, 267, 394
Jacobs, George F., 395
Jacobs, Visconti and Jacobs, 403
Jacoby, Russell, 193
Jakobson, Leo, 240, 348, 404
James, Willie, 303
James Madison Memorial High School, 197–198, 204, 237, 238, 283, 284, 285, 333, 335, 386, 387
James Madison Park, 128, 185, 223, 291, 343–344, 344
Jardine, John, 375
Javid, Manucher, 23
Jenkins, Lowell "Gooch," 125
Jensen, Ellis, 57
Jews, 4, 9, 42, 52, 76, 80, 81, 93, 144, 179–181, 198
Johansen, Gunnar, 132
John Muir Elementary School, 290, 334
John Nolen Drive. *See* Monona Causeway
Johns, Joshua, 126
Johns, Richard, 126
Johnson, Bob, 234
Johnson, Gary, 381
Johnson, Jean Sue, 172
Johnson, Lyndon, 154, 169, 199, 279, 316, 326
Johnson, Walter K., 10, 159
Johnson Street, 28, 31, 95, 243, 275
Joint City-State Downtown Planning Committee, 159
Joint Committee to Study Disruptions, 363, 377
Jolly, Carlos, 257, 264
Jordan, A. C., 268
Jordan, Pallo, 268
Jorgensen, Niels, 342
Julian, Percy L., Jr., 248, 252, 255, 264, 304

Kalb, Danny, 40, 53, 83
Kalb, Johnny, 279
Kaplan, Bill, 309, 378, 380
Karp, Gary, 299
Kassabaum, Thomas, 305
Kastenmeier, Robert, 73, 97, 99, 174, 217–218, 232, 326, 400

Katz, Leonard, 288
Kauffman, Joseph E., 191, 209, 211, 221, 248, 254, 256, 257, 281, 324
Kaufmann, Bruce, 230
Keene, David, 170, 174, 374
Kehl, Leo T., 297
Kellman, Norris J., 146
Kelly, Robert C., 203
Kennedy, Edward, 32, 131, 218–221, *218*
Kennedy, John F., 9, 20, 32–33, *33*, 35, 48–49, 99, 116, 157–158, 197, 199, 238; assassination, 131–133; memorial service, 132–133, *133*
Kennedy Manor, *xiv*, 31, 63
Kincaid, Charles, 51, 340
Kind, Walter, 306
King, Martin Luther, Jr., 79, 179; assassination, 301–303, 335; memorial service, *300*, 302–303, *302*; scholarship fund, 309, 383
Kink, Marcella, 379
Kirchhoff, Roger C., 37
Kissinger, C. Clark, 107, 126–127, 143, 153
Kissinger, Henry A., 56, 278
Klairmont, Alison, 364
Klauser, James R., 328–329, 390
Knowles, Warren, 155, 177, 195, 211, 222, 250, 260, 279, 302, 320, 332, 333, 345, 356, 359, 362, 373, 377, 380, 382, 383
Knox, Bruce, 320
Koepcke, Bruce, 132
Kolicsh, Rudolph, 132
Konnak, Harold A., 77
Kopp, Richard, 67, 69, 104–105, 118, 131, 138–139, 163, 175, 184, 202, 275, 316, 348
Korten, Patrick, 373–374
Kreisman, Irv, 197
Kresge's (department store), 7
Krider, Douglas, 157
Ku Klux Klan, 9, 25, 147

Lackore, Irv, 294
Ladinsky, Jack, 116
La Follette, Bronson, *218*, 238, 273, 340–341
La Follette High School. *See* Robert M. La Follette High School
Lake Park Corporation, 141, 188, 232, 289, 337, 403
Lake Wingra Community Council, 161, 336
Land Tenure Center, 378
Landau, Saul, 5, 21, 22, 235
Landgraf, Richard J., 395
Langer, Rudolph E., 332
Larson, Bryce, 381
Latimer, James, 383
Lauri, Carl, 238

Lauterbach, Ann, 53

law and order. *See* crime; Madison Police Department

Law, Law, Potter and Nystrom, 292

Law Park, 2, 185, 223–224, 266, 393

Law Park Auditorium, 267, 322

Lawton, John, 137

League of Women Voters, 32, 136, 336

Leahy, James, 321

Leahy, Maurice, 321

Lease, David, 51

Le Bosquet, Charles R., 382

Lee, Clifton, 304

Lee, Janet, 109

Leidner, Roberta, 284, 295

Lemberger, Annie, 99

Leonard, Jerris, 194, 236

Lescohier, Mary, 1

Leslie, Vernon "Jack," 253, 349, 364, 368

Levin, Sol, 47, 73, 139, 140, 141, 187, 232, 337, 338, 403

Levitan building, *xiv*

Levy, Marc, 378

Leymann, Richard A., 384

Liberace, 51

Liberace, Salvatore "Sam," 51

Liberace, Zona, 51

Licari, Joseph, 16, 47, 73

Lipp, Jonathan, 335

Lippman, Walter, 217

Lipsky, Suzanne, 310

litigation, 27, 30, 229–230, 295, 318, 334, 341–342; annexation, 94, 161; auditorium, 1–3, 35, 38, 67, 71, 129, 147–149, 183–184, 225, 266, 322; bus lane, 278, 401; urban renewal, 10–11, 16, 48, 131; UW, 255, 320

Local Committee on Urban Renewal, xi, 15–16, 44, 73

Loftsgordon, Herman, 297

Longenecker, G. William, 376

Longfellow Elementary School, 72; PTA, 73

Lowell Hall (dorm), 58

Loyal Order of Moose, 228–229, 385

Luberg, LeRoy, 6, 8, 22, 54, 80, 82, 152

Lucey, Patrick J., 102, 104, 218, *218*, 219, 370, 402

Luedtke, Kenneth, 182

Lysaght, Paul, 26

MacDonald, Betty, *102*, 103, 104, 107, 141, *141*

MacDonald, James B., 196, 335

Madison, WI, ix–xii, *xiv*, 31, 62, 66, *100*, *130*, *134*, *168*, *191*, *208*, *246*, *274*, *354*, *405*; area, x, 28, 59, 62, 92, 129, 158, 203, 239, 289, 291, 342, 402; budgets, xi, 25, 272–274, 347, 349, 389, 396; city administrator, 347; curfew, 390; demographics,

xi–xii, 4–5, 17, 28, 29, 42, 62, 92, 106, 129, 158, 186, 189, 203, 239, 289, 342, 402; flag, 97, *97*; maps, *9*, *406–410*; parks, 129, 203, 343–344, 402 (*see also individual parks*); taxes, xi, 44, 117, 187, 239, 271–274, 284–285, 288, 337, 347, 349, 388, 395, 396, 399; and UW, 19, 57, 175, 183, 191, 192, 250, 277, 317, 323–324, 329, 331, 338, 371; valuation, 29, 60, 62, 92, 94, 187. *See also specific city entities, e.g.,* Common Council

Madison (town), x, 161, 344, 403

Madison Area Technical College, 286, 334, 383, 394. *See also* Madison Vocational, Technical, and Adult Schools

Madison Art Association, 123, 165

Madison Art Center, 165, 325, 343, 394

Madison Board of Realtors, 46, 102, 104, 116, 139, 161, 226

Madison Bus Company, x, 27, 163, 197, 204–205, 242–243, 293–295, 346, 358, 368, 398, 400, 401

Madison Business College, 108

Madison Chamber of Commerce, 30, 92, 102, 107, 108, 165, 294, 348; nativity scene, 52

Madison Citizens Committee on Anti-Discrimination in Housing, 41, 78

Madison Citizens for a Vote on Vietnam, 253, 254, 315

Madison Citizens for Fair Housing, 101, 103

Madison Citizens for Peace in Viet Nam, 192

Madison Civic Music Association, 165, 393

Madison Club, *36*, 76, 179–181

Madison Committee for Civil Rights, 108, 144

Madison Community Center, 37

Madison Conference on Afro-American Letters and Arts, 325

Madison Council of Parent-Teacher Associations, 30, 334

Madison Education Association, 156

Madison Federation of Labor, 25, 107, 197, 271

Madison Federation of Teachers, 156

Madison Fire Department, 26, 52, 93, 127, 245, 348, 349–350, 367, 381, 395, 396, 399

Madison Gas & Electric, *xiv*, 46, *100*, 205

Madison General Hospital, 15, 72, 92, 231

Madison Home Owners Association (MHOA), 114–115, 136, 140, 186, 188, 289, 336

Madison Hotel, *66*, *168*, 204

Madison Housing Authority (MHA), 13, 15, 42–45, 47, 73–74, 75, 110, 111, 136, 139, 140, 185, 186, 188, 231, 232, 240, 289, 336, 338, 399

Madison Jewish Council, 180

Madison Kaleidoscope (newspaper), 374

Madison Medical Center, *187*, 231, *288*

Madison Municipal Airport, x, 50, 117, *118*, 162, 163, 205, 243

Madison Musicians Association, 30

Madison Mustangs Football Club Inc., 202

Madison Neighborhood Centers Inc., 15, 26, 42, 186, *187*, 226, 306, 344, 396

Madison Peace Center, 121, 143

Madison Police Department, 25–27, 60, 61, 125, 126–127, 201, 206, 287, 339, 340–342, 348, 356, 358, *358*, 370–371, 377, 390, 391; black members, 271, 304, 306, 383, 384; and blacks, 270–271, 303–304, 306, 308, 312, 384–385; and Mace, 287, 340–341; and university students, 22, 57, 86, 155, 170, 172, 173, 175, 211, 217, 234–235, 254, 255–261, *259*, 263, 275–276, 318, 328, 356, 363, 364–368, *365*, *366*

Madison Police Union, 287

Madison Professional Policemen's Association, 340, 341

Madison Properties Inc., 158, 160, 203

Madison Public Library: Carnegie library, 93, *100*, 130, *130*, *159*, 240–241, *241*; central library, 30, 49, 50, 51, 93, 117, 129, 130, 204, 241, 244; Lakeview branch, 241; Monroe Street branch, 93; Sequoya branch, 30; Silas U. Pinney Library, 241

Madison Public Schools, xi, 24–25, 59–61, 89–91, 94, 122–124, 156–158, 195–198, 227, 236–239, 270, 283–286, 290, 333–336, 386–390; achievement tests, 60, 156, 196; budget, xi, 25, 60, 237, 272–273, 286, 349, 389; building program, xi, 89, 91, 123, 124, 157, 196, 238; Christmas programs, 198; curriculum, 157, 335, 388; discipline, 61, 156, 286, 334, 387, 389; dress code, 334–335, 386–387; human relations, 335–336, 387; minority students, 196, 333, 387; pledge of allegiance, 285; redistricting, 123; segregation, 196; state aid, 284; statistics, xi, 24, 59, 89, 91, 122, 156, 157, 162, 195, 236, 283, 285, 333–334, 335, 386, 387; student misconduct, 30, 60, 123, 156, 196, 197, 238, 284, 285, 286, 303, 383; teacher salaries, 25, 91, 156–157, 196, 239, 284, 286, 336, 389; teachers, 25, 60, 91, 108, 123, 156, 196, 238, 239, 285, 286, 335–336, 386, 387–388; unified school district, xi, 285, 286, 389. *See also* Board of Education

Madison Redevelopment Authority (MRA), xi, 9–17, 42–48, 57–58, 72–75, 101, 110–114, 115–116, 117–118, 135–138, 186, 187, 188, 231, 232, 288, 289, 336–337, 399, 402, 403; ethics issues, 139–140

Madison Sun (newspaper), 226, 398

Madison Teachers Inc., 284, 336, 389

Madison Tenant Union (MTU), 397–398

Madison Theater Guild, 185

Madison Vocational, Technical, and Adult Schools, *xiv*, 25, 51, *66*, 118, 124, *130*, 157, *159*, 182, 195, 227, 236–237, 286, 334; statistics, 25, 108, 157. *See also* Madison Area Technical College

Madison Youth Council, 163

Makagon, Jim, 172

Malloy, Mike, 65

Maloney, Norris, 2, 3, 35, 48, 229, 341

Manchester, Morgan, 158–159, *159*, 165, 203

Manchester's (department store), *xiv*, *66*, *100*, *130*, 158, 159, 164–165

Mansfield, Arthur "Dynie," 25, 37, *90*, 198, 237, 272, 284, 334, 388

Mansion Hill (neighborhood), 112

Maple Bluff, WI, 94, 346

Mapleside, 403–405, *404*

Maraniss, Elliott, 23

Marcus, Herbert, 238, 285

Marfyak, Jan, 76–77

Marks, James, 17, 107, 113–114, 141, *141*, 248

Marquette Area Redevelopment Study, 114, 136

Marquette Neighborhood Association, 401

Marshall, James, 52, 63, 123, 296, 343, 402

Marshall, Nancy, 119

Marshall Dairy Laboratory, 43, 44

Marti, Merlin, 86

Martin's Tailor Shop, *161*

Masonic Temple, *130*

Mass Transit Study Committee, 27

Matthews, Charles, 70

Matthews, John A., 336

Matush, Thomas E. "Pete," 265

May Second Committee, 164

Mayer, Oscar F., 206

Mayer, Oscar G., Jr., 85, 206, 239

Mayor's Commission on Human Rights (MCHR), 5, 8, 16–17, 25, 40–41, 76, 101, 103, 109, 133, 141

Mazursky, Bernard "Bernie," 321

McBurney, Floyd, 296–297, 331

McCarthy, Eugene, 253, 315, 326, 347

McCarthy, Thomas, 234, 259, 364, 367

McCauley, Tom, 313

McClinnon, Dorothy, 198

McCollum, John P., 15

McCormick, Lawrence, 117, 273

McFarlane, James, 328–329

McGinnis, Albert, 14, 43, 44, 45, 48, 74, 75, 101, 111–112, 113, 117–118, 136, 196, 231, 237, 335, 387

McGovern, George, 192, 250

McGovern, Susan, 250

McGrath, John, 40–41, *102*, 103, 104, 106, 107, 141–142, *141*, 144, 145, 157

McGraw, Ralph A., 127, 245, *245*, 348, 349–350

MCHR. *See* Mayor's Commission on Human Rights (MCHR)

McMaster, John D., 234

McMillin, Miles, 78, 261

McMurray, Robert, 223

McParland, Leland, 261

McVicar, Angus, 167

McWilliams, Jim, 8

Mead and Hunt Inc., 96

Meadowood-East, 203

Meek, Clara, 301

Memorial High School. *See* James Madison Memorial High School

Memorial Union, *58*, 280, 311, 319, 329–330, 374

Mermin, Samuel, 314, 317

Methodist Hospital, *100*

Metzner, Carroll, 1, 2, 103, 182, 198, 225, 266, 322

Meuer, William J., 207

Meyer, Frederick J., 64

Meyer, Robert, 171, 207

Meysembourg, Daniel Lloyd, 321

MHA. *See* Madison Housing Authority (MHA)

MHOA, 114–115, 136, 140, 186, 188, 289, 336

Mickelson, Donald, 61

Middleton (town), x

Midland Realty, 203

Midwest Planning and Research Inc., 290

Mifflin-Bassett (neighborhood), 403

Mifflin Street block party riots, 364–371, *364*, *365*, *366*, *367*

Mifflin Street Community Co-op, 349, 366, 370, 396–397, *397*

military service: National Guard, 51, 162, 209, 260, 359–361, *359*, 378; recruiting, *161*, 253, 314, 315, 319; Reserve Officer Training Corps (ROTC), 20, 121, 316, 319, 354, 376, 378, 380, 381. *See also* draft

Miller, Lorenzo, 205–206

Miller, Marjorie "Midge," 253, 347

Miller, Steve, 121, 323, 373

Mitby, Norman, 25, 195, 286

Mohr, Charlie, 23–24, *23*

Mohs, Frederick J., Jr., 63, 337, 402

Mollenhoff, David, 401

Monona, WI, 182, 306, 346

Monona Avenue, *62*

Monona Basin, *266*; master plan, 225

Monona Basin Foundation, 393

Monona Causeway, x, 49, 50, 95–96, *95*, 117, 118, 128–129, 163, 205, 242, *246*, 290, 293

Monona Golf Course, 60, 63

Monona Terrace. *See* auditorium

Montgomery, Dudley, 207

moral issues and government, 164–165, 199, 229, 325, 374. *See also* censorship

Moran, Thomas H., 297

Moratorium to End the War in Vietnam, 378–380, *379*, *380*

Morgan, James, 303

Mosse, George, 7, 170, 212, 215, 361, 377

Mother Jones Revolutionary League, 377

Mott, Roger, 331

Mount Zion Baptist Church, 73

movies: advertising, 52, *97*; censorship, 125; "Madison's Black Middle Class," 307; "To Find a Home," 41, 78–79, 104, 105, 109

MRA. *See* Madison Redevelopment Authority (MRA)

MTU, 397–398

Mucks, Arlie, Jr., 179–180, 373

Muir Woods, *19*, *110*

Murphy, Donald R., 109

Murphy, Robert B. L., 348

Murray Mall, 188–189, *191*, 232, 289

National Association for the Advancement of Colored People (NAACP), 5–6, 39, 43, 44, 73, 76, 78, 101, 157, 196, 336

National Coordinating Committee to End the War in Viet Nam, 172, 175

National Guardian Life Insurance Company, 129, 159, 160, *168*

National Organization for Women (NOW), 226

National Student Association (NSA), 5, 6, 21, 56, 147, 178, 252

Neighborhood House, 15, 72, 99, 110, 135, *138*, 186, *187*, 324, 336

Nellen, James, 277, 281, 282, 374, 376

Nelson, Gaylord, 7, 20, 40, 55, 92, 99, 109, 152, 182, 326

Nelson, Tracy, 144, 153, 172, 200, 325

Nemec, William, 139

Nestingen, Ivan, 1, 2, 15, 17, 25, 26, 29, 32, 33, 35, 48–49, 70, 95, 105, 225

Neubauer, James R., 222

Neuman, Mark W., 265

Neviaser, Daniel, 403–404

Newhouse, Eric, 177

Nichols, Paul, 396

Ninneman, Terry, 280

Nissley, J. E., 203

Nixon, Richard, 9, 22, 33, 296

Nolen, John, 70, 95

North Hall, 234

Norvell, Merritt, 202, 231, 304, 305, 307, 337, 382

NOW, 226

NSA, 5, 6, 21, 56, 147, 178, 252

Nuckles, Robert, 36, 49–50, 138–139

Oberdorfer, Michael, 264

Obey, Dave, *8*, 9

O'Connor, William P., 98, 295

Odana School, 285

O'Donnell, Cletus Francis, 295

Ogg Hall (dorm), *150*, *191*

Olbrich Park, 344

Old Market Place (neighborhood), 44, 45

Old Red Gym, 191, 281–282, *354*

Olin Park, 70, 96, 185, 223–224, 267, 393

Olip, George, *141*

Olshanski, Hank, 202

Olson, C. E., 316

Onsager, Douglas M., 388
Orchard Ridge Elementary School, 284, 285
Orpheum Theater, *v*, *xiv*, *34*, *66*, *352*
Oscar Mayer and Company, 132, 206–207, 239, 351
Oshkosh State University, 311–312, 355, 361, 362
Osterloth, Richard C., 205–206
Over, William "Bill," 126
Ozanne, Larry, 147

Page, Edward J., 127
Panhellenic Council, 369, 383
panty raids, 56–57, 85–86, 276
Papadopulos, P. F., *186*
Park Hotel, *xiv*, 62, 63, 129, 168
Park Motor Inn, 63, 129, *168*
Parkinson, Christine, 245, *245*
Parkinson, Daniel P., Jr., 245, 348
Parks, Eugene, 109, *109*, 163, 164, 177, 280, 308–309, 326, 349,
    365, 367, *367*, 369, 370, 385, 386, 394–395, 399
Parks Commission, 63, 123, 128, 164, 295, 296
Parkwood Hills, 204
Pasch, Maurice, 16, 47, 48, 55, 154, 221, 244, 325, 329, 374
Paster, Rob "Zorba," 280, 373
Peabody, Arthur, 155
Penn, Nolan E., 363
Penn Park, 289
Pepper, Lew, 366
Peter Pan (theater production), 330–332, *331*, 395
Peters, William Wesley, 2, 3, 36, 37, 38, 148, 183–184, 223–225,
    266–267, 322–323, 392, 393
Peterson, A. W., 57, 137, 188, 192
Peterson, Franklynn, 5
Peterson, Martha, 209
petitions, 383; auditorium, 2–3, 35; bus service, 294; Central
    High School, 196; gun control, 340; housing, 103; liquor
    licenses, 16–17; Madison Club, 180; urban renewal, 114, 136;
    UW, 80, 314, 361; Vietnam, 171, 217, 254, 315–316
Petrovich, Michael, 215
Pfankuchen, L. E. (Mrs.), *39*
PFC. *See* Police and Fire Commission (PFC)
Pfefferle, James, 229–230, 231, 237
Philip H. Falk Elementary School, 124
Phillips, Wendell, 28
Picket Line News (newspaper), 126
Pieper, August, 61
Pierson, William C., III, 381
Plaenert, Walter, 16
Plan Commission, x, xi, 47, 63, 131, 159, 161, 203, 224, 242, 344,
    403
planning and development, 28–30, 62–63, 70, 92–94, 129–131,

158–162, *159*, *160*, *161*, 203–204, 239–242, 289–292, 342–345,
    402–403. *See also* urban renewal
Plecity, James Donn, 265
Plumbers Union, 290
Police and Fire Commission (PFC), 25–26, 127, 271, 287, 367, 371,
    383, 384, 399
Pommer, Matt, 327
Pomraning, Fred, 143
Ponty, Michael, 287
Poorman, Norman, 51, 92
Porter, Leonard, 47, 131, 141, *141*
Potter, Leonard, 45
Potter, Van R., 152, 185, 223–224
Powless, John, 327
Pregler, George, 9
Pregler's Addition, 9; map, *12*
Pritchard, Richard, 76, 101, 302–303, 349, 391
privacy, 41, 78–79, 104, 109, 144
Proctor, Samuel D., 310, 312, 361
protests. *See* demonstrations; riots
PSC. *See* Public Service Commission (PSC) *under* Wisconsin
public access: hearings, xi, 3, 4, 13–14, 16, 47, 48, 96, *102*, 104–105,
    143, 159, 174, 186, 267, 268–269, 270–271, 272, 304–305, 334,
    340, 389, 395; open meetings, 127, 200
Public Facilities Associates, 337, 338, 402
Purdy, Carol Ann, 331–332
Puro, Naomi, 317

Quinn, Pat, 366
Quixote (literary journal), 193, 235, 255, 279, 280

race relations. *See* civil rights; discrimination
Radosh, Ron "Ronny," 22, 53, 54
Randall, John T., 305
Randall's (women's clothier), *130*
Raskin, Marcus, 171
Rauschenbush, Walter, 147
Ray-O-Vac, 343
Red Gym, 191, 281–282, 354
Reddan, William G., 403
Redding, Otis, 297–299
Reese, Bernard, 298
Reese, Gordon, 111, 112, 113
referenda, xi; auditorium, 1, 2–3, 35, 36, 37–38, 67–69, 90, 185;
    mayoral term, 348; public housing, 42, 74; transportation,
    346, 400; urban renewal, 114–115, 136–137, 188; UW, 175,
    252, 316, 324; Vietnam, 175, 253, 254, 315–316. *See also* bond
    issues
Reger, George, 106, 182
Reichardt, Rick, 153

Reichenberger, Al, 391

Reichenberger, Tom, 391

Reierson, Owen H., 109, 132, 133

Reindahl, Amund, 292

Reinke, Ronald, 265

Remeika, Fran, 114, 137, 186

Remington, Frank, 235, 253, 327

Renk, Walter, 314, 319, 325

Renk, Wilbur, 20

Rennebohm, Oscar, 20, 30, 55, 332–333

Reott, Charles, 306

Reynolds, Anna Gault, 49

Reynolds, Edward, 49

Reynolds, Henry, 56, 124, 135, *141*, *160*, 165, 199, 204, 235, 244, 348; and annexations, 94, 123; appointments, 76, 138; and auditorium, 2, 36–38, 50, 67–71, 129, 148–149, 183, 184, 272, 322, 392; and civil rights, 43, 101–102, 104, 105–107, 178, 180, 200, 313; mayoral elections, 36, 49–50, 101, 111–112, 113, 117–118, 398–399; and police department, 61, 127; and transportation, 50, 64, 95–96, 128, 205, 293; and urban renewal, 44, 45, 47, 48, 50, 58, 73, 75, 111, 113, 130, 136, 137, 138–141, 185, 186, 203; vetoes, 50, 68, 140–141, 183

Reynolds, John, 110, 124, 153, 155, 158–159, 161

Reynolds, Robert "Toby," 138–139, 141, 145, 180, 188, 202, 223, 273, 275, 296, 316, 398–399

Reynoldson, John, 239

Rice, William Gorham, 78, 124, 125, 170, 287

Richter, Pat, 55, *84*, *85*, 86, 121

Rieder farm, 151, *151*, 161, 235

right-to-work laws, 174

riots, 155, 258–261, *259*, *260*, 303–304, 306, 364–371, *364*, *365*, *366*, *367*, 377, 381, 384–385; panty raids, 56–57, 85–86, 276; riot-control training, 378

Risser, Fred A., 99, 121, 221, 372

Ritcherson, Lew (student), 230, 313

Ritcherson, Lewis "Les" (coach), 230, 304, 313, 314, 375

Ritchie, Douglas S., 157, 197, 272, 285, 286, 329, 334, 335, 336

Robb, Chuck, 263

Robert M. La Follette High School, 60–61, 89, 122, 124, 157, 195, 236, 283, 303, 333, 386, 387, 389

Roberts, Clifford S., 96, 144–145

Roberts, Joseph, 43

Robinson, Jackie, 8–9, *8*

Rohr, Harold E. "Babe," 138, 238, 290, 350; and alcohol sales, 30; and auditorium, 2, 3, 71, 267, 322, 392; and civil rights, 16–17, 43, 47, 48, 76–77, 104, 105, 106–107, 141, 144–145, 200, 229, 230, 269, 304, 386; elections, 50, 76–77, 96, 111–112, 118, 144–145, 182, 306, 348; and gun control, 339–340, 390; and urban renewal, 113; and Vietnam, 174

Romnes, Bjarne, 93, 140, 336, 338

Roseleip, Gordon, 195, 362

Rosen, Cheryl, *264*

Rosen, Laura, 316

Rosen, Michael, 312, 326

Rosenberg, Gilbert S., 203

Rosenthal, Harold, 158

Ross, Frank, 69

Rosser, J. Barkley, 122, 376

ROTC. *See* Reserve Officer Training Corps (ROTC) *under* military service

Rothschild, Christine, 342

"Roundy Says," x, 32, 99, 164, 234; auditorium, 69, 129, 225; demonstrations, 253, 369; skywalks, 234; UW athletics, 121, 193, 225, 253, 280, 369, 372, 373, 375

Rowen, James, 248, 376, 379

Rupnow, Roger, 11, 13, 15, 44, 45, 46, 47, 72, 73–74, 75, 116, 135–136, 139–140, 187, 231

S. S. Kresge Company, 7

Sachtjen, William, 229, 264, 314

St. Joseph's Catholic Church, *115*

St. Raphael's Cathedral, 98, *100*

St. Thomas Aquinas School, 283

Samp, Helen S., *90*, 167

Sampson Enterprises, 232

Sampson Plaza, 43, 72, 109–110, 137, 288

Samuel L. Gompers Elementary School, 25

San Francisco Mime Troupe, 255, 256

Saunders, Lawrence, 226, 304

Scaggs, Boz, 121

Schaller, Lyle, 11

Schenk's Corners (neighborhood), 241–242, 290

Schesch, Adam, 398

Schiro, Dominic, 206

Schiro, George, 127, 340

Schiro, Vito, 111

Schmidt, Pete, 137, 200, 269, 348

Schmiege, Herbert J., *90*, 196, 198

Schmitz, F. Edwin, 351

Schmitz, Walter J., 132

Schmock, Leonard "Smoky," 396

School Board. *See* Board of Education

Schreiber, Martin J., *218*

Schueler, Donna, 275, 276

Schwartz, Sam, 231

Schwerner, Michael, 147

Scoon, Darwin, 102

Scudder, Bourtai, 143, 146, 172, *173*, 217–218, 248, 250

SDS. *See* Students for a Democratic Society (SDS)

Sears, Roebuck and Company, 94, 142–143, *143*

Second Baptist Church, 43, 73

Segoe, Ladislas, 70–71

segregation. *See* discrimination *under* housing

Sellery, George C., 88

Sellery Hall (dorm), 82, *119*

Senior Citizens of Wisconsin Inc., 31, 63

Sennett, Ray, 25, *90*, 237, 388

Sewell, William, 87, 171, 252, 253, 254, 257, 260, 261, 262, 281, 301–302, 309, 314, 315, 317, 318, 323–324, 327, 328

Shade, Don, 56

Shapiro, Marshall, 349

Shaw, Alfred P., 71

Shaw, Robert, 140

Shaw Metz & Associates, 71

Shesky, John H., 126

Shew, Dennis W., 382

Shivers, Dimetra, 46

Shivers, Stanley, 46

shopping centers, 29–30, 92, 94, 111, 151, 158, 161, 187, 231, 240, 241–242, 290, 291, 337, 344, 402–403

Shor, Ira, 263

Shorewood Hills, WI, 94, 182, 346

Sidran, Ben, 119, 121, 279, 373

Siegrist, Bob, 174, 194

Silver Springs School, 60

Sinykin, Gordon, 179, 181

sixties: defined, ix

Sklar, Marty, 79

Skloot, Robert, 331

Skornicka, Joel, 256

Skuldt, Robert, 97, 162

skywalks, 58, 158–160, *160*, 187, 203, 253, *288*, 373

Slavney, Morris, 127, 294

Slichter, Charles S., 283

Smith, Betty, 399

Smith, Don, 202

Smith, Newell, 57

Smith, William Bradford, 51, 75, 105, 157–158, 182, 217, 218, 250, 272

smoking, 162–163, 197, 386

Smolen, Phyllis, 51

SNCC, 153

Soglin, Paul: as alderman, 316, 320, 341, 348, 350, 365–370, *365*, 378, 390, 399, 400, 403; as mayor, ix; as student, 192, 214, 220, 251, 253, 255, *258*, 261, 262, 263, 276, 278, 281

Somerfeld, Warren, 243

Somers, Andrew, 314, 344, 348

sororities: black, 310; civil rights, 8, 80–81, *80*, 146–147, 369; statistics, 21, 280

South Central Federation of Labor, 317

South Madison (neighborhood), 4, 101, 144, 163, 178, 197, 226, 238, 271, 306; urban renewal, 13, 74, 110, 116, 136, 137, 187, 189, 289, 337

South Shore Methodist Church, 43

Spanish-Americans, 311, 326, 333, 336

Special Committee on Minority Housing, 102

Special Five-Year Program for Tutorial and Financial Assistance, 230, 310, 311–313, 359, 382

Spencer, David A., 386, 389

Spitzer, Robert, 173

Spurley, James V., Jr., 382

Stark, Evan, 143, 170, 172, 173, 175, 215, 216, 218, 254, *255*, 257, 261, 262, 315

State Street, *ii, vi, viii*, x, 34, 61, 64, *66*, *88*, 92, 117, 160, 164, 201, *201*, 205, 242, 276, 292, *352*, 401; demonstrations, 6, 8, 85–86, 300, 301–302, 312, 320, 368, 371, 379, *380*; fires, 52, 245; pedestrian mall, 400

State Street Association, 28

Staven, Roger W., 395

Stavrum, Thomas, 16, 51

Steelworkers Local 1401, 343

Steenbock, Harry, 283

Steiger, William, 7

Stein, Bruno, 180

Steiner, Allison, 335

Stephens, Glenn W., *90*, 124, 156, 197, 198, 238

Sterling Court, *119*, *191*

Sterling Hall: bombing, 381

Stich, Vernon J., 265

Stickels, Jack, 196

Stielstra, Jonathan, *258*, 260, 366

Stock Pavilion, *68*

Stoflet, Gordon Wayne, 265

Stolen, Ole, 99

Stone, Dennis, 97

Stone, Frances, 97

Stone, Patrick, 199

Stone, Rick, 97

Strand, John, 129

Straub, William, 243, 276, 293–295, 346

streets and highways, x, 27, 28, 50, 63, 64, *64*, 95–96, *95*, 128–129, 151, *151*, 163, 204, 205, 242–243, 246, 275–278, 288, 290, 291, 292, 345, *345*, 400–402; expressways, 64, *64*, 95, 163, 164, 181, 243, 398; statistics, 64, 401. *See also individual streets*

strikes, 63, 92, 126–127, 199, 254, 271, 283, 290, 293–295, 334, 343, 346, 399; rent, 397–398; sick-ins, 349–350, 399; students, 262–263, 312, 318, 353–363, *357*, *358*, *359*, *360*

Stuck, Howard, 28

Student Council for Civil Rights, 8, 40, 41, 42, 102

Student Life and Interests Committee, 81, 85, 120, 121, 221

Student Nonviolent Coordinating Committee (SNCC), 153

Student Peace Center, 20, 121, 122, 153, 172, 175, 279

Students for a Democratic Society (SDS), 126–127, 143, 153, 171, 210, 211, 211, 218, 247–250, 251, 252, 253, 254, 279, 311, 314, 318, 319, 320, 335, 358, 377, 378- 379, 380, 381

Students for Peace and Disarmament, 119, 121, 122

Studies on the Left (journal), 79

Studt, Robert, 185

Stuhledreher, Harry, 375

Styles, Emery (Mrs.), *39*

Suhr, Frederick W., 206

Sundt, Guy, 372

Supernaw, J. S., 27

surveys, 42, 45, 107, 115–116, 163, 175, 240, 252, 285, 324, 325, 404

Swan, Alfred Wilson, 78, 133, 302

Swarsensky, Manfred, 164, 177, 302

Swenson, Ellsworth, 105, 139, 145, 316, 348, 399

Sykes, James T., 123–124, 177, 384

Symon, Mary Louise, 102, 268, 269, 307, 383, 399

Tabankin, Margery, 353, 357, 378

Taliaferro, Odell "Tally," 5–6, 7, *39*, 43, 44, 46, 76, 143

Taliesin Associated Architects, 2

Tandler, Marty, 210, 252

Tanzman, Harriet, 164

taxes, xi, 44, 117, 187, 239, 271–274, 284–285, 288, 337, 347, 349, 388, 395, 396, 399

Taychopera Foundation, 348, 403–405

Taylor, Robert, 330

Taylor, William "Willie," 60, 175, 216

Teaching Assistants Association, 262

Teamsters' Union, 92, 283, 293–295, 346

Temple Beth El, 164

Tenney building, *66*

Tenney-Lapham (neighborhood), 13

terrorism: arson, 317, 319, 361, 368; bombing, 378, 381; cross burning incidents, 307, 383; firebombings, 268, 309, *310*, 317, 381

Thiede, Wilson B., 309, 362

Third World Liberation front, 361

Thirty on the Square, *168*

Thoma, Charles, 264–265

Thomas, Herman, 125, 143, 206, 271, 304, 364–365, 367, 370, 371, 377, 382

Thomas, Nathan Lee, 206

Thompson, Leonard D., 265

Thompson, Tommy G., 99, 174

Thorstad, Clarence, 245

Thorstensen, Gerald, 304, 306

Thronson, Lowell, 112

Tiffany, Jackson, 79

"To Find a Home" (movie), 41, 78–79, 104, 105, 109

Torphy, Michael, 244

Towell, Arthur, 137

Towers (dorm), *66*

Traffic Commission, 27–28, 164, 205, 276, 293, 346

transportation, x, 27–28, 163–164, 204–205, 242–243, 292–295, 345–346, 398, 400–402; air travel, x, 50, 163, 205, 243; bicycles, 164, 205; bus service, x, 27–28, 60, 163, 182, 197, 204–205, 238, 242–243, 275–278, *276*, *277*, 283–284, 293–295, 346, 358, 368, 398, 400, 401–402; motorcycles, 242, 292; parking, 62, 93, 94, *94*, 129, 152, 158–160, 163, 240, 242, 267, 292, 323, 345, 392, 400, 401; railroads, x, 27, 82, 205; UW, 82, 151, 152, 193, 234–235, 275–278, *276*, *277*, 345, *345*. *See also* streets and highways

Travanti, Daniel, 22, 55

Triangle urban renewal project, 9, 10–16, *10*, 42–46, 72, 73–75, 93, 110–111, 115–116, *115*, 135, 136, 137, 185–187, *186*, *187*, 205, 231, 287–288, *288*, 337, 402; demographics, 4, 17, 42, 186; map, 12, 14, 72

Trotter, Zachary, 16–17, 47–48, 73

Truax, Thomas L., 162

Truax Air Field, 51, 97, 169, 172–173, 399; closing, 157, 162; housing, 5, 41, 42

Truax Park apartments, 45, 73, 74

Tucker, Ardinette, 302

Tuesday Night Committee, 103, 104

Turville, Henry, 240, 291

Turville Park, 291

Tuschen, John, 366–367

UAW, 126–127, 343

UCA, 218, 248, 252, 254, 278, 309, 361

Uhr, Leonard, 275, 277

Underhill, Fred, 5, 7, 53, 54

unemployment, 62, 96–97, 127, 189, 204, 290

Union (UW), *58*, 280, 311, 319, 329–330, 374

Union Forum Committee, 230, 353

Union Literary Committee, 120

Union Music Committee, 373

United Auto Workers (UAW), 126–127, 343

United Campus Action, 218

United Migrant Organization Services, 336

United States government: Central Intelligence Agency, 248, 252, 253, 254; Federal Housing Administration, 93, 140, 231, 287, 288, 336; House Un-American Activities Committee, 56, 85, 195; Housing and Home Finance Agency, 10–11, 13, 57, 140, 189; Housing and Urban Development, 289, 337; National Labor Relations Board, 127; Selective Service System,

174, 209, 210, 215, 253, 281, 319, 386; Supreme Court, 318; Urban Renewal Administration, 15, 16, 45, 73, 74, 110
University Avenue, x, 28, 31, 118, 163, 164, 242, 243, 274, 292; bus lane, 275–278, 401–402; urban renewal, 137, 141, 160, 191, 232, 289, 337, 403
University Book Store, 339, 354, 371, 400
University City project. *See* General Neighborhood Renewal Program (GNRP)
University Community Action (UCA), 218, 248, 252, 254, 278, 309, 361
University Community Co-op, 280, 373
University Heights (neighborhood), 112, 145, 272, 345
University of Wisconsin, xii, 19–24, *19*, 52–58, 81–89, *110*, 118–122, *119*, 149–155, *149*, *150*, 190–195, *191*, 233–236, 274–283, *274*, 323–333, 353–381, *354*; affirmative action, 230, 312; antiobstruction policy, 220, 221, 250, 251, 254, 256, 262–263, 312, 319, 320; athletics, 19–20, 21, 23–24, 55, 56, 83, 84–85, *84*, 86, 107, *120*, 121, 131–132, *149*, 153, 154, 192–193, 230, 234, 235, 279, 313–314, 324, 327, 356, 361, 372, 373, 375; bequests, 38–40, 77; Black Studies Department, 309–311, 355, 362–363; Board of Regents, 7, 20, 48, 55; budget, 221, 251, 279, 309, 373; building program, 21, 52, 57–58, *58*, 81, 82, 110, 118, 119, 129, 149, 150, *150*, 154–155, 190, 233, 274, 289, 290, 323, 353, 372, 375 (*see also* urban renewal); and civil rights, 38–40, 41, 42, 77, 80–81, *80*, 107, 108, *108*, 145–147, 176–177, 178–179, 230, 269, 308–314; compulsory military training, 20, 316, 319, 376; confidentiality, 209–215, 252, 253; curfew, 20, 85, 120, 193, 324, 325, 329, 374; dormitories, 19, 21, *31*, 57, 58, 82, 119, *119*, 129, 150, *150*, 191, *191*, 233, 234, 274, *354*, 372; dress regulations, 193; Faculty Assembly, 319; farms, 151, *151*, 161, 235; housing regulations, 21, 81, 121, 152, 279, 324, 325, 374; out-of-state students, 22–23, 54, 233, 373; photo id cards, 381; Protection and Security Department, 119, 190, 247, 248, 253, 311, 315, 374, 390, 391; public relations, 172–173, 174, 175, 214, 221, 320, 323–324, 329, 363, 369, 373; research, 118, 131, 283, 376, 379; statistics, xii, 19, 21, 22, 52, 81, 118, 145, 149, 150, 152, 178, 190, 233, 236, 274, 310, 323, 325, 353, 371; transportation, 82, 151, *152*, 193, 234–235, 275–278, *276*, *277*, 345, *345*; urban renewal, 13, *19*, 57–58, 74, 85, 112–113, *113*, 135, 136, 137, 140–141, 188–189, 232, 337, 403; western campus, 151, 191, 235–236
University of Wisconsin–Extension, 41, 78, 105, 109
University of Wisconsin Socialist Club, 5, 9, 22, 54, 83, 122, 143
University Park Corporation, 85, 137, 141, 188
University Students for the Abolition of HUAC, 85
Urban League, 196, 269, 336, 383
Urban Planning Consultants, 189
urban renewal, 9–18, 40–41, 42–48, 72–75, *72*, 93, 109–116, *115*, 135–141, *138*, 178, 185–189, *186*, *187*, 231–232, 287–289, *288*, 290–291, 336–338, 402–403; clearance/rehabilitation, 11–13,

15, 46, 58, 73, 111, 289, 337; eminent domain, 10–11, 240, 343; federal regulations, xi, 72, 73, 116, 231, 337; joint housing and redevelopment authority, 47, 73, 188, 338; land acquisition policy, 46; maps, *9*, *12*, *113*; UW, 13, *19*, 57–58, 74, 85, 112–113, *113*, 135, 136, 137, 140–141, 188–189, 232, 337, 403. *See also specific projects*
Urich, John, 400, 403

Valdes, Luis, 54
Vander Kelen, Ron, 55, 86
Vander Meulen, August, 124, 285
Van Hise, Charles, 68, 86, 91, 155
Van Hise Elementary School, 285
Vann, George W., *108*, 177–178
venereal disease, 51, 200, 234
Versace, Humbert "Rocky," 207
Vesey, Richard W., 167
Veterans for Peace in Vietnam, 295
Victor, Meyer, 160
Viet Nam Dissenters, 175
Vietnam, 83, 119, 121, 122, 154, 164, 169–175, 182, 190, 192, 199, 207, 209–222, 247–265, 295, 296, 314–321, 376, 378–382, 389
Vilas, William Freeman, 31, 39, 42, 63; mansion, *31*, 63, 93, *100*, 129
Vilas Park, 31, 63, 295, 344; zoo, 31, 32, 127, 243–244
Vilas Towers, 31, 63, 93, 111, 129
Vitale, Frank, 16, 17
Vitale, Peter, 46
Vogel, Ken, 378
Voight, Floyd, 291
von Metterheim, Jack, 302
Vukelich, George "Papa Hambone," *98*, 307, 341
Vultaggio, Joseph W., 388

W. T. Grant Inc., 6, 7, 29
Wagner, Dave, 373
Waisman, Harry, 131
Walk for Development, 395
Walker, Charles "Rut," 361
Walker, William E., 65
Wallace, George, 145, 152, 153
Waller, Carl H., 60
Walsh, John, 23
Wapenduzi Weusi, 312, 355, 358–359
Ward, Walter, 230
Warner Park, 202, 344
Warren, Jennifer, 53
Watson, Roth, 341
WDRU, 248, 250, 311, 318, 319, 320, 325, 342
We Want No Berkeley Here Committee, 250, *251*

weapons, 156, 162, 238, 285, 339, 377; gun control, 61, 339–340, 342, 390

Weatherly, Bruce, 25–27, 98, 125, 287

Weatherly, Inez, 98

Weber, Mary Jane Frances (Sister), 65

Weisfeld, Neil, 353

Weiss, Lee, 164, 405

Weiss, Leonard, 164

Weissberg, Eric, 53, 234

Weissman, Gary, 5

welfare, 42, 75, 96–97, 127, 228, 250, 269, 306, 396

Weller and Strang Architects, 130

Wendt, Donald, 387

Wendt, Kurt E., 58, 75, 151, 154, 282

Werner, A. Matt, 77

West High School, 24, 59, 60, 89, 91, 122, 123, 156, 157, 195, 197, 218, 236, 283, 285, 333, 334, 335, 386, 388, 389

West High Times (newspaper), 386

West Side Businessmen's Club, 161

Wexford Village, 402

WHA (radio station), x

WHA (television station), x, 32

Wheeler, Jan, 348, 390

White, Fredrick A., 41

White, Helen C., 282–283

Wiegner, Edward A., 51, 58

Wil-Mar Center, 344

Wilkie, Edwin, 11, 266, 322

Wilkie, Horace, 48, 77, 99, 266

Williams, Carolyn, 383

Williams, David, 365, 366

Williams, Samuel, 39

Williams, Sloan, 25

Williams, William Appleman, 170–171, 174, 212, 214, 215, 318, 372–373

Williamson, Ivan "Ivy," 234, 235, 313, 372, 375

Williamson, Kenneth, 359

Williamson-Marquette (neighborhood), 13, 114, 137, 344–345

Wilson, Richard, 32, 51, 197

Wimmer, James, 40

Winfield, Bill, 349, 396

Wingert, Emmett, 370

Winograd, Richard W., 170

Winston, Johnny E., 383

Wisconsin: Employment Relations Board, 127, 293; Equal Rights Council, 382; Highway Commission, 95, 164; Industrial Commission, 26–27, 107, 228, 229, 295; legislature, 1, 11, 101, 103, 146, 236, 261, 277, 279, 328–329, 334, 358, 362, 363, 372, 373, 376, 391, 399; Public Service Commission (PSC), x, 96, 128, 163, 205, 294, 346; State Building Commission, 57, 137,

191; state capitol, *xii*, *52*, *62*, *66*, *165*, *168*, *208*, *360*, *401*; State Industrial Commission, 107, 142, 143, 229; Supreme Court, 129, 376

Wisconsin Alliance Party, 349, 394–395, 398

Wisconsin Alumni Association, 173, 234, 320, 373; Alumni House, 58, *58*

Wisconsin Alumni Research Foundation, 24, 181, 283

Wisconsin Civil Liberties Union, 9, 78, 124, 125, 287

Wisconsin Conference on Afro-Arts, 325

Wisconsin Draft Resistance Union (WDRU), 248, 250, 311, 318, 319, 320, 325, 342

Wisconsin Film Society, 331

Wisconsin High School, 60, 91, 236

Wisconsin Life Insurance, *xiv*, *130*, 168

Wisconsin Players, 22, 55

Wisconsin Power and Light, *xiv*, *66*

Wisconsin Professional Police Association, 287

Wisconsin Realtors Association, 102, 226

Wisconsin State Historical Society, 31, *58*

Wisconsin State Journal (newspaper), *109*, 202; advertising, 52, 104, 183; and auditorium, 3, 50, 68, 184, 224, 267; and civil rights, 105; and demonstrations, 77, 173, 174; and elections, 50, 77, 117, 145; and transportation, 96; and urban renewal, 45, 75, 110, 136. *See also* "Roundy Says"

Wisconsin Student Association (WSA), 8, 21, 40, 161, 170, 215, 220–221, 252, 309, 311, 323, 324, 361, 369, 374; Student Senate, 6–7, 78, 175, 192, 212, 251, 253, 278, 316, 357, 368; symposia, 20, 54, 82, 152, 190, 233, 278, 324, 362, 372

Wisconsin Telephone Co., *xiv*

Wisconsin University Building Corporation, 188

Witte, Edwin E., 24

Witte Hall (dorm), *119*, *150*

WKOW (radio station), 347

WMTV (television station), 158

Wolf, David, 177

Wolff, Kubly & Hirsig (hardware store), *xiv*

women, 85, 119, 153, 164–165, 193, 226, 250, 253, 316; discrimination, 50, 77, 200, 229–230, 295, 317, 382–383; liberation, 153, 226, 317, 375

Women Strike for Peace, 121

Women's International League for Peace and Freedom, 99, 217

Women's Liberation Conference, 375

Woodington, Neil, 158, 203

Woodward, Vern, 23

Woolworth's (department store), 5–6, *6*, *7*, *130*

work relief program, 96–97, 127

Wright, Frank Lloyd, 1–2, 35, 42, 70, 93, 167, 183, 225, 267, 323, 393, 394

Wright, James C., 102, 103, 107, 141, 144, *178*, 226, 268–269, 302, 304, 307–308, 335, 385

Wright, Peter, 396
WSA. *See* Wisconsin Student Association (WSA)

YAF, 170, 174, 261, 358, 373–374
Yasko, Karel, 57
Yelinek, Keith, 335
YMCA, *xiv*, *100*, 153, 280, 337
Yost's-Kessenich's (department store), *xiv*
Young, Edwin, 87, 310, 311, 312, 316, 320, 324, 327–328,
    329–330, 331, 353–354, 355, 356–363, 372, 374, 379, 400
Young, F. Chandler, 337, 355
Young, M. Crawford, 362–363
Young Americans for Freedom (YAF), 170, 174, 261, 358,
    373–374
Young Democrats, 6, 122, 169, 175, 218, 230, 253, 278
Young Republicans, 7, 169, 194, 213

Young Socialist Alliance, 122, 133, 377, 378
Younger, A. H., *90*, 196
YWCA, *xiv*, *130*, *159*, 348, 375

Zaleski, Michael, 329
Zander, Arnold, 131
Zander Northport Apartments, 131
Zeitlin, Maurice, 154, 170, 251, 254, 302, 315–316
Zeldin, Lea, 143, 172, 217, 220, 248, 250, 261, 286, 334
Zeldin, Robin, 286, 334, 335
Ziegler, Bernard C., 325, 330
Zmudzinski, Chester, 15, 16, 43, 44, 45, 46, 47, 73, 135, 141, 344,
    396
Zmudzinski, Florence, 15, 44, 46, 47, 73, 74–75, 111, 116
Zweifel, Gary, 215, *215*
Zwicker, Robert, 211, 247, 248, 252, 318, 369

About the Author

TERESE BERCEAU

Stuart D. Levitan, an award-winning print and broadcast journalist and long-time local official, has been a mainstay of Madison media and government since 1975. He is the author of *Madison: The Illustrated Sesquicentennial History, Vol. 1*, has written extensively for local and national newspapers and magazines, and produces the *Madison in the Sixties* podcast on WORT-FM. As a downtown Dane County Supervisor in the mid-1980s, he wrote the ordinances establishing the fair housing code, Sensitive Crimes Commission, and newspaper recycling program. Since 1989, he has chaired the Madison Community Development Authority, Landmarks Commission, Plan Commission, and several other city and nonprofit boards. A graduate of the UW Law School, he spread labor peace and imposed industrial justice as a mediator-arbitrator for the Wisconsin Employment Relations Commission from 1987 to 2015. He became a Deadhead at age sixteen, in 1970.